EVALUATING BASEBALL'S
MANAGERS

Evaluating Baseball's Managers

A History and Analysis of Performance in the Major Leagues, 1876–2008

CHRIS JAFFE

McFarland & Company, Inc., Publishers

Jefferson, North Carolina, and London

Library of Congress Online Catalog data

Jaffe, Chris.
Evaluating baseball's managers : a history and analysis of
performance in the major leagues, 1876–2008 / Chris Jaffe.
p.   cm.
Includes bibliographical references and index.

ISBN 978-0-7864-3920-1
softcover : 50# alkaline paper ∞

1. Baseball managers— Rating of— United States.
I. Title.
GV875.7.J34   2010   796.357'64 — dc22   2009049187

British Library cataloguing data are available

On the cover: (*top, left to right*) Harry Wright, Frank Selee, Connie
Mack, John McGraw; (*bottom*) Casey Stengel, Tommy Lasorda,
Bobby Cox. Background ©2010 Shutterstock

Manufactured in the United States of America

*McFarland & Company, Inc., Publishers
Box 611, Jefferson, North Carolina 28640
www.mcfarlandpub.com*

With love to my parents,
Ed and Liz Jaffe

There is one indispensable quality of a baseball manager:
The manager must be able to command the respect of his players.
This is absolute; everything else is negotiable.

— Bill James, *The Bill James Guide to Baseball Managers.*

What do managers *really* do?

Worry.

Constantly.

For a living.

— Leonard Koppett, *The Thinking Fan's Guide to Baseball.*

Acknowledgments

If I were to name all the people who deserved thanking for the creation of this book, these acknowledgments would run longer than the entire rest of the book. My name goes on the copyright page, but many others played a vital role in the creation of the present work.

First and foremost, I owe a heartfelt thanks to Phil Birnbaum. Without him, this book would have been impossible. Eons ago I thought one could learn a lot about managers by comparing how players performed with them versus the rest of their careers in some systematic way. Figuring out such a system was so laughably beyond my mathematical and computer skills that this thought remained a pipe dream. Then Phil created a database that allowed me to examine this question. I thank him not only for that, but also for his willingness to help me out over the years. Please realize he created the database to examine luck, not managers. He is still not entirely convinced that it does enlighten us about skippers, yet that never stopped him from running and re–running his numbers as needed for this study. If Phil explains the database in his own words in Appendix I, and for that, again, my heartfelt thanks.

Second, I need to thank Jim Furtado and Dan Szymborski, who are respectively the owner and chief editor at the Baseball Think Factory website. They thought enough of my early work on managers to publish a trio of my articles on their server space in the summer of 2006. Those articles first gave me the inklings that perhaps I could build up my investigations into an entire book.

Also deserving hearty thanks are David Smith and Sean Forman, the forces behind the two greatest websites in the world: Retrosheet and Baseball-Reference.com. Without those sites, this book either would not exist, or be far worse. Phil Birnbaum's work may have inspired and jumpstarted my research, but the information at those sites provided much of this study's meat. Speaking of thanking the people who run wonderful websites, I also gladly thank Dave Studenmund of *The Hardball Times*. He recruited me as a writer there in 2007, and never complained and protested when I had to back out of several articles over the last year because I was busy putting this together.

The annual conventions of the Society for American Baseball Research also helped, giving me a sounding board to test out some of my ideas. (I presented early versions of this book's first three chapters at SABR's national conventions from 2006 to 2008.) The feedback I received at these get-togethers was most gratifying.

The late Dick Thompson, via his book, *The Ferrell Brothers of Baseball*, also inspired some of my research. Though we never met (and some of our online exchanges were contentious) his awareness that managers intentionally matched pitchers up against particular opposing squads, which affected their value to the team, proved quite important for this study. Thompson's notions are as important to Chapter 3 as Birnbaum's study is to Chapter 1. In both cases, it sparked my subsequent research.

There are so many others worth mentioning that space requirements prevent me from doing more than just a cursory mention of their names. These individuals offered all sorts of help, ranging from sharing ideas, proofreading, offering an insight into a particular manager or managers, computer help, or any number of other little favors that aided me in this undertaking. Among those deserving mention: Jeff Angus, Richard Barbieri, Bill Baer, John Brattain, Paul Brewer, Cliff Blau, Craig Calcaterra, Eric Chalek, Warren Corbett, Jon Daly, Chris Dial, Joe Distelheim, Mike Emeigh, David Geisler, Sherif Geleil, Anthony Giacalone, Scott Goldstein, Janis Greene, Brian Gunn, Ed Jaffe, Eriq Jaffe, Liz Jaffe, Mike Jezioski, Vinay Kumar, Dan Markham, Mike McCullough, Matt Rauseo, Greg Spira, Steve Treder, Bryan Tsao, Mike Webber, Geoff Young, and Will Young.

Once this book has gone to print, I am sure I will think of several others I forgot. To them I apologize. As I noted at the outset, thanking everyone who helped with this book would take a book in and of itself.

Table of Contents

Preface

The purpose of this book is to use sabermetric methods to appraise the overall performance and particular tendencies of baseball's field generals—its managers. Although this is not
the first sabermetric study of managers to be done, it is a bit different from much of what has
come before it. Most other attempts to quantify managerial performances focused on the in-
game decisions made. Individuals much smarter than myself have looked at very specific decisions managers make—such as sacrifice bunting, issuing intentional walks, attempting to
steal, etc.

These studies normally focus on how managers manage the game, but the people skills
and basic management portions of the jobs are generally ignored. This includes responsibilities such as dealing with players, setting and enforcing rules, motivating and teaching as
needed, assessing talent, handling the stress of being one of the most second-guessed men in
the metropolis, delegating authority to coaches while still retaining ultimate authority, having an effective working relationship with the front office, handling the fans, putting up with
the media, and balancing one's personal life and professional obligations.

This limited level of research is especially striking given that for many people in and out
of the game, the areas neglected by sabermetrics are often more important than the in-game
tactical decisions. There is a good reason for this focus of interest. None of those softer, people skills can be proven to exist solely by using statistical methods, thus the sabermetric
research into these areas dies before it even begins.

The disinclination to quantify these more amorphous portions of the job is reminiscent
of the old analogy of the hedgehog and the fox. The hedgehog knows one thing, but understands it extremely well. The fox lacks the depth of the hedgehog in any given field, but makes
up for it with a far greater breadth of knowledge. This comparison was first applied to Rus-
sian literature (Fyodor Dostoyevsky is the hedgehog, and Leo Tolstoy the fox), but it works
for many things worthy of study. It should never be taken as a value judgment—both Tolstoy and Dostoyevsky were tremendous writers, after all—but a way of noting different
approaches.

Many of the sabermetricians who have studied managers are hedgehogs. They are
strongest when dealing with numbers, so they sensibly focus on that. However, while numbers are *a* source of knowledge, they are not *the* source. When practically every single person involved in baseball for a century or more feels that the people and coaching skills exist
and are vital to a manager's job, but quantitative studies alone cannot prove their existence
or import, that means either all of baseball is clueless about its skippers or the softer side of
managing reveals limitations in the sabermetric hedgehog approach. I believe the latter is the
case in this instance, and thus take a fox-like approach.

The central theory of this book is that managers are primarily managers of men, not of
the game. The on-field decisions matter, but ultimately are of only secondary importance. It
is perfectly true that neither of those contentions can be proven using just math. That is fine,

1

though. This book incorporates sabermetrics—in fact, there are several new stats thrown out for your reading pleasure—but it is not a purely quantitative exercise. Its approach is more art than science.

I hope that this book can add to people's knowledge of the game's managers, but it is not intended to be the last word on managers. Instead, it is hoped to be the first word in a new approach on the subject.

PART I
ANALYSIS

    This book has a fairly basic goal: try to understand managers better, largely through the use of statistics. Though the heart of this book thus focuses on individual managers themselves, it is necessary to first explain some of the numbers before moving on to the skippers. Consequently, this book features two parts: an analytical one that presents the various techniques for evaluating managers, and a commentary section that discusses the careers of 89 of baseball's most important managers based on the tools described in the first part.

    Part I consists of three chapters, each of which introduces a different analytical track. Chapter 1 covers the Birnbaum Database, which gauges managerial performance. Chapter 2 introduces the Tendencies Database, which looks at a huge array of proclivities and interests for managers. Though it is a short chapter, it forms the real core for Part II, the book's commentary. The third chapter examines and quantifies a long-lasting (though now dormant) practice managers had for using their starting pitchers—leveraging them against specific opponents.

1

Evaluating Managerial Performance

What makes managers important? There are some obvious parts of the job. Managers handle in-game strategy and fill out the lineup cards. They figure out who should bunt, and when they should do it. They call steals. Managers decide if pinch-hitters or pinch-runners should be used, and if/when defensive replacements enter the game. More importantly, they decide which players start. Some platoon while others use a set lineup. Some skippers prefer veterans while others are more willing to give kids a shot. With pitchers, managers decide how long to leave the starter in, which relievers to use, and assign roles to each person in the bullpen.

When people call the local sports radio station or post on their favorite blog about their team's manager, these and a million other similar issues are the typical discussion topics as in-game decisions are the most visible parts of a manager's job. To be sure, they make up a vital part of what managers do—but there is more to it than that.

Several years ago ESPN.com writer Rob Neyer asked some general managers what attributes they sought in a manager and what topics they discussed in interviews with job candidates. He learned GMs did not focus on baseball tactics or strategy, but instead they centered on communication. One GM confided that retired ballplayers were satisfied with their physical preparation, but wished they could have been more successful at getting themselves in the right mental state to play. It is not simply a matter of effort as trying too hard can lead to pressing.

Along those lines, while taking part in a panel discussion at the 2008 national convention of the Society for American Baseball Research (SABR) in Cleveland, Mark Shapiro, Indians general manager said the three most important qualities for a manager were communication, self-awareness, and the ability to prioritize. The first point was what Neyer's column noted. For self-awareness, a manager had to recognize how the players reacted to him in order to properly communicate and have the desired impact on them. With prioritization, all clubhouses have 75 fires that need to be put out, but a manager only has time to handle three or four. He needs to take care of the worst ones, so they do not wreck the season for the squad.

Both Neyer's column and Shapiro's statements have a common point—a skipper's main duty is not managing the *game*, but the *players*. Focusing only on strategic decisions not only misses part of managing—it also misses the job's central task. How one handles the entire clubhouse and particular individuals is more important than bunting or intentional walks. Basic coaching—helping players master the finer points of their games—still matters, but much of that is taught in the minors or by the hitting and pitching coaches. The manager can have a broader effect on his players based on how he handles the game's psychology and culture.

The manager should handle his charges in a way that ensures they produce as much as they are capable of. To do that, players should be put in the best frame of mind so that when they stand on the field, they are as focused and determined as possible. These things are not matters of conscious choice as people rarely (if ever) choose to have a particular emotion at a given time. Feelings are messy things. A manager can prod one player, challenge another, baby a third, and leave a fourth entirely alone — handling each in such a way as that all do the best they can on the field. The most famous example of a coach effectively prodding his players comes from college football when Notre Dame's Knute Rockne gave his "win one for the Gipper" speech. A big league baseball manager handling mature adults will rarely be that maudlin, but the central point remains true: how a manager treats his players can have a noticeable impact on how they play and their level of performance. Adding to this, a manager must establish boundaries, set up rules, and ensure that they are properly respected and enforced.

Despite being important, to date this portion of managing has received scant attention from the sabermetric community. Its focus has been on in-game strategy, which makes sense as this is the easiest managerial responsibility to quantify. Numerous fine studies on issues like bunting and filling out the lineup card — perhaps most notably in *The Book* by Mitchel Lichtman, Tom M. Tango, and Andy Dolphin — have advanced our understanding of these areas. However, little has been done on the softer people skills of managing. The existence of managerial impact on players is virtually impossible to prove by math alone, because numerous issues muddy the waters. It is necessary to separate the manager from the coaches, trainers, players' own motivations, random happenstance, aging, and God only knows what else. Thus the researchers who focus solely on what can be proven by the numbers have shied away from the more amorphous parts of the manager's job.

Despite this, a few attempts to quantify managerial impact on players have been tried. In the *2003 Baseball Prospectus* annual, the section on the San Francisco Giants contained an examination of how manager Dusty Baker affected his hitters, concluding that batters improved by 8 percent under his watch. To date, that is the only statistical study that takes an in-depth look at how players improve or worsen under a particular manager.

Also, two similar studies have centered on pitching coach Leo Mazzone, formerly of the Braves and Orioles. Sabermetric researcher J. C. Bradbury did an investigation, included in his book *The Baseball Economist*, showing pitchers improving their ERA by 0.64 under Mazzone during his Braves tenure. Second, at the 35th annual SABR convention in 2005, a presentation titled "The Leo Mazzone Effect" by Peter Bendix and Matt Gallagher concluded that pitchers improved so much under Mazzone that he was more valuable than many of the game's biggest stars.

Shortly after those studies, James Click — then of Baseball Prospectus and currently employed by the Tampa Bay Rays— examined managers as a whole. In the book *Baseball Between the Numbers* by the Prospectus crew, Click performed a brief study about what impact managers have on their players, ultimately concluding that skippers had no meaningful effect on player performance. However, whatever the study's merits, he spent barely one page introducing, summarizing, and concluding the entire matter before moving on. Dismissing the existence of coaching requires a bit more time than that.

Ultimately, I have a much broader point of contention with Click's study. He never provides an argument to explain his study's results or a rationale to help the skeptical understand why his study is right and the opinions of a century's worth of people in and around the game are wrong. There is a sense that all one needs to know is the proper equation to understand the matter. This strikes me as misguided. It is necessary to provide such a rationale unless a person thinks that only quantitative information matters.

I have an admitted bias: I believe managers matter. To convince me otherwise would take more than an equation, no matter how brilliant its math. I need a clear and coherent argument based on ideas and thoughts instead of double regression studies and metrics. It takes words, not numbers, to convince me otherwise. Paragraphs make better arguments about human interactions than equations. Click never even tries to move beyond numbers, thus I reject his approach. I do not take issue with his formulas (in fact, I cannot even rebut them) as much as I do his mindset.

Fortunately, I do not think it is necessary to pick between words or numbers. One can have formulas whose underlying principles make sense to someone who does not have an advanced degree in math. For example, one could attempt to study all managers the way Bradbury and Bendix/Gallagher approached Mazzone, or how Prospectus examined Dusty Baker. Ideally, a database would compare how all players did each particular season to the surrounding ones, and determine if they over- or underachieved by a sensible mathematical formula. Fortuitously, a man named Phil Birnbaum did just that.

Enter the Birnbaum Database

At the 2005 SABR convention (the same one in which Gallagher and Bendix gave their presentation), Phil Birnbaum introduced a database he had created. He designed it to measure ways teams under- or overachieve in a given year, most notably performances by individual hitters and pitchers. For both batters and hurlers, Birnbaum created algorithms that determined how they should have done in a given season based on what they did in surrounding years. Birnbaum's algorithms are a huge breakthrough because you can grasp with some precision how a player met his expectations in a season. Running everyone who played under a manager through these algorithms should provide an idea how well he did at coaching and leading his men. While an appendix in the back of the book provides all the details on how the algorithms work, the next two paragraphs offer a brief summation.

Let's say you wanted to see if Tony Gwynn under- or overachieved in 1999. Birnbaum's hitting algorithm calculates the tech version of Bill James's Runs Created statistic in the four surrounding seasons (1997, 1998, 2000, and 2001) and adjusts the results for park and league. Armed with those numbers, you can estimate how many Runs Created that Gwynn should have had in 1999 by finding a weighted average of those surrounding seasons. In compiling this average, weight the campaigns immediately before and after (1998 and 2000 in this example) twice as much as the others. After weighting the seasons, regress to the mean. The result is an estimation of how many Runs Created that Gwynn should have tallied in 1999. From there, just pro rate the estimation based on Gwynn's real playing time to see if he under- or overachieved that year based on his performances in surrounding seasons. As an added bonus, the database's structure adjusts for where a person resides on the aging curve. A young player on his upswing is not just compared to his previous, lesser performances, but also to his upcoming seasons when he reaches his prime. Similarly, for someone declining there are factors against what he once was and what he would soon become.

Birnbaum created a similar algorithm for pitchers. The metric of choice is another James stat, Component ERA. Introduced in his *Win Shares* book, James described it as the Runs Created by the opposing hitters off a particular pitcher. The algorithms works the same basic way — take the four surrounding years, weigh the inner seasons twice as much, adjust for park and league, and regress to the mean.

These algorithms can cover almost all of baseball history. At one end, the Birnbaum Database has to stop two years before the most recently completed season to make the algorithms work. This book comes out after the 2008 campaign, so the Birnbaum Database ends in 2006. It starts in 1896 because when using Runs Created, you need all the stats that make up its formula, and 1894 was the first year baseball tabulated sacrifice hit data.

I initially tried to adapt Runs Created to make it work without sacrifice hits, but it broke down badly. The game underwent such drastic changes in the nineteenth century that any adjustments made for the mid–1890s would not effectively apply to major league ball in the early 1890s. As is, the little corner of the nineteenth century used by the algorithms yield its most questionable results. James never intended Runs Created to be used for pre–1900s baseball. Though the numbers for 1896–1900 are a tad fuzzier, the results work tolerably well.

In these algorithms, managerial influence is not the only factor affecting player performance. Luck is the most obvious other element coming into play. In fact, Phil Birnbaum initially put his database together in an attempt to measure luck (though he agrees it is a good tool to use for examining anything that can cause teams to under- or overachieve). Looking solely at one season, the database primarily notes a team's luck. Then again, the larger the sample size, the more luck evens out. If players continually exceed expectations under a particular manager, that is not luck. Thus, the longer a manager lasts on the job, the more the Birnbaum Database tells us about him.

For the moment, everything so far alleged on behalf of managerial influence has been solely theory and belief. To see if this has any merit, it needs to be tested and verified.

Testing It

Fortunately, there is a nice, quick 'n' dirty way to check if managers have an impact on these algorithms. First, divide all games from the Birnbaum Database into four categories: decisions where the skipper piloted teams at least 2,000 times (the "2000s"), games from managers who lasted 1,000–1,999 contests (the "1000s"), decisions by managers who lasted 500–999 games (the "500s"), and 1–499 games (the "499s"). After that, see if any difference exists in the scores in the different groups. If the longer groups do better, that is a sign that tells us something about managers.

This rests on the assumption that some correlation exists between managerial ability and length of service. As assumptions go, that one seems unusually safe and sensible. It is no accident that Maury Wills failed to last as long as Bobby Cox, or that Terry Bevington's tenure was less than that of Earl Weaver. Though obviously not all 2000s are better than the 1000s, nor are the 1000s all better than the 500s, but on the whole they should be better. Before getting to the results, let's stop and think about what they should look like if these components primarily tell us about luck or skill:

Luck	Skill
The 499s should do worst	The 499s should do worst
The 2000s should be the most average	The 2000s should be best
The gap between the 1000s and 2000s should be smallest	The gap between 500s and 1000s should be smallest

Either way, the 499s should be the worst. If the result is because of skill, they are the least talented. However, if luck was the cause, they lost their jobs because they were the unluckiest, hence that is a wash. Once you move beyond the 499s, things change. Again, the larger the sample size, the more luck should even out. Though luck does not always perfectly even out, over 2,000 games it should be mighty close to even. Please realize 2,000 is just the minimum number of games for the top group — many are over 3,000 or even 4,000 games. They should really be the most average. But if it is talent, they should definitely be the best. Since luck tends to even out over the longer runs, that means the gap between the larger groups should not be as great as the gap between the smaller groups. If, for example, the 499s score -4 runs per 162 games with individual pitchers, then maybe the 500s will come out at +2.5 runs, 1000s at +1.0 runs, and the 2000s at +0.5 runs. They are constantly coming closer to the middle, hence the gaps should be shortened. If it were skill, that would be the opposite of what one would expect. The 2000s should be dominated by the game's greats, the 499s should contain undue numbers of the worst, but the middle groups are each more average. Thus the results for the 500s and 1000s should be closest together.

However, something very important about the Birnbaum Database should be noted before moving on. It actually contains *five* separate components—the two algorithms along with three other areas of exploration. Phil Birnbaum's goal was to account for all ways teams under- or overachieve, not just player performance. Though his algorithms captured my attention, this study can run all five components. Reasonable arguments can be made that managers have an impact on the other areas as well.

Two of the components focus on team run scoring—one centers on team offense, the other on run prevention — which might tell us something about a manager's in-game strategic abilities. Even if his main job is to manage men, running the game is still a vital part of his job.

For offense, Phil Birnbaum compares how many runs a team scored with how many runs they would be projected to have scored based on their offensive accomplishments during the season. Plug the team's entire season's stat lines— their doubles, triples, sacrifices, stolen bases, and all the rest — into Bill James's Runs Created formula. Compare its results with how many runs the squad actually scored on the year. If a manager was especially adept at making tactical decisions, the team's runs could exceed their projection. Maybe he did an unusually good job calling for stolen bases on occasions when a single could and did drive the runner in. Proper timing matters in decision making. Perhaps he was especially efficient at filling out the lineup card. Alternately, if he did a bad job at these or other areas, his team could score fewer runs than one would expect, even if they hit the same number of doubles, triples, and had as many stolen bases as they would under a good manager. A manager is not the only thing that can create a differential between projected and actual run scoring, as other factors, most notably clutch hitting, affect the results. As was the case with the algorithms, one season's worth of sample size primarily indicates a team's luck—but that is why this study intends to look at larger stretches. Over a period of several years, things like clutch hitting should even out.

Birnbaum takes a similar approach with runs allowed. He uses Component ERA to compare actual runs allowed with projected runs allowed. Again, a single season tells us more about random happenstance than anything, but individual seasons are not this study's priority. A manager could conceivably affect a team's under/overachievement by how he runs his staff. If he knows when to take pitchers out, and who to bring in, it could determine things such as what percentage of inherited runners score.

The final component is even more contentious: Pythagorean formula. It is a classic sabermetric formula to gauge if a team under/overachieves. However, people ordinarily associate deviations from the Pythagorean record with luck. Birnbaum compared a team's actual win-loss record to a projected winning percentage using runs scored and allowed based on a variant of the Pythagorean formula known as pythagenpat. The classic Pythagorean formula everyone learned in math class squared the sides of a right triangle to find the length of the hypotenuse, and the traditional baseball variation of the Pythagorean formula squared runs scored and runs allowed to determine an approximate winning percentage: $RS^2/(RS^2 + RA^2)$. However, while an exponent of two is optimal for figuring out the relationship between sides of the triangle, it is not necessarily ideal for determining the relationship of runs and wins. An internet sabermatrician called Patriot figured out a formula considered by the acclamation of people far better at math than myself to be the ideal relationship of run scoring and wins. Rather than a constant exponent, it uses a variable one depending on the run environment. The exponent used for a given league is determined by the formula $(RS/G+RA/G)$ $^\wedge.287$. Though conventional wisdom contends that pythagenpat deviation is luck, it could not hurt to check. Besides, looking at the manager section in the *ESPN Baseball Encyclopedia* (which lists Pythagorean deviation for all managers in each season) reveals some skippers—such as Earl Weaver and Harry Wright—had strikingly consistent patterns for their careers. Personally, the algorithm-based components are the only ones I strongly feel say much about managers, but since it is possible the other three do as well and it is easy to check, this should be investigated.

Finally, before getting to the results of the 2000s/1000s/500s/499s test for all five components, one quick adjustment to the entire Birnbaum Database must be made: its numbers are not grounded at zero. Runs Created and Component ERA, like all stats, are imperfect and therefore do not perfectly capture the contours of run scoring for all periods of baseball history. For example, according to Runs Created, from 1994 to 2001 all teams combined to score 3,500 fewer times that they should have. That tells us more about the limitations of the stat than baseball in those years. Other eras have similar systematic problems. In some seasons a score of -7 runs can be more impressive than another year's mark of +6 runs. To compare across eras, everything should be centered at the same point, thus the results of all five components for each league in every year are re-centered at zero. This ensures a positive score always indicates an above average performance and negative scores consistently correlate with below average accomplishments. With that in mind, here are the results for all five components in runs per 162 games, all managers separated into 2000s/1000s/500s/499s:

Table I: Determining Managerial Impact

Category	2000s	1000s	500s	499s
Individual Hitting	+3.79	+0.34	−1.44	−8.21
Individual Pitching	+6.06	+1.34	−1.74	−15.20
Pythagenpat	+3.97	−1.58	−1.11	−6.07
Team Offense	+1.89	+1.31	−0.69	−5.94
Team Pitching	+1.84	−0.42	−0.29	−3.62
ALL	+17.55	+0.99	−5.27	−39.04

The results almost perfectly align with the notion of managerial skill. The 499s are always the worst and the 2000s always the best. The gaps between the 1000s and 500s are the smallest in four of the five components. A man who lasts fifteen to twenty years should not have shockingly more pronounced luck than someone who lasts eight years on the job; that flies in the face of reason. The Birnbaum Database indicates skill, not luck.

There are two results that go against the notion of skill—with pythagenpat and team pitching, the 500s narrowly top the 1000s. While these exceptions should be noted, I am hesitant to read too much into them. The difference between 1000s and 500s with team pitching is 0.13, which is the smallest gap in any component between two groups. The gap between 2000s and 1000s with team pitching is over seventeen times as large, and the 499s/500s gap is bigger still. The 0.47 gap between 1000s and 500s in pythagenpat is similarly paltry compared to the 2000s/1000s and 500s/499s in that component. There is an overall trend that cannot be missed—longer means better, in a way that confounds any notion of luck. Minor quirks in the data do not negate the overall result.

Moreover, the advantages the 500s bunching has over the 1000s in pythagenpat and team pitching component can be explained by a handful of managers right on the edge of 1,000 games itself. Of the 58 different individuals who managed 1,000 to 1,999 games from 1896 to 2006, Donie Bush managed the fewest games, with 1,036, and also scored -136 runs with team pitching. The other 57 managers in that group had a combined score of -79 runs in that component. If you move the boundary by just one manager, the 1000s top the 500s in team pitching. Also, Jack Hendricks, who managed 1,048 games, scored at -117 runs by this component. Alternately, of the 99 managers with 500 to 999 games managed, Roger Peckinpaugh, who managed 991 games (the most of anyone in the 500s cohort), had the best score with team pitching, at +134 runs. The superiority 500s have over 1000s in team pitching is a fluke caused by endpoint placements.

The same is also true of pythagenpat. The seven managers with the fewest games managed in the 1000s group combined to score -610 runs, while the seven skippers with the most games managed in the 500s scored +219 runs. Aside from those skippers, the 1000s scored -0.45 runs per 162 games at pythagenpat while the 500s post a mark of -2.46 runs. Please note there are no other gaps where the results from the above chart can be changed so easily. If I removed a handful of skippers just over and under 2,000 games managed, the 2000s would still easily best the 1000s in every component. The same is true of the 500s/499s border, and even the other components with the 500s/1000s boundary. Aside from the two occasions when the 500s top the 1000s, the gaps are too large to eradicate easily. Those two incidents do not negate the overall trend of the Birnbaum Database indicating managerial influence.

I cut up the data in a myriad of ways—divvying it into thirds, into sixths, into a litany of combinations. The results never quite came out perfectly, but they consistently refuted the luck storyline. That was especially true with the algorithms, which were the areas that first made me think the database could enlighten us about managerial performance.

Please note this chart falls far short of conclusive, purely mathematical proof that managers have an impact on any of these areas. It is evidence, but nothing definitive. However, I do not believe in limiting myself to mathematical rationales. This evidence beautifully corresponds to long-lasting and widely held notions that managers can and do have an impact on player performance. I therefore accept it.

The most extreme differences exist with individual pitchers, which intuitively makes sense. A manager who does not know what he is doing is more likely to ruin an arm through overuse while a savvier mind can keep him healthy. Even aside from health, knowing when to pull the starter can make a tremendous amount of difference. Also, managers need to decide who is best suited to the bullpen or the starting rotation. In the modern game, they also have to know what particular bullpen role best suits hurlers. These issues do not matter as much with hitters. Make someone a left fielder or a first baseman, and his offensive numbers should not be significantly affected.

Then again, the score with individual hitters is more extreme than any other component. That also makes sense. These results merely confirm the notion that the job is managing men first, and the game second. Apparently GMs like Mark Shapiro know what they are doing when they prioritize making sure their managers know how to handle the clubhouse first and foremost.

According to the above table, the difference between the best and worst managers is about 50–60 runs, or five or six wins per year. Then again, while there is a correlation between ability and length of career, it is not a perfect correlation. All baseball fans can name several long-lasting managers they think were terrible and others who deserved a better chance that they got. If this table indicates a five or six game split between the longest and shortest careers, the split between the best and worst should be even more substantial. Maybe just seven or eight or perhaps ten game difference between the elite and the dreadful.

Though pythagenpat failed to perfectly pass the above test, its results are still impressive. Prior to collecting this data, I expected this component to yield negligible results much more in tune with luck than skill. Instead, it generally shows managers playing a role in pythagenpat deviation. I am not as firm a believer that managers have an impact on pythagenpat deviation as I am that they affect how their hitters and pitchers play, but the results above are striking enough for me to give managers the benefit of the doubt that they play a role in this component as well. Frankly, the algorithm-based components are the only ones I am completely convinced indicate managerial skill, but the results from the 2000s/1000s/500s/499s chart make me fairly sure managers play a role with the other components.

This leads to the question of how managers could impact a team's pythagenpat differential. One way to exceed a pythagenpat projection is to have a remarkably consistent offense. In the summer of 2005, *Hardball Times* writer Dave Studenmund examined that year's White Sox squad, who were exceeding their pythagenpat projection. He noticed their secret was steadily scoring runs as they rarely scored ten runs in a game but were difficult to shut down entirely.

Let's think about this. If a team has scored nine runs in a game, getting a tenth run does not substantially alter their chances of winning. Squads almost always win after they scored nine runs, and number ten provides only a minute uptick in their chances of victory. Something similar exists at the other end. Teams have no chance to win when shut out, and minimal chance with only one run. That first run helps— more than the tenth run does— but does not make much of a difference. However, when a team moves from three to four runs, or from four to five, the chances of winning move up substantially. Adding on the third, fourth, and fifth runs normally means the most.

This means a consistent offense should exceed their win projection. To demonstrate this, let's use two extreme examples involving a pair of fictional teams that each averages six runs scored per game. One scores twelve runs in half their games and is shut out in the other half. That squad will finish .500 at best. They will lose all the games with no runs, and win all (or nearly all) the others. The other team, however, scores exactly six runs in each game. They will win most of their contests. When teams are consistent, they constantly score enough to give your team a chance to win. Studenmund discovered the 2005 White Sox's consistent offense kept finding that sweet spot on the runs scored slope.

A manager can have an effect on offensive consistency. He keeps the team ready on a day-in, day-out basis by keeping guys healthy, motivated, and playing well. It is up to the manager to ensure his players are properly rested. Though the skipper is not the only factor affecting offensive consistency, using sample size to control for other factors should shed light on this area.

In 2007, Diamondbacks manager Bob Melvin demonstrated another way a team can beat its projection. That season, Arizona won 90 games despite allowing more runs than they scored. That partially— though by no means entirely— stemmed from the way Melvin used his bullpen. When his team fell well behind, he consistently tapped his dreg relievers. Most managers try to avoid using their better arms when it does not matter, but few went as far as Melvin. On multiple occasions Melvin placed position players on the hill during blowouts in order to save Arizona's important arms. As a result of Melvin's bullpen usage, two things occurred. First, the Diamondbacks performed especially poorly in blowouts, because they had so many terrible arms pitch in those games. Despite possessing the league's best record, they went 20–26 in games decided by five or more runs. Second, they played great in close games, in part because Melvin made sure his best relievers were always available for tight contests. Result: Arizona beat their expected win-loss mark by eleven games. Luck also played a substantial role, but it was not the only factor. Ensuring the best arms are always on the mound in tight situations and ruthlessly reserving slop arms for unessential moments can help a team defy Pythagorean. In Melvin's case, his usage of his bullpen helped the team to beat their expected mark and win more games.

Special Problem with Team Pitching Component

One very important problem must be noted: a considerable flaw exists in the team runs allowed component. To calculate Component ERA, one needs doubles and triples by opposing hitters. This information only exists when the Retrosheet website has provided the public with all box scores for a season. In the Birnbaum Database, that is only 1960–onward. For earlier years, Phil Birnbaum used an estimator that figured approximate numbers so he ran them through his database. Now this is using one estimator to determine another—a second-generation guess. That is *terrible* math. It is tempting to throw out this component altogether. However, it still contains some validity. When looking exclusively at 1960–onwards (when the numbers used are real ones), managers who lasted 2,000 or more games in that period do better than the 1000s, who beat the 500s, who top the 499s, indicating the component's importance. The 1896–1959 info remains shaky, at best.

The goal becomes minimizing this component's distortion for the time before Retrosheet. Three elements can warp the stat — managers, luck, and stadiums. The last two variables need to be factored out as best as possible to shed light on the first one. The entire study has the same approach when dealing with luck: use sample sizes to neutralize it. If that is the case when examining managers who last five to ten years, then it should apply when adjusting for stadiums that lasted over a half-century. Thus, the correction focuses on parks, assuming luck works itself out.

Stadiums require an adjustment because the particular configuration of a ballpark can cause an unusual amount of doubles or triples to be hit there, making a mockery of Birnbaum's extra base estimator. A quick correction can lessen park effect. Take the Giants' old Polo Grounds, for example. From its construction in 1912, until the Giants moved out, the club averaged about +0.068 more runs per game than the formula expects them to; in other words approximately +11 runs per year. That is not necessarily all park, though. The whole point of this study is that managers have an impact as well. If John McGraw or Bill Terry had a pronounced trend, that could skew the data.

To adjust for the stadium, estimate that the Polo Grounds is responsible for half of that +11 runs a year, and adjust every season the Giants played there by about +5.5 runs. Why make the estimate half park and half manager? Frankly, it is a pure guess. Estimating that this is 75 percent one element and 25 percent the other opens up the possibility of being wildly off on both. This way, the margin of error is reduced.

From one perspective, this becomes ridiculous. I am making a guess, to fix a run approximation, to determine a third estimation. Math professors have burned people at the stake for less than this. Yet each estimation makes sense on its own, and improves the results. However, of all the five components, you should have the least faith in this one. If you ignore it entirely, I would not begrudge you.

Problems and Limitations of This Study

Before revealing how individual managers score in the Birnbaum Database, I should pause to note this study's broader shortcomings and quirks. First, some managers only last part of the year, getting hired and fired midseason. There is no perfect way to handle this. This study takes the number of games an individual managed in a season, divides it by the team's games played and then multiplies that by how they did in each of the five components. This approach acts if it made no difference whom the manager is, which completely negates the point of the study.

Two things minimize this problem. First, changing managers rarely causes extreme shifts in fortunes. A managerial change has an effect, but many managers are roughly similar in their capabilities. Second and more importantly, the longer a manager lasts, the greater a percentage of games he manages come from full seasons. Even Billy Martin, the patron saint of rapidly hired and fired managers, had over two-thirds of his games occur in complete campaigns.

Another concern is that this study does not correct a flaw in Phil Birnbaum's original presentation as much as it reverses one. Birnbaum believed his database only measured differences due to luck and ignored all else. Here, managers alone are held responsible. Obviously, luck still factors in, distorting the numbers. There is, alas, no pure way to distill a manager from his team. Sample size largely minimizes this problem as the odds on being lucky year after year are quite long, but that does not guarantee luck plays no role.

However, luck is not the only factor bleeding into the mix: team quality also does. A manager who scores +2 runs for a team with 100 losses had a fantastic year. Alternately, +2 for a 100-win team indicates a poor managerial performance. It is very rare for a manager to field continually negative scores for a team with consistent winning records; enough of a trend exists to indicate team quality affects the numbers. While better teams should have good managers, players are still by far the most important factor in a club's success. Ultimately, the longer a manager lasts the less likely he is to work continually for excellent or for horrid franchises. Also, since the main focus will be on the all-time leaders, it is mighty tricky to make a leaderboard unless one really does something right (or horribly wrong).

This study ignores still another key factor affecting player performance—coaches. Leo Mazzone, Johnny Sain, Charlie Lau, and Walt Hrniak do not exist according to this study, which cannot be right. Frankly, I have no idea how one would go about divvying up credit between the manager and his coaches. Even assuming it is possible (and that is by no means certain), it is beyond my capabilities.

Next, long-term player-coach relationships wash themselves out in Birnbaum algorithms for the first two components. How would one go about trying to separate Albert Pujols from Tony LaRussa? Every game in his career has been under LaRussa. If LaRussa seriously affected Pujols, whether positive or negative, it will not show. No good solution exists for this. It should be noted this facet is unaccounted for.

Also, this study overlooks entire aspects of a manager's job. For example, it assumes a manager will play the right person, and keep the proper people on the bench. That is not always the case, but this study makes no value judgments on that subject.

The Main Problem: Statistical Analysis and the Nature of the Job

Some of the above listed problems, such as how this study ignores coaches, hint at the central defect in this study: it is a false notion that credit for coaching/managerial impact can ever be perfectly doled out appropriately to individuals. Therefore, any attempt to try—such as this one—will be flawed.

For example, the 1990–2005 Braves were extraordinarily successful in getting production from their pitchers. Hurlers without much success would come, flourish, and return to their bad old ways upon departure. This tendency for pitchers to suddenly improve themselves in Atlanta was so pronounced for such a long period of time that it strains credulity to claim it was luck. Team manager Bobby Cox found success with pitchers previously in his career, but nothing that approached the success of these clubs. General manager John Schuerholz assembled a terrific pitching staff in his previous job running the Royals, but that team's success also paled in comparison to the Atlanta miracle. Thus pitching coach Leo Mazzone received much credit for this "Mazzone Effect." However, when Mazzone served as pitching coach for the Orioles from 2006–07, the result was a disaster. The team's pitching worsened, bottoming out in the last 40 games of 2007 when the staff had an ERA of 7.47, the worst stretch for that long a period by any team since at least the 1930s. The Mazzone Effect cannot be pinned on anyone, even the man it is named after.

There is a word that can describe what is going, and it is often a dirty word in sabermetrics: chemistry. It was not Cox, Mazzone, nor Schuerholz—but how they all worked together. And not just how they interacted and reinforced each other, but how they all interacted with the players and the trainers, and how all these elements worked together. I once heard an illuminating comment from an Atlanta fan on how he thought the Cox/Mazzone system worked. Cox and Mazzone began with total authority and no star pitchers. They nurtured two, John Smoltz and Tom Glavine, who both accepted their lead, and the club signed Greg Maddux who also supported Cox and Mazzone, greatly enhancing their authority. Further aiding this stature was an effective working relationship with each other and the front office. All these factors made it far less likely for any other pitcher to challenge or question them. Therefore they could continue to press their way with minimal problems. The Braves fan concluded that if Mazzone went elsewhere his success would not be duplicated because all the circumstances beyond his control would not follow him. This makes sense, though good luck trying to quantify it.

Ultimately, coaching is an *art* and this study treats it as a *science*. Trying to create a coaching staff and front office is like forming a music group. It does not matter how great the bass player or drummer or guitarist is if they are unable to play together. If a great manager has a fabulous pitching coach, and they are both under a world class GM, the team will suffer if they are not all on the same page. This study treats managers in a strictly reductionist way that misses the nuances. The manager is a key — the key, in my opinion — but they are all also creatures of the circumstances in which they worked.

Overall though, the Birnbaum Database works well. While it has its limitations and imperfections — Phil Birnbaum would be the first person to agree to that — imperfect is not a synonym for useless. Ultimately, it makes a very effective, quick 'n' dirty attempt to gauge how managers succeed or fail. Besides, no statistical formula will ever be perfect, and this works rather well. Sometimes you have to settle for good enough, and the Birnbaum Database is full of Good-Enoughedness.

The Fun Stuff: Results

So much for the background. Now for the main event — the results. First I will go component by component, and then present the combined totals.

Component I: Individual Pitchers

The most important parts of the database are Phil Birnbaum's algorithms for how players under/overachieve, also referred to as the coaching components. Let's start with the pitching algorithm because that had the most extreme splits between 2000s and 500s. First, here are the top twenty managers from 1896 to 2006 with individual pitchers:

List 1: Best with Individual Pitchers, 1896–2006

1.	Joe McCarthy	+649 runs
2.	Bobby Cox	+607 runs
3.	Al Lopez	+472 runs
4.	Walter Alston	+459 runs
5.	Tony LaRussa	+455 runs
6.	John McGraw	+415 runs
7.	Earl Weaver	+409 runs
8.	Bill McKechnie	+402 runs
9.	Fred Clarke	+395 runs
10.	Paul Richards	+342 runs
11.	Billy Southworth	+336 runs

List 1: Best with Individual Pitchers, 1896–2006 (continued)

12.	Frank Selee	+331 runs
13.	Tommy Lasorda	+306 runs
14.	Jimy Williams	+305 runs
15.	Pat Moran	+276 runs
16.	Whitey Herzog	+256 runs
17.	Billy Martin	+234 runs
18.	Frank Chance	+232 runs
19.	Mike Scioscia	+214 runs
20t.	Bucky Harris	+206 runs
20t.	Jack McKeon	+206 runs

Any study should do two things. First, it should normally align with conventional wisdom. While not perfect, popular perceptions on the best and worst are more right than wrong. Second, when the study veers from accepted belief, it should be able to explain itself.

The Birnbaum Database does both. This list has the right names on top. Bobby Cox had a great reputation with pitchers. Walter Alston won for twenty years with super moundsmen. Bill McKechnie won pennants with three separate teams by emphasizing pitching. Paul Richards earned the nickname "The Wizard of Waxahachie" for his ability to work with pitchers. The surprises also make sense. The most obscure name above is Pat Moran, a forgotten manager from the 1910s and 1920s. Looking at his record, though, pitchers routinely improved when they played for him. Frank Chance and Fred Clarke are remembered more as players than managers, but both had tremendous success with pitchers. In particular, both used pitchers differently from most of their peers. Rather than relying heavily on one or two, both Chance's Cubs and Clarke's Pirates spread out the innings among several starters, assuring that they had fresh men on the mound more often.

Atop the leaderboard two managers dominate all the others: Joe McCarthy and Bobby Cox. McCarthy's Yanks are remembered for their awe-inspiring offenses, but he received good production from his pitchers as well. The most famous turnaround for him was Red Ruffing, who transformed from a scuffling starter to a Hall of Famer upon joining McCarthy's Yankees. Cox scores so well largely because from 1990 to 2005, when partnered with pitching coach Leo Mazzone, the Braves scored at +598 runs, which is the best sixteen-year stretch any team has ever had. This list underestimates Cox because Maddux, Smoltz, and Glavine served under him for an extended period of time, eating up 40 percent of the team's innings each year, and as previously noted, long-term player-manager relations wash themselves out. Cox might deserve to rate higher than McCarthy when that is included.

That was the good. Now for the bad — here are the twenty worst managers at coaching individual pitchers:

List 2: Worst with Individual Pitchers, 1896–2006

1.	Don Baylor	−530 runs
2.	Connie Mack	−419 runs
3.	Art Fletcher	−361 runs
4.	Burt Shotton	−348 runs
5.	Jimmie Wilson	−315 runs
6.	Zach Taylor	−313 runs
7.	Jim Marshall	−291 runs
8.	Buddy Bell	−285 runs
9.	Clint Hurdle	−279 runs
10.	Jim Leyland	−278 runs

List 2: Worst with Individual Pitchers, 1896–2006 (continued)

11.	Fred Tenney	−251 runs
12.	Tom Kelly	−249 runs
13t.	Fred Haney	−233 runs
13t.	Dave Bristol	−233 runs
15.	John McNamara	−224 runs
16.	Rogers Hornsby	−218 runs
17.	Jerry Narron	−211 runs
18.	Frank Robinson	−165 runs
19.	Terry Francona	−193 runs
20.	Fred Hutchinson	−185 runs

This list reveals a significant problem with the Birnbaum Database: its difficulty handling Denver's Coors Field. Only four men have ever managed the Rockies: Don Baylor, Jim Leyland, Clint Hurdle, and Buddy Bell—all of whom make the list's bottom ten.

A couple of factors explain this oddity. First, Denver is such an extreme environment that it is impossible to account for it perfectly. To refresh, Component ERA does not always treat each run scoring environment the same. Normally, this is only a serious concern when comparing across eras—which is why each year for every league is normalized at zero. Park factors exist, but they generally have a minor impact. Coors Field (and Mile High Stadium, where the Rockies played for their first two seasons) are exceptions. Park factor in Denver is so extreme that it essentially rivals the effect an era can have on Component ERA. If the rest of the league averages five runs a game, then Coors will be around seven. Thus its park factor creates significant distortions in the Birnbaum Database.

Second, even if one adjusted for the supersized park factor, that would not adjust for how the park gets inside a pitcher's head. For example, curveballer Darryl Kile nearly ruined his career by pitching for Denver in 1998–99. His curve flattened out in the mountain air, causing him to lose confidence. He stopped throwing the ball over the plate, nibbling at the corners instead. His strikeouts plummeted and walks skyrocketed—both at home and on the road. It totally disrupted how he approached the game, which explains why simply adjusting for park factor will not solve this. There is not much a manager can do about that; he cannot lower Denver.

Though Coors warps the numbers for Denver managers, the Colorado quartet also finished so badly because the Rockies hire managers who are not very good at handling pitchers. Everyone except Hurdle has worked outside of Denver, and they all score quite poorly at sea level. Buddy Bell, for example, presided over the 1996 Tigers, who allowed more runs than any other team since the 1930s.

Don Baylor truly was the worst at handling pitchers. While Coors Field unfairly lowers his number, another factor unduly aids him. While managing the Cubs in 2001, his pitchers scored +51 runs. They were Baylor's only staff to exceed expectations—and he had nothing to do with their success. The pitchers loudly gave as much credit as possible to the team's pitching coach, Oscar Acosta, whom Baylor canned late in the season due to internal politics. The pitchers were horrified, and there was even talk some pitchers wanted to refuse to pitch the next game in protest. That never happened, but clearly Baylor's only quality staff thought very little of him. Aside from 2001, Baylor scores -581 runs for his career, far worse than anyone else. Watching him manage made it clear he had no idea how to handle a staff. Some managers determine if a pitcher is tiring by noticing how his trailing leg looks in his follow-through, or how his back looks when pitching. Others use the radar gun or track pitch counts. Baylor used no discernable method. Pitch counts could be high, the fastball could lose speed, and the hurler could be clearly melting on the mound and Baylor would leave him in. With the Cubs, Baylor was in charge of Kerry Wood when the young fireballer returned from Tommy John surgery. Baylor's handling of Wood was utter madness as he kept Wood in when he was clearly on fumes. Coors or no Coors, Baylor had no clue how to handle his pitchers.

Two factors beyond Jim Leyland's control mar his score. One was the Coors Field effect as his stint in Colorado came precisely when Darryl Kile collapsed. The 1999 Rockies scored -184 runs in Leyland's only Colorado season. Leyland's second qualifying factor was his managing the 1998 Marlins. That year team owner Wayne Huizenga held a giant fire sale, sending virtually all his quality players to the winds, because he was upset that the local community refused to grant him a new stadium deal. Under the theory that front office and coaching staff chemistry matters, it was almost impossible to imagine any manager in the world could succeed in that situation. That team scored -132 runs with this component. Aside from those two years, Leyland is +38 runs.

That is all true, but one should not let Leyland off the hook too much. Not only was his one year in Colorado the worst season the Rockies have ever had, but it is the worst any team did in this component since 1900. Yes, there was the ballpark and the Darryl Kile Effect, but that does not absolve the century's worst mark. While one year's total primarily indicates luck, the worst score of modern times can only mean that everything went wrong for the team — including the manager's performance. Besides, Leyland's numbers were also bad in Pittsburgh. Also, while his score is positive when those two terrible seasons are deducted, that may not be the case for much longer. While with Detroit in 2006, Leyland scored +114 runs, (easily the best of his career) partially because the team's arms wilted so badly in 2007–08. When those years are added to the Birnbaum Database, Leyland's score will suffer, possibly pushing him into the bottom five. The 2006 Tigers stick out as the aberration, not the Rockies. Leyland is not as bad with pitchers as the Birnbaum Database indicates, but that does not mean he is good.

A problem similar to the Denver effect could distort the score for managers who worked in Philadelphia's old Baker Bowl. Though it initially performed as a neutral field from its opening in the 1890s, once the rest of the teams constructed larger edifices in the early 1910s the small bandbox became the NL's most extreme hitters park, a claim it routinely held from 1912 to 1937. Art Fletcher, Burt Shotton, and Jimmie Wilson, who each make the bottom five in this category, all managed in that facility.

While Baker Bowl likely was partially responsible for lowering their scores, it is doubtful it was nearly as significant a factor as the stadiums in Denver. First, Baker Bowl's park factor was not nearly as severe. Baseball-Reference.com often lists Coors Field with a park factor around 120, while Baker Bowl generally hovered at 110. While that is significant, it is closer to 1970s Fenway Park than Denver. Also, from 1915 to 1918, Pat Moran managed in that stadium, yet scores as the fifteenth best manager with individual pitchers. To be fair, Baker Bowl was not as extreme a hitter's park as it later became, but in 1918, when the stadium was easily the league's worst place for pitchers, Moran scored +19 runs in this component.

If a lurking variable hurts the Phillies' managers, it is more likely team quality. Between Pete Alexander and Robin Roberts, the Phillies lodged sixteen consecutive seasons with losing records, went 78–76 in 1932, then posted another fourteen straight sub -.500 seasons. If one combines their best April, May, June, July, August, and September/October records they ever recorded in that 31-year stretch, the resulting sum would still not be good enough to win most NL pennants in that period; stop and think how bad a team must be to "achieve" that. They experienced a dozen 100-loss seasons, and eleven more containing 90 to 99 defeats. They never finished higher than seventh the entire time Franklin Delano Roosevelt served as president.

The above covers not only years in the Baker Bowl, but the club's initial Shibe Park experience. Doc Prothro, the club's first post–Baker Bowl manager, nearly makes the bottom list with a score of -158 runs despite a career that lasted only three seasons. Club quality likely unfairly skews the Phillie managers downward, but odds are the club also hired bad managers. After all, they fielded a series of rotten pitchers, dismal gloves, and forgettable hitters— why would one expect much from their managers? Shotton, Fletcher, and Wilson do not necessarily all belong in the bottom five, but that leaves them plenty of room in the bottom twenty.

Leaving Denver and Philadelphia behind, there are some other interesting names listed. Connie Mack was a creature of extremes. In his good stretches, his career through 1914 and the 1925–32 A's, he scores +357 runs. In his other years, he did as badly as anyone in history. In a testament to how important handling individual pitchers is to a manager's job, not only is Connie Mack the only Hall of Fame skipper in the bottom twenty, but he is also the only immortal with a negative score at all. The next worst is Sparky Anderson at +22 runs. Clearly, a skipper ought to know how to handle his pitchers in order to manage his way into Cooperstown.

The biggest shock is Fred Hutchinson, a well-regarded former Reds manager. The first team he managed for a full season, the 1953 Tigers, murders him. Their ERA was 5.25, a full point higher than the previous season. Going by Adjusted ERA, a stat in the *ESPN Encyclopedia* that adjusts for ballpark and league, the 1953 Tigers were baseball's worst pitching staff since World War II.

Tom Kelly is another unexpected entrant; his failing was to trust pitching long after it made any sense to do so. The most obvious example was his handling of LaTroy Hawkins. Kelly gave him twenty starts in 1997, and the pitcher responded with a 5.84 ERA. That did not faze Kelly, who let Hawkins start all 1998. The pitcher improved, to a point, with a 5.25 ERA. He kept him in the rotation throughout 1999 as a result, despite a 6.66 ERA. There is a fine line between being supportive and foolhardy. That was fairly typical for Kelly, though. He let Jim DeShaies start all year for the 1994 Twins, despite a 7.39 ERA. Mike Smithson had a 5.94 mark in 1987. All those horrific innings ruin his score.

Component II: Individual Hitters

Now for the other half of the Birnbaum's algorithms. These managers got the most out of their hitters:

List 3: Best with Individual Hitters, 1896–2006

1.	Joe McCarthy	+550 runs
2.	John McGraw	+344 runs
3.	Lou Piniella	+300 runs
4.	Billy Southworth	+298 runs
5.	Bruce Bochy	+270 runs
6.	Sparky Anderson	+259 runs
7.	Tony LaRussa	+240 runs
8.	Bucky Harris	+230 runs
9.	Leo Durocher	+225 runs
10.	Casey Stengel	+224 runs
11.	Davey Johnson	+209 runs
12.	Tris Speaker	+201 runs
13.	Earl Weaver	+183 runs
14.	Miller Huggins	+178 runs
15.	Billy Martin	+177 runs

List 3: Best with Individual Hitters, 1896–2006 (continued)

16.	Joe Cronin	+174 runs
17.	Joe Torre	+166 runs
18.	Gene Mauch	+163 runs
19.	Danny Ozark	+160 runs
20t.	Mel Ott	+154 runs
20t.	Ty Cobb	+154 runs

Joe McCarthy is the greatest manager in baseball history. It is the perfect storm: put the best manager ever on the best franchise with the best front office and a great farm system and the result is comically high scores. Then again, even away from New York he did exceptionally well. Though he scores +434 runs with individual hitters in New York, the remainder of his career would make him 27th best; not bad considering that was around seven years worth of games.

The biggest jolt is Lou Piniella finishing third. His score is primarily caused by his time with the Mariners and Devil Rays. The 2001 Mariners, whom Piniella managed, scored +131 runs in this component, the highest by any team in the database. For that accomplishment, everything must have gone right for the team — including how Piniella handled the hitters. The rest of his managerial career shows the 2001 campaign was no fluke. Alex Rodriquez was only eighteen when he debuted under Piniella. One can easily imagine a scenario where a skipper mishandles his young, highly talented charge, either letting him rot on the bench or disdainfully throwing him to the wolves. While in Seattle, Piniella nurtured Rodriquez, and looked after his interests on the field. By age twenty, A-Rod was the MVP runner-up. Piniella received the most from his offensive core, which included Ken Griffey Jr., Edgar Martinez, and Jay Buhner. Piniella also oversaw an All-Star Game appearance from journeyman middle infielder Joey Cora, oversaw Mike Cameron's development at the plate, presided over Mark McLemore's unlikely mid–30s offensive surge, and got the most from Paul Sorrento. In Tampa, his most famous decision was calling for 21-year-old Rocco Baldelli's promotion, even though he had only played 40 games above Class A ball in the minors. The move, criticized at the time, worked out very well.

Piniella's stint with the Cubs has not yet affected his score, but it will drive him into second place. The club had come next-to-last in runs scored in 2006 just before he arrived. Just two years later, they led the league, with 50 runs more than the runner-up. A half-dozen men who qualified for the batting title had an OBP over .350, which last happened to the Cubs in 1935.

One surprising absence is Piniella's predecessor in Chicago, Dusty Baker. As noted at the outset of the chapter, Baker's uncanny ability to get the most out of his hitters in San Francisco caused the first serious statistical survey of a manager's effect on his players. Looking exclusively at his tenure with the Giants, he scored +217 runs, easily enough to qualify. Chicago did not go nearly as well for him, though, especially 2006, his final season. Through 2005, Baker had a career mark of +175 runs, which would be worth sixteenth place on the above list, but 2006 knocked him down to +119 runs, in 26th place. Everything went wrong in 2006, not just with the Cubs but also Baker. He spent all year sending out a vibe that he was unhappy and did not want to be there. Few things hurt an organization, baseball or otherwise, than to hear their leader sound despondent. Chemistry matters in managing, and it cost him in Chicago.

Tris Speaker, Ty Cobb and Mel Ott are all known as great hitters, but rarely thought of as managers, let alone particularly good ones. Speaker was extremely successful, guiding the Indians to their first ever world title in 1920. His handling of the team's offense was a main reason why they won that title, as he extensively platooned his hitters, allowing him to get the most out of his bats. Thus it makes sense to see him here. Cobb did not know how to run his pitchers, but his lifetime devotion to the art of hitting helped him coach the Detroit batters. Catcher Johnny Bassler and first baseman Lu Blue both emerged as solid offensive threats under Cobb. Bobby Veach and Cobb himself had late-career surges when he became manager. Harry Heilmann had his first Hall of Fame–caliber season in Cobb's inaugural season as skipper. Donald Honig's *Baseball When the Grass Was Real* recounts how Cobb also nurtured a young Charlie Gehringer for the Tigers. Ott also was at his best with individual hitters. In 1947, he managed a Giants squad that hit 221 homers, shattering the existing team record. Only one other baseball team that year was within 100 of them, and no NL squad bested Ott's squad until the 1997 Rockies. Ott had problems with every other aspect of the job, but he could get his hitters to produce.

Here are the worst at effectively handling their hitters:

List 4: Worst with Individual Hitters, 1896–2006

1.	Jimmy Dykes	−219 runs
2.	Wilbert Robinson	−178 runs
3.	Luke Sewell	−175 runs
4.	Hal McRae	−170 runs
5.	Dave Bristol	−168 runs
6.	Clint Hurdle	−158 runs
7.	Lloyd McClendon	−151 runs
8.	Buck Rodgers	−150 runs
9.	Connie Mack	−149 runs
10.	Bill McKechnie	−145 runs
11.	Bobby Cox	−141 runs
12.	Billy Gardner	−139 runs
13.	Jim Riggleman	−133 runs
14.	Frank Selee	−127 runs
15.	Cookie Lavagetto	−119 runs
16t.	Rene Lachemann	−118 runs
16t.	Jim Marshall	−118 runs
18.	Bob Boone	−115 runs
19.	Del Baker	−114 runs
20.	Lee Fohl	−112 runs

Baseball lore contends that Connie Mack let his coaches do much of the actual managing in his final years. Fittingly, one of those coaches was Dykes, who appears atop the list while Mack places ninth. Mack remained above average until 1942, but fell hard.

Several Hall of Fame–caliber managers make this list — Frank Selee, Bobby Cox, Wilbert Robinson and Bill McKechnie — who all won with pitching and defense. Since the Birnbaum Database's individual pitcher scores are more extreme than its individual hitters marks, it shows a manager who has trouble with hitters has a greater chance of success than one who cannot work with pitchers. Selee reveals how one could be successful without necessarily doing a good job with hitters. Going by Pete Palmer's batting runs statistic, Selee's long-time first baseman Fred Tenney exploded as soon as Selee left Boston. Making it all the more remarkable, Tenney's rapid improvement came as soon as he reached his 30s, when he should have been declining. The career of Jimmy Collins, Selee's Hall of Fame third baseman, followed a similar pattern. Tommy Tucker produced far more with his bat at age 33 in Washington than he had in the previous several years in Boston.

Jim Marshall is also worth discussing. Amazingly, he was one of the twenty worst with both individual hitters and pitchers despite managing only three and a half years. His problem was the 1979 A's, a club that combined the worst aspects of the 1998 Marlins with the less pleasant features of a raiding Visigoth horde. Oakland owner Charles Finley was always difficult to put up with, but at least in the early days his teams could focus on their talent. By 1979 free agency had wrecked his dynasty, and Finley lacked the economic resources to remain competitive. He went out of his way to ruin the atmosphere just for its own sake. There's one story of a new employee walking into the main club lobby and instead of a secretary at the desk, there was just a sign telling him where to get coffee. The team public relations man wanted to write a letter to all remaining season-ticket holders and found all their names and addresses fit easily on a sheet of paper. Then again, Marshall was a bad manager. His previously managed the Cubs, and they got noticeably worse when he began and improved by approximately ten games upon his departure.

Component III: Pythagenpat

The first two components are the most important, but the next three are also worth exploring. The following managers did the best at exceeding their team's win-loss records:

List 5: Best at Pythagenpat, 1896–2006

1.	Bill McKechnie	+330 runs
2.	Joe Torre	+278 runs
3.	Bobby Cox	+264 runs
4.	Walter Alston	+245 runs
5.	Wilbert Robinson	+243 runs
6.	Bobby Valentine	+237 runs
7.	Felipe Alou	+228 runs
8.	Hughie Jennings	+225 runs
9.	Ralph Houk	+220 runs
10.	Dick Howser	+202 runs
11.	Clark Griffith	+201 runs
12.	Sparky Anderson	+197 runs
13.	George Gibson	+195 runs
14.	Ron Gardenhire	+187 runs
15.	Jimmy Dykes	+185 runs
16.	Al Lopez	+183 runs
17.	Lum Harris	+182 runs
18.	Billy Martin	+179 runs
19.	Jack McKeon	+176 runs
20.	Don Zimmer	+174 runs

To be clear, pythagenpat projections are normally listed in terms of wins, not runs, but using the standard sabermetric shorthand of ten runs per win, this can be adjusted as shown above to keep this component in line with the others.

Ron Gardenhire's inclusion on the list points to another way for managers to exceed their expected pythagenpat records—by winning extra-inning games. Gardenhire's Twins are 69–47 (.595) in them, a feat which is not merely luck, as Gardenhire has done a superlative job developing a strong bullpen in Minnesota. Extra-inning games are frequently bullpen endurance competitions.

Looking at the list of names above, it is striking how many big names are on this list. Almost all of these men have good reputations. Seven of these men are Hall of Famers or will be upon their retirement, and Earl Weaver just misses this list, coming in 21st place at +173 runs. Billy Martin is one of the best managers not currently inducted, and Clark Griffith may have made it as a manager if he had not become an owner. Gardenhire has been splendid managing the Twins. If beating pythagenpat projections were just luck, the list of names would be more random. Even if the extra wins given them by this component are stripped away, these men would remain terrific managers with impressive records. Altogether, they are 3,300 games over .500; adjust for their pythagenpat deviation and they were still over 2,800 games better than .500. Certainly, it contains more big names here than the worst at pythagenpat, who are listed below:

List 6: Worst at Pythagenpat, 1896–2006

1. Bucky Harris	−332 runs
2. Jimmie Wilson	−296 runs
3. Jimy Williams	−254 runs
4. Hugh Duffy	−227 runs
5t. Buddy Bell	−207 runs
5t. Eric Wedge	−207 runs
7. Preston Gomez	−204 runs
8. Tommy Lasorda	−200 runs
9. Jim Riggleman	−199 runs
10. Bobby Bragan	−198 runs
11. Joe Kelley	−190 runs
12. Larry Dierker	−171 runs
13. Dallas Green	−148 runs
14. Mel Ott	−138 runs
15t. Leo Durocher	−134 runs
15t. Phil Garner	−134 runs
17. Doug Rader	−133 runs
18t. Clint Hurdle	−132 runs
18t. Sam Mele	−132 runs
20. Tris Speaker	−126 runs

There are some impressive names here — most notably three Hall of Famers — but those names are lost among a sea of Hugh Duffys and Doug Raders. Instead of eight Hall of Fame–caliber skippers in the top 21, one has to forage beyond the bottom 100 to find five more immortals. If someone wants to argue that managers have little impact on this component, I would not argue against them as vigorously as I would with Birnbaum's algorithm-based components, but one should not try to create a stark black/white dichotomy. It is not a matter of managers versus luck with pythagenpat deviation. Just because luck is the most important determinant in this component, that does not mean it is the only factor.

Component IV: Team Offense

The final two components are the strategic ones, showing which managers made the best decisions at the right times. The fourth component analyzes which offenses scored more runs than they should have:

List 7: Best at Team Offense, 1896–2006

1. Leo Durocher	+333 runs
2. Tony LaRussa	+297 runs
3. Frank Chance	+274 runs

List 7: Best at Team Offense, 1896–2006 (continued)

4. Fred Clarke	+237 runs
5. Dick Williams	+216 runs
6. Joe McCarthy	+190 runs
7. Bucky Harris	+188 runs
8. Frank Selee	+186 runs
9. Frankie Frisch	+182 runs
10. Bill McKechnie	+169 runs
11. Tom Trebelhorn	+167 runs
12. Walter Alston	+156 runs
13. Fielder Jones	+155 runs
14. Hugh Duffy	+152 runs
15. Phil Garner	+151 runs
16. Pat Moran	+140 runs
17t. Buddy Bell	+135 runs
17t. Casey Stengel	+135 runs
19. Donie Bush	+130 runs
20. Art Howe	+124 runs

It is striking how many listed in the top ten are reputed to be amongst the sharpest and savviest minds in baseball history. Durocher was known for always looking for the angles, as were Dick Williams and former boy wonder Bucky Harris. LaRussa has been called a genius so many times it is a cliché. Beyond them you have McCarthy, McKechnie, Selee, Clarke, and Chance. Also, it is worth noting that when James Click evaluated managers in *Baseball Between the Numbers* he ran another study in which he looked at how managerial strategic decisions impact run scoring. It showed that Dick Williams was among the best.

If one drew up a list of the masters of baseball strategy, many of these men would top it, which is what should happen. Managers can cause a team to score more or fewer runs than the projection would estimate for them by knowing when it is most advantageous to deploy those bits of strategy. For example, according to some sabermetric estimates, a stolen base is worth approximately 0.3 runs. However, that is an average value for the play. In some instances it might be worth more. Depending on the quality of the hitter at the plate or the number of outs already recorded in the inning, a stolen base can mean more than it typically would. *When* a manager uses a bit of strategy can have a pronounced impact.

The following skippers scored worst with this component:

List 8: Worst at Team Offense, 1896–2006

1. Lou Piniella	−233 runs
2. Lou Boudreau	−210 runs
3. Branch Rickey	−171 runs
4. Ned Hanlon	−169 runs
5. Patsy Donovan	−163 runs
6. Wilbert Robinson	−133 runs
7. Bill Virdon	−129 runs
8t. Chuck Tanner	−128 runs
8t. Connie Mack	−128 runs
10. Nap Lajoie	−111 runs
11t. Joe Morgan	−105 runs
11t. Lee Fohl	−105 runs

List 8: Worst at Team Offense, 1896–2006 (continued)

13.	Larry Bowa	–96 runs
14.	Jimmie Wilson	–94 runs
15t.	Dusty Baker	–93 runs
15t.	Johnny Oates	–93 runs
15t.	Pie Traynor	–93 runs
18.	Terry Francona	–92 runs
19.	Ray Miller	–87 runs
20t.	Cito Gaston	–86 runs
20t.	Jimy Williams	–86 runs

The single most inexplicable finding on any of these lists is Ned Hanlon's fourth-worst score here. Going purely by reputation, he was as sharp a manager as Leo Durocher, Dick Williams, and the other skippers listed atop the good list for this component. If anything, that understates Hanlon, who was not just good at in-game tactics, but damn near the father of modern baseball managing. No one else had a collection of disciples as impressive as Hanlon did. John McGraw, the ultimate manager, learned from Hanlon, as did fellow Hall of Fame skipper Wilbert Robinson. Hughie Jennings, who won three pennants in a decade-plus stint as Tigers manager, also played for Hanlon. Over a century later, virtually all managers are in some way or another descendants of Ned Hanlon. His Baltimore Orioles had a reputation of looking for any way — fair or foul — to try to improve their odds of scoring that extra run. Yet he sits near the top of the wrong list.

A few things should be kept in mind. These results do not include Hanlon's entire career, possibly hurting him. Also, Bill James only intended Runs Created to go back to 1900. However, the 1890s were not Hanlon's problem. He managed until 1907 and his twentieth century scores are terrible. From 1900 onward, Hanlon scores -101 runs, which by itself would be the thirteenth worst of all time. This result completely refutes his managerial reputation.

To make an analogy, when Bill James initially provided Win Shares results in the *New Historical Abstract* he mentioned how Fielding Win Shares confirmed the reputation of all the first basemen with great defensive reputations, except for George Sisler. He took that as a mark against Sisler rather than against his system. Obviously, he cannot look over old footage of Sisler to explain why he was not as strong as his reputation, but the overall sensibility of the results should not be ignored. No one would want to argue that popular perception is always correct. Perhaps Hanlon was better at coming up with new ideas than implementing them. Protégé Wilbert Robinson is also in the bottom ten. John McGraw scores decently at +86 runs in this component, but that was actually one of his worst scores.

Moving past Hanlon, the names here normally make sense. In *Veeck as in Wreck*, former Indians owner Bill Veeck criticized the in-game managerial abilities of Cleveland's longtime manager, Lou Boudreau. Veeck argued that the skipper's moves were solely based on reactions to what had just happened, rather than any thoughts on what he would like to see start to happen. He made a move not because he thought it would work, but because he felt he had to do something. Chuck Tanner and Wilbert Robinson both had reputations as nice guys rather than as especially deep thinkers. Dusty Baker is another whose strength is people skills. In games, he screwed up double switches, and once had his players bat out of order. With the 2005 Cubs, Baker spent much of the year with Corey Patterson's .254 OBP batting leadoff, and Neifi Perez's .298 OBP in the #2 hole; no wonder why #3 hitter Derrek Lee, despite hitting 46 homers and 50 doubles, could barely amass 100 RBIs. Larry Bowa's strong point is supposed to be motivation rather than brilliance. His proponents will claim he improves teams more by sheer willpower than by outsmarting opponents.

Several other interesting names appear on the list. Lou Piniella's bleak results are rather surprising, but the Yankees, Reds, Mariners, and Devil Rays all scored negatively for him. Like Bowa, he was more a motivator than strategist. Branch Rickey may have a reputation as the smartest man in baseball history, but his brains were best applied to the front office, not the dugout. Connie Mack was above average until the mid–1930s.

Component V: Team Pitching

Finally comes the most questionable component of all. Scores for post–1960 managers should be fine — but beware earlier scores:

List 9: Best Team Pitching, 1896–2006

1.	Charlie Grimm	+332 runs
2.	Tom Kelly	+255 runs
3.	Bill McKechnie	+242 runs
4.	Joe Cronin	+215 runs
5.	Frank Robinson	+204 runs
6.	Fred Clarke	+188 runs
7.	Mike Hargrove	+182 runs
8.	Joe McCarthy	+169 runs
9.	Miller Huggins	+165 runs
10.	Jim Leyland	+153 runs
11.	Don Zimmer	+142 runs
12.	Roger Peckinpaugh	+134 runs
13t.	Sparky Anderson	+133 runs
13t.	John McGraw	+133 runs
15.	Al Lopez	+123 runs
16.	Gabby Street	+118 runs
17.	Frank Chance	+108 runs
18.	Jerry Narron	+107 runs
19t.	Bill Terry	+103 runs
19t.	Billy Gardner	+103 runs

Due to the shoddy math on pre–1960 guys, Charlie Grimm's results are extremely questionable. Then again, luck by itself is unlikely to get anyone this high. His teams always did well at this component. In the eighteen seasons he managed at least 50 games, his squads scored above average seventeen times. That is a trend.

Many of the other men on this list innovatively used their pitchers. John McGraw used the game's first relief specialist in Doc Crandall. Frank Chance and Fred Clarke, as mentioned earlier, spread out the innings among starters to keep everyone sharper. Sparky Anderson gained the nickname Captain Hook for his willingness to yank his starters. All these guys would rather take their pitchers out one pitch too early rather than one too late. And if there were runners on base, that one pitch too many could have unusually serious repercussions. Altogether, this list has seven who managed their way into Cooperstown. Just off the list is an eighth immortal, Ned Hanlon at +101 runs.

Now for the worst at this most questionable component:

List 10: Worst at Team Runs Allowed, 1896–2006

1.	Felipe Alou	−205 runs
2.	Lee Fohl	−196 runs
3.	Tommy Lasorda	−186 runs
4.	Dusty Baker	−154 runs

List 10: Worst at Team Runs Allowed, 1896–2006 (continued)

5t.	Bobby Cox	–144 runs
5t.	Jimmy Dykes	–144 runs
7.	Donie Bush	–136 runs
8.	Jerry Manuel	–135 runs
9.	John McCloskey	–133 runs
10.	Bob Lillis	–130 runs
11.	Patsy Donovan	–126 runs
12.	Tony LaRussa	–118 runs
13.	Jack Hendricks	–117 runs
14.	Hughie Jennings	–116 runs
15.	Bruce Bochy	–115 runs
16.	Fred Tenney	–113 runs
17.	Tom Loftus	–106 runs
18.	Charlie Fox	–103 runs
19.	Herman Franks	–99 runs
20.	Jeff Torborg	–97 runs

Most of these managers are since 1960, so the information should be more reliable. There are some big names near the top, but generally there are good reasons for their placement here. Lasorda was always more a motivator than strategist. Bobby Cox is a surprise, given Atlanta's great reputation for pitching, but getting men to pitch better is not the same as handling them optimally. James Click did yet another brief manager study in the *Between the Numbers*— this one looking at how good a job managers did deploying pitchers. In his results, Bobby Cox came off as one of the worst in recent decades.

Tony LaRussa is a highly regarded recent manager who has a solid reputation for handling pitchers. His usage of Dennis Eckersley in Oakland is seen as the harbinger of the modern three-out closer. His score here is almost entirely a product of his pre–Oakland career as White Sox manager. Since 1988, when Oakland's glory run began, he has actually been above average, scoring +42 runs over the last two decades.

Lee Fohl is exactly who belongs near the top of this list. He lost his job managing the Indians in 1919 for his clueless handling of pitchers. He ceded this duty, allowing center fielder Tris Speaker to decide when to bring in relievers and which ones should be used. On July 18, while the Indians protected a late lead against the Red Sox in Cleveland, Speaker signaled to Fohl to warm up a particular reliever. Fohl misread Speaker and warmed up a different one. Speaker was not sure if he should call time and tell Fohl who to start or if the manager had overridden him, something that rarely happened. The wrong pitcher faced Babe Ruth, who promptly hit a game-winning home run. That was Fohl's last game as Indians manager. He had no one to blame but himself for his firing as he let someone do his job for him, and did not bother to think about what he heard. He detached himself from the game.

The Best and Worst Managers of All Time

Now, for the main show — best and worst when you put it altogether. Since these are the main lists, I will present the top 30:

List 11: The Best, 1896–2006

1.	Joe McCarthy	+1,451 runs
2.	Tony LaRussa	+1,012 runs
3.	Bill McKechnie	+998 runs

List 11: The Best, 1896–2006 (continued)

4.	Walter Alston	+904 runs
5.	John McGraw	+853 runs
6.	Al Lopez	+836 runs
7.	Earl Weaver	+744 runs
8.	Billy Martin	+715 runs
9.	Frank Chance	+686 runs
10.	Fred Clarke	+672 runs
11.	Bobby Cox	+655 runs
12.	Billy Southworth	+653 runs
13t.	Dick Williams	+526 runs
13t.	Sparky Anderson	+526 runs
15.	Leo Durocher	+513 runs
16.	Miller Huggins	+512 runs
17.	Pat Moran	+510 runs
18.	Paul Richards	+496 runs
19.	Casey Stengel	+487 runs
20.	Buck Ewing	+494 runs
21.	Joe Torre	+475 runs
22.	Joe Cronin	+474 runs
23.	Ron Gardenhire	+430 runs
24.	Whitey Herzog	+404 runs
25.	Davey Johnson	+386 runs
26.	Jack McKeon	+381 runs
27.	Frank Selee	+367 runs
28.	Bobby Valentine	+356 runs
29.	Mickey Cochrane	+355 runs
30.	Bruce Bochy	+354 runs

Again, the results confirm the overall validity of the Birnbaum Database. It consistently either confirms common perception or has a good explanation for its differences. Pat Moran is no one's idea of a household name, but checking how his teams performed makes it clear he knew what he was doing. The two clubs he managed, the Phillies and Reds, improved as soon as he showed up and declined when he left. If he lived longer, he would have been a Hall of Famer.

Buck Ewing managed only a handful of years in the 1890s, making his 20th place showing rather improbable, but the man could manage. He generally had the fifth or sixth most talented team in the twelve-team NL, but kept piloting them to third or fourth place. He is the best manager ever to have such a short career.

Ewing's biggest competition for that title are player-manager Mickey Cochrane and current Twins skipper Ron Gardenhire. Cochrane managed only 598 games, but claimed the pennant in his first full year, and won the World Series in his second. He never managed another full campaign again, though he managed for a few partial seasons afterwards. His playing career cut short by a beaning that nearly killed him, he had trouble adjusting to managing without being able to get in the game himself. If he left the game on his own terms, he might have enjoyed a long, productive managerial career. Gardenhire's Twins consistently win more games than anyone expects them to year after year. His score is inflated because the Twins suffered through a rotten 2007 campaign under him. When it qualifies for the Tendencies Database after another year, his score will go down. Then again, Minnesota's 2008 campaign, when Gardenhire nearly took a talent-deprived unit to the post-season, will likely help his score more than 2007 hurts it.

Only one manager on the list has a losing record — Bruce Bochy in 30th place. Bochy never received much attention from the nation but he performed an admirable job in San Diego, most notably getting terrific production from his veteran hitters. Unfortunately, even when San Diego fielded good teams under Bochy, they normally wilted in the postseason, ensuring he would be overlooked. Bochy's strong showing partially derives from a terrific pythagenpat score of +155 runs. If you want to discount that, the next best performances by managers with losing records are George Stallings, who is in 36th place at +274 runs, and Gene Mauch in 41st place at +225 runs. Both were widely heralded as brilliant managers when they worked, despite their lackluster clubs.

At the top, Joe McCarthy easily trumps the competition. Bill James called him the game's greatest manager. In their book *Baseball Dynasties*, Rob Neyer and Eddie Epstein said McCarthy's 1936–39 Yanks were the greatest clubs of all time. McCarthy has the best winning percentage of anyone in the record book with more than a smattering of games managed. John McGraw might be the more iconic manager, but Joe McCarthy is the gold standard.

To realize how much he dominates his competition, one can compare his value to the greatest players in history. Using a standard ten runs to one win ratio, McCarthy was worth 145 wins. According to Pete Palmer's total player rating, that is more than Babe Ruth was worth. It is more than Mickey Mantle and Lou Gehrig are worth *combined*. Take Bob Gibson, add Tom Seaver and Joe DiMaggio to the mix, and it still falls short of McCarthy's score here. Want a foursome? Well, then try Eddie Murray, Jim Palmer, Roberto Clemente, and Cap Anson. They add up to 140.8 wins — not quite McCarthy. An infield consisting of Mark McGwire, Jackie Robinson, Ernie Banks, and George Brett garners five fewer wins than McCarthy. He also beats an outfield of Mel Ott, Reggie Jackson, and Al Kaline, or a starting rotation of Phil Niekro, Juan Marichal, Robin Roberts, Fergie Jenkins, and Stan Coveleski. It is absurd how well he scores, as he tallied almost seven wins per 162 games. Again, it is unfair to give all the credit to McCarthy as he relied on coaches, front office, others, and the interaction between them all. Though a confluence of factors occurred, McCarthy was the best manager.

Current second place skipper Tony LaRussa might fall into third, as many managers trail off in their final years. Casey Stengel rose as high as +991 runs before taking charge of the Mets. Al Lopez should have stayed retired after 1965, as should have Earl Weaver after 1982. Dick Williams lost 100 runs with Seattle, his final managerial tenure. The man LaRussa's currently jostling with, McKechnie, topped +1,100 runs after the 1944 season. LaRussa will be hurt by 2007, and aided by 2008, but it is hard to say what will happen after that. Odds are, Tony LaRussa — like almost all great managers — will drop a bit at the end. However, barring an epic collapse he will retire as baseball's best manager since World War II.

According to the Birnbaum Database, here are the worst managers of all time:

List 12: Worst, 1896–2006

1.	Jimmie Wilson	−823 runs
2.	Connie Mack	−668 runs
3.	Don Baylor	−568 runs
4.	Art Fletcher	−496 runs
5.	Fred Tenney	−482 runs
6.	Buddy Bell	−442 runs
7.	Rogers Hornsby	−411 runs
8.	Billy Meyer	−404 runs
9.	Clint Hurdle	−390 runs
10.	Zach Taylor	−387 runs

List 12: Worst, 1896–2006 (continued)

11.	Doc Prothro	−350 runs
12.	Burt Shotton	−326 runs
13.	John McCloskey	−457 runs
14.	Russ Nixon	−316 runs
15.	Lee Fohl	−315 runs
16.	Fred Haney	−282 runs
17.	Preston Gomez	−279 runs
18.	Cookie Lavagetto	−278 runs
19.	Patsy Donovan	−274 runs
20.	Dave Bristol	−269 runs
21.	Hugh Duffy	−262 runs
22.	Pat Corrales	−245 runs
23.	Lloyd McClendon	−237 runs
24t.	Dan Howley	−225 runs
24t.	Jim Marshall	−225 runs
26.	Bill Dahlen	−212 runs
27.	Ray Miller	−202 runs
28.	Terry Francona	−195 runs
29.	Chuck Tanner	−193 runs
30.	Hal McRae	−182 runs

Ten of the bottom thirteen were out of the business a half-century ago, and the remaining trio all worked for Denver. Regardless of the Coors Field effect, that club hires bad managers. Clint Hurdle is not nearly as bad as he appears here as Colorado's surprise pennant in 2007 hurts his scores in the 2005–06 seasons. However, even after adjusting for 2007 and the Coors effect, Hurdle still scores poorly. Sadly for him, Buddy Bell's final season in 2007 will not help him, though it is unlikely to hurt him so badly he falls into the bottom five. Don Baylor is the anti–LaRussa — the worst manager since World War II.

Jimmie Wilson is the anti–McCarthy, the worst manager in baseball history. Like McCarthy, circumstances amplify his score. He had the misfortune to manage the interwar Phillies, who were, as previously noted, in the midst of the worst extended stretch any franchise has ever had. Burt Shotton, Art Fletcher, and Doc Prothro were the only others to spend much time with the club in those years, and all end up on this list. It was a bankrupt team playing for uncommitted owners before indifferent crowds. However, even if one adjusts for the franchise, Wilson stank, as a comparison with Burt Shotton (his immediate predecessor in Philadelphia) makes clear. In six seasons managing the Phillies, Shotton averaged almost -100 runs a year, while Wilson averaged nearly -120 runs per year in five campaigns. Philadelphia improved with Shotton, but declined the longer Wilson lasted. Shotton performed well when given a second chance as a manager, but Wilson flopped in his second go-around when the Cubs gave him a chance in the 1940s. They fired him in 1944 and won the pennant the next year. Every time Wilson managed more than 10 games, his teams underachieved by at least -50 runs. Since he consistently got the least out his squads, Wilson was an all-too-appropriate choice to manage pathetic clubs.

Terry Francona is the most surprising inclusion on this list. Though Boston won a title under him during the time span of the Birnbaum Database, it does not give him much credit. It claims that since Francona joined the Red Sox as manager in 2004, the team has underachieved by -96 runs. As far as the database is concerned, the Red Sox success is a triumph of the front office. Like Clint Hurdle, Francona is hurt by 2007, when the Red Sox won the pennant. If that season pulls him out of the bottom 30, Jerry Narron, at -178 runs, would take his place.

Even if Francona stumbles out of the bottom 30, he will likely possess the worst mark by any manager with a winning record after 2007 factors into the Birnbaum Database. (Through 2006, Francona's record was slightly under .500). As it stands, the "honor" of worst scoring with a good record by anyone who lasted 500 games belongs to Billy Hitchcock. He scores at -171 runs despite a .514 record from his stints leading the Braves and Orioles in the 1960s. Though both squads won more than they lost under Hitchcock, each improved as soon as he left and went to the postseason two years after his departure. The next worst is Joe Morgan, who was -134 runs despite a .534 winning percentage with the Red Sox. The worst manager with a winning record and over 1,000 games under his belt was Fred Hutchinson, who was -115 runs with a .501 winning percentage.

Most managers on the above list had a fairly short career, which makes sense. The worse someone is the harder it is to keep his job. In fact, the real worst manager of all time is someone who did not even qualify for this list. Only three men with 2,000 games on the job make the list — Leyland, Connie Mack, and Chuck Tanner. Leyland has some extenuating circumstances minimizing his score, and Mack was a great manager who held on too long. That leaves Chuck Tanner as the worst to ever last so long on the job.

For what it is worth, among those who managed at least 500 games, eight men score above average in all five components — Joe Altobelli, Mickey Cochrane, Buck Ewing, Davey Johnson, Al Lopez, Billy Martin, George Stallings, and Dick Williams. They are the game's most well-rounded skippers. Five men are on the opposite end of the spectrum, below average in all areas — Bill Donovan, Rogers Hornsby, Dan Howley, Billy Meyer, and Jimmie Wilson.

Further Combinations

The five components can be looked at in different ways. For example, the first two, working with individual hitters and pitchers, have a similar underlying foundation. Both focus on getting the most out of the players. Call those the coaching components. The following managers did the best at them:

List 13: Best at Coaching, 1896–2006 (continued)

1.	Joe McCarthy	+1,199 runs
2.	John McGraw	+759 runs
3.	Tony LaRussa	+695 runs
4.	Billy Southworth	+634 runs
5.	Earl Weaver	+592 runs
6.	Walter Alston	+527 runs
7.	Al Lopez	+512 runs
8.	Bobby Cox	+466 runs
9.	Bucky Harris	+436 runs
10.	Paul Richards	+424 runs
11.	Tommy Lasorda	+417 runs
12.	Billy Martin	+411 runs
13.	Fred Clarke	+371 runs
14.	Jimy Williams	+336 runs
15.	Tris Speaker	+318 runs
16.	Leo Durocher	+316 runs
17.	Mike Scioscia	+303 runs
18.	Casey Stengel	+300 runs
19.	Joe Torre	+287 runs
20.	Sparky Anderson	+281 runs

It is impressive that despite scoring sixth-worst at handling hitters, Bobby Cox still makes the top eight in overall coaching. The top nine are either in Cooperstown or will be as soon as they retire. In the early 1960s, Paul Richards gave up managing to work in the front office, costing him a plaque. If Stengel had never taken the job with the Mets, he would have topped Al Lopez for seventh place. Among Hall of Famers, only Connie Mack and Wilbert Robinson score negatively. At the top of the list, the gap between Joe McCarthy and John McGraw is larger than the scores of all but eight managers in baseball history. Contemporary skipper Bruce Bochy appears in a tie for 27th place at +227 runs.

Here are the worst at handling players:

List 14: Worst at Coaching, 1896–2006

1.	Don Baylor	−612 runs
2.	Connie Mack	−478 runs
3.	Art Fletcher	−462 runs
4.	Clint Hurdle	−437 runs
5.	Jim Marshall	−409 runs
6.	Dave Bristol	−401 runs
7.	Zach Taylor	−393 runs
8.	Jimmie Wilson	−383 runs
9.	Jim Leyland	−380 runs
10.	Tom Kelly	−356 runs
11.	Fred Tenney	−345 runs
12.	Buddy Bell	−330 runs
13.	Rogers Hornsby	−322 runs
14.	Fred Haney	−309 runs
15.	John McNamara	−297 runs
16.	Burt Shotton	−294 runs
17.	Billy Meyer	−262 runs
18.	Cookie Lavagetto	−245 runs
19.	Darrell Johnson	−242 runs
20.	Luke Sewell	−234 runs

Anytime Hurdle or Leyland appears on these negative lists, I want to apologize. Just because this study focuses on the Birnbaum Database does not mean I have to shut my brain off and declare it omniscient. As mentioned at the outset, it is good enough, but far from perfect. Still, Don Baylor really was a terrible coach and Buddy Bell failed everywhere he managed. Among non–Denver managers, Jim Marshall achieved the dubious distinction of averaging about -100 runs per year at coaching.

Other combinations are worth making. The last two components, team pitching and offense, also have a similar underlying philosophy: both deal with how managerial decisions affect the team. Call these the strategic components. When they are combined, the follow do the best:

List 15: Best Strategy, 1896–2006

1.	Fred Clarke	+425 runs
2.	Bill McKechnie	+411 runs
3.	Frank Chance	+382 runs
4.	Joe McCarthy	+359 runs
5.	Charlie Grimm	+357 runs
6.	Tom Kelly	+335 runs

List 15: Best Strategy, 1896–2006 (continued)

7.	Leo Durocher	+330 runs
8.	Dick Williams	+267 runs
9.	Phil Garner	+251 runs
10.	John McGraw	+219 runs
11t.	Art Howe	+218 runs
11t.	Frank Robinson	+218 runs
13.	Casey Stengel	+208 runs
14.	Jim Leyland	+207 runs
15.	Luke Sewell	+198 runs
16.	Gabby Street	+195 runs
17.	Joe Cronin	+193 runs
18.	Mickey Cochrane	+180 runs
19t.	Clint Hurdle	+179 runs
19t.	Tony LaRussa	+179 runs

This list is notable because Joe McCarthy does not top it. There are other surprises, such as Frank Robinson, who is tied for eleventh. He did not have the best reputation towards the end of his days, appearing more as a cranky caretaker for the Expos when the commissioner's office took charge of that franchise. However, when younger he was respected enough to become the game's first black manager, and was also a highly regarded coach for Earl Weaver's Orioles. Phil Garner, in ninth place, is another surprise, but each of the three clubs he managed (Milwaukee, Detroit, and Houston) performed well in these categories. In eleven full seasons, his squads score negatively overall in these components only twice.

Appearing on both the best strategy and best coaching lists are Joe McCarthy, John McGraw, Fred Clarke, Leo Durocher, Casey Stengel, and Tony LaRussa.

Next are the worst managers at strategy:

List 16: Worst Strategy, 1896–2006

1.	Lee Fohl	−301 runs
2.	Patsy Donovan	−289 runs
3.	Tommy Lasorda	−262 runs
4.	Dusty Baker	−247 runs
5.	John McCloskey	−211 runs
6.	Lou Boudreau	−208 runs
7.	Felipe Alou	−191 runs
8.	Lou Piniella	−177 runs
9.	Bill Virdon	−169 runs
10t.	Pie Traynor	−164 runs
10t.	Fred Tenney	−164 runs
12.	Tom Loftus	−163 runs
13.	Connie Mack	−160 runs
14.	Nixey Callahan	−157 runs
15.	Branch Rickey	−147 runs
16t.	Jack Hendricks	−144 runs
16t.	Jimmie Wilson	−144 runs
18t.	Doc Prothro	−137 runs
18t.	Wilbert Robinson	−137 runs
20.	Billy Meyer	−133 runs

A lot of these guys, especially the more famous of them, are known more for leading by emotion. Wilbert Robinson had kids crawl on the Dodger bench creating a better mood for the players. Over seventy years later, Baker did the same thing with the Giants. Tommy Lasorda took a more boisterous approach, but still was more a motivator than strategist. They lasted as long as they did because their strengths at handling players outweighed whatever problems they may have had. Others here held on too long, like Connie Mack.

These components can be mixed and matched a bit differently. For example, one coaching and one strategy component deals with offense (individual hitters and team offense). Put those two together and you can see which skippers got the most and least overall out of their offenses.

Here are the leaders:

List 17: Best Overall Offense, 1896–2006

1.	Joe McCarthy	+740 runs
2.	Leo Durocher	+558 runs
3.	Tony LaRussa	+537 runs
4.	John McGraw	+430 runs
5.	Bucky Harris	+418 runs
6.	Casey Stengel	+359 runs
7.	Bruce Bochy	+357 runs
8.	Dick Williams	+352 runs
9.	Billy Martin	+251 runs
10.	Gene Mauch	+238 runs
11.	Billy Southworth	+236 runs
12.	Frank Chance	+235 runs
13.	Walter Alston	+224 runs
14.	Davey Johnson	+222 runs
15.	Fred Clarke	+213 runs
16.	Mickey Cochrane	+206 runs
17.	Hank Bauer	+199 runs
18.	Tris Speaker	+198 runs
19.	Mel Ott	+190 runs
20.	Sparky Anderson	+174 runs

This provides a list of the game's most offensively-minded managers. Several of these men were big platooners. During the glory day of the strategy, Speaker utilized it, and at the mid-century Southworth and Stengel helped repopularize it. Mauch was a firm advocate of getting that lefty-righty advantage whenever he could. Most of these men are names already seen before, which is as it should be.

The managers with the game's least effective offenses were:

List 18: Worst Overall Offense, 1896–2006

1.	Wilbert Robinson	−311 runs
2.	Connie Mack	−277 runs
3.	Lee Fohl	−217 runs
4.	Rene Lachemann	−187 runs
5.	Hal McRae	−177 runs
6.	Rogers Hornsby	−170 runs
7.	Bob Melvin	−166 runs
8.	Bill Dahlen	−164 runs

List 18: Worst Overall Offense, 1896–2006 (continued)

9.	Jimmie Wilson	−162 runs
10.	John McCloskey	−159 runs
11.	Billy Gardner	−157 runs
12.	Frank Lucchesi	−155 runs
13.	Del Baker	−152 runs
14.	Red Schoendienst	−150 runs
15t.	Billy Meyer	−146 runs
15t.	Bill Virdon	−146 runs
17t.	Fred Tenney	−145 runs
17t.	Lloyd McClendon	−145 runs
19.	Buck Rodgers	−131 runs
20.	Cito Gaston	−127 runs

Almost all these men were unsuccessful managers, generally very unsuccessful. Cito Gaston probably had the best bunch of hitters, but then again he is the last man listed above.

There is one final combination to make — tally up the coaching and strategic pitching components (individual pitchers and team pitching). The following men got the most from their pitching staffs:

List 19: Best Overall Pitching, 1896–2006

1.	Joe McCarthy	+818 runs
2.	Bill McKechnie	+644 runs
3.	Al Lopez	+595 runs
4.	Fred Clarke	+583 runs
5.	John McGraw	+548 runs
6.	Bobby Cox	+463 runs
7.	Earl Weaver	+461 runs
8.	Charlie Grimm	+457 runs
9.	Walt Alston	+435 runs
10.	Billy Southworth	+389 runs
11.	Frank Chance	+340 runs
12.	Tony LaRussa	+337 runs
13.	Jimy Williams	+323 runs
14.	Frank Selee	+306 runs
15.	Paul Richards	+295 runs
16.	Pat Moran	+286 runs
17.	Billy Martin	+285 runs
18.	Joe Cronin	+271 runs
19.	Mike Scioscia	+260 runs
20.	Buck Ewing	+257 runs

Two contemporary managers appear in 22nd and 23rd places: Ron Gardenhire at +230 runs and Phil Garner at +228 runs.

Nine men appear on both the best overall pitching and best overall offense lists—Joe McCarthy, Fred Clarke, John McGraw, Tony LaRussa, Billy Southworth, Walter Alston, Frank Chance, Billy Martin, and Frank Selee. Clarke, McGraw, LaRussa, and McCarthy are the only ones among the top twenty with all combinations—team pitching, team hitting, coaching, and strategy. McCarthy, LaRussa, and McGraw are not surprising as they are all among the top five managers of all time, but Clarke is "only" eleventh best. His weakness comes in pythagenpat. Remove that component, and the four best managers of all time are McCarthy, McGraw, LaRussa, and Clarke.

Finally, these managers do the worst when you find the sum of team pitching and individual pitchers:

List 20: Worst Overall Pitching, 1896–2006

1.	Don Baylor	−492 runs
2.	Connie Mack	−451 runs
3.	Jimmie Wilson	−365 runs
4.	Fred Tenney	−364 runs
5.	Buddy Bell	−325 rims
6.	Zach Taylor	−314 runs
7.	Art Fletcher	−310 runs
8.	Jim Marshall	−291 runs
9.	Burt Shotton	−263 runs
10.	Billy Meyer	−249 runs
11.	Patsy Donovan	−229 runs
12t.	Roger Bresnahan	−228 runs
12t.	Dave Bristol	−228 runs
14.	Rogers Hornsby	−224 runs
15.	Dusty Baker	−216 runs
16.	Charlie Dressen	−214 runs
17.	Terry Francona	−207 runs
18.	Doc Prothro	−209 runs
19t.	Fred Haney	−196 runs
19t.	Fred Hutchinson	−196 runs

With a few exceptions, this list is a role call of the damned. By that standard, the right man tops it.

A Final Note

One other study should be considered. A few years ago, when I first applied the Birnbaum Database to managers, I shared the results with some others in the sabermetric online community. It helped inspire David Gassko to do his own study, titled "Do Managers Matter?" which looked at all skippers who lasted at least 1,000 games from 1876 to 2007. Appearing in the *2008 Hardball Times Baseball Annual*, it was similar to James Click's study in that it used advanced math to see if managers impacted player performance at all.

Two features distinguish it from Click's one-page blurb. First, it lasted multiple pages—six to be exact. Second, and more importantly, he reached a different conclusion, as his numbers indicated managerial influence on players existed. There were some very considerable surprises in his study. Most notably, it argued that Joe McCarthy was a below average manager, a rather stunning result. Forget the Birnbaum Database for a second. McCarthy never had a losing season in a quarter-century of managing, and owns the highest career winning percentage of any person in Gassko's study. How in blazes could he be bad? Gassko openly admits the proper score for McCarthy might be between his study and this one. However, Hall of Famers Walter Alston, Bucky Harris, Miller Huggins, Frank Selee, and Casey Stengel also score negatively by Gassko's system.

A study should confound some expectations, but more importantly, it should explain those surprises. Otherwise the unexpected result does not throw conventional wisdom into question; it makes the study suspect. Is it really explaining anything about baseball, or just about math? An advantage of the Birnbaum Database is that the unexpected men it pushes forth as the best managers— such as Pat Moran — really do look terrific upon closer inspection. David Gassko is a first-class researcher with a brilliant intellect who does great work, and possesses mathematical capabilities light years beyond mine, but this particular study of his does not pass the smell test. I prefer it to Click's piece (admittedly, this preference is largely because it provides results I find more agreeable), but overall the Birnbaum Database reigns supreme.

Ultimately, I have the same problem with Gassko as I do with Click. There is no way to argue baseball with their results. They deal with math and numbers instead of ideas and words. Extremely counterintuitive results, such as McCarthy being a bad manager, need explanations offered. Otherwise, it is just a quantitative exercise. The Birnbaum Database has an understandable argument backing up its math. Gassko and Click may provide better mathematical formulas, but that is all they provide. A formula whose results cannot be explained has less value.

Complete Results: Birnbaum Database

For those who really are interested in the numbers— here they are. Below, in alphabetical order are the complete and full Birnbaum Database results for everyone who managed at least 500 games from 1896 to 2006. The list includes manager name, games managed in the years in question, the five components in the same order they are listed in this chapter, and their full results. Enjoy diving into the numbers!

Manager	Games	Indiv. Hit.	Indiv. Pit.	Pythag.	Offense	Pitching	TOTAL
Felipe Alou	2055	-14	182	228	11	-205	202
Walter Alston	3653	68	459	245	156	-24	904
Joe Altobelli	844	108	7	56	4	55	230
Sparky Anderson	4028	259	22	197	-85	133	526
Bill Armour	729	34	4	118	-65	21	112
Del Baker	779	-114	96	-41	-38	-6	-91
Dusty Baker	2203	119	-62	87	-93	-154	-103
George Bamberger	936	-48	-38	-6	-44	2	-134
Dave Bancroft	574	2	-49	29	-24	-51	-93
Ed Barrow	630	82	14	-90	25	51	82
Hank Bauer	1138	106	26	-37	93	5	193
Don Baylor	1321	-82	-530	33	-27	38	-568
Buddy Bell	1081	-45	-285	-207	135	-40	-442
Yogi Berra	928	-74	60	73	55	58	172
Ossie Bluege	769	88	1	143	-15	-86	131
Bruce Bochy	1926	270	-43	155	87	-115	354
Bob Boone	815	-115	7	45	5	-24	-82
Lou Boudreau	2386	92	30	-55	-210	2	-141
Larry Bowa	855	7	32	-74	-96	7	-124
Bobby Bragan	921	87	17	-198	32	7	-55
Bob Brenly	565	-3	119	-22	-17	-96	-19
Roger Bresnahan	760	71	-133	22	55	-95	-80
Dave Bristol	1421	-168	-233	16	111	5	-269

Manager	Games	Indiv. Hit.	Indiv. Pit.	Pythag.	Offense	Pitching	TOTAL
Donie Bush	1036	-55	75	-17	130	-136	-3
Nixey Callahan	852	-17	-19	63	-77	-80	-130
Bill Carrigan	989	-88	-67	169	-35	16	-5
Frank Chance	1594	-39	232	111	274	108	686
Fred Clarke	2782	-24	395	-124	237	188	672
Ty Cobb	923	154	-21	52	2	-61	126
Mickey Cochrane	598	112	53	10	94	86	355
Jimmy Collins	831	-19	59	8	45	-85	8
Terry Collins	878	-38	-56	50	81	84	121
Pat Corrales	1206	-32	-97	-120	87	-83	-245
Bobby Cox	3857	-141	607	264	69	-144	655
Harry Craft	845	-74	53	73	9	-96	-35
Roger Craig	1475	-18	35	-108	73	-90	-108
Del Crandall	833	-16	-85	-68	7	2	-160
Joe Cronin	2291	174	56	51	-22	215	474
Bill Dahlen	606	-101	60	-85	-63	-23	-212
Alvin Dark	1948	8	-46	-65	79	6	-18
Larry Dierker	783	112	115	-171	-4	65	117
Bill Donovan	546	-17	-24	-38	-16	-5	-100
Patsy Donovan	1563	91	-103	27	-163	-126	-274
Red Dooin	762	3	-86	95	53	75	140
Chuck Dressen	1981	61	-164	126	76	-50	49
Hugh Duffy	1206	-111	6	-227	152	-82	-262
Leo Durocher	3717	225	91	-134	333	-3	512
Eddie Dyer	771	-55	89	-16	62	92	172
Jimmy Dykes	2947	-219	114	185	104	-144	40
Lee Elia	538	-35	-122	-88	-6	77	-174
Buck Ewing	623	9	169	130	87	88	483
Art Fletcher	620	-101	-361	-62	-23	51	-496
Lee Fohl	1505	-112	123	-25	-105	-196	-315
Charlie Fox	748	84	-65	-38	10	-103	-112
Terry Francona	1134	-11	-193	115	-92	-14	-195
Herman Franks	1126	-75	183	155	75	-99	239
Jim Fregosi	2122	38	37	-76	41	-79	-39
Jim Frey	610	34	-25	99	-44	79	143
Frankie Frisch	2216	-33	-113	30	182	-55	11
Dave Garcia	618	32	-38	112	8	-53	61
Ron Gardenhire	809	38	164	187	-25	66	430
Billy Gardner	747	-139	-80	-42	-18	103	-176
Phil Garner	1908	-35	106	-134	151	100	188
Cito Gaston	1319	-41	135	-22	-86	-18	-32
George Gibson	757	-14	110	195	-57	-70	164
Kid Gleason	756	-44	13	79	11	25	84
Preston Gomez	875	-64	-32	-204	-42	63	-279
Joe Gordon	613	-18	27	-32	58	4	39
Dallas Green	932	77	-49	-148	52	38	-30

Manager	Games	Indiv. Hit.	Indiv. Pit.	Pythag.	Offense	Pitching	TOTAL
Clark Griffith	2858	-32	151	201	-13	-2	305
Charlie Grimm	2354	-102	125	-46	25	332	334
Fred Haney	1386	-76	-233	-9	-1	37	-282
Ned Hanlon	1710	102	153	-95	-169	101	92
Mike Hargrove	2283	-77	-38	9	-28	182	48
Bucky Harris	4375	230	206	-332	188	-62	230
Lum Harris	954	18	-48	182	-83	11	80
Jack Hendricks	1048	8	146	-52	-27	-117	-42
Whitey Herzog	2406	-6	256	137	65	-48	404
Pinky Higgins	1116	124	-25	25	-83	-6	35
Billy Hitchcock	535	-88	-66	-32	-5	20	-171
Gil Hodges	1413	-58	99	62	23	-61	65
Rogers Hornsby	1513	-104	-218	-17	-66	-6	-411
Ralph Houk	3150	87	39	220	-67	29	308
Art Howe	2266	-8	-63	65	124	94	212
Dan Howley	921	-59	-28	-35	-38	-65	-225
Dick Howser	932	139	49	202	-65	-55	270
Miller Huggins	2547	178	43	150	-23	165	513
Clint Hurdle	788	-158	-279	-132	80	99	-390
Fred Hutchinson	1657	-24	-185	141	-36	-11	-115
Hughie Jennings	2179	15	-53	225	39	-116	110
Darrell Johnson	1062	-72	-170	32	-26	93	-143
Davey Johnson	2036	209	54	97	13	13	386
Walter Johnson	961	-79	157	41	55	-14	160
Fielder Jones	1265	13	53	-51	155	8	178
Eddie Kasko	640	-51	-74	48	3	55	-19
Johnny Keane	748	6	61	-101	0	51	17
Joe Kelley	659	29	82	-190	99	-7	13
Tom Kelly	2384	-107	-249	96	80	255	75
Bob Kennedy	542	20	-24	27	-67	25	-19
Kevin Kennedy	582	107	-146	79	35	-47	28
Bill Killefer	1146	-55	-158	46	80	42	-45
Rene Lachemann	977	-118	71	-20	-69	42	-94
Nap Lajoie	686	32	65	-2	-111	59	43
Gene Lamont	1115	87	134	-101	5	-62	63
Tony LaRussa	4283	240	455	138	297	-118	1012
Tommy Lasorda	3038	111	306	-200	-76	-186	-45
Cookie Lavagetto	655	-119	-126	-41	30	-22	-278
Jim Lefebrve	859	40	8	-7	-61	0	-20
Bob Lemon	833	124	45	-66	14	23	140
Jim Leyland	2362	-102	-278	17	54	153	-156
Bob Lillis	537	59	41	-24	4	-130	-50
Tom Loftus	552	14	-65	42	-57	-106	-172
Al Lopez	2414	40	472	183	18	123	836
Fred Lucchesi	715	-104	76	73	-51	39	33
Ken Macha	648	-9	99	86	31	16	223

Manager	Games	Indiv. Hit.	Indiv. Pit.	Pythag.	Offense	Pitching	TOTAL
Connie Mack	7525	-149	-419	60	-128	-32	-668
Charlie Manuel	735	26	-53	2	-27	-4	-56
Jerry Manuel	971	2	86	41	65	-135	59
Marty Marion	728	-67	48	-66	-31	34	-82
Jim Marshall	555	-118	-291	146	38	0	-225
Billy Martin	2266	177	234	179	74	51	715
Gene Mauch	3939	163	56	-59	75	-10	225
Jimmy McAleer	1624	-32	-45	-86	-40	51	-152
Joe McCarthy	3458	550	649	-107	190	169	1451
Lloyd McClendon	782	-151	35	-39	6	-88	-237
John McCloskey	476	-81	5	-31	-78	-133	-318
John McGraw	4711	344	415	-125	86	133	853
Bill McKechnie	3619	-145	402	330	169	242	998
Jack McKeon	1950	5	206	176	-15	9	381
John McNamara	2415	-73	-224	82	-53	94	-174
Hal McRae	872	-170	-11	52	-7	-46	-182
Sam Mele	960	-48	119	-132	13	-51	-99
Bob Melvin	648	-87	14	-16	-79	6	-162
Billy Meyer	769	-79	-183	-9	-67	-66	-404
Ray Miller	563	64	-113	-95	-87	29	-202
Fred Mitchell	1037	-40	49	-66	49	38	30
Pat Moran	1334	-23	276	107	140	10	510
Joe Morgan	563	23	-41	4	-105	-15	-134
Danny Murtaugh	2065	76	145	-93	-50	74	152
Tony Muser	748	-52	-89	-81	95	-40	-167
Jerry Narron	551	33	-211	-30	-77	107	-178
Russ Nixon	578	-77	-55	-109	18	-93	-316
Johnny Oates	1543	44	9	59	-93	88	107
Steve O'Neill	1861	54	74	-3	17	-15	127
Mel Ott	994	154	-143	-138	36	-26	-117
Danny Ozark	1160	160	-32	-2	-52	59	133
Roger Peckinpaugh	991	60	-113	53	-57	134	77
Lou Piniella	2939	300	-85	12	-233	56	50
Frank Quilici	567	17	-1	-60	-84	-43	-171
Doug Rader	805	-109	85	-133	4	67	-86
Paul Richards	1824	82	342	171	-52	-47	496
Branch Rickey	1261	89	-44	-28	-171	24	-130
Jim Riggleman	1084	-133	45	-199	77	51	-159
Bill Rigney	2560	-28	50	47	-1	-67	1
Frank Robinson	2241	40	-207	168	14	204	219
Wilbert Robinson	2797	-178	47	243	-133	-4	-25
Buck Rodgers	1557	-150	182	67	19	43	161
Red Rolfe	534	3	18	46	-19	-1	47
Pete Rose	785	69	-4	130	23	-23	195
Pants Rowland	586	-1	51	-121	84	18	31
Eddie Sawyer	813	-34	148	54	-33	28	163

Manager	Games	Indiv. Hit.	Indiv. Pit.	Pythag.	Offense	Pitching	TOTAL
Bob Scheffing	845	24	-16	-93	10	6	-69
Red Schoendienst	1996	-102	169	-11	-48	31	39
Mike Scioscia	1134	89	214	1	-38	46	312
Frank Selee	1333	-127	331	2	186	-25	367
Luke Sewell	1250	-175	-59	-88	111	87	-124
Bill Shettsline	670	19	23	128	4	-4	170
Burt Shotton	1461	54	-348	-57	-60	85	-326
Buck Showalter	1715	111	0	-89	-17	-39	-34
Mayo Smith	1274	16	45	34	20	-43	72
Billy Southworth	1748	298	336	28	-62	53	653
Tris Speaker	1137	201	117	-126	-3	-52	137
Jake Stahl	533	-34	52	-38	71	22	73
George Stallings	1777	110	55	18	39	52	274
Eddie Stanky	902	65	113	-45	-18	-34	81
Casey Stengel	3747	224	76	-21	135	73	487
George Stovall	689	-4	41	-5	-30	-47	-45
Gabby Street	697	59	-31	-106	77	118	117
Chuck Tanner	2733	47	-114	-57	-128	59	-193
Zach Taylor	645	-80	-313	1	6	-1	-387
Birdie Tebbetts	1453	41	6	-24	-18	6	11
Patsy Tebeau	651	4	57	-42	-24	94	89
Fred Tenney	604	-94	-251	27	-51	-113	-482
Bill Terry	1484	-59	-6	21	36	103	95
Joe Tinker	612	61	146	-113	-16	-76	2
Jeff Torborg	1352	31	-61	-28	86	-97	-69
Joe Torre	3639	166	121	278	-6	-84	475
Jim Tracy	972	3	189	73	73	-36	302
Pie Traynor	863	-16	59	1	-93	-71	-120
Tom Trebelhorn	932	-47	60	-84	167	-62	34
Bobby Valentine	2189	76	151	237	-18	-90	356
Bill Virdon	1916	-17	157	-9	-129	-40	-38
Harry Walker	1234	-12	12	-66	20	-34	-80
John Wathan	646	-22	-48	-19	35	26	-28
Earl Weaver	2540	183	409	173	-73	52	744
Eric Wedge	648	111	107	-207	-38	-9	-36
Wes Westrum	626	0	-97	63	20	7	-7
Dick Williams	3022	136	51	72	216	51	526
Jimy Williams	1700	31	305	-254	-86	18	14
Ted Williams	637	90	-40	-94	29	29	14
Jimmie Wilson	1228	-68	-315	-296	-94	-50	-823
Ned Yost	647	9	48	38	-35	-59	1
Don Zimmer	1779s	37	-151	174	-52	142	150

2

Evaluating Managerial Tendencies

While the Birnbaum Database provides an overview of managerial performance, it does not enlighten anyone about the inclinations and peculiarities of individual skippers. To really understand a manager, comprehending such details is vital. Ideally, one would know who preferred veterans and who used kids; which ones bunted and which did not; who relied on contact hitters and who depended on power; which manager relied on his bench and who used his starters; who went to the bullpen and who relied on his starters, and so on.

These issues and many similar ones can be answered using the basic statistical record, but the raw stats can be deceptive because they provide information about both the manager and when he managed. For example, say one wanted to find out which managers had the most or least interest in using relief pitchers. All current skippers use relief pitchers more than anyone previously. However, this does not mean that placing any modern manager, whether it is Ron Gardenhire or Mike Scioscia or whoever, back in the 1930s that he would use the same number of relievers as he did in 2006. Managers are always influenced by their era.

Before judging managers across era, it is necessary to first compare them to their contemporaries. In his book on managers, Bill James had a few pages showing which managers' clubs led the league in various categories the most often. That approach can be taken a bit deeper. Instead of relying only on first-place finishes, it would be better to account for every ranking a manager had in a given category.

The Tendencies Database

Sticking with relief pitchers, manager Buck Ewing was one of the game's leading users of the bullpen in the 1890s. He used a few dozen relievers a season, which is nothing by current standards, but consistently put him among the league leaders of his day. Ewing possessed good pitching staffs so necessity did not cause this usage pattern; it was his managerial inclination. Here are the teams Ewing managed, how many relievers he used, and where he ranked as a result:

Year	Team	RP	Rank
1890	NYP	23	2nd of 8 teams
1895	CIN	35	2nd of 12 teams
1896	CIN	26	5th of 12 teams (tied)
1897	CIN	38	1st of 12 teams
1898	CIN	27	1st of 12 teams (tied)
1899	CIN	28	3rd of 12 teams (tied)

Two problems exist with this data. First, there are several ties. Ideally, Ewing should be cleanly separated from those surrounding him. Second, and far more importantly, there is a considerable difference between ranking second in eight- and twelve-team leagues. Looking purely at rank distorts more than it illuminates.

Fortunately, both problems can be solved. For ties, you can use relievers per game instead of relief pitchers used. In baseball's early decades, teams frequently finished the season having played slightly different numbers of games owing to rainouts and darkness. Nowadays that is rarely the case, but the much greater number of relief appearances makes ties considerably less common. Using relievers per game has a second and much more important advantage: it makes the results more precise.

To adjust for league size, divide a squad's rank by the number of teams in their league. For example, coming in second in the eight-team 1890 Players League would be worth 0.250 (2/8), and 0.167 in the twelve-team 1895 National League (2/12). From there, one can figure out a career average. Apply both adjustments to Ewing and here are the results:

Year	Team	Rank	League	Average
1890	NYP	2nd	8 teams	0.250
1895	CIN	2nd	12 teams	0.167
1896	CIN	5th	12 teams	0.417
1897	CIN	1st	12 teams	0.083
1898	CIN	2nd	12 teams	0.167
1899	CIN	4th	12 teams	0.333

The lower the score, the more a manager used relievers; the higher the score, the less inclined he was. Ewing's score is above average at 0.236. That is low, but what does it mean? Well, coming in second in an eight-team league was 0.250, so he was a bit more extreme than that.

Seems nice, but a quirk needs to be resolved. The midpoint shifts based on league size, which causes the average score to fluctuate. That is incredibly noteworthy because to examine managers across all eras, it is necessary to have them centered the same. If managerial scores float in space, with no constant fixed point of reference for all of them, comparisons across the decades are impossible.

Take an eight-team league like the 1890 Players League. To figure its midpoint, average up all the scores: one-eighth plus two-eighths plus three-eighths up to eight-eighths divided by eight. The midpoint averages out at 0.5625, which is precisely halfway between four-eighths (0.500), and five-eights (0.625). Similarly, in a twelve-team league like the 1895 National League, the midpoint is again halfway between the two middle markers. However, this time those are sixth-twelfths (0.500) and seven-twelfths (0.583). Thus the 1895 NL has a midpoint of 0.5417, a bit lower than that of the Players League.

It seems odd that the leagues would have different midpoints, but it makes sense. Ultimately, no matter what the league size is, last place will always be the same — eight-eighths is one, as is twelve-twelfths, and sixteen-sixteenths. Alternately, first place constantly changes. One-eighth is 0.250 and one-twelfth is 0.167. If one endpoint always moves and the other never does, the center shifts.

Fortunately, a simple fix exists. Take Ewing's score for each year, and divide it by the league average. For 1890, that is 0.5625. For the other years it is 0.5417.

Year	Team	Rank	League	Average	Lg.Avg	Final
1890	NYP	2nd	8 teams	0.250	0.5625	0.444
1895	CIN	2nd	12 teams	0.167	0.5417	0.308
1896	CIN	5th	12 teams	0.417	0.5417	0.771
1897	CIN	1st	12 teams	0.083	0.5417	0.154
1898	CIN	2nd	12 teams	0.167	0.5417	0.308
1899	CIN	4th	12 teams	0.333	0.5417	0.617

Ewing's score works out to be 0.434 with relief pitchers—still better than coming in second place in an eight-team league.

With this method, an average score is *always* one; that is how the math works when you always divide by league average. League size no longer causes the midpoint to float. This formula can allow for comparisons between different managers across the generations. Better yet, it does not just work for relief pitchers used. One can use this method for anything. Just choose a stat, and plug it in. I created a database to handle this—the Tendencies Database.

Guidelines for the Tendencies Database

First, the Tendencies Database only examines those who managed in the major leagues ten or more seasons. (By this, I mean he should have managed the majority of a season at least ten times). The shorter the career, the less the database tells you about the manager and the more it tells you about the particular group of players under his care. Playing talent always matters the most in determining what happens in a season, but over the years managers shape and guide a team in a manner that suits their tendencies. For example, if a manager really believes in contact hitting, team strikeouts should decline. Strikeout rate will play a larger role in determining playing time, which will cause players to minimize striking out. The manager can coach the hitters to make contact and/or hire a hitting coach to do that. In the old days the manager would make roster decisions that general managers currently cover. Even to this day managers who last a long time on the job usually have good working relationships with their bosses; that relationship includes input into roster construction. Thus managers can have a considerable effect on stats containing no obvious managerial influence.

Several oddities arise in the Tendencies Database. For one, based on the way the database is set up, the man with the most relievers (or any other stat) ends up with the lowest score. That might seem backwards, but it makes sense. The Tendencies Database is not accounting for the *raw number*, but the *rank*. Teams with the most relief pitchers used, or home runs hit, or sacrifice bunts are always ranked first—the lowest ranking of all.

What really matters is how far a number is from one. This can be shown conclusively if the Buck Ewing relief pitcher example is flipped around. If you think the person who used the most relievers should have the largest score, put him in last every time he used the most, second-to-last when he used the second most and so on. Putting that through the Birnbaum Database yields a score of 1.566, which is equally far from one as Ewing's actual score of 0.434. Ultimately, it makes no difference which end is up.

Some clear patterns determine which way to point the rankings. Whenever possible, follow the logic of the leaderboards. Most stats have a clear and obvious quality dimension to them. For example, any team would like to rank first in batting average. Some clubs prioritize other aspects of the game—whether it is power, or walks, or pitching—but no club would mind having the highest batting average. The lower score means you did a better job. Alternately, teams want to finish last in some categories—for example, no squad wants to allow the most walks. Since fewer walks allowed are inarguably better, the team with the smallest raw number ranks first, and hence gets the lowest score in the Tendencies Database.

Some issues are a bit more contentious. Take sacrifice hits, for example. Some managers love bunting the runner over and try to lead the league in them, while others think they are terrible and intentionally avoid them. In this case the team with the most sacrifices will rank first, and hence have the lower score. Again, the Tendencies Database follows the logic of leaderboards. The same thing holds true for relief pitchers. Using more puts you higher on the leaderboard, though it does not necessarily mean teams aspire to use more relievers. Sometimes the issue is completely arbitrary. Should a team with the most batting orders rank first or last? No obvious answer exists and the leaderboards do not help. That is a coin flip.

Fortunately, such issues are rare. Again though, what really matters is how far removed a score is from one.

The Ewing example also showcases the importance of adjusting for context, which should be done whenever possible. For example, when looking at sacrifice hits, the raw number can be misleading. For a sacrifice to occur, a runner must be on base. If one team with a .350 OBP performed 100 sacrifice hits, and another squad with a .310 OBP had 95, the latter liked to bunt more. As was the case with relief pitchers, the Tendencies Database adjusts for context whenever possible, which both makes the results more precise and reduces ties.

However, there is a difference between reducing and vanquishing ties. This is particularly true because not all stats can be easily converted into context-based percentages. However, while minimizing ties is appropriate, one should not unduly fret about them. Ultimately, ties make surprisingly little difference. Think it through. Since the Tendencies Database only applies to men who lasted ten years or more, the worst case scenario would be someone that barely lasts a decade ties in a particular category five or six times, and by random happenstance he is listed first in each tie. That could screw up his score. How realistic is that, though? First, it is highly unlikely someone will tie in any given category that frequently, especially when you consider that most of the stats in the database have been converted to a percentage. Even if a manager found himself in that many ties, the odds he would be the listed first in the tie every time are slim. Coin flip logic says there is a one in 32 chance in the case of five ties, one in 64 for six.

However, even if it happens— and this is the real key point — it is still not worth worrying about. If someone ties that many times in a given category, it means he was constantly in the middle of the pack, which is where ties most commonly occur. The results from the Tendencies Database listed in this book are from the extremes. Replicating many of the studies in the Tendencies Database would cause minor differences to emerge because of occasional ties, but that is the point — the differences would be minor. A person's exact score matters less than the general picture it provides.

Managers who last only part of the season are another sore spot for the Tendencies Database. After all, teams routinely fire their skippers in midseason. In those situations, a manager will be added into the database if he lasted at least half of the season. This is not a perfect solution, but frankly perfection is not an option. This approach works well as it is very rare that a manager lasts 51 percent or 49 percent of a season.

In baseball history, 77 managers lasted at least a decade on the job, and thus qualify for the Tendencies Database. However, not all statistics have been recorded for all baseball history, causing fewer managers to qualify for some particular studies. For example, sacrifice hit totals are only known since 1894; only 72 managers lasted a decade since then. Some stats, based on Retrosheet's gamelogs, go back to only the mid–1950s, thus a reduced number of managers are eligible. The Tendencies Database can be used to help formulate commentary for managers with shorter careers given in this book — whether it was Pat Moran's interest in using his frontline starters, Gil Hodges's adoration with using his bench, or Roger Craig's fixation on the double play — but they are ineligible from the leaderboards.

Tendencies Database: Overview of the Results

Dozens of stats have been run through the Tendencies Database. The point in generating the numbers was to learn more about the individual managers, so the results will be sprinkled throughout the second part of the book. Still, it is worth providing an overview of what the results look like, especially in some facets of the game that managers have particular influence over. Thus the rest of this chapter contains several lists to familiarize the reader with the Tendencies Database.

Relief Pitchers Used

Since the example given at the chapter's start focused on relievers, that will be the first item examined. As noted already, instead of using relief pitcher appearances, it is relievers per game. Without question the quality of starting pitchers plays a role, but it is very difficult to make these leaderboards without clear managerial preference for calling on relievers. Here are the results:

Most Relievers Used		Fewest Relievers Used	
Burt Shotton	0.378	Bill Virdon	1.609
Jimy Williams	0.440	Ralph Houk	1.608
Lou Boudreau	0.458	Earl Weaver	1.566
Whitey Herzog	0.551	Jimmie Dykes	1.522
Joe Cronin	0.607	Cito Gaston	1.520

Shotton's score reveals how athletic talent and managerial temperament both play a role. Shotton ran the 1928–33 Phillies, who had no quality pitchers. Naturally, he led the league in relief pitchers used every season he managed in Philadelphia. There was more to it than that, though. His 1928 Phillies completed only 42 games, easily the fewest ever to that point in history. The previous record was 49, by an 1876 club that played 60 games. All previous twentieth century pitching staffs had at least 52 completions, and no club dropped under 42 until 1941. Though Shotton had a bad rotation, by itself that does not explain the tremendous drop-off in complete games. Years later he managed a Dodger team that had a decent staff who finished in the top three in relievers per game every year but one under Shotton. They used the most relief pitchers in 1947 despite winning the pennant.

On the other side, it is very interesting to see Virdon and Houk virtually tied for first. Though both men were known for relying on their starters, if you asked 100 serious baseball fans which managers avoided their bullpens the most, not many would say those two. It helps to crunch the numbers.

Sacrifice Hits Frequency

The Tendencies Database also can adjust for numerous offensive stats. Sacrifice hits are good to look at because they involve a strategic choice about which managers have wildly divergent opinions. Since the number of sacrifice hits depends on having base runners, raw numbers are not used. Instead, sacrifice hit frequency is figured as SH/(H+BB+ROE+HBP-HR-2B-3B). Doubles and triples are subtracted because a large majority of all sacrifice hits come with a runner on first base. That skews the data if some managers are more likely to call them in unusual circumstance, but the error would be greater if doubles and triples were not subtracted in the denominator.

Since sacrifice hits data only exists from 1894 onward, a handful of ancients are cut off from this inquiry. Some of the stats in the equation, such as ROE (reached on error), do not go that far back, but are used when they exist. The teams that sacrifice the most often will rank first, and hence have the lowest scores:

Biggest Sacrificers		Least Likely to Sacrifice	
Gene Mauch	0.440	Bruce Bochy	1.655
Billy Southworth	0.463	Buck Showalter	1.606
Tommy Lasorda	0.517	Tom Kelly	1.547
Felipe Alou	0.554	Jimmy McAleer	1.455
Joe Cronin	0.563	John McGraw	1.443

Baseball lore always claimed Gene Mauch was a leading advocate of bunting. It is nice to confirm that.

The list of managers opposed to bunting contains some interesting surprises. John McGraw has always been associated with the old Baltimore Orioles school of playing inside ball and always looking for that extra edge. But McGraw—both as a player and manager—also believed trying to put his batters on base. He guarded his outs jealously and was not about to give them up voluntarily. From 1911 to 1927 he was last or second-to-last in the Tendencies Database's sacrifice hit equation every year except 1916, when he was third-to-last. Bruce Bochy may not get much attention as an opponent of bunting, but he was consistently one of the least likely to employ the strategy. Conspicuously absent is Earl Weaver, famous for opposing the sacrifice. However, he bunted as often as most managers for the first half of his career. It was only in 1977 that he made his big turn away from sacrifices.

Stolen Base Frequency

Like sacrifices, managers have different opinions regarding stolen bases. Some build their game around basepath speed, and others think the risk of a caught steal negates the reward of a successful attempt. Since stolen bases are also a product of times on base, a similar formula is used to the one above: (SB+CS)/(H+BB+HB+ROE-HR-2B-3B). This formula includes doubles and triples for the same reason the previously noted sacrifice hit equation did: though teams occasionally attempt to steal third and home, the overwhelming majority of attempted swipes occur at second base.

Stolen bases only go back to the 1880s, so the four earliest managers are cut off. Here are the most extreme results for the rest:

Most Likely to Steal		Least Likely to Steal	
Whitey Herzog	0.358	Bill Terry	1.600
Red Schoendienst	0.491	Danny Murtaugh	1.506
Walter Alston	0.507	Jimy Williams	1.500
Clark Griffith	0.538	Johnny Oates	1.493
Mike Hargrove	0.569	Buck Showalter	1.442

Anyone shocked by Whitey Herzog's score did not live through the 1980s. Red Schoendienst, who preceded him in St. Louis, was the man who unleashed Lou Brock on the bases. Alternately, only once did Bill Terry have a runner steal more than ten bases in his decade running the Giants (Burgess Whitehead swiped fourteen in 1936).

Hit and Run

The above examples are straightforward. However, with the Tendencies Database, there were times I was more ambitious and tried to use the available data to make the best estimate for stats unknown. The hit and run is a good example of this. You do not find stats for this play for most of baseball history. What if you want to judge how recent managers compare to their predecessors in this strategy?

Time to think it through. A main reason teams call the hit and run is to avoid the double play, so grounding into double plays can serve as a rough approximation for it. The formula GIDP/(ROE+BB+HB+H-2B-3B-HR-SH-SB-CS) is double plays divided by the number of times someone made it to first without moving past the bag. In other words, double plays divided by chances to be doubled up. Admittedly, the hit and run is not the only thing that would cause teams to hit into or avoid double plays. How many right-handed hitters are used plays a role, as would the number of groundball hitters. However, over a decade or more—usually on multiple teams—those things often even out. As always, it is exceptionally unlikely to end up at either extreme in the Tendencies Database unless a manager had a pronounced interest in or antipathy toward the hit and run. This is an imperfect guess, but perfection is not attainable, and running this formula through the database provides a reasonable approximation. GIDP data goes back to 1939 for the AL and 1933 for the NL. Since 54 of the 77 managers lasted at least ten years during this time, here are the results:

Most Interest in the Hit and Run		Least Interest in the Hit and Run	
Birdie Tebbetts	0.548	Tom Kelly	1.467
Billy Southworth	0.606	Connie Mack	1.389
Al Lopez	0.639	Frank Robinson	1.323
Sparky Anderson	0.647	Mike Hargrove	1.316
Davey Johnson	0.664	Bill McKechnie	1.302

Not only does Tom Kelly score high at the right side, but his replacement — Ron Gardenhire — has a similar score (1.429) over seven seasons. Gardenhire coached under Kelly for a decade, and they clearly agree on this strategy.

Season Pace

While the hit and run is one of the more ambitious portions of the Tendencies Database, it has the benefit of being a well-known play. The database also allows one to check items that have drawn less attention. One such issue is how a manager paces his team over a season. Baseball-Reference.com lists the first and second half winning percentages for every team in baseball history. Put them both in the database, and divide the former by the latter to see whose teams improved or declined as the campaign wore on.

A manager should influence pacing to some degree. He keeps the team motivated, prepared, and most importantly of all, healthy. Pitcher arms can turn to dust through overuse or grow rusty if not called on often enough. Position players can also be overworked or underutilized. The manager has to rest his hitters often enough so that little aches and pains do not become full-blown injuries or nagging problems that can deplete their strength as the year continues. Clearly managers are not the only factor that affect team pacing, but the larger the sample size, the more important their role becomes.

Improved as Year Went on		Worsened as Year Went on	
Al Lopez	0.646	Joe Cronin	1.393
Frank Chance	0.667	Bill Terry	1.289
Jimy Williams	0.734	Johnny Oates	1.280
Ned Hanlon	0.734	Danny Murtaugh	1.222
Billy Martin	0.744	Miller Huggins	1.216

One important fact should be noted. In the Tendencies Database, "half" does not literally mean the first 50 percent of games played. Baseball-Reference.com's schedule uses the All-Star break from 1933 onward as the halfway mark. Previously, it picks a date that occurs around midseason. Technically saying "half" is inaccurate, but it is a reasonable shorthand description

Aside from that quirk, one key problem exists with this list — managers do not always last a full season on the job. This is especially important with Billy Martin. He gets full credit for the Yankees late season, pennant-winning explosion in 1978 despite the fact that it came after the franchise replaced him with Bob Lemon. That said, Martin's teams generally improved later in the season. The sixth best score for in-season improvement belongs to Earl Weaver, at 0.800.

Teams managed by men such as Lopez, Williams, and Chance virtually always played better as the year progressed. Alternately, Cronin and Terry's teams melted in the dog days of summer almost every year of their careers.

Starter Percentage

This is a simple concept — add together plate appearances by the starting eight batters (or nine in a league with the designated hitter) and divide that by the team's total plate appearances. Like season pace, this has not been studied, but ought to be. Some managers prefer a set lineup while others platoon or mix-and-match their starters. As always, managers are not the only factor affecting the results. Player health is the most important one in an individual season. Over a decade or more, however, injuries should even out. If a manager has a pronounced tendency to appear among the league leaders in using his starters or his bench, then you know quite a bit about how this manager liked to use his players.

Use Starters the Most		Use Bench the Most	
Frank Selee	0.580	George Stallings	1.387
Dick Williams	0.584	Frank Robinson	1.381
Danny Murtaugh	0.600	Jim Fregosi	1.290
Joe McCarthy	0.657	Paul Richards	1.258
Ralph Houk	0.658	Casey Stengel	1.242

Pat Moran, who only managed nine years, scored 0.543 in this query. Moran served as a backup catcher for list-leader Frank Selee at the turn of the century. Looking at their scores, one can easily imagine Moran sitting on the bench next to Selee, soaking up wisdom.

It is perfect that George Stallings tops the list on the right. As manager of the 1914 Miracle Braves he did more to popularize platooning than any other manager in baseball history. That strategy fell out of style, only to be reinvigorated in the 1950s when Casey Stengel used it while winning five straight world titles with the Yankees. Fittingly, Stengel also appears in the right-hand column.

Finally, note that Gil Hodges, who died after managing nine seasons, posted a mark of 1.667, which means Hodges was almost *twice* as far from average as Stallings. Hodges could have used his bench the least of any manager for several years and still comfortably topped everyone.

Top Three Pitchers

It would be nice to have a pitching version of starter percentage: something that indicates which managers relied the most on their frontline hurlers and who liked to spread the innings around. A cursory examination of baseball history reveals that some managers treated their aces like pack animals while others evenly doled out the work. For example, in the first decade of the twentieth century John McGraw squeezed every inning he possibly could out of Christy Mathewson and Joe McGinnity while rival skipper Frank Chance parceled out the innings among his arms more evenly. Distributing innings is not simply a matter of starters versus bullpens, either. For much of baseball history, managers used pitchers in both roles. Aces — including Carl Hubbell, Lefty Grove, and Mordecai Brown — led the leagues in saves. Besides, starter/bullpen inning splits only go back to the 1950s.

No perfect way exists to distinguish between the McGraws and the Chances with the Tendencies Database. However, when perfection is unattainable, one should make the best imperfect approximation. There is an effective, albeit rough, way of reckoning who leaned the most/least on their main arms. Go through every team in baseball history, find each squad's top three leaders in innings, add together their workload, and divide by the team's total innings pitched. Why focus on the top three workhorses? Making it just the ace or top two pitchers would cause the results to be excessively dependent on a team with a dominant hurler. Broadening it out to four or five pitchers primarily reveals the overall depth of the rotation rather than the manager's predilections. Three provides a nice middle ground. Quality of the ace and staff depth each blend in, but both are more subdued.

Pitching staffs from the 1870s and 1880s require tiebreakers, because many teams had three or fewer individuals perform all their pitching. The first tiebreaker is percentage of innings by the top two pitchers, and the next is percentage by the ace.

Rely on Main Pitchers		Spread Out the Innings	
Tommy Lasorda	0.429	Frank Robinson	1.331
Earl Weaver	0.435	Gus Schmelz	1.322
Bobby Cox	0.443	Jack McKeon	1.285
Al Lopez	0.588	Jimy Williams	1.279
Frank Selee	0.599	Frank Chance	1.273

John McGraw scores a 0.823 with this stat. Once McGinnity faded away, McGraw eased up on his main starters quite a bit, a tendency that increased when Mathewson waned.

Staff quality clearly influences these totals, but there is more to it than that. Bobby Cox regularly pushed his starters hard even before Greg Maddux, Tom Glavine, and John Smoltz were at his disposal. Weaver and Lasorda were known not only for having great rotations, but for also relying on their starters as much as possible. Alternately, from the column on the right, both Jimy Williams and Frank Chance oversaw spectacular staffs.

Frank Selee not only heavily relied on his front line talent, but his protégé Pat Moran had a score of 0.519. Clearly, these men had some similar thoughts on how to run a team. Then again, Selee's first baseman with the Cubs was Frank Chance, who obviously took a very different approach to handling his pitchers. Sometimes managers emulate those they played under, as Moran did with Selee. Other times they move in the opposite direction, as was the case with Chance.

Small Ball

All the above examples of the Tendencies Database look at one stat at a time. However, since all of the database's results are centered at one, they can be combined rather easily. Some statistics have an underlying philosophical similarity, and combining them gives you a better appreciation of how managers approached their job. For example, sacrifice hits, stolen bases, and the hit and run are all classic parts of "small ball"—doing the little things to manufacture one run at a time. Combining their Tendencies Database scores reveals which managers were the biggest advocates and opponents of this approach.

However, for now, this examination will only add steals and bunts. (Note: An average score is 2.000, not 1.000, because two items are under examination.) The hit and run tendency is a much hazier estimate. Also, it only goes back to the 1930s, while virtually all managers are included in the other two metrics. Add together the Tendencies Database's results for sacrifice hits and stolen base frequency to solve the ancient riddle—who most loved and hated playing for one run?

Small Ball Backers		Small Ball Opponents	
Walter Alston	1.133	Buck Showalter	3.048
Frank Chance	1.334	Jimy Williams	2.927
Whitey Herzog	1.345	Jimmy McAleer	2.849
Paul Richards	1.348	Ralph Houk	2.698
Jack McKeon	1.455	Johnny Oates	2.693

Historically, Red Sox managers did not play for one run. If this list included all the men who lasted at least six years as managers, four of the top seven anti-smallballers would be Red Sox men. Aside from Jimy Williams, there would be Pinky Higgins (3.004), Terry Francona (2.751), and Jimmy Collins (2.741). Among their shorter lasting managers, Billy Herman (2.936) and Joe Morgan (3.022) were all-time great opponents of this strategy, and Eddie Kasko (2.731) was close behind them. Also, Ralph Houk ended his days there. Joe Cronin, with a score of 1.526, is the most notable exception to the franchise's overall trend.

Here are the leaders since the 1930s, including the hit and run estimate (since three stats are added together, an average score is 3.000):

Small Ball Backers		Small Ball Opponents	
Whitey Herzog	2.105	Jimy Williams	4.028
Billy Southworth	2.106	Danny Murtaugh	3.931
Walter Alston	2.201	Buck Showalter	3.929
Al Lopez	2.229	Tom Kelly	3.787
Birdie Tebbetts	2.293	Ralph Houk	3.780

When Ralph Houk finished his managing career, he became a special assistant to the Twins, where he served as a strong influence on the team's new manager, Tom Kelly.

Batting Orders

Finally, beginning in the 1950s, several entirely new avenues of exploration emerge thanks to the wonder and glory of Retrosheet, which provides team splits for all squads since then. As an added bonus, Baseball-Reference.com has taken this splendid data and produced even more intriguing information. Batting orders are one example of this. Baseball-Reference.com includes how many batting orders every team in the last century has used in the course of a season. (Actually, it gives two separate numbers—with and without pitchers included. The Tendencies Database uses the sans-pitchers version.)

I am being intentionally cagey when saying "the 1950s." Specifically, the Tendencies Database includes Retrosheet info from 1956 onward. By the time you read this book, Retrosheet will have made some more years prior to 1956 available. However, when the Tendencies Database was assembled for this book, that was all that was available from Retrosheet.

This sample size includes 39 managers. Here are the men who use the most and fewest batting orders in a season:

Fewest Batting Orders		Most Batting Orders	
Cito Gaston	0.320	Felipe Alou	1.520
Bobby Cox	0.448	Tom Kelly	1.449
Dick Williams	0.522	Tony LaRussa	1.435
Johnny Oates	0.573	Bill Rigney	1.314
Ralph Houk	0.637	Al Dark	1.302

However much influence Houk had on Kelly, that does not make the one-time Twins skipper a clone. He was his own man and made his own decisions, as the above tables note. An underlying philosophical unity exists between Cox's score here and his use of his front-line pitchers. A greater reliance on the same starters leads to fewer batting orders. In both cases Cox wanted to use his most talented players as much as he could in as reliable a manner as possible.

Conclusion

Hopefully these little tables made sense, because the second part of the book is littered with them. (A complete list of all Tendencies Database inquiries used in this book can be found in Appendix II in the back.) The same principles hold true for them all: the center is always 1.0 (unless multiple items are combined, of course); the important part is how much a tendency veers from that center point, not if it is high or low; adjust for context whenever possible; and if there is no perfect way to answer a question (as is the case with hit and run) do the best you can with the info at hand. The Tendencies and Birnbaum Databases are based on the overriding belief that good enough trumps nothing when perfection is not an option.

3

Managers and Starting Pitchers

As their series opened at Comiskey Park on August 8, 1960, the New York Yankees peered out of the visitors' dugout and witnessed an all-too-familiar sight: White Sox ace Billy Pierce warming up on the mound. This would be the fifth time they had seen him that year — and these teams still had two more series to play after this one. The Yankees had faced Pierce seven times the year before and at least five times every season since 1955. That day would be Pierce's 70th start against New York. Given that he had barely 350 starts with Chicago, that was far more than one would expect. In the eight-team AL, only one-seventh of his starts — 50, not 70 — should have come against the Yankees.

It strains credulity to think random happenstance caused Pierce's penchant for performing against the Yankees. Instead, it was the design of Chicago's manager, Al Lopez, who sought to have his ace on the mound for key contests. First-place New York held a one and a half game lead over the White Sox when that August 1960 series began, so it was vital Pierce start. He could pitch in the series opener because Lopez refrained from using Pierce in the preceding five-game series against Washington. The Senators were also-rans, so those games were not as important. Pierce would not have consistent rest, but then again he never had a set pitching schedule. Instead, flexibility defined how Lopez used Pierce, as the skipper even used his ace southpaw from the bullpen several times a year.

Lopez was not the only manager to use pitchers this way. In fact, he was not the only manager in the stadium that day who did so. Casey Stengel had Yankee immortal Whitey Ford warming up in the bullpen past the outfield fence. The White Sox were as sick of him as the Yankees were of Pierce. These two constantly squared off against one another; that day would be their sixteenth duel.

Nowadays, starting pitchers are used in a highly regimented manner with every team's starters pitching in a predetermined order of rotation. It is easy to think that this has been the case since time immemorial. In fact, it is a relatively recent invention. For most of baseball history managers tinkered with their starters rather than giving them a consistent rest period. The game situation, most notably the opposing team's identity, often determined who pitched. In short, managers leveraged their pitchers as best fit the existing circumstances. Individual managers varied in how much they leveraged — some went whole hog for this practice while others were considerably more muted — but it was a key strategic concern for managers for nearly a century.

However, pitcher leveraging has been the subject of minimal research from baseball historians and analysts. Dick Thompson in, *The Ferrell Brothers of Baseball*, touched on how this managerial strategy affected Wes Ferrell. However, Thompson looked at merely one pitcher. The only other substantial investigation of leveraging came in a series of articles that I penned at *The Hardball Times* website in 2007, which laid out the basic approach to studying leveraging followed in this chapter. However, this chapter does more than simply regurgitate those articles. Most notably, the sample size under examination has been significantly expanded, allowing for a better and more complete understanding of this practice. When those articles were published, about 70 percent of all starts from the years leveraging occurred (from the 1870s to 1960s) had been examined. Now, 92 percent of all starts from 1876 to 1969, including every time any pitcher started at least ten games in a season, are accounted for. The enlarged sample size provides both a clearer picture of the course of leveraging and a better understanding of exactly how and why it ended. What follows is a new and improved version of those articles.

Quantifying It: AOWP+

Noting leveraging's existence is one thing; quantifying it is another matter entirely. To do that, I created a stat called AOWP+, which can be best explained with an example. In 1909, Cubs ace Mordecai "Three Finger" Brown started 34 games for manager Frank Chance. Below are how many starts came against each rival, and the teams' winning percentages:

Team	GS	Pct
PIT	8	.724
NYG	9	.601
CIN	4	.503
PHI	3	.484
BRK	4	.359
STL	2	.355
BOS	4	.294

Now *that* is leveraging. Half of Brown's starts came against the two rivals with the best winning percentage.

To quantify this leveraging, multiply the number of starts Brown had versus each opponent by their winning percentage, add the results together, and divide by total starts in order to discern the average record for the teams Brown opposed.

Team	GS		Pct		Result
PIT	8	×	.724	=	5.792
NYG	9	×	.601	=	5.409
CIN	4	×	.503	=	2.012
PHI	3	×	.484	=	1.452
BRK	4	×	.359	=	1.436
STL	2	×	.355	=	0.710
BOS	4	×	.294	=	1.176

The numbers on the right add up to 17.987. Divide that by the 34 starts that Brown had in 1909, and the result is a .529 Average Opponent Winning Percentage, or AOWP for short. That is a remarkably high AOWP, especially when you realize the Cubs had a .680 winning percentage themselves. In fact, applying the same process to the Cubs as a whole that was just used on Brown (take games played against each individual team times their winning percentage, then average it) produces a result of .475. That is TOWP (Team's Opponent Winning Percentage). To determine the way a pitcher was leveraged, divide AOWP by TOWP, multiply by 100, and round to the nearest integer. The result is called AOWP+, which best indicates the degree a particular starting pitcher was leveraged in a season. In 1909 Mordecai Brown had an AOWP+ of 111 (.529/.475*100); which is the highest AOWP+ since 1876 by anyone with at least 30 starts.

The only credible explanation for Brown's score was that Frank Chance intentionally reserved him for series against Chicago's best rivals. However, that begs a question — at what point does AOWP+ indicate intentional leveraging, and when is it just random happenstance? A 111 is the product of design, but what about a 107 or 105 or 103? There is no perfect answer; instead of a black and white line, a substantial shade of gray exists. However, a few points can be noted based on the research I have done. It is virtually impossible to get an AOWP+ of 105 or higher (or 95 or lower) without intentional leveraging. In a rare once in a while it might occur, but it is needle in a haystack territory. An AOWP+ of 104 almost always indicates leveraging, but some exceptions exist. Scores become increasingly murky at 103 and especially at 102. Those marks can indicate moderate leverage, but they are increasingly likely to be achieved through the luck of the draw. An AOWP+ of 101 or 99 tells you virtually nothing; it is essentially luck.

This analysis breaks down a little bit in the very early days of baseball. Through the mid–1880s, teams occasionally had one pitcher start every day for weeks on end, and then take him out for an extended stretch. It could indicate leveraging, or that the pitcher had been benched. For example, if you look at the National Association, Tommy Bond received an AOWP+ of 122 in 1875. However, he was not leveraged, he just happened to join the team midseason after they had finished playing the creampuffs. By the mid–1880s this problem fades away.

Applying to Managers: LPA+

The above is nice, but this book is not entitled *Evaluating Baseball's Pitchers*. Mordecai Brown and his teammates on the 1909 Cubs demonstrate how AOWP+ can be applied to managers. Here are the marks for everyone on that staff with at least ten starts:

Pitcher	AOWP+	GS
Mordecai Brown	111	34
Ed Reulbach	105	32
Orval Overall	101	32
Jack Pfiester	89	25
Rube Kroh	82	13

Clearly Cubs manager Frank Chance loved to leverage his starters. Brown and Reulbach had 27 starts against the top two rivals, but only eleven against the worst pair. Meanwhile, Jack Pfiester faced last-place Boston as often he started against the three best opponents combined: seven times.

To quantify managerial inclination, first assign every pitcher a value based on how far his AOWP+ ranges from 100. An AOWP+ of 100 is worth zero points. Call this zero Leverage Points (LP). If someone has a score of 99 or 101, credit him with one Leverage Point. From that point, add two LPs for every integer the AOWP+ moves from 100:

AOWP+	LP
100	0
101, 99	1
102, 98	3
103, 97	5
104, 96	7
105, 95	9
106, 94	11
107, 93	13

As anyone can easily notice, the first gap is worth only one LP, but all subsequent ones are worth two. This is because the first step from 100 is the least important, hence the comparative devaluing of that gap.

After calculating LP for every pitcher with at least ten starts, take their LP and multiply by games started. Add that together and average out for the entire staff. For the 1909 Cubs, the calculation looks like this:

Pitcher	LP		GS		Result
Mordecai Brown	21	×	34	=	714
Ed Reulbach	9	×	32	=	288
Orval Overall	1	×	32	=	32
Jack Pfiester	21	×	25	=	525
Rube Kroh	35	×	13	=	455
ALL			136		2,014

Divide 2,014 by 136, for a result of 14.81 LP per start, a very high total. That is Chance's LPA — Leverage Points Average. This can be applied to every team in each season for all managers. Only pitchers with at least ten starts are considered for LPA because it is very easy to pile up a tremendous number of LP if a pitcher only has a small number of starts even if he was not intentionally leveraged. Including those scrub starters creates unduly high LPAs for squads that contained an unusually high number of spot starters. (Admittedly, managers often leveraged their tertiary arms, often lining them up against the league's worst squads, but the cons outweigh the pros when it comes to including them in LPA.)

However, two quirks need to be addressed. First, LPA only examines pitchers in the years 1876–1965. This cutoff has been made due to the results of the research on pitcher leveraging. As noted earlier, this study has looked at every time a pitcher started ten or more times in season through 1969. As a result, I can say with considerable confidence that leveraging ceased to exist by the mid–1960s. To be sure, an additional 35,000 starts since 1970 were also checked — primarily starts by the ace pitchers who would have been the most likely to be leveraged. It is abundantly clear that leveraging never recovered as a meaningful strategy after the mid–1960s. Since this is a study of leveraging, it is best to focus on the years the practice actually occurred. If a manager began his career before that breakpoint and stayed on the job after that, this study ignores his future career when calculating LPA and LPA+.

Second, when someone pitches for multiple teams in a season, that campaign is not included in a manager's LPA. It messes up TOWP because maybe the team faced an unusually hard or easy schedule when he was on their roster. Besides, guys who only pitched for one team in a season while having at least ten starts account for almost 85 percent of all games started from 1876 to 1965.

Here are the most extreme LPAs among the 75 skippers with the longest careers in the leveraging era:

Leverage Kings, 1876–1965		Anti-leveragers, 1876–1965	
Frank Chance	7.78	Pat Moran	2.27
Pie Traynor	6.60	Bill Rigney	2.59
Mel Ott	6.13	Horace Phillips	2.63
Walter Johnson	5.91	Tom Loftus	2.65
Frankie Frisch	5.88	Luke Sewell	2.69

Frank Chance leveraged like nobody else. Pat Moran actually played for Chance from 1906 to 1909, but Moran clearly came to completely different conclusions on how to run a pitching staff. Moran's inclusion reveals a main philosophical divide in handling starting pitchers. The main concern for managers like Chance was making the innings count by putting their ace on the mound in every important series: the *quality* of innings mattered most. Moran had a different priority —*quantity*. As noted in Chapter 2, he leaned on his main starters as much as possible, having them throw as many innings as possible. In order for them to achieve such hefty workloads, Moran used them with minimal concern for the opposing team's identity.

Managers who frequently leveraged had trouble maximizing innings from their most important arms. By its very nature, leveraging causes a manager to give his ace extra rest sometimes. For example, from 1906 to 1912, when Chance managed the Cubs, Mordecai Brown had two 300-inning seasons and the rest of the staff had one, but the other seven NL teams combined for 36 different 300-inning performances in that period.

One technique minimized leveraging's quantity problem — relief work. Chance did not just use Brown as his ace, but also made him the bullpen fireman. Though no one tracked it back then, Brown led the league in saves every year from 1908 to 1911, becoming the first man to crack double digits with thirteen in 1911. At one point, Brown was baseball's career save leader. Chance was extreme, but far from unique, in using his starters like this. Actually, it is not entirely accurate to call someone like Brown a starter as that word creates an image of a stark split between relievers and starters. No such firm distinction existed, either in 1909 or 1960. As late as the 1960 American League, every pitcher with at least twenty starts had at least one relief appearance. In contrast, of the 1,100 occasions a pitcher started twenty or more games from 2000–08, 769 (70 percent) performed exclusively as starters.

However, though relief work minimized leveraging's quantity dilemma, it did not solve it. Despite being used so frequently in relief, Brown racked up relatively few innings for an ace hurler in his era. The best leveraged pitchers and the hardest worked starters were historically two separate groups.

A problem exists with the lists of managers with the most extreme LPA scores: era bias. For various reasons to be covered later, leveraging had its ebbs and flows over time. One of the main goals of the last chapter was to contextualize a manager's tendencies within his era, and we will do that in this chapter as well.

Pat Moran, who managed from 1915 to 1923, can serve as an example of how to adjust LPA for era. First, figure out his LPA. Excluding pitchers who played on more than one team in a season, 42 different times one of Moran's hurlers started at least ten games in a season for him, which produced, as noted previously, an LPA of 2.27. Next, calculate the LPA for Moran's era. In other words, take every occasion a pitcher started at least ten games from 1915 to 1923, determine the LPA for each one, and figure the overall LPA for major league baseball in the years Moran managed. Based on that approach, baseball's LPA was 3.60 in that period. Divide Moran's LPA into major league baseball's overall LPA from 1915 to 1923, multiply by 100, and round to the nearest integer. For Moran, 2.27 divided by 3.60 times 100 equals 63. Upon completing this formula to adjust a manager's propensity to leverage by era, the resulting statistic will be centered at 100. Thus a manager whose leveraging perfectly suited the period's inclinations will have a mark of 100, one who leveraged more will have a higher score, and a lower score indicates the skipper did it less than his peers. Call this number LPA+. Its leaders were:

Leverage Kings, 1876–1965		Anti-leveragers, 1876–1965	
Frank Chance	178	Horace Phillips	60
Bill Killefer	143	Luke Sewell	61
Walter Johnson	137	Pat Moran	63
Mel Ott	132	Tom Loftus	70
Pie Traynor	130	Frank Bancroft	70

While many names are repeats from the LPA leaderboards, new faces appear and some of the old ones drop off. For example, Killefer managed during a lull in the practice that occurred in the early 1920s. Various circumstances caused the ebbs and flows of leveraging over time. While Appendix III covers baseball's LPAs over the years, the next section provides a brief summary and explanation for leveraging's ups and downs over the decades.

A Very Brief History of Leveraging

In major league baseball's infancy, teams used only one pitcher. His job was to toss the ball to the batter and let him put it in play. Since the pitcher's job was far less stressful than it currently is, he could pitch practically all the time. For example, Jim Devlin pitched every single inning for the 1877 Louisville Grays. If the pitcher needed a day off, his team often started a position player. However, this system did not last forever, as the playing season expanded from 60 to 80 games, then to 100 and beyond. Concurrently, the art of pitching evolved, causing hurlers to put increasing strain on their arms. They could still throw huge number of innings, but the Devlin days had passed. By the early 1880s, teams needed multiple pitchers.

Pitcher leveraging had its murky origins in these years. In researching the creation of leveraging, ideally an "A-ha!" moment would be found, when you could say the practice began when Manager X leveraged Pitcher Y on Team Z in the year Q. Alas, no such moment exists because leveraging predates teams possessing multiple starting pitchers. That sounds strange, but it is true. When teams featured only one starter, they were more likely to rest him against a dreadful opponent; this similar to how a twenty-first-century team might rest a star hitter against a weaker opponent so he will be ready for a crucial series. For example, in 1877 Boston hurler Tommy Bond started 57 of his team's 60 games, missing only three contests against the last-place Cincinnati squad.

When teams began using multiple pitchers, some of the most impressive AOWP+s were low scores from secondary arms. The ace still started a large majority of games, making it impossible to get an AOWP particularly different from the squad's TOWP. However, secondary arms could and did pile up a noteworthy AOWP+, as teams frequently relegated them to facing off against the least impressive opponents. For example, when Providence ace John Ward recorded an AOWP+ of 103 in 60 starts in 1879, teammate Bobby Mathews had an AOWP+ of 91 in the team's 24 remaining contests.

In the 1880s, leveraging became whom an ace pitcher faced instead of rested against. The most impressive achievement of the decade occurred in 1888 from the American Association's third-place Philadelphia Athletics. Team workhorse Ed Seward started 57 of their 136 games. Eleven came against the first-place St. Louis club, ten versus second-place Brooklyn, and eleven against fourth-place Cincinnati for an AOWP+ of 108, miraculous for someone who started so frequently.

In the early 1890s, leveraging temporarily declined. The American Association collapsed after 1891, and the NL absorbed some of its squads, expanding to a twelve-team league. This lessened the appeal of leveraging because teams normally only saw each other twelve games a year, making the strategy less useful. Though leveraging fell into temporary eclipse, the 1890s witnessed a massive rule change that eventually aided the strategy's popularity. In 1893, a change in baseball's rules moved pitchers to the present distance of 60 feet 6 inches from the plate. Previously they had thrown from a pitcher's box whose front line was closer to the batter. Overnight, innings pitched totals plummeted. Pitchers not only stopped throwing 500 innings in a season, but quickly fell below 400 as well. By making a team less dependent on one or two arms, this rule change opened the door for more leveraging once the league contracted to eight teams in 1900.

When teams began playing each other 22 times a season in 1904, leveraging soon attained a prominence heretofore unknown. In 1907, baseball had an overall LPA of 4.96, the highest mark in almost twenty years. Two years later, it rose to 6.48, the largest total the game had seen up to that point. As leveraging developed, it was not a simple matter of ace vs. good teams. Sometimes, a manager just liked the way a particular pitcher matched up against a specific opponent. For example, in mid–1909 the A's acquired Cy Morgan, a serviceable right-handed pitcher. He started 90 games for his new team, 26 of which came against the Indians. Heaven only knows why Connie Mack loved starting Morgan against Cleveland, but he clearly did.

A far more important variation emerged — platoon leveraging, which was arguably more widespread than standard leveraging. Teams hid their southpaws against exceptionally right-handed lineups (or ballparks not favorable to them) and started them against squads laden with left-handed hitters. Though platoon leveraging predated the twentieth century, the late nineteenth and early twentieth centuries witnessed an upsurge in quality lefty arms, causing this method to expand. In theory, AOWP+ does not measure this, but in practice it usually does. After all, the teams most likely to be platoon leveraged against were those with the best right- or left-handed offenses. Not surprisingly, teams with first-rate offenses are typically good squads. It was especially common for teams to start their southpaws against clubs containing the Cobbs and Ruths of the world. Since fewer left-handed pitchers existed, the ones worth spotting against specific teams experienced platoon leveraging far more often than righties did. Lefties as a whole have superior AOWP+ totals throughout baseball history.

After World War I, a combination of factors led to another decline in leveraging. Since platoon leveraging had rapidly become a vital part of managerial strategy, the rise in offensive platooning caused a downturn in overall pitcher leveraging. In 1914, the Miracle Braves won the World Series, largely thanks to manager George Stallings's penchant for platooning his hitters. Other teams copied Stallings's technique, inaugurating the golden age of offensive platooning, which lasted until approximately 1930. Aside from that, the surge in run scoring in the early 1920s put a crimp into leveraging. As home runs became far more common with the rise of Babe Ruth, pitchers had to bear down on each hitter more, increasing the strain and stress every start put on a pitcher's arm. Previously, a mistake would be considerably less likely to leave the park. The lesser strain of deadball era pitching allowed managers to use pitchers on shorter rest with greater frequency, increasing the scenarios in which pitchers could be leveraged. The new offensive environment limited flexibility for handling pitchers, and flexibility was the lifeblood of leveraging. Yearly LPA scores, which had consistently been well over 4.0 when Chance managed, fell to around 3.0 in the early 1920s, dipping down to 2.73 in 1918 and again in 1923.

Around 1930, as Bill James and others have noted, offensive platooning declined, causing a corresponding increase in both platoon and regular pitcher leveraging. In 1928, baseball's overall LPA cracked 4.0 for the first time in nine years. By the late 1930s, LPAs hovered over 5.0 on a regular basis. The huge individual AOWP+ totals hurlers like Mordecai Brown posted were in the past, but teams consistently placed particular pitchers against specific rivals, and posted their southpaws against the most fearsome left-handed hitters. This continued fairly steadily prior to World War II. In 1942, yearly LPA reached its one-year zenith at 7.07. This was something of a fluke, as unusually disparate win/loss records can lead to unexpectedly large AOWP+s, and that season the Cardinals won 106 games, the Dodgers won 104, and the Phillies lost 109.

The next year, the military draft began to take a serious toll on baseball. Until the regular players began returning, leveraging fell into relative disuse, as teams barely knew who their own best hitters and pitchers were, let alone those of the opposition. In 1944, baseball had a total LPA of 2.46, the lowest single season in nearly a half-century.

After the war, leveraging again revived. In fact, the strategy encountered its greatest stretch since the deadball era, arguably ever. Five of the seven highest post–1920 LPAs occurred between 1946–55, and baseball's only back-to-back LPAs over 6.0 occurred in 1953–54. This new wave of enthusiasm can be largely attributed to Casey Stengel. Even before Ford and Pierce began dueling, Stengel was a big proponent of pitcher leveraging. Eddie Lopat's uncanny ability to defeat the Indians in the early 1950s was so pronounced that Cleveland owner Bill Veeck held a special "Beat Eddie Lopat" night at the ballpark. Since Stengel captured five consecutive world championships, others adopted his methods. In 1954, baseball had an overall LPA of 7.07 (though technically tied with 1942 for the best ever, but taken to the thousandths decimal, 1942 tops 1954). Fourteen different pitchers posted an AOWP+ of at least 105. On the Yankees alone, Stengel had Ford, Lopat, and Allie Reynolds post AOWP+s of 112, 109, and 107 for a team-wide LPA of 16.52, the highest by any squad in the twentieth century.

By this time leveraging had been used longer than anyone in the game could remember, was firmly entrenched, popular, and had the game's best-regarded manager clearly advocating it. Yet the concept was on its last legs. In the mid–1960s, baseball's yearly LPA fell below 2.0 for the first time ever, and with the exception of the occasional flukish one-year blip, it has stayed there. It is the damnedest thing.

The End of Leveraging

Several factors caused the rapid demise of this long-lasting pitching practice. One of the first noteworthy blows to the old strategy came in the 1959 World Series, in which Al Lopez's White Sox faced the Dodgers. That Dodger bunch, which possessed a lower winning percentage than any previous National League pennant winner, did not belong in the postseason. Their offense had declined considerably from their mid–1950s heyday and the pitching tandem of Sandy Koufax and Don Drysdale was a few years from its prime. However, the Dodgers handily beat the White Sox in six games. Chicago fans did not have to look far to find a reason to be upset: Lopez, for reasons many could not fathom, opted not to start staff ace Billy Pierce. Instead, Pierce threw a mere four inconsequential innings in relief, spending the rest of the Series as a bystander.

From the point of view of leveraging, Lopez made a sound decision. Pierce was not just an ace — he was also a lefty. In the 1950s, teams rarely pitched their southpaws against the Dodger hitters, because right-handed hitters dominated their lineup. In 1957, for example, lefties started only six games against Los Angeles. In some ways, Lopez was just behind the times, as the 1959 Dodgers were no longer as loaded with righties as in previous seasons. Rather than trusting his best arm, Lopez out-thought himself in October. The Pat Morans of the world were aghast.

The following World Series delivered another blow to leveraging. The Yankees famously lost to the Pirates in seven games despite outscoring them 55–27. Again, the most obvious oddity was a manager who refused to trust his ace southpaw. Stengel, noticing that the first two games were in Pittsburgh's Forbes Field, a ballpark hard on southpaws, reserved Whitey Ford for Game 3 in Yankee Stadium. As a result of this decision, Ford started only two games that October. Making a mockery of Stengel's strategy, he twirled shutouts in both contests, including one at Forbes Field. Like Lopez before him, Stengel became an easy target for critics. Both men had overanalyzed the situation. Fans groused, Pat Moran spun in his grave, and the Yankees fired Stengel.

Neither the 1959 nor 1960 World Series was a story about classical leveraging; in both cases there was only one opposing team. Yet the decisions Lopez and Stengel made unmistakably came from a leveraging mindset. Both wanted to place their aces in situations where the quality of their work would be most advantageous. To that end, they willingly sacrificed quantity.

The 1961 season further hastened leveraging's demise. Instead of showing the limitations of emphasizing quality, the baseball world witnessed an impressive demonstration of the advantages of prioritizing quantity. Though new Yankee manager Ralph Houk had played and coached for Stengel, he belonged to the Moran school when it came to handling his pitchers. Under Stengel, Whitey Ford had started more than 30 games in a season only once, and last topped 29 in 1956. Stengel had pressed him into bullpen service every year, up to a half-dozen relief appearances a season. Ford may have been one of the most leveraged pitchers in the game, but he also averaged barely 200 innings a year, and had never won twenty games. Houk ended that, and under his guidance Ford led the league with 39 starts and 283 innings pitched in 1961. He never pitched in relief, only appearing when it was his turn in the starting rotation. As a result, Ford went 25–4 to earn the Cy Young Award. Behind the Houk-ized pitching staff, the Yankees won 109 games— the franchise's most since the 1927 Murderers Row squad — and easily captured the World Series. They repeated the following October, for New York's first back-to-back titles since 1949–53.

The moral of the story was simple: put your best pitcher out there as often as possible. Preferably he should have a set amount of rest so he can consistently perform his best. In order to do that, managers should use their starters in a steady and consistent manner in which they not only take the mound in regular turns but are also not used out of the bullpen. Trust in the pitchers' talent rather than the manager's brains, and the team will win more games. The 1960 AL was the final time every starter in the league with at least twenty starts also appeared in relief. It would be a gross oversimplification to claim that the arrival of Ralph Houk forced the change, but the Stengel-Houk shift more than anything else embodied the revolution in pitcher-usage patterns.

A background factor aided this transition: expansion. From 1904 to 1960, teams routinely played each opposing squad 22 times per year. As late as 1959, Don Drysdale pitched nearly 70 innings in nine games against the Braves. With the move to ten teams in the AL in 1961 and the NL the following year, teams faced each other in only a half-dozen series. In the 1890s, a similar process had diminished leveraging.

In 1962, Don Drysdale and Johnny Podres started 81 of the Dodgers's 165 games for manager Walter Alston. The previous decades had almost no precedent for two pitchers starting such a high percentage of a team's games. The Spahn and Sain Braves reached a similar point in the late 1940s, but the next most recent example came with Pat Moran's Reds in the early 1920s. Alston achieved this by putting them on a set schedule and making them almost exclusively starters. Admittedly, Drysdale had two relief appearances, but revolutions are rarely pure breaks with the past.

The next year, Drysdale and Sandy Koufax started 82 of the team's 163 games without any relief appearances. This had never occurred before — but it nearly happened to another team that same year. Juan Marichal and Jack Sanford of Los Angeles's archrival Giants combined for 82 starts, but with one relief appearance. A revolution was underway, and the best teams in baseball were at its forefront.

This revolution quickly reverberated across baseball, with a structural element aiding its rapid adoption. If the Dodgers or Giants developed a pitcher, the franchise indoctrinated him into pitching on regular rest. Maybe once in a while he would receive a short start and days off could cause him to have extra rest, but typically he grew accustomed to appearing on a regular turn. Thus it became part of his physical and mental approach to the game. If the Dodgers traded him to a team that leveraged, he would have to make a tremendous adaptation. Not only would he have to retrain his arm to pitch on varying days rest, but also (and more importantly) he would need to adjust himself psychologically. His arm might get sore, and/or his confidence could erode, causing his numbers to decline. The new team would be better off treating him as the Dodgers did. This does not mean the new generation could not be used in the Frank Chance method, but that it is difficult and dangerous to retrain some-one unnecessarily. Alternately, a pitcher joining the Dodgers would not have any correspon-ding difficulties. Even if he had been the most heavily leveraged pitcher in the world, he had experience pitching on three or four days rest, even if it had not been exclusively the case. It was like bad money driving out good: the very existence of some standardized rotations forced the destruction of all leveraged starters.

People like to think that the standard four-man rotation existed for decades, but that is not true. If that were the case, pitchers would have regularly started 38 or 39 times in the course of the 154-game season. Instead, there were plenty of times prior to 1960 when 35 starts led the league. Sometimes 34 sufficed. In the 1953 NL, Robin Roberts was the only man to start more than 33 times. From 1920 to 1960, no Cub pitcher had more than 36 starts in a sea-son. Cleveland's great staffs of the early 1950s provide a good example of how differently teams handled their pitchers in days before a strict four-man rotation. With Early Wynn, Bob Lemon, Bob Feller, and Mike Garcia, Cleveland had the most solid rotation baseball had seen it decades, yet it looked nothing like Walter Alston's 1960s staffs. Even when all four Indians were healthy and productive they usually each started 30–35 games a year while also making occasional relief appearances. As he would in Chicago, Indians manager Al Lopez had a flexi-ble approach to pitching, giving his main arms varying days of rest throughout the early-to-mid 1950s. Though Cleveland possessed four main starters, they never pitched in a fixed, rotating order.

The 1964 NL pennant race provided another nail in leveraging's coffin. In one of the most infamous collapses in the annals of sports, Gene Mauch's Phillies blew a six and a half game lead with a dozen contests left to play by dropping ten straight decisions. In that dis-astrous stretch, Mauch made the controversial decision to start his hurlers on short rest. When the losses kept mounting, the move immediately became second guessed and for some symbolized the entire Phillie collapse. Just like the 1959–60 World Series, this move was not technically an example of classical leveraging as Mauch's pitchers still pitched in a set order. In fact, Mauch had never been much of a leverager (though he had dabbled in the practice a little with the Phillies). However, the notion of short starting them harkened back to lever-age's central premise: the way a manager used his pitchers mattered the most.

From a storytelling purpose, it would be perfect if no teams leveraged after the great Phillies Phlop. Reality has a nasty habit of being slightly messier than one would like it to be, however. Though leveraging essentially ended after 1964, one last gasp provided a final coda to the nearly century-old practice as Senators' manager Gil Hodges noticeably leveraged some of his pitchers in 1965. Most notably, swingman Bennie Daniels recorded an AOWP+ of 108 in 18 starts. Only three of his starts came against the four opposing teams with losing records. Alternately, he had five against the second-place White Sox and three versus the pennant-winning Twins. Southpaw swingman Frank Kreutzer had an AOWP+ of 95 over fourteen starts, while rotation warhorse Phil Ortega had a mark of 94 in 29 starts. Even with Hodges's rotation, major league baseball had an overall LPA+ of 2.46, one of the lowest ever. In 1966, it fell to 1.68, the first time ever that is was lower than 2.0. With the exception of the occa-sionally flukishly high mark, baseball-wide LPA+s have stayed under 2.0 ever since. By the mid–1960s, leveraging ceased to exist as a meaningful practice.

Even on the rare occasion in contemporary baseball when a manager tries to specifically match up a starter against an opponent, it is a far cry from the days of Stengel and Chance. Nowadays, a manager would only adjust his pitcher's day off, while still maintaining a rota-tion. Stengel and Chance never had a rotation. When leveraging starters, a set rotation is impossible. Leveraging is dependent upon fluid pitcher usage, and a rotation requires a reg-imented pattern. In the early to mid 1960s, the latter pushed out the former. To date, the pen-dulum has never swung back.

PART II
COMMENTARY

Part II applies everything discussed in Part I to specific managers. Since the goal is to cover the most important managers, this part includes everyone who served at least ten years as the primary manager for a major league team. Also, a dozen of the most notable skippers with shorter careers also are examined.

I divided managerial commentary into eras. The breaks between periods correspond with key changes occurring in the managerial profession and baseball in general. Sometimes judgment calls must be made when trying to decide which manager belongs in what era. Managers typically go where they spent the most time, but that is just a general guideline, not a fixed law. A manager might spend 60 percent of his career in one era, but be best remembered for the remaining 40 percent of his career, in which case he would be placed in the latter period. The idea is to put them where they fit best, not to build a monument to consistency. At times it is a little arbitrary deciding who goes where, but that is unavoidable.

Also, a few items are included at the outset for all managers:

- Win/loss record
- Teams managed
- Score in the Birnbaum Database
- Characteristics of their teams
- Combinations of multiple inquiries.
- LPA and LPA+ (only for those that managed from 1876 to 1965)

The list of teams managed has been divided into three categories: squads managed the entire season, majority of the season, and minority of the year. The first two groups affect their scores in the Tendencies Database, but the third does not.

Birnbaum Database information is only included if the manager had at least 500 games under his belt from 1896 to 2006 (the period covered by the database) and those games make up over half his career. For other managers, this information obscures more than it illuminates. As a result, Birnbaum Database results will not be found in Chapter 4 at all, or for Ozzie Guillen in Chapter 9.

Team characteristics cover some interesting and important overall information about each manager. Two main sources exist for this information: the Tendencies Database and a series of searches performed with Baseball-Reference's Play Index. The latter source generated information such as which manager oversaw the most 200-hit seasons or never had a 20-game winner. Sometimes other facts that did not fit in anywhere else are also included in team characteristics.

Sometimes statistics will be discussed in an ahistorical manner. For example, the concept of the save did not exist until the 1960s, so managers prior to then could not have had that specific stat in mind when using their teams. Saves for previous teams were determined well after the fact, but this study refers to teams and pitchers from well before 1960 setting save records, as if they knew what that was. This is done in part for the sake of convenience.

Referring to saves as a future creation each time it was brought up in the next three chapters would be needlessly cumbersome. More importantly, even if the saves were retroactively determined, the stat still says something vital about how managers differed in their approaches to running pitching staffs. Other stats, such as Defensive Efficiency Ratio (DER) and Win Shares, are handled in a similar manner.

4

Primordial Managers, 1876–1892

Nineteenth century managers were an odd lot. By twentieth century standards, a great many would never have been hired. To comprehend them and their role in the game, one should understand how baseball has evolved as a business.

For example, look at Bill Cammeyer, who managed the National League's New York Mutuals in 1876. He was a very important person in the game's history because he introduced profitability to baseball; more precisely, he institutionalized it. Specifically, he introduced the fence — two fences actually. He built one around the field, and the second at the outskirts of the property itself (which he owned). Then he made people pay money to get past the latter so they can sit behind the former to watch the game. They call Cammeyer's creation the stadium. Sometimes the simplest revolutions are the most important.

Before Cammeyer, teams would pass around the hat at a contest's conclusion for their money. This system was not especially dependable. People walked away during the game and cheapskates could leave little. The stadium was a shrewd move on Cammeyer's part, but it had nothing to do with managing. That idea qualifies one to be a top front office executive or the eager young beaver in marketing — something like that. There is no evidence he had any real idea how to handle pitchers or a clubhouse.

Cammeyer's managerial career was no aberration. Several of the game's early skippers — Charlie Byrne, Jim Hart, Jimmy Williams, and Bill Sharsig — were like that. Some, like Cammeyer, were the owners and planting themselves on the bench saved money. They were business managers, not baseball managers. The most successful business manager was Jim Mutrie, who won two pennants and ended a nine-year stint with a .611 winning percentage. He left most baseball decisions to team captains John Ward and Buck Ewing.

One of the more intriguing managers was Cincinnati skipper O. P. Caylor. Prior to taking over the Reds, he was a local sportswriter. Caylor used that position to argue on behalf of a club returning to Cincinnati after the NL revoked the town's franchise after 1880. It is impossible someone like that would become a manager today. The best current comparison would be if the Washington Nationals pegged Thomas Boswell to run their club — but Boswell would be lucky to be the 10,000th person on the National's list of possible managers.

In short, the people listed in the encyclopedias as this period's managers undertook very different responsibilities than current ones do. While they ignored many core elements of modern managing, primordial skippers often performed a variety of different tasks that nowadays are considered the responsibilities of traveling secretaries, clubhouse attendants, and other lesser regarded roles, such as taking care of the team's inventory and supplies, counting the receipts, arranging transportation and lodging, and so forth. There was not enough money in and around baseball in 1880 to justify separate jobs, so the manager did them. The game's finances were very precarious in these early years. In the first fifteen years of the

National League, eighteen teams went out of business—and that was the game's most successful league. At least it survived, unlike the National Association, Union Association, Players League, or American Association.

With their numerous responsibilities, about the only thing managers did not do was manage the game. In fact, when the NL began, in-game strategy was largely an undiscovered country. Fielders backing each other up and bits of classic baseball play that most learn in Little League nowadays were still being worked out. With less strategy, teams had minimal interest in paying someone who focused on that. Instead, managers needed to make sure the economic entity that was their team survived the road trip; whether or not they outmaneuvered the opposition was not their main concern.

To be fair, not all managers were like Cammeyer. There were always some players who also managed, such as Cap Anson or Harry Wright. They helped invent the ideas that became received wisdom to all subsequent generations—though they still contended with the irregular obligations of the job. They were the ultimate jacks-of-all-trades: playing, managing, and doing all the unglamorous jobs as well.

Things began changing around 1890. Some of the team captains and player-managers who were still effective at handling their dugout responsibilities retired. They moved the job from its primordial origins to a more fully evolved position as they determined strategy even though they did not actually play themselves. As the game's financial health became more profitable, the petty little jobs that took up the time from the original batch of managers began to be assigned to others. Once the NL stabilized, the position of manager could come into its own. The old Cammeyer-Caylor type of manager vanished. A new crop of managers emerged—men like Ned Hanlon and Frank Selee. They still had to sort out some off-field issues, but the focus changed from being a business manager to a baseball manager. In-game tactics became more advanced and refined, causing that portion of the job to gain greater importance. Almost all the first generation of managers had been swept away by 1895. Some of the sharpest baseball minds, like Charles Comiskey, were rising up the chain and would become owners. Others had been drummed out of the sport.

Fittingly, this occurred just as the game's central rules became established. The 1880s saw the legalization of overhand pitching and the creation of the four-ball, three-strike count. When pitchers had to work from 60 feet six inches in 1893, modern baseball had essentially emerged, more common to the 2008 game than its 1876 version. Similarly, managers like Ned Hanlon had more in common with Mike Scioscia than O. P. Caylor.

CAP ANSON

> **W-L Record**: 1296–947 (.578)
> **Managed**: Full Seasons: Chicago (NL) 1879–97
>   Majority in: (none)
>   Minority of: New York 1898
> **Team Characteristics**: Anson's teams had terrific offenses which heavily relied
>   on set starting lineups. They played well in one-run games, posting
>   a 275–225 (.550) record in those affairs. Chicago won a majority of
>   those closest of contests in ten straight seasons.
> **LPA**: 4.46   **LPA+**: 107

Arguably the best player of his generation, Anson was one of the first managers who took an active role during the game itself. He mocked opposing players from the sidelines and baited umpires. Though this made him one of the more volatile managers of the 1880s, by the 1890s—when rowdyism reached its peak—his act seemed downright tame. His in-game orneriness was not an act, either. A natural and forceful leader, Anson ruled his players firmly off the field as he possessed a temper that could make people think twice before crossing him.

He did not rule entirely by temperament, though. Anson insisted his players have the best accommodations when they traveled. Since the White Stockings (as the Cubs were called back then) was one of the most profitable teams in the league, they could live comfortably on the road. As early as 1886 he took his team to Arkansas for spring training, and by the early 1890s (if not earlier) Anson established an informal scouting network that allowed him to keep tabs on players possibly worth picking up. He occasionally had open tryouts for these young hopefuls who wanted a crack at the big leagues. This approach gave Anson tremendous success early on as manager, winning five pennants from 1880 to 1886.

By the 1890s, Anson was far less successful, primarily because he did not have the same caliber of players. That always matters the most. Even aside from that, Anson was less effective. Although the practices listed above helped put him ahead of the game in the 1880s, the playing field evened out when other squads did likewise. With franchises no longer folding every year, others could afford to invest more in their teams.

As the resources gap narrowed, the generation gap widened, further hurting Anson. When players began a union effort in the late 1880s, the elder Anson forcefully backed the owners. (In fact, by this time Anson personally held a small stake in the Chicago franchise.) The players formed their own league in 1890, taking most of the NL players with them, including almost all of Chicago's lineup — but not Anson. When the new league faltered, players returned to the NL, but they were angry. In fact, some contemporaries thought the Cubs lost the 1891 pennant due to this widely-felt animosity toward Anson. When the Boston Beaneaters won eighteen consecutive games late in the season to overcome a six and a half game lead held by Anson's Cubs, rumors swirled that players had intentionally dumped games against Boston to help the Beaneaters capture the flag. Though the rumors were never substantiated, the fact that they existed indicated considerable animosity towards the league's best-known name. After the 1891 campaign, Anson's club never factored in another pennant race.

Not only did Anson have trouble relating to players, but he also fell behind the times in his approach to the game, a fact exemplified by his handling of pitchers. In 1880, Anson became the first NL manager to evenly and intentionally split the work between two pitchers on a regular basis. Up to that point in time, teams generally relied as much as they could on one arm. For example, in 1879 Will White started almost every game for Cincinnati, and Boston ace Tommy Bond blew out his arm after starting 35 consecutive games. Teams that featured more than one pitcher generally used the second man as an emergency spot starter while the ace went out as often as possible. By divvying up Chicago's work between Larry Corcoran and Fred Goldsmith in 1880, Anson helped change how teams used their pitchers.

Later in the 1880s, as the schedule lengthened and all teams started using at least three pitchers, Anson began holding back, relying on his ace more than most. From 1885 to 1892, a National League pitcher threw over 520 innings nine times; five came under Anson, including three of the four times a hurler topped 600 innings. The manager once at the cutting edge of inning distribution was falling behind the times with the increased schedule.

Thus Anson was especially ill suited to handle the change that came in 1892–93. When the pitcher was moved from 50 feet to the present distance from the plate, workloads dropped drastically for hurlers. From 1876 to 1892, every NL innings leader threw at least 483 innings, a feat no one has ever since matched. Complete games dropped as well — from 86.4 percent of all starts in 1892, to 81.2 percent the next year. Anson had trouble making this shift. Rather than adapting, he dug in his heels. Anson's teams had been rather low in complete games beforehand, but from 1894 to 1897 Chicago led the league in complete games every year, usually by a healthy margin. In 1897, with a mediocre staff, he had his pitchers complete 131 of 138 games, which was Chicago's highest percentage of completed starts since 1885.

Anson took a similar backwards step with his bullpen. In reality, it is impossible to speak of a bullpen back then because in the 1880s teams would bring in relief pitchers only a handful of times a year at most, and some not at all. Anson, however, was one of the men most willing to do it in those days. In 1885, his squad had more saves than the rest of the league combined (four to three). Given that they only won the pennant by two games, those few saves may have provided the difference for Chicago. Under Anson, Chicago led the league in saves three more times by 1890. Yet in the Great Change of 1892–93, Anson pulled back. The NL went up from averaging two saves per team in 1892, to three by 1894, and four in 1895. From 1894 to 1897, Anson's team lodged three saves— not per year, but in total.

Anson was only 41 when the league pushed the pitchers back, which by modern standards is young for a manager. At the time, however, he was unusually old. Of the game's dozen skippers in 1893, only two were older than him, both of whom departed by 1894.

In some ways Anson's tendencies remained the same. Anson's clubs always centered their offenses around power. In fact, using isolated power (slugging percentage minus batting average) as a shorthand gauge for how much teams relied on offensive muscle, the Tendencies Database shows that Anson's squads rank with the most extra-base reliant in baseball history:

Most Reliant on Power

Joe McCarthy	0.364
Sparky Anderson	0.478
Jimy Williams	0.486
Cap Anson	0.529
Hughie Jennings	0.556

Chicago led the league in isolated power six times in a row in the 1880s and ranked first eight times in Anson's nineteen years as manager. In his final year as skipper, Chicago ranked third in isolated power in a twelve-team league. The year before they had been runner-up. In his managerial career, Anson's batters slugged 194 more homers than his pitchers allowed, easily the best home run differential in pre–Ruth baseball. By the end of World War II, the differential was still the fifth best, behind only Joe McCarthy, Miller Huggins, John McGraw, and Bill Terry. Four times Anson's Chicago squad had at least a twenty homer advantage, a remarkable achievement in the nineteenth century.

At the end of 1896, Anson surpassed Harry Wright to become the game's all-time leader in managerial victories. He held that title for almost twenty years, until 1914 when both Connie Mack and John McGraw passed him.

BILL BARNIE

> **W-L Record:** 632–810 (.438)
>
> **Managed:** Full Seasons: Baltimore 1883–91; Louisville 1893–94; Brooklyn 1897
> Majority in: (none)
> Minority of: Washington 1892; Brooklyn 1898
>
> **Team Characteristics:** Losing. Barnie's teams rarely threatened to win any pennants while often coming in last. He managed some quality pitchers, but his teams really could not hit. They also had shoddy defense backing up his hurlers. Barnie used his bench a lot, especially in the infield.
>
> **LPA:** 3.63   **LPA+:** 84

Barnie was a likable, funny man whose popularity was entirely out of line with his team's results. He was the only manager for the American Association's Baltimore franchise and the city loved him despite his squad's wretched performance. Like many managers of the day, he was essentially a front office figure. He attended numerous league business meetings and at one point he was vice president for the entire AA. After it disbanded, he took part in an aborted attempt to revive it. Instead, he ended up managing Louisville, one of the NL's cash-strapped franchises. He would never manage nowadays.

His squads' problem was hitting. Barnie's teams routinely finished near the bottom of the league in runs. They possessed speed and could steal bases— the 1887 squad was credited with 545 thefts (it was a very different game back then). However, they could not steal first. His squads had historically bad rankings in on-base percentage, the league's worst OBP four times, and second worst three other times, a fact the Tendencies Database confirms:

Worst OBP

Billy Barnie	1.401
Felipe Alou	1.349
Bill McKechnie	1.324
Jimmy McAleer	1.273
Patsy Donovan	1.268

Since he possessed minimal talent, Barnie used the few good players on hand as much as possible, especially with his best pitchers. Of the 21 times a pitcher tossed at least 500 innings in the AA, five happened under Barnie. He was also responsible for nine of the 41 greatest single-season innings totals in league history. He was not simply relying on one super workhorse either; a half-dozen starters contributed to those nine seasons. Barnie's heavy usage of his aces was not nearly enough to overcome the lack of quality position players. In an era when pitchers constantly blew their arms out, his hurlers had an especially bad track record staying healthy. As a result, he frequently had extremely young staffs. His 1887 squad had an average pitcher age of 21.2 years old. Admittedly, it was a time when pitchers as a whole were very young, but that staff was *young*.

CHARLES COMISKEY

W/L Record: 840–541 (.608)
Managed: Full Seasons: St. Louis (AA) 1885–89, 1891; Chicago (PL) 1890;
      Cincinnati 1892–94.
      Majority in: (none)
      Minority of: St Louis (AA) 1883–84.
Team Characteristics: Comiskey's teams featured terrific fielding. The offenses
      consisted of good contact hitters who stole plenty of bases. He over-
      saw nineteen different occasions when one of his players stole at least
      50 bases in a season, more than any other manager in baseball his-
      tory. Comiskey helped break in four pitchers who won 200 games in
      their careers: Bob Caruthers, Silver King, Jack Stivetts, and Clark
      Griffith.
LPA: 5.20   **LPA+:** 122

There are six managers who won four consecutive pennants in any major league:

Manager	League	Years
Harry Wright	NA	1872–75
Charles Comiskey	AA	1885–88
John McGraw	NL	1921–24
Joe McCarthy	AL	1936–39
Casey Stengel	AL	1949–53, 1955–58
Joe Torre	AL	1998–2001

While people best remember Comiskey as an owner, he was also a well-known player in his day, and probably the greatest manager of his generation. As a skipper, he created a baseball philosophy that not only brought his teams success, but was later adopted by many other clubs in the ensuing decades.

Comiskey's four-peat with the American Association's St. Louis Browns (who later changed leagues and team colors to become the modern-day Cardinals) came about from the strategy he employed. It was a very simple design that rested on two pillars: (1) pitchers who could keep the ball in the strike zone and (2) defenders who could field their positions. By combining these two features, Comiskey ensured his team's strengths complemented each other, making the whole greater than the sum of its parts.

Prior to his becoming St. Louis's full-time manager, the franchise's pitchers had mediocre control. In terms of walks allowed per inning, the Browns finished third out of six teams in their inaugural campaign in 1882. Next year, they were fourth out of eight squads in this stat, and in 1884 they finished sixth among thirteen teams. In 1885, with Comiskey firmly entrenched as field general (he ran the team for a mere few weeks in each of the two previous seasons), St. Louis walked the fewest batters in the league despite a staff entirely consisting of men who pitched there in 1884. In the five consecutive years Comiskey ran the squad, the Browns never finished worse than second best in this statistic. St. Louis's staff maintained this consistency with their control despite the fact that all its pitchers on the 1885 club had departed by 1889. Among the six franchises that played in the AA from 1885 to 1889, Comiskey's squads overwhelmingly dominated the league in this facet of the game, with second place closer to last than to Comiskey's bunch:

Team	Walks Allowed
STL	1,458
LOU	1,762
BRK	1,814
PHI	1,866
BAL	1,886
CIN	1,912

St. Louis typically was not particularly good at striking out opponents or avoiding gopher balls, but that was fine by Comiskey. It was the deadball era — batters rarely belted home runs anyway. His pitchers just needed to avoid making mistakes, and rely on their defenders to make the outs.

Comiskey made sure they could rely on the defenders by fielding a tremendous defensive unit. According to both Defensive Efficiency Ratio and Bill James's Fielding Win Shares, Comiskey possessed the league's best bunch of gloves. St. Louis twice paced the circuit in DER and routinely came near the top in Comiskey's other seasons there. The Browns performed even better at Win Shares, leading the league four times in Comiskey's five consecutive seasons with the franchise, tying for second best in the remaining campaign. As was the case in walks allowed, Comiskey's squad dominated the league in Fielding Win Shares and DER from 1885 to 1889, as the lists below reveal:

Team	FWS	Team	DER
STL	216.0	STL	.673
CIN	197.6	BRK	.655
BRK	180.5	CIN	.652
PHI	161.8	BAL	.636
LOU	147.6	PHI	.634
BAL	140.5	LOU	.626

Note: Cumulative DER is figured by averaging team Baseball-Reference.com's annual DER for the teams in this period.

One of the main reasons for St. Louis's tremendous defensive performance was centerfielder Curt Welch. Though he struggled through a rookie season with the AA's Toledo franchise in 1884, Comiskey recognized Welch's prowess in the field. According to Jon David Cash's book on the nineteenth century Browns, *Before They Were Cardinals*, Comiskey insisted that St. Louis owner Chris Von der Ahe acquire him. After von der Ahe acquiesced, Welch quickly gained a reputation as one of the greatest fielders of his generation. Bill James's Win Shares agrees with that perception, listing Welch as an A+ glove.

In fact, in Comiskey's ten complete seasons as manager, his teams constantly fielded first-rate defenses. His teams had the most Fielding Win Shares seven times, finished second another time, and tied for second a ninth time. Bill James capped the amount of Fielding Win Shares a team could attain at 0.32375 per game played, and Comiskey's teams reached that level in all but one of his ten seasons as a squad's primary manager. No other prominent manager in baseball history can make that claim.

By possessing fielders and pitchers whose strengths meshed together so well, Comiskey's teams expertly prevented opponents from scoring runs, a fact to which the Tendencies Database can attest. The table below, which looks at how teams did at park-adjusted runs allowed per game, demonstrates the effectiveness of Comiskey's teams over his entire managerial career:

Fewest Runs Allowed, Park-Adjusted

Frank Selee	0.408
Charles Comiskey	0.415
Al Lopez	0.513
Bobby Cox	0.527
Cito Gaston	0.560

St. Louis played in one of the game's best hitters' parks, partially hiding the effectiveness of Comiskey's approach. Yet, even with their bandbox the Browns kept teams from scoring. When they won four consecutive pennants from 1885 to 1888, they held opponents to 4.40 runs per game even though the AA as a whole averaged 5.75 runs in that span. Control pitching plus great defense equaled a dynasty for St. Louis in the 1880s.

How much credit should Comiskey be given for devising this strategy? Looking at the historical record, this philosophy originated in St. Louis in the 1880s. There were virtually no deep strategic concerns for the game prior to this period. As late as the 1890s, elemental bits of baseball fundamentals such as the cutoff play had not been worked out. Bill James, in his book on managers, noted that people paid little attention to managerial strategy until the turn-of-the-century, because strategic thinking had not yet become central to the game. Instead, teams put their best players on the field, and may the most talented bunch win. That was one reason why franchises frequently hired individuals such as O. P. Caylor as managers. Other teams may have contained control pitchers and good fielders before, but none intentionally built their game around these twin pillars of run prevention until St. Louis.

If the notion of complementary fielders and pitchers developed in St. Louis, and it apparently did, then Comiskey deserves credit for it. Unlike modern managers, Comiskey only reported to one person — team owner Chris Von der Ahe. Though one of the most colorful owners of his day, Von der Ahe was not a brilliant baseball thinker, to put it mildly. According to one anecdote, Von der Ahe once told reporters that his field possessed the game's biggest diamond. After Comiskey took the owner aside and explained all fields had the same-sized diamonds, Von der Ahe returned to the reporters to clarify: he meant he had the biggest infield of them all. Clearly, Von der Ahe was not a baseball savant. Conversely, Comiskey, in his half-century in baseball, earned a reputation as one of the sport's smartest men. In his playing days as a first baseman, Comiskey was often given credit for being one of the first to play off the bag, giving the position greater defensive range. He was one of the great success stories, rising up from humble player to owner of the White Sox from their inception until his death in October 1931.

In fact, Comiskey's White Sox consistently practiced the same baseball philosophy that made his St. Louis squads so successful. They lacked power and impressive batting averages, but they made up for it with control pitching and superlative defense. In the 31 years Comiskey ran the franchise, they had the most overall Fielding Win Shares, best Defensive Efficiency Ratio, and fewest walks allowed in the American League, as the tables below reveal:

Team	Walks Allowed	Team	FWS	Team	DER
CWS	12,551	CWS	1,288.0	CWS	.694
BOS	12,996	BOS	1,229.8	BOS	.692
NYY	13,398	CLE	1,226.2	NYY	.689
CLE	13,830	PHI	1,207.4	PHI	.688
WAS	13,918	NYY	1,177.8	WAS	.687
STB	14,358	WAS	1,163.8	STB	.686
DET	14,775	STB	1,121.2	DET	.685
PHI	14,950	DET	1,116.9	CLE	.684

While one rarely thinks of the White Sox as one of the game's great franchises, prior to 1930 they had won more regular season games than any other franchise in American League history.

The White Sox were rarely the best defensive unit in the league, but they were typically among the best, finishing in the top half of the league in Fielding Win Shares 24 times in their first 28 seasons. Chicago's pitchers were more impressive, as their staffs allowed the fewest walks per inning ten times under Comiskey's reign, and were runner up another four times. This approach created wins. Most famously, the 1906 "Hitless Wonders" managed by Fielder Jones won a world title with pitchers who threw strikes performing before terrific defenders. The White Sox appropriated the old 1880s St. Louis Browns strategy.

Furthermore, while many teams in the early twentieth century delegated considerable authority to their managers, Comiskey appears to have been the mastermind behind the White Sox. In contrast to powerful skippers like John McGraw with the Giants or Connie Mack with the A's, Comiskey's managers tended to be faceless cogs in his machines. He hired thirteen different managers, ten of whom had never managed previously, and only three of whom ever managed after leaving Chicago. Pants Rowland won a world title with the White Sox in 1917 and compiled a .578 career winning percentage with the club, but after Comiskey fired him no other major league team ever hired him as manager afterwards. Rowland's successor, Kid Gleason, also failed to get another team to hire him despite claiming a pennant in Chicago (though his pennant winner tarnished his reputation, as it was the World Series–throwing

1919 Black Sox). Aside from Clark Griffith and Fielder Jones, two of the team's first three managers, Chicago won with forgettable field generals

The similarities between Comiskey's Browns and White Sox do not end with control pitching and superlative fielding. As St. Louis's manager, Comiskey's run-prevention program contained another key trait: leaning heavily on his most important pitchers. All nineteenth century innings pitched totals look incomprehensible by modern standards, but even compared to his peers Comiskey worked his starters like dogs. As usual, the 1885–89 St. Louis squad illuminates Comiskey's interest in working his main pitchers hard. The following table lists innings garnered by the top three pitchers for the clubs that existed in the AA throughout the 1885–89 period:

Team	IP
STL	5,296
BAL	5,096
CIN	4,910
BRK	4,792
LOU	4,765
PHI	4,659

In 1885, Comiskey's squad became the last team in baseball history to use only three pitchers all season long. Two of them threw almost 90 percent of those innings that year, with ace Bob Caruthers starting almost half of their games. After the team sold Caruthers to the Brooklyn franchise, Silver King became St. Louis's ace, throwing 585 innings in 1888; no other hurler was within 50 innings of King's mark that year and only two were within 100 innings. The next year Comiskey reduced King's workload, but St. Louis still had two of the league's top six in innings thrown, one of whom was King.

When Comiskey went to the Players League's Chicago franchise, King came with him, throwing 460 innings. That was the second most in the league, behind only his teammate Mark Baldwin, who tossed over 500 innings. No one else in the league had more than 400. After 1890, Comiskey never ran his starters nearly as hard, but then again in the rest of his managerial career he no longer had a starter he trusted as much as Caruthers or King.

White Sox hurlers never threw King-ian levels of innings under Comiskey, but they resembled his old St. Louis team because their main arms were pushed harder than the aces on rival clubs. The table below, which lists the total innings thrown by the top three arms for each AL squad every year from 1901 to 1931, demonstrates the similarity in the deployment pattern of White Sox hurlers with the 1880s Browns:

Team	IP
CWS	25,133
WAS	23,922
BOS	23,631
PHI	23,622
DET	23,522
CLE	23,222
STB	23,160
NYY	23,021

The difference between Chicago and Washington is greater than the difference between Washington and New York.

In 1908, White Sox ace Ed Walsh became the last man to throw 400 innings in a season. He led the league in innings pitched four times in six years. When he missed part of the 1909 season with an injury, teammate Frank Smith topped the league in innings. When they departed, Eddie Cicotte twice led the league in innings. After major league baseball banned Cicotte from the game for his role in the Black Sox scandal, Red Faber led the league in innings, throwing 352 innings in 1921. Only one other pitcher topped 300 in the AL that year. When he declined, teammate Ted Lyons once led the league outright in innings pitched and tied with fellow White Sox Tommy Thomas another time. As long as Comiskey lived, Chicago centered on defense, control, and rubber-armed pitchers.

A common theme existed in Comiskey's teams: fielders meant more than pitchers. Both were important, but pitchers were more replaceable. Comiskey needed a hurler with control who could constantly take the mound, but if he wore out that was fine. Comiskey could always replace him with another hurler, so there was no point in being gentle.

This approach was especially well suited to the period Comiskey managed. Think about it: how was it possible that pitchers could throw 400–500 innings year after year without destroying themselves? Simple — they were not expected to put too much "oomph" on each pitch. Thus the fielders were more important in stopping the opponents. With the big change in 1893, this relationship between fielders and pitchers began to shift. (It shifted further in the 1920s with the liveball, but that is getting ahead of the story.) Comiskey intelligently adapted to the conditions.

However, the above paragraph does not give full credit to Comiskey's strategy because it was much more than an approach that worked in 1880s baseball. Though one could not ask a pitcher to throw the gargantuan inning totals achieved by Silver King, the basic approach still worked, as evidenced by Comiskey's White Sox. Pitchers and fielders who complemented each other was an effective way to stop opponents from scoring, and it allowed teams to push their starters harder.

Most important of all, Comiskey's formula was not merely something he personally utilized; it may be the most commonly replicated route to success in baseball history. In particular, the effort to place control pitchers before terrific fielders was adopted by numerous managers in the years since Comiskey left the dugout. This style of baseball became *the* style of play from 1893 to 1920, as skippers such as Fred Clarke, John McGraw, Pat Moran, Buck Ewing, Frank Selee, and Frank Chance owed varying degrees of debt to Comiskey's system. It remained a vital template for lively ball era managers, including Bill McKechnie, Joe McCarthy, Billy Southworth, Paul Richards, Al Lopez, Walter Alston, Earl Weaver, Whitey Herzog, Tom Kelly, Bobby Cox, and Ron Gardenhire, who all used variations on this approach. Some focus on pitchers more, or do not lean on their starters as much, or put more emphasis on the offense. All, however, fostered a symbiotic relationship between their pitchers and fielders. The former would not put men on and the latter would take care of the rest. Moran, McKechnie, Lopez, and Weaver most closely followed Comiskey's theory of run prevention. They all prioritized superb gloves playing behind control pitchers who ate up tremendous numbers of innings.

Charles Comiskey created one of the greatest approaches to winning in baseball history.

CAL MCVEY

W/L Record: 91–64 (.587)
Managed: Full Seasons: Cincinnati 1878–79; plus some time in the National
           Association
           Majority in: (none)
           Minority of: (none)
Team Characteristics: He engaged in a highly innovative and influential strat-
           egy for using pitchers.

Cal McVey is easily the most important manager to last fewer than 160 games. He revolutionized the sport. Virtually no one knows this, but it is true — Cal McVey is the godfather of platooning.

That might sound strange since plenty of work has been done on the origins of platooning, and no one has ever mentioned McVey as playing a role. In the original *Historical Baseball Abstract*, Bill James included a lengthy write-up on this tactic's origins. He figured that it began in 1906 with the Detroit Tigers platooning their catchers under manager Bill Armour, and came of age when the Miracle Braves extensively platooned en route to the 1914 title. Other researchers have dug back further and found examples of the practice existing in the late nineteenth century. James himself noted in the *New Historical Abstract* that a platoon arrangement existed on the 1887 NL's Indianapolis franchise. In *Game of Inches*, baseball historian Peter Morris collected the evidence of several nineteenth century platoons, going so far as to say the Miracle Braves merely reestablished the practice. However, the creation of offensive platooning was less invention than inversion. It was a reaction to a method for handling pitchers begun by Cal McVey.

The time is 1878. The place is Cincinnati. As new manager, Cal McVey is in a peculiar, though not unique position: he has two pitchers. The better pitcher is clearly Will White, destined to win over 200 games in his career. The other hurler is Bobby Mitchell, a lackluster holdover from the previous season's last-place squad. Aside from Boston, where Tommy Bond started every game for the squad in 1877, teams had more than one starter. Normally, though, squads put their second pitcher on the mound only because their ace needed a day off. McVey, however, had another idea.

Though Mitchell was inferior to White, he had one advantage over his teammate: Mitchell was a southpaw. Though the game was still in its infancy, a burgeoning recognition existed that a left-handed hitter had an advantage when facing a right-handed pitcher because of the way the ball curved as it reached the plate. Conversely, a southpaw should have an advantage over his fellow lefties, but be hindered against the game's righties. The game had even produced its first noteworthy switch-hitter, Bob Ferguson. In 1878, the same year McVey became manager, a rookie right-handed pitcher on the Providence Grays named John Ward opted to hit left-handed.

McVey came up with a simple but exceptionally influential plan for handling his pitchers. The more left-handed bats an opposing team had, the better the odds were Mitchell would start. Mitchell had only nine starts on the year, but four came against Providence, which featured two great hitting left-handed outfielders in Dick Higham and Tom York, plus first baseman Tim Murnane and pitcher Ward. No other team trotted out that many lefties. Chicago, Indianapolis, and Milwaukee also had some lefties, so Mitchell started against them when White needed a break. The one team he never faced, Boston, was the one team without any lefties in its batting order. McVey had introduced the concept of platoon starting his pitchers.

Harry Wright, manager of Boston, must have noticed this. The next year, when the schedule expanded to make multiple pitchers a necessity on all teams, Wright added southpaws Curry Foley and late season addition Lee Richmond. They combined to start 17 games, a dozen of which came against Chicago, Cincinnati, and Providence, the teams that had the most impressive left-handed offensive firepower.

McVey's brand of platoon pitching initially caught on slowly, because there were not that many southpaws in the game. However, the practice gained steam. A breakthrough came with the 1890 Players League's Buffalo Bisons. Their lineup contained seven left-handed hitters. If opposing teams used their southpaws randomly, the Bisons would have faced them 26 times on the year. Instead, lefties started against them in 48 games. The notion of platoon starting had clearly come of age. An increasing number of left-handed pitchers in the following years allowed the practice to expand. In response to its expansion, the offensive platoon emerged.

The 1906 Tigers reveal how pitcher platooning led to offensive platooning. From the outset of the AL, Detroit's lineup featured numerous left-handed bats. In 1902, their entire starting outfield hit from the left side, and the next year they nabbed Sam Crawford, one of the best left-handed hitters in the game. Due to this impressive left-handed offense, rival teams frequently pushed southpaws against the Tigers. By 1906, Tiger manager Bill Armour faced a dilemma. Along with Crawford, Detroit's offense contained an even more promising left-handed bat, teenaged Ty Cobb. That year would be the fifth consecutive season southpaws started over 30 percent of all games against them, something no team had previously experienced. Faced with this unprecedented flurry of southpaws, Armour began platooning his catchers.

In his examination of platooning's origins, Bill James noted how surprised he was that the origins of this vital baseball strategy were so poorly known; it even lacked an origin myth explaining its beginnings. This is why platooning's start was so murky: it was not a revolution, but a reaction. Platooning hitters was a response to the existing practice of platooning pitchers. Even in 1906, few of the old-timers could remember back to the 1870s.

Since then, it has been inverted again, with modern-day bullpens. Most teams now have a LOOGY — a Lefty One Out GuY. This is the most recent chapter in a story that began with Cal McVey. Jesse Orosco and his fellow LOOGYs are the grandchildren of Bobby Mitchell.

GUS SCHMELZ

> **W/L Record:** 624–703 (.470)
> **Managed:** Full Seasons: Columbus (AA) 1884; St. Louis (NL) 1886; Cincinnati
>   (AA) 1887–89; Columbus (AA) 1891; Washington 1894–96
>   Majority in: Cleveland 1890
>   Minority of: Columbus (AA) 1890; Washington 1897
> **Team Characteristics:** Schmelz's teams hit for power and frequently struck out.
>   He used his bullpen quite a bit, and leaned even harder on his starting catchers. In 1895, Deacon McGuire played every game behind the backstop, a superhuman achievement in the days before shin guards.
> **LPA: 4.01   LPA+: 87**

Gus Schmelz was one of baseball's great innovators. He changed baseball and in the process made the manager a far more important part of the game. His lackluster career winning percentage reflected the talent he had to work with, not his personal capabilities.

First, Schmelz was a big proponent of practicing. In 1884, his first season managing, he opened a preseason training camp for his team. Within a few years, other teams caught on, and spring training became an annual rite of passage. A few years later, as Cincinnati's manager, Schmelz began extensively drilling his players in their sliding technique. This again put him at the forefront of coaching.

Schmelz made perhaps even more significant changes in the realm of in-game strategy. Teams rarely engaged in much in-game maneuvering in the 1880s— which was one reason managers frequently let their captains run the games. Then came Schmelz. According to baseball historian Peter Morris, Gus Schmelz was the first man to capitalize on bunting as a weapon. In 1891, the periodical *Sporting Life* referred to the habit of bunting as "the Schmelz system" of baseball. That journal also noted that managers all across the game rapidly adopted his system. This change, perhaps more than anything else, really heralded the end of the business manager as strategy became a vital part of the game. Teams needed a manager who could outthink the opponent instead of someone who just let his players do what they wanted on the field.

Unfortunately, sacrifice hit data for the late 1880s and early 1890s— when Schmelz revolutionized the game — does not exist. Baseball only tabulated the stat from 1894 onward, when Schmelz managed in Washington. At the risk of ruining a good story, his teams rarely bunted. It is the damnedest thing. In 1894, he bunted less than anyone else with 56 sacrifice hits, and his bunt totals remained below average the rest of his career. The press at the time gave him credit for it, but the numbers make him look positively anti–small ball.

The world will probably never really know what happened, but a possible explanation can be floated. Bunting is usually a way to play for one run. Beginning in 1893, baseball witnessed an offensive explosion that possibly diminished Schmelz's interest in playing for one run. Also, the team he managed was absolutely terrible. They were more likely to be down by far more than one run than practically anyone else. Alternately, perhaps Schmelz's imitators took the technique farther than he envisioned.

Looking solely at his team's stats, Schmelz appeared to disdain playing for one run at a time not only because of his low sacrifice hit totals, but also because his offenses consistently prioritized slugging. Columbus had the second best isolated power in the league his only year there. In three years, the Reds were always in the top two in isolated power.

Schmelz's experience in Washington best demonstrated his commitment to a bashing brand of baseball. In 1894, Schmelz came to Washington to manage the downtrodden Senators franchise (which should not be confused with future downtrodden Senators franchises; this one ceased to exist after 1899). The year before, they finished ninth in the twelve-team NL in isolated power. Gus Schmelz found a 34-year-old named Ed Cartwright who had only played one year in major league ball — way back in 1890 — and made him the everyday first baseman. He hit 60 extra-base hits, including twelve homers—a high number for the day. Schmelz took Bill Joyce, who had been out of the majors the year before, and put him at third. Joyce hit seventeen homers, second best in the NL. Schmelz noticed a 27-year-old on the bench named Charlie Abbey who had barely played 30 games in the majors. Made a starting outfielder, he hit eighteen triples. Schmelz gave an opportunity to a 22-year-old Kip Selbach, who hit seventeen triples as a rookie. Roaring Bill Hassamaer, a career minor leaguer nearing age 30, joined Abbey and Selbach in the outfield and also hit seventeen triples. While Washington remained a perennial loser under Schmelz, they consistently had some of the best power in the league.

That was impressive, but exactly the opposite of what one would expect from the Father of the Bunt. He died over 80 years ago, so it is a little late to pick his brains over his baseball philosophy. Whatever the story, he was one of the game's greatest forgotten innovators. By stressing a manager's role in coaching, conditioning, and thinking, he ensured the extinction of the O. P. Caylors and opened the door for the Ned Hanlons.

HARRY WRIGHT

> **W/L Record:** 1225–885 (.581)
> **Managed:** Full Seasons: Boston (NA) 1871–75; Boston (NL) 1876–81; Providence 1882–83; Philadelphia 1884–89, 1891–93
> Majority in: (none)
> Minority of: Philadelphia 1890
> **Team Characteristics:** Wright liked to use his starters. In fact, his 1878 Boston team set the NL record for lowest percentage of plate appearances by the bench. It featured one back up, who played exactly two games in the outfield. That was it for the entire year for the squad's bench. Wright's teams had terrific fielding. He had a terrific record in one-run games, 282–207 (.565), including the National Association.

LPA: 5.15   **LPA+:** 123

Harry Wright invented managing. He was reportedly Connie Mack before Connie Mack: a teacher who did not criticize his players after a defeat. Instead, he talked to them after things went well.

Including the National Association, Wright managed a major league team every year for 23 straight seasons. The only others in baseball history who can say that are John McGraw, Connie Mack, Walter Alston, Gene Mauch, Sparky Anderson, and Tony LaRussa. Mighty cozy club.

Wright was flexible with his pitchers. At times he was perfectly willing to go to his bullpen. For instance, in 1876 he pulled his starting pitcher from the game 21 times even though the other seven teams did that 26 times combined. He used relievers in 30 percent of Boston's games, a record that stood nearly 30 years. However, it would be a mistake to portray Wright as the game's first great advocate of the bullpen. Immediately after that season, he aggressively shifted directions, not using a single relief pitcher in 1877. For Wright, calling on a reliever was less a goal than a survival strategy. When he trusted his starters, he left them in, but if he had little faith in them he was willing to pull them. In 1876, he had no good pitchers, but the next year he had Tommy Bond, probably baseball's best pitcher in the 1870s. Wright avoided relievers until Bond ruined his arm.

The two most important books about managers—*The Bill James Guide to Managers* and Leonard Koppett's *The Man in the Dugout*—both examine managerial family trees. In an attempt to see the lines of descent across the generations, the authors note who the main influences on each manager was. Koppett begins his trees in 1900, with John McGraw, Connie Mack, and Branch Rickey (who managed for several years before joining the front office). James goes back a bit further, to 1890s Hall of Famers Frank Selee and Ned Hanlon. Neither goes to the beginning. That gap should be examined.

Any attempt to look at the first generation of managers must begin with Harry Wright. What mark did he leave? Initially, he left a huge one as a slew of his former players became managers in baseball's early years. He managed numerous eventual skippers, including Cal McVey, John Morrill, Jim Manning, Al Spalding, Jim O'Rourke, Pop Snyder, John Ward, Arthur Irwin, Deacon McGuire, Kid Gleason, and his brother George. It was an impressive start.

Unfortunately, that was nearly where it ended as most of those men left no managerial footprint. John Ward was a successful manager, but Wright only managed him for one season, and that came two years after Ward's managerial debut. Maybe the most impressive future manager of the bunch was Kid Gleason, who managed the Black Sox. When he stepped down in Chicago, two of his former players, Eddie Collins and Ray Schalk, managed the Sox through 1928. One of their former players, Ted Lyons, ran them from 1946 to 1948. That was it, though. Ultimately, longtime White Sox skipper Jimmy Dykes should have been a bigger influence on Lyons than those two. Frankly, it is not clear Gleason should be classified as a Wright guy, as he played for Wright in only four of his 22 years.

Wright's lack of a sustained imprint on future managers indicates how the nature of the job changed. It was a more hands-off role until the Schmelz revolution. That was true not only for the business-managing receipt-counters like Billy Barnie, but also for the legitimate baseball men like Wright. Thus his impact on twentieth century managers was almost nonexistent.

Almost. Wright has one solid link to the next century. In the National Association, he managed Al Spalding. When the NL began, Spalding became his own manager for a little bit, before moving into upper management. From that position, he tapped Cap Anson, one of his former players to run the team.

Anson's influence itself was not spectacular since most of his protégés lasted only a short while on the job. For example, his longtime middle infielder Tom Burns replaced him, running Chicago in 1898–99. Though Anson's strand was thin, it contained one key man — Clark Griffith.

He came up in 1891 with Comiskey in St. Louis, but in midseason went to the AA's Boston's club under Arthur Irwin — whom Wright had managed for five seasons. Griffith's breakthrough came when the Cubs grabbed him in 1893. He served under Anson, and then Burns — all members of Clan Wright. For those Wrighters, Griffith became one of the game's most reliable pitchers.

When the AL formed in 1901, Griffith became manager, a position he held for twenty years, by which time he had entered the ownership ranks in Washington. He managed future skippers Fielder Jones (who won a World Series title in 1906), Nixey Callahan, Walter Johnson, and Bucky Harris. Plus, as owner he left a continuing mark on Washington until his death in 1955, and his family owned the team until 1984. The franchise was always willing to give new managers a try — Bucky Harris, Walter Johnson, Joe Cronin, Ossie Bluege, Cookie Lavagetto, Sam Mele, Billy Martin, and Billy Gardner all first filled out a line-up card for the Griffith family's squad. When the family sold the team, Tom Kelly was a coach in Minnesota.

Of course, that takes things a bit too far. When examining lines of managerial descent, the strand becomes thinner the farther from the source you go. That is especially true when Wright's prodigies were so few and those of other managerial family trees so many. Others influenced Tom Kelly, and it is a stretch to claim he modeled himself on the team's aging owner.

However, the Wright-Griffith connection makes sense. In his book, Koppett classified just about every notable manager in baseball history into the Mack, McGraw, or Rickey families in which Mack stood for tactics, McGraw control, and Rickey organization. However, Koppett made an exception for Griffith, not including him in any of those families. Griffith had more of an even keel, merging the other traditions, picking and choosing from them. That above-the-fray mixture might be the lingering influence of Harry Wright on the managerial world. While Wright may have no real influence on Tom Kelly, as long as Clark Griffith picked new managers for his Senators franchise, some lingering trace of Wright remained.

5

Rise of the Fundamentalists, 1893–1919

The importance of managers peaked at the turn of the century. They inhabited a specific period in the evolution of baseball between two crucial metamorphoses of the game. First, in the late nineteenth century, field generals like Gus Schmelz and Ned Hanlon caused the rise of the modern manager and the extinction of the old business manager. By placing a premium on the preparation of players before contests and handling strategy during them, the position of manager came into its own. A generation later, the rise of the front office diminished the manager's position by serving as a rival power source within the franchise. Between these transformations, managerial power in the sport crested. Managers ascended into the ranks of ownership with greater frequency than at any other time in baseball history, as there were fewer steps between themselves and owners. Even those who did not own a share of the club frequently had considerable autonomy. When John McGraw became Giants manager, he told the owners which players to keep or remove from the roster, indicating who called the shots for that franchise. Not all managers wielded such authority in this era, and many held considerable power in the future, but they had their strongest opportunity to control the entire franchise at the turn of the century.

Managerial power also reached its zenith because coaching was more important in this period than any other. Old-time baseball is often remembered as a glory era, when players dedicated themselves to the craft of the game in a way that modern players with their supposedly softer attitudes never could. Though this attitude is very frequent in the modern day, ideas that the old-timers were better, wiser, and more dedicated are as old as the game itself.

People look at John McGraw and his devotion to those precious fundamentals. He ordered his players to come to the park to practice and work out for several hours every day, making the athletes perform precisely in accordance with his formidable will. Other managers, like Frank Chance, made a similar fervent push for sound ball. Chance's Cubs had a well-earned reputation as the sharpest players in the league.

However, not only was the deadball era far from being the golden era of fundamentals, but the evidence used to make it seem like a Mecca of proper execution are the very facts that indicate otherwise. John McGraw did not want his players practicing constantly because they were so committed, but because those who earned a spot in major league baseball commonly displayed poor fundamentals. The book *Crazy '08* by Cait Murphy provides an interesting window into baseball during the 1908 NL pennant race. Despite focusing on teams that diligently practiced their basics—McGraw's Giants and Chance's Cubs—examples of shoddy play litter the book. It was not a matter of errors; the gloves and conditions of the day made muffed grounders understandable. The problems went deeper. Virtually every game contained at least one boneheaded play that could not be blamed on the conditions. Flies landed between fielders. A baserunner would be doubled off on a popup. An outfielder would misplay a grounder for an inside-the-park home run. These plays still happen, but not nearly as often. If the Cubs and Giants played like that, imagine how the doormats played. There were also some extremely smart plays, but the floor for proper conduct was much lower in 1908.

It seems strange that teams that practiced so religiously played so poorly, but think for a second. Much of what is now received wisdom was still being worked out. In the last quarter of the nineteenth century, players slowly began figuring out how to work together, or back each other up. For example, what should a catcher do when a baserunner is caught in a rundown between first and second? Where should the shortstop go when the runner on first heads for third on a single to right? People are not born knowing the answers.

Look at it from the point of view of someone born in 1879 earning a roster slot in 1900. He grew up in a world where even the best players at the highest levels were still learning the core basics. It did not trickle down to Iowa's cornfields or Pennsylvania's coal mines overnight. Neither TV nor radio existed to teach him how the pros acted. Odds were very good he had never seen a big league game, and may not know anyone who has. Sandlot baseball has always been self-regulating, but there is usually at least some fundamental knowledge for kids to rely on. When he starts playing semipro ball, his manager was likely another player, probably under 30 years old himself. That man hopefully has some exposure to the basics being threshed out, but that was not guaranteed. Even if the skipper had basic knowledge of fundamentals, perhaps he cannot coach well. Depending on the club's finances, he might be a business manager. If a kid could hit or possessed a strong arm, he would receive playing time, no matter how ignorant he was of fundamentals.

Thus you end up with the following story told by baseball historian Fred Stein. In 1897, a rawboned young buck called Honus Wagner began playing for the Louisville Colonels. His manager, a not yet 25-year-old Fred Clarke, told the kid to "lay one down" in his next at bat. Instead, Wagner hit a home run. Appreciative of the result but curious as to why the rookie ignored his instructions to bunt, Clarke asked Wagner what happened. Shamefacedly, the future Hall of Fame shortstop admitted he had never heard the phrase "lay one down" before. He had no idea what his manager was talking about. This was the situation Clarke, McGraw, and Chance contended with.

Fundamentals first have to be developed. Then they diffuse. Next, their instruction becomes institutionalized. Once the lessons become second nature to one generation, the next wave can be fully and immediately immersed in them. Nowadays, high-schoolers are better versed in solid fundamentals than many big-leaguers were a century ago. After enough years and decades go by, fundamentals are so ingrained even Little Leaguers learn them, and you assume that everyone getting paid to play the game knows them by heart. Even a poor kid from the Dominican Republic has access to more knowledgeable adults and coaches than was the case for an 1890s Wisconsin farm boy.

This might oversell the point. At SABR's annual convention in 2007, I heard Cait Murphy talk about what she learned from researching her book, and she was surprised at how advanced the level of play sometimes was. Examples of intelligent play existed—for instance the Cubs had worked out an impressive system of defensive signals amongst each other. However, such plays coincided with embarrassing miscues, as the floor for acceptable play was quite low. A wide discrepancy existed in the quality of fundamental ball played in these years. The more advanced examples of shrewd gamesmanship were often the result of major league managers instilling those values into their charges.

This explains why coaching fundamentals mattered so much for this generation of managers. The basic ideas of how to play had been worked out, now it was a time to diligently instruct them to the players. McGraw, Chance, and their ilk focused on the fundamentals because their players so sorely lacked knowledge that these pointers could significantly improve squads.

A century later, in his bestseller *Moneyball*, Michael Lewis introduced the phrase "market inefficiency" to baseball fans. He argued the 2002 A's won 103 games despite a low payroll because they realized the baseball world undervalued the importance of on-base percentage. By exploiting this gap between reality and perception, A's GM Billy Beane made his team a winner. A century earlier, the market inefficiency was fundamentals. The best managers, such as McGraw and Chance, were those who could transform raw clumps of talent into majestic creations. One should not underestimate how important sound play was back then. In the early twentieth century some teams made 100 fewer errors a year than their rivals. Combined with improved baserunning, solid mental play, and all those other little things, proper fundamentals were worth many wins.

FRANK CHANCE

> **W/L Record:** 946–648 (.593)
> **Managed:** Full Seasons: Chicago (NL) 1906–12; New York (AL) 1913; Boston
> (AL) 1923
> Majority in: Chicago (NL) 1905; New York (AL) 1914
> Minority of: (none)
> **Birnbaum Database:** +686 runs
> Individual Hitters: -39 runs
> Individual Pitchers: +232 runs
> Pythagenpat Difference: +111 runs
> Team Offense: +274 runs
> Team Defense: +108 runs
> **Team Characteristics:** Overall, Chance oversaw very solid teams, which especially excelled at run prevention. His squads had world-class defense. His pitchers were also quite good at striking out hitters, further improving their ability at run prevention. On offense, his teams frequently stole and bunted.
> **LPA:** 7.78   **LPA+:** 178

People frequently claim that none of the members of baseball's most famous double-play combination — Joe Tinker, Johnny Evers, and Frank Chance — belong in Cooperstown. While Chance's playing career was slender, if one factors in his managing, he certainly belongs.

The Cubs performed as well under Chance as any team ever has in baseball history. In his first full season, they set a record with 116 wins. Over the ensuing seasons they set highs that still stand for the most wins over two years (223), three years (322), four years (426) and five years (530). Yet, the 1906–10 Cub rosters were far less impressive than their records. They were exceptionally solid, but not obviously spectacular as Mordecai Brown was their only clear-cut immortal. Chicago's unprecedented results indicate that Chance earned his nickname "the Peerless Leader." In less than eight years managing Chicago, the Birnbaum Database gives Chance a score of +826 runs.

Chance mastered the implementation of smart, heads-up play, causing Chicago's amazing success. For example, his squad made greater use of delayed steals than any other team. In this play, the runner on first broke for second when the catcher returned the ball to the pitcher. That type of play could regularly succeed only if the opponents had poor fundamentals (as many did back then) and Chance's squad mastered expert execution. The Cubs could implement that play frequently because Chance drilled his team harder than most of his peers. According to baseball historian Peter Morris, Chance was one of the first managers to have his pitchers and catchers report early for spring training. Intensive training begot sounder baseball, creating more wins for the franchise.

Despite his emphasis on practice, however, Chance did not want automatons on the field merely following instructions. He prioritized smart players who thought on their feet. He believed the best way to gain the measure of a man was to watch him play poker. Chance sought risk takers who tempered their boldness with intelligence. He had that in savvy players like Johnny Evers and Joe Tinker. By combining street smarts with learned skills, the Cubs played a far more effective brand of baseball than anyone else. Early in *Crazy '08*, Cait Murphy provides a snapshot of Chance's infield at work. The defenders silently gave each other a series of signals just before the pitcher threw the ball, so they all knew what pitch was coming, and how to defend the ball if the hitter made contact with it. They were the savviest team baseball had ever known up to that point.

Chance reinforced the team's successes with his own unswerving will to win. After one tough loss his wife reminded him that regardless of what happened on the field, he still had her. Chance replied that he would have traded her for some good clutch hitting late in the game. The story's importance lay not in its accuracy (which is questionable), but that people retold it. Those who knew Chance thought it reflected on a pronounced character trait of his.

Just as Charles Comiskey had done with his 1880s St. Louis squads, Chance centered his teams around defense. In fact, his Cubs might be the greatest defense unit ever assembled. One good way to measure defense is with a stat called Defensive Efficiency Ratio (DER), which determines what percentage of balls in play become outs. The 1906 Cubs recorded a .736 DER while the rest of the league had a combined DER of .694, meaning the Cubs allowed a hit fewer per game off balls in play than an average squad. The Cubs constantly finished at or near the top in DER and in Fielding Win Shares as long as Chance managed them. He honed their raw defensive talent until they mastered the game's nuances. As soon as Chance left they fell to the middle of the pack in DER and near the bottom in Fielding Win Shares.

A great defense made Chance less reliant on one or two main arms. Unlike Comiskey, who kept trotting out the same man as often as he could, Chance distributed innings much more widely. His staffs consistently had the best ERAs while rarely finding any of its members among the league leaders in innings pitched, an oddity in any era. In 1906, the Cubs had the best ERA in the league by nearly a half-run, but none of their hurlers appeared in the top ten in innings pitched. The following year they posted a 1.73 ERA, the lowest by any team in history — again without the benefit of a single hurler among the league leaders in innings.

By not using his aces especially often, Chance was able to become the game's greatest leverager of starting pitchers. During his entire term as Cubs manager, their main rivals were the Pirates and Giants. Of Mordecai Brown's 182 starts from 1906 to 1911, 40 percent came against either New York (42) or Pittsburgh (33). Brown was just the tip of the iceberg. In 1906, for example, Jack Pfiester won twenty games for the Cubs largely because of how Chance handled him. While Brown took the lion's share of starts against the Pirates and Giants, nearly half of Pfiester's starts occurred against two cellar dwellers, Boston and Brooklyn.

When Chicago won its second straight pennant in 1907, Jack Taylor, Brown, and Carl Lundgren each had an AOWP+ of 105, quite impressive as they combined for over 40 percent of Chicago's starts. They started 38 games against the three opponents with winning records, but only 27 against the remaining four clubs. This allowed the rest of Chance's pitchers to whip the hell out of the little teams of this earth. Orval Overall went 23–7 that year, largely because Chance consistently slated him against the league's lesser squads. He recorded only two starts against the second-place Pirates alongside sixteen starts against the three worst teams. Even still, Overall's AOWP+ of 97 was better than Ed Reulbach's 95 or southpaw Jack Pfiester's 94. Pfiester had more starts (seven) against the 65–83 Dodgers than against the entire first division (five).

The next year, with Taylor gone, and Lundgren only able to start fifteen games, Chance gave Pfiester a meatier role. Pfiester gained a reputation as a Giant killer, with eight starts against them. He and Brown were responsible for over half of the team's starts against the Giants and Pirates. Orval Overall became the king of garbage time, with an unfathomably low AOWP+ of 91.

As Chapter 3 demonstrated, in 1909 Chance maintained his manic leveraging. Reulbach joined Brown atop the staff. They combined for fourteen starts against the pennant-winning Pirates and thirteen against the Giants. Pfiester still had his share of starts against the Giants with five, but otherwise found himself relegated to facing second division squads.

In 1910, Chance did not leverage quite as much, but still possessed some clear preferences. That was the only time Mordecai Brown took on all comers fairly evenly, leading to a 103 AOWP+. King Cole, however, largely repeated Orval Overall's 1907 season. Cole went 20–4 in 29 starts while facing the second-place Giants only twice, and third-place Pirates thrice. Orval Overall himself remained on garbage patrol, with ten of his 21 starts come against two of the league's worst teams, Boston and Brooklyn. Chance ensured his southpaws faced the Giants. Four of Pfiester's thirteen starts came against them. Rube Kroh, a marginal southpaw with only four starts all season, faced the Giants in three of them. Mordecai Brown, Harry McIntire, and midseason acquisition Lew Richie started sixteen of the club's 22 starts against the Pirates. The next year, Richie became one of Chance's favorites, posting an AOWP+ of 106, nearly equal to Brown's mark of 107.

When Brown lost almost all of 1912 to an injury, Chance's penchant for leveraging reached its all-time pinnacle. Richie inherited the ace role, sporting an inhuman AOWP+ of 117. Since 1876, that was the highest mark by anyone with at least twenty starts. Alongside him, Jimmy Lavender earned a 109. In some ways that was equally impressive. It is hard to get that high an AOWP+ under normal circumstances, let alone when a teammate sets the all-time record. Since those two hurlers accounted for 58 of the team's 152 starts, staff workhorse Larry Cheney's AOWP+ of 98 in 37 starts was remarkable. Aside from that trio, no one on the staff faced a good team all year. Here was how Chance used his Big Three and the remainders in 1912:

Opponent	Pct.	Richie	Lavender	Cheney	The Rest
NYG	.682	10	9	3	1
PIT	.616	6	4	8	3
CIN	.490	3	4	2	13
PHI	.480	2	5	6	7
STL	.412	4	5	6	7
BRK	.379	2	1	5	14
BOS	.340	0	3	7	12

On three separate occasions Richie faced the Giants twice in the same series. Lavender did it twice. In fact, in one four-game series in late July, they each took two turns against McGraw's squad. Chance squeezed in Cheney when they could not perform, but that was rather rare. Mordecai Brown, who only had eight starts all year, had the sole leftover turn against New York. Meanwhile, Reulbach had only one of his 19 starts come against a team with a winning record.

Chance also leveraged his pitchers by using his ace in key relief situations. Mordecai Brown was the game's all-time save king until the mid–1920s. In 1910, he set a baseball record with 26 relief appearances in one season. Chance wanted Brown on the mound in all the most important situations, whether it be a start against the Giants or preserving a close lead against the heart of the order at the end of a contest. This maneuver worked for Chance as his teams were 264–190 in one-run games over his career. His .581 winning percentage in those contests is one of the best in baseball history. Though a manager who nearly won sixty percent of all his contests should have a good record in close games, .581 is still better than one would expect.

Fred Clarke

> **W/L Record:** 1,602–1,181 (.576)
> **Managed:** Full Seasons: Louisville 1898–99; Pittsburgh 1900–15
>   Majority in: Louisville 1897
>   Minority of: (none)
> **Birnbaum Database:** +672 runs
>   Individual Hitters: -24 runs
>   Individual Pitchers: +395 runs
>   Pythagenpat Difference: -124 runs
>   Team Offense: +237 runs
>   Team Defense: +188 runs
> **Team Characteristics:** Clarke managed well-rounded teams. His position players were strong hitters and terrific defenders. (Obviously, the presence of Honus Wagner helped on both points.) Clarke's pitchers threw strikes and kept the ball in the park. He showed a willingness to spread out the work among his main starting pitchers.
> **LPA:** 3.62   **LPA+:** 89

It is fitting that Fred Clarke and Frank Chance appear close to each other alphabetically as they shared several other traits. They were contemporary National League player-managers for teams that competed for the pennant every year. Clarke stopped managing when he finished playing and the important part of Chance's managerial career occurred when he played. Both would do anything to win and hated their players fraternizing with the opposition. Along with Chance, Clarke popularized a new kind of pitching staff, one with the innings more spread out among various men. During the Pirates glory run of 1901–10, only Vic Willis threw 300 innings in a season, and he did that only twice. The other major league teams had 140 different 300-inning seasons in that span. Longtime rotation stalwart Sam Leever peaked at tenth on the innings pitched leaderboard. Deacon Phillippe, Leever's perennial pitching partner, never rose higher than ninth.

A fundamental difference existed in the approaches of Chance and Clarke, however. While both had splendid pitchers and fielders, Chance emphasized gloves and Clarke prioritized arms. The early twentieth century Pirates had four pitchers with distinguished careers—Sam Leever, Deacon Phillippe, Jesse Tannehill, and Hall of Famer Jack Chesbro. Pittsburgh later acquired Hall of Famer Vic Willis, and developed Babe Adams, a high quality pitcher. At the end of Clarke's tenure, Wilbur Cooper began his noteworthy career. None of Clarke's hurlers were as talented as Mordecai Brown, but all were better than the second best pitcher Frank Chance ever had. Clarke's pitchers threw 250 innings (39) more frequently than Chance's threw 200 (34). With so much talent, Clarke presided over 27 different twenty-win seasons; only Connie Mack, John McGraw, and Frank Selee managed more.

Clarke wanted pitchers with superb control. His clubs were always among the leaders in fewest walks per nine innings, topping the league in it seven times from 1899 to 1910. In 1900 and 1901, Phillippe and Tannehill came in second and third place in fewest walks per nine innings. In 1902, they improved to first and second. Phillippe led the league in it five times, all under Clarke's watch. Tannehill was one of the greatest control pitchers of all time, aver-

aging 1.65 walks per nine innings in his career. Yet under Clarke, it was still drastically better, averaging 1.30. Chesbro finished in the top ten once in his career, which occurred in one
of his only seasons with Clarke. Leever walked 122 batters in 1899, just prior to teaming up
with Clarke. Under Clarke, he never issued half as many free passes in a season. Instead,
Leever finished in the league's top ten in walks per inning eight times as a Pirate. Vic Willis
walked a batter every four innings when he pitched with the Pirates, but in the rest of his
career, he issued a free pass every third frame. The fewest walks Willis ever issued in his nine
non–Pirate seasons was 78. The most he ever gave up for Clarke was 83. A lesser Pirate pitcher,
Howie Camnitz, twice finished in the top ten in walks per nine innings. As soon as he lost
his control the Pirates dumped him. Clarke gave Babe Adams his first real major league shot,
and Adams developed into the best control pitcher of his generation.

With so many quality pitchers, Clarke had less interest in leveraging them than Chance
did. Clarke's LPA+ of 89 was remarkably low, given how he distributed his work. He leveraged a little, but rarely to a substantial degree. From 1900 to 1902, when the Pirates had their
four aces, Phillippe was treated like the ace. Of his 95 starts in that period, 30 came against
either the best or second best rival squad, while only nineteen came against the two weakest
teams in that three-year period. Conversely, Chesbro, Leever, and Tannehill had no meaningful leveraging patterns in that period. Given Clarke's interest in control, it was understandable he would treat Phillippe as the ace. With a career average of 1.25 BB/9IP, Phillippe had
the best control of any pitcher since 1893. Perhaps Clarke's most pronounced form of leveraging was to use a particular starting pitcher against second division teams. Toward the end
of their productive years, both Phillippe and Leever found themselves relegated to regularly
facing bottom feeders. Leever had an AOWP+ of 93 in 1908 and Phillippe had a score of 88
the next year.

Impressive fielding aided the pitching talent. While Clarke's Pirates did not emphasize
gloves as much as Chance's squads did, the worst that can be said about Pittsburgh's defense
is that they were not as good as Chicago's unit. In sixteen years running the Pirates, Clarke's
teams led the league in Defensive Efficiency Ratio "only" three times, but came in second (usually behind the Cubs) in eight more seasons. In shortstop Honus Wagner and third baseman
Tommy Leach, the Pirates had two of the best defensive players of their generation backing
up the pitchers.

Clarke modified Charles Comiskey's approach to running a baseball team in two ways.
Though both managers combined control pitching and solid defending to win by run prevention, Clarke led with pitching instead of defense, and he did not rely heavily on his main
arms the way Comiskey did.

While Clarke liked to rest his starting pitchers, he was not as considerate toward his
catchers. In 1909, Pittsburgh's George Gibson played 150 games at backstop, establishing a
league record that lasted until World War II. He caught 140 games the year before and worked
another 143 behind the plate the year after. For perspective, the entire time Clarke managed
there were only two other times an NL catcher worked at least 140 games. Predictably, Gibson collapsed due to overuse in 1911. Given the catching gear of the day, he deserved a monument built in his honor.

Random fact: Clarke patented one of the first pairs of flip-down sunglasses that players
wore on the field.

PATSY DONOVAN

> **W/L Record:** 684–879 (.438)
> **Managed:** Full Seasons: Pittsburgh 1897; St. Louis (NL) 1901–03; Brooklyn
> 1906–08; Boston (AL) 1910–11

Majority in: Pittsburgh 1899; Washington 1904
Minority of: (none)
Birnbaum Database: -274 runs
Individual Hitters: +91 runs
Individual Pitchers: -103 runs
Pythagenpat Difference: +27 runs
Team Offense: -163 runs
Team Defense: -126 runs
Team Characteristics: Donovan had very young teams. His hitters drew walks but that was one of his team's only positives. His defenders could not field, and his pitchers could not do anything. Donovan was one of only a handful of managers whose career W/L mark once fell 200 games under .500. He was the only one who rallied back from that point prior to his retirement. None of his hitters ever walked 75 or more times in a season.
LPA: 4.71   **LPA+:** 110

Donovan had one of the worst winning percentages for anyone who managed at least a thousand games. At a time when many managers won via run prevention, his teams were especially bad at stopping their opponents, allowing the most runs in the league three times. If you adjust run scoring for park effects, he had the worst squad four times. Donovan was the anti–Comiskey as his teams combined bad control with shoddy defense. They only had the worst control once but routinely finished in the back half of the league. Similarly, by every defensive metric his teams routinely floundered.

However, Donovan's personal reputation was out of line with his teams' performances. The baseball community thought enough of his acumen to hire him five times as manager. He was not blamed for their failings because the squads were known to be horrible. Brooklyn played .405 for him, but they were .316 the year before he arrived and .359 after getting rid of him. The Washington Senators were 1–16 when they hired him in early May 1904. Donovan's distinguishing feature was his uncanny ability to be repeatedly and almost exclusively hired by doormats.

It was not a coincidence that marginal franchises hired him. The same thing that drew them to Donovan was what made them futile in the first place — money. Donovan spent almost his entire career as a player-manager. In fact, he had one of the longest careers of any player-manager in history. From the franchise's point of view, a major advantage of a hyphenated manager is one man can do two jobs for less cost than it would take to hire separate individuals. Teams that could not afford a real manager were unlikely to spend enough money on players.

Donovan once said he would love to run a team backed with enough cash to compete. That finally happened with the Red Sox, which ultimately proved to be his professional undoing. They declined each year under him, and as soon as Donovan left improved by almost 30 games, taking the World Series. Though they had a winning record under Donovan, the Birnbaum Database scores Donovan at–53 runs in Boston; rather bad given the quality of the teams. Thus the only good team Donovan ran became his last stop.

BUCK EWING

W/L Record: 489–395 (.553)
Managed: Full Seasons: New York (PL) 1890; Cincinnati 1895–99
Majority in: (none)
Minority of: New York (NL) 1900

Birnbaum Database: +483 runs
   Individual Hitters: +9 runs
   Individual Pitchers: +169 runs
   Pythagenpat Difference: +130 runs
   Team Offense: +87 runs
   Team Defense: +88 runs
Team Characteristics: Ewing's teams contained their share of veteran players. His position players played great defense and put the ball in play when batting. They also stole bases and bunted. Ewing's squads did quite well in one-run games, posting a 124–97 (.561) lifetime record for him in those affairs.
LPA: 4.81   **LPA+:** 111

Buck Ewing is one of the most underrated managers in baseball history. He consistently got the most from the talent available. Look at the cumulative records for the best NL teams from 1895 to 1899, when he managed Cincinnati:

Team	W-L	Pct
Baltimore	449–237	.655
Boston	435–260	.631
Clev/StL	398–291	.578
Cincinnati	394–297	.570
Philadelphia	367–327	.529
Chicago	362–326	.526

The two best teams, Boston and Baltimore, both contained Hall of Fame managers and star-laden rosters. Buck Ewing's Reds rivaled the Cleveland/St. Louis concoction as best of the rest. (Why Clev/StL? In the 1898–99 off-season, the Cleveland Spiders owners bought the floundering St Louis Cardinals franchise — while maintaining control of Cleveland. They shipped all the talent to the larger St. Louis market, making it the real successor to the Spiders.) Though Cincinnati and Cleveland possessed similar records, they had very different rosters.

Cleveland's best pitcher was Cy Young, obviously one of baseball's greatest hurlers, who was in his prime at this time. Their best hitter, Hall of Famer Jesse Burkett, was one of the leading bats of the decade. Infielder Bobby Wallace provided a third future Hall of Famer for the roster. Though primarily inducted for his career value, Wallace was an excellent glove in his prime, and from 1897 onward was also a very good hitter. He was actually a quality pitcher through 1896 before transferring to an everyday position.

Backing up Cleveland's trio of Hall of Famers, Cupid Childs manned second base. He was on pace for the Hall of Fame only to fall apart completely in his early 30s. A fine defensive player with lots of steals and a high OBP, he was Roberto Alomar with a shorter career. Cleveland also had Chief Zimmer, one of the decade's better catchers, and Ed McKean, a very good hitting shortstop. Alongside Cy Young, Cleveland possessed hurler Nig Cuppy, one of the best second fiddles of his day. When he faltered, the team produced Jack Powell, who went on to win 245 games. Overall, they contained an excellent core of talent, plus numerous quality players providing depth.

The Reds could not come close to matching Cleveland. Admittedly, Cincinnati also had three Hall of Famers on its roster, but they were far inferior to Cleveland's trio. The most famous was Ewing himself. Though he was the best catcher of his day, that day had passed. He played only 175 games, all at first base, before retiring after 1897. He was replaced by Jake

Beckley, whom the Veterans Committee later voted into Cooperstown. He only joined the squad in mid–1897, however. Bid McPhee was the only immortal to play for Cincinnati the entire time Ewing managed them. However, he was only two weeks younger than Ewing, and only gained his Cooperstown plaque in 2000, well after the death of everyone who ever saw him play.

Cincinnati's main pitcher was Frank Dwyer, whose 76–54 win-loss record from 1895 to 1899 was not quite as good as Nig Cuppy's 81–50 mark in these years. Maybe the most talented pitcher Ewing had was Ted Breitenstein, who arrived in 1897. He was probably the best pitcher of the 1890s to end his career with a losing record. While a pitcher must be quite talented to win that honor, he cannot be too talented. The Reds also possessed Pink Hawley, who is Breitenstein's main competition for that dubious distinction. Filling out their roster, third baseman Charlie Irwin and catcher Heine Peitz provided solid defensive though minimal offensive value. One of their better offensive players, outfielder Dusty Miller, was merely adequate.

The best player on the Reds in these years would be the fifth or sixth best on Cleveland. Cincinnati had no one who could touch Cupid Childs, let alone Burkett and Young. Yet they ended up with nearly identical records.

Forget Cleveland for a minute. Did the Reds have as much talent as Chicago? Aside from the aging Cap Anson at first, the Windy City squad contained two of the greatest players denied entry into Cooperstown in shortstop Bill Dahlen and center fielder Jimmy Ryan. The latter was there the entire time, and the former only missed one year. They also had Bill Lange, a center fielder who was terrific in the field and at the plate. On the mound, staff ace Clark Griffith constantly won twenty games. Alongside him they got help at various points in time from Adonis Terry, Iron Jack Taylor, and Nixey Callahan. Chicago arguably possessed a better infield, outfield, and pitchers than Cincinnati. Yet the Reds won 32 more games.

The highest compliment you can pay a manager is that one cannot imagine his team performing any better than they did given the talent they had. There are few managers in baseball history who deserve that praise more than Buck Ewing. Cincinnati's achievements were wildly out of line with their capabilities.

They succeeded because Ewing had pitchers and fielders who complemented each other. His teams had great defense. Going by any defensive metric—Fielding Win Shares, DER, or fielding percentage—Ewing's Reds were consistently superior with their gloves. For example, the 1896 squad made approximately 100 fewer errors than most teams in the league while also doing the best job in the league turning batted balls into outs. Their lack of errors was especially important because the pitchers rarely struck out opposing batters. Like Comiskey (who he replaced as Cincinnati's manager), Ewing wanted his pitchers to focus on control. The gloves would ensure outs came.

Ewing had an offensive philosophy that meshed with his defensive approach. He liked hitters who put the ball in play. In 1896, his hitters were baseball's second hardest team to fan—an especially impressive achievement since they never faced their own pitchers, who recorded the fewest strikeouts. Cincinnati's offensive philosophy allowed more batters to reach base not only through hits but also errors, as they could take advantage of the primitive fielding equipment and shoddy fundamentals endemic in the 1890s.

Just like Chance and Clarke a decade later, Ewing realized good defense allowed him to spread his innings around instead of heavily relying on one or two arms. The most innings ever thrown by one of his starters, 331, was the National League's 47th highest total from 1895 to 1899. That was especially remarkable since Ewing's staffs were consistently well above average. Though people who study baseball history often comprehend that Frank Chance and Fred Clarke diffused their team's innings in the 1900s, it is less well known that they adopted Buck Ewing's strategy, rather than developed it themselves.

Ewing spread out the innings two ways. First, he never had anyone on the Reds start 40 games in a season. They were the only team from 1895 to 1899 who can claim that. Second, as noted in Chapter 2, Ewing was his day's biggest user of relief pitchers. Only five men had a dozen relief appearances in a season in those years, three of whom pitched for Buck Ewing. In 1897, Red Ehret set a single-season major league baseball record with fifteen relief appearances.

By easing up on his pitchers and putting them in front of a good defense, his pitchers remained fresher, healthier, and thus better. When Ewing came to Cincinnati in 1895, he brought Billy Rhines and Frank Foreman with him. They had combined for eight wins from 1892 to 1894. Under Ewing, they went 73–52. Ewing inherited a solid veteran in Frank Dwyer. When Ewing cut his innings, Dwyer responded with the strongest stretch of his career. When Breitenstein and Hawley arrived, both appeared to be on the downward swing in his career. With the Ewing treatment, Breitenstein posted back-to-back 20 win seasons, and Hawley's ERA dropped by almost 1.50 in his first season in Cincinnati.

Riding this philosophy, Ewing scores preposterously high in the Birnbaum Database. According to it, he was one of the twenty best managers of all time. That cannot possibly be the case since Ewing only lasted six seasons—only four of which are in that database. While the score might look like a reason to condemn the Birnbaum Database for how it handles the 1890s, Ewing's results demonstrate the database's validity. Though it exaggerates how good Ewing was, the Birnbaum Database recognizes a forgotten great.

CLARK GRIFFITH

> **W/L Record:** 1,491–1,367 (.522)
> **Managed:** Full Seasons: Chicago (AL) 1901–02; New York (AL) 1903–07;
>   Cincinnati 1909–11; Washington 1912–20
>   Majority in: (none)
>   Minority of: New York (AL) 1908
> **Birnbaum Database:** +305 runs
>   Individual Hitters: -33 runs
>   Individual Pitchers: +151 runs
>   Pythagenpat Difference: +201 runs
>   Team Offense: -13 runs
>   Team Defense: -2 runs
> **Team Characteristics:** No player of his ever had a 100 RBI season or a .500 slugging percentage. He *easily* had the longest managerial career without either achievement happening, let alone both. Only once did a player even slug .450 under him. Conversely, Griffith's teams constantly stole, averaging more swipes per season than any other prominent twentieth century manager. Based on the limited evidence available, Griffith's runners had a terrific success rate on the base paths. Though his teams never had any power, he rarely used sacrifice hits. Then again, he often received credit with helping popularize the suicide squeeze.
> **LPA:** 4.31   **LPA+:** 107

The baseball world has a term used to describe a particular person: redass. A redass is someone full of fire—someone so desperate to win that he fumes after every loss. As manager, Griffith was something of a redass, becoming one of the game's most ejected managers. Perhaps that is not the best term for him, though, as the word redass conjures up an image of a man who has more fire than brains—Larry Bowa, for instance. Clark Griffith was as brainy as they came. Sometimes he tried to predict the next pitch while watching the game from the bench, and his former players said that he was right 90 percent of the time. He had enough smarts to pull one of the game's first known double switches in 1906. Revealing his smarts, he rose from player to owner with manager serving as the key stop along the way.

As manager, Griffith had a pronounced interest in trusting his bullpen. Prior to 1905, no pitcher had ever made more than fifteen relief appearances in one season. The New York Highlanders (as the Yankees were called at the time) had two pitchers break the record that season (one was Griffith himself, nearing the end of his splendid career as a major leaguer pitcher). A third hurler had fourteen relief appearances despite being traded late in the year. The next season, one of Griffith's pitchers made sixteen trips from the bullpen while the manager himself netted fifteen. No other American League pitcher exceeded a dozen relief appearances. In 1913, Washington pitcher Bert Gallia set an AL record with 27 games from the bullpen. A teammate of his made 24 relief appearances that year.

As a result of Griffith's willingness to go to the bullpen, his teams had comparatively few complete games. In each of the five years that Griffith ran the Highlanders, they finished last in completions despite featuring quality staffs. In 1904, they recorded 123 complete games while the next lowest squad finished 134. The next year New York completed only 88 starts, almost 30 fewer than anyone else. Prior to them, no team had ever completed fewer than 70 percent of its starts, yet they finished fewer than 60 percent. The Tendencies Database corroborates Griffith's willingness to give his starters the hook by noting what percentage of pitcher starts were completed by all teams. The following managers, relative to their peers, were the least likely to use only one pitcher in a game:

Fewest Complete Games

Jimy Williams	1.523
Burt Shotton	1.489
Gus Schmelz	1.366
Clark Griffith	1.357
Bill Rigney	1.335

From Schmelz's departure until Shotton's arrival nearly forty years later, Griffith was the king of yanking his starters. Actually, the numbers undersell Griffith's interest in the bullpen. Schmelz and Shotton make the list in part because they ran horrible pitching staffs. Clark Griffith managed Walter Johnson, who completed more games than anyone else in the twentieth century.

Griffith made the above table because he did not treat his starters equally. In 1914, Johnson led the league with 33 complete games, but his teammates had only 42. At a time when pitchers completed half of their starts, Doc Ayers—Washington's second best pitcher—finished only eight of 32. In 1918, Johnson completed all of his starts—something no pitcher had done in ten years—but none of Washington's other primary hurlers completed half of their starts. Griffith's Senators finished last in complete games only once, but they were normally near the bottom despite Johnson's presence. In 1904, Griffith had something similar happen in New York. As noted, that team had the fewest complete games in the league. Incredibly, they did so despite staff ace Jack Chesbro setting a post–1893 record for most complete games, with 48 in his 51 starts. His teammates finished only 72 percent of their starts while the rest of the league's starting pitchers completed nearly nine-tenths of their contests.

Griffith frequently combined two features that rarely go together—very good starting pitching with comparatively few innings by the starters. The best modern parallel is the man topping the list above—Jimy Williams. When Williams ran the Red Sox, he kept Pedro Martinez on the mound for seven or eight innings every chance he could in order to give his middle relievers a breather, and then pulled the rest of his starters very early. Clark Griffith had the same approach: rely on your main guy and rest the lesser starters. Pedro Martinez was never the workhorse that Johnson was, but was among the league leaders in innings for three of his four seasons under Williams.

Oftentimes a manager who starts his career as one of the game's more bullpen-reliant skippers will fall back when he gets older. Throughout virtually all baseball history there has been a gradual erosion of innings thrown by starters and it is tough to remain ahead of this curve. Both Leo Durocher and Sparky Anderson began their careers with reputations for quick hooks only to have the league catch up with them and then surpass their interest in using the bullpen. However, Griffith avoided this fate. In 1919, his penultimate season as manager, his squad was last in complete games. In a scenario reminiscent of 1904, Walter Johnson and teammate Jim Shaw completed 50 out of their 66 starts, while the rest of the staff finished only 18 of 76. Even after Griffith left the dugout to become a full-time executive, his Senators stayed at the cutting edge of using relievers. In the mid–1920s, Washington's Firpo Marberry emerged as the game's first true relief ace. One can only wonder what influence Griffith had from the front office.

Griffith also used his aces differently than his other starters. For Griffith, the goal was to get quantity out of the ace and as a result Walter Johnson was one of the period's least leveraged aces. As with Griffith's decision to give Johnson so many complete games, matching him up against a specific opponent was not the main priority; maximizing his innings was. Griffith's LPA+ of 107 came because he leveraged his secondary pitchers so much. Quantity was only a concern with the ace. In Cincinnati, where Griffith lacked a dominant pitcher, he was especially prone to leveraging. Thus Fred Beebe posted an AOWP+ of 108 in 1910, and Bobby Keefe a 106 in 1911.

A common theme exists in Griffith's leveraging and bullpen usage. It was all about trust. The ace should stand strong in any circumstance. Thus Chesbro and Johnson logged as many innings as possible, regardless of the situation. Circumstances mattered with his lesser arms. Since Griffith had less faith in them, he felt it necessary to match them against particular teams, and to pull them in the middle of a game as needed.

NED HANLON

> **W/L Record:** 1,313–1,164 (.530)
> **Managed:** Full Seasons: Pittsburgh (PL) 1890; Baltimore 1893–98; Brooklyn 1899–1905; Cincinnati 1906–07
>   Majority in: Pittsburgh 1891; Baltimore 1892
>   Minority of: Pittsburgh 1889
> **Birnbaum Database:** +92 runs
>   Individual Hitters: +102 runs
>   Individual Pitchers: +153 runs
>   Pythagenpat Difference: -95 runs
>   Team Offense: -169 runs
>   Team Defense: +101 runs
> **Team Characteristics:** Hanlon's offenses could get on base, slug, steal bases, draw walks— you name it. They rarely hit many home runs, but blasted enough other extra-base hits to make up for it. For such a prominent manager, his pitchers did not possess very good control. He used his bench infrequently.
> **LPA:** 3.51   **LPA+:** 89

Chapter 2's study of team pacing noted which managers' teams improved and declined the most over the year. A case can be made that a manager belongs on neither list. If his team trails off over the course of a season, it means he does not know how to pace them. Then again, if they get considerably better in the second half, then what was he doing in the first part of the year?

Another way of looking at it is to see which teams paced themselves the most evenly. Take all teams in a league, figure which clubs' first and second half winning percentages are the most similar, and rank them accordingly. Churn them through the Tendencies Database and see the results:

Most Even Pace

Charles Comiskey	0.562
Frank Selee	0.702
Bill Virdon	0.757
Ned Hanlon	0.758
Fred Clarke	0.765

Hanlon's place on this list is unexpected because in Chapter 2, he appeared among those whose teams improved the most in the second half, with a nearly identical score to this one, 0.734. Neat trick. Hanlon's teams almost always played better as the year wore on but rarely played exceptionally better. In eighteen years as a team's primary manager, his squads improved fifteen times in the second half. However, they had the league's biggest improvement only once, in 1892. Interestingly, that was the only season of the eighteen where Hanlon replaced another manager in midseason. Meanwhile, three times his teams had the most even, and twice the second most even performance. Though fairly evenly paced, his teams typically enjoyed a modest boost in their records in the second half. In his sixteen full seasons as manager, Hanlon's squads posted a 592–531 (.527) first-half record and a 621–483 (.563) second-half mark. While 38 points is a substantial discrepancy over a career, over a single season that would be a mild difference. Hanlon's uncanny consistency allowed him to make both the most improved and most even pace lists.

Chapter 2 also revealed which managers liked to rely on their starters or bench the most. That brings up the question: what is the most any team relied on its starting lineup in a single season? The best way to answer this question is to divide up teams by decade because over the years, as major league baseball has expanded its schedule and increased its roster sizes, the percent of plate appearances by starting lineups has declined. Also, since the designated hitter gives American League squads a structural advantage in recent decades, only plate appearances by the starting eight position players will be looked at. Based on that, the following clubs gave the largest share to their main batters in each decade:

Year	Team	League	Pct.	Manager
1878	BOS	NL	89.2%	Harry Wright
1882	BUF	NL	87.2%	Jim O'Rourke
1894	BAL	NL	85.1%	Ned Hanlon
1905	PHI	NL	83.7%	Hugh Duffy
1915	NEW	FL	82.5%	George Stovall
1926	CLE	AL	83.0%	Tris Speaker
1938	PIT	NL	83.1%	Pie Traynor
1949	BOS	AL	79.9%	Joe McCarthy
1950	PHI	NL	82.5%	Eddie Sawyer
1962	MIN	AL	82.3%	Sam Mele

Year	Team	League	Pct.	Manager
1978	MON	NL	81.8%	Dick Williams
1989	STL	NL	80.5%	Whitey Herzog
1996	TEX	AL	76.4%	Johnny Oates
2000	PHI	NL	78.9%	Larry Bowa

Hanlon's 1894 Orioles leaned on their starters more than any team that played 100 or more games in a season. They are the only such squad to top 85 percent; in fact no other team who played that long a schedule topped 84 percent. For what it is worth, Hanlon also managed the squad with the second highest total of plate appearances given to any bunch of starters in the 1890s—the 1890 Pittsburgh Players League squad, at 81.5 percent. Conversely, his 1892 Baltimore squad featured the smallest percent of plate appearances by any starting lineup that decade, 52.1 percent, as he immediately tried to remake the team in his image when he took over in midseason.

That being said, Hanlon, most famous as the man who taught John McGraw how to manage, scores surprisingly poorly in the Birnbaum Database. He has a positive score, but a middling one. Two main reasons explain this. First, the Birnbaum Database only goes back to 1896, missing much of Hanlon's peak. His Orioles won it all in 1894 and 1895. Given the nature of Birnbaum's algorithms, that should deflate the scores of the first two components in 1896–97. For the years in his prime that are scored, Hanlon performed exceptionally well. From 1896 to 1903, Hanlon has a mark of +566 runs, one of the best stretches of any manager in history. Earl Weaver's best eight-year stretch, 1973–80, scores at +554 runs. Tony LaRussa's highest period of that length, 1988–95, is worth +513 runs. Advantage: Hanlon.

Second, the last four years of Hanlon's career kill him. With Brooklyn in 1904–05 and Cincinnati in 1906–07, he scored a cumulative -474 runs. The Dodgers had been a winning club for years under him, but collapsed at the end. In 1905, they went 48–104 (.316), the worst season in franchise history. When Hanlon left, they rebounded by 18 games. Cincinnati had been a consistent winner before he arrived, but came in sixth place both years with him. Their two worst campaigns from 1902 to 1912 were his pair of seasons.

Hanlon would not be the only manager who lost his touch. For example, Casey Stengel clearly slipped by the end when he managed the expansion Mets. Still, Stengel was 75 when he retired—Hanlon was only 49 when he departed from the dugout, and 46 when the game passed him by. Since when is 46 years too old for a manager? Actually, back then it was old. When Hanlon's career collapsed in 1904, most of his peers were far younger. The NL had only two other managers over 36, Al Buckenberger and Selee. Both would be out of the business by mid–1905. Fred Clarke, who had already managed for almost a decade, was only 31. The oldest AL manager was 41-year-old Connie Mack.

By the first decade of the twentieth century there was minimal precedent for a successful manager in his 40s. The oldest pennant-winning manager of all time was Jack Chapman at 47 in the 1890 American Association. However, that league was on the verge of collapse. The next oldest was 43-year-old Harry Wright. Only one other 40-something had accomplished it—Ned Hanlon himself. Life spans were considerably shorter then, and the game itself was still getting established. It was a young man's sport. Fred Clarke stopped managing in his 30s, and Frank Chance won his final pennant before he was 35. Connie Mack was the outstanding exception, as in 1913 he became the oldest man to win a pennant at age 50. Not until 1914 would both pennant-winning skippers be older than 40. In contrast, 1935 was the last time both World Series skippers were in their 30s.

In his prime "Foxy Ned" was historically great. With Baltimore, he was credited with revolutionizing managing. He wanted his players always looking for any angle they could. Sometimes this meant rather unsavory behavior, such as tripping opposing base runners, or hiding an extra ball in the poorly maintained playing field. Hanlon's Baltimore groundskeeper, Thomas Murphy, banked the baselines to either help or hurt bunting, depending on who the opposing team was. He spread soap into the dirt on the mound to make the enemy pitchers' hands slippery. Murphy also created a hard spot before home plate, which became the source for the Baltimore chop. If the other squad had lefthanders, he would dig up that corner of the pitching rubber and soak it to ruin the opponent's footing. Hanlon was one of the first managers to have his pitchers throw from a mound — back then the rubber was usually at ground level. He put opponents' benches in the sun so they would boil on those hot summer days, forcing baseball to create a rule mandating that dugouts have roofs. While W. C. Fields said never give a sucker an even break, Hanlon lived this ethos.

More important than ethically dubious shenanigans, Hanlon's brand of baseball meant engaging in a higher level of in-game strategy than had been common. The goal was to win, and cheating was one possible route to that destination The Orioles are well remembered for playing "inside baseball" trying to do those little things to move runners over. Hanlon was credited with helping to popularize the hit-and-run. He also emphasized fielders backing each other up. Supposedly his squads began the practice of taking pitches when the count was 3–0 or 3–1. The O's were consistently one of the most felonious teams on the bases under him, and in 1894–95 also bunted more than their share of times. However, Hanlon retreated from bunting, declining from 151 in 1894 to 72 three years later. He went from being one of the most to one of the least frequent sacrificers.

It is a guessing game as to why Hanlon backed away from the bunt, but a few thoughts can be hazarded. First, this was reminiscent of Gus Schmelz's bunting history. Credited by contemporaries with inventing the practice of the bunt as an offensive weapon, Schmelz had very low sacrifice hit totals by the time the NL began recording that stat in 1894. Both possibly began bunting as a way to get an edge on the opposition. Perhaps they used the bunt more for on-base purposes with the sacrifice as an accepted secondary outcome. Doing what the opposition was not expecting and/or unable to defend, could give a team a better chance at getting on base. As teams defended it more, and the likelihood of bunting for a hit declined — especially with a runner on first base — Hanlon backed away from it, not willing to trade a base for an out. As Chapter 2 showed, John McGraw, Hanlon's prize protégé, was historically averse to the sacrifice hit. Hanlon and Schmelz were looking for that extra edge, and if bunting provided it, use it. If not, move along. The result, not the process, mattered most.

Hanlon had another innovation. His 1894 Orioles became the first team to record double-digit saves in a season, with eleven. Given that they won the pennant by three games, those relief stints might have been especially important. The second highest team save total from the nineteenth century was nine, by Hanlon's 1899 Brooklyn club. Normally, Hanlon's squads did not lead the league in saves, but he was flexible in his approach to the bullpen.

HUGHIE JENNINGS

> **W/L Record:** 1,184–995 (.543)
> **Managed:** Full Seasons: Detroit 1907–20
> Majority in: (none)
> Minority of: New York (NL) 1924–25
> **Birnbaum Database:** +110 runs
> Individual Hitters: +15 runs
> Individual Pitchers: -53 runs
> Pythagenpat Difference: +225 runs
> Team Offense: +39 runs
> Team Defense: -116 runs

Team Characteristics: His teams could hit, but not field. Jennings presided over some of the most well rounded offenses of any manager. His hitters scored above average at virtually every facet of the game: they had power, hit for average, were difficult to strike out, drew walks, and could steal. He oversaw 39 separate 20+ sacrifice-hit performances; only Connie Mack had more.

LPA: 5.46   **LPA+:** 127

Hughie Jennings and Ralph Houk were the only two managers to win a pennant in each of their first three seasons. Neither ever claimed another.

Jennings played for one of baseball's greatest offensive juggernauts, Ned Hanlon's 1890s Baltimore Orioles. Jennings's teams were similar, as more than any other manager of the early twentieth century, his squads centered on offense. Detroit was either first or second in Hitting Win Shares almost every year Jennings ran them. The centerpiece, obviously, was Ty Cobb, who gave Jennings a great deal of credit for his early success. Jennings let him run wild on the bases from the early days, bolstering his confidence. In a more recent parallel, A's manager Billy Martin allowed a young Rickey Henderson to average nearly a stolen base attempt per game under his watch. While Cobb and Henderson would have both been great basestealers regardless who their manager was, that does not mean all skippers would have trusted their talented but untested players as much as Jennings or Martin did.

Jennings's Tigers had an Achilles heel, however: below-average defenses. This was odd given that Jennings, a former shortstop, had been possibly baseball's best defender during his peak in the mid–1890s. Still, no matter what metric one prefers—fielding percentage, DER, Fielding Win Shares—his squads finished below average. Only 14.8 percent of his squads' Win Shares were allocated to their fielders, the lowest total for anyone in this book. They were especially bad at turning double plays. The Tendencies Database gauges this with the formula: DP/(H+BB+HB-SH-2B-3B-HR-SB-CS); this is essentially double plays divided by opportunities to turn them. Not all that data exists for every year, but it gives the best idea how often a runner stood on first base, making a twin killing feasible. The following managers scored the worst:

Worst at Turning Double Plays

Hughie Jennings	1.540
Wilbert Robinson	1.439
Alvin Dark	1.357
Felipe Alou	1.276
Bobby Valentine	1.264

Not only does Jennings top the list, but no one seriously challenges him. Jennings's teams scored last nine times in his fourteen years. The 1911 Tigers did the worst job turning double plays of any team in the deadball era, with 78 turned in 1,812 opportunities by the formula above. (Actually, that is the worst score by any team since 1884. However, it is not fair comparing the 1911 Tigers to more recent teams because if caught steals data for 1911 were known, they likely would pass some squads.) The third worst score of the decade belongs to the 1910 Tigers, with the 1919 Tigers coming in fourth worst. The 1920 Tigers had the lowest score of the 1920s.

Detroit's defensive problems were especially crucial because their pitchers struck out few hitters. Placing poor defenders behind pitchers who rely on their fielders represents a fundamental failure of roster construction. It caused Jennings's Tigers to consistently have trouble preventing their opponents from scoring. For evidence, look at the results when the Tendencies Database examines runs allowed per game, adjusted for park:

Most Runs Allowed, Adjusted for Park

Hughie Jennings	1.365
Patsy Donovan	1.336
Frank Robinson	1.278
Billy Barnie	1.253
Bruce Bochy	1.218

Jennings's high score is exceptional as he is the only one listed with a winning record. Sometimes people knock Cobb for the squad's inability to win a pennant after 1909. It was not his fault, though. Pitching and middle infield were not his responsibilities.

Also, middle infield glove work wasn't the only stark disparity between Jennings' teams and the way he played. In his day, Jennings was the king of getting hit by a pitch, and he still owns both the single-season and career HBP records. Over his career, pitchers plunked him once every 20 plate appearances. Jennings' offensive approach centered on reaching base and the HBP was a key tool he used to reach that end. Yet his Tigers never took advantage of this option. From 1907 to 1920, no Tiger ever received more than a dozen HBP in a season, even though that happened over 60 times on other clubs. Meanwhile Jennings' pitchers routinely hit more than their share of opposing batsmen. Detroit's pitchers tallied more hit batsmen than the HBP totals of their own hitters' in each of the fourteen seasons Jennings managed the Tigers, which is the longest such streak in major league baseball history. Comparing the overall total of hit batters on Detroit with batsmen hit by Tiger pitchers, Jennings' clubs had the worst negative HBP differential of those of any manager, as the list below makes clear:

Worst HBP Differentials

Hughie Jennings	-232 HBP
Lou Piniella	-164 HBP
Jim Leyland	-150 HBP
Bruce Bochy	-145 HBP
Branch Rickey	-139 HBP

Note: the numbers above are not exact, because for partial seasons this chart covers only seasons in which the skipper managed a majority of the season, and he gets full credit for those. Regardless, Jennings's lead is overwhelming.

There is a logic behind the disparity between Jennings' playing and managing career when it comes to HBP. In his playing prime, Jennings was one of the game's brightest talents, but taking so many fastballs in the ribs greatly shortened his career. In order to help his team score 10 to 15 runs per year, Jennings shaved perhaps 1,000 games from his career. Looking at how he managed, Jennings did not think the tradeoff had been worth it. Though the HBP might be an offensive weapon, the main casualty was the guy getting hit. He made sure that never happened to his players.

FIELDER JONES

W/L Record: 683–582 (.540)
Managed: Full Seasons: Chicago (AL) 1905–08; St. Louis (FL) 1915; St. Louis (AL) 1916–17
  Majority in: Chicago (AL) 1904
  Minority of: St. Louis (FL) 1914; St. Louis (AL) 1918
Birnbaum Database: +178 runs
  Individual Hitters: +13 runs
  Individual Pitchers: +53 runs

Pythagenpat Difference: -51 runs
Team Offense: +155 runs
Team Defense: +8 runs

Team Characteristics: Jones's teams contained veteran players who lacked power. Only twice did someone who qualified for a batting title under him post a slugging percentage over .410. On 22 different occasions, one had an isolated power below .050, which is nearly the most by any manager in history (Connie Mack had 23, and Harry Wright had 25). That is an amazing achievement given that Jones's career was so short. Alternately, none of his pitchers allowed more than six home runs in a year. By the standards of his day, Jones leaned heavily on his main pitchers and even harder on his catchers.

LPA: 4.54   LPA+: 110

More than any other manager in history, a clear unity exists between Fielder Jones the player and Fielder Jones the manager. The same attributes that made him a quality player were precisely the factors that caused his teams to be successful.

As a player, Jones knew the value of a walk, as he finished among the top ten in the league in that stat nine straight years. In his five years managing the White Sox, Chicago led the league in walks four times and came in second once. In 1908, they collected 95 more walks than any other American League offense. Later, in Jones's only full season in the Federal League, his St. Louis squad again paced the league in walks. In 1916, he took over a Browns squad that had been sixth in the league in walks the year before. They vaulted to first place, with 83 more free passes than the runner up.

That is only half the story, though, as Jones's pitchers walked few men. In 1903, before he took over in Chicago, the White Sox were fifth in the league in walks per nine innings. Jones moved them up to third in 1904, and second the following year. In all his remaining seasons, Chicago's pitchers had the best control in the league. The 1915 St. Louis Terriers surrendered the fewest walks in the Federal League. The Browns shot up from the second worst control to the third best when Jones arrived.

When walks drawn and allowed are factored together, few managers gained more from free passes than Jones. The 1906 White Sox drew 198 more walks than they gave up, the best differential by any AL team that decade. The 1908 squad came in third place with a 179-walk advantage. In his first six full seasons as manager, Jones's teams drew 2,978 walks while allowing 2,047; giving him an advantage of 931 walks in 942 games. In the Tendencies Database, teams ranked first in both walks drawn and allowed on 52 occasions. Only two men managed more than two of those squads—Jones and John McGraw—who each had four. However, McGraw lasted four times as long in baseball as Jones. It makes one wonder what went wrong in 1917, Jones's last year on the job. The Browns pitchers had the second-worst control and his hitters finished last in walks.

As a player, center fielder Jones was one of the most sensational fielders of his day. Bill James's Win Shares system rates Jones an A+ for his fielding ability. Jones's teams followed in his footsteps, leading the league in Fielding Win Shares on two occasions. Twice the Tendencies Database lists them leading the league in turning double plays, adjusted for opportunity. They led in fielding percentage and DER four times each. When they did not lead, they normally finished in the top half. According to baseball historian Peter Morris, Jones was one of the first managers to position his outfielders during games. Again the 1917 Browns are an aberration, finishing last in DER and fielding percentage. Given their un–Jonesian performance and that it was his last year, one can wonder how attentive he was to the team that season.

With this approach, Jones's teams achieved noteworthy success. His most famous team was the 1906 Hitless Wonder White Sox, who—despite hitting only .230 with seven home runs on the season — shocked baseball by defeating the 116-win Cubs in the World Series. The White Sox overcame their obvious deficiencies by mastering the parts of the game Jones loved. They led the league in walks for a respectable, albeit below average, on-base percentage. Their pitchers walked far fewer men than an average team did, and the defense ensured they would not surrender many hits. The combination of control pitching and defense was well established by the time Jones became a manager. In fact, his employer — White Sox owner Charles Comiskey — invented it. However, Jones broadened it by using the walk as an offensive weapon.

Jones possessed another interesting tendency as manager: he was the all-time champ at an especially extreme form of pitcher leveraging. Since 1893, there have been only fourteen times when a pitcher started ten or more times in a season against a specific opponent. Six occurred under Jones:

Year	GS	Opponent	Pitcher
1904	10	Boston	Nick Altrock
1904	10	New York	Doc White
1905	10	Detroit	Doc White
1907	10	Boston	Nick Altrock
1907	10	Philadelphia	Ed Walsh
1908	11	Senators	Doc White

Ed Walsh was Jones's main workhorse, which paradoxically explains why he only shows up once. Since he pitched the most, Jones did not spot him intensely against particular teams. Instead, Jones targeted his southpaws, Altrock and White, at particular teams with an intensity unmatched by any other manager in baseball history. In Altrock's 134 starts under Jones, 39 came against the Red Sox. Meanwhile, from 1904 to 1907 he faced the Senators only four times.

That was moderate compared to how Jones managed Doc White. After facing New York ten times in 1904, he saw them nine more times the next year. When Detroit's left-handed Ty Cobb emerged as the game's next great hitter, Jones used White against the Tigers at every possible opportunity. In 1907–08, White saw them in 18 of his 72 starts. Alternately, for three years, White never faced Washington. On July 30, 1907, in his 115th start under Jones, he finally took the hill against them. The next year, coinciding with the emergence of left-handed hitting outfielder Clyde Milan in Washington, Jones constantly had White face them. That was the only time any twentieth century pitcher started eleven games against one rival.

CONNIE MACK

W/L Record: 3,731–3,948 (.486)
Managed: Full Seasons: Pittsburgh 1895–96; Philadelphia (AL) 1901–36, 1938, 1940–50
　　　　Majority in: Philadelphia (AL) 1937, 1939
　　　　Minority of: Pittsburgh 1894
Birnbaum Database: -668 runs
　　　　Individual Hitters: -149 runs
　　　　Individual Pitchers: -419 runs
　　　　Pythagenpat Difference: +60 runs
　　　　Team Offense: -128 runs
　　　　Team Defense: -32 runs

Team Characteristics: Mack liked pitchers who could overpower hitters, and was less concerned if they had the best control. His staffs led the league in strikeouts well over a dozen times, including almost every season in the A's two glory stretches.

LPA: 3.44   LPA+: 81

Question: How long should one consider Connie Mack's legitimate managerial career to be? On the face of it, the answer is obvious. He managed until 1950, end of story. True, but he lasted so long because he was not only the manager, but also the owner. At a certain point he became more a figurehead than manager. He lasted until age 87; no one else has lasted beyond age 75 in the job. According to baseball lore, coaches Al Simmons and Jimmy Dykes handled most of the real responsibilities in Mack's later years. Mack supposedly fell asleep on the bench during contests and would call out the names of retired players to enter the game.

Mack clearly lasted too long on the job. Since he wore both the hats of manager and owner, one can ponder what motivated him to stay in the dugout as long as he did. According to *It Ain't Over 'til It's Over* by Baseball Prospectus, Mack once claimed he could earn more with a last-place team than a pennant winner as he made his money by pinching pennies. Leaving himself as manager was a great cost-cutting maneuver, something especially important for his club's financial health in the dark days of the Depression. Afterwards, during World War II, teams across baseball were reluctant to fire their managers. The last few seasons, when Dykes and friends ran the show, it looked like Mack just wanted to last 50 years. Perhaps had it not been for the nation's fiscal calamity and war Mack, like his contemporary Clark Griffith, may have excused himself from the dugout. Perhaps not, as he survived the team's dismantling after 1914, but the final years were clearly a sad coda that would never have happened if anyone else controlled the franchise.

With that in mind, one can draw a line after the 1933 season, which was Philadelphia's last winning campaign for quite some time. Mack ended that year with over 5,200 games managed, still more than anyone else in baseball history. The Birnbaum Database gives Mack a score of +481 runs through that point, which would be the 21st highest career score. That serves as a far more appropriate score than what Mack ended up with. It may even be low, given that his first seasons as Pittsburgh's skipper predate the database. From 1934 onward, when the game slipped away from him, he scored –1,149 runs, the worst stretch in baseball history.

Double plays demonstrate how difficult it can be to separate Mack's real managerial career from his caretaker years. Going by the information available, the Tendencies Database says his teams grounded into double plays like none other. This uses a different GIDP-based formula than the one presented in Chapter 2, which studied the hit and run. Since this one aims at the double play itself, items such as stolen base attempts and sacrifice hits are not factored out because one reason managers call for those plays is to avoid the double play. With a formula of GIDP/(H+BB+HBP+ROE-2B-3B-HR), here are the managers whose squads did the least to avoid double plays:

Most Double Plays Grounded Into

Connie Mack	1.426
Tom Kelly	1.413
Danny Murtaugh	1.365
Frank Robinson	1.317
Don Zimmer	1.225

A savvy student of the game can immediately spot a problem: American League GIDP info only goes back to 1939. The above only highlights Mack's bench-napping days. Guess that means it is useless, right? Well, maybe not. The double play is an interesting part of the game. Some managers pay considerable attention to this play, making it a central part of their baseball philosophy and strategy. Though on the surface managers have no obvious involvement in double plays, the teams run by some skippers consistently pull off more double plays than they hit into. That was true of Casey Stengel and Gene Mauch, for instance. Players came and went, but these managers continued making the play work for them. Others, such as Tom Kelly, consistently punt the play, accepting a double play gap the same way a slugging team accepts strikeouts or a team centered on fielding accepts lackluster offense.

Using the same double play formula listed in the Hughie Jennings comments, Mack's teams always had trouble turning double plays, even when they were good. Mack apparently made double plays a low priority. In 52 years on the job, his squads performed the best at the pivot only twice. Mack's teams came in the top half of the league only sixteen times, including his last three seasons when he had the least connection to the game. Alternately, he had a dozen last-place finishes and ten next-to-last showings. Half of those dismal showings came when the A's were good.

Going by the Tendencies Database's double plays formula, Mack's A's had at least one team in the bottom ten of twin killing turned in almost every decade. From 1900 to 1909, the 1905 A's did the second worst job in major league baseball turning double plays based on opportunities and the 1904 A's were fifth worst. The 1920 A's were eighth worst in their decade. The 1933 A's were fourth worst and the 1938 A's fifth worst in their stretch. The 1942 A's had the ninth worst season of the 1940s. Mack's A's did not feature one of the ten worst during the 1910s, but the 1919 squad was the eleventh worst in that span. A consistent half-century long pattern of neglecting the double play exists. It certainly fits with Mack's score in grounding into double plays.

Improbably, however, a Connie Mack team actually set the record that still stands for most double plays turned in a season, with 217. In fact, Mack managed two of the only twelve seasons in which a team topped 200 double plays turned. However, those occasions came at the very end of his career, when he was manager in name only. The 1949 and 1950 Philadelphia defenders made 217 and 208 double plays, respectively. Revealing how marginal Mack was to that effort, the Athletics pulled off 204 more double plays in 1951, when Jimmy Dykes managed them. That was the only time in history a team had three consecutive 200+ double play seasons. Prior to 1945, Mack's defenders exceeded 157 double plays only once.

If the Tendencies Database's two double play based scores are added together, Mack comes off dreadfully:

Worst at Combined Double Plays

Connie Mack	2.625
Bobby Valentine	2.431
Bruce Bochy	2.421
Frank Robinson	2.413
Tom Kelly	2.409

Even if the sad final seasons of his career are adjusted for, Mack did not prioritize this part of the game.

Walks were another part of the game Mack apparently had little interest in. Mack's offenses never led the league in walks drawn. Similarly, going by walks per inning, his pitchers only had the best control twice, in 1928 and 1944. Alternately, his hitters drew the fewest walks in the league thirteen times and were runners up in eight other seasons. His pitchers possessed the league's worst control a dozen times, and the second worst in another dozen campaigns. The 1915 A's allowed 391 more walks than they earned, easily the worst differential in baseball history. Second worst belongs to the 1916 A's who drew 309 fewer walks than they handed out. Mack's teams allowed 100+ more walks than they garnered fifteen times. They had a 100+ walk advantage only four times, all between 1927–32. Looking at every season a manager lasted over half a season, the following skippers had the worst career walk differentials:

Worst Walk Differentials

Connie Mack	-2,862 walks
Lou Boudreau	-1,229 walks
Casey Stengel	-972 walks
Alvin Dark	-884 walks
Buddy Bell	-837 walks

Those numbers are not exact due to partial seasons, but the results are rather telling. Mack's differential equals a walk every third game for a half-century. From 1901 to 1950, the A's allowed more walks than any other American League franchise, and earned the second fewest number of offensive walks.

Unlike double plays and walks, relief pitchers interested Mack. He did not lead the charge for the bullpen like Clark Griffith, but Mack carved out an interesting niche for himself. He is the game's all-time champion of swingmen, pitchers that could be used either as starters or relievers. Steve Treder, a writer for The Hardball Times website, did a series of columns on swingmen in 2008, in which he classified swingmen as hurlers who appeared in 40 or more games with at least fifteen starts and fifteen relief appearances. By that reasonable definition, Mack presided over 25 swing seasons, easily the most in baseball history. The next two highest skippers, Bill Rigney and Miller Huggins, managed that many combined. Mack had none in his first several years managing because no one did back then. The bullpen was not developed enough to allow for this phenomenon. The first swing seasons came in 1908, and Connie Mack had one, with Rube Vickers starting 34 games while relieving another nineteen. With swingmen Chief Bender and Byron Houck, Mack's 1913 A's became the first team to ever have more than twenty saves in a year. Mack was especially active with swingmen in the early-to-mid 1920s. From 1922 to 1925, the A's had eight swingmen, the highest total any franchise has had in such a short time. Mack also used some of his best pitchers in that role. His favorite swingmen were Eddie Rommel and Lefty Grove, at three and four seasons apiece.

In his prime, Mack's astuteness earned him the nickname "The Tall Tactician." With the sharp mind of his younger days, Mack was known for being a master of reading other team's signs. He was one of the first men to use advance scouts to check on opposing teams. He also was effective at correcting the mental mistakes of his players. He had a gentlemanly way of handling it. If they made a mental miscue, Mack would wait until a day or two had passed before quietly discussing the mishap with the player behind closed doors. Mack got his message through and also earned the respect of his players for preserving their dignity. They tried to play better because they wanted to win for Mr. Mack. He was not the first to treat his players in a respectful manner, as Buck Ewing and Frank Selee had also done so, but Mack was the most famous for it. Mack had rookies sit by him on the bench, talking to them about the game, making them more aware of its fine points. Decades later, Joe McCarthy adopted a similar strategy with young infielders like Phil Rizzuto. That may not be a coincidence as Mack biographer Norman Macht noted that McCarthy idolized Mack while growing up near Philadelphia.

JIMMY MCALEER

W/L Record: 735–889 (.453)
Managed: Full Seasons: Cleveland 1901; St. Louis (AL) 1902–09; Washington 1910–11

Majority in: (none)
Minority of: (none)

Birnbaum Database: -152 runs
Individual Hitters: -32 runs
Individual Pitchers: -45 runs
Pythagenpat Difference: -86 runs
Team Offense: -40 runs
Team Defense: +51 runs

Team Characteristics: McAleer's pitchers were not too bad, but his hitters were horrible. In one-run ballgames, he had a career mark of 233–273 (.460), worse than everyone else in this book except Billy Barnie. McAleer's teams played better in the second half, though still poorly. Even by the standards of his time, McAleer used few relievers. Define a relief pitcher as someone with at least 25 appearances with a majority occurring from the bullpen, he was the only prominent twentieth century manager with none.

LPA: 3.38   **LPA+:** 77

McAleer won more games than any other manager in St. Louis Browns history. He also lost the most. He was perhaps the best indicator of how ripe the period was for managers to advance themselves in baseball. Despite his lackluster results in the dugout, he briefly became a minority owner in the Red Sox before a dispute with AL President Ban Johnson forced him out.

The central failing of McAleer's teams was their historically dreadful hitting. If runs scored per game are adjusted for park, and put into the Tendencies Database, his teams had the least punch of all:

Fewest Runs Scored Per Game, Park Adjusted

Jimmy McAleer	1.333
Jimmy Dykes	1.290
Billy Barnie	1.281
Paul Richards	1.280
Felipe Alou	1.261

McAleer never ranked last in any season, but repeatedly had the second or third worst offenses. His teams could not hit and were mediocre at drawing walks, giving them an overall weak OBP score. When someone got on, McAleer's teams were unable to move him around the bases. They had no power, and rarely bunted or stole that much. An inability to do anything right on offense created a whole that was less than the sum of its parts.

Cait Murphy, in *Crazy '08*, tells an interesting story about McAleer. In 1908, he hit upon one of the unlikeliest — yet strangely successful — strategies of all time. Toward the end of a summer road trip, he ordered everyone to get drunk. He threatened a $50 fine to anyone who arrived at the hotel that night sober. The players followed this commandment without protest. The following day the blotto bunch wobbled their way to victory, sparking a run where they went 12–2 over the next fortnight. That was the best fourteen-game stretch in McAleer's managerial career.

JOHN MCGRAW

W/L Record: 2,763–1,948 (.586)
Managed: Full Seasons: Baltimore (NL) 1899; Baltimore (AL) 1901; New York (NL) 1903–23, 1926, 1928–31

Majority in: New York (NL) 1924, 1925, 1927
Minority of: Baltimore (AL) 1902; New York (NL) 1902
Birnbaum Database: +853 runs
Individual Hitters: +344 runs
Individual Pitchers: +415 runs
Pythagenpat Difference: -125 runs
Team Offense: +86 runs
Team Defense: +133 runs
Team Characteristics: McGraw's teams were generally built around offense as they hit for average, had power, drew walks, and stole bases. However, McGraw loathed the sacrifice hit, so his teams hit relatively few of them. His pitchers had good control, and he used more relievers than most of his peers. He generally presided over younger teams.
LPA: 4.51   LPA+: 111

John McGraw contained two pronounced, well-documented personal tendencies that fit well together. He was the ultimate control freak, and his strong point was working with young talent.

His desire for authority was legendary. Leonard Koppett, in his book *The Man in the Dugout*, argued that McGraw personified the notion of control. Christy Mathewson wrote that the Giants won the 1904 pennant with McGraw calling every play from the bench. He would go over the meal tickets from the team hotel to ensure that all his players ate right. Anyone who failed to meet McGraw's dietary guidelines contended with McGraw, which was not a pleasant experience. His longtime coach, Arlie Latham, once said, "McGraw eats gunpowder for breakfast and washes it down with warm blood." With McGraw, it was his way, and his way alone.

He also loved giving untried players a shot. He gave more kids their first big break than any other manager in history. Here is an all-star team of the men who got their first legitimate crack under McGraw:

McGraw's All-Prospect Team

C	Roger Bresnahan
1B	Bill Terry
2B	Frankie Frisch
SS	Travis Jackson
3B	Fred Lindstrom
OF	Mel Ott
OF	Ross Youngs
OF	George J. Burns
SP	Carl Hubbell
SP	Joe McGinnity
SP	Rube Marquard
SP	Freddie Fitzsimmons
SP	Red Ames

That just scratches the surface. Beyond them are Fred Merkle, Chief Meyers, George Kelly, Larry Doyle, Art Devlin, Art Fletcher, Jo-Jo Moore, Dave Roberston, Hooks Wiltsie, Harry Howell, Bill Keister, Jeff Tesreau, Ferdie Schupp, Bill Walker, and Virgil Barnes. Christy Mathewson does not quite qualify because he had one full season under his belt before McGraw came to the Giants, but he flourished under the new manager. McGraw always had a project, usually a hitter, on the bench to teach.

McGraw had greater control when dealing with players trying to prove themselves, hence his tendencies meshed well together. The best modern parallel might be legendary college basketball coach Bobby Knight. In his years at Indiana and Texas Tech, he demanded absolute authority, succeeding while subjecting his young charges to a level of dictatorial control grown men would likely not tolerate. The most comparable modern baseball manager to McGraw would be Dick Williams, another stubborn cuss who was willing to break in young talent and demanded people do things his way.

Though McGraw produced a bountiful supply of quality young players, he rarely guided truly great talents. Great players are irreplaceable, and the only man indispensable in McGraw's system was himself. He would rather have someone who fit into his method. The parallel with Knight continues, as he had only one future NBA star, Isiah Thomas, on his many great teams. McGraw had Christy Mathewson, and they forged a great working relationship as they made each other's reputation in the early twentieth century. For similar reasons McGraw had little trouble with Joe McGinnity, whose Hall of Fame pitching career began during McGraw's inaugural managerial season. The best hitter McGraw ever had was Mel Ott, the greatest of all his projects, who debuted at age 17. McGraw kept Ott beside him on the bench for the better part of two years, molding him. However, when McGraw retired Ott was still only 23 years old. McGraw only broke in two or three other obvious Hall of Famers. Aside from Ott, McGraw's best position players were Frankie Frisch and Bill Terry. McGraw traded the former away and was not on speaking terms with the latter for several years. He started Carl Hubbell, but the Meal Ticket reached his prime after McGraw left.

McGraw won ten pennants in 30 years based on his ability to work with players like Fred Merkle and Fred Snodgrass. McGraw coaxed four consecutive pennants out of a team led by Ross Youngs, George Kelly, Dave Bancroft, and a foundling Frisch from 1921 to 1924. In comparison, Connie Mack had Lefty Grove, Jimmie Foxx, Mickey Cochrane and Al Simmons in their primes at the same time — yet that squad only won three pennants. McGraw had a plan, found the guys who fit into it, and pushed them relentlessly.

While McGraw held fixed ideas on power relations, he was always looking for a way to win the game. According to baseball historian Peter Morris, McGraw was an early main proponent of pinch-hitting, and received much credit for helping to popularize that strategy in the early twentieth century. Years later McGraw made Sandy Piez the first pinch-runner.

McGraw also innovated with his pitching staff, most notably by serving as an early adherent of relief pitching. In 1906, New York Giant George Ferguson became the first person to have more than twenty relief appearances in a season, with 21. The next year Giant teammates Red Ames and Joe McGinnity tied for the NL lead in relief appearances. Doc Crandall set a new record in this stat for five straight seasons, from 1909 to 1913. McGraw's teams often led the league in saves. Then again they routinely won more games than other squads, and more wins should lead to more saves. The Tendencies Database adjusts for this, using the formula of saves divided by wins (which is roughly saves divided by opportunity). Here are the results:

Most Wins Saved

Bruce Bochy	0.546
Burt Shotton	0.578
John McGraw	0.600
Felipe Alou	0.673
Bill Rigney	0.679

The Giants claimed the NL's highest percentage of wins saved every year from 1903 to 1909 despite possessing two of the game's great workhorses in Mathewson and McGinnity.

In 1904, when the Giants recorded fifteen saves, the rest of the league combined for fifteen. That season New York broke the old record of eleven saves held by the 1894 Orioles, whom McGraw played for. In 1905, the Giants again collected fifteen saves, while the rest of the NL had eighteen. In 1906, the Giants set a new mark with eighteen saves, a figure they matched in 1908. Some franchises would not reach that mark until the 1930s. All of McGraw's teams from 1903 to 1909 had at least thirteen saves. The most by any rival NL squad in that period was twelve. In all, his team recorded far more saves than any opponents:

Total Saves, 1903–09

Giants	102
Cubs	54
Pirates	39
Phillies	31
Dodgers	28
Reds	28
Cards	18
Braves	10

Though the Giants ceased to dominate the league in saves in the 1910s, McGraw remained at the forefront of relief pitcher usage. In 1909, he turned scrub starter Doc Crandall into a new type of pitcher: the relief specialist. Though far from the first man to appear in relief, he was the first whose primary employment was for that purpose. From 1909 to 1913, he appeared in 185 games for the Giants, but only started 48.

Glancing at Crandall's stat lines, it appears he primarily pitched in garbage time. From 1909 to 1913, despite finishing 119 of the 132 games he relieved, Crandall rarely picked up the decision or save. Examining Retrosheet's gamelogs for 1911 makes it clear that McGraw used him differently from what one would now expect from a relief ace. After nearly blowing a lead on May 2, McGraw did not let him pitch with a lead for over a month. Crandall protected a one-run lead only three times all year. Instead, his saves came in odd situations. For example, Crandall lodged a save by pitching the final three innings to protect an eleven-run lead on August 9. He claimed another save in his last appearance when, upon being asked to protect a 13–4 lead in the ninth inning, he allowed a slew of runs to make it close.

McGraw's usage of Crandall was a reaction to New York's performance immediately prior to Crandall's move to the bullpen in 1909. In 1908, the Giants blew a four and a half game lead in the final two weeks of the season in part because their starting pitching collapsed. McGraw had been short on reliable arms all year long, forcing him to push those he trusted heavily. In the final weeks, those few good starters completely wore down. Even the great Christy Mathewson suffered after starting eight games in less than three weeks. Learning from that painful experience, McGraw clearly sought a way to keep his starters effective the entire season. He did not want to cut back on starts—he lacked enough solid hurlers to go around in the first place. Instead, McGraw made sure the least important moments did not sap his most important pitchers' arm strength. McGraw placed Crandall into the newly created relief role as a result. He existed to eat New York's useless innings. When Crandall left the team after 1913, McGraw found new hurlers for this role. McGraw's Giants continued to use relief pitchers, but without racking up many saves, even by the standards of the time.

Crandall's most telling experience came in the 1912 World Series, one of the most closely fought contests in the history of October. He pitched only once, when the Giants trailed by a pair of runs in Game 1. McGraw refused to use him in Game 2, even though New York blew leads in the eighth and ninth innings. Crandall rusted in the bullpen in Game 3, when the Red Sox almost came back to win in the ninth inning. In the all-important Game 8 (Game 2 ended in a tie, causing an eighth contest to finish the Series), Crandall remained a spectator when the Giants blew the game in the bottom of the tenth inning. Those were the situations McGraw least wanted Crandall to pitch.

Beginning in 1917, McGraw again trusted his relief pitchers with leads more often. As had been the case in 1909, recent experience dictated his move. After staying in the pennant hunt every season for a decade, the Giants slipped to last place in 1915, and could only rise to fourth in 1916. Christy Mathewson was gone and McGraw needed a new approach as his old ones stopped working. Beginning in 1917, the Giants led the league in saves for eight consecutive seasons. They racked up 119 overall from 1917 to 1924. The next highest was the Cardinals, with 76 saves.

While McGraw was innovative, he engaged in some typical practices for his time. McGraw, like Fred Clarke and Fielder Jones, preferred pitchers who threw strikes. Christy Mathewson's control was legendary, but even after he retired McGraw's staffs had the league's best control several times. The Tendencies Database (which examines the issue as unintentional walks allowed per nine innings) thinks very highly of the ability of McGraw's teams' to avoid handing out free passes:

Best Control Staffs

Patsy Tebeau	0.476
John McGraw	0.514
Al Lopez	0.537
Tom Kelly	0.587
Fred Clarke	0.596

Patsy Tebeau possessed one huge advantage in this category — he managed Cy Young in the 1890s. In his career, Young led the league in fewest walks per inning thirteen times — the most any player has led the league in any category in baseball history. He threw one-third of all innings for Tebeau from 1891 to 1900. Adjust for how Young affects Tebeau's numbers, and McGraw did the best job having his pitchers throw strikes.

This disinclination to surrender walks complemented McGraw's offensive strategy. As a player, he was especially adept at drawing bases on balls, having led the league in walks drawn twice and coming in the top five seven times (despite appearing in 100 games in only five seasons). McGraw made sure his hitters understood the importance of the free pass. On the 31 teams he managed for all or most of the season, McGraw's hitters earned a combined total of 13,605 walks while his pitchers allowed 11,248. The 2,357 differential between those two figures was historically great, as the list below demonstrates:

Best Walk Differentials

John McGraw	+2,357 walks
Joe McCarthy	+2,320 walks
Joe Torre	+2,306 walks
Earl Weaver	+1,729 walks
Sparky Anderson	+1,646 walks

McGraw's teams gave more walks than they received only four times, including each of his last pair of full seasons. From 1905 to 1913, the Giants had an advantage of 1,439 walks in 1,397 games, which is the best stretch any team ever had with walks.

Walks were not the only thing McGraw's teams excelled at, as they also posted the greatest HBP differential in baseball history:

Best HBP Differentials

John McGraw	+708 HBP
Al Lopez	+270 HBP
Joe McCarthy	+246 HBP
Earl Weaver	+203 HBP
Bobby Cox	+190 HBP

Due to partial seasons these numbers are never perfect, but McGraw clearly made the HBP work for him. McGraw's first full season as New York manager began a streak of 27 consecutive positive HBP differentials for the franchise, easily the best in baseball history. Interestingly, McGraw was an old teammate and friend of Hughie Jennings, who tallied the largest negative HBP differential ever. Both future managers took numerous balls in the ribs in their playing day (though Jennings took considerably more). Unlike Jennings, McGraw apparently had no regrets about that approach. As a player, getting on base was McGraw's strength, and he emphasized that approach while managing as well. Not only did his clubs post history's best walk and HBP differentials, but they also claimed baseball's best hit differential, by a fairly healthy margin.

Best Hit Differentials

John McGraw	+3,113 hits
Joe McCarthy	+2,527 hits
Jim Mutrie	+1,883 hits
Frank Selee	+1,879 hits
Walter Alston	+1,650 hits

This primarily indicates the quality of talent on McGraw's clubs, but it is part of an overriding theme indicating how McGraw constructed his squads: teams that get on base more often win. In all, McGraw's teams posted an aggregate on-base differential of +6,178. Not only is that the best ever, but only Joe McCarthy and Joe Torre come within half of that, and Torre only barely. McGraw's managerial career predated on-base percentage as a popular statistic, but he believed in it as a philosophy more than any other manager in baseball history.

PAT MORAN

W/L Record: 748–586 (.561)
Managed: Full Seasons: Philadelphia (NL) 1915–18; Cincinnati 1919–23
        Majority in: (none)
        Minority of: (none)
Birnbaum Database: +510 runs
        Individual Hitters: -23 runs
        Individual Pitchers: +276 runs
        Pythagenpat Difference: +107 runs
        Team Offense: +140 runs
        Team Defense: +10 runs
Team Characteristics: Moran rode his starting position players and main pitchers as much as humanly possible, only using his bench when the situation forced it upon him. He preferred veteran hitters. Like Fielder Jones, Moran relied on hitters who took pitches, pitchers who worked the strike zone, and fielders who caught everything.
LPA: 2.27   **LPA+:** 63

Pat Moran might be the most underrated manager in baseball history. The Birnbaum Database loves him and he had a tremendous record, yet few have heard of him. It is understandable why he has been forgotten — he managed only nine seasons before dying over 80 years ago. However, in that brief stretch Moran was clearly on pace for Cooperstown:

- From the dawn of time until 1950, the Phillies only claimed one pennant. That came in 1915, during Pat Moran's rookie season as manager.
- From creation until 1939, the Reds nabbed a sole pennant. That came in 1919, when Pat Moran took the reins in Cincinnati. He also won that year's World Series, one of only two the franchise won prior to 1975.

Nice tidbits to have on the resume. Aside from his two pennants, Moran had a quartet of second-place finishes. Alas, Moran was an alcoholic (nicknamed "Whiskey Face") whose liver gave out before his fiftieth birthday. Otherwise he would be in the Hall of Fame

Moran made the most of the talent he had. Though his teams featured only one legitimately great player, Pete Alexander, they consistently competed. The Phillies improved by sixteen games when Moran arrived. When he left, their winning percentage dropped by over 100 points. Meanwhile, Cincinnati's winning percentage improved by 150 points his first season, and their record declined by seven and a half games after his liver failed. Moran helmed only two losing seasons. One came in 1918 after Philadelphia's owners sold superstar Pete Alexander. In response to that deal, Eppa Rixey, their second best hurler, left to help the US war effort. Moran's other dismal season came in 1921, when his three best hitters — Heine Groh, Jake Daubert, and Edd Roush — all suffered injuries.

Moran put his own distinctive stamp on his ball clubs, which largely caused their success. As a backup catcher in the early century, Moran had played under Frank Selee and Frank Chance. Those men prioritized sound play and fantastic defense. Moran adopted those ideas, demanding attention to detail and thorough practice. When he became Phillies manager in 1915, he made his players walk to and from the playing field, two miles from where they stayed, for extra exercise. He sometimes held two-a-day practices, making his players walk twice as much. His spring trainings consisted of endless hours of practicing plays — pickoffs, cutoffs, bunt fielding, backing up teammates. He did not want to lose because of the details.

His techniques paid immediate dividends. In 1914, Defensive Efficiency Ratio, Fielding Win Shares, and fielding percentage all agree the Phillies' defense was horrible. For example, their .666 DER was almost 30 points behind the second worst squad. Under Moran in 1915, they topped the league in DER. They also committed over 100 fewer errors than the year before while leading the NL in Fielding Win Shares. They remained no worse than average in DER and Fielding Win Shares his entire time there. As soon as he left, Philadelphia fell to last place in both categories. Cincinnati had been seventh in DER for three successive seasons before Moran arrived, but he vaulted them atop the league in 1919. They experienced a similar surge in Fielding Win Shares and fielding percentage. The Reds committed 192 errors in 1918's war-shortened 129-game season. With Moran, they committed barely an error a game.

This improved defense had a pronounced impact on his hurlers. Philadelphia's team ERA went from worst to first from 1914 to 1915, dropping nearly a full point along the way. *Every* pitcher's ERA dropped. Seven of the eight hurlers who spent all year with the Phillies set new personal bests in ERA. Of the seventeen seasons Pete Alexander qualified for an ERA title, three came under Moran: they were the first, second, and fourth best ERAs of his career. When Moran went to the Reds in 1919, the scenario repeated itself. Despite having several veteran pitchers, a majority of the hurlers posted new career-best ERAs.

It was not just defense causing this improvement, either. Moran involved himself preparing his pitchers. When pitchers warmed up before games, he stood behind the catcher and yelled situations for the pitcher to imagine himself in. Moran began the practice where catchers flashed a series of signs to the pitcher instead of a single sign.

Not only did Moran improve the performance of his pitchers, he did it while making them throw more innings. As noted in Chapter 3, his aversion to leveraging stemmed from a desire to get as much production as he could from his most important hurlers. The 1916 Phillies possessed three of the NL's top nine leaders in innings pitched. Pete Alexander threw over 375 innings every year he was under Moran. He never did that in any other seasons. In Philadelphia's first 32 years of existence, its pitching staff led the league in complete games once. They did it in both of Moran's first two seasons there.

When the liveball caused pitchers to throw fewer innings, Moran could no longer have one man throw nearly 400 innings, as Alexander had. Moran still worked his horses as hard as anyone, though. Moran's 1921 Reds contained half of the league's 300-inning men. By the end of his career, he essentially adopted a four-man staff, plugging in his main starters as often as possible. Here are how many innings each NL team gathered from their four main pitchers in 1922–23:

Team	1922	1923	Total
CIN	1,080	1,124	2,204
BRK	962	1,042	2,004
PIT	945	982	1,927
CHC	871	908	1,779
NYG	830	829	1,758
STL	867	873	1,740
PHI	869	761	1,630
BOS	799	828	1,627

Furthermore, Moran, like so many managers before and since who centered their game on run prevention, prioritized pitchers with control instead of those who could overpower hitters. The fielders would make outs, pitchers were just to avoid putting men on. A third of Moran's teams led the league in fewest walks per inning. Another third came in second place. Alternately, most of his teams came in the bottom half of the league in strikeouts per inning.

Slim Sallee's 1919 season embodied many of the characteristics Moran's teams based themselves on. With a 21–7 record and 2.06 ERA, it was the best season of Sallee's career. He set a new personal best by completing 22 of his 28 starts. In the process, Sallee racked up some of the strangest peripherals in baseball history, ending the season with only 20 walks and 24 strikeouts. A heavy workload, superlative control, reliance on defense, and success at run prevention were the classic hallmarks of a Pat Moran pitcher.

With his hitters, Moran loved using his front line talent. Few prominent managers in baseball history were as disinclined to use their bench as he did. Six times his starting players gobbled up the highest percentage of team plate appearances of any NL squad. In 1916, half the Phillies starters missed eight games or fewer. Two years later, five starters missed a combined seven games. Under Moran, Philly first baseman Fred Luderus put together one of the decade's longest consecutive-game playing streaks. When Cincinnati won the 1919 pennant, four players missed eight games between them. In 1922, three played in every contest.

This tactic for using players stood in stark contrast with the practice of platooning, which reached its zenith in popularity when Moran managed. Moran's disinclination to platoon revealed two key strategic traits he held. First, position players were more important for their defensive value than their offense. His best fielders were the same no matter what the handedness was of the opposing pitcher.

Second, his indifference to platooning reveals what he thought won games. It was the preseason drilling and endless fixation on sound fundamental play that determined winners. For Moran, as had been the case for his mentor Frank Selee, the in-game tactics and lineup card calculations were not terribly important. Managers earned their pay with the prep work before the games getting their charges ready to play, not during the game with Napoleonic tinkering. His almost complete disinclination toward pitcher leveraging might be the best sign of this way of thinking. Train your players as best as you can, put the best ones out there as often as possible, and trust them to execute what they learned. That was how Moran won.

WILBERT ROBINSON

> **W/L Record:** 1,399–1,398 (.500)
> **Managed:** Full Seasons: Brooklyn 1914–31
>   Majority in: Baltimore 1902
>   Minority of: (none)
> **Birnbaum Database:** -25 runs
>   Individual Hitters: -178 runs
>   Individual Pitchers: +47 runs
>   Pythagenpat Difference: +243 runs
>   Team Offense: -133 runs
>   Team Defense: -4 runs
> **Team Characteristics:** Robinson's middle infielders could not turn the double play, coming in last in turning it per opportunities to do so ten times. He generally had veterans. His teams relied on their main starting pitchers. A former catcher himself, Robinson gave his catchers plenty of rest.
> **LPA:** 4.44   **LPA+:** 118

Why is this man in the Hall of Fame? People recognize who are the least deserving players in Cooperstown. One can easily check the stats and notice that Tommy McCarthy and Chick Hafey were mistakes. Poorly made decisions on non-players are not as scrutinized, though. Wilbert Robinson won only two pennants. Among the other immortals, only Al Lopez and Bucky Harris can make that claim. Lopez had a slew of second-place finishes (to Casey Stengel's Yankees), and Harris had the third most wins of any manager in history until the mid–1990s. Robinson only won 1,399 games, fewer than any Cooperstown-bound twentieth century manager except Billy Southworth (who had one of the greatest winning percentages ever). Robinson also lost 1,398 games for a .5002 winning percentage. Only Harris and Connie Mack, who both had much longer careers, had sub–.500 records. Someone who ranks near the bottom of every key category has no business being in Cooperstown. The Birnbaum Database agrees with this assessment, giving Robinson a negative score for his career.

Achievements did not propel Robinson toward the game's highest honor, however. He got in because he was a kindly, lovable old guy who lasted forever. He was so popular that for a while the public nicknamed Brooklyn the Robins after him. Regardless, Cooperstown is not supposed to be a popularity contest. The most similar modern manager to Robinson is Dusty Baker, except that such a comparison is a disservice to Baker. After fifteen years of managing, Baker has a winning percentage of .527. Robinson was at .497 after a similar stretch of time. Robinson had an extra pennant, but then again he managed in an eight-team league, not the modern sixteen-team one. Both were well liked by their players and had success as a manager for a while. Neither had a reputation as a great in-game thinker. They are similar, but Baker is better. After 2008, in order to equal Robinson's career win-loss record, Baker would have to go 163–269 (.377). Another similar manager is Chuck Tanner, whose congenial nature was his most widely touted feature. Tanner was worse than Robinson in terms of games managed, wins, and winning percentage, but they were more alike than different. Robinson is midway between Baker and Tanner, which ought to place him well south of Cooperstown.

Robinson's Cooperstown enshrinement highlights a problem in how baseball remembers its managers. Once a skipper fades into the past, people remember him more for his personality than his accomplishments. Even now, for people that are interested in baseball history, Robinson exists as more than just a name. He is far better remembered than Bill McKechnie, though he was not nearly as good a manager. McKechnie was one of the greatest managers in baseball history, but he was also decidedly colorless, causing his accomplishments to drift into the past. Similarly, Al Lopez is rarely on the tips of people's tongues when people think of the greatest manager of all time, though he should be. Alas, like McKechnie, he was quiet.

Admittedly, overrated is not a synonym for useless. Robinson had some positives. Most notably, he got far more from veteran pitchers than anyone could reasonably imagine. Dazzy Vance was the greatest example of a veteran who excelled under Robinson. A veteran minor leaguer who could not retain a slot in the major leagues until he was in his 30s, Vance ended up with a Hall of Fame–caliber career. That one largely fell in Robinson's lap, though, as an elbow surgery cleaned up his arm just before he became a great pitcher. However, Robinson also had success with journeymen like Jeff Pfeffer and Jesse Petty. Burleigh Grimes made the Hall of Fame for his performance under Robinson.

Vance also points to the other main strength of Robinson's staffs—they struck men out. Vance himself was a force of nature in this regard. In 1924, he fanned 262 men; only one other pitcher in the league had more than 90. That hurler was his teammate, Burleigh Grimes, with 135. Aided by Vance, Robinson scores among the best when strikeouts per inning are put through the Tendencies Database:

Most K/9IP

Jimy Williams	0.460
Davey Johnson	0.484
Walter Alston	0.498
Bobby Valentine	0.506
Wilbert Robinson	0.538

Vance aids Robinson's score, but then again Sandy Koufax helps Alston, and Pedro Martinez bumps Williams up. In every case, it was more than just one pitcher. Vance started for Robinson beginning in 1922, but every year from 1918 onward Robinson's staffs were in the top three in strikeouts per inning. In 1920 and 1921, two different Dodger pitchers took turns leading the league in strikeouts per inning.

FRANK SELEE

W/L Record: 1,284–862 (.598)
Managed: Full Seasons: Boston (NL) 1890–1901, Chicago (NL) 1902–04
        Majority in: (none)
        Minority of: Chicago (NL) 1905
Birnbaum Database: +367 runs
        Individual Hitters: -127 runs
        Individual Pitchers: +331 runs
        Pythagenpat Difference: +2 runs
        Team Offense: +186 runs
        Team Defense: -25 runs

Team Characteristics: Fittingly, the man who managed Pat Moran lived and died with pitching and defense. His teams had good offenses, but they did not earn Selee his plaque in Cooperstown. He used his benches as sparingly as possible.

LPA: 4.04   LPA+: 106

Frank Selee might be the game's first modern manager. He was neither a business manager nor a player-manager. In fact, he never played major league baseball at all. Widely considered one of the sharpest minds in the game, the Boston club hired him because of his track record as a minor league manager. He made them look brilliant, compiling a Hall of Fame record for the Braves and Cubs over the next sixteen seasons before a lethal case of tuberculosis forced him to retire.

However, there are major differences between him and current managers. He was only 30 years old when he first arrived in Boston, far younger than any current managers. He also wore a suit in the dugout. No one does that anymore, but at the time others did likewise, including George Stallings and Connie Mack. Selee was like Connie Mack in another way — he had a reputation for treating his players with quiet respect, believing that accommodating players will cause them to respond positively.

Selee had an exceptional eye for talent. For example, with the Cubs he noted a young catcher with a promising bat who had trouble fielding. Selee switched the young Frank Chance to first base, where he became a star. Similarly, he moved third baseman Joe Tinker to short, and shortstop Johnny Evers to second. If not for Selee, poetry's most famous double play combination would never have existed.

As a manager, Selee lived for defense. A very good argument can be made that the Tinker-Evers-Chance Cubs was the best defensive team of all time. Selee constructed its formidable defense. If those Cubs were not the greatest fielding unit ever, the 1890s Boston squads might have been. Selee assembled their gloves as well. Boston featured historically great fielders Jimmy Collins and Herman Long manning third base and shortstop, respectively. In Bill James's *Win Shares* book, in which he assigns a letter grade to every key defensive player in baseball history, both Collins and Long receive an A+. Numerous other fine gloves filled out Boston's lineup. For example, their 1897 starters included three A+s, four A-s, and a B+ in *Win Shares*. Few teams in baseball history can claim seven As and a B+ on their defense. The Tendencies Database rates Selee's defenses very highly. When Defensive Efficiency Ratio goes through the Tendencies Database, the following managers score best:

Best DER

Earl Weaver	0.410
Frank Selee	0.458
Frank Chance	0.505
Bill McKechnie	0.589
Joe McCarthy	0.596

Selee's teams had the best DER seven times, and were twice runner-up.

Selee did not rely just on talent, but like virtually all the great managers of this era, he emphasized fundamentals. He was one of the greatest practitioners of team play on defense. According to Peter Morris, the 1895 Boston squad was the first to practice the cut-off play, ensuring that the ball could get from the outfield to the appropriate base in an efficient and timely manner. Selee's Boston teams were also reputedly the first to master the 3–6–3 double play.

His pitchers usually had good control and an above average ability to fan hitters, but neither tendency was as pronounced as it was for many of the other managers who centered their teams on defense. Then again, by being above average at both pitching peripherals, his squads did not have to focus so heavily on control.

Like his pupil Pat Moran, Selee leaned as heavily as he could on his core players. Chapter 2 showed which managers had the highest percentage of plate appearances come from their starting lineup, and also whose main starting pitchers gobbled up the most innings. Combine those two results from the Tendencies Database to find out which managers relied the most on their main players:

Heaviest Use of Frontline Players

Frank Selee	1.179
Earl Weaver	1.278
Bobby Cox	1.364
Tommy Lasorda	1.379
Al Lopez	1.397

Moran scored a 1.062 in his nine years, so had it not been for his untimely death he would stand atop this list with Selee.

The managers listed above tended to emphasize fielding. It makes sense such individuals would score highly here — the optimal offensive lineup might change from day-to-day, but the best gloves remain the same. Also, by relying on fielders to prevent runs, a manager can use his pitchers as workhorses, allowing them to rack up the most innings.

In each of Selee's first six years as manager, at least one player appeared in every game. When this streak was finally snapped in 1896, a pair missed only one game each. Oftentimes multiple players missed only a handful of games for Selee. On the 1899 Boston starting lineup, only the catcher missed more than eight games. Johnny Kling, starting catcher on the 1903 Cubs, played in 132 of their 139 games. Given the equipment of the time, that pushed the limits of human endurance.

Most of the managers who learned the trade under Selee clearly replicated many of his trademarks. Aside from Moran, longtime Boston infielders Jimmy Collins and Fred Tenney became managers. Collins revealed a strong Selee-streak when he became the inaugural manager for the American League's Boston franchise. Collins pushed his main players very hard. In five full seasons, he had fourteen batters play in every game, and a half-dozen others miss only one or two contests. In 1904, six of his starters appeared in at least 155 of the team's 157 games while his pitchers completed a record 148 starts. In 1901, his starting eight accounted for 83.3 percent of all plate appearances, which is the third highest total by any team that played over 120 games in a season.

Fred Tenney, Collins's old teammate, exhibited similar characteristics. In his four seasons as manager, Tenney's top three pitchers twice accounted for the largest share of innings on any pitching staff in the league. In 1905, three of the NL's top five leaders in innings pitchers performed for his team. Vic Willis won and lost twenty games that year, something no NL pitcher would do again until Phil Niekro. In 1906, on an otherwise untalented team, he rode his starting pitchers so hard that they became the only staff in baseball history to contain four different twenty-game losers.

Collins, Tenney, and Moran have another commonality — none leveraged their starters. Moran had an LPA+ of 63, Tenney 64, and Collins 81. Curiously, founding father Selee did leverage his pitchers as often as most of his peers. Actually, Selee's willingness to leverage is an oddity in his career, even aside from the record of his pupils. Those who rely on their main starting pitchers as much as Selee usually leverage less often. Prioritizing the quantity of innings usually leads to a corresponding decline in quality. Selee performed an impressive balancing act by trotting out his most important pitchers as often as he did while maintaining an LPA+ of 106. His protégés apparently could not match that, instead focusing on maximizing quantity of innings exclusively.

However, the Selee family tree soon withered. Moran and Selee died relatively early, and neither Collins nor Tenney lasted 1,000 games. Collins's abbreviated career was especially odd. After claiming two pennants and the first modern World Series title with Boston, he was jettisoned as soon as the team foundered in 1906, and no other squad ever tabbed him as their manager. The firing was understandable but his inability to land a new job appears unusual given his pair of pennants.

The key to understanding why Selee's disciples failed to last long in the profession lay with his most successful descendent, apostate Frank Chance. In the nine full seasons he ran a club, Chance never had someone play every game. Likewise, he spread out the innings among his starters, and leveraged them more than anyone else in baseball history. Chance enjoyed the longest and most successful career of anyone Selee sired.

This tells us something about what teams wanted from their managers during the early twentieth century: they sought someone who would be active in running the game. Selee's men were too passive, perhaps even reminiscent of the pre–Schmelz managers. Selee himself was an innovator, but once other teams learned how to work the cutoff play, it took more than that to be seen as an effective manager. Managers who took a hands-off attitude toward in-game maneuvering needed to aggressively enforce pre-game practice — like Moran did — to be seen as effective at the job. The managerial position was at its height of power, and teams wanted someone who did something with the authority entrusted to him.

George Stallings

> **W/L Record:** 879–898 (.495)
> **Managed:** Full Seasons: Philadelphia 1897; Detroit 1901; New York (AL) 1909;
>   Boston (NL) 1913–20
>   Majority in: New York (AL) 1910
>   Minority of: Philadelphia 1898
> **Birnbaum Database:** +274 runs
>   Individual Hitters: +110 runs
>   Individual Pitchers: +55 runs
>   Pythagenpat Difference: +18 runs
>   Team Offense: +39 runs
>   Team Defense: +52 runs
> **Team Characteristics:** Stallings avoided using relief pitchers whenever possible. His hitters knew how to draw walks. His teams were fairly young. Last, but certainly not least, he was a big proponent of offensive platooning.
> **LPA:** 4.45   **LPA+:** 110

George Stallings's best managerial comp from the second half of the twentieth century is Gene Mauch. Baseball pundits lauded both as terrific strategic minds who ultimately ended their careers with losing records. They might be the two best managers with career records under .500. As an added bonus, both began their careers managing the Phillies, though Mauch lasted much longer there.

One final bit of serendipity exists between Stallings and Mauch — each was the leading proponent of platooning in their respective generations. Stallings, more than anyone else, helped popularize it in the late deadball era. In 1914, Stallings's Boston Braves shocked the world by rising up from last place on July 4 to win the World Series. When people looked for reasons for Boston's unexpected success, platooning was the key strategy they noted. Since Stallings's teams wildly exceeded expectations, others soon adopted Boston's practice, allowing it to enter its golden age, from approximately 1915–30.

Stallings mixed his platooning with an interest in defense. He wanted his best gloves on the field, so he generally preferred a set group of starters in the infield while platooning the outfield. The Miracle Braves exemplified how he handled his lineup. None of its outfielders had 400 at bats. They moved in and out of the lineup based on the opposing pitcher. With this vigorous platooning, Boston finished third in the league in offensive Win Shares, the franchise's best showing since the nineteenth century. However, Stallings's starting four infielders gobbled up 36.5 percent of the entire team's plate appearances, more than any other squad in the NL that year. Also, at a time when most starting catchers played approximately 100 games a year, Boston's Hank Gowdy appeared in 128. That was how Stallings normally ran the Braves. In eight years on the job in Boston, his trio of starting outfielders had the league's smallest percentage of the squad's plate appearances five times, and had the second fewest two other times. Meanwhile, Boston's infielders and catchers routinely worked more frequently.

Platooning was not Stallings's only noteworthy tendency with the Braves, as he also rode his main starting pitchers quite hard. From 1913 to 1920, Brave hurlers completed 774 games, the most for any franchise. In those years, the other fifteen clubs averaged over 100 fewer complete games. The Braves' pitchers completed at least 105 games three times under Stallings; no other NL team topped 102. Twice a Boston hurler led the league in completions. As a result of Stallings's reliance on starting pitchers, his 1918 Braves were the only club since 1906 to not record any saves. Only twice did one of his Boston relievers make at least twenty relief appearances. Major league baseball had 118 such occurrences from 1913 to 1920. As many managers since the time of Charles Comiskey have realized, prioritizing defense allows managers to push their arms quite hard.

Another factor played a key role in Boston's turnaround under Stallings—walks. His teams lived and died on the base on balls, especially on offense. The Tendencies Database notes this using the formula of bases on balls minus intentional walks divided by plate appearances (intentional walks do not affect Stallings, as that information is not available for his era, but they change the numbers for more recent managers). Based on that, these managers did the best job coaxing their hitters to draw free passes:

Best Offensive Walk Rate

Joe McCarthy	0.354
Sparky Anderson	0.447
George Stallings	0.502
Earl Weaver	0.538
Art Howe	0.599

McCarthy, Anderson, and Weaver led imposing offenses that made opposing teams want to pitch around their main batters. Howe managed the A's, whose front office prioritized landing players who worked the count. Stallings's squads had to earn their walks. The 1901 Tigers had the second most walks in the AL. He left and they regressed. In 1908, prior to his arrival, New York drew the fewest walks of any AL squad. Two years later they topped the circuit. Stallings's most impressive achievement came in Boston where an immediate improvement in walks taken occurred upon his arrival. In terms of walks per plate appearances, Boston had been among the NL's top two only once in the previous seventeen seasons. They finished first or second every year from 1913 to 1918 under Stallings.

Like Fielder Jones, walks were not just an offensive concern for Stallings. He tried to keep his pitchers from issuing free passes. Stallings's 1910 Yankees had the fewest walks per nine innings of any AL team; that was the only time in their first quarter-century of existence they did that. Detroit's control declined when he left. Boston's staff, which had not appeared in the top half of the league in walks per inning since the nineteenth century, consistently finished in the top three during Stallings's first half-dozen seasons. As a result, his teams benefited tremendously from walks. If one combines the scores for walks per nine innings in the Tendencies Database — well, actually it is (BB-IW)/IP in the database — and offensive walk rate, Stallings did a historically great job making the base on balls work for his teams:

Best at Walks — Combined

Patsy Tebeau	1.162
Al Lopez	1.191
Earl Weaver	1.280
Joe McCarthy	1.293
George Stallings	1.368

Fielder Jones scored at 0.972 in his eight seasons—0.634 excluding his final year. Stallings's teams drew more walks than they allowed ten times in twelve campaigns. Three times they had at least a walk advantage in excess of 100, topped by a +183 performance by the 1915 Braves. In all, Stallings's teams came out 693 bases on balls ahead. An old story claims that when Stallings was on his deathbed a friend asked what was killing him. "Oh, those bases on balls!" responded the former manager. He may not actually have said that, but he should have given how much emphasis he put on that play.

Also, Stallings was the perfect manager for Boston's miraculous 1914 campaign because he had a personal tradition of having teams play very differently in the second half from how they performed in the first half. If Ned Hanlon's teams had maintained a strikingly even pace from first to second half according to the Tendencies Database, Stallings's squads were only consistent in their inconsistency:

Most Uneven Pace

Don Zimmer	1.258
George Stallings	1.226
Paul Richards	1.207
Jimmy Dykes	1.162
Bill Terry	1.156

What makes Stallings special was that sometimes his teams got much better (as happened in 1914), and other times they got much worse. He had the league's biggest second-half collapse only once (in 1920), but three times they had the second largest decline. In fact, that happened with three separate franchises— the 1897 Phillies, 1910 Yankees, and 1918 Braves. Conversely, Stallings oversaw the biggest second-half improvement three times, and was runner-up another three times. From 1914 to 1917, the Braves consistently had one of the biggest improvements in the second half each year, performing 131–156 (.456) in the first half and 207–116 (.641) afterwards.

Stallings was a highly intense man. A graduate of a military institute, he ran his clubs like boot camp, approaching the game as an all-out war. He wore out numerous pairs of pants sliding along the dugout bench, trying to cope with his nerves. He tried to assuage the stress caused by his internal pressure with superstitions. If the team started a rally he would not move from his position, as if he were a statue.

His intensity caused him to wear out his welcome despite his tendency to improve squads. The Phillies revolted on him. He alienated star pitcher Brewery Jack Taylor, who—true to his nickname — responded by showing up to the park drunk. The Tigers dumped Stallings after just one year, and declined by 22 games after he left. He managed the Highlanders, who went 51–103 prior to his arrival. Two years later he had them in second place. However, in one of the worst decisions ever, management decided they would be better off with their morally corrupt first baseman, Hal Chase. Stallings finally succeeded in latching on for a prolonged period with Boston. Winning a surprise world title created some job security, but even that squad eventually let him go.

PATSY TEBEAU

> **W/L Record:** 726–583 (.555)
> **Managed:** Full Seasons: Cleveland (NL) 1892–98; St Louis 1899
> Majority in: Cleveland (NL) 1891; St Louis 1900
> Minority of: Cleveland (PL) 1890
> **Birnbaum Database:** +92 runs
> Individual Hitters: +102 runs
> Individual Pitchers: +153 runs
> Pythagenpat Difference: -95 runs
> Team Offense: -169 runs
> Team Defense: +101 runs
> **Team Characteristics:** Tebeau's hitters drew plenty of walks. Complementing that, his pitchers rarely gave them up. His teams drew more walks than they allowed in every season he managed a majority of the year. From 1891 to 1900 he posted a +1,332 walk differential, one of the best by any manager.
> **LPA:** 3.47   **LPA+:** 93

This chapter previously noted that Buck Ewing's Reds posted similar win-loss records to Tebeau's squads despite a considerable talent disparity. While that was seen as a positive for Ewing, it can be flipped around. The real question might be why Tebeau's Spiders lost as many games as they did.

Forget the Reds for a second, and compare Tebeau's teams to Frank Selee's Boston club. Each franchise had one of the best pitchers in the game — Cy Young in Cleveland and Kid Nichols with Boston. A solid sidekick flanked both aces. Cleveland had first Nig Cuppy then Jack Powell, while Boston had 200-game winner Jack Stivetts. Cleveland's lineup centered on Jesse Burkett, Cupid Childs, and Bobby Wallace, while Boston had Hugh Duffy, Billy Hamilton, Jimmy Collins, and Herman Long.

The advantage goes to Boston, but the gap was not as great as their win-loss record. The Birnbaum Database gives Tebeau a score of +92 runs, which is actually underwhelming given the circumstances. From 1896 onward — the years the Birnbaum Database examines — his teams posted a .547 winning percentage. Almost everyone with higher winning percentage scored better than +92 runs, usually significantly better.

Tebeau's reputation explains why Cleveland underachieved. Find any book about 1890s ball and it will give you the same paragraph about Tebeau. In a time of rowdy baseball, Tebeau's teams led the league in hooliganism. He once denigrated those who played a more gentlemanly style of ball as "milk-and-water, goody-goody" players and wanted nothing to do with them.

Being an obnoxious roughneck is not a problem as many have proved that a jerk could successfully manage a ball club. However, Tebeau became so caught up in the process he forgot about the results. The means became his ends as he focused so much on what he did he forgot why it was done. Ned Hanlon's Baltimore Orioles had an unsavory reputation, but even their critics acknowledged they used every trick in order to win. However, Cleveland was known for playing nasty, not smart. When baseball cleaned up its rowdiness at the turn of the century, there was no reason for any team to want Tebeau as their manager. McGraw and Hanlon survived because they were known for intelligent — if unethical — play. Tebeau was only known for his behavior.

He ended up owning a bar in St. Louis before killing himself when his wife left him. Jimmy McAleer, who also managed a major league baseball team in St. Louis at the turn of the century, also committed suicide after his baseball career had ended. Between them, it appears some sort of curse on Gateway City skippers existed a century ago. McAleer even played center field for Tebeau's Cleveland squads.

6

Managing in the Lively
Ball Era, 1920–1950

While the deadball era saw managerial power in its ascendancy, the early lively ball period witnessed its power gradually erode. In both periods, an underlying trend caused the ebb and flow of managerial importance: the development of the business of baseball. Managers had gained power when the sport reached a point in which their role could be separated from that of business manager; however, beginning around 1920 a new transformation clipped into their job — the rise of the front office. Though no overnight thunderclap occurred, a revolution slowly altered the profession.

The most famous aspect of this change came from Branch Rickey and the St. Louis Cardinals. While managing the club from 1919 to 1925, he sought a cheap way to ensure a steady supply of quality young players. His solution was the farm system, in which the Cardinals established special relationships with pre-existing, minor league teams to funnel talent to St. Louis. Scholarship has shown that Rickey was not the first to engage in this endeavor, however, he pushed it further and more aggressively than anyone before. It was such a difference in scope that it amounted to a difference in kind. Rickey did for the general manager what Gus Schmelz had done for the manager — he put the position on the map. Rickey's departure from the dugout after the 1925 season to become a full-time general manager signified this shift. Initially, the GM only took responsibility for developing talent. General managers, including Rickey, allowed managers to decide which veterans belonged on the squad. Slowly, using their position, GMs took greater power over the entire roster in the ensuing decades.

As Branch Rickey moved into his new role, another incident confirmed the division of authority between manager and front office. In 1925, the Pirates won their first championship in fifteen years under the quiet and effective Bill McKechnie. Normally, such an achievement guarantees job security. Unfortunately for McKechnie, the previous skipper to lead the Pirates to glory, Fred Clarke, was still around. Though he was officially team vice president, Clarke sat on the bench during games, and tongues wagged that he wanted to manage again. In August 1926 the situation came to a crisis point when some veteran players publicly picked sides in the Clarke-McKechnie quagmire. The owner did not want the players calling the shots, so he got rid of those who had spoken publicly on the matter. These were not fringe players: team captain and future Hall of Famer Max Carey went to waivers, while Babe Adams, who had been playing for Pittsburgh for almost twenty years, was released. The team floundered late in the season, and the Pirates fired McKechnie at its conclusion. Clarke stayed with the club, but never appeared on the bench again, nor would he ever get another shot to manage. It was a complete fiasco for everyone involved.

From this incident teams learned that a crucial difference exists between front office and managerial roles, and it would be wise not to mix them. In the short run, this incident could be seen as a victory for the manager as executives were banished from the bench, leaving the skipper in uncontested control of the dugout. In the wider sense, this spelled a decline in managerial authority. Since this separation of powers came just when the GM position was in ascendancy, the McKechnie-Clarke imbroglio guaranteed managers would not benefit from the farm system revolution. A new layer of authority existed above the manager, one that assumed some of his old responsibilities. Though individuals simultaneously served as GM and manager as late as the 1980s, they were the exception rather than the rule.

While managers lost some of their old power, they could still retain considerable authority if they learned how to work with the new front office dynamics. For example, in 1925 an ongoing feud between New York Yankees manager Miller Huggins and star slugger Babe Ruth came to a head over the Bambino's refusal to heed Huggins's commands. The situation climaxed when Huggins suspended Ruth and fined him $5,000 — ten times the largest fine previously decreed in baseball history — for violating team rules. Ruth raised Cain about it, protesting to Yankee GM Ed Barrow and owner Colonel Jacob Ruppert about the situation. His pleas fell on deaf ears, because Huggins, prior to levying the staggering fine, had consulted with Barrow and been assured front office support in any showdown. This alliance forced Ruth to back down. With his best player chastised, Huggins gained control of the clubhouse. While the manager won the battle, his strength came from the decision to consult with Barrow in advance. Managers retained authority because important front office personnel wanted them to have that authority, not because it was inherent in their position.

The 1920s also witnessed another important change for managers; this one did not affect their power, but what they did. The lively ball era began. Run scoring skyrocketed in the 1920 AL and the following season in the NL, and remained high for the rest of the decade. A series of ideas that had been built up over the previous generation about how the game ought to be played and the proper strategic guidelines for it suddenly became outdated. People either adapted to the new baseball environment, or fell by the wayside.

Some veteran managers claimed a great deal of success as John McGraw won four straight pennants in the early 1920s, and Connie Mack built his second dynasty later in the decade. However, while they found victory, another very curious phenomenon played out. A trio of the most prominent managers of the first two decades of the twentieth century — George Stallings, Hughie Jennings, and Clark Griffith — all left the major league dugout after 1920, just as the new day dawned. This could simply be a coincidence. Certainly, there is no evidence that they left because of baseball's brave new world. However, in baseball history there have been three great moments of managerial retirement — 1920, 1950–51, and 1976 (the latter two will be discussed in subsequent chapters), all of which coincided with three of the biggest changes managers ever contended with.

After 1920, Jennings left the Tigers and never seriously sought out another managerial opening again. He contently sat on the Giants bench alongside his old chum, John McGraw. Jennings filled in as manager when health issues affected McGraw, but it was clear who the real boss was. Griffith, as Washington's owner, could have stayed in the dugout as long as he desired — his contemporary Connie Mack did just that — but Griffith opted to let others handle the players and in-game decisions. Of the three departing skippers, only Stallings wanted to continue managing, but he was stuck in the minors for the rest of his days.

Even if the 1920 group departure was purely coincidental with the game's massive change, it was an especially appropriate coincidence. The new ball created a change in how managers went about their jobs. Previously, many of the game's best managers won by emphasizing a combination of great defense and control pitching. Charles Comiskey, Fielder Jones, Frank Chance, George Stallings, Pat Moran and others used this approach to win pennants. In the lively ball era, with the notable exception of Bill McKechnie, that approach was not nearly as pronounced. The most successful manager of the day, Joe McCarthy, prioritized hitting first and foremost.

LOU BOUDREAU

W/L Record: 1,162–1,224 (.487)

Managed: Full Seasons: Cleveland 1942–50; Boston (AL) 1952–54; Kansas City
    1955–56
    Majority in: Kansas City 1957; Chicago (NL) 1960
    Minority of: (none)

Birnbaum Database: -141 runs
    Individual Hitters: +92 runs
    Individual Pitchers: +30 runs
    Pythagenpat Difference: -55 runs
    Team Offense: -210 runs
    Team Defense: +2 runs

Team Characteristics: Boudreau's lineups featured young bats and plenty of
    power. His teams routinely allowed more walks than they gained.
    The 1955–57 A's surrendered 647 more walks than they earned,
    becoming the only team to have three consecutive 200-walk-differ-
    ential seasons.

LPA: 4.50   LPA+: 93

With apologies to Pete Rose, Lou Boudreau was the last significant player-manager in baseball history. That does not necessarily mean he was a good manager, however. Clearly the Birnbaum Database thinks little of him with his overall score of -141 runs is largely the result of his historically bad team offense score, indicating that he was not very good at in-game maneuvers.

The Tendencies Database also corroborates Boudreau's inability to make shrewd decisions during contests. While Chapter 2 looked at one aspect of stolen bases, how often teams ran, another avenue can be explored — success rate on the bases: SB/(SB+CS). Since major league baseball began tracking caught steals, only 53 managers have had at least ten years on the job. According to the Tendencies Database, the following managers' teams had the worst success rates, compared to their peers:

Least Successful at Stealing

Bobby Valentine	1.305
Miller Huggins	1.293
Ralph Houk	1.274
Lou Boudreau	1.250
Frank Robinson	1.237

Unlike the others listed, Boudreau attempted to steal slightly more than average for his day, with a stolen base frequency score of 0.903. Taking that into account, Boudreau hurt his teams with steals more than anyone else listed, except perhaps Bobby Valentine, whose 1.050 frequency score is closest to that of Boudreau. In his managerial career, Boudreau's teams stole 681 bases while the opposing catchers nabbed them 641 times (In his partial seasons, those numbers include only the games he managed, not the full campaigns). When he managed Cleveland, the three players who ran the most for him (Dale Mitchell, Otis Hockett, and the player-manager himself) all successfully stole bases in less than half of their attempts.

Boudreau was his generation's biggest believer in the bullpen. He led the league in most relievers used eight times in sixteen seasons, and always finished in the top half of the league. In 1944, when Boudreau called on 200 relievers, no other AL squad had more than 150. Four times one of his pitchers led the league in appearances; it was a different hurler on each occasion. The bullpen was the key to Cleveland's 1948 pennant. Only six men in the league had at least 40 relief appearances, but Boudreau had two of them. That duo—Russ Christopher (who led the league in saves), and Ed Kleiman (who led it the year before)—combined for a 2.73 ERA in 89 appearances. Boudreau also had veterans Steve Gromek, Bob Muncrief, and the legendary Satchel Paige work as swingmen.

Like Clark Griffith, Boudreau was willing to rely heavily on a trusted starter despite his plentiful use of relievers. In 1946, Bob Feller completed 36 games, which was the most in a season since the days of Pete Alexander and Walter Johnson. The rest of the staff, however, completed only 27. When Bob Lemon later developed, he also led the league in complete games for Boudreau.

Though Boudreau scores poorly overall in the Birnbaum Database, it is possible a lurking variable unfairly skewed his numbers downward. As noted in Chapter 1, every component for all leagues in each season is normalized at zero. While that minimizes any bugs in Runs Created or Component ERA, it introduces a new possible error. Keeping all leagues centered at the same point assumes that managerial talent is fixed and constant, which is not necessarily true. Like any position, sometimes an unusually large amount of talent will appear at one time. For example, the 1930s AL had Lou Gehrig, Jimmie Foxx, and Hank Greenberg at first base.

The 1950s AL was to managers what the 1930s AL was to first basemen as a trio of skippers performed brilliantly: Casey Stengel, Al Lopez, and Paul Richards. Considering that there were only eight teams, that makes it quite difficult for anyone else to score well. To see if the great managers skewed Boudreau's Birnbaum score downward, here are the results for individuals who managed over 500 games in the 1950s AL. Included are their games managed for the decade along with their raw and per 154 game Birnbaum scores for the period. For comparison, the total scores for all remaining managers are also listed.

Name	Games	Birnbaum	Per 154 Games
Casey Stengel	1,537	+650 runs	+65 runs
Al Lopez	1,386	+596 runs	+66 runs
Paul Richards	1,374	+445 runs	+50 runs
Pinky Higgins	689	+81 runs	+18 runs
Bucky Harris	1,076	-16 runs	-3 runs
Jimmy Dykes	753	-91 runs	-19 runs
Lou Boudreau	1,026	-124 runs	-19 runs
Marty Marion	574	-134 runs	-36 runs
Everyone Else	3,893	-1,407 runs	-56 runs

Even by the standards of short-lived managers, those who managed less than 500 games scored terribly in the 1950s AL. It looks like they bore the brunt of the Big Three's brilliance. Even ignoring Stengel, Lopez, and Richards, Boudreau scores rather poorly. Perhaps they hurt him a little, but it is doubtful Boudreau would score well anyway.

JOE CRONIN

W/L Record: 1,236–1,055 (.540)
Managed: Full Seasons: Washington 1933–34; Boston (AL) 1935–47
        Majority in: (none)
        Minority of: (none)
Birnbaum Database: +474 runs
        Individual Hitters: +174 runs

Individual Pitchers: +56 runs

Pythagenpat Difference: +51 runs

Team Offense: -22 runs

Team Defense: +215 runs

Team Characteristics: Cronin had terrific offenses that hit for high average. Despite having quality bats playing in a run-inflating ballpark in a high offense era, Cronin loved to bunt the runners over. He had a 374–310 (.547) record in one-run games, so apparently he did a good job playing for one run. He consistently was among the league leaders in most relievers used.

LPA: 4.68   LPA+: 100

The most famous part of Cronin's managerial career was something he could not control. While playing for the Senators, he married the daughter of club owner Clark Griffith. Desperately needing cash during the Great Depression, Griffith sold his son-in-law to Boston's wealthy and free-spending new owner, Tom Yawkey, after the 1934 season. One wonders how Griffith's daughter reacted to the news.

Whatever Cronin's strengths as manager, as Chapter 2 noted, pacing was not one of them as his teams consistently played worse in the second half of the year. Here are the first and second-half winning percentages for every club he managed as well as the percentage increase/decrease after the All-Star break:

Team	Year	First	Second	Dif.
WAS	1933	.653	.650	-0.46%
WAS	1934	.507	.360	-28.99%
BOS	1935	.521	.500	-4.03%
BOS	1936	.553	.410	-25.85%
BOS	1937	.556	.506	-8.99%
BOS	1938	.582	.598	+2.75%
BOS	1939	.632	.554	-12.34%
BOS	1940	.569	.500	-12.13%
BOS	1941	.548	.543	-0.91%
BOS	1942	.605	.618	+2.15%
BOS	1943	.473	.423	-10.57%
BOS	1944	.539	.461	-14.47%
BOS	1945	.527	.400	-24.10%
BOS	1946	.701	.649	-7.42%
BOS	1947	.535	.542	+1.31%
CAREER		.566	.515	-9.01%

Only three of Cronin's teams improved in the second half, in 1938, 1942, and 1947; all experienced meager increases. Alternately, substantial declines litter his career.

Examining Cronin's career season-by-season, Boston appeared to look for an excuse to quit. For example, in 1937 they made a brief run after the All-Star break, winning twelve consecutive games in late July and early August. However, the front-running Yankees also kept winning during that period, and Boston only gained two games. Frustrated, they dropped nearly two-thirds of their remaining contests.

In 1938, Boston played like a team afraid of first place. They began the year with a 16–8 record, jumping into first. Then they dropped eight of their next eleven, falling into fourth place. They fought their way back into the thick of things, only to experience another sustained losing streak at the end of May. By early August, the Red Sox were again poised for a pennant push, with a 55–38 record, six and a half games behind the Yankees with a pair of upcoming series against league doormats Philadelphia and Washington. The Red Sox proceeded to drop six straight to the second division clubs and never threatened again.

In 1939, Boston replayed their 1937 season. Beginning with their last game in July, the second-place Red Sox began a huge push against the first-place Yankees. They went 17–7 over the next few weeks, pushing their overall record up to 72–41. For all that, they had only gained a game and a half on the similarly surging Yankees. Disappointed, the Red Sox suffered a sweep at the hands of the middling White Sox. That series pushed Boston further from first than they had been prior to their glory run. One can just imagine the players in the clubhouse shaking their heads in frustration and dismay. They played less than .500 ball the rest of the way. When adversity hit, they expected to fold. It became a self-fulfilling prophecy.

Perhaps their most ignominious moment came in 1940. In the late 1930s, the Yankees were so strong it was quite unlikely the Red Sox could have captured the pennant no matter how they played down the stretch. In 1940, however, the pennant was up for grabs. When the sun rose on July 17, 1940, the Red Sox stood in third place, a pair of games behind the Indians and Tigers, who were tied for first. Even better, that day the Red Sox swept a doubleheader against Detroit in Fenway Park. Combined with an Indian loss, Boston found itself a mere half-game out of first place with a 47–33 record. The Red Sox would play two more games against the Tigers, and then Cleveland came to Boston for a three-game showdown. The Red Sox, masters of their own fate, dropped all five contests. Put in a desperate situation, they fell back on what they knew best —collapsing. After that home field deflation, they traveled to Chicago, where the White Sox swept them. That eight-game losing streak effectively ended Boston's season. The Red Sox limped along the rest of the season, barely playing .500 afterwards.

Circumstances beyond Cronin's control contributed to Boston's annual flop. Under Yawkey, the Red Sox had the reputation as a soft, cushy place to play. One can argue Cronin was the victim of circumstance, with ownership creating a culture of complacency in which players could slack off. While Yawkey was partially to blame for Boston's second-half floundering, that does not let Cronin off the hook. As manager, he was the point man between the club and the players. He was the one they had to contend with and thus the man with the most responsibility for ensuring that the team did not settle for second best. A generation later, rookie Red Sox manager Dick Williams proved this rather conclusively. No one complained about a culture of complacency under his watch, as he led Boston to its first pennant in over twenty years in 1967. Clubhouse atmosphere falls on the manager's shoulders.

JIMMY DYKES

> **W/L Record:** 1,406–1,541 (.477)
> **Managed:** Full Seasons: Chicago (AL) 1935–45; Philadelphia (AL) 1951–53;
>   Baltimore 1954;
>   Majority in: Chicago (AL) 1934; Detroit 1959–60; Cleveland 1961
>   Minority of: Chicago (AL) 1946; Cincinnati 1958; Cleveland 1960
> **Birnbaum Database:** +40 runs
>   Individual Hitters: -219 runs
>   Individual Pitchers: +114 runs
>   Pythagenpat Difference: +185 runs
>   Team Offense: +104 runs
>   Team Defense: -144 runs

> **Team Characteristics:** Dykes played small ball, but his teams rarely had good offenses. He loved starting pitchers with good control. Defining a swingman as a pitcher who appears in at least 40 games with fifteen coming in relief and fifteen others as a starter, Dykes is the only prominent manager from the rise of real relief pitching around 1910 until expansion in the 1960s to never have a swingman season.

LPA: 4.45   LPA+: 97

As a manager, Dykes is best known for his failures, as for eons he held the record for most seasons managed without a pennant. Gene Mauch eventually broke it, but at least Mauch managed in the 1986 postseason and threatened to make October several other times. Dykes never finished higher than third, and came within sixteen games of first place only once. As a result, Dykes never received much respect, which was not fair because he never had much talent at his disposal. A majority of his tenure came with the White Sox, where he did a spectacular job with what he had. The Birnbaum Database gives him a score of +227 runs for those years, despite Chicago attaining a flaccid 899–940 (.489) record.

The best example of his ability occurred in 1940, when he pulled his underwhelming White Sox team into a third-place tie with Joe Cronin's Red Sox. For comparison's sake, here are both clubs' frontline players:

Pos.	White Sox	Red Sox
C	Mike Tresh	Gene Desautels
1B	Joe Kuhel	Jimmie Foxx
2B	Skeeter Webb	Bobby Doerr
SS	Luke Appling	Joe Cronin
3B	Bob Kennedy	Jim Tabor
OF	Taffy Wright	Doc Cramer
OF	Mike Kreevich	Dom DiMaggio
OF	Moose Solters	Ted Williams
SP	Johnny Rigney	Jim Bagby Jr.
SP	Thornton Lee	Lefty Grove
SP	Eddie Smith	Denny Galehouse
SP	Ted Lyons	Fritz Ostermueller
RP	Clint Brown	Jack Wilson

Five of the Red Sox are in Cooperstown, and several others were star players. Some were still blossoming, like Williams, or past their primes, like Grove, but Williams hit .406 the following campaign and an aging Lefty Grove was still formidable. The White Sox featured two Hall of Famers in Appling and Lyons, and some quality athletes such as Thornton Lee, but a comically large gap in talent existed. Yet both clubs finished 82–72. This was not a fluke for Chicago, which was about as good in 1939 and 1941 despite possessing the same lackluster core.

After Chicago fired Dykes, he became a coach for Connie Mack, and when Mack retired after 1950, Dykes succeeded him as Philadelphia's manager. Dykes's A's improved by eighteen games his first year, and another nine the next, giving them a winning record of 79–75. The team flopped in 1953, costing Dykes his job. Firing him did not help, though, as the franchise's next winning season came in 1968.

Another team immediately hired Dykes after Philadelphia dumped him. Unfortunately for him, it was another doormat, the Orioles, who were in their first year after relocating from St. Louis. They lost 100 games under Dykes—the fourth time they did that in six years—and fired him. Baltimore replaced him with Paul Richards, one of the best managers of the decade.

Yet Richards could only improve them by three games the first year, and it took him a half-dozen years to get them over .500.

Dykes finally landed on teams with some talent at the end of his career; however, none had pennant-contending talent. Also, by then, it had been a quarter-century since he began managing. Virtually all managers are past their primes by that point.

Though Dykes began as a player-manager, he was in his 60s before his lineups featured quality bats like Frank Robinson and Al Kaline at his disposal. Prior to then, the only Hall of Famers he commandeered were Luke Appling, Ted Lyons, and the last quality campaign from Al Simmons. That was a rather meager haul over the course of nearly 2,500 games. Dykes's typical stars were players like Thornton Lee, Ferris Fain, Eddie Yost, and Gus Zernial, which explains why he never won a pennant.

Dykes relied on starting pitchers, especially those who threw complete games. Seven times Dykes used the fewest number of relief pitchers per game, and five other times he was next-to-last. His 1941 White Sox completed 106 games, the most by any team since 1920. Longtime Chicago ace Ted Lyons completed nearly 80 percent of his starts under Dykes. In Dykes's first full season as manager, Lyons completed 19 of his 22 starts. In 1942, at age 41, Lyons went 14–6 with a 2.10 ERA while completing all twenty of his starts. Lyons and Walter Johnson in 1918 are the only ERA qualifiers in the last 100 years to finish all their starts.

Lyons's career best shows how Dykes got the most out of his starting pitcher. Lyons lasted forever because Dykes made him a Sunday pitcher for much of his career. A Sunday pitcher was a veteran who started once a week, in the team's regularly scheduled doubleheader, thus ensuring the extra game did not affect the rest of the staff. Lyons was the best known and most successful of the Sunday pitchers. Dykes put him in that role.

On offense, Dykes's squads contained a striking number of veterans. Baseball-Reference.com provides average ages for every team's offense, rounded to the tenths decimal. Running those numbers through the Tendencies Database, the following managers fielded the oldest lineups:

Oldest Offenses

Jimmy Dykes	1.632
Al Lopez	1.499
Earl Weaver	1.490
Dusty Baker	1.456
Wilbert Robinson	1.427

Dykes does not just top the list, he laps the field. The gap between first and second is wider than the difference between second and sixth place (Bruce Bochy, at 1.389). In the nineteen times Dykes managed a majority of the season, his teams had the league's oldest offense ten times, and second oldest six times. All his squads were in the older half.

Dykes was not entirely responsible for the preponderance of veterans. The first three franchises that hired him had abysmal farm systems. Connie Mack, for instance, refused to build up a Branch Rickey–style minor league system. The Sox and Browns/Orioles were also behind the curve in creating effective pipelines to the majors.

However, that does not totally absolve Dykes for the lack of youngsters. When he managed the White Sox, they consistently featured the oldest lineups. Upon his arrival in Philadelphia, the A's possessed older hitters than everyone else, including the White Sox. The pattern repeated itself in Baltimore. In the 111 occasions a player qualified for the batting title under Dykes, only five were younger than 25 years old. One of those seasons came from Al Kaline, who was already an established star before Dykes arrived in Detroit. Alternately, 71 of those seasons came from players in their 30s. Dykes liked known quantities.

His batters rarely hit home runs. The White Sox never hit 100 homers in a season for him — in fact, they never hit 75. They launched only 22 in 1945, the fewest by any AL team since the mid–1920s. In 1944, they hit only 23, and two years before that knocked out 25. Dykes's Baltimore squad blasted 52 homers, the second fewest by any team in the 1950s. In his nineteen seasons as a squad's primary manager, his teams hit more homers than they allowed exactly once. That was an advantage of only nine, by the 1960 Tigers, who Dykes managed for only 96 games. Dykes presided over fifteen different twenty-homer performances by his hitters, and 22 occasions a pitcher allowed at least twenty home runs. (The latter was the most by any manager when Dykes retired). Noting the difference in home runs hit and allowed for Dykes's entire career indicates his squads suffered a historic disadvantage from the long ball:

Worst Home Run Differentials

Tom Kelly	-710 home runs
Jimmy Dykes	-594 home runs
Bruce Bochy	-393 home runs
Bucky Harris	-374 home runs
Phil Garner	-362 home runs

These numbers are not perfect, since managers get full credit for teams they managed for most of a season, and no credit when they lasted a minority of a year. Still, with results this striking, one should not quibble. Most of the managers on the list are from modern times, when players hit more long balls overall. When Dykes retired in 1961, his -594 differential was more extreme than the combined sum of the next two worst: Bucky Harris at -374 home runs and Bill Killefer at -179.

Dykes's teams tried to make up for the damage long balls caused by centering themselves on balls in play on both defense and offense. Dykes's pitchers rarely blew opposing hitters away. The White Sox never finished higher than fourth in strikeouts per inning when he managed them. They needed the fielders behind them to make plays. Similarly, Dykes's offenses put as much pressure as possible on opposing defenses. They possessed neither power nor the ability to draw many walks, but according to the Tendencies Database Dykes's batters were among the toughest to strike out in baseball history. The best formula for determining this is K/(AB-H), because, unlike strikeouts per plate appearance, teams that do a good job hitting are not given an unfair advantage. All teams have to make three outs an inning. Based on that premise, here are the managers with the hardest teams to fan:

Teams Most Difficult to Strikeout

Bill Virdon	0.402
Felipe Alou	0.476
Jimmy Dykes	0.592
Phil Garner	0.635
Bill Terry	0.644

Under Dykes, Philadelphia was a little better than average at avoiding the whiff, but as soon as he left the A's became one of the worst in the league. When Dykes left Baltimore, their offense struck out over 100 more times.

Centering a team on balls in play can work, but it has to be done right. Teams need either hitters with extremely high averages or fielders who gobble up everything hit at them. Dykes's dreadful offenses put the onus of winning squarely on his defenders. It was too much for them.

LEE FOHL

W/L Record: 713–792 (.474)

Managed: Full Seasons: Cleveland 1916–18; St. Louis (AL) 1921–22; Boston (AL) 1924–26

Majority in: Cleveland 1915, 1919; St. Louis (AL) 1923

Minority of: (none)

Birnbaum Database: -315 runs

Individual Hitters: -112 runs

Individual Pitchers: +123 runs

Pythagenpat Difference: -25 runs

Team Offense: -105 runs

Team Defense: -196 runs

Team Characteristics: Fohl's scores in the Tendencies Database are extraordinarily ordinary; almost all are between 0.900 and 1.100. He used plenty of relievers, and in 1915, Sad Sam Jones set a record with 39 relief appearances with Fohl's Indians club. In 1917, Ray Chapman had 67 sacrifice hits for Fohl, still baseball's single-season record. Fohl also gave his catchers noticeably more playing time than his contemporaries.

LPA: 3.27   **LPA+:** 91

The first part of the book mentioned that Fohl lost his job in Cleveland when he not only delegated responsibilities for handling his pitching staff to center fielder Tris Speaker, but completely abrogated personal oversight. Fohl's experience shows some persistence with nineteenth century managers as the old-time business managers of the 1870s and 1880s openly let their team captains call plays. Thus the 1890s revolution pioneered by Gus Schmelz did not force a complete break with past practices. Some of the most successful twentieth century managers wanted the thoughts and input of their players. Connie Mack, for instance, had a brain trust with veteran players such as Harry Davis with whom he discussed strategy and tactics. A vital distinction existed in the styles of Mack and Fohl, however. Mack still led the decision making process, even though he allowed others to have input. Fohl wanted Speaker to do the thinking so he could avoid doing so. Unlike 30 years earlier, the public held the manager accountable for in-game decisions. Fohl's ouster in mid–1919 demonstrated conclusively that the buck stopped with the manager.

Throughout his career, Fohl depressed his teams' win totals. Even clubs that were successful under him were better off when he was not around. Cleveland had a good record for Fohl, but after firing him in mid–1919 they won two-thirds of their games the rest of the way, nearly capturing a pennant. The following year they won the franchise's first flag.

In St. Louis, Fohl scored -66 runs in the Birnbaum Database despite their 226–183 (.553) record. They had the greatest collection of talent in Browns' history with Hall of Famer George Sisler at first; Baby Doll Jacobson, Jack Tobin, and Ken Williams forming one of the greatest outfields in baseball history; a rotation featuring Urban Shocker, the best pitcher the Browns ever had, and a fine starter in Elam Vangilder. All were in their primes, yet, aside from 1922, they barely finished .500 for Fohl.

He only lasted three years with the Red Sox, but in that time the club managed two of its worst three winning percentages in franchise history. Admittedly, they were a terrible team before and after he arrived, but they still managed to play worse under him. From June 18, 1932, until the same date the following year, the Red Sox went 41–112, in which opponents outscored Boston by over two runs per game.

An obvious trend existed. Teams that hired Lee Fohl performed as poorly as one could reasonably fear. That is the biggest indictment one can hurl at a manager.

FRANKIE FRISCH

>   **W/L Record:** 1,138–1,078 (.514)
>
>   **Managed:** Full Seasons: St. Louis (NL) 1934–37; Pittsburgh 1939–45; Chicago (NL) 1950
>
>   Majority in: St. Louis (NL) 1938; Pittsburgh 1946; Chicago (NL) 1949, 1951
>
>   Minority of: St. Louis (NL) 1933
>
>   **Birnbaum Database:** +11 runs
>
>   Individual Hitters: -33 runs
>
>   Individual Pitchers: -113 runs
>
>   Pythagenpat Difference: +30 runs
>
>   Team Offense: +182 runs
>
>   Team Defense: -55 runs
>
>   **Team Characteristics:** Frisch's teams stole bases, but rarely bunted. He gave his starting catchers plenty of rest. In his twelve full seasons as manager, no catcher ever played in 120 games for him; back then about half the teams asked their catchers to play at least that often. Partially as a result of that, Frisch became the first manager to last a decade on the job despite never having his starting eight batters gobble up three-fourths of the team's plate appearances in any season.
>
>   **LPA:** 5.88   **LPA+:** 126

As the last two chapters showed, several managers have centered their teams on fielders who could turn batted balls into outs. The question arises which manager had the worst collection of gloves. Defensive Efficiency Ratio, which notes what percentage of balls in play the defense turned into outs, is one of the best ways to check:

Worst DER	
Don Zimmer	1.437
Frankie Frisch	1.393
Billy Barnie	1.345
George Stallings	1.257
Burt Shotton	1.244

Frisch's teams never finished higher than fourth and finished last four times. That was not the only problem for Frisch's defenses. They also made numerous errors, as the following table shows:

Worst Fielding Percentages	
Art Howe	1.373
Wilbert Robinson	1.357
Patsy Donovan	1.329
Frankie Frisch	1.319
Clark Griffith	1.275

Frisch is the only manager on both lists. His teams had trouble getting to balls, and frequently flubbed them when they did. Lovely combination. Making it even worse, his pitchers had trouble striking batters out. Under the circumstances, it is surprising Frisch attained a winning career record.

Though player-manager Frisch won a world championship in his first full managerial season in 1934, he never made it to another World Series. Once he stopped playing he never seriously threatened to claim a title. Yesterday's genius turned into today's journeyman. That made him an archetypal figure: the player-manager who lost his touch once he hung up his spikes. Many player-managers seemed to lose their zest for the job once they de-hyphenate their job title. It happened to Fred Clarke and Frank Chance a generation before, to Frisch and Bucky Harris in the lively ball era, and to Lou Boudreau after World War II.

However, in his book on managers, Bill James concluded this notion on player-manager aging was fundamentally flawed because a distortion mucked up people's perceptions. Normally, a manager needs some early success if he hopes to last a long time on the job. Since maintaining success is difficult, most peak early. What happened to Frisch, Boudreau and company also happened to many who never played while managing, such as Ralph Houk or Alvin Dark. If a player-manager succeeds once he stops playing, as happened to Miller Huggins, no one thinks of him as a player-manager. Thus a distortion created the illusion that player-managers age especially poorly.

While a good point, it should not be taken too far. Even if conventional wisdom is generally wrong on a point, that does not mean it is never right; Frankie Frisch serves as a case in point. Evidence indicated the job flatly bored him as he aged. According to John C. Skipper's *Biographical Dictionary of Major League Managers*, Frisch once let a heckler manage a game for him in Pittsburgh. Cubs owner Phil Wrigley supposedly fined him for reading a book during a game. *The Biographical History of Baseball* claims Frisch lost his job with the Cubs when a team official overheard him tell a fan that the GM had been robbed in a recent trade. A manager does not say that if he cares about keeping his position. If ever a person fit the stereotype of player-manager losing his zest after retiring from the diamond, it was Frisch.

Aside from boredom, Frisch's other main trait as post-playing manager was his disdain for players. Frisch routinely treated them coldly. He was not a disciplinarian, he was just mean. When an attempt was made to start a players union at mid-century, Frisch's Pirates were the first recruitment center as the union backers wanted to capitalize on the team's widespread antipathy toward the manager.

Frisch succeeded as a player-manager because he had a sense of belonging with his teammates. Even if he had a superior position to them, the bond he had forged with them as their teammate endured. This connection survived any problems they caused Frisch when he managed them. In 1934, he suspended Dizzy Dean in a highly public dispute pitting the team versus its star. Despite that, Frisch retained a certain fondness for his biggest headache. Though Dean could be a royal pain, he was one of the men Frisch played and bled with on the field. Frisch ended up telling loving anecdotes about Dean for the next 30 years. Once he stopped playing, Frisch had little affection for those he managed. He spent the rest of his life bellyaching about young players, even though none gave him as much grief as Dean.

Frisch's career highlights a crucial difference between a manager and a player-manager. The former understands from the moment he takes the job that he is not one of the boys. Joe McCarthy, for example, always kept his distance from the players. A player-manager could feed off the energy that was never available to the un-hyphenated. Therefore, he faced an extra adjustment as he aged. Some could not make that shift, including Frisch.

Don Baylor serves as the best modern comparison for Frisch. Like Frisch, Baylor had a forceful personality with a strong reputation as a natural leader. Communication skills were supposedly Baylor's strongest point. He played on three different clubs from 1986 to 1988, all of which won the pennant, further heightening the belief that Baylor was a splendid leader who helped out behind the scenes. If player-managers had been common in the 1980s, Baylor would have been one, just as Frisch had been a half-century earlier.

Yet as a manager, Baylor was not only excruciatingly bad, but his weakest point was his once vaunted communication skills. He could lead the players when he identified with them, but lost interest when he hung up his spikes. By the end, Baylor's sole strong point was his willingness to badmouth his players to the media. The symmetry with Frisch was uncanny.

CHARLIE GRIMM

> **W/L Record:** 1,287–1,067 (.547)
>
> **Managed:** Full Seasons: Chicago (NL) 1933–37, 1945–48; Milwaukee 1953–55
>   Majority in: Chicago (NL) 1938, 1944; Boston (NL) 1952
>   Minority of: Chicago (NL) 1932, 1949, 1960; Milwaukee 1956
>
> **Birnbaum Database:** +334 runs
>   Individual Hitters: -102 runs
>   Individual Pitchers: +125 runs
>   Pythagenpat Difference: -46 runs
>   Team Offense: +25 runs
>   Team Defense: +332 runs
>
> **Team Characteristics:** Grimm's teams were rarely exceptional at any single facet of the game, but above average in almost all of them. They featured very good pitching bolstered by solid fielding and hitting. He liked starting pitchers who could strike out the opposition. When Grimm managed the 1955 Braves, Roberto Vargas became the first pitcher to average less than an inning per appearance while appearing in at least 25 games. Grimm's 1946 Cubs gave only 47.9 percent of its plate appearances to its starting eight batters. They are the only team in baseball history below 50 percent.
>
> **LPA:** 5.07   **LPA+:** 104

Charlie Grimm came incredibly close to making the Hall of Fame; if just one or two things broke differently for him, his plaque would be in Cooperstown. That may sound surprising given that people never mention Grimm among the greatest managers, but he consistently got the most out of his clubs. He won multiple pennants with the Cubs and very nearly went to the postseason with the Braves. If he had won a Series with Chicago and taken a pennant in Milwaukee, his place in history would have been assured. Grimm came exceptionally close to both objectives.

He first became manager when the Cubs fired Rogers Hornsby in August 1932. The squad began the year hoping to win the pennant, but instead they had played .500 since early May. Technically in second place, the Cubs stood closer to fifth than first. Once Grimm took over, they began a hot streak, winning 24 of 29. They took the pennant and Grimm, with only 55 games on the job, became history's least experienced World Series manager. Chicago ran into a buzz saw, getting swept by the 107-win Yanks, but Grimm's career was off to a flying start.

Three years later, the Cubs won another pennant for him, capped off by an amazing 21-game winning streak in September. The Cubs should have won that World Series—they had a superior record to pennant-winning Tigers and had peaked late in the season. Instead, Chicago lost the World Series in six games with two of the defeats occurring in heartbreakingly close fashion. Had they won just one of those, they would have forced a Game 7 where the Cubs would have possessed a distinct edge in pitching.

In 1938, when the Cubs won another pennant, Grimm managed them for most of the season. In a reversal of 1932, however, he was the one replaced in mid-season. That was a very strange departure, coming shortly after a seven-game winning streak. Grimm resigned due to disagreements with the front office, and instead successfully managed a Milwaukee minor league team run by Bill Veeck.

The Cubs continued to respect Grimm's baseball acumen, a fact they proved by rehiring him as manager in 1944 after a rough 1–10 start. Though the club's last winning season occurred five years previously, Grimm kept them over .500 the rest of the year, and then led them to the pennant the following season. Facing off against the Tigers again, the 1945 World Series went seven games. Alas for Grimm, the Cubs came up short. The franchise entered its post-war torpor and Grimm departed in 1949. The Cubs continued to get worse without him. Grimm went back to the minors, winning *The Sporting News* Minor League Manager of the Year Award in 1951.

In mid–1952, Grimm landed a dream job managing the Braves, who were clearly putting together something special. Young Lew Burdette established himself on the staff while Warren Spahn provided consistent ace-quality work. The offense had a budding star in 20-year-old third baseman Eddie Mathews, and a quality infielder in Johnny Logan. Under Grimm's watch the next two years, they added Hank Aaron, Joe Adcock, Bob Buhl, Del Crandall, and Bill Bruton. Grimm gave them all their first opportunities and watched them blossom while Mathews, Logan, and Burdette continued to improve. They averaged over 90 wins in 1953–54 despite being one of baseball's youngest teams.

With dynasty potential, they merely needed a skipper who would not screw things up for them to claim considerable postseason glory.

Unfortunately for Grimm, he did not last long enough to enjoy the franchise's moments of glory. Expectations were high in 1955, but the Dodgers effectively ended the pennant race in mid–May by winning 22 of their first 24 games. Milwaukee finished second, thirteen and a half games back. In 1956, the pressure was on Grimm to deliver. The Braves began the year playing well, leading the league in early June. Then they dropped ten of fourteen, which was enough to cost Grimm his job. Milwaukee recovered, and finished in second place that year. Their glory began immediately afterwards as the Braves won the world title in 1957, took the pennant in 1958, and nearly won another pennant the following year. Grimm was likely past his prime by the time he ran the Braves, but then again he was still better than Fred Haney, his replacement. Bill James once argued that while helming the Braves Haney did the worst job any manager has ever done running a quality team.

Just think how close Grimm came. He was just a few innings away in either 1935 or 1945 from a World Series ring. Had it not been for one ill-timed slump in 1956 he could have been there for Milwaukee's glory run. If Lady Luck was on his side, he may have claimed a half-dozen pennants and a ring or two divided up between two franchises. He did 95 percent of the work to achieve that, but that last 5 percent separates a Hall of Famer from a managerial afterthought in baseball history.

BUCKY HARRIS

> **W/L Record:** 2,157–2,218 (.493)
> **Managed:** Full Seasons: Washington 1924–28, 1935–42, 1950–54; Detroit
>   1929–32, 1955–6; Boston (AL) 1934; New York (AL) 1947–48
>   Majority in: Detroit 1933, Philadelphia (NL) 1943
>   Minority of: (none)
> **Birnbaum Database:** +230 runs
>   Individual Hitters: +230 runs
>   Individual Pitchers: +206 runs
>   Pythagenpat Difference: -332 runs

Team Offense: +188 runs

Team Defense: -62 runs

Team Characteristics: Harris's teams stole their share of bases, but bunted infrequently. His offenses were centered on young contact hitters. Home runs were a continual sore spot and his squads consistently allowed more than they hit. He managed for over a quarter-century before any of his staffs led the league in fewest walks allowed per inning. Harris presided over more 200-hit seasons than any other manager in history — eighteen. That was more than Bobby Cox, Leo Durocher, Whitey Herzog, Tony LaRussa, Al Lopez, Bill McKechnie, Casey Stengel, Earl Weaver, Dick Williams, and Harry Wright combined.

LPA: 3.97   **LPA+:** 86

Loyalty: it is a trait people prize immensely in those around them, particularly in spouses, friends, and cocker spaniels. It is not, however, always the most appropriate characteristic for a manager to display. Bucky Harris twice demonstrated that, at opposite ends of his lengthy career.

The first example occurred in Game 7 of the 1925 World Series. Walter Johnson had already won two games against the Pirates in that Fall Classic, and Harris wanted him to notch a third. However, Johnson was not feeling his best. He had a sore leg, which the day's muddy field conditions aggravated. Noting this, the Pirates began a bunting campaign to discomfort Johnson further. As the game wore on, it became apparent to everyone in the park that Johnson's pain hindered his performance. Harris kept him in anyway, though Johnson surrendered fifteen hits, including several for extra bases. He blew a two-run lead in the bottom of the seventh, and when the Senators scored the next inning, Johnson allowed three more runs to lose the game. Pundits pilloried Harris as soon as the game ended. No less a person than AL founder and president Ban Johnson weighed in, deplored that the game had been lost for sentimental reasons. It was nice of Harris to show faith in Johnson, but he let loyalty override common sense.

In 1948, Harris found himself in the midst of another pitcher controversy. The year before, when Harris piloted the Yankees to his first pennant since 1925, one of the team's most important stars was relief ace Joe Page. After earning considerable accolades for his bullpen fireman duties in 1947, Page could not maintain the same level of performance the next year, losing as many as he won for the Yankees in close and late situations. However, Harris was determined to keep Page in that role. He told reporters Page had proven himself the year before and he was going to stick with him, come what may. The Yankees finished two and a half games behind the pennant-winning Indians, fired Harris, and brought in Casey Stengel, who was willing to remove players regardless of their previous achievements.

Harris's problem was that while managing entails a personal relationship between the man and his players, it is fundamentally a professional relationship; everyone is on the job. Developing a rapport with players can be beneficial, but it cannot be unconditional. If loyalty to a player becomes so strong that a manager refuses to let performance determine how a person should be used, that is disloyal to the franchise as a whole. Harris had trouble tempering allegiance with accountability. Ultimately, Harris's brand of loyalty was an inverted version of a manager who refused to play someone because of the doghouse. It is two sides of the same coin, both basing workplace decisions on personal sentiments.

Despite flaws, Harris could manage, as he possessed a strong command of baseball strategy. Stolen bases are the best example of his acumen, as his teams enjoyed tremendous success on the base paths. When SB/(SB+CS) enters the Tendencies Database, the following managers had the best idea when to steal:

Best Stolen Base Success Rate

Cito Gaston	0.347
Red Schoendienst	0.457
Whitey Herzog	0.465
Bucky Harris	0.587
Jim Fregosi	0.632

Harris made this list the hard way. All the men above Harris possessed at least one great basepath thief: Gaston managed Roberto Alomar, Devon White, and Otis Nixon in Toronto; Schoendienst led Lou Brock; and Herzog possessed the greatest basestealing corps of all time with the Cards. Harris oversaw only one great basepath thief, George Case, who played for him in only six seasons. Also, one team dominated the managerial tenures for all the managers listed except Harris. Schoendienst and Gaston only managed one team, and Herzog spent most of his career with the same squad. Even Fregosi had almost half his career with the Phillies. Harris has 28 seasons in the Tendencies Database, but he never managed with one team for longer than eight years. Altogether, seven different tours of duty are represented (it would be eight but caught stealing information is unknown for his time with the Phillies).

Harris kept building up his running game time and again, finding legs that could steal and judging when it was best to run them. Harris's teams led the league in success rate nine times, finished second six times, and third another half-dozen times. His score is not as impressive as those above him, but his achievement was. His success was especially notable given that he stole somewhat regularly. He was not as avid a runner as Schoendienst and Herzog were, but his 1932 Tigers and 1940 Senators topped the league in both success rate and frequency of attempts adjusted for opportunity.

Harris's overall Birnbaum score falls short of the game's greatest managers because of his exceptionally bad pythagenpat underperformance. One of two culprits normally cause teams to fall short in this area: squads perform either especially poorly in close games, or unexpectedly well in blowouts. Harris's teams played 1,354 one-run games, in which they went 649–705 (.479), quite a bit below what one would expect.

How well should they have done? In his entire career, Harris had a .493 winning percentage. That is about the same as the winning percentage for a team that went 76–78 in the old 154-game schedule, or 80–82 nowadays. In major league baseball history, 36 teams have ended the season with one of those records, and they went 866–860 in one-run games, for a .502 winning percentage. If Harris's teams achieved a .502 winning percentage in those contests, they would have won 30 more games, making his pythagenpat score about average. His career win-loss record would have been exactly one game under .500, but his Birnbaum score would have been +530 runs, among the fifteen best of all time.

It was odd that Bucky Harris would have done so poorly in those games. Though luck is the conventional and most important reason given for teams under- or overachieving their run-based record, unusually good performances in close and late situations should cause a team to win an unexpectedly large percentage of one-run games. A team can achieve that by either hitting or pitching especially well in close and late situations. Managers cannot control the former appreciably, but they choose who appears on the mound in the game's crucial late moments. Interestingly, Harris was at the forefront of relief pitcher usage. In his first tour with Washington, he turned Firpo Marberry into the game's first real star reliever. A quarter century later, he reinvigorated the notion of a stud relief pitcher with Joe Page. As a result, Harris is the last sort of manager you would expect to do horribly with pythagenpat.

A key word in the last paragraph explains this paradox — reinvigorated. The position of relief ace had to be resurrected because everyone went away from it after Marberry — including Bucky Harris. It was the damnedest thing. The best modern analogy would be if Billy Beane turned away from statistical analysis after the A's posted consecutive 100-win seasons in 2001–02. More than anyone else, Harris should have realized how important a man like Marberry could be, yet after leaving Washington he did not try recapturing that old magic until Joe Page. After Page, the position remained established. Relief pitcher Jim Konstanty won National League MVP in 1950, and shortly afterwards perennial relief specialists like Elroy Face emerged. Harris scored well with pythagenpat when he had Marberry, +63 runs. Perhaps if he had continued to defy baseball convention he would have had a much better record in the close games.

MILLER HUGGINS

    W/L Record: 1,413–1,134 (.555)
    Managed: Full Seasons: St. Louis (NL) 1913–17; New York (AL) 1918–28
                       Majority in: New York (AL) 1929
                         Minority of: (none)
    Birnbaum Database: +513 runs
                         Individual Hitters: +178 runs
                         Individual Pitchers: +43 runs
                         Pythagenpat Difference: +150 runs
                         Team Offense: -23 runs
                         Team Defense: +165 runs
    Team Characteristics: Huggins's teams did not bunt or steal frequently. He usually leaned fairly heavily on his main starting pitchers. For example, the 1922–23 Yankees became the last franchise to post consecutive seasons with over 100 complete games. However, "usually" does not mean always. The 1916 Cardinal pitchers completed 58 games, the lowest by any modern team at that point. His squads hit far more homers than they allowed. The 1927 Yankees hit 116 more (158 to 42), which is still baseball's best single season home run differential. Of the 77 managers who lasted at least a decade on the job, Huggins is the only one who never had a pitcher strike out 140 batters in a season.
    LPA: 3.20   **LPA+:** 89

The Yankees have won almost all of their championships under four different managers: Miller Huggins, Joe McCarthy, Casey Stengel, and Joe Torre. Miller Huggins created the mold they all fit into.

Huggins managed prior to the Yankees. All four did. As it happens, all his managing came in the NL. That is true of the entire quartet — Huggins with the Cardinals, McCarthy the Cubs, Stengel the Braves and Dodgers, and Torre the Mets, Braves, and Cardinals. In fact, Huggins never even played in the AL. Again, none of them had. Huggins got his start as a player-manager. McCarthy was a player-manager in the minor leagues with Louisville before becoming a full-time manager. Stengel briefly served as player-manager as well, in 1925 for the Braves' minor league team in Worcester. Even Joe Torre began as a player-manager (barely, with two plate appearances after becoming Mets manager in 1977).

Finally, everyone but McCarthy had been previously unsuccessful before arriving in the Bronx. Check that. They appeared to be unsuccessful. Joe Torre was more than 100 games below .500. Stengel had washed out with two teams. Huggins, in six seasons in the Gateway City, possessed a record of 346–415 (.455). This reveals the problem of judging managers solely by their win-loss records. All were quality managers toiling for substandard franchises prior to claiming the Yankees' job.

Take Miller Huggins, for example. Despite his .455 record with St. Louis, the Birnbaum Database rates him as +136 runs, which might be the greatest disconnect ever between winning percentage and Birnbaum score. Eleven managers in the Birnbaum Database possessed winning percentages between .445 and .465, and they averaged -182 runs, over 300 worse than Huggins's mark.

Huggins had exactly one noteworthy player with the Cardinals, Rogers Hornsby, who was only 21 years old when Huggins left. Aside from the future Hall of Famer, Huggins's best threats were Walton Cruise and Jack Smith. There is a reason you never heard of them. Yet Huggins coaxed a pair of winning seasons from that squad.

Huggins won in St. Louis with pitching. He did not possess great pitchers, but solid ones. He had a mix of youngsters trying to establish themselves like Bill Doak and Lee Meadows alongside tested veterans such as Red Ames and Slim Sallee. Normally, Huggins had three men he trusted. Their names changed from year-to-year, but Huggins routinely used a trio of dependable starters. Huggins took a middle course with them, never aggressively leveraging them, nor working them too hard. Every St. Louis pitcher with at least 20 starts in a season under Huggins had an AOWP+ between 98 and 102, but none appeared among the top five in the league's innings pitched leaders. He mixed regular pitching with rest to ensure hurlers remained productive without blowing their arms out. Huggins resembled a modern manager, except he occasionally used his starters as relievers.

In fact, pitching was the focus of Huggins's early New York teams as well. One always expects the Yankees to be batter-oriented, but from 1919 to 1923 the Yankees led the league in Pitching Win Shares four times, finishing second the other year. Meanwhile, they led in Hitting Win Shares "only" twice and never came in second. Babe Ruth may have been the most important addition in those years, but all the other prominent ones were pitchers. The Yankees claimed spitballer Jack Quinn, who had only started five games in the majors since the demise of the Federal League, and saw him become one of the staff's best pitchers. Aside from Quinn, New York largely reassembled the late 1910s Boston Red Sox staff. The Yankees purchased Carl Mays from Boston, and he won 53 games in two years for his new team. Future Hall of Famer Herb Pennock arrived in another sale. A traditional trade with Boston landed 20-year-old future Hall of Famer Waite Hoyt, who became one of only sixteen lively ballers to win 150 games before his thirtieth birthday. In another Boston trade the Yankees scored both Sad Sam Jones and Bullet Joe Bush, who each enjoyed 20-win seasons with their new team. They later flipped Bush to the Browns for Urban Shocker, one of the AL's best pitchers of the decade.

The early 1920s staffs may be the best in Yankees history. New York won three consecutive pennants from 1921 to 1923 even though the best non–Ruth hitters were players like Wally Pipp and Bob Meusel. Ruth missed 44 games in 1922, but the Yankees still won the pennant, largely due to their tremendous pitchers. Prior to the emergence of Lou Gehrig during 1925–26, seven of the eight most important pickups they made were hurlers. This was a time when managers still held tremendous input into the roster. Yankee general manager Ed Barrow did not arrive until 1921, by which time they already had terrific pitching.

As had been the case in St. Louis, Huggins used his starting pitchers in ways reminiscent of modern skippers. For example, the 1922 Yankees essentially had a five-man rotation. Hoyt, Bush, Mays, Jones, and Bob Shawkey each started 28 to 34 times, for a combined 152 of the squad's 154 games. All their AOWP+s were between 98 and 102. The next year Huggins again evenly distributed almost all of New York's starts among a quintet of arms. They also appeared in relief, but the overall pattern is far more similar to a 21st-century rotation than one would expect.

Though Huggins's Cardinals hitters were not as talented as the Yankee ones, a common theme links them — offensive strikeouts. Using the same K/(AB-H) formula explained in the Jimmy Dykes comment, these managers had the most whiff-friendly lineups in baseball history:

Most Offensive Strikeouts

Miller Huggins	1.634
Sparky Anderson	1.450
Joe McCarthy	1.374
Burt Shotton	1.356
Art Howe	1.335

A substantial gap separates first and second place. Huggins's teams featured the highest strikeout rate ten times, including thrice in St. Louis. In fact, by the strikeout formula listed above, Huggins managed three of the seven easiest NL teams to fan from 1893 to 1945: the 1915 to 1917 Cardinals. However, in a sign of how the game has changed, none of Huggins batters ever fanned 100 times in a season.

Due to his tolerance for offensive strikeouts, Huggins was an ideal manager to handle Ruth. In the Bambino's final season in Boston in 1919, he was second in the league in strikeouts with 58. He topped that mark every year under Huggins, including 1925 when he missed 60 games. Ruth struck out 80 or more times in seven different seasons during the 1920s; no one else did it more than twice that decade. This is the downside of swinging for the fences. Many other managers would have fought with Ruth to change his approach at the plate. Though his home runs gave the team an undeniable aid, decades of offensive philosophy taught managers to prioritize putting the ball in play. Huggins's pre–Ruth career shows a distinct tolerance for swinging and missing. His fights with Ruth dealt with off-field behavior, never on-field activity. Once Huggins had won his war with Ruth in 1925, the Sultan of Swat never had to worry about changing or even moderating his approach at the plate. Huggins's baseball philosophy enabled Ruth to reach his fullest potential.

WALTER JOHNSON

> **W/L Record**: 529–432 (.550)
> **Managed**: Full Seasons: Washington 1929–32; Cleveland 1934
>   Majority in: Cleveland 1933, 1935
>   Minority of: (none)
> **Birnbaum Database**: +160 runs
>   Individual Hitters: -79 runs
>   Individual Pitchers: +157 runs
>   Pythagenpat Difference: +41 runs
>   Team Offense: +55 runs
>   Team Defense: -14 runs
> **Team Characteristics**: Johnson's teams had terrific pitching. They avoided home
>   runs, did not walk many opposing batters, and struck out more than
>   their share. A typical position player for Johnson would be a good
>   fielder who lacked power but could put the ball into play.
> **LPA**: 6.13   **LPA+**: 137

Walter Johnson was an exceptionally underrated manager. Popular thoughts about him reveal the power of perception, as people were so sure he was too nice to be a quality manager, that they missed how effective he actually was.

He spent a year managing in the minors to prove the critics wrong and claimed enough success that his old owner, Clark Griffith, picked him up. In Washington, where he replaced the two-time pennant-winning manager Bucky Harris, critics repeated the old charges that Johnson was too nice. Johnson failed to win any in four years, causing a round of "I-told-you-so"s. Griffith let him go after 1932, and the Senators won the 1933 pennant, which entrenched conventional wisdom. The Indians hired Johnson. They had been good but not great for years, and Johnson was unable to put them over the hump. That was all the proof baseball needed; Walter Johnson never managed again.

All of the above facts are true, but the derived conclusions are a complete disservice to Johnson. Looking at the record, he got as much out of his teams, especially in Washington, as one could reasonably hope for. The expectations placed on him were unreasonably high.

For example, the main charge against him in Washington was that — unlike the managers who came immediately before and after him — he never won a title. Well, how could he? The year he took over, Connie Mack's second great dynasty entered its prime. They won three straight pennants from 1929 to 1931, averaging more than 104 wins. Johnson's teams "failed" to top that, but no team in the history of the Senators/Twins franchise history ever won that many games in a season. Mack's squad featured Lefty Grove, Al Simmons, Jimmie Foxx, Mickey Cochrane, and Jimmy Dykes. Johnson possessed Joe Cronin, Heinie Manush, Sam Rice, General Crowder, and Sad Sam Jones. Advantage: Philadelphia. In 1932, Babe Ruth's last great season propelled the Yankees to a 107-win season. Johnson's personality did not prevent Washington from winning 108 games.

As it was, the Senators performed very well under him. After a year settling in, Johnson led the franchise to three consecutive seasons of at least a .597 winning percentage. In their six decades in Washington, they accomplished that only three other times. In the trio of non–Johnson years, however, Washington took the pennant because no all-time monster stood in their way. When Cronin led the Senators to the 1933 World Series, the best rival team was the 91–59 (.607) Yankees. Johnson's teams played at that level. Admittedly, Washington's winning percentage was slightly under .607 in all but one of his seasons. Then again, the 1929–32 Washington squads had to play eighteen games against a historically great team, while no 1933 team did. Johnson failed to capture a pennant with Washington because of the period he managed in, not due to his demeanor.

In Cleveland, perception again colored people's minds so they could not observe Johnson's accomplishments. In 1934, his only full season there, Cleveland finished in third place, their highest finish in five years. Their 85–69 record was one of their best between the fall of Tris Speaker in the early 1920s and the emergence of Bob Feller as a workhorse in the late 1930s.

Win-loss records are blunt instruments for evaluating managers, but they indicate something important about Johnson. He did not have more talented rosters than preceding or succeeding managers had, but he did more with them. Strong pitching was the hallmark of his team. He provided Firpo Marberry with more save opportunities than he had since the mid-1920s while still finding more times for him to start games than any other manager ever had. Marberry logged 32 saves — more than any other reliever in those years — with a 58–24 record. Johnson gave a chance to Monte Weaver, a minor leaguer getting a little too old to be considered a prospect, and Weaver responding by winning 22 games for the 1932 Senators. Johnson also received good work from Lloyd Brown, General Crowder, and Bump Hadley. Washington always had one or two men emerge from the pack and have a good year under Johnson's care.

Joe McCarthy

W/L Record: 2,125–1,333 (.615)
Managed: Full Seasons: Chicago (NL) 1926–29; New York (AL) 1931–45; Boston (AL) 1948–49

Majority in: Chicago (NL) 1930
Minority of: New York (AL) 1946; Boston (AL) 1950
Birnbaum Database: +1451 runs
Individual Hitters: +550 runs
Individual Pitchers: +649 runs
Pythagenpat Difference: -107 runs
Team Offense: +190 runs
Team Defense: +169 runs
Team Characteristics: McCarthy's teams score well at practically everything. His defenses were good, pitchers were terrific, and offenses were the cream of the crop. If you could quantify batboy performance, McCarthy probably would rate the best with them as well. Most notably, his teams possessed great offenses. Bill James noted that McCarthy managed nine of the fourteen highest scoring teams of the twentieth century. Admittedly six were Yankees squads, but McCarthy also managed three of the five highest scoring non–Yankee teams. Neat trick.
LPA: 3.89　　　**LPA+**: 86

Joe McCarthy won seven pennants in eight years, and never had a losing season in a quarter-century on the job. McCarthy's success allowed him to publish his Ten Commandments for Baseball:

1. Nobody ever became a ballplayer by walking after a ball.
2. You will never become a .300 hitter unless you take the bat off your shoulder.
3. An outfielder who throws in back of the runner is locking the barn after the horse is stolen.
4. Keep your head up and you may not have to keep it down.
5. When you start to slide, SLIDE. He who changes his mind may have to change a good leg for a bad one.
6. Do not alibi on bad hops. Anyone can field the good ones.
7. Always run them out. You can never tell.
8. Do not quit.
9. Try not to find too much fault with the umpire. You cannot expect everyone to be as perfect as you are.
10. A pitcher who hasn't control hasn't anything.

Notably, only the tenth item dealt with pitchers. Several items are common sense bits that apply to all players, but this list primarily focuses on position players. That was appropriate because everyday players made McCarthy's teams peerless.

Despite his fantastic career record, he managed virtually no great pitchers. When McCarthy arrived in Chicago, the Cubs had Pete Alexander, but McCarthy had him traded away after seven starts. McCarthy also had Lefty Gomez and Red Ruffing with the Yankees, but both have their critics who think neither belongs in Cooperstown. Aside from that, McCarthy's only immortal hurlers were Burleigh Grimes and Herb Pennock. Not only were both questionable Hall of Fame selections, but each was also on the cusp of retirement when playing for McCarthy. He achieved a .615 winning percentage without top tier pitching.

Conversely, one can fill out a lineup of nothing but Hall of Famers from his position players and have enough leftovers for an extra team or two:

Joe McCarthy's First Team

C	Gabby Hartnett
1B	Lou Gehrig
2B	Rogers Hornsby
SS	Phil Rizzuto
3B	Joe Sewell
RF	Babe Ruth
CF	Joe DiMaggio
LF	Ted Williams

McCarthy's best pitchers—Gomez, Ruffing, Charlie Root, Mel Parnell, and Johnny Allen—would make an excellent staff, but are clearly outclassed by the above position players. In fact, they are nowhere near as good as the offensive B-team:

Joe McCarthy's Second Team

C	Bill Dickey
1B	Charlie Grimm
2B	Joe Gordon
SS	Frankie Crosetti
3B	Red Rolfe
RF	Kiki Cuyler
CF	Hack Wilson
LF	Charlie Keller

That still does not exhaust the offensive stars who batted for McCarthy. Beyond them are Tony Lazzeri, Bobby Doerr, Woody English, Vern Stephens, Johnny Pesky, Earle Combs, Tommy Heinrich, Ben Chapman, and Riggs Stephenson. Not surprisingly, the Tendencies Database believes McCarthy had tremendous offenses. Here are its results for park-adjusted runs per game:

Most Runs, Park-Adjusted

Joe McCarthy	0.404
Hughie Jennings	0.429
Davey Johnson	0.460
John McGraw	0.478
Sparky Anderson	0.591

McCarthy's squads almost always finished first or second in the league in scoring. While McCarthy possessed great offenses, his squads excelled in some areas more than others. They bunted and stole infrequently. Also, despite his bevy of Hall of Famers, the Tendencies Database ranks McCarthy "only" twelfth at batting average. Instead, McCarthy focused on the "take'n'rake" approach in which his hitters practiced plate discipline while looking for a pitch to drill. Thus despite his lackluster (by his standards) performance in batting average, his squads still did a great job getting on base his teams were first or second in OBP nearly a dozen and a half times as the Tendencies Database reveals:

Best OBP

Joe McCarthy	0.414
Hughie Jennings	0.476
John McGraw	0.526
Burt Shotton	0.578
Billy Southworth	0.593

With fantastic position players, McCarthy merely needed durable pitchers who would not give the game away. Red Ruffing exemplified a McCarthy pitcher. Ruffing had a career like none other. He initially played for a perennial sad sack Red Sox franchise, yet still lost games at a greater frequency than his teammates. Upon arriving with the continually contending Yankees, he suddenly won at a better clip than the squad. At first glance, it does not make sense. The key to unlocking Ruffing's secret lies in the only pitching aspect of McCarthy's Ten Commandments: control. In his Red Sox life, he walked 3.68 batters per nine innings, but as a Yankee he walked only 3.03.

McCarthy did not merely instruct Ruffing and his other pitchers to throw strikes, he made his hurlers more comfortable throwing the ball over the plate by emphasizing defense. Five times his bunch led the league in fielding percentage. From 1934 to 1945, the Yankees finished first the league in Defensive Efficiency Ratio every year except 1940, when they came in second. Six times his squads topped the AL in Fielding Win Shares, and they came in second place a half-dozen more times. McCarthy normally had defense-first players in the middle infield, like Rizzuto and Crosetti. Ruffing trusted the solid gloves behind him, allowing him to attack the batters, and throw balls over the plate. With fewer hits and walks allowed, Ruffing suddenly became a better pitcher. He relied on his supreme attribute — durability. That was all McCarthy needed.

A similar philosophy existed in McCarthy's approach to hitting and pitching. His hitters prioritized walks and home runs, and relying on fielders meant pitchers had to keep walks and homers in check. McCarthy's teams clubbed more home runs than they surrendered in each of the 22 seasons he managed. The odds on that happening by random happenstance are one in 4,194,304. His record with walks was nearly as impressive. His squads drew more free passes than they surrendered every year except 1944 (when they allowed only nine more than they earned) and with a few of his Chicago squads. Overall, his squads belted 2,891 long balls while allowing 1,711, a difference of 1,180. As the list below shows, McCarthy gained more benefit from the home run than any other manager:

Best Home Run Differentials

Joe McCarthy	+1,180 home runs
Bobby Cox	+828 home runs
Miller Huggins	+533 home runs
Tommy Lasorda	+506 home runs
Earl Weaver	+465 home runs

This includes only years in the Tendencies Database, so partial seasons make the results slightly inaccurate, but McCarthy's dominance is overwhelming. When he retired, only Huggins and John McGraw (+232) exceeded the 200 mark. McCarthy also possessed the second best walk differential of all time.

Years ago, ESPN writer Rob Neyer invented a stat called the "Beane Count" to look at how teams performed with walks and homers at both ends of the game (Neyer named it after Oakland A's GM Billy Beane, whose teams excelled at all these aspects in the early 21st century). It is a simple stat — take how teams rank in home runs and walks received and given, and find the sum of how they rank in these categories (which the Tendencies Database examines on a per inning and plate appearance basis). Here are baseball's most Beane Count-friendly managers, which shows only one manager is close to McCarthy:

Best at Beane Count

Joe McCarthy	2.505
Earl Weaver	2.641
Al Lopez	2.937

Best at Beane Count (continued)

Jimy Williams	3.004
Tommy Lasorda	3.021

A sound baseball philosophy was not enough to explain McCarthy's exceptional record; he was also exemplary at implementing his notions. McCarthy had a reputation as someone who could see problems coming two years in advance and adjust accordingly. There were some occasions when he did not read the tea leaves properly — most notably his decision to stick with aging shortstop Frankie Crosetti in 1940, a move that likely cost New York the pennant; but that was the exception, not the rule.

McCarthy not only knew when to break in kids, but also how to do it. When Phil Rizzuto first came up, McCarthy sat him on the bench next to him for several weeks early in the season. McCarthy quizzed the kid, making sure Rizzuto stayed alert at all times. He pointed out various intricacies to the young shortstop, making sure Rizzuto absorbed as much knowledge as possible. When McCarthy put him in the lineup to stay, Rizzuto was considerably surer of himself than he otherwise would have been. Rizzuto later concluded that this was McCarthy's standard practice for breaking in young players. Rob Neyer investigated Rizzuto's claims in his book *Baseball Legends*, and determined that although several other rookies (Crosetti, Joe Gordon, and Dixie Walker) had prolonged gaps as starters early in their rookie season, it did not happen often enough to qualify as McCarthy's modus operandi.

The question arises, if McCarthy used this system repeatedly (as he apparently did), why would not he do it more often? Think it through: to have a player sit next to McCarthy on the bench for that much time entailed a considerable investment in the prospect. McCarthy would not spend that much time with a player unless he expected the foundling to spend many years in the starting lineup. Those players do not come along every year. Also, while the kid has to have enough potential to be a fixture, the prospect cannot be so exceptionally talented that he has to be played right away. McCarthy would not keep Joe DiMaggio on the bench. Furthermore, as Yankee manager, McCarthy possessed one of the most solid lineups in baseball, and thus fewer openings than others. Finally, it is worth noting most of the guys McCarthy established in this manner were infielders. By virtue of the geography of the baseball diamond, such players have to be a bit more aware of the game's finer points. When McCarthy had the chance to break kids in by this method, he did so.

McCarthy's method of handling rookies indicates an overriding attitude he prioritized — professionalism. He preferred, though not necessarily demanded, a level of proper conduct among his players. Early in his tenure with the Yankees he destroyed a clubhouse card table to make his point on how they should act. He also instituted a dress code and ordered his men to be clean-shaven. When a player misbehaved in New York, McCarthy told him to act like a Yankee. He did not just set down rules, but also enforced them. That was why shortly after becoming the Cubs' manager McCarthy immediately got rid of Pete Alexander, a hard drinker who followed the beat of his own drummer.

That being said, McCarthy was not inflexible. His Chicago center fielder, Hack Wilson, was possibly an even bigger drinker than Alexander. However, McCarthy established a prodigal son relationship with Wilson. Rather than destabilize the team, Wilson's problems strangely fit into the system as he always accepted McCarthy's authority. After all, McCarthy gave him a starting job in center field after John McGraw banished him to the American Association. With the Cubs, Wilson became the exception that made the rule. Similarly, when he came to the Yankees, McCarthy also accepted Ruth's bravado. After all, there was only one Ruth.

Still, it is telling that McCarthy's career really took off once his squad had been cleared of any Wilsons or Ruths. Before 1936, he finished in second five times in the previous six seasons. Then, with a lineup full of business-like professionals such as DiMaggio, Crosetti, Bill

Dickey, and Tommy Heinrich, McCarthy won six championships and seven pennants in eight years. Their average margin of victory in those pennant-wining seasons was fourteen games. Their closest scare was 1942, when they won by nine games.

McCarthy's emphasis on professionalism paid dividends. By stressing proper conduct, and gathering a core of players who embodied the character traits he extolled, he created an espirit de corps. Players came to live up to McCarthy's Ten Commandments not because their manager told them to, but because they wanted to, and they saw those around them doing so. Yogi Berra once reminisced that when he first joined the Yankees, he failed to run out a routine grounder because he knew the throw would beat him. Upon returning to the dugout, the great DiMaggio came up to him, and asked the rookie if something was wrong with his legs. Another vet chided him for not running it out. Berra was a scared kid to whom the star center fielder had barely spoken. Berra finally had the attention of the Yankee Clipper, only to be upbraided. More importantly, Berra knew DiMaggio was right. He violated McCarthy's Seventh Commandment: always run them out. The story happened after McCarthy had left the franchise, but it showed the mindset he instilled.

That professional demeanor helped McCarthy's Yankee squads greatly in the postseason. In his seven world titles, New York went 28–5 in the Fall Classic. Even including the 1942 contest against the Cards—the only time his Yankees lost to the NL—they still went 29–9. While this would be an incredible achievement under normal circumstances, against the best clubs in baseball it was almost impossibly good.

Stonewall Jackson once remarked that an army conditioned to victory will become invincible. They will endure greater burdens while maintaining faith and order under the direst conditions. They can fight more resiliently than their opponent because they believe their sacrifices will not be in vain. That was the case for McCarthy's Bronx Bombers. Their ultimate postseason moment came in Game 4 of the 1941 World Series against the Brooklyn Dodgers. The Yankees, who led the series two games to one, trailed 4–3 in the top of the ninth in this contest. With two outs, two strikes, and no one on base, batter Tommy Heinrich swung and missed for an apparent game ending strikeout, but the ball squirted away from catcher Mickey Owen. Heinrich made it to first on a wild pitch. Given an inch, the Yankees took a mile. They ripped off a furious rally and won, cutting the hearts out of Brooklyn. They had followed with McCarthy's Fourth Commandment—play with your head up. When the right players with the right attitude are under the right manager, the results can be miraculous.

BILL MCKECHNIE

> **W/L Record:** 1,896–1,723 (.524)
> **Managed:** Full Seasons: Pittsburgh 1923–26; St. Louis (NL) 1927–28; Boston
> (NL) 1930–37; Cincinnati 1938–45
> Majority in: Newark (FL) 1915; Pittsburgh 1922; Cincinnati 1946
> Minority of: St. Louis (NL) 1929
> **Birnbaum Database:** +998 runs
> Individual Hitters: -145 runs
> Individual Pitchers: +402 runs
> Pythagenpat Difference: +330 runs
> Team Offense: +169 runs
> Team Defense: +242 runs
> **Team Characteristics:** Fielding. McKechnie just needed gloves backing up
> pitchers who kept the ball in the park, had good control, and com-
> pleted their starts. He did not use his bullpen much, but when he

did he often relied on one man. From 1920 to 1970, only three squads had one reliever record all their saves. McKechnie managed two, the 1935 Braves and 1942 Reds.

LPA: 4.23   LPA+: 98

Bill McKechnie is the anti–Wilbert Robinson. While Uncle Robby left a mark on the game far in excess of his accomplishments, McKechnie has been unfairly overlooked. In both cases personality caused the discrepancy between profile and performance. McKechnie was the lowest key of the great managers. Nicknamed "the Deacon," he abstained from drinking, cussing, and did not even raise his voice. Instead, he used superb listening skills to interact with his players. People expected their manager to be louder and more aggressive, confusing volume with substance. Since McKechnie stayed in the background, he received considerably less credit for victories than he deserved, and was often quick to be blamed for losses.

That was one of the reasons he became the first man in baseball history to win pennants for three teams. No matter that he delivered Pittsburgh its first pennant in sixteen years or gave St. Louis its best single-season winning percentage since the days of Charles Comiskey; both franchises sent him packing even though he never had a losing season with either. As noted at the introduction of this chapter, the Fred Clarke controversy further hurt McKechnie in Pittsburgh. St. Louis demoted him to the minors after he led the team to the 1928 World Series because they had been swept by the Yankees in October. Mind you, the Yanks had swept the NL champion in 1927 as well. McKechnie did not receive the respect he deserved until claiming back-to-back pennants with Cincinnati in 1939–40.

His approach to the game was basic — run prevention. McKechnie used the old Comiskey method of having pitchers who threw strikes stand before fielders who caught everything. Others have adopted this philosophy, but no one ever implemented it as effectively or thoroughly as McKechnie. One of his patented techniques was to have an infield consisting of three shortstops and a first baseman. He placed his best glove at short, and the others at second and third. In Pittsburgh, he had Glenn Wright at short, moved the aging Rabbit Maranville to second, and put Pie Traynor (who had previously split his time between third and short) strictly at third. When McKechnie arrived in Boston, he did the same thing. He would also stack his outfield with multiple men capable of playing center field. Even his first basemen could field.

A person who could hit but not field had no place in McKechnie's clubhouse. It was the misfortune of Hank Sauer, a Reds' prospect when McKechnie managed in Cincinnati, to prove this. Sauer averaged over 32 home runs a year from 1948 to 1954 in the NL, but could not land a regular spot on a big league roster until he was 31 years old, because McKechnie let Sauer rot in the minors due to his inability to field his position. Sauer did not get his break until after McKechnie's managerial career concluded.

Naturally, McKechnie's ceaseless focus on defense paid dividends on the field. In his 23 seasons as a team's primary manager, his squad had the best Defensive Efficiency Ratio eight times. They came in the top three eighteen times. Every team he managed for at least one full season topped the league in it. McKechnie's squads led the league in fielding percentage five times, and had an equal number of runner-up finishes. According to Win Shares, 19 percent of his squads' value came from fielding, the highest percentage of any manager who lasted more than ten years. McKechnie's infielders did a very good job turning the double play, especially in Pittsburgh.

Since McKechnie possessed superlative fielders, brilliant pitchers were not required. Aside from a forty-something Pete Alexander, he never had any. McKechnie only needed pitchers who would not short-circuit their defenders. None of his teams ever came in last in either walks or home runs allowed per nine innings. In fact, none ever finished next-to-last in either. That is a truly remarkable achievement in four decades of managing with five separate franchises. Alternately, McKechnie had five last-place finishes in strikeouts per nine innings. A pitcher only had to be solid in order to achieve spectacular results with McKechnie's array of defensive wizards. With this approach, McKechnie coaxed twenty-win seasons from nearly a dozen men, including "luminaries" Lee Meadows, Bill Sherdel, Ben Cantwell, Lou Fette, and Elmer Riddle. Someone named Johnny Morrison won 25 games for him in 1923. In all, McKechnie oversaw seventeen different twenty-win seasons. In the last 90 years, only Earl Weaver presided over more.

McKechnie prized durability with his pitchers instead of brilliance. Each of the five teams he managed led the league in complete games at least once. The Reds paced the NL five times from 1939 to 1944. When they completed 86 starts in 1939, no other team in the league had more than 72. The next year Cincinnati's starting pitchers completed 91 games, 40 percent more than what the rest of the NL averaged. Seven times a McKechnie pitcher led or tied for the league lead in complete games. From 1939 to 1941, Bucky Walters completed 87 of his 107 starts and teammate Paul Derringer finished 71 of 100. No other NL hurler completed more than 57 starts in those years. Derringer was the ultimate McKechnie hurler. He led the league in fewest walks per inning twice, including a minuscule 35 walks allowed in 301 innings in 1939. That was the best control by any NL pitcher from 1925 to 1970.

McKechnie generally preferred veteran pitchers who had proven they could handle pitching a full season without breaking down. Baseball-Reference provides average ages for all pitching staffs in baseball history, rounded to the tenths decimal. When pitcher age is run through the Tendencies Database, McKechnie had some of the oldest units of all time:

Oldest Pitchers

Al Lopez	1.564
Wilbert Robinson	1.427
Bill McKechnie	1.420
Bobby Valentine	1.384
Joe Torre	1.383

McKechnie possessed one of the two oldest staffs in the league a dozen times; he never had one of the two youngest. All but two of his twenty-game winners were in their 30s, while the youngest was 27 years old. His 1935 Brave pitching staff had an average age of 33.2, which was the oldest of the twentieth century. Seventeen of his 23 staffs had an average age of 30 or older, a level only one-fourth of teams reached in those days.

Not only did McKechnie's teams rarely feature great pitchers, but his position players were even less impressive. The best position player McKechnie ever managed was second baseman Frankie Frisch, but that was for less than two seasons. Otherwise, McKechnie's best position players were Ernie Lombardi, Pie Traynor, Rabbit Maranville, Jim Bottomley, Kiki Cuyler, Chick Hafey, and Max Carey. While all are in Cooperstown, they are typically considered either borderline selections or outright mistakes. Together, they are not as talented as Joe McCarthy's third-string team. An All-Star team from McKechnie's entire career might not be as formidable as the 1939 Yankee lineup.

McKechnie did not need great players because he knew how to get the most from the talent available. His experience with Boston, the one National League team he never led to October, best exemplifies his ability to extract the maximum from his teams. Boston never finished higher than fourth under McKechnie because their rosters were exceptionally weak. Here are the core players for the 1933 Braves:

Pos.	Player
C	Shanty Hogan
1B	Buck Jordan

Pos.	Player
2B	Rabbit Maranville
SS	Billy Urbanski
3B	Pinky Whitney
OF	Randy Moore
OF	Wally Berger
OF	Hal Lee
SP	Ed Brandt
SP	Fred Frankhouse
SP	Ben Cantwell
SP	Huck Betts
RP	Leo Mangum

Anyone who can recognize more than three of those names should be considered an expert on baseball history. Anyone who cannot is not missing much.

Yet the 1933 Braves went 83–71. That was no fluke: they went 78–73 the next year and had gone 77–77 in 1932. In eight campaigns with the team, the Braves went 560–666 (.457) for McKechnie. Despite that, the Birnbaum Database gives him an overall score of +166 runs for that period. That rivals Miller Huggins's achievement with the Cardinals for the Birnbaum score for most impressive discrepancy between what the database says and the team's winning percentage. McKechnie turned seventh-place talent into fourth-place finishes.

McKechnie also knew how to manage the game. His credo was that if you worked the percentages, the percentages would work for you. In his own quiet way McKechnie exquisitely implemented tried and true baseball wisdom. For example, caught stealing data exists from the NL for only three years he managed (1923–25), but his teams had the league's best stolen base success rate each time. He bunted and stole more than opposing teams, a sensible option for him. When a team has minimal chances for the big inning, it needs to score when it can.

While he was a brilliant manager, circumstances beyond his control aided him. As a keen reader may have noticed, few managers in the 1920s and 1930s based their games on defense and control. It had been the preferred system for roster construction in the deadball era, but the new scoring environment made offense more important. This opened a gap for McKechnie to exploit. Since few rival clubs fought for gloves, there were more first-rate defenders available. A market inefficiency existed, just as it did with fundamentals at the turn of the century. If multiple teams collected defenders, the edge this system gave McKechnie would have been a liability.

McKechnie's approach had its limitations. Prioritizing gloves caused his offenses to suffer. His teams were not very good at drawing walks, had minimal power, and could not hit very well. When batting average, the preferred performance metric of McKechnie's times, goes through the Tendencies Database, his teams appear historically bad:

Worst Batting Averages

Art Howe	1.526
Billy Barnie	1.461
Frank Robinson	1.297
George Stallings	1.282
Bill McKechnie	1.266

The other managers listed had losing records, while McKechnie earned a .524 mark.

McKechnie's emphasis on defense eventually crippled his teams. After the 1940 championship, teams looked especially vigilantly for ways to beat McKechnie's Reds, ultimately using McKechnie's roster construction against him. His interest in fielding meant his lineup had little effective left-handed hitting, so teams stopped using southpaws against them. From 1941 to 1945, the most southpaw starters the Reds faced in a single season was sixteen. The fewest such starts any other NL team had was also sixteen. To put this into perspective, the table below shows how many times southpaws started against the Reds that year, and how many overall starts the other seven NL teams gave their lefties. If left-handers had been used evenly, 14.3 percent of their starts would have come against McKechnie's Reds. That clearly did not happen:

Year	vs Cin	All	%
1941	16	241	6.6%
1942	2	250	0.8%
1943	13	237	5.5%
1944	13	231	5.6%
1945	12	234	5.1%

The 1942 Reds faced fewer southpaws than any team since 1884. McKechnie's single-minded focus on defense not only left his team wide-open to this response, but prohibited him from reacting to it. His offenses, never especially good in the first place, worsened. This explains why he scores so poorly with individual hitters in the Birnbaum Database — he put them in poor situations, and did not get them out of it. By 1946, the Reds were terrible and not worth platoon leveraging against anymore.

McKechnie did a subpar job at the end, but that was normally the case. From Ned Hanlon to Casey Stengel, the greats depart not with a bang but a whimper. Overall, though, Bill McKechnie was the best manager in National League history, with the possible exception of John McGraw.

STEVE O'NEILL

W/L Record: 1,040–821 (.559)
Managed: Full Seasons: Cleveland 1936–37; Detroit 1943–48; Boston (AL) 1951;
        Philadelphia (NL) 1953
        Majority in: Boston (AL) 1950, Philadelphia (NL) 1952, 1954
        Minority of: Cleveland 1935
Birnbaum Database: +127 runs
        Individual Hitters: +54 runs
        Individual Pitchers: +74 runs
        Pythagenpat Difference: -3 runs
        Team Offense: +17 runs
        Team Defense: -15 runs
Team Characteristics: O'Neill's teams contained fantastic pitching staffs. They
        also had good hitters, but O'Neill's teams were centered on pitch-
        ing. His squads went 300–243 (.552) in one-run games. He used a
        set lineup and leaned on his ace pitchers.
LPA: 4.18   LPA+: 90

O'Neill managed for all or part of fourteen seasons, posting a winning record every time. Only Joe McCarthy, with 24 seasons, tops that. Every other skipper with more than five seasons had one with a losing record. Rather appropriately, when Joe McCarthy resigned as Red Sox manager mid-season in 1950, the team tapped O'Neill as his replacement. Al Lopez misses this exclusive club on a technicality. After managing for fifteen full seasons, he came out of retirement as an interim manager for the White Sox twice and narrowly had losing records both times. Earl Weaver posted a winning record in each of his first sixteen seasons only to blow it in his seventeenth and final one.

Joe McCarthy. Al Lopez. Earl Weaver. Steve O'Neill. Which one of those names does not belong? Clearly O'Neill is the weak one in that pile, but in some ways his achievement was the most impressive of all. He managed four franchises, more than the others.

O'Neill preferred basing his teams around strong starting pitchers, especially young ones—a fact the Tendencies Database can attest to:

Youngest Staffs

Burt Shotton	0.378
Patsy Donovan	0.522
Steve O'Neill	0.598
Billy Barnie	0.644
Felipe Alou	0.666

Most of these individuals ran clubs that could not compete financially and had to sell off their players, such was the case with Donovan, Barnie, and to a lesser extent Shotton. Alou's Expos lost them to free agency. No similar reason explains why O'Neill's staffs would be among the youngest, but they were. He presided over ten separate twenty-win seasons, half of which came from hurlers 26 years old or younger. Only one came from someone in his 30s.

Only sixteen pitchers in the last 90 years won 150 games before their thirtieth birthday; four of them played for O'Neill—Bob Feller, Mel Harder, Hal Newhouser, and Robin Roberts. That was partially a coincidence—Harder's biggest seasons came before O'Neill arrived, and Feller did not become a full-time starter until after O'Neill left. However, it sheds light on how O'Neill managed. He relied on his best arms as much as possible. Newhouser never pitched 200 innings in a season until O'Neill came to Detroit. From 1944 to 1947, he averaged over 300 per year. O'Neill's aggressive usage caused Newhouser to win 188 games before turning 30, the most of anyone since 1920. Robin Roberts had already established himself as both an ace and a workhorse before O'Neill, but O'Neill pushed him harder than ever. In their only full year together, Roberts threw 346.7 innings, the most by any NL pitcher since Pete Alexander. When O'Neill lost his job midway through 1954, Roberts was on pace to throw over 350 innings. In each of O'Neill's three campaigns with the Phillies, Roberts threw more innings than any of his other sixteen seasons.

Those are merely O'Neill's most prominent pitchers. In 1944, Detroit's Dizzy Trout became the first pitcher in over twenty years to exceed 350 innings. He and Newhouser threw 47.5 percent of Detroit's innings that year, the highest percentage by any twosome since 1920. Under O'Neill, Phillies hurler Curt Simmons received some of the highest workloads of his twenty-year career. In half of O'Neill's seasons, his teams led the league in complete games.

O'Neill also had notable success with pitchers that were not worked to the maximum. In 1936, O'Neill oversaw Johnny Allen's only 20-win season. The next year Allen went 15–1 for O'Neill. Mel Parnell, Virgil Trucks, Fred Hutchinson, and Tommy Bridges also provided good work for O'Neill. He converted Ellis Kinder into a relief pitcher, a job Kinder flourished in.

Pitchers were central to O'Neill's run prevention program. His staffs excelled at the three stats—strikeouts, walks, and homers—that are independent of the defenses behind them. When these pitching peripherals are run through the Tendencies Database (which looks at each on a per-inning basis) and the results added together, O'Neill's staffs look fantastic:

Best Pitcher Peripherals

Jimy Williams	1.758
Tommy Lasorda	1.772
Steve O'Neill	2.000
Paul Richards	2.093
Davey Johnson	2.187

O'Neill's squads led the league in best control almost as often as they did in complete games. Also, prior to coming to Philadelphia, his staffs were always in the top three in the league in strikeouts per inning. They were generally effective against the long ball.

With superlative pitching, O'Neill prioritized hitting over fielding from his position players. His teams led in Fielding Win Shares only once, fielding percentage once, and Defensive Efficiency Ratio never. Instead, his teams almost always produced a solid on-base percentage. His teams were good at drawing walks, and tough to strike out. He only had one genuinely great offense—his 1950 Red Sox were the only team to hit over .300 since the 1930s—but he usually had formidable lineups. Of the 70 occasions a hitter qualified for the batting title under O'Neill, 54 had a mark superior to the league average. O'Neill often coaxed league-leading performances from his players. In 1936, Hal Trosky led the league with 162 RBIs under O'Neill. A decade later, Hank Greenberg topped the AL with 127 runs batted in. In 1950, Red Sox teammates Vern Stephens and Walt Dropo tied for the RBI crown with 144. O'Neill also presided over three hit leaders, two home run champions, one batting average title claimant, a pair of bases of balls champions, a stolen base king, two runs leaders, a couple slugging average winners, and a pair of on-base percentage leaders.

Despite his success, O'Neill has been forgotten. His teams were good, but nothing more than that. He was the king of third place. Detroit was his best club, but it captured only one pennant. That came in 1945, when many of the best players had been drafted. Also, that team only won 88 games, rather unimpressive for a squad in the World Series. They nearly won the pennant the year before, only to lose a close race to the Browns. The 1946 Tigers had potential, but that year the Red Sox won 104 games. O'Neill's Hall of Fame what-if is not nearly as strong as that of Charlie Grimm. What most hurts O'Neill was a late start. He was 43 when he got his first shot as a manager. He was major league baseball's fifth oldest manager at that time, junior only to some Hall of Famers—Casey Stengel, Bill McKechnie, Connie Mack and Joe McCarthy. Aside from Stengel, those men had won at least one pennant before turning 43. When O'Neill left in 1954, only Casey Stengel was his senior, by merely a year.

BURT SHOTTON

> **W/L Record:** 697–764 (.477)
> **Managed:** Full Seasons: Philadelphia (NL) 1928–33; Brooklyn 1949–50
>   Majority in: Brooklyn 1947, 1948
>   Minority of: Cincinnati 1934
> **Birnbaum Database:** -326 runs
>   Individual Hitters: +54 runs
>   Individual Pitchers: -348 runs
>   Pythagenpat Difference: -57 runs
>   Team Offense: -60 runs
>   Team Defense: +85 runs
> **Team Characteristics:** Shotton had the youngest teams relative to the league of all managers with at least a decade's experience. His offenses put up terrific numbers, though parks (especially Philadelphia's tiny Baker

Bowl) played a role in that. He still holds the NL record for most 40-double seasons occurring under his watch, with eleven. He used plenty of relievers, but not many bench players.

LPA: 3.34   LPA+: 74

As noted throughout this book, many managers won by making sure their pitchers throw strikes. However, not all teams can rank among the best in control. The Tendencies Database also notes which staffs walked the most per inning:

Worst Control

Burt Shotton	1.600
Casey Stengel	1.387
Dusty Baker	1.351
Jim Fregosi	1.350
Lou Boudreau	1.292

Burt Shotton "wins" in a landslide. He oversaw five last-place finishes in ten years along with a trio of next-to-last place results. Admittedly, the Phillies featured terrible staffs before and after Shotton, but they were far less adept at throwing strikes for him.

Shotton's inaugural squad in 1928 possessed the worst control of any team in the 1920s, allowing 4.48 walks per nine innings. The year before they averaged barely three in nine innings. To this day, 1928 reigns as the highest walks allowed rate in franchise history. In fact, it is the third worst mark by any NL team in the twentieth century. From 1913 to 1937, only one other NL team averaged worse than 3.70 walks per game; that was Shotton's 1929 Phillies, at 4.11. Brooklyn had similar problems under Shotton. Each of his four years with the club ranks among the franchise's dozen worst walk rates since 1900.

Failure marked Shotton's Philadelphia, and for a long time it looked like he would never be given another chance to manage. His gap between jobs was one of the longest in history. Shotton owed his managerial resurrection to three factors: his relationship with Dodger GM Branch Rickey, a bizarre suspension of Leo Durocher, and his willingness to work with young players.

Shotton played for Rickey when the future Hall of Famer managed the Browns. The pious Rickey refused to manage on Sunday, instead letting Shotton handle the chore for him. That relationship came in handy because immediately prior to the beginning of the 1947 season, new commissioner Happy Chandler suspended Brooklyn manager Leo Durocher for the year. The specific reasons for the decision were strange and did not justify the punishment. Durocher was a controversial jerk, and hung out with gamblers (though he had already agreed to stop doing that). The suspension primarily gave the new commissioner a chance to assert his authority. Not only was a new campaign about to begin, but that season Rickey intended to debut Jackie Robinson, breaking the game's color barrier. Rickey needed someone trustworthy who would play kids.

Shotton perfectly fit that description. The Tendencies Database notes that he had the youngest batters of any manager in history:

Youngest Offenses

Burt Shotton	0.467
Dick Williams	0.580
Art Howe	0.656
Miller Huggins	0.667
Lou Boudreau	0.694

Shotton oversaw 68 occasions when a hitter had enough plate appearances to qualify for the batting title. Only seven came from batters older than 30.

The Phillies were bad, but improved under Shotton, largely because of the young hitters who blossomed under him. He installed Hall of Famer Chuck Klein in the outfield and saw him win a Triple Crown. Shotton successfully broke in a pair on infielders in his first year, Pinky Whitney and Don Hurst. Shotton also turned Spud Davis from a Cardinals washout into one of the best hitting catchers in the game. Lefty O'Doul had a breakthrough as a hitter as soon as he played for Shotton. Altogether, it was an impressive record.

That was precisely what Rickey sought. Aside from Robinson, Rickey had Duke Snider and Gil Hodges waiting in the wings. Furthermore, Rickey intended to promote more Negro League stars, such as Roy Campanella. Rickey was impressed enough with Shotton's work as emergency fill-in during 1947 that he arranged for Durocher to go to the Giants in mid–1948 so Shotton would be Brooklyn's full-time manager.

Shotton successfully broke them in, not flinching when they had troubles. Jonathan Eig's book about Jackie Robinson's rookie season, *Opening Day*, provides a snapshot of Shotton at work. When Robinson slumped in April, Shotton ignored calls to bench him. Instead, the skipper kept his own logbook in which he recorded every hard out Robinson made, saying they were hits to him. He recognized that Robinson kept making solid contact, but the balls were not dropping. Robinson rewarded Shotton for that trust by winning the Rookie of the Year Award.

Unfortunately, while Shotton's subdued demeanor endeared him to Rickey, the press reacted differently. To them, Shotton appeared to be a cog in Rickey's machine. Sportswriter Dick Young bestowed the nickname "Kindly Old Burt Shotton" on him, giving Shotton the image as a well meaning but out of touch old fart. It did not help that Shotton refused to wear a uniform, choosing a suit instead. The only other manager to do that was the aged Connie Mack, who by then was an out of touch old fart. When the talented team lost two World Series, fans demanded a change, ending Shotton's career.

BILLY SOUTHWORTH

> **W/L Record:** 1,044–704 (.597)
> **Managed:** Full Seasons: St. Louis (NL) 1941–45; Boston (NL) 1946–48, 1950
>   Majority in: St. Louis (NL) 1929, 1940; Boston (NL) 1949
>   Minority of: Boston (NL) 1951
> **Birnbaum Database:** +653 runs
>   Individual Hitters: +298 runs
>   Individual Pitchers: +336 runs
>   Pythagenpat Difference: +28 runs
>   Team Offense: -62 runs
>   Team Defense: +53 runs
> **Team Characteristics:** Southworth's teams were very good at almost every phase of the game. Southworth was the preeminent bunter of his generation. He prized durable pitchers who threw strikes and batters who could hit for average. He normally did very well in one-run games, 289–253 (.533) for his career, but dropped twelve of his last thirteen. He relied on his starting catcher more than most. He was the last important manager who neither had a pitcher record ten saves nor 40 relief appearances in a season.
> **LPA:** 5.40   **LPA+:** 119

In 1918, Bill McKechnie, Casey Stengel, and Billy Southworth all played for the Pirates, which was the greatest concentration of future managerial talent ever assembled on one roster. McKechnie won pennants with three franchises, Stengel collected five consecutive titles, and Southworth's 1942–44 Cardinals became the only team to win 105 games three straight seasons. Even the 1890s Orioles with John McGraw, Hughie Jennings, and Wilbert Robinson cannot match that. Unlike that squad, which had Hall of Famer Ned Hanlon calling the shots, the Pirates had Hugo Bedzek, who lasted a mere 356 games as skipper.

Southworth had a most unusual career path for a Hall of Fame manager. He first managed the Cardinals in 1929. He was familiar with many of the players, having been their teammate in 1926–27. However, that closeness proved to be his undoing. Southworth tried to show he was not one of the boys anymore by aggressively asserting his authority, but the predictable friction with the vets cost him his job. Throughout his career, Southworth always worked better with kids.

Three issues prevented him from getting another major league managerial job in the 1930s. First, getting fired midway through one's first season is a horrible way to start a career. Second, the Great Depression caused a return to player-managers, who were cheaper, limiting Southworth's opportunities. Finally, Southworth developed a drinking problem. He overcame it (for a time), winning three pennants for St. Louis's minor league squads before the Cardinals promoted him to the big leagues.

With the exception of Casey Stengel, no one took such full advantage of his second chance as Southworth. He had a great stretch, though it was short-lived. Southworth returned to the bottle when his son died in 1945, and by some accounts nearly had a nervous breakdown with the Braves. Despite managing less than a dozen years, Southworth gained a plaque in Cooperstown (albeit well after his death) by revitalizing two franchises.

However, the Birnbaum Database and his win-loss record each overrate him. Southworth was a great manager, but World War II exaggerated his capabilities. The armed forces drafted many players, giving an advantage to two types of franchises: those with the deepest talent pools and any who fortuitously had their stars drafted later rather than sooner. Both elements favored Southworth's Cardinals. Defensive whiz Marty Marion, already an established player, spent the entire war in St. Louis. Enos Slaughter got drafted early, leaving before the 1943 season, but the club called up Harry Walker, who possessed enough talent to win the 1947 batting title, to replace him. When the draft board knocked on Walker's door, St. Louis installed Johnny Hopp, a supersub who had earned MVP support in 1941, as an everyday starter. On the pitching staff, ace Mort Cooper stuck around until early 1945, when the team traded him for Red Barrett, who won twenty games that year. Veteran hurler Max Lanier lasted until the spring of 1945 with the club. St. Louis kept long-time starter Harry Gumbert until mid–1943, when they sold him. When the pitchers started to thin, St. Louis simply called up from the minors Harry Breechen, who starred for the rest of the 1940s.

Similarly, the club added three new hitters in 1942, all of who were legitimate call-ups: Whitey Kurowski, Walker Cooper, and Stan Musial. Kurowski, a hard-hitting third baseman, was talented enough to make the All-Star team in 1946 and 1947. Catcher Cooper became an eight-time All Star who played until the late 1950s. Musial was, with the possible exception of Albert Pujols, the most talented player in franchise history. Kurowski played for the team during the entire war while Musial and Cooper joined the armed forces only in the last year.

In other words, through 1944, most of St. Louis's lineup consisted of men who possessed enough talent not only to start under regular conditions, but also to star as well. Given how the draft affected other teams, Southworth's win-loss record and Southworth's Birnbaum Database score were inflated.

Still, Southwoth was a fantastic manager. Flexibility was one of Southworth's strengths, a fact especially shown by the very different ways he handled his pitchers in St. Louis and Boston. With the Cardinals, he had one workhorse he knew he could count on, first Lon Warneke and then Mort Cooper. Southworth used them on a regular basis, with only minimal interest in who they opposed.

Conversely, he intentionally matched the rest against specific teams, to an almost unprecedented degree. His cumulative LPA and LPA+ for 1940–45 were 6.55 and 156, each among the largest scores by anyone not named Frank Chance. The most extreme example came in 1942 with southpaw Max Lanier. Seven of his twenty starts came against the Dodgers, who won 104 games, while he faced the Reds, Braves, Pirates, and Phillies a combined total of four times. Lanier ended the year with an AOWP+ of 114, the highest for a pitcher with at least twenty starts since the First World War. In his 105 starts from 1940 to 1945, 51 came against either the Cubs or Dodgers while he faced the Phillies and Reds only a half-dozen times each. Lanier averaged one start per season against the Braves from 1940 to 1942, and then in a remarkable about face, started against them eleven times in 1943 to 1944. In 1942, Howie Pollet had seven starts against the Giants; a rather remarkable achievement since he only began thirteen games. Pollet was a lefty and Southworth liked the platoon match up against New York. In 41 starts in 1941 to 1942, southpaw Ernie White never faced the Phillies, and saw the Reds only three times. Southworth did not relegate leveraging exclusively to southpaws. Five of Harry Breechen's thirteen starts as a rookie came against Pittsburgh, three more were versus Brooklyn. Two years later, in 1945, he saw the pennant-winning Cubs more times (six) than he saw the three worst teams combined (five). In Red Barrett's twenty-win 1945 campaign, he frequently faced the league's three worst teams.

However, in Boston Southworth abruptly shifted away from leveraging. He used Warren Spahn and Johnny Sain on a regular basis, with little concern for who the opponent was. In the 1948 pennant race, Southworth used them both on short rest on a regular basis to claim the league title (hence the famous slogan "Spahn and Sain and pray for rain"). With multiple trustworthy starters, quantity was the central concern. By 1949, he found a third man, Vern Bickford, to use similarly, and the Braves became the first NL team to give three men at least 36 starts each since the 1923 Reds (managed by Pat Moran). In 1950, Southworth's threesome each started 37 or more games, something even Moran never did. Boston's top three pitchers accounted for nearly two-thirds of all innings thrown, more than any other 1950s squad. Also, unlike his habits in St. Louis, Southworth almost never used his Boston starters in relief. Southworth's Braves became a forerunner for the modern pitching staff, drawing a clearer divide between starter and reliever, and using his starters on a regular basis. Perhaps it was a coincidence, but Braves starter Johnny Sain became the greatest pitching coach of his generation.

In both towns Southworth worked with what he had. He had more reliable starters in Boston, so he trusted them. In St. Louis, he picked spots for them instead. Southworth's Boston LPA and LPA+ were 3.61 and 73 respectively. It would have been lower, but he usually reserved one marginal starter for use against second-division squads (Si Johnson had LPAs of 91 and 93 in 1946 and 1947; Red Barrett posted a 92 in 1948).

On offense, Southworth was one of the greatest practitioners of counter-clockwise baseball of all time. Hitters made it on base, and kept moving in a never-ending loop around the bags. First, they had to get on base. Southworth's teams drew their share of walks, but base hits were their bread and butter. While both a hit and walk can get men on, only a hit ensured that the runners would move on their counter-clockwise course. According to the Tendencies Database, his teams were historically great at batting average:

Best Batting Averages

John McGraw	0.490
Billy Southworth	0.519
Hughie Jennings	0.540
Danny Murtaugh	0.550
Red Schoendienst	0.607

In 1946, Southworth's first year in Boston, the Braves finished second in the NL in batting average. They had not done that well since 1911. Next year they led the league in batting for the first time since 1877. In 1948, they repeated as batting average champs for the only time in franchise history. Southworth's teams came in first or second in batting average every year from 1940 to 1948.

Once he had a player on base, Southworth was determined to move him around. More singles helped. Southworth's squads also had plenty of mid-range power, hitting numerous doubles. Of the ten NL teams that hit the most doubles in the 1940s, Southworth managed five (three in St. Louis, two in Boston). Southworth was not about to just wait for hard hit shots; instead he bunted constantly. In the 1940s, only a dozen teams had at least 125 sacrifice hits in a season, Southworth managed seven—four in St. Louis, three in Boston. In his managerial career, only once did a player who qualified for the batting title go an entire season without a sacrifice hit (Johnny Mize, 1940). In Chapter 2's list of the biggest proponents of the sacrifice hit, Southworth ranked third.

Though those sacrifices cost him outs, they served multiple purposes for Southworth. First, they put a runner in scoring position, where one of the squad's plentiful doubles or singles could score him. Second, they eliminated the chance the runner would be lost to a double play, which was a key concern for a team counterclockwising its way to glory. Going by the Tendencies Database, Southworth did a fantastic job ensuring his base runners did not get doubled up. The table below, which uses the formula discussed in the Connie Mack comment last chapter, reveals how hard it was to double up a Southworth squad:

Least Likely to Hit Into Double Plays

Billy Southworth	0.505
Birdie Tebbetts	0.570
Al Lopez	0.606
Whitey Herzog	0.632
Davey Johnson	0.657

Only once did a member of Southworth's teams ground into more than eighteen double plays. For context, that occurred 90 times across major league baseball from 1940 to 1950.

In 1945, St. Louis had 1,175 singles, 515 walks, and 26 times hit by pitch, but hit into only 75 double plays. That was less than one in 22 times someone was on first base, the best ratio in baseball history. That low ratio was aided by the poor quality of defensive play during World War II, but it was also a testament to the importance Southworth placed on avoiding the double play.

BILL TERRY

W/L Record: 823–661 (.555)

Managed: Full Seasons: New York (NL) 1933–41
    Majority in: New York (NL) 1932
    Minority of: (none)

Birnbaum Database: +95 runs
    Individual Hitters: -59 runs
    Individual Pitchers: -6 runs
    Pythagenpat Difference: +21 runs
    Team Offense: +36 runs
    Team Defense: +103 runs

Team Characteristics: Terry's offenses blasted homers, but rarely stole bases
    or struck out. In fact, none of his batters fanned more than 71 times

in a season. His teams also had groundball pitchers. Though precise groundball-to-flyball ratios do not exist for those days, it can be roughly determined with the formula A/(PO-K) as flies rarely result in assists but grounders typically do. Plugging that into the Tendencies Database, Terry had the most groundball-oriented staffs of all time.

LPA: 3.84   LPA+: 82

In June 1932, Bill Terry replaced John McGraw as Giants manager, beginning the greatest infusion of new managerial talent in baseball history. In the next 26 months, Charlie Grimm, Joe Cronin, Frankie Frisch, Mickey Cochrane, Casey Stengel, Jimmie Wilson, Jimmy Dykes, Pie Traynor, and Charlie Dressen joined Terry as debuting skippers. Combined, they managed almost 20,000 games while claiming 23 pennants and 10 world titles. They dominated baseball for decades, with four plying the trade until the 1960s.

This unprecedented avalanche of managerial timber was not caused by random happenstance. It happened in the darkest days of the Great Depression, when financially damaged teams most needed to save money. One simple way was to replace a manager with a player-manager. Franchises paid the player more to take on the extra responsibility, but not as much as a full-time manager would cost. Most of baseball history has been a move away from player-managers, but the 1930s are the great reverse step. From 1911 to 1931, player-managers won only one NL pennant. In the AL, Bucky Harris was the only player-manager to claim a pennant from 1922 to 1931. In 1931, there was only one real player-manager in the game. However, by 1934, a majority of teams employed hyphenated managers. From 1932 to 1938, Joe McCarthy was the only *non*–player-manager to win a pennant. Not all of the 1932 to 1934 new managers played, but a majority did.

Terry faced the most daunting task of the new generation, replacing the game's most legendary manager. Those who replace towering figures are often reduced by their predecessors' long shadows, but not Terry, who lasted a decade on the job before stepping down. When McGraw told Terry he wanted the veteran infielder to succeed him as manager, Terry would not accept unless some conditions were met. He would only be the boss if he really *was* the boss. McGraw was not to look over his shoulder. In response, McGraw told Terry (and later the press) that he would only return to the dugout if invited. He never was. With power firmly established, Terry immediately fired the team's trainer, whom the players widely believed to be McGraw's clubhouse spy. It also helped Terry that the Giants were in last place when McGraw resigned 40 games into the 1932 season.

As a manager, Bill Terry was quite comparable to Joe Cronin. Both infielders became player-managers within a year of each other and won a pennant in their first full season. In fact, they faced each other in the 1933 World Series. Also, as noted in Chapter 2, the Tendencies Database lists Cronin and Terry as the two worst managers in history when it came to pacing a club over a season. Below are the pre– and post–All Star break records for the Giants in Terry's full seasons as manager:

Half	W-L	Pct
First	385-255	.602
Second	383-347	.525

Terry's teams did not falter as regularly as Cronin's did (giving Terry a less embarrassing score in the Tendencies Database), but when they collapsed, they fell apart like no other. They had the worst second-half fall-off in the league four times: 1935, 1938, 1940, and 1941.

From 1933 to 1941, the years Terry managed a full season, the biggest second-half fade by any NL team came from the 1940 Giants. They went 40–28 before the All-Star break, only to stagger 32–52 the rest of the way. The second-worst fade by any NL team in those years was another Giants squad, the 1935 bunch. At the All-Star break, the pennant looked to be theirs, as they possessed a seven-game lead with a 48–21 record. After pushing their mark to 51–21, they soon collapsed, playing .500 ball the rest of the way, ending up in third, eight and a half games behind Charlie Grimm's Cubs. The fourth-worst fade in this period was by yet another Terry team, his 1938 team (the 1935 Braves possessed the third-worst flop, for what it is worth). Terry's 1938 squad started out 45–25, on pace for their third straight pennant, but instead they lost most of their remaining games. In a league without any really strong teams, the Giants settled for third place.

It was rather fitting that the most famous moment of Terry's managerial career came when his team blew a lead. In 1934, the Giants led the Cardinals by seven games with less than four weeks to play. The Giants went 8–13 while the Cards staged an 18–5 pennant sprint. That collapse is better remembered than the others because Terry impolitely dismissed the pennant chances of the local rival Dodgers by asking the press, "Is Brooklyn still in the league?" The Dodgers responded by knocking the Giants out of postseason contention in a season-ending series. Then again, people still recall the choke precisely because it was not as bad as their other late season failures. If the 1934 Giants played like the 1938 squad, they would have lost their lead well before the Brooklyn series.

Terry's pacing problem centered on run prevention. It is tricky to observe simply by looking at raw numbers, as the game's annual temperature curve always affects run scoring month-to-month. However, when comparing New York's first half-runs allowed per game to the second half, and then see how that corresponds with other teams, the Giants performed terribly. Their staff did the worst job holding up five times in his nine full seasons. Terry, as manager, needs to take some blame for this. It was his job to pace the team and handle his staff appropriately.

The Giants also suffered offensive letdowns in the second half. It was not as severe as their annual pitcher wilting, but it existed. One factor that probably hurt the Giants was Terry's unwillingness to rest his backstops. During Terry's reign, the most games caught by any catcher in the NL was Gus Mancuso, who had 144 for the Giants in 1933, Terry's first full season. That was one of four times Mancuso led all National League catchers in games played under Terry. His successor, Harry Danning, paced the senior circuit's backstops in three more seasons. While Terry's use of catchers does not explain all of the late summer offensive malaise, it did not help.

7

❖

The Modern Manager
Emerges, 1951–1976

The second, and perhaps most impressive, bunching of managerial retirements happened in the early 1950s. On June 18, 1950, the Boston Red Sox, who began the year expecting to compete for the pennant, dropped their fifth straight game, falling to 31–28. Manager Joe McCarthy clearly had seen enough, as he resigned, ending his illustrious career. Almost exactly one year later, Billy Southworth — managing Boston's other team, the Braves— reached a similar conclusion, and also retired from the profession. Perhaps the biggest news of all occurred between those departures when Connie Mack belatedly put himself out to pasture after a half-century running the A's. It was the only time in baseball history three Cooperstown-bound managers left the game in such short order. Also, two more pennant-winning managers left the profession after 1950: Eddie Dyer of the Cardinals and Burt Shotton with the Dodgers. Finally, barely a month after Southworth stepped down, the Chicago Cubs fired former world champion manager Frankie Frisch, ending his dugout career. That sextet had won 26 pennants, 16 World Series titles, and over 9,000 games between them.

As was the case in 1920, these departures corresponded with a crucial change in the game. In the 1920s, run scoring blossomed while the relationship between managers and the front office transformed. After World War II, managers experienced a considerable shift in the way they related to and dealt with their players. Traditionally, managers not only examined their players' performance on the field, but also their lives outside it. Managers enforced codes of conduct dictating off-hours behavior, such as nighttime curfew rules. That largely (though not entirely) fell by the wayside as a national cultural change engulfed baseball.

Over ten million young men had gone off to fight in the war, in some cases for several years. Upon coming home, that generation wanted more leeway in controlling their destiny, especially outside of work. Additionally, the affluence of the postwar nation furthered desires for personal autonomy. Alongside the economic boom, the automobile became more pervasive than it had been previously, helping people achieve greater control of their day-to-day existence. Both prosperity and the car gave people a greater sense of control, and desire to exercise individual autonomy. America had enjoyed years of prosperity before the war, but nothing compared to the boom that came afterwards. The new cultural environment affected those too young to have fought in the war. The younger generation, like the veterans, also wanted this greater degree of personal choice in their lifestyle. While America was hardly a wide-open society in the 1950s, it was certainly a far less chaperoned place that it had previously been.

Managers needed to adjust to this new reality. There was no singular moment when the game shifted to a more hands-off policy toward its players. Some skippers had ignored curfews before the war and others enforced those policies well after 1945, but a tipping point occurred, and the 1950–51 managerial exodus serves as the best approximation for this change in manager-player relations. Some managers, including several who retired at the mid-century mark, experienced considerable turbulence in relations with their players after the war, despite generally unremarkable relations beforehand. Southworth, after years of running young Cardinal clubs without any major incidents, suddenly had nonstop friction with a veteran Braves unit. Frisch constantly carped about the youth of America. Even McCarthy, long considered a gentleman manager, became quite a bit more agitated. A generation after losing power to the GM, managers began to lose control of their players as well.

At the same time managers experienced this significant social change, the entire sport (and entire nation) underwent a much vaster revolution that managers also had to contend with: integration. By and large, managers handled it effectively. The nature of the sport helped the process go more smoothly in it than across society as a whole. A team is easier to integrate than a nation because baseball's goals are much easier to define. The purpose is to outscore the opponent in order to win, while the purpose of life is far less clear. Since the goal of a game is obvious, even some bigots could work with blacks. For example, in 1901 spring training, John McGraw tried to break the game's racial segregation by passing off a black player named Charley Grant as an Indian. Though McGraw was willing to play blacks, he was hardly without prejudice. At an exhibition game in Springfield, Illinois, in 1908, local citizens presented him with a piece of rope that had been used to lynch a black man in town earlier that year. Ghoulishly, McGraw said he was honored and kept it as a keepsake for the rest of the season.

Though the game was easier to integrate than the nation, some managers still proved unable or unwilling to adjust at the mid-century. However, the worst cases rarely lasted long on the job. When the St. Louis Browns signed a pair of black players in 1947, manager Muddy Ruel made no effort to welcome them. After Willard Brown, one of the pioneers, hit an inside-the-park home run, Ruel did nothing when outfielder Jeff Heath responded by destroying Brown's bat in front of the entire team. Ruel prioritized race over talent in what proved to be his only season as big league manager. Ben Chapman, who managed the Phillies in the late 1940s, gave Jackie Robinson the nastiest bench jockeying the infielder ever received. Chapman lost his job in mid–1948 and was never hired again as a big league manager. Whatever their personal feelings, for purposes of job security managers had to at least grudgingly accept integration.

Rumors have long swirled that certain clubs and managers used quotas on the number of blacks they would let on the roster and/or put on the field simultaneously. There are clear reasons to think this occurred with different teams at various points in time, but it is hard to pin down. Neither Retrosheet nor Baseball-Reference.com lists a player's race, so it would be excruciatingly time-consuming to determine if a particular manager consistently refused to start more than a certain number of blacks in a game. Though integration had a much larger impact on the game and society as a whole, the shift in off-field relations between players and managers had a greater impact on the nature of the job.

Finally, at mid-century, another difficult to pin down development occurred — managers lost control over the roster. Branch Rickey's generation had given the front office power over player development, but managers initially had discretion over which veterans were on the team. It is impossible to determine when the shift toward the front office occurred, because it happened at different times for various franchises. Bill James argued the first time a GM took complete control was likely Larry MacPhail with the early 1940s Dodgers, and their executives followed MacPhail's lead. The mid-century departure of numerous respected managers makes an appropriate a marker for this shift as anything.

Once managers lost control of the roster and their players' nightlife, they just had to focus on the game and the clubhouse. This marked a decline in managerial authority, which two events in 1960 signified. First, the Tigers and Indians traded their managers: Jimmy Dykes and Joe Gordon. In the early 1900s that would have been as unthinkable as a trade of GMs would be in the early 2000s. Second, the Cubs made an even more telling internal move. They swapped their manager, Charlie Grimm, for their broadcaster, Lou Boudreau. Instead of being the franchise's master architect, a manager was now a well-regarded functionary. He still played an important role, but his powers were not as expansive as in the past.

By the early 1950s, the modern manager had finally emerged. He looked after the players, provided he knew his limits in monitoring them after hours. While his formal powers may have declined, managers still were the central authority figure all players contended with in the increasingly diverse clubhouse.

WALTER ALSTON

> W/L Record: 2,040–1,613 (.558)
> Managed: Full Seasons: Dodgers 1954–75
>   Majority in: Dodgers 1976
>   Minority of: (none)
> Birnbaum Database: +904 runs
>   Individual Hitters: +68 runs
>   Individual Pitchers: +459 runs
>   Pythagenpat Difference: +245 runs
>   Team Offense: +156 runs
>   Team Defense: -24 runs
> Team Characteristics: He generally practiced small ball. He did not like to replace his starters, whether it be a pitcher or position player. Alston leaned heavily on starting pitchers, presiding over ten 300-inning seasons— no other skipper since 1920 tops six. A pitcher won twenty games for Alston on thirteen different occasions, the most by any NL manager since World War II. He loved pitchers who could blow opponents away, as 22 different 200-strikeout seasons occurred during his tenure. No other manager oversaw more than eleven.
> LPA: 3.11 (through 1965 only)   LPA+: 82 (through 1965 only)

For much of his career, Walter Alston received minimal respect as people viewed him as a cog in the Dodger machine. When he became Brooklyn's manager in 1954, every circumstance conspired to reduce his public stature. First, New York's other managers greatly overshadowed him. The Yankees employed Casey Stengel, who had just won his fifth consecutive world title. The Giants had Leo Durocher, who delivered that franchise's first world title in 21 years during Alston's rookie season. Moreover, not only were Stengel and Durocher established successes, but both were also outspoken, vibrant personalities who made good copy for the reporters. In contrast, the colorless Alston had played one game of major league baseball and had spent most of his adult life as a minor league manager. He appeared bush league.

The way the Dodgers hired Alston further diminished him. The Dodgers shocked much of baseball when they refused to re-sign Charlie Dressen, the cocky man who had won two pennants in Brooklyn. When Dressen demanded a multiyear contract, owner Walter O'Malley refused; instead he hired Alston, who accepted a one-year deal without qualm. Further minimizing Alston's stature, he became baseball's first great manager who never had control over the roster. Leo Durocher did not have control when he ran Brooklyn in the 1940s, but he was given a free hand to remake the Giants in the early 1950s. Many believed Alston was nothing more than O'Malley's lackey.

There was some truth to the criticisms of Alston. He not only lacked control of the roster, but he even lacked full control of his coaching staff. O'Malley would hire established baseball men (including both Dressen and Durocher at different times) for "creative tension." Alston never received a multiyear contract, instead surviving on 23 consecutive single-season deals. Even his own club seemingly viewed Alston as replaceable.

However, that does not preclude him from being a good manager. In fact, that does not preclude him from being a great manager. It merely means he had a very different role to play than the best managers who preceded him. Though he did not control the roster, he did an excellent job utilizing it. If a cog, he was the most efficient one possible.

The best way to explain Alston's success is with an analogy: he was to baseball what Michael Curtiz was to the movies. Curtiz was a longtime director for Warner Brothers in the first half of the twentieth century. His greatest film was easily *Casablanca*, but he made a host of others that are still watched and beloved, including *Yankee Doodle Dandy*, *White Christmas*, *Angels with Dirty Faces*, *The Adventures of Robin Hood*, and *Mildred Pierce*. His strengths and weaknesses as a director mirrored Alston's as manager. A Hollywood historian once noted Curtiz would never have survived in the current Hollywood environment. Now directors are expected to be artists who create and develop projects into motion pictures. Curtiz was purely a craftsman, who took projects assigned to him and did his best to flesh them out. He was a cog in the studio's machine.

Still, he was a great director. Take *Casablanca*, for example. Roger Ebert once noted that no one ever talks about great camera shots in Casablanca—there are none. It is the most beloved film that lacks any memorable directorial flourishes. Despite lacking overt zest, no serious film buff ever says, "You know what would've made *Casablanca* better?" It is *Casablanca*—it could not be better. With a cast and script that good, all Curtiz had to do was focus on telling the story as efficiently as possible without trying to look like a genius. His sense on when to cut to reaction shots, when to switch scenes, and how to handle different characters was perfectly appropriate. He never needed to impress people because he was so good at all the basic parts of directing that the general public fails to notice.

That was Alston. He managed a great franchise with the best farm system in the game. He did not need to shock the world with managerial ingenuity, he just had his team play smart baseball. He trusted his players, guided them as well as he could, and played the percentages. Along the way, the Dodgers won more World Series titles for him than they have for all the other managers in franchise history combined. Only John McGraw captured more National League titles.

Alston's secret was to not try to be a genius. Rather than amaze the world with his brilliant plans, Alston flexibly adapted his strategies based on the talent at hand. Initially, he had a strong offensive team, so he let them hit. In the 1960s, when a new crop emerged that relied more on speed, pitching, and defense, Alston shifted his approach. His team continually ran the bases and bunted runners over, engaging in more small ball activity than other squad of the day. Under the circumstances, it was sensible. Offensive scoring was down across the game as a whole; Dodger Stadium further depressed runs. Alston's hitters were not the type who would slug their way to a pennant. With pitchers like Sandy Koufax and Don Drysdale routinely taking the mound, the Dodgers did not need a blizzard of runs to win most games. Furthermore, he selectively practiced small ball by becoming the king of the eighth-inning bunt. In the last half-century, only five teams have had more than twenty sacrifices in that frame: Alston managed four of them. When one run could decide a game late, he lunged at it, trusting his pitchers to hold the fort.

Maury Wills's experience in Los Angeles best demonstrates how Alston adeptly handled his team. Wills was 27 years old when he first played over 100 games in a season. Yet in that season Alston had him attempt more stolen bases than any NL player in 35 years. Many managers would have let the speedy Wills run, but few would be that fearless with an aging unknown quantity. Alston did, and two years later Wills established a new twentieth century record with 104 stolen bases in a season.

Alston was also flexible with his starting pitchers. When Alston arrived in the big leagues, leveraging was a well-established practice, and he initially went along with it. To acclimate his young starters, he had them routinely face lousier opponents and avoid the most dangerous lineups. For example, in Koufax's first three seasons he only had one start against the Braves, who were the best rival team. Meanwhile, he faced the doormat Cubs in nearly 30 percent of his starts.

Leveraging starters helped Alston win the 1959 pennant. Don Drysdale, though not yet in his prime, was already the team's best pitcher, as he led the league in strikeouts. Alston had Drysdale face the defending pennant-winning Braves whenever possible. In eight starts and a six-inning relief outing, Drysdale personally accounted for 5 percent of all innings thrown against them that year, with 69.3. No pitcher since then has thrown that many innings against one rival. The Dodgers and Braves ended the season tied, with Los Angeles winning the best-of-three playoff. With other pitchers on the mound, Alston's squads likely would have lost at least one more regular season game to the Braves and not forced the playoff.

Despite that experience, Alston was at the forefront of moving to a set rotation. In 1959, he only had one dependable starter. With the emergence of Koufax (and later Claude Osteen, Don Sutton, and others), it made more sense to put his arms out there as often as possible with regular rest. Alston became a great champion of the four-man rotation, with pitchers starting 40 or more games for him fifteen times, a half-dozen times more than any other twentieth century manager. As the Dodgers continued producing more solid pitchers from their farm system, Alston later helped create the five-man rotation. Pitchers on the 1973 Dodgers started games on four days rest 111 times, which set a (since eclipsed) record. Rather than wed himself exclusively to specific strategies, Alston did what best fit the talent on hand.

Throughout it all, Alston was best served by his trademark trait, patience. He knew he had superior talent, so he did not panic when things went awry. His patience paid off not only over the course of a season, but also with players. He stuck with Koufax for a half-dozen years while the flame-throwing lefty floundered. In Koufax's seventh year, he had his typical underwhelming start, allowing 54 baserunners in 37.3 innings for a 4.58 ERA in early 1961. Alston did not blink, and Koufax finally responded, developing into a very good pitcher that year and a great one afterwards. Similarly, Don Sutton trudged through his first five seasons, posting a 66–73 record while his teammates went 350–320. Alston left him in the rotation, allowing Sutton to come into his own. First baseman Wes Parker had a disastrous sophomore campaign, hitting .238 with eight homers. Alston kept him in the everyday lineup and he rebounded. In 1959–60, Johnny Roseboro hit .224 at ages 26 and 27. Alston kept the faith, slotting Roseboro in the everyday lineup for seven more years, in which he improved noticeably. Not only did Alston stick with these players in the downward turns, but the club kept winning in the process. He successfully balanced the demands for winning today with patience required to win down the road.

Alston's patience could cost the Dodgers, as it infamously led to the most famous mistake of his career. He blew the 1962 pennant when, in the final game of a best-of-three playoff against the Giants, he held Don Drysdale in reserve to start the first game of the World Series, a game which never came for LA. Admittedly, Drysdale threw 102 pitches the day before, but with the game slipping away in the ninth, the fastballer twice asked Alston if he should warm up, only to be told he would start in the World Series the next day instead. While that was not a good plan for such a high stakes game, in the marathon of the season Alston kept his team playing as well as they could.

Alston never tried to be a genius. Thus he topped almost everyone who thought they were.

ALVIN DARK

> **W/L Record:** 994–954 (.510)
>
> **Managed:** Full Seasons: San Francisco 1961–64; Kansas City 1966; Cleveland 1968–70; Oakland 1974–5
>
> Majority in: Kansas City 1967; Cleveland 1971; San Diego 1977
>
> Minority of: (none)
>
> **Birnbaum Database:** -18 runs
>
> Individual Hitters: +8 runs
>
> Individual Pitchers: -46 runs
>
> Pythagenpat Difference: -65 runs
>
> Team Offense: +79 runs
>
> Team Defense: +6 runs
>
> **Team Characteristics:** He had young lineups. The 1967 A's, whom he ran for most of the season, were the youngest team of the twentieth century. Dark's teams usually stole their share of bases and he liked to issue intentional walks and go to the bullpen. His squads generally played worse in the second half, especially his pitchers. The starting players (including designated hitter) accounted for 88.3 percent of all plate appearances on the 1975 A's, the highest percentage attained by any team with a DH.
>
> **LPA:** 3.63 (through 1965 only)   **LPA+:** 105 (through 1965 only)

Dark garnered as little respect as is possible while leading one team to a world title and another to a pennant. In fact, both squads he took to the World Series, the 1962 Giants and 1974 A's, undermined his reputation.

The Giants contained so much talent—with a core that included Willie Mays, Juan Marichal, Orlando Cepeda, Willie McCovey, and Felipe Alou—that Dark received little credit for their success. Instead, he drew attention to himself in a most unwanted manner, publicly stating that black players lacked guts and Hispanics had a poor work ethic. Making the situation worse, many of San Francisco's minorities did not get along with Dark. Orlando Cepeda remembered that Dark once took all the Hispanic players aside and told them to stop speaking Spanish in the clubhouse. Willie Mays stopped speaking to Dark for the final months of 1964. Nowadays, it is hard to imagine any team would hire him to manage after that, yet Dark was hired four more times. That partially occurred because Dark changed. For example, Felipe Alou had some trouble with Dark when he played under him with the Giants. However, according to Cal Fussman's *After Jackie: Pride, Prejudice, and Baseball's Forgotten History, An Oral History*, Alou later said he came not only to appreciate Dark, but also to love him after Dark grew as a person. Cepeda let go of his bitterness after receiving a heartfelt apology note from Dark.

The next time Dark had a really good team, with Oakland, he found himself in a very volatile situation. In 1974, Charles Finley, the franchise's megalomaniac owner, hired Dark to replace Dick Williams. Oakland had already won two consecutive titles, so Dark would not be credited with any future successes they attained. Even worse, the dynamic between Finley and the team was poisonous. Over the years Finley had gone out of the way to humiliate, bully, and alienate his players. The situation bottomed out during the 1973 World Series when he coerced second baseman Mike Andrews into signing a fraudulent medical report claiming he was injured. It was Finley's way of punishing Andrews for making some game-losing errors earlier in the Series. The public discovered and protested, and the players were openly sickened. In this environment, Williams, fed up with Finley, announced to the team he would not return to manage Oakland in 1974. Williams further displayed his personal independence and bolstered anti–Finley feelings in the dugout by letting Andrews pinch-hit, despite Finley's explicit order to not use the infielder again.

Dark arrived in this mess, appearing subservient to the detested owner. Dark would joke to reporters about running his lineup cards past Finley for approval, making clear he did not want to ruffle his boss's feathers. Finley had previously ordered Williams whom to start, but Williams never seemed as obsequious about it. Even while obeying, Williams's rugged demeanor gave him a certain sense of independence. Besides, after the Mike Andrews incident, the club was less willing to tolerate Finley's guff. As a result, the players openly disdained Dark. For a while it looked like he would have a player rebellion, but it was not to be. The team had too much pride, and wanted to prove to the world and themselves they could win a third World Series. They accomplished their goal, but never showed love for Dark in the process.

CHARLIE DRESSEN

    W/L Record: 1,008–973 (.509)
    Managed: Full Seasons: Cincinnati 1935–37; Brooklyn 1951–53; Washington
                    1955–56; Milwaukee 1960; Detroit 1964
                 Majority in: Milwaukee 1961; Detroit 1963, 1965
                 Minority of: Cincinnati 1934; Washington 1957; Detroit 1966
    Birnbaum Database: +49 runs
                 Individual Hitters: +61 runs
                 Individual Pitchers: -164 runs
                 Pythagenpat Difference: +126 runs
                 Team Offense: +76 runs
                 Team Defense: -50 runs
    Team Characteristics: Dressen's teams featured strong offenses, but were below
                 average at run prevention. In his later years at least, he made plenty
                 of in-game substitutions for his position players. He rarely handed
                 out intentional walks. His starting catchers received more rest than
                 most of their peers did.
    LPA: 4.83   **LPA+:** 112

Perhaps even more than Wilbert Robinson, Charlie Dressen reveals the role personality plays in the public's perception of managers. Dressen's most famous managerial stint came with the Dodgers in the early 1950s. His predecessor, Burt Shotton, had won two pennants but had never earned much respect from the fans. Branch Rickey's system delivered a tremendous amount of talent to the Dodgers and Shotton seemed like a mere caretaker. Dressen also won a pair of pennants, just as Shotton had, yet the public heralded him as a savant. They had the exact same talent; if anything Dressen had the advantage as more men entered their prime under him. Alston, who succeeded Dressen, basked in the shadows and repeatedly needed to win the World Series to avoid getting fired after he became Dodger manager. There was little difference between the regular season successes they enjoyed, but the quiet men received minimal credit.

Dressen was anything but quiet. He may be the cockiest manager in baseball history. There is an anecdote about him, usually dated from his days in Cincinnati, that summarizes his demeanor. Early in a game, his team returned to the dugout after getting shellacked. Dressen told them not to worry — just keep it close and he would think of something to win it. He sincerely believed his brains meant more than their brawn. During the sizable gap in his managerial career, he served as Leo Durocher's assistant coach with the Dodgers. Dressen made sure that the media recognized that many of Durocher's maneuvers were his ideas. Between his self-promotion and his genuinely formidable intellect, most who encountered Dressen thought highly of him.

Ultimately, however, people are better off recognizing the limits of their capabilities. Alston did, which was why he had a much more successful career. Dressen's maneuvers led his squads to victory when correct, but could also cause defeat when faulty. Most notably, he made a terrible decision in the finale of the 1951 three-game playoff against the New York Giants that cost the team the pennant. Bobby Thomson concluded the contest by hitting baseball's most famous home run off of reliever Ralph Branca, whom Dressen had just brought into the game. Sitting in the front office watching the game, Branch Rickey's numbers cruncher Allan Roth noted that Thomson owned Branca, having hit multiple homers off him. Checking with Roth would have been an anathema to Dressen's style, however.

After the 1953 season, Dressen was so sure his brilliance won the ballgames instead of his players' abilities that he refused to sign with the Dodgers unless they gave him a multi-year contract. They refused, and Dressen spent the rest of his career learning the hard way that the quality of players meant more than managerial intelligence.

In his final full season as manager in 1964, Charlie Dressen presided over the final great moment in the history of starting pitcher leveraging. Here are the starts for Hank Aguirre and Mickey Lolich, two of Detroit's most important arms, against opposing teams that year, along with the winning percentages for those squads:

Team	Pct	Aguirre	Lolich
NYY	.611	6	5
CWS	.605	4	6
BAL	.599	5	4
LAA	.506	3	3
CLE	.488	4	5
MIN	.488	2	5
BOS	.444	0	1
WAS	.383	1	2
KCA	.352	2	2

In all, Aguirre had an AOWP+ of 109, and Lolich's was 106. These men had barely a third of the team's starts, but they had a majority of the turns against the Yankees and White Sox and exactly half against the Orioles. Conversely, they accounted for less than 15 percent of all starts against the three bottom teams.

From a purely storytelling perspective, it would be perfect if this was the end of leveraging in baseball. The practice should have died out with an aging manager at the end of his time. Alas, as noted in Chapter 3, Gil Hodges mucked up the narrative by engaging in some leveraging with the 1965 Senators. Still, Hodges primarily spot started his ancillary arms, while Dressen made leveraging crucial to using central pitchers—something that never happened again. Dressen was the perfect manager for leveraging to end on. The strategy provided managers a sense of control, that his wits meant more than anything else in determining the team's success. That was always Dressen's hallmark.

LEO DUROCHER

W/L Record: 2,008–1,709 (.540)

Managed: Full Seasons: Brooklyn 1939–46; New York (NL) 1949–55; Chicago (NL) 1966–71; Houston 1973

Majority in: New York (NL) 1948; Chicago (NL) 1972
Minority of: Brooklyn 1948; Houston 1972
Birnbaum Database: +512 runs
Individual Hitters: +225 runs
Individual Pitchers: +91 runs
Pythagenpat Difference: -134 runs
Team Offense: +333 runs
Team Defense: -3 runs
Team Characteristics: Durocher's teams had strong offenses. He avoided using his bench as he preferred a set lineup and did not use many pinch-hitters or mid-game replacements. He used plenty of relief pitchers relative to his peers, but as he grew older that ceased to be true. Ultimately, Durocher became the last prominent manager to never have a closer record twenty saves in a season.
LPA: 5.35 (through 1965 only)   **LPA+:** 107 (through 1965 only)

Only three men in baseball history have managed in five different decades: Connie Mack (who managed in seven), John McGraw, and Leo Durocher. Currently, Joe Torre, Tony LaRussa, and Bobby Cox threaten to join that club.

Unlike the others listed above, Durocher's career contained a decade-long gap, which serves as an appropriate breakpoint for evaluating him. On one side of it, he was one of the savviest and sharpest managers in the game. Afterward, he was a past-his-prime codger surviving on his reputation and self-promotional skills.

Blasting Durocher for his tenure with the Cubs sounds odd. After all, Chicago, which had been a doormat for twenty years before Durocher arrived, reeled off six consecutive winning seasons under him, and then flopped once he left. However, the team was successful despite, not because of, him. Durocher receives a score of -155 runs from the Birnbaum Database for his Chicago sojourn. The franchise had a winning record in those years, making his score that much more striking. It is extremely difficult to score negatively in those circumstances, especially when the stretch is entirely surrounded by extended losing periods. Only two other managers in the 1960s had similarly negative scores while piloting consistently quality squads: Dave Bristol with the Reds and Sam Mele with the Twins. That is not the company one wants to keep.

Durocher did not elevate the Cubs. Instead scouts like Buck O'Neill, who signed Billy Williams and Lou Brock, did. Durocher happened to be the manager of record for the Cubs when their best crop of young players in decades reached its prime. That Cub bunch is often pointed out as a squad that could have been a winner, but failed to live up to its potential. Looking back, the Cubs falling short in 1969 was less striking than their inability to seriously threaten in the surrounding seasons. Despite a core of Williams, Fergie Jenkins, and Ron Santo, they only had one other campaign that topped 84 victories, and that was only 87 in 1967.

Several years ago I read two books back-to-back: Durocher's autobiography, *Nice Guys Finish Last*, and *Jocks* by Leonard Schecter. It was an interesting contrast as Schecter peeled back the self-promotion that lay beneath *Nice Guys*. Though Durocher did not pretend to be a nice guy in his book, he wanted to convince the public that he embodied a particular ideal: all-out effort. In his first chapter, titled "I Come to Kill You," he claimed he would run over his mother for a win, a sentiment that pervaded the rest of the book. He argued that his drive led his teams to success in his early days, but caused him difficulties in his later years. By the 1960s, Durocher contented that the players lacked the same fire in the belly, preferring to be pampered instead.

Alternately, Schecter's book contained a two-page section that in many ways demolished the image Durocher conveyed. It was a biting composite character called the Big League Manager that Durocher fit all too well. The Big League Manager was working for his third team. He told everyone that he was in it for the love of the game, but that was just a line. In reality, he had developed a love for finery and the high life as a player, and remaining in baseball was the only way he could afford it. He had a girl in every city, and wives who came and went, furthering his need for money. Though he complained about the modern player, he personally was on autopilot. When *Jocks* came out, Durocher was with the Cubs, his third team. In Durocher's autobiography, his wives arrive and disappear with regularity. He openly admits he loved the expensive lifestyle as a player, living beyond his means at times. He certainly complained about baby boomer players frequently.

Durocher's days with the Cubs indicate that he was on autopilot. In 1968, Chicago catcher Randy Hundley played 160 games, which remains the most games any catcher has been asked to appear in during one season. In one of the least shocking developments in the history of cause and effect, Hundley melted as the season wore on. After hitting .252 in the first half, he trudged his way to an anemic .201 average along with an on-base percentage of .264 and a slugging percentage of .283 in Chicago's last 81 games—all of which he played in. Durocher had always preferred a set lineup, but with the Cubs he crossed the line into somnambulant behavior. This mistake was especially damning for Durocher, whose managerial reputation was built on outthinking the opponent.

Hundley's experience reveals the ways Durocher's managerial tendencies had changed by hardening. In each of Durocher's first three seasons with the Cubs, the starting eight players had 76 percent of the team's plate appearances, something Durocher's teams had only done that twice in his seventeen New York campaigns. Starters for the 1969 Cubs accounted for "only" 74.5 percent of the team's plate appearances, but that was because the club had a gaping hole in center field. The Cubs offenses consistently melted down on him as the season wore on. From 1966 to 1971, the Cubs scored 4.41 runs per game before the All-Star Game, but only 4.06 afterwards. The game's annual temperature curve partially explains this decline (NL-wide run scoring declined from 4.07 to 3.94 after the break), but not most of it. In 1969, the Cubs had the league's most proficient offense for most of the season, but barely scored three runs per game in September.

One of the most obvious signs of his unwillingness to make proper moves centered on Ernie Banks. Though, Durocher did not think Banks could play very well by the mid-to-late 1960s due to his chronic knee problems, he still played Mr. Cub 150 games a year for three straight seasons. In his autobiography, Durcoher lamely claimed that there would be revolution in Chicago's streets otherwise. Fear of fan criticism is not only a dubious excuse, but also entirely out of line with Durocher's self-created mythology.

Despite Durocher's later limitations, in his earlier phase he had been a legitimately great manager. The Birnbaum Database gives him a score of +591 runs in his stints with the Dodgers and Giants. Both by that database and by reputation, his strongest point was always his in-game maneuvers. He declined at the end, but almost all managers do; 1968 was 27 years after his first pennant. In all baseball history, only Connie Mack won pennants more separated than that (29 years between 1902 and 1931).

Durocher always had a reputation as an obnoxious human being, but even his critics readily acknowledged his impressive acumen. One story (that has nothing to do with baseball) simultaneously embodies Durocher's intelligence and controversial nature. Durocher said that when on a first date with a girl, early in the evening he would firmly pat her rump. One of two things would happen. Either she would not mind, in which case Durocher knew right away he was in store for a fun evening. Alternately, she could be upset, in which case she was not the girl for him anyway, and he had the entire night before him to find someone else. That story is crass, rude, and seedy—yet downright brilliant. In other words, it was quintessentially Durocher.

Gil Hodges

W/L Record: 660–753 (.467)
Managed: Full Seasons: Washington 1964–67; New York (NL) 1968–71
        Majority in: Washington 1963
        Minority of: (none)
Birnbaum Database: +65 runs
        Individual Hitters: -58 runs
        Individual Pitchers: +99 runs
        Pythagenpat Difference: +62 runs
        Team Offense: +23 runs
        Team Defense: -61 runs
Team Characteristics: Hodges used his bench as much as he could, in part because he oversaw terrible offenses that were routinely among the league's least effective at scoring runs. He went to his bullpen frequently, and his relievers were generally better than his starters. He was usually among the league leaders in intentional walks. His teams suffered far more strikeouts than they inflicted.
LPA: 4.32 (through 1965 only)   **LPA+**: 151 (through 1965 only)

More than any other manager in baseball history, Hodges relied on his bench. Four times—in 1964, 1965, 1967, and 1969—three of his reserves played in at least 100 games. On all other teams from 1963 to 1971, 183 rosters in all, only seven had a trio of backups appears in 100 games. In 1966, two of Hodges's backups played in 100 games and a third was in 94. The 1971 squad featured three reserves who played in at least 97 games. In all, he had twenty bench players appear in 100 games in his nine campaigns, twice as many as typical. In part this was because Hodges had underwhelming lineups, but he also made sure all his starters had days off, even his rare quality ones. In nine years on the job, only twice did one of his players appear in 155 games. From 1963 to 1971, the other teams had 285 occasions where a starter played in that many contests. Only eight times did one of Hodges's players appear in 150 games. Other baseball teams averaged that 2.45 times per season. Hodges's second baseman played 130 games once. He never had a first baseman do that. None of his right fielders ever played 140 games.

Hodges generally adopted a similar approach with his pitchers. Rather than rely too much on his starters, he heavily involved his bullpen. In 1965, Ron Kline tied an American League record with 29 saves. In 1966, the Senators became the first baseball team with four men with at least 50 relief appearances. In 1967, Hodges again had four men with 50 relief appearances, alongside a fifth man with 46 relief stints and a sixth with 38. Hodges used fewer relievers with the Mets, but then again Tom Seaver and Jerry Koosman anchored his rotation.

Hodges's poor career winning percentage reflected his rosters, not his managerial acumen. It is likely that no manager since World War II was given two jobs in as dreary circumstances as Hodges. The Senators finished last in run scoring three times for Hodges and the Mets' hitters were only slightly better. Hodges never oversaw a player who recorded 100 RBIs, or drew 100 walks, or slapped out 200 hits in a season. He only presided over one 30-home-run campaign from his players, one .400 OBP, and two .300 hitters. None of his batters ever hit more than 30 doubles.

His first job came with the Washington Senators in mid–1963. They had just completed back-to-back 100-loss seasons in their first two seasons, and were off to an even worse start, going 14–27 before Hodges appeared. Washington's record improved every year Hodges served as their manager. By 1967, he pushed Washington into sixth place with a 76–85 record despite the club possessing the league's worst offense and a dismal pitching staff. Still, improvement came too slowly for the front office, which sold him to the Mets for a prospect and $100,000. The next year Washington dropped into last place. Hodges's tenure was the franchise's best stretch until the mid–1970s.

Prior to Hodges's arrival in New York, the Mets had lost over two-thirds of the games in franchise history. It was a moral victory that they lost only 196 games in 1966–67. However, this squad actually had some of the makings of a quality team as Seaver and Koosman formed a dynamic one-two punch in the rotation. Unfortunately, Hodges had very little else. Shifting gears from his Washington days, he leaned heavily on his two main starters and delivered the Mets their first 70-win season in 1968. That was Hodges's last losing season. The Mets famously shocked the world by winning it all under Hodges in 1969, but even after the miracle faded he kept them over .500 in the next pair of seasons. Three of the five best pre–Davey Johnson Mets clubs came under Hodges.

RALPH HOUK

W/L Record: 1,619–1,531 (.514)
Managed: Full Seasons: New York (AL) 1961–63, 1967–73; Detroit 1974–78;
        Boston 1981–84
        Majority in: New York (AL) 1966
        Minority of: (none)
Birnbaum Database: +308 runs
        Individual Hitters: +87 runs
        Individual Pitchers: +39 runs
        Pythagenpat Difference: +220 runs
        Team Offense: -67 runs
        Team Defense: +29 runs
Team Characteristics: Houk relied on his starting pitchers, whom he used on a set rotation. Similarly, he used a set starting lineup with his position players and avoided making in-game substitutions for them. Houk had above average offenses that rarely played small ball. In 1973, the Yankees had only 27 sacrifice hits, a new record low. His pitchers had good control as only two ever walked 100 batters in a year. One of Houk's hitters qualified for the batting title without ever stealing a base seventeen times; the highest total for any manager.
LPA: 2.45 (through 1965 only)   **LPA+:** 71 (through 1965 only)

In his first season on the job, Ralph Houk won 109 games, the all-time record for a first-year manager. (Earl Weaver had 109 in his first full season, but he managed half of the prior year.) Houk's 1961 squad won the World Series, repeated as world champions the following season, and claimed the pennant in 1963. It was the greatest start any manager ever had, but instead of the beginnings of a Hall of Fame career, Houk never managed in another Fall Classic.

Anyone who begins his career with such a bang will draw attention to himself. That is why Houk's refusal to leverage his starting pitchers, as discussed in Chapter 2, was so influential. Also, Houk's treatment of his players influenced a generation of managers. In *The Man in the Dugout*, Leonard Koppett noted Houk would not publicly criticize his players. Casey Stengel had done so to motivate his athletes, and assert his authority. Houk felt the new generation would respond better to milder treatment. Along with Walter Alston, who similarly treated his players, Houk ushered in a different approach for the triangular relationship between manager, players, and media. That may sound like an overstatement given that Houk was far from the first to refrain from publicly criticizing his players. Managers as far back as Connie Mack had done likewise. Also, numerous managers since Houk blast their players in the press. However, the game experienced a shift in the prevailing way managers negotiated this aspect of the job in the 1960s, and Houk was at the change's forefront.

To ensure players respected his command, Houk relied on his personality. Nicknamed "the Major," Houk exuded authority. His nickname came from the rank he earned upon discharge from the army during World War II. That background gave him the ability to make timely and appropriate decisions, focus on what really mattered, and not sweat the small stuff — which caused people to defer to his leadership.

Houk's significance as a manager lay in his handling of pitchers. He made Johnny Sain New York's pitching coach. Though Sain had served in that role for one year with the A's, his experience with the Yankees launched his career. He became the most heralded hurler-handler of his day. It is especially interesting such a prestigious pitching coach would establish himself under Houk, given that his team ushered in the popularity of the standardized rotation in those years.

Houk's use of starters had a corollary impact on his bullpens. Standardized starters forced the men in the bullpen to be used in more settled patterns as well. In 1961, Luis Arroyo set a major league record with 29 saves under Houk. Eleven years later, Sparky Lyle set an AL record with 35.

When Houk inserted a reliever, that pitcher was to finish the game. In fact, his relievers lasted longer per outing than anyone in baseball history. Using the splits available at Baseball-Reference.com, the following teams had the most innings per relief appearance of any squad since 1956:

Year	Team	IP/RA	Manager
1974	DET	2.73	Houk
1973	NYY	2.68	Houk
1982	BOS	2.51	Houk
1976	DET	2.51	Houk
1975	DET	2.45	Houk

There are three different franchises in the top finishers, but only one manager. Just think how difficult it must be to average seven or eight outs per appearance. There are always going to be times a reliever has no stuff and needs to be yanked immediately. Some days Houk would bring a new reliever into the game with only one inning left. Yet he still averaged almost three innings per appearance a few times. Forget averaging nearly three innings per relief appearance for a season — when was the last time you saw a reliever do that in one game?

An era bias exists, as all of the sixteen highest finishes, and 35 of the top 36, come from the 1973–82 AL, its first decade with the designated hitter. Yet even among that bunch Houk dominates, as the above list attests. He is the entire top five, and seven of the longest sixteen averages. Also, the 1982 Red Sox performance was completely out of step with how managers handled relievers in the early 1980s. That year only one other club cracked the two innings per appearance barrier.

If you put innings per relief appearance in the Tendencies Database, here are the results:

Most IP Per Relief Appearance

Ralph Houk	0.325
Jack McKeon	0.551
Davey Johnson	0.585
Lou Piniella	0.598
Walter Alston	0.600

Only 39 managers lasted long enough to qualify, but Houk clearly owns first place. His mark of 0.325 is the lowest score of any Tendencies Database inquiry in this book. DH or no DH, Houk liked his relievers to last forever.

With the 1973 Yankees, Lindy McDaniel threw 138.3 innings in 44 calls from the bullpen. Most impressively, on August 4, he pitched an incredible thirteen innings in relief. Three days later he threw 3.7 innings more. Another three days later he lasted four innings. Lyle's teammate, Fred Beene threw 65.7 in fifteen relief games, including an eight-inning appearance in July, and a nine-inning stretch the next month. In 1982, in only 48 appearances, Bob Stanley threw 168.3 innings out of the bullpen. Only 1970s iron man Mike Marshall has topped that. Stanley averaged 3.51 innings per relief appearance in his big season. There have been 4,951 times in baseball history a pitcher has appeared in 25 or more games without ever starting any games. None of the other 4,950 occurrences topped three innings per appearance, let alone Stanley's 3.51.

Due to Houk's tendency to leave relievers in games for prolonged stretches, he virtually never used them on back-to-back days. Adding together innings pitched by men on zero days rest with those who pitched in the second game of a doubleheader after appearing in the first, and plug that into the Tendencies Database, the following managers had their hurlers pitch the least on no rest:

Fewest IP on No Rest

Ralph Houk	1.625
Jim Leyland	1.589
Earl Weaver	1.560
Cito Gaston	1.453
Buck Showalter	1.397

In nineteen years as a manager, Houk used pitchers on back-to-back days 307 times. In comparison, Nationals manager Manny Acta did it 226 times in 2007–08. In 1982, the Red Sox staff threw only 8.7 innings on zero days rest, the lowest total for any team since 1956. Two years later they threw only 17.7 such innings, along with two-thirds of an inning tossed by a man who pitched in both ends of a doubleheader.

FRED HUTCHINSON

W/L Record: 830–827 (.501)
Managed: Full Seasons: Detroit 1953–54; St. Louis 1956–57; Cincinnati 1960–63
　　　　　Majority in: Detroit 1952; St. Louis 1958; Cincinnati 1964
　　　　　Minority of: Cincinnati 1959
Birnbaum Database: -115 runs
　　　　　Individual Hitters: -24 runs
　　　　　Individual Pitchers: -185 runs
　　　　　Pythagenpat Difference: +141 runs
　　　　　Team Offense: -36 runs
　　　　　Team Defense: -11 runs
Team Characteristics: Whenever possible, Hutchinson made sure his offenses
　　　　　had a platoon advantage. He liked to pinch-hit and have runners
　　　　　steal bases, but his teams rarely bunted. He used relievers about as
　　　　　often as most, but he rarely had them appear on consecutive days.
　　　　　As a result, Hutchinson is the only prominent manager whose career

began after World War II to never have a pitcher make 60 relief appearances in a season. He did not like to issue intentional walks.

LPA: 3.71   LPA+: 90

Fred Hutchinson is a rarity — a big league pitcher who became a manager. Hutchinson, Tommy Lasorda and Clark Griffith are the only ones to last a decade on the job. Roger Craig just missed at nine years, and Walter Johnson deserved a longer shot. Hutchinson was also distinctive by being the last hurler to serve as player-manager. For what it is worth, Craig and Lasorda — the two most prominent pitchers-turned-managers since Hutchinson — were also two of the oldest rookie managers who went on to have memorable careers.

Thus it is especially striking that Hutchinson scores so wretchedly with pitchers in the Birnbaum Database. The problem lies with the Detroit Tigers. Hutchinson's first full season running the team, 1953, was a complete disaster for the pitching staff. In the 1952–53 off-season the Tigers traded away rotation anchor Virgil Trucks for a trio of forgettable position players. That opened up a void in Detroit's rotation that turned into a black hole, sucking in the rest of the pitchers. Adjusted for park, only one man on the entire staff had an above-average ERA. That was Hutchinson himself, who threw under ten innings in his career's swan song. Three men anchored the staff: Ted Gray, Billy Hoeft, and Ned Garver. Combined, they threw nearly 600 innings with an ERA of 4.63. The year before they had a cumulative ERA of 4.01.

Perhaps the black hole simile is inappropriate. That makes it sound like the staff slowly imploded as the season went along. In reality, Detroit began the year disastrously, allowing ten runs in the season opener and eleven in the second contest. The Tigers started the year 6–20, allowing 181 runs in that stretch while the other AL clubs averaged 97 runs allowed. Hutchinson began his career with a record of 33–76; rarely has a successful manager had such an inauspicious start. After 1953, he scores positively in the Birnbaum Database, with an overall mark of +112 runs, though his mark with individual pitchers remains negative.

Hutchinson had a very good reputation when he managed. His main claim to fame comes from the 1961 Reds, who won a surprise pennant. However, as Bill James noted in the original *Historical Abstract*, general manager Bill DeWitt deserved much of the credit for that squad. DeWitt had a tremendous off-season, pulling off a series of moves that turned the also-ran into a perennial contender, most notably landing Gene Freese and Joey Jay, who both made the 1961 All-Star team. DeWitt's achievement glanced off the public's skull, so much of the reputation Hutchinson earned that year belonged to the GM.

Fans thought the Reds could have won the pennant in 1964, and they likely have a point as the squad just missed making the World Series. The Reds actually played better when Hutchinson was away, but the problem was that Hutchinson, dying by inches as the year went on, was not able to give the game and team as much attention as he otherwise would. That was especially costly because his toughness had been one of his strong points. He was known as a strict but fair man, with no tolerance for lazy play.

Al Lopez

W/L Record: 1,410–1,004 (.584)
Managed: Full Seasons: Cleveland 1951–56; Chicago (AL) 1957–65
          Majority in: (none)
          Minority of: Chicago (AL) 1968–69
Birnbaum Database: +836 runs
          Individual Hitters: +40 runs
          Individual Pitchers: +472 runs

Pythagenpat Difference: +183 runs

Team Offense: +18 runs

Team Defense: +123 runs

Team Characteristics: Lopez's teams were solid in all phases of the game, though they were a bit better at run prevention than scoring. He leaned heavily on his starters, though he gave his catchers plenty of rest.

LPA: 4.11   LPA+: 104

Lopez's career helps trace the course and extinction of starting pitcher leveraging. In Cleveland, he oversaw one of the best collections of starting pitchers in history with Early Wynn, Bob Lemon, Bob Feller, and Mike Garcia. Such impressive pitching quality and depth put Lopez in an ideal position to adopt the Pat Moran approach of maximizing innings—but he did not. The table below lists what percentage of each of the Big Four's starts came against rival squads during Lopez's tenure (and all four aces pitched in Cleveland during that span). The teams are ordered from most to least wins accumulated from 1951 to 1956:

Team	Lemon	Wynn	Feller	Garcia
NYY	17.8%	19.2%	8.3%	13.8%
CWS	15.6%	14.8%	14.0%	11.7%
BOS	14.6%	13.8%	14.9%	13.8%
DET	15.6%	13.3%	13.2%	13.8%
WAS	13.2%	12.3%	13.2%	13.3%
A's	9.8%	13.8%	20.7%	16.8%
St/B	13.7%	12.8%	15.7%	16.8%

The results do not indicate an especially impressive degree of leveraging, but it is noteworthy that any existed given the overall quality and depth of Lopez's starting rotation. Clear trends are discernable, especially against the Yankees and A's. Wynn and Lemon most frequently faced the best available teams and least often go up against the worst. Conversely, Feller and Garcia saw the bottom pair of teams the most often.

The table minimizes Lopez's leveraging to some extent because his habits for using individual pitchers evolved over the years (Bob Feller started regularly against the Yankees in 1951–52, for example). Lopez also liked to reserve one pitcher to start against the league's dregs. From 1953 onward, an aging Bob Feller filled the role. In his final seasons, Feller faced the Yankees only once while over 20 percent of his starts came against last-place squads, for a cumulative AOWP+ of 93 from 1953 to 1956. Though Lopez was not as extreme a leverager as Frank Chance, he still engaged in the practice.

When Lopez came to Chicago, he maintained this approach, using ace Billy Pierce frequently against top rivals. As noted in the first part of the book, Lopez's decision to not start Pierce against the Dodgers in the 1959 World Series helped bring about the end of starter leveraging. However, Lopez did not immediately back away from the practice. For example, when old warhorse Early Wynn struggled towards his 300th win in 1962, Lopez helped him by giving him a slew of starts against the last-place Senators and the dismal Boston Red Sox. As late as 1963, Lopez continued to engage in some leveraging. That year, Juan Pizarro and Ray Herbert, his two best established starters, posted AOWP+s of 103 and 104. In the dreg role, spot-starter Dave DeBusschere had a 93 AOWP+ in ten contests. In 1964, Lopez changed. The reform that had blown across the baseball world over the previous few years finally came to Chicago.

Lopez centered his teams on durable starting pitchers with good control. Succeeding bullpen-happy Lou Boudreau as Cleveland's manager, Lopez's Indians led the league in complete games five times in six years. It did not take a genius to realize that the starting rotation was Cleveland's strength, but Lopez kept them performing as effectively as could be hoped. When he went to Chicago, the rotation was not as good, but the general pattern of leaning on his top starters continued. Over his career, Lopez oversaw sixteen different twenty-game winning seasons, which ties him with Clark Griffith for third most in American League history behind Connie Mack (38) and Earl Weaver (22).

Like many of the deadball era managers of yore, Lopez lived and died on the base on balls. His teams drew more walks than they allowed in each of his fifteen full seasons. The odds on that happening by luck of the draw are one in 32,768. Six times they had a 100+ walk advantage; half came in Cleveland, and the other half in Chicago. Four times they had a 150+ edge in walks; again those seasons were evenly divided between his two teams. In Lopez's full seasons as manager, his squads issued 7,639 walks and collected 9,013, for a 1,374 edge. Like another White Sox manager, Fielder Jones, Lopez combined strong defense, solid starting pitcher, and the walk to ensure consistent winners. Lopez showed the classic Comiskey formula remained a viable way to win ballgames in the 1950s and 1960s.

From 1951 to 1965, Lopez's teams never even came close to posting a losing record, as all his squads cleared the .520 mark. He once went six years without a losing month. Adding up his worst April, May, June, July, August, and September/October to create the worst of all Lopez seasons sums up to a 64–88 (.421) record. A losing mark to be sure, but still noticeably better than most teams in or near last place. In Lopez's full seasons, his teams had losing records in nine of 90 months. Conversely, they won twenty or more games in sixteen different months.

Despite this consistency, his teams rarely maintained the same pace all year. Instead, Al Lopez had that special knack for improving his teams' play as the season progressed. Ignoring 1968–69, when he only managed for snippets as an interim skipper, here are his team's monthly records:

Month	W	L	Pct
April	109	78	.583
May	240	184	.566
June	246	201	.550
July	267	176	.603
August	283	179	.613
Sept/Oct	236	154	.605

Through June 30, Lopez's teams played .562 ball. Afterwards, they achieved a .607 mark. Only twice, in 1956 and 1957, did his squads perform worse in the second half. His teams never had a losing August or September/October.

The second half improvements by Lopez's teams were remarkably consistent as both his hitters and pitchers took part in the improvement. For example, the 1960 White Sox scored 4.61 runs per game in the first half of the year, and 5.03 in the second half, an improvement of 9.1 percent, which was the largest offensive second-half surge by any American League team that year. Meanwhile, the pitchers experienced the second-largest reduction in runs allowed after the All-Star Game, from 4.23 to 3.77 runs per contest. In all, nine of Lopez's pitching staffs had one of the league's three best second-half improvements, and nine of his offenses did likewise.

A manager can do several things to make sure the team improves as the year goes on — most importantly monitor his players' health. A manager needs to keep both hitters and pitchers maintaining their best over the course of the season by knowing when it is best to push them harder and when the team is better served to ease up on them. One has to decide what dings and muscle pulls a player can tolerate and what require some rest. Even something minor in and of itself can affect a player as the season wears on, because injuries do not exist in isolation. One sore joint can affect a player weeks later when he feels a minor pull somewhere else, and then jams a finger shortly after that. Over time, accumulated problems, even those individually negligible, make someone increasingly pained as the season wears on. Anyone who plays 154 or 162 games in six months cannot feel his best all the time.

There is no single "magic bullet" strategy a manager can employ to help his players as the season goes on. Lopez apparently had the knack for weighing various factors to help his players over the course of the season. One example helps illuminate how Lopez used the game's details to keep his players healthy and productive. Lopez, unlike other AL skippers, noted the weather and temperature when decided how much he should lean on his starting pitchers. The below table notes what percentage of starts resulted in completion for the White Sox from 1957 to 1965 (when Lopez managed them) in comparison to the rest of the league:

Month	CWS	Other AL
April	25.7%	26.2%
May	25.3%	26.4%
June	28.0%	25.6%
July	28.4%	26.1%
Aug.	34.7%	27.1%
Sept/Oct	24.6%	27.7%

This list reveals that the rest of the league's pitchers started games on a regular basis throughout the season, but Lopez's White Sox were less likely to finish games in the colder months. This looks like sensible player management on Lopez's part. The colder the weather, the harder it is for the muscles to warm up (this is especially true after sitting down for a half-inning). An arm that was not fully warmed up risked a greater chance of injury or at least ineffectiveness. The changes are not incredibly dramatic from one month to the next, but then again temperature was just one factor Lopez had to account for. By maintaining an awareness of when to push or ease up on his players, Lopez's squads could thrive instead of wilt as the year went on. While it is not reasonable to expect a team to be at 100 percent after 100 games played, if one squad is at 95 percent and the opposition at 85 percent, a clear edge exists.

Lopez had another rather pronounced trait — he preferred veterans. The Tendencies Database, as one might expect, can verify this by using Baseball-Reference's average offensive and pitching ages for all teams (which are rounded to the tenths decimals). When both are put through the database and their scores summed together, the following managers had the oldest teams:

Most Veteran Teams: Combined Hitters and Pitchers

Al Lopez	3.063
Wilbert Robinson	2.854
Earl Weaver	2.809
Jimmy Dykes	2.789
Bill McKechnie	2.686

According to the Tendencies Database, Lopez oversaw the oldest pitching staffs of any manager and the second-oldest collection of hitters, which is why his lead is so substantial when those studies are combined. Lopez managed the teams with the oldest hitters and pitchers five different times: 1954, 1957, 1958, 1960, and 1961.

Due to his preference for older players, Lopez never broke in a single Hall of Famer despite the overall high quality of his squads. The best players Lopez ever debuted were Rocky Colavito, Herb Score, Joe Horlen, Gary Peters, Al Smith, Pete Ward, Jim Landis, Don Buford, and Floyd Robinson. Fine players all, but that was a meager catch given Lopez's fifteen-year winning stretch. Compare that with the record of Earl Weaver, who had a virtually identical career winning percentage and career length to Lopez. Weaver, who also tended to play veterans, had a far greater haul of kids. He introduced two Hall of Famers—Cal Ripken and Eddie Murray—and also debuted Bobby Grich, Ken Singleton, Doug DeCinces, Don Baylor, Al Bumbry, Dennis Martinez, and Mike Flanagan. Weaver had seven or eight guys better than Lopez's second best.

Even Colavito, the best player Lopez ever produced, required several events to ensure him regular playing time. In 1956, Colavito began the year on the bench, and only received his first real chance at sustained playing time when left fielder Gene Woodling suffered an injury. Al Smith moved to left and Colavito took Smith's place in right. Rather than Colavito winning the job outright, Cleveland traded for veteran Preston Ward in mid–May. Ward was a disaster, playing his way out of a starter's slot in weeks. Colavito still had to fight for playing time until mid-summer with Smith and another veteran, Sam Mele. The right field logjam eventually worked itself out. Mele, in his final year, soon played his way onto the bench. Also, Lopez shifted Smith to center to replace the floundering Jim Busby. Colavito started only 88 games that year, most of which came in August or September. To crack the starting lineup, Colavito needed an outfield's worth of vets—Mele, Ward, and Busby—to be tried and found wanting.

This raises the question what role Lopez played in the most infamous off-season in White Sox history. After winning the title in 1959, Chicago engaged in a horrific series of trades, dumping prospects Norm Cash, Johnny Callison, Johnny Romano, Don Mincher and Earl Battey—who all earned slots to multiple All-Star teams in the 1960s. Those trades netted them a 33-year-old Roy Sievers, a 26-year-old Gene Freese, and Minnie Minoso, who returned to Chicago at age 34.

By 1959, managers had lost final authority over all roster decisions to the front office, but they usually retained some say in the matter. The more successful the manager, the more input he typically had in these decisions. Lopez had just won the franchise's first pennant in 40 years and had finished no worse than second place in nine straight seasons. He was at the pinnacle of his power, and apparently preferred veterans. The front office still bears ultimate responsibility for the trades (in his autobiography, Veeck noted that he hankered for Sievers), but it looks like a series of trades Lopez would support. The Sox missed the 1964 pennant by one game and in 1967 by three; the departed players would have come in handy those years. If Lopez helped push for a series of trades that cost the Sox multiple pennants, it should be held against him.

The 1959–60 off-season fiasco possibly caused Lopez to moderate his ways. He broke in more prospects in the last third of his career than the entire previous decade. Floyd Robinson received support in Rookie of the Year voting in 1961 under Lopez. Two years later Gary Peters won that award for Lopez's White Sox. In between, Joe Horlen established himself in the rotation. Pete Ward, Don Buford, Tommy McCraw, Ken Berry, and Bruce Howard also received considerable playing time in the early-to-mid 1960s from Lopez. In part, this certainly reflected what talent Lopez had on hand as the White Sox had a booming farm system. One cannot help but wonder about the shadow of the 1959–60 trades, though. As early as 1960, Callison and Battey established themselves as productive players for their new teams. In 1961 Romano made the All-Star team while Cash had a season for the ages, hitting .361 with 41 home runs and 132 RBIs. Perhaps other factors explain why Lopez played more kids in the 1960s, but he must have been aware of how poorly those trades had gone.

GENE MAUCH

W/L Record: 1,902–2,037 (.483)

Managed: Full Seasons: Philadelphia 1960–67; Montreal 1969–75; Minnesota
    1976–79; California 1982, 1985–87
    Majority in: Minnesota 1980; California 1981
    Minority of: Philadelphia 1968

Birnbaum Database: +231 runs
    Individual Hitters: +163 runs
    Individual Pitchers: +56 runs
    Pythagenpat Difference: -59 runs
    Team Offense: +75 runs
    Team Defense: -10 runs

Team Characteristics: Befitting his reputation, Mauch loved playing inside
    baseball. His teams bunted constantly, focused on platoon advantage,
    and had numerous in-game substitutions and pinch hitters. He did
    a little bit of pitcher leveraging early in his career (most notably Jim
    Owens had an AOWP+ of 106 in 22 starts in 1960), but he never did
    it that much.
    LPA: 2.73 (through 1965 only)   **LPA+**: 80 (through 1965 only)

Few men have been as widely heralded for their ability to manage the game as Gene
Mauch. Though he had the longest managerial career without a pennant, even his detractors
acknowledged that his mind contained a comprehensive understanding of the game. He was
one of the game's leading tinkerers, always looking for that little extra edge on the opponent.
Three tendencies especially stand out.

First, Gene Mauch loved to bunt. He would have anyone bunt: from 1967 to 1980, everyone with at least 300 plate appearances in a season for him had at least one sacrifice hit. Seven
players on his 1979 Twins cracked double digits in sacrifices. The team's second basemen (not
just the starter, but the total performance from everyone playing that position) combined for
36 sacrifice hits. Since 1956, no other team's second basemen have cracked 28. That squad's
third basemen had twenty bunts, tied for the most by any squad in the Retrosheet era. Similarly, the most bunts ever attained by a team's catchers came from Mauch's 1982 Angels, with
24. Only one other team had more than nineteen. Bob Boone, Mauch's starting catcher that
year, bunted more times than in his previous six seasons combined. Since 1956, at least one
of Mauch's teams rank in the top five in sacrifice bunts from shortstop, designated hitter, and
right field. Incredibly, none of his pitching staffs are in the top 140. For other managers, the
bunt was a default move. For Mauch, it was a weapon — hence the difference with pitchers.

By reputation, Mauch was the all-time champion of bunting to move the runner into
scoring position. Thanks to Retrosheet's work, this can be verified. One split generated by
that website's data shows what all teams did with a runner on first and the remaining bases
empty. Looking at how likely teams were to sacrifice in that situation (sacrifice hits divided
by total plate appearances in that split), Mauch's dominance is overwhelming. He managed
nine of the 23 most bunt-prone squads, and sixteen of the top 64 (out of 1,316 teams since
1956).

Over his career, Mauch called 86 percent of his bunts with only a runner on first, which
is the highest percentage by any manager who lasted four or more full seasons in the last half-
century. That should not happen. Across all baseball, most bunts occur with a runner on first
and no one else on. By bunting more than anyone else (not just in this split, but overall as
well), it should be that much harder for Mauch to be the manager with the highest percent-

age of bunts called with a runner on first and the remaining bases empty. Clearly, Mauch was passionate about bunting his runners into scoring position.

Bunting a player from first to second provides a crucial advantage: it removes the possibility of a double play. The twin killing was also something Mauch had an intense interest in. Not only did he try to prevent his batters from hitting into them, but he wanted his defenders performing them. As noted in the Hughie Jennings commentary, the following formula in the Tendencies Database determines which defenses did the best job turning double plays based on opportunity: DP/(H-2B-3B-HR+BB+HB-SH-SB-CS). It is double plays turned divided by the times someone should have been on first base. The following managers' squads were the most adept at turning two:

Most Double Plays Turned

Danny Murtaugh	0.497
Earl Weaver	0.531
Gene Mauch	0.591
Casey Stengel	0.667
Whitey Herzog	0.670

Murtaugh scores the highest, but he had uber-whiz Bill Mazeroski at second base. Earl Weaver also benefited from spending his entire career with one team and a core of defensive specialists up the middle. In contrast, Mauch, constantly created new double play combinations. Account for that, and Mauch may have been baseball's best at coaxing double plays from his fielders. He found the best gloves he could, coached them to focus on the double play, and had them positioned so they could pull it off. Mauch took advantage of whatever little nooks and crannies existed for the manager to increase the number of double plays turned. On several occasions, Mauch famously used a defensive alignment featuring five infielders and two outfielders, a maneuver that greatly aided the likelihood of a double play.

By the Tendencies Database's double play formula, Gene Mauch ran the two best teams in history at this play. Incredibly, they were separate franchises with completely different middle infielders—the 1979 Twins and 1985 Angels. Both turned a double play in 14.9 percent of all opportunities while no other units are over 14.7 percent. Mauch managed two of the only seven teams in the last half-century that turned over 200 double plays. With each of the four teams he managed, he set franchise defensive records that still stand for most double plays in a season: 179 with the 1961 Phillies, 193 with the 1970 Expos, 203 with the 1979 Twins, and 202 with the 1985 Angels.

Delving into team splits data makes Mauch's interest in players who could make the double play even more apparent. Add together splits at Baseball-Reference.com that includes a runner on first base (a runner only on first, runners on first and second, runners on the corners, and bases loaded), and use the formula DP/(PA-K-BB-HR-HB-SB-CS-PK) to determine how successful squads were at turning this play when they had the opportunity. Six Mauch teams led the league; those squads featured five different starting second baseman and four shortstops. Another half-dozen Mauch-managed clubs came in second place.

Due to his intense focus on the double play, Mauch's teams greatly benefited from this play. Only once did his batters hit into more than 140 double plays in a season while Mauch's defenders pulled off at least 141 double plays every season except his rookie campaign and the strike-shortened 1981 season. Each one of the 26 teams Mauch managed pulled off more double plays than they hit into.

However, the previous sentence is not quite as impressive as it sounds. League-wide, double plays turned are always higher than those grounded into. That sounds impossible— because for every double play hit into, another is turned—yet that is the case. Baseball has three main statistical reference sources: the *ESPN Baseball Encyclopedia*, Baseball-Reference. com, and Retrosheet. The ESPN book gives defensive double plays, but not offensive ones hit into. Retrosheet has team totals for GIDP, but not DP. (Retrosheet does provide double plays for the years they have game logs, but not earlier, and the game logs from the 1950s onward are sometimes incomplete.) Baseball-Reference alone features both. Its GIDP info matches Retrosheet and its team DP numbers are the same as ESPN's book, yet Baseball-Reference's league-wide DP are *always* higher than their GIDP. Sometimes, every single team in a league has more DP turned than hit into. My best guess for this discrepancy is that the GIDP counts only those double plays grounded into, and not outfield flies, or strike out/throw out double plays.

That puts us in a quandary. Mauch clearly benefited from double plays on both sides of the ball, yet it is difficult to put the two halves together. There is no perfect way to solve this riddle, but an effective rough approximation exists. Take the 1961 NL, for example: every team in that league supposedly turned more double plays than they hit into, for a combined difference of 294 DPs. At eight teams, that was a difference of 36.75 double plays per club — so adjust all teams in the league by that. In 1961, Mauch's Phillies grounded into 130 double plays while their defenders turned 179. That difference of 49 becomes 12.25 when adjusted by the league average differential ($49 - 36.75 = 12.25$). Once the same adjustment is made for all teams in each league in every season, estimated double play differentials can be determined for all managers. The following had the best career marks:

Best Adjusted Double Play Differentials

Casey Stengel	+537 double plays
Gene Mauch	+423 double plays
Roger Craig	+326 double plays
Whitey Herzog	+285 double plays
Sparky Anderson	+283 double plays

Only one other manager is over +200 (Phil Garner at +212). By this reckoning, Mauch had 22 teams benefit from double plays. Only once (1973 Expos) did he have a team do worse than -10.

Mauch also fixated on platoon advantage, a fact Retrosheet's splits can verify. Those splits contain righty/lefty breakdowns for all teams' pitching staffs and offenses for the last half-century. Determine what percentage of each teams' plate appearances contained the platoon edge, and likewise for the batters faced by their pitchers. Run both items through the Tendencies Database, and add them together to determine which managers since 1956 had the greatest overall interest in ensuring their squads had the platoon advantage working in their favor:

Combined Platoon Advantage

Gene Mauch	1.098
Bruce Bochy	1.332
Whitey Herzog	1.354
Frank Robinson	1.402
Bill Virdon	1.420

Mauch dominates this list. He scored best overall with pitchers, and second with hitters. Whitey Herzog beats him in the latter category, but only because he possessed numerous switch-hitters in St. Louis. Five times Mauch's hitters had the platoon advantage in the highest percentage of plate appearances in the league. His pitchers topped the league nine times.

One aspect of Mauch's managerial style appears out of place with the overall thrust of his career: he had little interest in the stolen base. His teams were not historically averse to stealing, but it is not what one would expect from such a staunch supporter of the game's details. However, Mauch's interest in the bunt negated the point of stealing. Most steals are of second base, and his teams bunted their way there. To steal, a team needs players with speed, but nearly anyone can be taught to bunt competently.

SAM MELE

> **W/L Record:** 524–436 (.546)
> **Managed:** Full Seasons: Minnesota 1962–66
>   Majority in: Minnesota 1961
>   Minority of: Minnesota 1967
> **Birnbaum Database:** -99 runs
>   Individual Hitters: -48 runs
>   Individual Pitchers: +119 runs
>   Pythagenpat Difference: -132 runs
>   Team Offense: +13 runs
>   Team Defense: -51 runs
> **Team Characteristics:** His teams had terrific offenses centered on plate discipline and power. They succeeded despite rarely having the platoon advantage. He had veteran pitchers with good control. The Twins played better in the second half under him.
> **LPA:** 3.10 (through 1965 only)   **LPA+:** 94 (through 1965 only)

Sam Mele is the worst manager to win a pennant. He ran a mid–1960s Twins squad with dynasty potential. Their offense featured Harmon Killebrew, Tony Oliva, Bob Allison, Earl Battey, Don Mincher, Zoilo Versailles, Jimmie Hall, Cesar Tovar, and Rod Carew. Minnesota's starting rotation contained Jim Kaat, Jim Perry, Camilo Pascual, Mudcat Grant, Dean Chance, and Dave Boswell. Al Worthington and Johnny Klippstein provided one of baseball's best bullpens. Not everyone played at the same time, but all provided quality work for Mele. Yet they only made it to one World Series, which they lost. That is not a mark in his favor

As soon as the Twins ran into some bad times, they fired Mele. Clearly the team itself did not give him much credit for their success. Even more damning, no other team ever hired him, showing how little respect he had earned around the game for helming the franchise to its first pennant in over 30 years. Still, that is merely circumstantial evidence against Mele.

Delving into the details hurts Mele even more. The Birnbaum Database gives him a woeful score. Ordinarily, a mark of -99 runs would not be too bad, but team quality affects the database's results, and Mele possesses one of the most striking disconnects between his winning percentage and Birnbaum score. Among managers who lasted at least 500 games, Mele has the highest career winning percentage of anyone with a negative Birnbaum score. There are only four managers with a winning percentage over .510 with lower career marks than his in the database.

It gets still worse when looking more closely at the data. Mele's best mark came with individual pitchers, where he scored +119 runs. However, good reason exists to think Mele deserves little credit for his pitchers' improvement. From 1965 to 1966, Johnny Sain served as pitching coach, a role in which he possessed a peerless reputation. Mele scored +88 runs with pitchers in that pair of seasons, accounting for almost all his positive score in this component. However, Mele butted heads with his star coach, eventually causing Minnesota to fire Sain after 1966. In the ensuing controversy, staff ace Jim Kaat publicly blasted the decision, saying that if the manager could not get along with Sain, the team should fire the manager instead.

Moving away from the Birnbaum Database, Mele continues to look bad. He had no idea what to do with his players, a fact best illustrated by his treatment of Jim Perry. Mele consistently refused to recognize Perry would make a fine starting pitcher, using him as a swingman instead. Shortly before coming to Minnesota, Perry had led the league in wins. Within a few years of Mele's firing, Perry posted back-to-back twenty-win seasons for the Twins. Bill James once noted that had Perry been used appropriately throughout his career, he could have made the Hall of Fame. Though Mele was not the only manager to use him as a spot starter, he was the one most responsible for Perry's mid-career blip.

In fact, Perry consistently pitched better as a starter than in relief under Mele. After the Indians traded him to Minnesota in mid–1963, Perry had an ERA of 3.61 in 25 starts while posting a 6.23 mark in ten relief appearances. Naturally, next year Mele made him a full-time reliever. That 1964 squad had some very serious problems with the back of their rotation, but Perry pitched poorly in the only start Mele trusted him with, so Perry's previous 136 career starts were ignored.

In 1965, Perry got a larger chance due to continued rotation problems. In nineteen starts, he posted a 2.45 ERA, which was superior to all Minnesota's regular starters. He threw enough innings to qualify for the ERA title, and despite being weighed down by his less impressive performance in the bullpen, Perry finished eighth in the league. However, Mele had already made up his mind on Perry. In mid–September, Perry went back to the bullpen and only had one start the rest of the year.

Perry's most frustrating season was 1966. Despite his success the year before, Perry started only three of the team's first 53 games. Once he finally got a shot to prove himself Perry again demonstrated his ability. He ended the year with a 2.54 ERA, fourth best in the league. Purely as a starter, he had a 2.43 ERA. If anyone had any concerns about his arm strength, Perry put them to rest by getting stronger as the year went longer, tallying a 2.15 ERA over the last three months. It should have been blindingly obvious he was one of baseball's best starting pitchers.

Preposterously, Mele refused to notice. He intended to open 1967 with a four-man rotation that included ace Jim Kaat, stud prospect Dave Boswell, and Mudcat Grant, who had won twenty games in 1965. Perry deserved the fourth slot. (Frankly, he deserved at least the third over the rapidly declining Grant.) Instead, at Mele's urging, Minnesota filled a non-existent void, sending their best trade bait—first baseman Don Mincher and outfield Jimmie Hall—to the Angels for ace pitcher Dean Chance. To be sure, Chance was a fine pitcher. However, the holes Minnesota needed to address were at catcher and shortstop. Instead, Mudcat Grant was a disaster, the club's glaring weaknesses at short and catcher remained, and Minnesota lost one of the closest pennant races in history.

Though failure to properly handle talent was Mele's most glaring error, it was not his only one. His in-game decisions were inappropriate for the club as well. For example, in 1964 his club was among league leaders in willingness to bunt. There is nothing wrong with that in theory, but it was a bad fit for the club. It was the sort of maneuver that made sense for Walt Alston's clubs, but not Mele's squads, who specialized in knocking the stuffing out of the ball. Furthermore, in his first few years Mele led the league in most mid-game substitutions for position players. If anyone had just cause to trust his starters, it was he.

Despite this willingness to substitute men, his offenses consistently finished at or near the bottom of the league in platoon advantage. Only once did he finish better than ninth best in the ten-team AL. Mele's mishandling of Perry helped create this situation. Both Mincher and Hall were left-handed hitters, and trading them for Chance amplified Minnesota's platoon disadvantage. Platoon advantage was a problem Mele had on both sides of the ball. His pitchers also were among the league's least likely to have the platoon advantage favor them. Even in 1965, when he used relievers fairly frequently, the Twins were next-to-last in giving their pitchers that little edge. From 1961 to 1964 the Twins were last or next-to-last at both versions of platoon advantage every year.

Mele also did a terrible job filling out the lineup card. The on-base percentage from his leadoff slot was routinely a little lower than the team-wide OBP, and the OBP from the #2 slot was even worse still. From 1963 to 1966, the batters in the #2 slot always had a lower OBP than the team, and the leadoff men did every year except 1966. Mele ensured the heart of his order would bat with empty bases as often as possible.

In all, he did a bad job handling his players, running the game, gaining respect from his team, other clubs, and at least one of his coaches. Sam Mele helped turn one of the decade's best rosters into a one-pennant wonder.

DANNY MURTAUGH

> **W/L Record:** 1,115–950 (.540)
> **Managed:** Full Seasons: Pittsburgh 1958–64, 1970–71, 1974–76
>   Majority in: (none)
>   Minority of: Pittsburgh 1957, 1967, 1973
> **Birnbaum Database:** +152 runs
>   Individual Hitters: +76 runs
>   Individual Pitchers: +145 runs
>   Pythagenpat Difference: -93 runs
>   Team Offense: -50 runs
>   Team Defense: +74 runs
> **Team Characteristics:** Murtaugh's offenses were built around balls in play. His hitters did not strike out much and walked even less. Murtaugh relied heavily on his main offensive starters. He loved to issue intentional walks.
> **LPA:** 4.02 (through 1965 only)   **LPA+:** 129 (through 1965 only)

The Pirates thought the world of Danny Murtaugh's managerial ability, but they kept pulling him out of the dugout because he had a weak heart, giving him less stressful jobs such as scout and director of player operations instead. However, since they thought he was the best manager around, they kept bringing him back. Murtaugh spent almost his entire adult life working for the franchise in various capacities.

As manager, he was one of the last of the leveragers. When Murtaugh came to Pittsburgh, the club had two established workhorses— Bob Friend and Vern Law. Murtaugh had them go out as often as they could, regardless who the opponents were, leveraging his tertiary starters instead. For example, in 1958, when the Pirates finished second behind the Braves, twenty starts came from Pittsburgh's swingmen and marginal pitchers. None of those games came against the Braves. Instead, that group faced the last-place Phillies seven times.

In 1961, an injury to Vern Law forced Murtaugh to scramble. He continued to have the ever-ready Bob Friend face all comers, while matching others against particular teams. Hurler Earl Francis provided the most obvious example of this tactic. From 1961 to 1963 he started 51 games for the Pirates, none of which came against an opponent that finished last. Instead, Francis started nine times against the Dodgers, the NL's winningest team in those years. He also had eight against both the Reds and Giants, who were the next most successful franchises. The Braves, who had a winning record every time in those years, also saw Francis eight times.

His overall AOWP+ for the period was 107. Alternately, in 1961 Murtaugh used veterans Harvey Haddix and Vinegar Bend Mizell almost exclusively against league doormats. They combined for 39 starts, only one of which came against the perennially contending Dodgers and three versus the pennant-winning Reds. Nearly 60 percent of their turns came against the three worst rivals in the league — Phillies (seven), Cubs (nine), and Cardinals (seven). Murtaugh slowly backed away from leveraging as the 1960s progressed. When he returned to Pittsburgh for his second full-season try at managing in 1970 the notion of leveraging had died, and Murtaugh did nothing to revive its corpse.

Murtaugh had another noteworthy tendency in using his pitchers: he was an early proponent of the bullpen. In the late 1950s, Pittsburgh's Roy Face became one of baseball's first consistent star relievers. In 1962, when Face recorded 20+ saves for the third time, no one else had ever had two such seasons. Face briefly served as the game's career leader in saves, and once held the NL single-season save record. When Murtaugh came back in the early 1970s, Dave Giusti was his bullpen ace. In 1971, he became the seventh man in history to log 30 saves in a season. The year before he had 26, giving him the third highest two-year total that baseball had then seen.

Symmetry exists between managers who leverage and those who rely heavily on the bullpen. In both cases he plays field general, trying to use his acumen and instincts to put the right men in the right place at the right time. Murtaugh bridged the gap between these two approaches.

Murtaugh's interest in strategically using his pitchers contrasts with his usage of hitters. On offense, Murtaugh took a minimalist approach, preferring a set lineup and rarely making mid-game replacements. Four times his teams led the league in greatest percentage of plate appearances allotted to starters. Twice they finished second. Seven times he led the league in complete games by position players. He rarely pinch-hit. Murtaugh had a bit of Frank Chance in him when it came to handling pitchers, but he was pure Pat Moran with his offense.

Murtaugh had another fixed managerial trait — he believed in the intentional walk. According to the Tendencies Database, which calculates it on a per-inning basis, he was the all-time leader at this maneuver:

Most Intentional Walks Issued

Danny Murtaugh	0.383
Frank Robinson	0.435
Art Howe	0.464
Sparky Anderson	0.465
Don Zimmer	0.527

In his entire career, Murtaugh issued over 1,000 intentional walks. He handed out nine in his first nine games as manager in 1957. On June 25, 1975, he called for five intentional walks in one contest. His teams led the league in IW/9IP in three different decades.

His willingness to walk batters reflected an overall disinterest toward the base on balls as a weapon. Murtaugh's hitters were consistently terrible at drawing free passes. The Tendencies Database, which looks at what percentage of plate appearances resulted in walks, reveals his squads' disinclination to take pitches:

Fewest Walks Drawn

Danny Murtaugh	1.665
Tom Kelly	1.484
Don Zimmer	1.407
Felipe Alou	1.400
Bill Virdon	1.396

The gap between first and second places is greater than the difference between second and sixth (Red Schoendienst at 1.306). In Murtaugh's twelve seasons as full-time manager, the Pirates finished last or next-to-last in walks per plate appearance eleven times.

Instead, Murtaugh prioritized batting average. The Pirates were in the top half of that category every year he ran them. Murtaugh's hitters generally were not home run threats, but they knew how to make contact. When BABIP (batting average on balls in play — essentially offensive DER) goes through the Tendencies Database, Murtaugh again appears at the extreme end:

Best BABIP

Danny Murtaugh	0.403
Red Schoendienst	0.451
Billy Southworth	0.500
Hughie Jennings	0.556
John McGraw	0.557
Whitey Herzog	0.557

Murtaugh led the league in it four times and came in second in five more seasons. He comes in first or second in nearly a dozen categories in the Tendencies Database lists, which is as often as any manager.

PAUL RICHARDS

W/L Record: 923–901 (.506)
Managed: Full Seasons: Chicago (AL) 1951–53, 1976; Baltimore 1955–60
            Majority in: Chicago (AL) 1954; Baltimore 1961
            Minority of: (none)
Birnbaum Database: +496 runs
            Individual Hitters: +82 runs
            Individual Pitchers: +342 runs
            Pythagenpat Difference: +171 runs
            Team Offense: -52 runs
            Team Defense: -47 runs
Team Characteristics: Richards loved to tinker. He not only had plenty of pinch hitters, but he would pinch-hit for his position players in the early innings more than anyone else year after year. He bunted, stole, and always sought the platoon advantage.
LPA: 5.56 (through 1965 only)   **LPA+:** 129 (through 1965 only)

Paul Richards is the most obvious example of how aging affects managers. During the 1950s, he had a reputation as the "Wizard of Waxahachie" (named after his hometown) — someone who approached the game like a chess match, always thinking three innings ahead. After a fifteen-year hiatus, Bill Veeck brought him back to manage the White Sox for one disastrous season during which Richards proved he was not the same manager he had once been. In his prime, Richards had been actively involved in the game, always looked for that little edge, constantly making moves. For example, every year he ran the Orioles, they had the league's fewest complete games by position players. Five times he topped the league in sacrifice hits per opportunity. Conversely, in 1976, Richards not only made fewer changes, but literally fell asleep on the bench during games. Had it not been for 1976, Richards would have ended his career with a score of +640 runs, the thirteenth best of all time.

Richards had a career winning record despite managing teams that never had overpowering lineups. One of the best ways to judge offensive muscle is isolated power, which is the difference between slugging and batting averages. According to the Tendencies Database, the following managers had the least power from their bats:

Lowest Isolated Power

Bruce Bochy	1.565
Jimmy McAleer	1.535
Paul Richards	1.516
Phil Garner	1.441
Jimmy Dykes	1.417

The Orioles finished last place in isolated power five consecutive years under Richards. His squads also had below average batting averages and rarely drew walks. They just could not hit.

Richards made up for this, though, with his handling of pitchers. He was willing to give young pitchers a shot. In Chicago, Billy Pierce emerged as an ace under Richards. In Baltimore, he oversaw one of the largest collections of young arms to emerge for one team simultaneously. In 1960–61, a quartet of pitchers—Milt Pappas, Steve Barber, Chuck Estrada, and Jack Fisher—combined to throw over half the teams' innings both seasons. Estrada, the oldest of the bunch, was born in February 1938.

More impressive was Richards's track record with veterans that other teams had no interest in. The best example occurred in August 1958, when the Orioles landed 35-year-old Hoyt Wilhelm, who had just been waived by two teams in less than twelve months. Though his ERAs were always fantastic, Wilhelm's knuckleball was so hard to catch that his teams consistently allowed numerous passed balls, leading to unearned runs. Additionally, baseball has always underrated knuckleballers. Richards, himself a former catcher, designed a comically large mitt to handle Wilhelm's pitch and had him throw it as often as possible. Even when the mitt was not employed, Richards insisted Wilhelm toss the knuckleball. Energized by his manager's confidence, Wilhelm made the All-Star team multiple times for the Orioles.

Wilhelm was not Richards's only reclamation project. Wilhelm's main bullpen companion in Baltimore was George Zuverink, another waiver-wire find. In five seasons, he posted a 3.15 ERA for Baltimore. In 1955, the Orioles claimed 30-year-old former major league pitcher Hal Brown from the Pacific Coast League. He developed into a surprisingly effective swingman for Richards. Joe Dobson had been a fine pitcher throughout the 1940s, but seemed to be on his downward arch when he came to the White Sox. However, in 1952, at age 35, he posted a 2.51 ERA, easily the best of his career. The next year Richards took a chance on 30-year-old rookie Connie Johnson, a former Negro Leaguer. Few Negro Leaguers that old got a shot to play in the majors unless they were prominent stars like Monte Irvin. After Johnson provided quality innings as a spot starter in Chicago, Richards took him to Baltimore where he briefly served as a rotation anchor. Furthermore, the Orioles lifted Arnie Portocarrero from the A's. He had won only eighteen games over the previous five seasons, but went 15–11 for Richards in 1958.

To ensure that his pitchers did well, Richards prioritized defense, since solid fielding always makes hurlers look better. His squads featured the league's best Defensive Efficiency Ratio three times and topped the league in Fielding Win Shares five times. Unlike other pitching-defense specialists, such as Bill McKechnie, Richards accepted pitchers with tepid control. Instead, he wanted power pitchers who kept the ball in the park. His teams led the league in strikeouts per inning three times and fewest home runs allowed per inning six times. Richards is the only prominent manager in the last eighty years who never had a hurler allow more than twenty home runs in a season. It was not the classic Comiskey combination for run prevention, but it worked.

Also, Richards loved to match up his pitchers against particular opposing teams. For example, from 1951 to 1954 Billy Pierce posted AOWP+s of 105, 107, 104, and 108 because Richards constantly pressed him into service against the best opposing teams. That allowed Richards's secondary pitchers to face lesser teams. Joe Dobson's big 1952 season came when he had an AOWP+ of 95. The next year it dropped down to an almost impossibly low 84 in fifteen starts. When Richards arrived in Baltimore, Bill Wight inherited the Billy Pierce role, albeit in fewer starts. From 1955 to 1957, Wight had an AOWP+ of 106. Complementing Wight, Richards had a rotating cast of swingmen who took turns facing down the Yankees and White Sox. In 1956, Don Ferrarese and Erv Palica, with 28 starts between them, had marks of 109 and 106. In 1957, Billy O'Dell had an 108 in fifteen starts. This allowed other swingmen to fatten up against the rotten teams. When the crop of young arms arrived in 1960, Richards surprisingly retreated from leveraging.

Bill James noted Richards's teams never featured a twenty-game winner, which is unexpected given his success with pitchers. In fact, Richards was the first manager in baseball history to last ten years without ever presided over a twenty-game winner. This stemmed from his handling of pitchers. The downside of leveraging has always been a limitation of innings pitched among the main aces. Warren Corbett, a baseball researcher who has done extensive study of Richards, noted that the Wizard of Waxahachie had a pronounced disinclination to start a pitcher on short rest. From 1956 to 1961, Orioles hurlers started a game on three days rest or less 108 times. The seven other pre-expansion AL teams averaged 326 such starts. Since Richards wanted his starters to have a minimum four days rest, leveraging was entirely a function of holding his starters back an extra day or two. As a result, prior to the 1990s Richards was the only manager to last ten seasons without ever having a pitcher start more than 34 games in a season. Fewer opportunities resulted in reduced victories for his main hurlers. Billy Pierce was the only one with multiple seasons at 30 or more starts, but he constantly faced the league's best teams which deflated his win totals.

In Baltimore, Richards was the ultimate mix-master with his rotation. Seven times someone threw at least 220 innings for him. It was seven different pitchers. Twelve times someone tossed 200 innings for him. Ten hurlers combined to do that. Sixteen different pitchers had enough innings to qualify for the ERA title under him, but only Milt Pappas and Hal Brown did it three times—and Brown never exceeded 170 innings. Richards would have one group of pitchers anchor the staff one year and completely overturn them the following campaign. In 1958, a trio of pitchers—Portocarrero, O'Dell, and Jack Harshman—combined to throw half the team's innings. The year before they had thrown 140.3 innings for Baltimore. After 1958, only O'Dell tossed 100 innings in a season for Richards, and he only did that once. In the early 1960s, when Richards finally had a stable rotation in place, he left.

That was normal for Richards, who was a builder. Neither of the teams he managed had enjoyed noteworthy success in decades. In 1954, he gave the White Sox their first 90-win season since the days of Joe Jackson. Prior to coming to Baltimore, that franchise had experienced four 100-loss seasons in the previous half-dozen years. Richards left both after they turned the corner. After Baltimore, he became general manager for the expansion Houston Astros, another chance to build from the ground up. The builder-manager has a proud tradition in baseball history, but other architects stuck around to reap the fruit of their labors. Richards did not, which made him unique. He was what would currently be called a serial entrepreneur; his fun came in the building rather than the result. A talented team does not need a genius manager to guide them to victory; someone who trusts the talent to win suits their needs. Richards wanted to prove his brilliance, thus explaining his unorthodox career choices.

BILL RIGNEY

W/L Record: 1,239–1,321 (.484)

Managed: Full Seasons: New York/San Francisco 1956–59, 1976; California
1961–68; Minnesota 1970–71;

Majority in: (none)

Minority of: San Francisco 1960; California 1969; Minnesota 1972

Birnbaum Database: +1 run

Individual Hitters: -28 runs

Individual Pitchers: +50 runs

Pythagenpat Difference: +47 runs

Team Offense: -1 runs

Team Defense: -67 runs

Team Characteristics: Rigney pulled off more than his share of suicide squeezes.
He used plenty of pinch-hitters and relief pitchers. Walks were his
longtime Achilles heel: his hitters did a poor job drawing them and
his pitchers offered up too many.

LPA: 2.59 (through 1965 only)   **LPA+:** 79 (through 1965 only)

The Walter Alston commentary noted that Don Drysdale threw 69.3 innings against the 1959 Braves, a total no one else can match in all the years since. While that is true, another pitcher that same year nearly equaled Drysdale's workload against Milwaukee. Toothpick Sam Jones, working for Rigney's Giants, tossed 68.3 innings against the Braves. Between them, Drysdale and Jones accounted for almost one-tenth of all of Milwaukee's outs. Drysdale is more famous, but Jones led the 1959 National League in wins and ERA. The Drysdale-Jones double-whammy was one of the many reasons the Braves lost the pennant that year.

Over his career, Rigney's handling of pitchers remained his most distinctive and important attribute. At the outset of his career, Rigney was the king of starting pitchers on two days rest. With the Giants in 1957, his pitchers started games with only two days rest 22 times. Four years later with the expansion Angels, they did it 23 times. Since the mid–1950s, only the Wilbur Wood–era White Sox top that. In 1958–59, the Giants had 35 more such starts, along with twenty starts on only one day's rest. Using the splits available at Baseball-Reference, which go back to 1956, the following managers gave the most starts to pitchers after exactly two days rest from their last outing:

Manager	GS
Bill Rigney	196
Chuck Tanner	148
Gene Mauch	146
Alvin Dark	115
Walter Alston	114

The numbers are not perfect due to partial seasons (managers get all the credit when they managed a full season but no credit when they helmed a squad for the minority of a campaign), but Rigney's dominance is overwhelming.

Rigney's antiquated notions of relief work caused those frequent short-rest starts. He thought all pitchers could be used in both relief and as starters, and starts on one or two days rest generally occurred after a hurler pitched an inning or two in relief. Many managers of yore had similarly lacked a fixed separation between bullpen and starters, but Rigney was the last of this breed. On the 1962 Angels, for instance, the half-dozen men with at least twenty starts all pitched from the bullpen as well, for a combined 54 relief appearances. In 1964,

Dean Chance won the Cy Young Award while mixing 35 starts with 11 relief appearances. Rigney was the last manager to use his ace as Frank Chance had worked Mordecai Brown

In other ways, Rigney pushed pitching staffs in a new direction by eschewing the complete game to an unprecedented degree. In 1961, his Angels set a new record for fewest complete games with 25. The next year they broke the mark with 23. They actually featured good staffs, so necessity did not dictate Rigney's pitcher usage patterns. In 1967, they tossed 19 complete games.

Instead, Rigney relied heavily on his bullpen, something the Tendencies Database confirms. Looking at Retrosheet's splits since 1956, the following managers had the largest percentage of innings eaten by their relievers:

Most Reliant on Bullpen

Jimy Williams	0.389
Frank Robinson	0.556
Bill Rigney	0.696
Felipe Alou	0.716
Tom Kelly	0.720

In the 1960s, most managers wanted their starters to pitch in the ninth. Rigney did too, just not necessarily in the games they started. He would rather take out one of his starters from a game that had already been wrapped up so he could finish a tighter contest some other time. With this approach Rigney helped push the bullpen to the fore, but it was a very different creature than anyone sees now. In was an entirely by-committee affair rather than one with clearly assigned roles. In 1962, seven of his men had at least 25 relief appearances. Even though they led the league with 47 saves (only one other team had more than 40), the team leader had nine.

Red Schoendienst

W/L Record: 1,041–955 (.522)
Managed: Full Seasons: St. Louis 1965–76
          Majority in: (none)
          Minority of: St. Louis 1980, 1990
Birnbaum Database: +39 runs
          Individual Hitters: -102 runs
          Individual Pitchers: +169 runs
          Pythagenpat Difference: -11 runs
          Team Offense: -48 runs
          Team Defense: +31 runs
Team Characteristics: Schoendienst's teams ran all the time, but aside from that Schoendienst did not really play much small ball. He rarely bunted and does not appear to have hit-and-run particularly often. Schoendienst generally did a good job putting high OBP near the top of the batting order. Of all the lively ball managers in this book, he is the only one who never presided over a batter who drew 80 walks in a season.
LPA: 3.63 (1965 only)   LPA+: 148 (1965 only)

Only once in baseball history has one team had three different managers who all won over 1,000 games in their careers: the 1990 Cardinals. Whitey Herzog began the year as manager, but departed at midseason. Schoendienst, a longtime institutional stalwart, served as interim manager for a few weeks, until the club settled on Joe Torre as their manager. Of that trinity, Schoendienst is clearly the least regarded.

He inherited a team that had won the World Series in 1964, and as a result, Schoendienst never received much credit for St. Louis's subsequent successes the rest of the decade. He was not necessarily regarded as a bad manager, just nothing special. The Birnbaum Database agrees, giving him a mildly positive score. Given that Schoendienst's career win/loss record was nearly 100 games over .500, his Birnbaum score is rather tepid. In comparison, Bobby Valentine, who had a slightly longer career with a lower (.510) winning percentage, scores at +356 runs. Jack McKeon managed almost 50 fewer games than Schoendienst and his record was a tad worse (.518), but still scored +381 runs. Yogi Berra, Hank Bauer, and Gabby Street share Schoendienst's .522 mark, but in the Birnbaum Database they come in at +172, +193, and +117 runs, respectively, all in shorter careers.

Schoendienst had his strengths as a manager. Most notably, he let Lou Brock run wild on the bases. Though Brock had never attempted more than 61 steals in a season under his previous managers, he attempted 90 swipes in Schoendienst's first year as manager. In the dozen years Schoendienst managed him, Brock made it to first on a single, walk, or hit by pitch 2,283 times. Looking at his offensive splits, he apparently tried to steal second base on approximately 900 different occasions, 40 percent of the times he was on first. Factor in that sometimes another runner was on second, Brock tried to steal second a majority of the times it was possible for a dozen years, indicating Schoendienst gave him a nonstop green light. It seems obvious in hindsight that he should have let Brock run at all times, but that is only clear because he was allowed to do so. Others would have been more conservative handling him.

More importantly, Schoendienst also played a key role in the bullpen's development. In 1967, he pioneered shorter relief outings for his relievers. Starting with 1956 (the first year Retrosheet info is available for this project), here are the teams (and their managers) with the fewest innings per relief appearance in history:

Year	Team	IP/RA	Manager
1956	PHI	1.500	Mayo Smith
1962	CHC	1.440	College of Coaches
1963	MIN	1.428	Sam Mele
1967	STL	1.333	Red Schoendienst
1968	HOU	1.313	Harry Walker
1971	CHC	1.312	Leo Durocher
1974	PHI	1.304	Danny Ozark
1987	PHI	1.275	Lee Elia
1989	STL	1.243	Whitey Herzog

The gap between the 1963 Twins and 1967 Cardinals is easily the largest one above. In fact, it is greater than the gap between the 1967 and 1989 Cardinals. Schoendienst's most important relievers that year threw a little over one inning per appearance. The main go-to bullpen arms were Ron Willis and Joe Hoerner; Willis pitched 81 innings in 65 appearances while Hoerner threw 66 in 57 games. Teammate Hal Woodeshick outdid both of them, throwing barely over 40 innings in 36 relief stints. No other team was even under 1.45 IP/RA with their relievers in 1967, and the rest of baseball averaged over 1.6. The Cards had nearly as many innings tossed by their bullpen as the Phillies or Giants, but in 60 more relief appearances.

The 1967 Cards were not an aberration for Schoendienst as his relievers habitually threw short outings. In Schoendienst's dozen years managing, his relievers averaged the fewest innings per appearance six times, and second fewest in four seasons. He was personally responsible for nine of baseball's 27 lowest marks from 1956 to 1976.

Schoendienst also used his starters a bit differently than his peers. More than anyone else in his day, he wanted his hurlers to start on four days rest. Based on the information at Baseball-Reference.com, the following squads from 1956 to 1969 featured the most starts by pitchers on exactly four days worth of rest:

Year	Team	GS	Manager
1967	STL	93	Red Schoendienst
1968	STL	93	Red Schoendienst
1968	NYM	93	Gil Hodges
1968	ATL	90	Lum Harris
1965	STL	89	Red Schoendienst

No other squad topped 78 starts on precisely that much rest until the 1970s. Since then, Schoendienst's style for using pitchers has become extremely common. In using both relievers and starters, Schoendienst was a harbinger of the future.

CASEY STENGEL

> **W/L Record:** 1,905–1,842 (.508)
> **Managed:** Full Seasons: Brooklyn 1934–36; Boston (NL) 1938–42; New York
>   (AL) 1949–60; New York (NL) 1962–64
>   Majority in: Boston (NL) 1943; New York (NL) 1965
>   Minority of: (none)
> **Birnbaum Database:** +487 runs
>   Individual Hitters: +224 runs
>   Individual Pitchers: +76 runs
>   Pythagenpat Difference: -21 runs
>   Team Offense: +135 runs
>   Team Defense: +73 runs
> **Team Characteristics:** Stengel is probably more famous for matching up his
>   pitchers against specific rival teams than any other manager in history. Others actually did it more often, but they did not win five consecutive pennants in the process. He platooned his hitters and used many pinch-hitters.
> **LPA:** 5.33   **LPA+:** 120

Once in a while I encounter someone who thinks managers have no meaningful impact on teams. (This is especially true when dealing with sabermetric types.) These people sometimes use Casey Stengel as an example of how overrated managers are. Stengel experienced unprecedented success with the Yankees, but he struggled in his various National League stints as field general. Stengel's best season in the NL was a mere 77–75 with the 1938 Braves. If Stengel was such a super-genius, then why could he not achieve more when he was away from the Yankees?

While managers have an impact, the quality of players is much more important. Stengel worked for one great franchise and three utterly dismal squads. The Birnbaum Database gives him a score of +53 runs in Brooklyn and +83 runs with the Braves; rather impressive achievements for such lackluster squads. Stengel had virtually no players to work with in those years. His leading lights were men like Van Mungo and Tony Cuccinello, which is not how clubs win pennants. As a result, Stengel found himself relegated to the Pacific Coast League, where he ran the Oakland Oaks during the 1940s. He had enough success there to land the Yankee job.

Stengel's pre–Yankee experiences formed the approach to the game than made him famous in the 1950s. In the NL, he never had any players worth depending on, so he avoided attachments. With Oakland, his most talented players were the ones most likely to be snatched up by the majors, so again he knew not to rely heavily on particular individuals. This outlook became central to how he ran the Yankees. For instance, the 1949 Yankees suffered a litany of injuries with Joe DiMaggio missing half the season, and only Phil Rizzuto playing in over 130 games. Stengel overcame these obstacles to capture the world title by mixing and matching the talent on hand.

There was no need for Stengel to be too loyal to individual players. If someone's skills declined or could no longer be counted on, he was shown the door. Since the Yankees had a great front office, Stengel could be assured they would land another suitable player to fit his needs. This forced his players to be that much more accountable. Everyone always tries their hardest regardless, but there is nothing like the pressure of imminent punishment to keep people on their toes. As Stengel kept winning, his stature grew so large that his players could not publicly tangle with him. The talent Stengel had on hand was not necessarily better than what Miller Huggins or Joe McCarthy had, yet they never won ten pennants in twelve years as Stengel did.

Examples of the "what have you done for me lately" attitude abounded on Stengel's Yankees. Second baseman Billy Martin had as close a relationship to Stengel as anyone on the team, having played for him as a teen in Oakland. In 1956, his career peaked when he earned a selection to that year's All-Star Game. The following year he got off to a slow start, so the Yankees traded him to the pathologically pathetic Kansas City A's. New York wanted to break in hot prospect Bobby Richardson and saw no need for patience with the declining veteran. Similarly, after a solid decade under Stengel, Hank Bauer had an off year in 1959. He was in another uniform in 1960. Phil Rizzuto was the anchor for Stengel's first teams, but once his skills diminished, Stengel would not give him many plate appearances for old-time's sake.

Pitching especially demonstrated Stengel's lack of sentimentality. Tommy Byrne won 30 games for the Yankees in Stengel's first two years. When he began 1951 poorly, the Yankees sent him to the Browns before the All-Star Game. Tom Sturdivant posted two consecutive sixteen-win seasons, but the club shipped him to Kansas City when an injury hampered him. Even Stengel's most tried and true warhorses were not immune. Among the three hurlers who served as the pitching nucleus for Stengel's five consecutive pennant winners— Vic Raschi, Ed Lopat, and Allie Reynolds— only Reynolds ended his days in the Bronx. The others were dismissed as soon as they faltered. Stengel's Yankees had to earn their roster spots everyday.

With the Mets, this same approach provided the opposite effect for Stengel. Instead of making a great team better, it made a horrible squad worse. He still had no qualms about moving players out of the lineup if they failed to perform. This time, however, he lacked quality replacements. Instead of breeding accountability, Stengel's technique fostered confusion, which led to apathy. Not only were they not any good, but the players could not get used to their roles. If the Yankees were an ideal situation for his management style, the Mets were the club least suited to it.

Also, by the 1960s Stengel had lost of a little of his mental edge. The six-month grind of a season demands a certain level of mental alertness and strength that is hard to maintain well into one's Social Security years. Only Connie Mack managed at an older age than Stengel, and he was utterly terrible in those seasons. As Mets manager, Stengel scored -504 runs in the Birnbaum Database. Had he retired after 1960, that system would rank him as the fourth best manager of all time. Instead, he fell to nineteenth place.

Though continuity existed with how Stengel managed the Yankees and his other clubs, that does not mean he lacked variation in how he handled his different teams. Stengel had engaged in one key strategic habit with the Yankees that was absent in his previous stints: he used a bullpen ace. None of his hurlers recorded more than eight saves in a season with Brooklyn or Boston, but Stengel became baseball's first manager to preside over ten different occasions in which a reliever logged at least ten saves in a campaign. When the Yankees narrowly won the 1949 pennant, fireman Joe Page earned 27 saves, the most in baseball history until the 1960s. Stengel's adoption of the fireman model signified a broader change in the game. Though teams had relievers in the 1930s, the concept of a relief ace who specialized in pitching in the most stressful situations did not gain particular attention until Bucky Harris used Joe Page to great effect with the 1947 Yankees. Stengel was one of the first to recognize the importance of what Harris had done, and helped popularize it.

Stengel treated his relievers the same way he did the rest of his players—with minimal sentimentality. Page helped the Yankees narrowly earn a pennant in 1949, but when he stumbled Stengel swiftly sent him packing. Due to his demanding nature, Stengel became the first manager to oversee three separate relievers log twenty or more saves in a season: Page in 1949, Johnny Sain in 1954, and Ryne Duren in 1958. Until the 1970s, only one other manager (Walter Alston) could make the same claim. Ultimately, eight different pitchers saved at least ten games in a season in Stengel's dozen campaigns with the Yankees.

In almost all his career, Stengel leveraged his starting pitchers. He was famous for it with the Yankees, but he engaged in it in his early days as well. In 1934, for instance, Stengel decided the best way to break in rookie Dutch Leonard was by having him face the league's dogs as often as possible; nine of his 21 starts came against the two worst teams in the league. In Boston and Brooklyn, Stengel was not always consistent the way he used pitchers from year to year. He had a belief in matching starters against particular opponents, but he had no arms he consistently trusted against the best squads. As a result, in 1940 Dick Errickson made eight of his ten starts against the three worst opposing squads for an AOWP+ of 84. Next year he faced the other half of the league for a mark of 106. While working as a swingman for Stengel in 1941–42, Tom Earley posted AOWP+s of 108 and 88.

Again, the Yankees' talent fit Stengel's managerial predilections. The table below lists what percentage of starts Stengel's Big Three of Reynolds, Raschi, and Lopez had versus all opponents during New York's 1949–53 five-peat. As was the case in a similar table given in the Al Lopez commentary, clubs are ordered from most-to-least wins attained in the period under question:

Team	Reynolds	Raschi	Lopat
CLE	16.2%	16.3%	20.6%
BOS	20.0%	18.1%	15.4%
CWS	10.0%	15.0%	11.0%
DET	12.3%	11.9%	11.0%
PHI	10.0%	18.8%	14.0%
WAS	15.4%	8.1%	14.0%
STB	17.7%	11.9%	14.0%

A few interesting patterns emerge. First, Stengel preferred using the Big Three against the best available squads. They combined for 75 starts against Cleveland, and 76 versus Boston, but no more than 62 against any other team. Aside from that, Stengel's usage differed. Reynolds loaded up on starts against the worst two opponents while Raschi almost never faced them. Lopat and Reynolds were more likely to skip turns against the middle class White Sox and Tigers instead of the dregs. Over the entire period, Lopat achieved an AOWP+ of 103, Raschi 102, and Reynolds 100. While none of those scores would be impressive single-season marks,

Lopat and Raschi's totals are rather impressive for a multi-year score. (Even Mordecai Brown ended with a career AOWP+ of "only" 104.)

With the Big Three gobbling up so many games against the Indians and Red Sox, Stengel could use less trustworthy arms against sad sacks. Tom Morgan was Stengel's favorite pitcher to deploy against the second division. As a 21-year-old rookie in 1951, Morgan posted an AOWP+ of 92. Next year it was 96. He did not play in 1953, but when he came back the following season, he set a new low of 91. Jim McDonald experienced similar treatment, with back-to-back AOWP+s of 90 and 85 in 1953–54. As a part-time rookie in 1950, Whitey Ford posted an AOWP+ of 89, though by the mid–1950s he emerged as the ace as Raschi, Reynolds, and Lopat went into eclipse.

In 1954, Stengel's Yankees, as noted in Chapter 3, achieved the highest single-season LPA by any squad in the twentieth century, 16.52. The chart below shows how many starts each of the seven Yankee pitchers with at least ten starts — Whitey Ford, Eddie Lopat, Harry Byrd, Bob Grim, Allie Reynolds, Tom Morgan, and Jim McDonald — had against each opponent, along with their AOWP and AOWP+ for the season:

Team	Pct.	WF	EL	HB	BG	AR	TM	JM	Remainder
CLE	.721	7	5	0	2	5	1	0	2
CWS	.610	6	6	4	2	2	1	0	1
BOS	.448	4	1	4	3	4	3	2	1
DET	.442	2	1	5	3	1	5	4	1
WAS	.429	5	4	1	5	0	1	0	6
BAL	.351	3	3	2	2	5	1	2	4
PHI	.331	1	3	5	3	1	5	2	3
AOWP		.533	.518	.439	.459	.508	.431	.403	
AOWP+		112	109	92	97	107	91	85	

Their record-setting LPA was aided by the league's extreme winning percentages, but inarguable preferences on matchups abound for every pitcher, except perhaps Bob Grim. Whitey Ford's AOWP+ of 112 is the best by any pitcher with at least twenty starts in a season since World War II. (There is no AOWP or AOWP+ for the remainders because that is the total for a collection of pitchers, whereas AOWP-type stats are meant to be assigned to individual hurlers).

However, Stengel virtually never leveraged his starters with the Mets. As much as Stengel loved to gain that extra edge, the little advantage gained seemed futile with his teams constantly finishing fifteen games out of ninth place. His final fling with leveraging came in 1962 when swingman Craig Anderson posted an AOWP+ of 107 in fourteen starts. Four teams won at least 90 games in the NL that year, and nine of his starts came against them. The Mets went 1–8 in those games, and Anderson allowed five runs in six innings in New York's sole victory.

Stengel also had a considerable interest in the double play, both on offense and defense. In his book on managers, Bill James noted that Stengel's teams constantly turned more double plays than one would expect, even when the middle infielders did not seem particularly impressive. Stengel's teams also generally avoided hitting into twin-killings. If you compare double plays fielded and recorded for all squads that information exists for, the following teams had the most advantageous single season double play disparity:

Year	Team	DP	GIDP	Difference	Manager
1956	NYY	214	102	+112	Casey Stengel
1952	NYY	199	93	+106	Casey Stengel
1954	NYY	198	94	+104	Casey Stengel
1966	PIT	215	111	+104	Harry Walker
1986	STL	178	83	+95	Whitey Herzog

The above does not take into account all the adjustments mentioned in the Mauch commentary. However, even with those refinements, the 1956 Yanks gained the greatest advantage from double plays of any squad in history, and Stengel managed three of the top four squads (the 1966 Pirates move into second place). Stengel's teams had the best double play differential in the league eleven times. With the Mauch adjustment, Stengel comes out 537 double plays ahead, easily the largest advantage in baseball history.

Perhaps Stengel's dominance in double play differentials is because he had such a long career. Another way of examining double plays is to add together what the Tendencies Database says about GIDP and DP. Based on that, the following managers score best overall with double plays:

Best at Double Plays — Combined

Whitey Herzog	1.261
Billy Southworth	1.357
Al Lopez	1.415
Casey Stengel	1.419
Gene Mauch	1.453

The men around Stengel all have a particular hook. Herzog was the king of the basestealers while Southworth and Mauch championed the bunt. Both strategies minimize double plays. Lopez benefited from several years managing one of baseball's greatest middle infields combinations, Hall of Famers Luis Aparicio and Nellie Fox. Stengel had neither any obvious strategic predilection nor historically brilliant defenders. He just did what he could to make the double play work for him, whether it was positioning his infielders or using groundball pitchers.

In Stengel's six years with the Braves, the team averaged over 155 double plays turned per year. In the franchise's previous 65 seasons, they reached that figure only three times. In his second season, they recorded 178 double plays, a franchise record that stood until the Braves moved to Atlanta. The Yankees averaged 186 double plays a year in Stengel's dozen years there. In the other 90+ campaigns in franchise history, they turned 186 in a season only two times. In Stengel's 25 years as manager — and GIDP data exists for all them — none of his batters ever grounded into twenty double plays in a season. He is the only manager who lasted over ten seasons since baseball began recording GIDP information who can make that claim.

Unlike the double play, Stengel had little interest in the base on balls. According to the Tendencies Database, of all managers who lasted at least a decade, only Burt Shotton's pitchers scored worse at walks per nine innings than Stengel. In his first year with the Yankees, Tommy Byrne set a franchise record that still stands with 179 walks. The next year he had 160. A few years, later teammate Bob Turley surrendered 177. The five highest single season individual walk totals in Yankee history all came under Stengel, as did one-third of all occasions a Yankee hurler gave up 100 walks.

Stengel also had tepid marks with offensive walks. Combine his Tendencies Database scores for hitting and pitching walks, and he got as little out of walks as any manager in history:

Worst with Walks — Combined

Patsy Donovan	2.549
Lou Boudreau	2.472
Bill Virdon	2.462
Casey Stengel	2.448
Bill Rigney	2.434

Stengel's teams earned more walks than they surrendered six times in 25 campaigns. Alternately, they had a -100 differential in half-dozen seasons. For his full career, his squads allowed nearly 1,000 more than they gave up.

Stengel's score with hitters, 1.061, is technically average, but a lurking variable distorts it: Mickey Mantle. In his decade under Stengel, Mantle constantly appeared among the league leaders in walks, averaging 100 per year in the 1950s. For that reason alone, Stengel should have scored above average. Aside from Mantle, Stengel had only a half-dozen times a batter garnered 80 walks in a campaign.

Stengel's walk imbalance partially explained his interest in the double play. Walks allow men to get on base, but are not very good ways to advance runners already on. Stengel would let them have first, provided he could figure out a way to make the next man ground into two outs.

BIRDIE TEBBETTS

> **W/L Record:** 748–705 (.515)
> **Managed:** Full Seasons: Cincinnati 1954–7; Milwaukee 1962; Cleveland 1963, 1965
> Majority in: Cincinnati 1958; Cleveland 1964, 1966
> Minority of: Milwaukee 1961
> **Birnbaum Database:** +11 runs
> Individual Hitters: +41 runs
> Individual Pitchers: +6 runs
> Pythagenpat Difference: -24 runs
> Team Offense: -18 runs
> Team Defense: +6 runs
> **Team Characteristics:** Tebbetts's teams had terrific fielding percentages, but none of the advanced metrics think much of their overall defense. His hitters were very good at avoiding grounding into double plays. He did a very good job making sure he had good OBP from the top of his batting order.
> **LPA:** 4.69 (through 1965 only)   **LPA+:** 120 (through 1965 only)

Tebbetts has been largely forgotten by history, and with good reason. His career was one of uncanny consistency as his teams always finished around the middle of the pack. His best showing was a third-place finish, and his worst was either a pair of sixth-place finishes in a ten-team league or a couple of fifth-place seasons in an eight-team league. Fittingly, the Birnbaum Database finds him to be an unusually bland manager, not especially good or bad at anything. He had the game's most extraordinarily ordinary managerial career.

Even Tebbetts's players tended to be a faceless bunch. No pitcher ever won twenty games for him. Prior to 1990, Richards and Tebbetts were the only managers to last ten campaigns who could claim that. Tebbetts also never oversaw a 200-hit season, or had one of his players steal 30 bases. Only once did someone walk 100 times for him or hit more than 40 doubles. There were only two .400 OBP under him. Tebbetts was the first manager in history to last a decade without ever having a player leg out ten triples in a season. Only two other managers (Jim Fregosi and Earl Weaver) have joined that small club. If it were not for power hitters like Ted Kluszewski, Frank Robinson, and Wally Post powering the 1956 Reds to a near-NL-record 221 home runs, Tebbetts would have possessed an outstandingly bland bunch of players.

Though their results were decidedly middling, Tebbetts's squads had some interesting tendencies. They excelled at some of the finer points of the game. Tebbetts made the leaderboard for the hit-and-run given back in Chapter 2. Largely as a result of this managerial tendency, his teams rarely hit into double plays. Only once did a Tebbetts hitter ground into twenty double plays in a season. His teams also shined at avoiding errors. According to the Tendencies Database, his teams boasted fantastic fielding percentages year-in, and year-out:

Best Fielding Percentages

Earl Weaver	0.365
Tom Kelly	0.516
Birdie Tebbetts	0.530
Charles Comiskey	0.532
Al Lopez	0.558

Weaver and Kelly each managed only one team while Tebbetts constantly moved from squad to squad, working with a different defensive core each time. The Reds had consistently performed well in this stat before hiring Tebbetts, but in 1957 they led the NL in fielding percentage for the first time since Bill McKechnie managed them. Next year, with Tebbetts on duty for three-quarters of the season, they repeated. The Indians had committed numerous errors before Tebbetts arrived, but under him they improved considerably. The Indians led the league in fielding percentage only once between 1955 and 2000; it was under Tebbetts in 1965.

Tebbetts had one other noteworthy trait — he was a great proponent of starting a pitcher on short rest. In 1956, his Reds combined twenty starts on two days rest with seventeen on one day's rest, and two on no days: that was a quarter of their games. In 1962, Cincinnati hurlers pitched 34 games on zero to two days of rest. In 1964–65, the Indians had 53 more such games. Since 1956, the following managers gave their pitchers the most starts on exactly one day's rest (again, partial managerial seasons make the results slightly off):

Manager	GS
Bill Rigney	79
Birdie Tebbetts	74
Walter Alston	57
Gene Mauch	56
Al Lopez	46

Rigney narrowly tops Tebbetts, but then again Rigney managed nearly twice as many seasons as Tebbetts in this period. Adjust for career length, and Tebbetts was the king of starting pitchers on one day's worth of rest.

This does not mean Tebbetts's pitchers threw complete games with only a one day window in between. Either someone would pitch in relief one day and start the next, or he would get shelled and taken out immediately the first day, leaving him suitably rested the next day. It happened much more frequently in the game as a whole back then, but Tebbetts still distinguished himself from his peers in this regard.

EARL WEAVER

> **W/L Record:** 1,480–1,060 (.583)
> **Managed:** Full Seasons: Baltimore 1969–82, 1986
>   Majority in: Baltimore 1968, 1985
>   Minority of: (none)
> **Birnbaum Database:** +744 runs

Individual Hitters: +183 runs
Individual Pitchers: +409 runs
Pythagenpat Difference: +173 runs
Team Offense: -73 runs
Team Defense: +52 runs

Team Characteristics: Earl Weaver's managerial tendencies are probably the best known of any manager since Casey Stengel. Weaver supported power, walks, defense, and strong solid pitching while having little interest in bunts and stolen bases. His teams also did very well in one-run games, 451–335 (.574) in his career (that counts the games he was on hand for in 1968 and 1985 but not the rest of those seasons). Casey Stengel and Earl Weaver are the only Hall of Fame managers who never presided over a 40-double performance from any of their hitters.

Earl Weaver was one of the most successful managers in baseball history. Some pilots succeeded by prioritizing run prevention, and others emphasized scoring. What makes Earl Weaver so unique was having clear, well-thought out approaches to both sides of the game that he successfully implemented.

Weaver was most renowned for his offensive philosophies, most especially as the leading proponent of the big inning in baseball history. Weaver believed that if a team played for only one run that is all they would get. Weaver's opposition to small ball is a bit overblown, however. In his earlier years he bunted and stole as much as most managers. It was only from 1977 onward that the Orioles constantly found themselves on the bottom of both those categories. From 1969 to 1976, the Orioles performed 548 sacrifice hits, fourth most among any AL franchise. After accounting for Baltimore's generally superior on-base percentages, they were still average in it. However, from 1977 to 1982, they issued only 192, tied with the Yankees for fewest by a junior circuit team in that period. A typical AL squad had approximately 100 more sacrifices in those years. Similarly, Baltimore cutback on their steals, declining from two swipes every three games from 1969 to 1976 to one every other game from 1977 to 1982.

Though he shifted away from small ball tactics in the middle of his career, Weaver always prioritized getting men on base throughout his entire career. To that end, he had an interest in the walk. From 1969 to 1982, the Orioles drew 8,131 walks. No other AL squad topped 7,500. With men constantly on base, his big hitters could collect more three-run homers.

When it came to run prevention, Weaver's strategy harkened back to giants like Comiskey, Moran, and McKechnie. Like them, he believed in working his starting pitchers as much as he could. The 1971 Orioles famously had a quartet of twenty-game winners. At least one pitcher won twenty games for Baltimore every year from 1968 and 1980, and one of Weaver's hurlers tied for the league lead in wins in the strike-shortened 1981 campaign. He presided over 22 occasions when a pitcher won twenty games, the most by any manager since World War I. Weaver oversaw 32 different 250-inning performances under his watch. Since 1920, only Walter Alston had more (36).

With his durable arms, Weaver wanted pitchers with good control, and was less interested if they could overwhelm opposing hitters. Under Weaver, the Orioles never finished better than third in strikeouts per innings and were in the league's bottom three every year from 1972 to 1977. No Oriole pitcher ever struck out 200 batters in any of Weaver's full managerial seasons.

Instead, Weaver's pitchers prioritized control. From 1969 to 1982, Baltimore pitchers issued 6,534 walks while an average AL club surrendered over 7,200 free passes in that span. Weaver's squads drew more walks than they surrendered in each of his 17 seasons: the odds of that occurring by random happenstance are one in 131,072. Also, Baltimore's pitchers normally did a good job keeping the ball in the park. Only twice did they give up more long balls than the team's batters hit, and the worst difference was -8 in 1986.

With durable pitchers who did not let runners on base, the Orioles needed quality gloves to prevent their opponents from scoring. Weaver successfully found numerous superlative defenders to aid his team, and was willing to use offensively challenged players such as Mark Belanger at key defensive positions.

All of that is certainly central to understanding Weaver, but another facet of his Baltimore squads is worth delving into: his teams consistently got better as the year went on. He does not score as well as Al Lopez in the Tendencies Database when it comes to second-half improvements, but in many ways what happened was more impressive. Whereas Lopez's teams just flipped a switch at midseason and played better, Weaver's teams kept improving all season long. This is especially true if you look at the years 1973–82, ignoring the strike-shortened 1981 season when the games were not played in every month. That might sound like selective endpoints, but for purposes that will be discussed later, there are reasons to isolate this period. Here are Baltimore's month-by-month records, runs scored and allowed per game for 1973–80 and 1982:

Month	W-L	Pct.	R/G	RA/G
April	78–86	.476	3.984	.15
May	128–115	.527	4.143	.87
June	147–101	.592	4.393	.89
July	154–103	.599	4.613	.96
Aug.	158–105	.601	4.403	.68
Sept/Oct	184–91	.669	4.873	.45

The longer the year went on, the better Baltimore played. Even if these endpoints were arbitrarily selected, you cannot produce a similarly impressive table for any other manager.

The Orioles had a losing record four times in April, thrice in May, twice in June, once each in July and August, but never in September. Their worst September record in this period, a .555 percentage (15–12) in 1979, was better than Weaver's overall pre–July record. Their best April record — a .609 (14–9) performance (also in 1979, interestingly enough) — was worse than their entire July 1-onward performance.

Not only did his teams do better as a whole, but both their hitters and pitchers improved virtually every month. Actually, that is misleading. Baseball has an annual temperature curve because the ball travels farther the warmer the weather becomes. To see how the pitchers and hitters did, one must account for this. This adjustment is fairly simple: first figure out AL-wide runs per game for every month for the years 1973–80 and 1982, then take Baltimore's accomplishments, divide by league average performance, and then adjust by Baltimore's park factor. To make it easier to read, I will center each result at 100 (in which 100 is an average result and higher means better, lower worse). Weaver's hitters and pitchers stack up as follows for the years in question:

Month	R/G	RA/G
April	94	101
May	100	106
June	104	107
July	108	106
August	106	112
Sept/Oct	119	117

In both cases, one backwards step occurs, but those are minimal declines. The Orioles constantly began the year tepidly but ended with the best hitting and pitching in the game. That raises the question — how did this happen? Perhaps Weaver benefited from having a core of guys who kept improving. That is unlikely given the extensive turnover on Baltimore's roster in these years, but it is worth checking.

Among pitchers, only Jim Palmer lasted the entire period. He pitched better in the second half, but only slightly so, with a 2.90 early season ERA compared to a 2.80 later one. Given that the entire AL had a similarly modest decline (4.38 runs per game through June 30, 4.34 afterwards), Palmer's improvement was essentially negligible. Among the other major Baltimore pitchers of this era, Mike Flanagan and Ross Grimsley normally pitched worse in the second halves of seasons in the course of their careers while Dennis Martinez, Scott McGregor, and Mike Cuellar improved. Perhaps these hurlers pitched better later in the seasons Weaver managed them. However, there is a difference between saying Weaver lucked into pitchers who inherently improved in the second half, and that pitchers improved in the second half when working for him. The first rationale indicates the players were responsible for the uptick, but the latter does not.

Weaver's offenses improved by almost a half-run a game after July 1: from 4.19 to 4.63. Only Al Bumbry stayed there the entire time. He got a bit better in the second half over his career (again, all numbers here are career, not just the Weaver years), but only a bit as his pre–All-Star Break OPS of 709 gave way to one of 736. Ken Singleton had more plate appearances for Weaver in the years under investigation than Bumbry. Singleton improved in the second half, but by an even slighter degree than Bumbry. Some hitters got noticeably better, such as Eddie Murray, and Doug DeCinces. Others, including Bobby Grich and Brooks Robinson, maintained the same level. A few, like Mark Belanger and Lee May, got worse as the year progressed. As was the case with his pitchers, it does not appear that Weaver benefited from having a large collection of men who just happened to improve as the season wore on. His hitters improved on the whole, but not enough to explain Baltimore's annual surge.

That leaves one obvious variable: Weaver himself. One of Weaver's hallmarks as manager was compiling as much information so he could put his players in the game at the most opportune circumstances. Weaver platooned, but rather than rely on merely left/right information, he included who hit groundball pitchers better, who hit fly balls, who had more success against the curve or the fastball and so on. That was exceptionally difficult because it required gathering and mastering those details, and then also staying on top of how they changed from year to year and week to week. Players develop or decline over time. Maybe someone who could not hit curveballs practiced harder over the winter, or the lefty-masher lost a bit of his stroke. Also, Weaver's roster changed every year, as did the rest of the league's lineups. It all took tremendous work to become an expert at all these little details of the game. This explains his teams' annual slow start. He had to catch up to speed on how the six months off had affected everyone. He learned and as the season went on had an ever-improving sense of exactly where to put all his players.

That being said, the real benefit of Weaver's super-specialized strategic usage of players may have been psychological. His tactics assured that everyone on his squad had a particular to role to play, knew what it was, and would neither be overused nor allowed to rust on the bench. Having their widely hailed boss tell them what particular situations they should play in could boost their confidence when they played. Leonard Koppett, in *Man in the Dugout*, theorized that the stats Weaver kept on individual players meant less to him than the sense of control it gave him. Weaver could tell a starter someone had to hit in his place that day because the numbers say so, and it was hard for the benched play to argue. Many people in the sabermetric community believe batter-pitcher matchups (which Weaver religiously tracked) can easily be overused, especially if the sample size of plate appearances is not particularly large. By this line of thinking, placing particular batters before each pitcher provides (at best) merely marginal returns. If true, Weaver's approach gave his team little strategic benefit. However, even if Weaver was primarily interested in psychological rather than strategic practices with his players, it was highly effective. His deployment allowed his teams to consistently improve as the season wore on.

Assuming that Weaver's strategies helped the Orioles play better as the season wore on, it may explain why the Oriole improvements existed in the years they did. From 1969 to 1971, Weaver possessed one of the most dynamite rosters in history. Their success depended on neither mastering the details of how each athlete hit left-handed curveball pitchers nor on any intensive psychological ploys with his players. In 1972, that ended, forcing Weaver to adapt, which he did from 1973 onward. The 1981 strike put a crimp in his plans.

Weaver's approach, whether tactical or psychological, took a lot of diligence, which relied on an intense level of passion. He did not have it with him when he returned in the mid–1980s. Instead, the 1986 Orioles experienced one of baseball's epic collapses. On August 5, they were 59–47, in second place, two and a half games back. For a typical Weaver team, this was the time to strike. Instead they dropped 42 of their last 56 games, finishing last. It was Weaver's only losing season, and he retired immediately afterwards.

DICK WILLIAMS

> **W/L Record:** 1,571–1,451 (.520)
> **Managed:** Full Seasons: Boston 1967–68; Oakland 1971–73; California 1975;
>   Montreal 1977–80; San Diego 1982–85; Seattle 1987
>   Majority in: Boston 1969; California 1974, 1976; Montreal 1981; Seattle 1986
>   Minority of: Seattle 1988
> **Birnbaum Database:** +526 runs
>   Individual Hitters: +136 runs
>   Individual Pitchers: +51 runs
>   Pythagenpat Difference: +72 runs
>   Team Offense: +216 runs
>   Team Defense: +51 runs
> **Team Characteristics:** Williams's Tendencies Database scores are surprisingly
>   moderate. His squads normally do well, but rarely superbly. His
>   teams usually played small ball, bunting and stealing. They received
>   far more intentional walks than they doled out.

The Al Lopez commentary noted which managers had the oldest teams when the Tendencies Database scores for pitcher and hitter ages are combined. By the same approach, the following managers had the youngest teams:

Youngest Teams: Combined Pitchers and Hitters

Burt Shotton	0.844
Patsy Donovan	1.261
Dick Williams	1.389
Felipe Alou	1.394
Frank Robinson	1.467

Three of these managers worked for financially hamstrung teams forced by circumstance to play young squads: Donovan's employers sold off their best players, and the Expos, who employed Alou and Robinson, lost them to free agency. Burt Shotton is the all-time champion of playing youngsters, but in some ways he had an easier chore than Williams. Shotton managed merely two teams. One can argue circumstances led him to play the kids. Williams, however, worked for a half-dozen franchises, making it difficult to the point of absurdity to claim that the situations he managed in forced him to play kids every time.

Dick Williams lived to break in fresh talent. On the 107 occasions a hitter had enough playing time to qualify for the batting title under Williams, 32 were age 24 or younger. Only nine were older than 30, almost all of whom were established stars Williams had no choice but to play. For instance, three were Tony Perez seasons in Montreal and two more were Steve Garvey campaigns in San Diego. Only six of the 61 pitchers who qualified for the ERA under him were older than 30, and three of those were only 31. He had nine ERA-qualifying seasons from hurlers age 22 or younger.

Williams went with the younger player whenever possible. He was fearless about putting kids in the game and would stand by them if he thought they had the talent, even if they initially faltered when establishing themselves. With that level of trust emanating from their authoritative skipper, rookies rarely fizzled on Williams. He not only gave prospects a chance, but more impressively he did it in a way that ensured they consistently reached their potential.

When Williams arrived in Boston in 1967, he gave 22-year-old Reggie Smith the starting center-field job. Smith had a rocky start, with his batting average below .200 (with few home runs or stolen bases) as late as June 24. As a rookie manager, Williams must have been under pressure to bench him for a veteran while the team hovered around .500. Williams never wavered. With that show of confidence, Smith warmed up, ending the campaign second in the Rookie of the Year voting, helping Boston win the pennant. He was the first of four Williams's players to finish in the top two slots in Rookie of the Year voting.

Also in 1967, Williams found room for another 22-year-old rookie, reliever Sparky Lyle. Before leaving Boston, Williams made Lyle the relief ace, a position Lyle thrived in for a decade. He also made 23-year-old Mike Andrews the team's everyday starting second baseman. Andrews played far better for Williams from 1967 to 1969 than he ever would for anyone else. In 1969, Williams also oversaw a 21-year-old pitcher named Mike Nagy, who went 12–2 for Boston.

In Oakland, Williams had less opportunity to break in new players. They had already installed their dynasty's nucleus—Catfish Hunter, Reggie Jackson, Rollie Fingers, Bert Campaneris, Sal Bando, and Joe Rudi. Even still, Williams figured out how to work in Gene Tenace and saw Vida Blue emerge as a star.

After leaving Oakland, he landed with the Angels. In the Angels' final game before Williams arrived in mid–1974, veteran pitcher Bill Stoneman started for them. He never pitched for California again. Always ready to give someone a shot, Williams gave Stoneman's rotation slot to rookie reliever Ed Figueroa, who won 73 games in the next four and a half years. Within a month Williams took a shine to a call-up named Bruce Bochte, who played in most of the games down the stretch. He lasted over a decade as a starting first baseman. Williams broke camp in 1975 with Jerry Remy, a 22-year-old rookie, as his starting second baseman. That summer he gave Dave Collins his major league debut as California's everyday left fielder, beginning a sixteen-year career. Before losing his job next year, he eased in Ron Jackson at third base, kicking off a ten-year career. There were always more established player Williams could have chosen. Remy replaced Denny Doyle, whom Williams benched. Instead, Doyle became Boston's starting second baseman for a few years. Collins took playing time from Leroy Stanton, who had been, and would be, a starting outfielder.

Williams's most impressive youth movement came in Montreal, who improved from 107 losses prior to Williams's arrival to consecutive 90-win seasons largely on the strength of the foundlings he found time for. Williams's first move was not to add a kid, but redeploy one.

Since arriving in the majors in 1974, Gary Carter had played almost as many games in the outfield as behind the plate. In the five years Williams ran the team, he played exactly one inning in the outfield.

By making Carter the catcher, Williams opened up a hole in the outfield, which he filled by installing a 22-year-old rookie Andre Dawson in center in 1977. Like Reggie Smith a decade earlier, Dawson began the year in a miserable slump. Near the end of May he was hitting only .222 with a paltry six extra-base hits. Rather than panic, Williams stuck with the kid. Dawson handsomely rewarded him, hitting almost .300 the rest of the campaign, demonstrating power at the plate and speed on the bases, claiming the NL Rookie of the Year Award. Alongside Dawson, Williams placed Warren Cromartie in left field, where he remained a Montreal fixture for several years. Toward the end of his Canadian sojourn, Williams found room in the outfield for Tim Raines, who finished second in 1981's Rookie of the Year voting.

Williams also allowed numerous young pitchers to get a chance in Montreal. In 1978, Dick Williams broke in two pitchers, 23-year-old Dan Schatzeder, who went on to pitch in over 500 games, and 21-year-old Scott Sanderson, who lasted twenty years. Both soon became regulars in Williams's starting rotation. While working as a swingman in 1979, 21-year-old David Palmer went 10–2 with a 2.64 ERA. In 1980, despite toiling in the midst of a pennant race, Williams willingly cast aside veteran starters Bill Lee and Ross Grimsley for 21-year-old Bill Gullickson and 23-year-old Charlie Lea. Gullickson placed second in the NL's Rookie of the Year voting, and went on to start nearly 400 games in his career. Lea started in an All-Star Game before ruining his arm. Between Palmer, Sanderson, Gullickson, and Lea, the 1980 Expos had four pitchers 23 or younger start a combined 90 games.

In San Diego, Williams again played those without status. As had been the case in Montreal, Williams created a starting rotation mostly consisting of those he inserted into the role. He took a trio of men in their mid–20s with minimal major league experience — Eric Show, Dave Dravecky, and Mark Thurmond — and converted them all into regular starters. He also broke in a young Andy Hawkins, who went 18–8 for Williams in 1985. That quartet started almost half San Diego's games under Williams. Rookie Luis DeLeon pitched very well in 1982, so Williams made him the club's fireman in place of veteran Gary Lucas.

Half of the regulars in his 1984 pennant-winning Padres lineup were those who got their first real chance to play under Williams. Upon his arrival in San Diego, Williams gave considerable playing time to Alan Wiggins, even though he initially had no position for him. When he settled on second for Wiggins in 1984, the infielder responded by stealing 70 bases and received some minimal MVP support. Also receiving token MVP votes in 1984 was Padre center fielder Kevin McReynolds, whom Williams had broken in the year before. McReynolds went on to have a nice decade–long run. Left fielder Carmelo Martinez came sixth in the Rookie of the Year voting in 1984. Last, but certainly not least, Hall of Fame right fielder Tony Gwynn began his career under Williams.

Williams's finale in Seattle showed some of his old eye for fresh talent. Immediately upon his arrival, he installed the slick-fielding Harold Reynolds at second base. Reynolds played almost every game Williams managed, earning selections to two All-Star games. Danny Tartabull also began his career in grand fashion under Williams, as he hit for both power and average in his first two full seasons.

That was as impressive a roundup of rookie successes any manager has had since John McGraw, made all the more noteworthy by the same pattern constantly repeating itself with different teams. It fit Williams's most pronounced personality trait: a desire for control. Throughout his entire career and life he demanded control. In Boston, his litany of petty fines and rules eventually caused his ouster just two years after the team's first pennant in decades. In Oakland, he voluntarily resigned after winning consecutive world titles due to owner Charles Finley's nonstop interference. In Williams's later stops his contentious, controlling nature kept causing him to wear out his welcome. Just as had been the case with John McGraw over a half-century before, a desire for control led to an interest in playing those with less leverage. Rookies are the least likely to rebel.

The above notes one clear difference between McGraw and Williams: McGraw stayed with one team for decades while Williams repeatedly wore out his welcome. However, that reveals more about how the job of manager had changed than it does about differences between the two men. The only person who outranked McGraw was the owner, who allowed him plenty of leeway (and eventually McGraw became a part owner himself). That was not the case for Williams, who butted heads with some of his superiors. When players got exasperated with Williams, they could appeal to upper management and have them intervene.

That being said, it would be a mistake to portray Williams as McGraw's managerial clone. He usually had at least one player on his teams that McGraw would never have been able to tolerate. In Oakland, it was Reggie Jackson with his vain public persona. With the Expos, Williams worked with veteran flake Bill Lee. Williams learned to adapt his personality to some extent, but he still preferred to work with young players whenever possible.

8

Managing in a New Era of Labor Relations, 1977–1997

Over a period of several months in 1976–77, baseball witnessed its third great wave of managerial retirements. In terms of sheer quantity, this shift was the most noteworthy single-season mass exodus ever as five prominent managers—Bill Rigney, Paul Richards, Danny Murtaugh, Red Schoendienst, and Walter Alston—left in a few brief months. That quintet claimed eleven pennants and won nearly as many games as Connie Mack and John McGraw combined.

As had been the case with the 1920 and 1950–51 departures, this retirement bunching coincided with the sport's reinvention. In 1976 we witnessed one of the most momentous changes in baseball history as starting pitcher Andy Messersmith left the Dodgers and joined the Braves. In and of itself, that was not terribly important, but what mattered was how he got there. The year before he had won free agency by successfully challenging the reserve clause, which for generations had prevented players from deciding for whom they could play. Beginning in 1976, the game's athletes could make their own choices on where to work. As soon as that happened, a generation of managers headed for the exits.

The departing skippers who had won world titles—Murtaugh, Schoendienst, and Alston—shed the most light on how free agency affected their profession. An underlying similarity united this trio: they were their generation's preeminent company men. As such, it is fitting that they moved on just as the old order collapsed. Murtaugh had spent the previous two decades bouncing in and out of the dugout for the Pirates, dutifully filling whatever role they thought best for him. Red Schoendienst spent virtually his entire life on the St. Louis payroll in one capacity or another. By his sunset years in the 21st century, he had become a venerable Redbird mascot. Twice after 1976 the team called on him to work as interim manager. He loyally fulfilled that duty, though his managing days effectively ended in 1976. Alston spent 30 years in the Dodgers organization before retiring. Team owner Walter O'Malley had installed him as manager in the big leagues when no one else considered him to be an important enough person for the job.

Murtaugh's departure was purely coincidental: he died in December 1976. With Schoendienst and Alston, it was more interesting. Not only were they company men, but they both worked for teams built around clear notions of hierarchy that free agency directly assaulted.

Under the O'Malley family, the Dodgers were a famously well-run and structured franchise. The franchise maintained the game's deepest farm system, ensuring a pipeline of players arrived in Los Angeles. Walter O'Malley was known for being the most powerful owner in the game, largely setting the agenda for league business. The Dodger success was based on a top-down sense of organization. This approach affected how the front office related to the manager, which manifested itself in contract negotiations with managers. As noted already, Alston became manager only after O'Malley refused to give incumbent manager Charlie

Dressen a multiyear contract. Alston, recognizing his place in the O'Malley hierarchy, accepted year after year of annual contracts. It was this hierarchical franchise that lost Messersmith at the beginning of free agency.

The Cardinals, owned by Gussie Busch, also felt free agency threatened their traditions. Baseball historian Anthony Giacalone delivered a presentation at SABR's 2007 national convention on the way Busch's Cardinals reacted to the new labor arrangements. Giacalone noted that Busch had always been generous to his players, as he financed the game's first million-dollar payroll and willingly helped players with other problems they had. However, his kindness was predicated on paternalism. To win his favors, an employee had to acknowledge his authority and acquiesce to its legitimacy. Schoendienst acclimated himself to this workplace culture. Busch's franchise found it considerably difficult adjusting to the changed labor relations. When Cardinals star Curt Flood became the first player to challenge the reserve clause, Busch felt personally betrayed. When young players like Steve Carlton and Jerry Reuss made demands Busch felt were inappropriate, he ordered his front office to unload them *immediately*. After an owners meeting, on the eve of a labor stoppage in 1972, Busch distinguished himself with his hardline attitude. While the other owners, not wanting to say anything that could unite the players, gave brief non-answers to reporters, Busch went up to the press and ripped into the union. Busch's sense of the sport's proper moral order was under siege.

The Pirates, Dodgers, and Cards all took very different approaches to the new era of player relations, and their choices signified the ways free agency had affected the game and the managerial profession.

The Pirates abrogated any oversight of their players. They replaced the late Murtaugh with Chuck Tanner, the game's most laissez faire manager. Though Pittsburgh initially responded by winning the world title in 1979, Tanner's approach had a dark side. With no authority figures guiding them, the team floundered and the Pirates' clubhouse devolved into cocaine central. Former MVP Dave Parker became addicted and suffered on the field. Relief pitcher Rod Scurry's drug problems eventually cost him his life.

St. Louis went to the other extreme, hiring Vern Rapp as manager. A career minor league manager, Rapp increasingly sullen and bitter after years of being passed over for promotion to the bigs. By 1977, his caustic and denigrating attitude toward the players perfectly complemented Busch's hostility to the union. Though the team improved in the standings, the players rebelled against Rapp, forcing Busch to fire him in early 1978.

The Dodgers successfully piloted a path between those extremes. They replaced Alston with Tommy Lasorda, immediately claiming back-to-back pennants and shortly afterwards winning a world title. Lasorda neither abdicated authority as Tanner had nor alienated his players like Rapp. He maintained his authority, but did so through personality and charisma. He built up a sense of common identity on the Dodgers, with himself as the leader. Lasorda lasted nearly as long on the job as Alston, and won enshrinement in Cooperstown immediately upon retirement.

These different experiences reveal how managing in the free agency period contained both change and continuity for the job. Pittsburgh's mistake was their inability to notice that the end of the previous order did not mean all authority had become null. Some level of control needed to be maintained. Yet, teams could not unilaterally impose their ways on players, which St. Louis learned that the hard way. Instead, managers had to work at establishing a relationship. That is why Lasorda succeeded. He recognized players wanted some level of authority, but it had to contain a personal relationship. Though a delicate balancing act, it could be achieved.

In some ways, Lasorda merely did what managers had been doing for generations. Few had ever been complete dictators. Free agency did not change the truism that it is easier to fire one manager than 25 players. In fact, one can argue free agency changed little for managers. Teams lost some authority to determine who was on their roster, but managers had lost that power to the front office decades earlier. From a certain view, free agency affected upper management, not the manager.

While free agency primarily affected the upper reaches of the ballclub, that spilled onto their managers. Though they wore a uniform, they were part of management, and that association aided their authority in the age of the reserve clause. An alliance between GM Ed Barrow and manager Miller Huggins allowed the skipper to prevail over Babe Ruth in their 1925 showdown, for example. With free agency, a manager had less sway over veterans. Though managers always had to negotiate their relations with players, free agency made it a much more sensitive affair. In baseball's brave new world, managers retained their power because their players were willing to let them have it.

Sparky Anderson

> **W/L Record**: 2,194–1,834 (.545)
> **Managed**: Full Seasons: Cincinnati 1970–78; Detroit 1980–95
>   Majority in: Detroit 1979
>   Minority of: (none)
> **Birnbaum Database**: +526 runs
>   Individual Hitters: +259 runs
>   Individual Pitchers: +22 runs
>   Pythagenpat Difference: +197 runs
>   Team Offense: -85 runs
>   Team Defense: +133 runs
> **Team Characteristics**: Anderson's teams featured power-hitting offenses, and fantastic defenses. He was a one of the biggest users of the intentional walk in baseball history. His 1989 Tigers issued 66 more intentional walks than they received, the greatest negative discrepancy ever.

One of the game's great unwritten rules is that a team should never steal a base late in the game when blowing out the opposition. Anderson abided by this code with an impressive tenacity. Since 1956, only 26 squads never attempted a steal all season long when one side led by more than four runs. Sparky Anderson managed three of those teams. Only Felipe Alou, with four, managed more. Fifty-one teams tried only one steal during blowouts. Anderson ran five of those teams. Six other Anderson-led squads did it only twice, and four more three times each.

He was also distinctive, especially in his early days, for how he handled his pitching staff. Anderson gained the nickname Captain Hook with the Reds for his willingness to yank starting pitchers. Not only did Cincinnati routinely lead the league in saves, but if saves are divided by wins (which roughly adjusts saves for opportunity to collect them) they still finished at or near the top throughout the 1970s. Anderson did not want his starters to pace themselves for a full nine innings, but give it everything they had for as long as they could. If they merely lasted seven, that was fine.

Over time, he treated his relievers differently. In 1970, Cincinnati fireman Wayne Granger recorded 35 saves, a new baseball record. Two years later, another Reds reliever, Clay Carroll, broke that mark with 37 saves, making Anderson the first manager to coax 30-save performances from multiple pitchers. However, in his remaining 23 years, Anderson never had another bullpen fireman reach 35 saves. Even though closers racked up increasing numbers of saves as the years wore on, only Willie Hernandez ever topped 30 saves for Anderson (32 in 1984 and 31 in 1985). In Anderson's seventeen seasons in Detroit, those were the only times his closer bested 25 saves. In all baseball, there were 185 occasions a pitcher had at least 25 saves from 1979 to 1995. It is one thing to not keep up with trends as a manager ages. It is another for a skipper to retreat from his own practices, but that was what Anderson did.

With starting pitching, Anderson played a role in a more important contribution. Perhaps more than any other manager, Anderson caused the shift to the five-man rotation. By using Baseball-Reference.com's splits, David Studenmund noted in an April 2008 column at The Hardball Times website that the great sea change from the four-man to five-man rotation occurred from 1975 to 1976, when starts on three days rest dropped across all major league baseball by almost 30 percent. In 1975, there were almost as many starts on three days rest as on four. By 1976, it was almost a two-to-one advantage for four days rest. The four-man rotation never recovered.

Several factors aided this change, but one of the most important occurred in Cincinnati. In 1975, the Reds won 108 games while their hurlers started a mere ten games on three days rest. Only one other team in either league had less then twenty starts on that little rest. Though Cincinnati won with hitting, others ape the most successful squad's distinctive characteristics. Baseball would have moved toward a five-man rotation anyway, but Anderson was the manager at the forefront of this change at the precise moment when the strategy began dominating the game.

It is ironic that Anderson helped revolutionize pitcher usage strategies because his teams were never known for their staffs. Instead, position players won games for him. Glancing at his pitchers' stats demonstrates how little Anderson's teams relied on superlative pitching. It has long been recognized that stats like walks, strikeouts, and homers allowed say quite a bit about pitcher quality because they are independent of fielding. When these three pitcher peripherals are entered into the Tendencies Database (which examines them all on a per-inning basis), and their scores combined, Anderson's pitchers come off quite poorly:

Worst with Pitcher Peripherals

Burt Shotton	4.067
Jim Leyland	3.640
Dusty Baker	3.616
Sparky Anderson	3.614
Patsy Donovan	3.559

Anderson's squads were the worst in the league in homers four times and at strikeouts a half-dozen times. They actually had about average control on the whole, but two rotten scores and a mediocre one put him near the bottom of all managers. The ultimate Sparky Anderson pitcher was Jack Morris, who never distinguished himself with power pitching or superior control. He was durable and adequate — exactly what Anderson wanted. Some say pitching wins games, but Anderson's 2,194 victories and trio of rings indicate other routes to glory exist. For Anderson, pitchers were supposed to keep the team in the game so hitters could win it.

Though he never had any great pitchers, he had an embarrassment of offensive riches. Anderson piloted seven squads that led the league in runs scored. The 1976 Reds may have been the best offensive squad of all time, as they led the league in batting average, on-base percentage, slugging percentage, hits, doubles, triples, homers, walks, stolen bases, and (of course) runs.

Anderson had possibly more great up-the-middle players than any manager, with perhaps the game's best catcher in Johnny Bench, arguably its greatest second baseman in Joe Morgan, and possibly baseball's most valuable middle infield combo in Alan Trammell and Lou Whitaker. Catcher Lance Parrish and shortstop Davey Concepcion were perennial All-

Stars. All those hitters were in their primes under Anderson. He also oversaw quality performances from center fielder Chet Lemon, shortstop Travis Fryman, and catcher Mickey Tettleton.

Anderson's offenses played for the big inning. The best way to gauge how much a team emphasized playing for crash-and-boom baseball comes from a study done by Clay Davenport in the Baseball Prospectus book *It Ain't Over 'til It's Over*. Davenport attempted to determine what team offensive statistics best correlate with the big inning approach (which he terms "static offense") and which best describe squads that play for one run at a time (termed "dynamic offenses" in his piece). Based on his analysis, Davenport concluded the three stats that best indicate how much a team employs the static approach are home runs, strikeouts, and walks. When scoring runs in bunches, home runs are the main objective, strikeouts are the byproduct of swinging for the fences, and walks occur because opposing hurlers are more prone to pitch around them. Putting that trio in the Tendencies Database and adding the results, it is clear Sparky Anderson preferred static offenses:

Most Static Offenses

Joe McCarthy	1.374
Sparky Anderson	1.447
Gus Schmelz	1.799
Miller Huggins	1.804
Earl Weaver	1.901

Anderson's lineups topped the league in walks and strikeouts ten times each, while belting the most home runs "only" eight times.

Between his hitters' willingness to whiff and his pitchers' inability to fan the opposition, Sparky Anderson had the worst strikeout differential of any managers in baseball history, as the list below reveals:

Worst Strikeout Differentials

Sparky Anderson	-2,942 strikeouts
Clint Hurdle	-1,256 strikeouts
Gil Hodges	-1,234 strikeouts
Casey Stengel	-1,192 strikeouts
Miller Huggins	-1,153 strikeouts

This differential list is not perfect because of partial seasons; but a cartoonishly large gap separates Anderson from the field. In Cincinnati, his hitters suffered 1,018 more strikeouts than his pitchers notched while in Detroit it was a difference of 1,924. Anderson's teams featured a positive differential only six times, peaking at +63 with the 1987 Tigers. His squads were -63 or worse sixteen times, including a dozen that were worse than -100. The 1991 Tigers hold the record with a -446 strikeout differential; no other squad is on the wrong side of -400.

That is not the only differential Anderson scored remarkably at. Anderson tended to issue intentional walks, causing his squads to give more than they received, as the following list makes clear:

Worst Intentional Walk Differential

Sparky Anderson	-497 intentional walks
Frank Robinson	-218 intentional walks
Bobby Cox	-213 intentional walks
Danny Murtaugh	-203 intentional walks
Gil Hodges	-198 intentional walks

Given how dangerous Anderson's lineups were, one would expect him to have a positive intentional walk differential. None of the other managers listed had nearly as much offensive firepower as he did, making Anderson's above score that much more staggering.

Maximizing his offensive talent, Anderson was especially adept at filling out the lineup card. Placing hitters at the top of the order who can get on base is one of the most important aspects in creating the batting order. If they do not get on, the sluggers in the heart of the order will have no one to drive in. Baseball-Reference's team splits is the best way to study which managers were the most effective at placing the proper men at the top of the order. Like Retrosheet's splits data, Baseball-Reference gives team-wide statistics for every slot in the batting order. Unlike Retrosheet, it also adds together the top two spots, giving aggregate statistical information for each teams' table-setters.

For the Tendencies Database, divide the top two slots' on-base percentage into the team's OBP to determine which managers best filled out the top of their batting order. OBP best describes the leadoff man's role. Divide by team OBP because the table-setter OBP by itself says more about the talent on hand than the manager. Some managers consistently have OBP at the top of their order worse than their team-wide mark; others are consistently better. That is the tendency under examination. By this system, Anderson appears brilliant at this part of the job:

Best at Putting OBP in Top 2 Slots

Sparky Anderson	0.572
Red Schoendienst	0.613
Bruce Bochy	0.753
Buck Showalter	0.801
John McNamara	0.814

Pete Rose and Joe Morgan gave Anderson the high score at this tendency every year from 1972 to 1975. He also had a terrific stretch with Tony Phillips and Lou Whitaker batting one-two for the Tigers in the 1990s. Whitaker and Trammell also had their moments in the 1980s.

ROGER CRAIG

W/L Record: 738–737 (.500)

Managed: Full Seasons: San Diego 1978–79; San Francisco 1986–92
           Majority in: (none)
           Minority of: San Francisco 1985

Birnbaum Database: -108 runs
           Individual Hitters: -18 runs
           Individual Pitchers: +35 runs
           Pythagenpat Difference: -108 runs
           Team Offense: +73 runs
           Team Defense: -90 runs

Team Characteristics: Craig, the apostle of the split-fingered fastball, is most famous for his work with pitchers. Despite having a weak collection of starters in San Francisco, Craig coaxed unexpectedly good work from veterans like Mike Krukow, Mike LaCoss, Scott Garrelts, and Vida Blue. Also, none of Craig's pitchers ever walked 80 batters in a season, a fact no manager with a longer career can claim. Craig liked to have his team steal when the game was close, but not at all otherwise. In his full seasons, only 28 of his squads' 1,590 attempted steals came when the game was more than four runs out of reach.

Known as "Humm Baby" for the nonsensical phrase he repeated as his own personal "Attaboy," Roger Craig paid as much attention to the double play as any manager in baseball history. When examining double plays turned per opportunity — DP/(H-2B-3B-HR+BB+HB-SH-SB-CS) — his teams were the best in the league three times, and were in the top four in all but one of his seasons. Craig does not qualify for the Tendencies Database leader list because his career lasted only nine years, but his score of 0.508 would be second only to Danny Murtaugh. That is amazing since Murtaugh's longtime second baseman was Bill Mazeroski, the Human Pivot himself. Also, both the Padres and Giants were among the worst in the league at turning double plays before Craig arrived.

Craig achieved his impressive record by placing the key defensive cog in the lineups of both teams he ran. In San Diego, he installed rookie shortstop Ozzie Smith in the lineup and played him virtually every game for the next two years. While Smith was obviously spectacular with his glove, it is easy to forget how heinous his bat was in those early days. Smith began 1979 with an 0-for-32 slump and by the last week of May his AVG/SLG/OBP was a pathetic .148/.233/.181. Many would have rested him more or possibly yanked him from the starting lineup. Craig refused. Though Smith did not crack .200 until August, he played almost every game that season. With the Giants, Craig gave the second base job to Robby Thompson, who was great at the pivot. Both San Diego and San Francisco set franchise single-season defense double play records under Craig that still stand: 171 with the 1978 Padres, and 183 with the 1987 Giants.

Craig's interest in double plays extended beyond defense; avoiding them was a central facet of his offenses. He loved the hit-and-run, a tactic employed to minimize the possibility for grounding into a double play. Using Chapter 2's hit-and-run estimation method, Craig receives a score of 0.427, while the best score of any man with at least ten years on the job was 0.548 by Birdie Tebbetts. Craig could have finished last in the league in a tenth season and still comfortably led the field. Also, Craig was a big believer in the bunt. Thrice he led the league in most bunts per opportunity and came in second place in another trio of seasons. Most of his bunts moved a runner from first to second, eliminating the possibility of grounding into a double play (though he was also willing to call suicide squeezes). None of Craig's hitters ever grounded into more than seventeen double plays in a season. In contrast, baseball contained 142 occasions someone grounded into eighteen or more double plays in the years Craig managed.

Between his interest in having infielders pull off the double play and his antipathy for hitting into them, Craig's teams scored one of the greatest advantages in double plays in history. In his years as manager, the Giants turned at least 134 double plays every season, but only hit into 100 double plays twice, peaking at 111. Admittedly, as noted in the last chapter, comparing raw GIDP and DP numbers can be misleading. Even when his totals are adjusted by the system listed in the previous chapter's Gene Mauch commentary, Roger Craig has the third greatest double play differential of all time, +326. The only managers ahead of Craig, Casey Stengel and Mauch, each had careers nearly three times as long as his. Craig's average advantage was 36.2 double plays per season, a far better rate than Mauch (16.9) or Stengel (21.5). Among all managers with at least six years of double play information, no one else exceeds 27 per season. From 1986 to 1992, the Giants grounded into 647 double plays while every other NL franchise hit into at least 700. In those same seasons, San Francisco's defenses pulled off 1,085 double plays, also the best in the league. Only one other team topped 1,000 twin killings.

Craig's focus on the double play had its downside as a batter swinging and missing on a hit-and-run results in an unintended stolen-base attempt. As a result, Craig's squads had subpar stolen-base success rates. San Diego had below average success despite the presence of speedsters like Ozzie Smith. Even less impressively, San Francisco finished in the bottom three in stolen-base success in each of Craig's seasons. Under Craig, Kevin Mitchell was 25 of 48 in stolen-base attempts, Matt Williams was 24 of 46, and Candy Maldonado 22 of 40. In 1987, Will Clark stole five bases in 22 attempts.

Given Craig's interest in the double play, it was clear he lost his touch in his final season, 1992. He appears to have called far fewer hit-and-runs, and that was the year his team grounded into 111 double plays. One Giants fan once told me that Craig looked so old in the dugout that year one just hoped he survived the season. As impressive as his double play inclinations were, they are watered down by that campaign.

JIM FREGOSI

> **W/L Record:** 1,028–1,095 (.484)
> **Managed:** Full Seasons: California 1979–80; Chicago (AL) 1987–88;
> Philadelphia 1992–96; Toronto 1999–2000
> Majority in: California 1978; Chicago (AL) 1986; Philadelphia 1991
> Minority of: California 1981
> **Birnbaum Database:** -39 runs
> Individual Hitters: +38 runs
> Individual Pitchers: +37 runs
> Pythagenpat Difference: -76 runs
> Team Offense: +41 runs
> Team Defense: -79 runs
> **Team Characteristics:** Fregosi did not like issuing intentional walks, but his pitchers gave out plenty of unintentional ones. His teams had very high success rates when they attempted to steal. On the 1991–96 Phillies, catcher Darren Daulton was 28 for 31 in steals, Jim Eisenreich was 32 for 35, Stan Javier 17 for 18, and Mark Whiten 20 for 23. Fregosi is the only manager to last at least ten years in the profession without ever having a batter belt at least eight triples in a season.

In his youth, many thought Fregosi was a natural leader, and widely considered him to be future managerial material. Once given the job, his career was a letdown as he turned into a journeyman skipper. His pre-managerial image allowed him more opportunities to ply the trade. Most managers with undistinguished performances in their first two hirings do not get a third try, but Fregosi did. Ultimately, he became the most forgettable four-decade manager since Roger Peckinpaugh.

Fregosi had his moment in the sun, though, as the Phillies won the pennant under his tutelage in 1993. That year Fregosi used numerous in-game substitutions to help out the team's defense. That was interesting because normally Fregosi rarely made mid-game switches of positional players. Retrosheet lists complete games for all players on a team for all the years it has game logs. Subtract pitcher completions from it, and it turns out that Fregosi was historically averse to removing his starters in the midst of a contest:

Most Complete Games by Position Players

Danny Murtaugh	0.311
Cito Gaston	0.320
Ralph Houk	0.389
Jim Fregosi	0.503
Don Zimmer	0.607

Fregosi led the league in position player complete games four times. He was in the top five almost every single season he managed. He only missed the top half once — his 1993 pennant winner. That was very strange for multiple reasons. First, managers usually repeat what they did in their most successful moments. Second, better teams are more likely to have complete games because they have a more solid starting unit. If Fregosi was willing to pull his best team, one would imagine he would yank the starters from his lesser squads. Yet that was not the case.

Though Fregosi let the same men play in an entire contest, he did not always start the same eight. At times, he liked to platoon. Other times, he just did not have much talent on hand, making it more difficult to come up with a set lineup. As a result Fregosi used his bench more than most managers, but the men who began the day on the bench could be certain they would end the day there. For example, in 1995–96, despite rarely allowing for using in-game substitutions, Fregosi's starting eight was near the bottom of the league in the percentage of plate appearances gobbled up.

Cito Gaston

W/L Record: 734–673 (.522)
Managed: Full Seasons: Toronto 1990–96
         Majority in: Toronto 1989, 1997, 2008
         Minority of: (none)
Birnbaum Database: -32 runs
         Individual Hitters: -41 runs
         Individual Pitchers: +135 runs
         Pythagenpat Difference: -22 runs
         Team Offense: -86 runs
         Team Defense: -18 runs
Team Characteristics: To Cito Gaston, "bunt" was a four-letter word. So were "pinch hit," "defensive replacement," and "young pitcher." His hitters had power and knew how to get on base, but struck out a ton. Pat Hentgen and Roger Clemens accounted for 36.6 percent of all innings thrown on the 1997 Blue Jays, the highest percentage by any team's top two hurlers in the last twenty years.

Cito Gaston belongs on a short list of baseball managers: he is one of only 21 who won multiple World Series. Thirteen of them made the Hall of Fame (all but Frank Chance as managers), and two others still managing assuredly will (Tony LaRussa and Joe Torre). A sixteenth, Terry Francona, is still in the midst of his managerial career. The others are Ralph Houk, Danny Murtaugh, Tom Kelly, Bill Carrigan, and Gaston. Carrigan voluntarily left the game to pursue other interests. Kelly also left the profession of his own free will. Heart problems shortened Murtaugh's career. Houk bounced between the dugout and front office for over twenty years before deciding to retire. That leaves Cito Gaston. After Toronto fired him in 1997, major league baseball took a collective pass on him for over a decade, until the Blue Jays tabbed him once more. Gaston is the only winner of multiple World Series titles unable to manage for as long as he wanted. Why did the lords of baseball continually pass on a man who had as many world championships as Earl Weaver, Leo Durocher, Al Lopez, and Wilbert Robinson combined?

There is an obvious elephant in the room — race. Baseball does not have a particularly good track record hiring managers who, like Gaston, were too dark to play before 1947. It took over 25 years before the hiring of Frank Robinson broke that color barrier. By 1987, only he and Larry Doby had run a squad — and Doby lasted only 87 games. That year Dodgers GM Al Campanis said on the television news show *Nightline* that blacks lacked the capabilities to be manager. Major league baseball responded to the furor Campanis created by setting up a program to aid the hiring of minority managers. Gaston was the first black manager hired after that incident.

This is obviously a touchy subject. No evidence exists that teams in the late twentieth century intentionally avoided hiring managerial aspirants due to their race. In fact, teams would definitely hire whomever they felt would be best. However, certain images and impressions — whether conscious or unconscious — can influence who they felt would be the best hire. To de-politicize this with an analogy, it is possible few pitchers become managers because people just are not used to hiring them in that role. The game's collective image of a manager is of a catcher or infielder, and pitchers are slotted almost exclusively as pitching coaches. A similar unintended bias can explain what happened here. After all, if teams were always willing to hire the most qualified individual, then why were no blacks chosen for decades? Certainly there must have been some blacks capable of managing from 1947 to 1987. These stains do not rub out overnight, so even after Gaston had broken through the glass ceiling, he could have trouble getting rehired. The game was changing. Dusty Baker, Don Baylor, Felipe Alou, Hal McRae, and Tony Perez had all become managers during Gaston's Toronto tenure, but transformations take time.

Also, Cito Gaston's managerial preferences hurt his chances at landing that next job. The ultimate minimalist, he had less interest in managerial razzle-dazzle than anyone else of his day. His teams were last in sacrifice hits per opportunity four times. Gaston used the fewest relievers in baseball five consecutive years. He also avoided using pinch-hitters. The 1993 world champs used only 30 all season, which is the fewest by a team in a full season since at least 1956. Even in strike-shortened seasons only the 1994 Orioles used fewer. Gaston was consistently among the bottom of the league in mid-game replacements for position players. In 1997, when he managed all but five games for the Blue Jays, 93.4 percent of Toronto's position players completed their starts — baseball's highest percentage in the 1990s. He used the same players day-in and day-out, only inserting bench players in case of emergency. He also did not issue intentional walks very often, though he was not quite as extreme about that as he was everything else. Most skippers avoid some of these maneuvers, but rarely does one completely distrust them all. In his book on managers, Bill James called Gaston inert.

There is an underlying philosophy: to succeed, a manager's best bet is always to trust his players' talent — especially the frontline players — more than his brilliance. Maneuvers like intentional walks and mid-game replacements just get in the way of victory. Ultimately, Gaston's passivity hurt his reputation. If a team had the talent to win, he would put it in place to earn victories. However, if a club did not have that much talent, then what? Most teams want to hire a manager who adds some value. Even teams that disdain small ball want a manager to help during the game.

During his latter years people began to doubt whether Gaston was good enough to be a tactical non-entity. Some of his later Toronto teams really underperformed, most notably the 1995 Blue Jays. When Phil Birnbaum debuted his database at SABR's annual convention in 2005, he used that squad as an example of a team that miserably underachieved. They won almost twenty fewer games than expected, according to Birnbaum's five components. Gaston's passive approach could easily be seen as a negative: he could not even bother to rearrange the deck chairs while the ship sank. By the time Toronto fired Gaston, several desultory seasons in Canada had tarnished his reputation.

Precedent exists for a manager with Gaston's success having trouble landing another job — Jimmy Collins, 1901 to 1906 manager of the Boston Red Sox. Like Gaston, Collins won back-to-back pennants as manager, winning every postseason series along the way. (In

Collins's case, there was no World Series after one of his pennants.) As noted in the Frank Selee commentary in Chapter 5, Collins was one of the most notable managerial minimalists of all time, as he rarely used his bench, kept his starters in as often as possible, and never leveraged his pitchers. Boston fell apart on him in 1906, just as Toronto did for Gaston 90 years later. Collins lost his job and no team ever hired him again, becoming one of the most successful managers to never get a second opportunity. His approach caused people to think he was a managerial cipher. It was Cy Young, Buck Freeman, and Chick Stahl that won it, not the manager. Similarly, people credited Toronto's success to a talent-laden roster featuring Roberto Alomar, David Winfield, and Joe Carter. Jimmy Collins and Cito Gaston may have run teams at opposite ends of the century, but they were each other's most similar manager.

Actually, one key exception to Gaston's minimalist ways should be addressed. He promoted an active running game in which his players not only frequently attempted steals, but recorded an impressive success rate as well. Adding together what the Tendencies Database says about frequency of attempted steals and success rate, the following managers got the most out of this tactic:

Stolen Base Success Plus Frequency

Whitey Herzog	0.833
Red Schoendienst	0.948
Cito Gaston	1.080
Walter Alston	1.286
Mike Hargrove	1.396

Gaston had as good a feel for when to let his players run as anyone in baseball history. In his original go-around with Toronto, the Blue Jays thrice led the league in stolen base success rate, came in second twice, and came in third twice. Their worst showing was fifth best. Admittedly they had a great core of baserunners with Roberto Alomar, Devon White, and Otis Nixon, but players routinely improved their stolen base success rate under Gaston. Below is a list of everyone with at least twenty steals on Toronto from 1989 to 1997, their success, total attempts, and success rate under Gaston; the same information away from Gaston; and the difference in their success rates:

	With Gaston		No Gaston		
Player	SB/SBA	Success	SB/SBA	Success	Difference
Roberto Alomar	206/252	81.7%	268/336	79.8%	+1.9%
Devon White	126/149	84.6%	220/295	74.6%	+10.0%
Otis Nixon	101/124	81.5%	519/682	76.1%	+5.4%
Joe Carter	78/104	75.0%	153/193	79.2%	-4.2%
Tony Fernandez	63/90	70.0%	183/294	62.2%	+7.8%
Paul Molitor	54/58	93.1%	450/577	78.0%	+15.1%
Mookie Wilson	46/54	85.2%	281/371	75.7%	+9.5%
Kelly Gruber	43/64	67.2%	37/49	75.5%	-8.3%
Alex Gonzalez	38/54	70.8%	59/91	64.8%	+6.0%
Junior Felix	31/51	60.8%	18/38	47.4%	+13.4%
Lloyd Moseby	24/31	77.4%	256/341	75.1%	+2.3%
Rickey Henderson	22/24	91.7%	1,384/1,717	80.6%	+11.1%
Shawn Green	21/27	77.8%	141/187	75.4%	+2.4%
Manuel Lee	20/27	74.1%	11/24	45.8%	+28.3%

Twelve out of fourteen improved. The worst fall was -8.3 percent by Kelly Gruber, who never stole that much anyway. Alternately, six improved by more than 8.3 percent. When Gaston returned to managing Toronto midway through the 2008 season he again oversaw a dramatic increase in basepath success. Prior to his arrival, they were 47 for 70 (67.1 percent) in stolen base attempts, but under Gaston, they were 33 for 37 (89.2 percent).

WHITEY HERZOG

> **W/L Record:** 1,281–1,125 (.532)
> **Managed:** Full Seasons: Kansas City 1976–79; St. Louis 1981–89
> 　　　　　Majority in: Texas 1973
> 　　　　　Minority of: California 1974; Kansas City 1975; St. Louis 1980, 1990
> **Birnbaum Database:** +404 runs
> 　　　　　Individual Hitters: -6 runs
> 　　　　　Individual Pitchers: +256 runs
> 　　　　　Pythagenpat Difference: +137 runs
> 　　　　　Team Offense: +65 runs
> 　　　　　Team Defense: -48 runs
> **Team Characteristics:** Herzog had some of the most extreme proclivities in
> 　　　　　history. His teams had bullpens, speed, and defense. He had a terrific
> 　　　　　record in one-run games, 410–354 (.537). That figure includes the
> 　　　　　games he managed in partial seasons, and only the ones he was
> 　　　　　responsible for in those years. He preferred control pitchers over
> 　　　　　dominating strikeout artists.

Whitey Herzog is so closely identified with a particular brand of baseball that the public nicknamed it "Whiteyball" after him. Most famously, Herzog was the biggest advocate of an effective running game in the last ninety years, possibly ever. In fact, Herzog's association with steals began when he was a coach. Herzog served as a coach on Dick Williams's 1975 Angels when that squad became the first team in over a half-century to steal more than 200 bases, with 220. Before Kansas City lured Herzog away at midseason, California averaged 2.5 stolen base attempts per game, but that rate fell by over half after Herzog's departure. In 1976, his first full season as manager, the Royals stole 218 while the Angels dropped back to 126 thefts. In the last 90 years, only 30 teams have reached 200 swipes in a campaign. Herzog managed ten of them — eleven if you count the 1990 Cards, whom he ran for 80 games. In the 1980s, St. Louis stole 2,045 bases. Since 1920, no other franchise has topped 1,700 in a decade. The impressive stolen base record of the Cardinals is especially noteworthy because Herzog served as the club's GM for a spell in the 1980s, giving him that much more input into the team's proclivities.

His squads not only stole frequently, but had an impressive success rate in their attempts. From 1983 to 1989, St. Louis featured one of the NL's top three stolen base success rates every season. When stealing as often as Herzog's clubs did, it should be that much harder to have an impressive success rate because the opposition always expects the swipe. Yet Herzog balanced quantity and quality with his teams' base thefts.

However, Herzog realized no one could steal first base. As a result, his Cardinals consistently ranked near the top of the league in OBP, and the Royals also did well by that metric. The Royals got on by getting hits, but the Cards mixed walks with their singles. Herzog rarely had a player who drew tremendous amounts of walks, but he had many who could draw at least 70 in a season. With the exception of Willie McGee, almost his entire regular Cardinal starters could be counted on to draw at least 50.

Whiteyball centered on a very active offense, with the ball constantly in play. In the same article (mentioned back in the Sparky Anderson commentary) in which Clay Davenport looked at the game's most static offenses, he also examined the most dynamic ones. He found three stats that best correlated with movement-oriented offenses: singles, triples, and steals. After plugging those three items into the Tendencies Database and adding their results together, the following managers had the most dynamic offenses:

Most Dynamic Offenses

Whitey Herzog	1.316
Red Schoendienst	1.470
Tom Kelly	1.910
Hughie Jennings	1.952
Clark Griffith	2.152

Only Schoendienst even approaches Herzog. Due to his fixation on movement-based baseball, Herzog was disinterested in the long ball. He allowed sluggers John Mayberry and Ted Simmons to depart Kansas City and St. Louis respectively. The St. Louis Cards never ranked higher than tenth in the league in isolated power from 1982 to 1989. The 1986 squad hit only 58 home runs, the fewest of any club in a full season all decade.

By placing a premium on baserunning, Herzog was interested in a set lineup, because the best basestealer did not change depending on the opponent. The 1986 Cards had the starting eight position players gobble up 80.5 percent of all plate appearances, the highest percentage of any team in the last 30 years.

Despite relying on the same players every day, Herzog remained attentive to platoon advantage by collecting switch-hitters. Again, in St. Louis this effect was at its most dramatic. Only three teams in the last half-century have had the platoon advantage in at least four-fifths of their plate appearances — the 1985–87 Cards, who score at 83.2 percent, 86.4 percent, and 80.0 percent respectively. Every team of his in St. Louis had the lefty/righty advantage over 70 percent of the time. Normally, only one team in 24 achieves that.

Herzog's prioritization of speed gave St. Louis a fantastic defense. Ozzie Smith exemplified this, as he stole dozens of bases a year while providing the most sensational glove work of his generation. Though no one matched Smith's innate defensive ability, his teammates could use their legs to run down more balls than average. As a result, Herzog's teams routinely scored quite well in Defensive Efficiency Ratio. Between Kansas City and St. Louis, his squads were in the top four on nine different occasions.

Superior fielding allowed Herzog to collect pitchers who were durable, but not overpowering. His Kansas City teams were average (at best) at strikeouts per inning. The Cardinals staff was even worse. From 1981 to 1989, they never ranked better than ninth in this category while coming in last four times. Overall, the Cardinals struck out 6,751 batters in those nine years, which was easily the smallest total by any National League team. The other eleven clubs averaged nearly 8,000 pitcher strikeouts and the team nearest St. Louis had an edge of more than 500 strikeouts (San Diego at 7,295).

Herzog never had a great pitcher. Instead he relied on guys like Joaquin Andujar, John Tudor, Dennis Leonard, and Larry Gura — solid, unspectacular workingman's pitchers. They were not supposed to win the game, just avoid losing it so the gloves and legs behind them could guide the squad to victory. As a result, Herzog's staffs, aside from his sole Texas campaign, were always in the top half of the league in fewest walks allowed per inning. Giving out free passes could lose the contest. Herzog added an unquenchable passion for theft to the formula invented by Charles Comiskey and perfected by Bill McKechnie.

Unlike McKechnie, Herzog dearly prized his bullpen. Nothing demonstrates the importance he placed on ace relievers better than the 1980–81 off-season. Right after he had become St. Louis's GM, he traded for two Hall of Fame closers: Rollie Fingers and Bruce Sutter. Herzog never intended to keep both, and in fact flipped Fingers for prospects by Opening Day, but it was the most aggressive push for frontline relievers any team has ever made. Herzog kept Sutter as his closer for several years, and when Sutter went to Atlanta, young Todd Worrell stepped into the role. Along the way St. Louis collected fabulous secondary relief pitchers such as Jeff Lahti and Ken Dayley.

A unified idea of how to build a ballclub runs through Herzog's teams. It starts with offense. Whiteyball was designed to be more consistent than average. Compare a Whitey Herzog team that averages four runs a game with a normal team that does the same. A normal team would have more power than a Herzog squad, resulting in more games where they scored large chunks of run. Correspondingly, the power-driven squad would have fewer runs to go around in the other games. Herzog, with an offense built to play for one run at a time would be harder to shut out altogether. The offense practiced a form of Chinese water torture. Instead of the drip-drip-drip driving someone mad, the swipe-swipe-swipe kept digging away on the scoreboard. The upshot: the offense consistently kept them in games. Similarly, his starting pitchers kept the team in the contest by not making mistakes and by relying on their defense. That let the bullpen decide the game. Herzog had designed the Cards so their superior bullpen would shut down the opposition, while his Chinese stealing torture continued. Thus they should hold leads and make comebacks. The 1985 Cards held every single ninth-inning lead they had all regular season. That is how Herzog designed them. There is a reason why his winning percentage in one-run games is even better than his overall record. If you check Herzog's results from the Birnbaum Database you will see his teams considerably exceeded their pythagenpat projections. With some managers that might be a fluke, but if that ever represents design, it was with Whitey Herzog's teams.

DAVEY JOHNSON

> **W/L Record:** 1,148–888 (.564)
> **Managed:** Full Seasons: New York (NL) 1984–89; Cincinnati 1994–95; Baltimore
> 1996–97; Los Angeles 1999–2000
> Majority in: Cincinnati 1993
> Minority of: New York (NL) 1990
> **Birnbaum Database:** +386 runs
> Individual Hitters: +209 runs
> Individual Pitchers: +54 runs
> Pythagenpat Difference: +97 runs
> Team Offense: +13 runs
> Team Defense: +13 runs
> **Team Characteristics:** His offenses were above average in almost every category in the Tendencies Database. They did especially well with power, but really, his offenses could beat opponents with everything except a sacrifice bunt. Davey Johnson thought the intentional walk a tool of the devil.

Davey Johnson is one of the most underrated managers in baseball history. He has his supporters, but the conventional wisdom across the sport does not give him enough credit. He had an impressive track record improving teams that hired him. Yet instead of earning job security, management showed him the door with considerable rapidity.

For over a decade prior to their hiring of Johnson, the Mets finished no higher than third. They performed no worse than second place every year Johnson was there. Yet a rotten quarter in 1990 was enough to cost him his job. In some ways Johnson was a victim of his own success, as the team had gotten used to competing. Johnson's failure to clear that last hurdle also hurt him, as the Mets racked up more second-place finishes than firsts. That was a fluke of divisional alignment. For whatever reason, baseball's powers believed St. Louis and Chicago belonged to the east, and Atlanta and Cincinnati in the west. In 1985 and 1987 the Mets won more games than any other team in the NL except the Cards. In 1984, the Mets would have won the division if the Cubs were in the geographically sensible locale. With a geographically appropriate realignment, the Mets would have won five consecutive division titles from 1984 to 1988, instead of settling for a pair of postseason appearances in 1986 and 1988.

Despite Johnson's success, it took a few years until another club claimed him. When Cincinnati finally gave Johnson another opportunity, he made the most of it. The Reds came in first place in his only two full seasons there, 1994–95. They have only one other first-place finish in the last 30 years. Team owner Marge Schott rewarded Johnson with a pink slip because she had previously promised Ray Knight the job. Her sense of loyalty outweighed doing what was best for the team. Cincinnati's winning percentage dropped by 90 points immediately after Johnson departed.

Johnson next landed with Peter Angelos's Orioles, taking them to the postseason in 1996 and 1997; those are Baltimore's only October appearances in the last quarter-century. However, Angelos is one of the most micromanaging contemporary owners, and Johnson has an ego. Again he lost his job despite his success. Baltimore's record declined by nineteen games in 1998 after that firing, and the franchise has not posted a winning season since.

Johnson's record was not as impressive in Los Angeles, but few well-traveled managers bring success to every squad they work for. Even still, Johnson's Los Angeles tenure was not bad. He still had an overall winning record there, albeit by the narrowest of margins. The Dodgers, like all of Johnson's previous employers, fired him.

Overall, in a dozen complete campaigns with four separate franchises, Johnson had exactly one losing record, which was only nine games under .500. He was at least ten games over .500 in every other full season.

No single clear reason explains why Johnson was so underrated. His frequent firings, however unusual the circumstances, could not have helped his reputation. Also, his teams had trouble in the postseason. Though they actually won more games than they lost in October (19–18), they only captured one pennant. That team, the 1986 Mets, had to endure two unexpectedly close postseason series to claim their championship despite rolling through the league with a tremendous 108-win team. The 1988 Mets lost the NLCS to a Dodgers team that they had defeated in eleven out of twelve regular season conquests. With less tangible achievements to his name and many short stints, Johnson's reputation suffered.

As manager, Johnson did whatever he could to coax more runs from his squads. The best example of this came with his handling of the shortstop position with the Mets. Starting shortstop Rafael Santana was a good-glove, no-hit player. They also had starting pitcher Sid Fernandez, an extreme fly ball pitcher who consistently placed among the league leaders in strikeouts. Putting two and two together, Johnson frequently gave Santana a day off when Fernandez pitched. In 1986, Santana appeared in 139 games on the year, but started only fourteen of the 31 games Fernandez took the mound. Instead, young Kevin Mitchell and the newly imported third baseman Howard "HoJo" Johnson got the starts. Neither belonged at shortstop, but their limitations with the leather would be less harmful with Fernandez pitching, and both represented considerable offensive improvements over Santana. For much of the summer of 1987, Davey Johnson again subbed HoJo for Santana when Fernandez pitched. When Kevin Elster, who was similar to Santana, became the starting shortstop in 1988, the arrangement continued as HoJo received almost half the shortstop assignments when Fernandez pitched.

While that was an inspired bit of roster management, Johnson's success with hitters primarily occurred because of his handling of players, not the lineup. For example, HoJo had already been drummed out of Detroit. Though HoJo's batting average was low, Davey Johnson was willing to look around that. Handed the third baseman's job in New York, HoJo took more pitches and began drilling those he did hit, becoming one of the best offensive third basemen in the game. While few improved as dramatically as HoJo did for Johnson, it was rare for anyone to underachieve on his watch, explaining his superb score with individual hitters in the Birnbaum Database.

With pitchers, Johnson worked his aces hard, which in the short term this led to impressive performances. Down the road, it created problems, as the career of Dwight Gooden revealed. Gooden was one of the greatest pitchers in baseball history before he was old enough to vote, but soon flamed out. Gooden also developed a drug habit that did him no favors, but neither did leading the league in complete games at age twenty. Alongside Gooden, the team simultaneously developed two other talented young pitchers, Ron Darling and Sid Fernandez. Both petered out by their thirtieth birthdays.

Johnson's most distinguishing strategic characteristic as manager also involved pitching — he loathed the intentional walk, as the Tendencies Database reveals:

Least Likely to Issue Intentional Walks

Davey Johnson	1.736
Casey Stengel	1.602
Tom Kelly	1.556
Felipe Alou	1.512
Tony LaRussa	1.479

Johnson's 1.736 is the most extreme mark in *any* category in this book. He was as militant in his aversion to this tactic as anyone has been to anything in baseball history. His teams were last in the league in intentional free passes six times, and thrice next to last.

The 1985 Mets received 52 more intentional walks than they dished out. Only four teams have ever had a bigger edge than that, two of which featured Barry Bonds. Johnson, over his career, had a tremendous edge in intentional walks, as the following differentials list makes clear:

Best Intentional Walks Differentials:

Tony LaRussa	+447 intentional walks
Dick Williams	+355 intentional walks
Davey Johnson	+312 intentional walks
Felipe Alou	+259 intentional walks
Walter Alston	+255 intentional walks

LaRussa has the largest overall advantage, but he managed twice as long as Johnson. In the years Johnson managed most of the season, his teams issued 442 intentional walks while receiving 754. Advantage: Johnson.

In his entire life, Johnson never issued an intentional walk that advanced the lead runner. Managers rarely like moving the runner forward, but three-fourths of all teams will do it at least once a season. It should be noted Felipe Alou can also make that claim (in a slightly longer career). Overall, however, Johnson remains the all-time enemy of the intentional walk.

Tom Kelly

W/L Record: 1,140–1,244 (.478)
Managed: Full Seasons: Minnesota 1987–2001

Majority in: (none)
Minority of: Minnesota 1986
Birnbaum Database: +75 runs
Individual Hitters: -107 runs
Individual Pitchers: -249 runs
Pythagenpat Difference: +96 runs
Team Offense: +80 runs
Team Defense: +255 runs
Team Characteristics: By most metrics, his teams had outstanding defenses. (Defensive Efficiency Ratio finds them average, but that could be a park effect.) His offenses centered on contact hitters who slapped out singles. He had little use for power hitters, and even less for bunts or the hit-and-run. His pitching staffs based their game on control.

Several years ago, ESPN.com columnist Rob Neyer invented the Beane Count in honor of Oakland A's GM Billy Beane's teams, which excelled at walks and home runs on both sides of the game. Tom Kelly's Twins took a different approach to baseball, eschewing the things that brought success to Oakland's early twenty-first-century clubs. When the Tendencies Database gets a hold of the Beane Count's four categories (all adjusted per plate appearances or innings pitched), these are baseball's most anti–Beane Count managers:

Least Interest in Beane Count

Tom Kelly	4.907
Burt Shotton	4.533
Jimmy Dykes	4.529
Fred Hutchinson	4.516
Jimmy McAleer	4.505

Kelly wins in a rout. Actually, that understates his tendencies because Kelly's pitching staffs were terrific at avoiding walks. With the remaining three components, Kelly scores nearly well enough (4.320) to crack the above list.

He was content to punt homers with Minnesota. After 1987, no Twin ever hit 30 homers in a season for Kelly, while baseball's other teams had 342 different 30-home run performances from 1988 to 2001. In only two of his fifteen seasons in Minnesota did the Twins hit more home runs than they allowed, both times by the narrowest of margins (151 to 146 in 1988, and 140 to 139 in 1991). From 1987 to 2001, Tom Kelly's Twins allowed 2,612 homers while blasting 1,902, which amounts to a home run differential of nearly -47 per season. For context, fewer than 130 teams (out of 2,500+) in baseball history have been -47 or worse in a season. Kelly's -710 homer differential is the worst in baseball history. Only one other manager (Jimmy Dykes) is below -400. Here are the worst single-season homer differentials in baseball history:

Year	Team	HR Differential	Manager
1996	MIN	-115 HR	Tom Kelly
1999	MIN	-103 HR	Tom Kelly
2000	MIN	-96 HR	Tom Kelly
1995	MIN	-90 HR	Tom Kelly
2006	KCR	-89 HR	Buddy Bell
2000	KCR	-89 HR	Tony Muser

A clear pattern exists. Please note 1995 was not a full season due to a labor stoppage. Those homer differentials reflect not only the available talent, but also Kelly's coaching tendencies. Former Twins' prospect David Ortiz once gave an interview explaining why his power erupted when he came to the Red Sox. He noted that in the minors his plate approach focused on hitting for power but when he came to Minnesota, they wanted him to shorten up his swing and approach the game the way everyone else on the team did. Thus a man with a pair of 30 home run seasons in the minors hit only one every nine games with the Twins. Upon arrival in Boston they let him go back to his old ways, and his homers, walks, and strikeouts all rose.

That story reveals the downside to Tom Kelly's managing, as he could be too inflexible for his (or the team's) own good. While Kelly was the worst manager for the David Ortizes of the world, he was not a net negative on the job. Kelly had a losing record in his career, but that was due to Minnesota's rosters. In the Birnbaum Database his score of +78 runs seems merely decent, but when circumstances are accounted for, he rises up. To compare: Kelly had +78 runs in 2,384 games with a .478 winning percentage while John McNamara scored at -174 runs in 2,415 games and a .484 winning percentage. The cigar-smoking Kelly had won four minor league manager of the year titles before getting his shot at the big league level.

Kelly punted Beane Count stats because his frame of reference centered on balls in play. The Twins were a difficult team to fan under Kelly. For example, from 1990 to 1993 the squad struck out 795 times per year. Other AL teams averaged over 900 whiffs per season during this span. Several players had their strikeout rates drop under Kelly. These improvements were consistent, though rarely dramatic. Gary Gaetti, Greg Gagne, and Corey Koskie were free swingers in their careers, yet none fanned quite as regularly under Kelly as they did away from him. The tendency was especially noteworthy with Kent Hrbek. The burly first baseman routinely had 80–90 whiffs a year, but once Kelly arrived he never had more than 60. A man who fanned more than once every seven at bats spent the rest of his career going down that way only one in nine times. Even Paul Molitor, who ended his 21-year career under Kelly, had his best single season strikeout rate under Kelly. From 1987 to 2001, no Twin struck out more than 130 times for him. The other AL teams had it happen to them on 112 occasions. Kelly's Twins made contact and legged out hits. In the Tendencies Database, Kelly had a higher score with batting average than Joe McCarthy (0.730 to 0.737).

With his kind of player, Kelly could be quite effective. Brian Harper was Kelly's kind of player. A back up journeyman catcher, Harper underwhelmed baseball by combining substandard defense with an inability to slug or work the count. Kelly focused on what Harper could do—put the ball in play—and made him Minnesota's starting catcher. From 1988 to 1993, in what should have been Harper's declining years, he developed into one of the game's best-hitting catchers, posting a .306 batting average while fanning once every twenty at-bats.

However, it would be wrong to consider Tom Kelly a small ball manager. He had no interest in the hit-and-run, for example. While a manager like Casey Stengel instinctively monitored the game to avoid possible double play situations, Kelly stoically resigned himself to double plays as a cost of doing business. In the 1990s, only thirteen teams hit into 150 double plays. Kelly managed five of them, and his 1999 Twins had 149. In 1996, the Twins grounded into 172, the second highest total in baseball history. As a result, double plays hurt Kelly more than any other manager in history. If you take team DP and GIDP, and give them the Mauch adjustments, Kelly possesses a sizable lead on the list of the worst career double play differentials:

Worst Double Play Differentials

Tom Kelly	-278 double plays
Mayo Smith	-222 double plays
Joe Torre	-210 double plays
Mel Ott	-189 double plays
Bruce Bochy	-184 double plays

When it came to run prevention, Kelly was a practitioner of the classic Comiskey philosophy of throwing strikes and playing sound defense. At the end of his career, he had one of the greatest defensive outfields of all time with the "Soul Patrol" of Torii Hunter, Jacque Jones, and Matt Lawton. The same squad had Gold Glover Doug Mientkiewicz at first. Ten of Kelly's teams were in the top four in fielding percentage. Twice they led the league in Fielding Win Shares, and were runner-up two other times. A manager can get away with minimizing the Beane Count approach by maximizing his team's quality on balls in play.

Even more than defense, though, control pitching typified Kelly's squads. Ten times they were in the top four in the AL in fewest walks per nine innings. The league averaged 3.5BB/9IP, but Kelly's Twins stayed under that every year except 1995. In the two dozen times someone threw at least 200 innings for him, nine times the hurler allowed less than two walks every nine innings.

This combination of solid defense with splendid control pitching allowed Kelly to minimize the importance of hurlers who blew opponents away. None of Kelly's starting pitchers ever struck out 200 batters in a season, rather unusual for a late twentieth-century manager. Only one-third of the pitchers who qualified for an ERA title under his watch struck out batters at a superior rate to the league as a whole. This fits into the philosophy pioneered by Comiskey and perfected by McKechnie: defense plus control equals less need for power pitching. Brad Radke was the ultimate Tom Kelly pitcher. He never struck fear in anyone's heart but he was durable and had great control. In 2001 he walked 1.04BB/9IP, the second lowest total by an American League pitcher since Walter Johnson.

With his lack of interest in the long ball and offensive walks, Kelly appeared to be a man from another era as the game's power numbers surged in the 1990s. Apparently Kelly thought so, because he voluntarily retired after 2001, despite only being 51 years old. In all baseball history, only one other person with at least 2,000 games managed who never served as a player-manager left at such a young age — Frank Selee, a century earlier. And that was not voluntary, as Selee was dying.

Tommy Lasorda

> **W/L Record:** 1,599–1,439 (.526)
> **Managed:** Full Seasons: Los Angeles 1977–95
>   Majority in: (none)
>   Minority of: Los Angeles 1976, 1996
> **Birnbaum Database:** -45 runs
>   Individual Hitters: +111 runs
>   Individual Pitchers: +306 runs
>   Pythagenpat Difference: -200 runs
>   Team Offense: -76 runs
>   Team Defense: -186 runs
> **Team Characteristics:** His teams revolved around starting pitching. He used them as much as he could and his bullpen as little as he could. Usually. Lasorda won the 1988 World Series largely thanks to an outstanding bullpen. He had nine different players win the Rookie of the Year Award. Lasorda has the longest managerial career in which none of his pitchers ever walked 100 batters in a season. He is the last prominent manager who never had a pitcher make 70 relief appearances in a season.

Lasorda is the most visible part of an impressive Dodger tradition — well-regarded managers. Of the nineteen managers currently in the Hall of Fame and three contemporary skippers (Tony LaRussa, Bobby Cox, and Joe Torre) destined for enshrinement, seven managed the Dodgers: Ned Hanlon, Wilbert Robinson, Casey Stengel, Leo Durocher, Walt Alston, Lasorda, and Joe Torre. The seven combined for approximately 80 seasons running the Dodgers; both figures are the tops of any franchise.

Lasorda is one manager I go back and forth about, veering from negative to sympathetic interpretations of his ability. Evidence can bolster either position. The darker take on his career notes that of the Cooperstowners, Lasorda is arguably the worst. Of those actually elected into Cooperstown, eighteen are in the Birnbaum Database (Harry Wright was too early). Most have among the all-time best scores, but three — Connie Mack, Wilbert Robinson, and Tommy Lasorda — have negative career marks. Mack was terrific but lasted far too long. Neither Robinson nor Lasorda has a similarly effective excuse for their tepid Birnbaum scores.

Robinson and Lasorda were similar in some ways. Not only did they achieve their most lasting fame running the Dodgers, but both personified the club. Lasorda spoke often about bleeding Dodger blue while fans nicknamed the Brooklyn club the Robins after Wilbert. Both are best remembered for their personalities, which overwhelm their public images. It is not a coincidence that the Birnbaum Database's two least favorite Hall of Famers were so personality-heavy. Personal charisma gives a manager more attention when he is employed, and makes for fonder memories after he retires.

Compare Lasorda to Dick Williams for a moment. They were contemporaries whose careers lasted almost as long as each other (an eighteen-game advantage to Lasorda), while each captured four pennants and two world titles. That achievement was frankly more impressive for Williams, since his pennants came with three separate franchises. Yet Lasorda went into Cooperstown as soon as he was eligible while Williams waited nearly two decades for enshrinement.

Lasorda had his warts. Most notably, he had a poor record keeping his best young pitchers healthy. They played very well for him — in the short term. Down the road, however, virtually every first-rate, tender-aged arm he got his hands on developed serious problems. In 1979, 23-year-old Rick Sutcliffe went 17–10 for the Dodgers to win the Rookie of the Year Award. He broke down badly the next year and only regained his form after escaping from Los Angeles. By that time, the franchise developed a much greater phenom, Fernando Valenzuela. The portly pitcher did not allow a single earned run in 17.7 innings as a nineteen-year-old in 1980, and began the next year with one of the greatest opening spurts in baseball history. Valenzuela won his first eight starts with an inhumanly good 0.50 ERA in 72 innings. He appeared destined for greatness, but petered out instead. After age 25, he was average at best. He had been the hardest-worked pitcher of his era, leading the league in innings and complete games at age twenty. Five years later he became the last man to complete twenty games in a season. Even before Valenzuela had flamed out, a new star had emerged — Alejandro Pena. In 1984, he led the league with a 2.48 ERA, but blew his arm out the next year. People scarcely noticed his absence because in 1985 Orel Hershiser went 19–3 with a 2.03 ERA in his first full-season as a starter. Hershiser led the league in innings every year from 1987 to 1989, tossing nearly 100 more innings than any other NL hurler while completing 30 percent of his starts. Then he too blew his arm out. When Hershiser went down, 22-year-old Ramon Martinez won twenty games, finishing second place in Cy Young voting. Like Valenzuela and Hershiser before him, he also led the league in complete games. After developing arm problems, he soon devolved into a journeyman. A pattern exists here, and it is not particularly flattering to Lasorda.

Pitchers get injured — that goes with the territory. It follows that not all injuries are the fault of the manager. However, when virtually all the best young arms under one manager's care go down, one has to wonder. There is nothing inherently wrong with a manager pushing his starting pitchers hard. Many had a great deal of success doing that. However, when guys keep breaking down on a particular manager the way they did for Lasorda, some of the blame will fall on his shoulders. Was Lasorda really a great manager, or just a loud personality who happened to be sitting atop a wealth of talent?

The above is one side of the debate, but much of it can be deconstructed. While Lasorda's overall Birnbaum mark is negative, he scores brilliantly with individual hitters and pitchers, which matches his reputation as a strong motivator. When added together, he is eleventh best of all time at the coaching components. Those are the two parts of the Birnbaum Database I have the most faith in. Lasorda's worst score comes with pythagenpat. On a purely gut level, it is easier for me to recognize the existence of coaching than to believe managers have a pronounced influence on their team's pythagenpat difference.

Lasorda's record with starting pitchers can be flipped in his favor as well. While he overworked Orel Hershiser, Lasorda was also the reason Hershiser became an ace in the first place. Hershiser had been a minor league reliever who Lasorda realized should start. Without Lasorda, Hershiser never would have collected 200 wins. Lasorda also made Pedro Astacio, who had not been a highly regarded prospect. However, after the 1992 Los Angeles Riot, the Dodgers played numerous doubleheaders that necessitated using any arm they could scrounge. Lasorda liked what he saw from Astacio in his start, and kept him around, nurturing him into a valuable pitcher. Many managers would not let him stick around on the basis of one game. Also, Lasorda should not be blamed for all the injuries as Pena was not worked very hard and Sutcliffe made a career out of falling apart and recovering. Frankly, even if Lasorda overworked his starters, that may be defensible under the circumstances. It was the free agent era, and he sat on a crop of quality arms— may as well ride them for all they were worth.

The record shows Lasorda got tremendous value from his starting pitchers. Teams need two things from starters—quantity and quality. Innings and park-adjusted ERA are respectively the best gauges of the former and latter. Run those two stats through the Tendencies Database, add them together, and discover which managers received the most from their starters since 1956:

Best Starting Pitchers: Quantity and Quality
Tommy Lasorda	0.945
Bobby Cox	1.155
Earl Weaver	1.157
Cito Gaston	1.213
Bill Virdon	1.266

Anyone who got more from his starting pitchers than Bobby Cox deserves the benefit of the doubt.

Given how much Lasorda used his starters, it is not surprising that his clubs had little interest in relief aces. When saves per win (saves divided by opportunities to tally them) are run through the Tendencies Database, the following managers had the least use for saves:

Fewest Saves Per Win
Tommy Lasorda	1.499
Billy Southworth	1.481
Charlie Grimm	1.429
John McNamara	1.411
Earl Weaver	1.392

Only once did someone save 30 games in a season for him — Todd Worrell with 32 in Lasorda's final campaign. During Lasorda's career 52 NL closers broke the 30 save barrier.

Only six times did Lasorda's closer get at least 20 saves, including none from 1978 to 1988. Instead, he had Valenzuela and Hershiser finish their starts.

Also, home runs were a strong point for Lasorda's teams. His staff, taking advantage of the pitcher-friendly Dodger Stadium, consistently surrendered among the fewest homers of any team. Despite the ballpark, Lasorda's offenses hit their share of blasts. Again, this can be verified by the Tendencies Database, which rates pitchers as homers allowed per inning and hitters as home runs per plate appearance. Based on the combined sum of that pair of formulas, here are the best results any manager has ever gotten from homers:

Homers and Homers Allowed

Joe McCarthy	1.212
Tommy Lasorda	1.278
Bobby Cox	1.291
Davey Johnson	1.330
Jimy Williams	1.338

From 1977 to 1995, the Dodgers hit 2,405 home runs and allowed 1,899, one of the biggest edges any manager ever had from the long ball. Only four times did his Dodgers allow more homers than they hit, and never by a margin greater than ten.

One final point should be noted on his behalf: the unlikely success of the 1988 Dodgers, one of the least talented teams to ever win the World Series. The most underwhelming rosters to win the Series almost always had terrific managers. George Stallings ran the 1914 Braves, Pat Moran the 1919 Reds, Bill McKechnie the 1940 Reds, Walter Alston the 1959 Dodgers, and Tony LaRussa the 2006 Cards. Even the 1987 Twins had the well-regarded Tom Kelly. It takes a great manager to win with second-rate talent, which is a sign in Lasorda's favor.

Ultimately, I find myself coming to the position that Lasorda is far better than the Birnbaum Database claims. He is overrated, but one can be quite good and overrated.

JIM LEYLAND

> **W/L Record:** 1,326–1,360 (.494)
> **Managed:** Full Seasons: Pittsburgh 1986–96; Florida 1997–98; Colorado 1999;
> Detroit 2006–08
> Majority in: (none)
> Minority of: (none)
> **Birnbaum Database:** -156 runs
> Individual Hitters: -102 runs
> Individual Pitchers: -278 runs
> Pythagenpat Difference: +17 runs
> Team Offense: +54 runs
> Team Defense: +153 runs
> **Team Characteristics:** Leyland's hitters are usually better than his pitchers. He
> gets plenty of innings from his bullpen, but he rarely works his pitch-
> ers on consecutive days. His pitchers are bad at striking out batters.
> At the conclusion of 2008, Leyland's record in one-run games was
> exactly .500: 408–408. Hitters qualified for a batting title 82 times
> under Leyland — and each one had at least one stolen base.

Jim Leyland's score is one of the most shocking finds in the Birnbaum Database. Despite possessing one of baseball's best reputations, Leyland rates quite poorly. The only prominent manager to score worse is Connie Mack, who the Birnbaum Database says was fantastic for his first 5,000 games.

Moving away from sabermetrics, Leyland's record is impressive. He came one at-bat away from having a guaranteed place in Cooperstown. Leyland took two franchises to the World Series, Florida and Detroit, and came achingly close with a third, Pittsburgh. The Pirates won three consecutive division titles from 1990 to 1992, and lost the last two NLCSs in seven games each. Only two managers won pennants with three clubs, and both are in Cooperstown: Bill McKechnie and Dick Williams. In Game 7 of the 1992 NLCS, the Pirates entered the bottom of the ninth leading by a pair of runs, but lost when pinch-hitter Francisco Cabrera capped Atlanta's rally by hitting a two-out single that drove in the tying and winning runs. Cabrera only had three hits the entire regular season and under 100 in a five-year career. Leyland came that close to guaranteed Cooperstown enshrinement.

A solid case for Leyland's induction can be made despite that disappointment. Pittsburgh floundered prior to Leyland's arrival, but posted a .595 winning percentage from 1990 to 1992, for the franchise's best three-year period since Honus Wagner's heyday. The Marlins never had a winning season before Leyland arrived and he took them to the Promised Land in his first year there. Detroit, which suffered through twelve straight losing seasons before Leyland came to town, captured a pennant upon his arrival. He did not have any success in Colorado, but even Dick Williams had his Seattle experience. In all, Leyland has five postseason appearances, three Manager of the Year Awards, two pennants, and one world championship. Yet the Birnbaum Database scorns him.

Two seasons ruin his score in the database: the 1998 Marlins (-127 runs) and 1999 Rockies (-211 runs). To understand why those seasons went so horribly wrong, it helps to look at the arc of Leyland's career. After presiding over Pittsburgh's revitalization, he remained for their demise. Almost all their best players fled via free agency for greener pastures causing Leyland, a man passionate about winning, to endure four straight hopeless seasons. Losing seasons at the start of one's career can be difficult to endure, but at least they can be viewed as a growing experience. Falling to the valley after reaching the mountaintop is harder to take. Thus being hired by Florida must have boosted Leyland's spirits. When the franchise hired him, it engaged in a massive spending spree that landed them the sort of free agents Pittsburgh could only dream of obtaining, such as Moises Alou, Jeff Conine, and Bobby Bonilla. After one season to savor the winning experience, the rug was pulled under from underneath Leyland. Team owner Wayne Huzienga, upset that local taxpayers refused to grant him he a new stadium deal, intentionally dismantled the team, deliberately dampening enthusiasm for the squad. It was one of the worst atmospheres any team has experienced in modern times. Leyland, freshly sucker-punched in the soul, could not build the energy to fight against it. He departed, only to find himself stuck with another rotten team in Colorado. When it soon became obvious that a high-atmosphere squad built around Darryl Kile's curveball had no chance, Leyland began commenting that he was exhausted and depressed. Little casts as heavy a pall on a club as a manager who does not want to be there. Denver stank. Leyland, desperately needing a vacation, left the game for several years to recharge.

That explains his low career score, but explaining is not a synonym for excusing. Other managers have gone through rough spells without floundering as badly. Leyland has a good Birnbaum score aside from those two years, but problems exist even there. Though the database gives him a tremendous score for Detroit's 2006 season (+93 runs) that was partially caused by Detroit's decline in 2007 and especially 2008. Those seasons will drag down Leyland's career score once they can be figured in Birnbaum's algorithms. The early part of Leyland's career helps him less than one would expect, too. Through 1997, he was +89 runs with a .503 winning percentage. That is nice, but similar to Mike Hargrove or Buck Rodgers; hardly Hall of Fame caliber. Also, since the Birnbaum Database is centered at zero, taking the two worst seasons out of someone's career should spring them over zero. Leyland does not get as much credit for his pre–1998 achievements as one might expect.

The problem lay with the Florida Marlins. The 1997 club is one of the few World Series champions to score negatively in the Birnbaum Database. While an individual season in the database should not be seen as telling us too much about the manager, in this case the 1997 Marlins' poor Birnbaum performance is striking because the club was so much worse in its surrounding seasons. As far as the math is concerned, GM Dave Dombrowski deserves the credit for assembling that team, not Leyland for running it.

Ultimately, Leyland's legacy will rest on what happens in Detroit. That is interesting because the Tigers strength is their pitching, and that has been Leyland's historic weakness. Detroit won the 2006 pennant behind terrific pitching as kids Justin Verlander and Jeremy Bonderman performed brilliantly while veteran Kenny Rogers was better than anyone could reasonably have hoped. However, Detroit's pitchers' performances have dramatically fallen since then.

Critics have always admonished the way Leyland handled his pitchers. For example, in April 1993 Leyland had knuckleballer Tim Wakefield throw 172 pitches in a game. That raised eyebrows even though nobody paid attention to pitch counts back then. Though it was high, it was not that unusual for Leyland. The year before Wakefield threw 290 pitches in his first two major league starts.

Leyland faced much more widespread criticism for his handling of Livan Hernandez, a superlative pitching prospect entrusted to his care. The 22-year-old Hernandez made a name for himself by striking out fifteen batters in one 1997 NLCS game. The next year, Leyland worked him as hard as possible. In midseason he endured successive starts with 131, 146, and 153 pitches thrown. Two outings later he threw 152 pitches. Two months later he hurled 136, 138, and 148 pitches in consecutive turns. A few years earlier this action would have gained little note, but two factors hurt Leyland: this came at the outset of the public concern over pitch counts, and much more importantly the bright, shining talent of the year before stumbled badly. Virtually all starting pitchers from the dawn of time until the mid–1990s were pushed harder than any current starters, therefore working someone hard is not inherently evil. However, when combined with little success developing pitchers—as is the case for Leyland—it looks bad.

Also, as wonderful as Detroit's 2006 rotation was, subsequent seasons have made that staff's performance seem like an aberration. Detroit, which looked like it could have the starting rotation of the decade, instead foundered. After leading the league with a 3.84 ERA in 2006, they fell to 4.59 in 2007, and in 2008 had a 4.91 mark, one of the worst in baseball. Relief ace Joel Zumaya got injured, Verlander regressed, and Jeremy Bonderman did both. Just two years after capturing the pennant, Detroit came in last, largely because their pitching staff was in shambles. Perhaps none of this is Leyland's fault. Young pitchers are always a gamble. However, as long as he has trouble developing his young arms, that mark will be held against him.

One other interesting feature about Leyland's pitching staffs is the lack of a dominating closer. Though not known as a critic of the role of closer, his actions indicate he thinks it is overrated. He either spreads saves out amongst his relievers or gives it to a second-rate arm, but he rarely uses his best arm exclusively in the ninth. In eleven years in Pittsburgh, only once did someone have more than 26 saves in a season (Jim Gott with 34 in 1988). Across all major league baseball, players posted 26 or more saves 135 times. During Pittsburgh's divisional threepeat, no one lodged over eighteen saves in a season for the franchise. In 1990, the main relief ace recorded only thirteen saves on a team that won 95 contests. No one on the 1994 Pirates had more than seven saves, even though the team won 53 games in that strike-shortened season.

The most obvious example of Leyland's treatment of relief aces came with Bill Landrum, who was the best closer Leyland ever had. Landrum recorded 26 saves with a 1.67 ERA in 1989, yet collected only thirteen of the club's 43 saves the following season despite posting a 2.13 ERA. Leyland was not using him as some sort of 1970s style fireman where others got all the cheap saves, he just removed Landrum from the role despite his brilliant pitching. On July 1, Landrum racked up his twelfth save and had an ERA of 1.62. After that, Leyland stopped using him in save opportunities. He was more likely to pitch in the eighth or when his team was done even though he was clearly the best arm in the bullpen.

Landrum was no aberration. Leyland frequently puts his best relievers in middle relief. This was especially apparent in Detroit where veteran plodder Todd Jones saved games while far superior performances came from Joel Zumaya, Bobby Seay, and Tim Byrdak. In Pittsburgh, Pat Clements clearly outpaced closer Don Robinson in 1986. When Jim Gott had 34 saves he was an average reliever. Dan Plesac's ERA was more than a run lower than that of nominal relief ace Dan Miceli in 1996.

BILLY MARTIN

> **W/L Record:** 1,253–1,013 (.553)
> **Managed:** Full Seasons: Minnesota 1969; Detroit 1971–72; Texas 1974; New York (AL) 1976–77, 1983; Oakland 1980–82
> Majority in: Detroit 1973; Texas 1975; New York (AL) 1978, 1979, 1985
> Minority of: Texas 1973; New York (AL) 1975, 1988
> **Birnbaum Database:** +715 runs
> Individual Hitters: +177 runs
> Individual Pitchers: +234 runs
> Pythagenpat Difference: +179 runs
> Team Offense: +74 runs
> Team Defense: +51 runs
> **Team Characteristics:** Martin's teams had superior batting average-driven on-base percentages. Their OBP was especially good at the top of the order. He relied as much as he possibly could on the front half of his pitching staff. He detested intentional walks.

Billy Martin was the most fearless manager in baseball history. In twenty years of managing, he never backed down from a challenge. As has been well documented by others, Martin consistently caused dramatic improvements to his squads immediately upon arrival by pushing them hard. The A's went from losing 108 games to fighting for .500. The Rangers, who had posted back-to-back seasons in which they had played .350 ball, suddenly won half their games when Martin arrived. The Twins and Tigers improved by eighteen and twelve games for him respectively. The Yankees won their first pennant in a dozen years under him. The Birnbaum Database gives him high scores for every stop along the way: +64 runs in Minnesota, +199 runs in Detroit, +91 runs in Texas, +142 runs with Oakland, and +219 runs in his various New York stops.

Martin's approach had its downside. He pushed his teams so hard they could not keep up with his pressure. Hiring Martin was like pushing too much voltage through a light bulb: for a brief while it burns brighter than otherwise possible, but it soon shatters unless the excess electricity is removed. Despite his impressive starts, Martin never lasted longer than three years in any managerial stint.

Though Martin is most famous for piloting the Yankees, his first managerial stint running the 1969 Twins best reveals his method and madness. The gutsy bravado and intensity to win that highlighted his career amply demonstrated themselves that year. Martin approached his rookie managerial season the same way a tough convict handles his first day in prison — determined to prove himself immediately as the cellblock's most dangerous man.

Martin's approach to the basepaths demonstrated how he wanted his team to play. In the second game he managed, Minnesota's Rod Carew stole home. This was no fluke — by the end of the month, Carew had three steals of home and by the season's conclusion he tied Ty Cobb's single-season record with seven such swipes. Three of them came on triple steals. On another occasion, Cesar Tovar stole home as part of a successful triple steal. Four triple steals are the most by any one team in the last half-century, and probably the most since the dead-ball era. On another occasion, opponents tagged Tovar out at the head of another triple steal — which Martin called when the Twins enjoyed a six-run lead. Graig Nettles, of all people, was once thrown out stealing home. Technically he was picked off of third and made a break for it, but he must have had a good-sized lead to draw a throw, as pitchers normally do not try picking runners off of third. Even slow-footed Harmon Killebrew, at age 33, stole eight bases that season. He had eleven in the rest of his career. Billy Martin truly did not fear a damn thing.

The ultimate Billyball moment came on May 18 when both Cesar Tovar and Rod Carew stole home plate, in the same inning — in the same at-bat. Carew stole his way around the bases in that plate appearance. At the plate during this maniacal baserunning was Harmon Killebrew. *Harmon Killebrew*! It boggles the mind — with one of the greatest home run hitters of that or any other generation up Martin wanted his men running wild.

One does not have to be particularly skilled at sabermetrics to know that according to the math everything just described was insane. Yet while the Minnesota experience was extreme, it was by no means atypical for Martin. Since 1956, the most stolen base attempts by any team with runners on second and third was seven, by the 1980 A's, whom Martin managed. Only four other teams had more than four — two with Martin at the helm (the 1977 Yankees and 1969 Twins). Stealing home is such a dangerous gamble it is rarely worth trying, and certainly not trying as often as Martin did it. By the numbers, Martin's moves were terrible.

Therein lies the rub. Instead of getting worse, his teams got dramatically better despite all these reckless maneuvers. If his moves should have hurt them, why did Martin's presence cause teams to improve dramatically? To solve the riddle of Martin, you have to take a step back from *what* he did, and understand *why* he did it. The basestealing makes him sound like a Whitey Herzog protégé. Not really. Carew, despite his thefts at the plate, only had nineteen swipes overall in 1969. For Martin, steals were not the ends but the means. He wanted to instill a specific mindset in his players: do whatever it takes to win every game. No manager had as little use for a second-place finish as Martin. Players gave it their best effort as a matter of routine, but that was the problem — it was a matter of routine. There is nothing quite like having a lunatic boss to cause employees to reach deeper within themselves. No one wanted to face a hostile Billy Martin in the dugout. Tellingly, almost all of the Twins' wild baserunning came in the first half of 1969. Carew's last home plate steal came in Minnesota's ninetieth game. Once Martin had installed the desired mindset in Minnesota, there was no need to run the risky home plate steals. For the rest of the season opponents played back on their heels, wondering what Minnesota would do next.

The man most comparable to Billy Martin was not Whitey Herzog, but Hernan Cortes, the Spanish conquistador who defeated the Aztecs. In 1519, he landed in Mexico to face the hemisphere's mightiest warrior nation with only 600 men. Upon arrival, he burned his boats, giving his men no way to leave. That move was pure Billy Martin. Safe to say, that in the military science version of sabermetrics a general would be poorly regarded for intentionally destroying his communication lines, supply routes, and exit strategy. It was possibly even worse than having two men steal home with Killebrew batting. However, like Martin, Cortes had an underlying rationale. The act was not the important part. All that mattered was the message it sent the men: there was no going back — they *needed* to win. He only cared about coming out on top and that move ensured his warriors must think likewise. They might lose and die, but with God as their witness no failure would stem from lack of effort on anyone's part. That was Billyball, sixteenth century style.

Martin's tactics against the 1969 A's demonstrated how he wanted his team to play. Minnesota hosted Oakland over Fourth of July weekend, with the A's leading the Twins by a game heading into the three-game series. In the first contest, the Twins exploded with an 8–0 lead after four innings. Rather than relax, Martin rubbed it in so everyone would know who was the big dog in the division. Martin twice ordered Tovar to steal second base even though the lead was safely iced. After his last steal, Tovar took such a big lead at second that Oakland's pitcher tried to pick him off. In frustration, he instead threw the ball into center. The rattled hurler immediately surrendered back-to-back doubles to the Twins, who romped to victory. Seeking revenge, the A's beaned Minnesota's leadoff batter the next day, which played right into Martin's hands. The beaning rallied Minnesota's troops, who scored four runs before the first out was recorded in what proved to be a 13–1 blowout. A come-from-behind victory the next day solidified their new division lead, which they never relinquished the rest of the season. Martin had not played to win; he came to castrate.

Martin's unsporting conduct could potentially motivate the opposition to try harder. Martin never cared about the downside, though. He knew repeated humiliation would cause the opponent's morale to collapse, while these tactics gave his team more confidence in their future fights. Prior to that series Minnesota had gone 5–4 against Oakland on the season. From that series onward, they won eight of nine games, outscoring the A's 85–37 in the process. In those future showdowns, Martin asserted Minnesota's supremacy by intentionally baiting Oakland. He once had a batter steal a base with the team leading 14–4 in the seventh inning. In their final showdown, Minnesota swiped a base when up by six runs. Animals who mark their territory by urination were subtler than Martin.

Billy Martin never saw moderation in pursuit of victory as a virtue. He would do whatever it took to win that day, and not worry about any possible negative side effects in the future. The best example came when he ran the A's in the early 1980s. They had a great stable of young pitchers whom Martin pushed as hard as he could. In 1980, they completed 94 games, the most by any team since the 1940s. Combined, his starters threw 1,261.3 innings, the most by any rotation since at least 1956. The second most in that span is 1,182 by the 1968 Giants, 79.3 innings behind (which is a difference of half an inning per game). For perspective, the second-place Giants are 79.3 innings ahead of the 75th place starting rotation since 1956. In 1981, the A's completed "only" 60 games, but a third of the season was lost to a strike. In fact, no other team of the 1980s completed that many games, despite Oakland only playing 109 games. No team in the last half-century averaged as many innings per start as the 1980 or 1981 A's. In 1980, at one point Oakland ace Rick Langford completed 23 of 24 games. In the remaining game he went 8.7 innings. The stretch ended in his final start of the season, when he went nine innings in a game that lasted ten. He began 1981 by completing eleven of his first twelve starts.

In the short run, it worked as Oakland produced the AL's best record in 1981. Then their arms fell off and they lost 94 games in 1982. Martin never considered the long-term repercussions. Then again, it was the only time he lasted three full seasons as manager. Martin was so concerned with seizing the day that he never considered what would happen tomorrow.

He always ran his pitchers hard. In Detroit, Mickey Lolich started 45 games, completed 29, and tossed 376 innings — the most by any AL pitcher since *Ed Walsh*. Lolich actually held up, but it was a dangerously relentless way to handle him. In 1975, when Martin replaced Bill

Virdon as Yankee skipper during the season, Catfish Hunter became the first AL pitcher to reach 30 complete games since Bob Feller. Though Virdon, who managed most of the season, worked Hunter hard, Martin pushed him more than anyone ever had, making Hunter complete all but one of his starts under Martin. Hunter was never the same, and four years later his career ended. In 1976, when Martin lasted the full season, New York's starters averaged 7.31 innings per season, the fourth highest total since 1956. In Texas, Fergie Jenkins completed 29 starts for Martin. He won twenty games, but was barely an average pitcher the following season.

Martin similarly handled his relievers. He wanted who he wanted when he wanted them without concern towards keeping their arms well rested. As a result, his bullpens consistently ranked among the league leaders in most innings pitched by men with zero days rest. The Tendencies Database can measure this using Baseball-Reference's team splits. That site informs us how many innings were thrown by pitchers who appeared the day before, or who took the mound in the second game of a doubleheader after appearing in the first one. When those splits are combined, the following managers used their relievers the most aggressively:

Most IP with No Rest

Billy Martin	0.574
Al Dark	0.586
Frank Robinson	0.659
Dusty Baker	0.674
Jimy Williams	0.731

Martin had unrested relievers gobble up the most innings four times, and was almost always among league leaders in that regard. On the 1974 Rangers, Steve Foucault threw 45 innings on a used arm; entire teams had fewer innings. In early May, he threw 2.3 innings in the first game of a doubleheader, then faced one man in the second game. The next day Martin had him toss 2.7 innings. The following day he threw a full three. In mid-season, he threw in six consecutive games, and eight out of nine. Due to Martin's aggressive usage, in 1974 Foucault became the only reliever between 1942 and 1996 to record all his team's saves. Though Foucault was fantastic that year, the load took its toll and he devolved into a sore spot in Texas's 1975 bullpen.

Whenever he saw an edge, Martin ruthlessly utilized it. His usage of Rickey Henderson demonstrates that. Henderson attempted 376 steals in 415 games under Martin. Given the young Henderson's speed and ability, any manager would have let him loose on the bases. However, there was no precedent for a player going that wild on the bases. Though Henderson had a long and fruitful career, most players who rack up huge number of stolen bases early in their career age rather poorly due to the wear and tear of all their swipes. Martin, true to form, was not concerned with down-the-road issues.

Martin was the perfect manager to hire if you wanted an immediate improvement, and the worst manager for a team seeking sustained success.

John McNamara

> **W/L Record:** 1,168–1,247 (.484)
> **Managed:** Full Seasons: Oakland 1970; San Diego 1974–76; Cincinnati 1979–81;
> California 1983–84; Boston 1985–87; Cleveland 1990
> Majority in: Boston 1988
> Minority of: Oakland 1969; San Diego 1977; Cincinnati 1982;
> Cleveland 1991; California 1996

Birnbaum Database: -174 runs
　　　　Individual Hitters: -73 runs
　　　　Individual Pitchers: -224 runs
　　　　Pythagenpat Difference: +82 runs
　　　　Team Offense: -53 runs
　　　　Team Defense: +94 runs

Team Characteristics: McNamara liked to bunt but had very little interest in stealing. He did a pretty good job filling out the lineup card, putting his better OBP guys in the top slots and making sure all the dross was at the bottom. That might sound like common sense, but many managers put terrible hitters in the #2 hole. His 1974 Padres issued 116 intentional walks, which is the all-time record. His 1988 Red Sox featured the best strikeout differential in AL history: their pitchers fanned 1,085 batters while Boston's batters whiffed only 728 times. The 1986 Red Sox contained the second best strikeout differential in league history.

McNamara's most famous managerial moment came in Game 6 of the 1986 World Series when his Red Sox, one out away from victory, blew a two-run lead by allowing three consecutive singles, a wild pitch, and an infield error. Fans often blame Bill Buckner's infamous botched grounder on McNamara because he did not insert defensive substitute Dave Stapleton for Buckner in that inning. That non-move defined McNamara as a managerial minimalist.

Perhaps the most telling moment in that game was not leaving Buckner in, but the bullpen meltdown. No manager has coaxed worse performances from his relievers than McNamara. Cumulative bullpen ERA, adjusted for park, serves as a good gauge for overall reliever quality. When that is plugged into the Tendencies Database, the following managers had the shoddiest bullpens in the Retrosheet years:

Worst Park Adjusted Bullpen ERA

John McNamara	1.357
Jim Leyland	1.307
Bruce Bochy	1.151
Al Dark	1.096
Tom Kelly	1.093

McNamara owns the dubious distinction of possessing the worst park-adjusted bullpen ERA with four different franchises: San Diego (1974), Cincinnati (1981), California (1983), and Boston (1987). He finished tenth or worse ten times.

Not coincidentally, McNamara has the worst record in extra-inning games of any prominent manager. (Note: this is based on information available at Baseball-Reference's expanded standings pages, which provide extra-inning records only since the 1950s.) In his career, McNamara's squads went 94–139 (.403) in marathon contests. If a good bullpen ever comes in handy, it is in these affairs. It is worth noting that the manager with the best record in overtime games of anyone in this book, Ron Gardenhire, possessed first-rate relief units. Only one of McNamara's teams exceeded .500 in these games. In his five partial seasons, that quintet of clubs went 9–26 in extra-innings games with McNamara, but 28–25 with someone else at the helm.

Actually, that 94–139 record is incomplete, because he was also 1–4 in post-season extra-inning games. Including those games, he had a .399 winning percentage, which translates to a record of 65–97 over a full season. Perhaps the real key signifying part of Game 6 was neither Buckner nor the bullpen, but the result.

John McNamara was also the game's archetypal journeyman manager. He helmed six different teams, tying a twentieth century record. He was fired mid-season by four clubs. Nothing says "hack manager" like many summertime pink slips. Since 1900, only Bill Virdon and Dick Williams can make the same claim. Williams's problem was his temperament. Virdon at least lasted eight years once; McNamara never lasted four years anywhere.

JOHNNY OATES

> **W/L Record:** 797–746 (.517)
> **Managed:** Full Seasons: Baltimore 1992–94; Texas 1995–2000
> Majority in: Baltimore 1991
> Minority of: Texas 2001
> **Birnbaum Database:** +107 runs
> Individual Hitters: +44 runs
> Individual Pitchers: +9 runs
> Pythagenpat Difference: +59 runs
> Team Offense: -93 runs
> Team Defense: +88 runs
> **Team Characteristics:** Oates's teams could hit, especially for power, but they rarely stole. He kept a set lineup and let his starters play all nine innings. His pitchers were control artists who did not strike out many batters.

Relief pitching was the key to Oates's managerial career as he presided over bullpen resurrections in Baltimore and Texas. Looking at managers who lasted at least a decade in the years Retrosheet splits are available, here are the ones with the best bullpens, as measured by park-adjusted ERA:

Best Park-Adjusted Bullpen ERA

Jimy Williams	0.641
Cito Gaston	0.653
Danny Murtaugh	0.685
Johnny Oates	0.693
Al Lopez	0.697

Oates may not be the most well known handler of bullpens, but he was quite successful. When he came to Baltimore, the team had never been known for its relief corps. He needed to change that as its starting pitching was below average. He inherited a solid closer in Gregg Olson, who promptly peaked under Oates. When Olson left in 1994, the Orioles replaced him with Lee Smith. The veteran Smith provided his typical solid and consistent work.

More importantly, Oates refurbished Baltimore's middle relievers. He had the knack for turning completely unheralded pitchers into late-game dynamos. Within a week of Oates's managerial debut, the Orioles called up minor leaguer Todd Frohwirth, whom the club had picked up from the Phillies the previous offseason at a discount price. Under Oates, Frohwith unexpectedly blossomed into perhaps baseball's best reliever over the next two years. He was one of baseball's only relievers to toss over 200 innings in 1991–92, a feat he achieved while posting a 2.18 ERA. Nearly matching him was teammate Alan Mills. Taken from the Yankees for a pair of players to be named later, Mills threw 100 innings in back-to-back seasons of high quality work.

An exceptionally strong middle relief team allowed Oates to rely less on his closer. Defining a relief ace as a pitcher with at least twenty saves in a season, no such individual had ever averaged under an inning per appearance prior to Oates's 1991 hiring. In the 127 games Oates ran the 1991 Orioles, closer Gregg Olson threw 46 innings in 47 appearances. Due to how Oates's predecessor handled the closer, Olson averaged slightly over an inning per appearance for the entire season, but Oates's major league managerial arrival heralded the rise of closer as a pitcher reserved for the ninth inning only. His closers had the shortest outing in all baseball three times with a trio of different relievers (Olson in 1991, Lee Smith in 1994, and Mike Henneman with Texas in 1996). Oates's closers had the second shortest average appearances in 1993 and 1995. Other managers came to adopt the model of reserving the closer for the ninth inning, but Oates was the first to do it from the outset of his career.

In Texas, Oates again revitalized his relievers. The Rangers had a rotten bullpen prior to his arrival. His first season saw the overall quality remain bad, though he had the glimmerings of his next relief pitcher revival in the admirable performances of hurlers Ed Vosberg, Jeff Russell, and mid-season pick up Dennis Cook. Joined by a few more arms the next year, an improved crew helped lead Texas to its first division title in franchise history. As had been the case in Baltimore, middle relief was the bullpen's strength. The 1996 Texas middle relief corps combined for a 4.16 ERA, which may not sound impressive but it came in the best hitter's park in a league with a 5.00 ERA. This served as a template for Oates's future teams in Texas. From 1996 to 1999, despite toiling in a hitter-friendly environment, their middle relievers had a combined ERA in 4.29 in leagues whose overall ERA was about a half-point higher. Beginning in 1997, Oates also possessed an outstanding closer in John Wetteland. Behind this unit, Texas captured three division titles in four years. In 2000, the bullpen imploded on Oates, and after the Rangers got off to a poor start the following season, he ended his managing career,

FRANK ROBINSON

> **W/L Record:** 1,065–1,176 (.475)
> **Managed:** Full Seasons: Cleveland 1975–76; San Francisco 1981–83; Baltimore
>   1989–90; Montreal/Washington 2002–06
>   Majority in: San Francisco 1984; Baltimore 1988;
>   Minority of: Cleveland 1977; Baltimore 1991;
> **Birnbaum Database:** +219 runs
>   Individual Hitters: +40 runs
>   Individual Pitchers: -207 runs
>   Pythagenpat Difference: +168 runs
>   Team Offense: +14 runs
>   Team Defense: +204 runs
> **Team Characteristics:** His pitchers did not strike out many batters and were
>   backed up by below-average fielders. He used his bullpen a great
>   deal, though the quality of his starters dictated that. With his position
>   players he also leaned on his bench a great deal. His teams
>   allowed more homers than they hit, but came out ahead on walks.
>   His clubs usually improved a bit after the all-star break.

One of the biggest surprises in the Birnbaum Database is how well it regards Frank Robinson, whose main managerial claim to fame was becoming the first black skipper in major league history. His win-loss record is unimpressive, though, with only two seasons over 83 wins, and a peak of 87. However, he consistently scored better than the franchises he managed. He earned +69 runs in Cleveland, +75 runs in San Francisco, and +119 runs in Montreal/Washington, all of which had losing records. It is rare for a manager to score so well for that many bad teams. His only negative mark came in Baltimore, -51 runs.

Looking at Robinson's teams, his performance in the Birnbaum Database makes sense. The franchises that hired him were laughingstocks in the midst of their worst stretch in decades. Oftentimes the worst clubs are the ones willing to break fresh sociological ground. This is true if you look at some of the first college football programs to hire black head coaches. In 1972, Macalester College, typically one of the worst football teams in the NCAA, became the first non–historically black college in the nation to hire a black coach. A few years later they began a 50-game losing streak. Northwestern hired future NFL coach Denny Green to run their squad in the early 1980s while in the midst of a 34-game losing streak. For these colleges, as long as they knew they could not field good teams they could at least be good citizens.

The Indians had been a doormat for several seasons before Robinson came aboard. The previous season the club had been so desperate to draw fans it had a Ten Cent Beer Night promotion that ended with a riot and forfeit. Under Robinson in 1975, the Indians finished 79–80, their best record in seven years. The next year he took them over the .500 hump, to 81–78. That was their best two-year stretch in a decade. After Cleveland fired Robinson for a slow start in 1977, the team played worse than it ever had under his watch.

The Giants were another franchise on the skids when they hired Robinson in 1981. They had only one winning season since dismissing Juan Marichal nearly a decade earlier. Shortstop Johnnie LeMaster, nicknamed "Johnnie Disaster" for his lackluster play, symbolized their futility. LeMaster appeared in nearly 1,000 games for the Giants because they lacked non-disastrous infielders. In 1981–82, Robinson delivered the franchise's first consecutive winning seasons since the Willie Mays era. When San Francisco declined, Robinson lost his job in mid–1984. The next year, the century-old franchise set its all-time record for losses in a season.

Early in 1988, the Orioles, who claimed the AL's worst overall record in 1986–87, hired Robinson. At the time of his hiring, Baltimore was in the midst of the longest losing streak in AL history. After a wretched 107-loss season in 1988, Robinson righted the ship, leading the Orioles to 87 wins in 1989. When he could not sustain that success, the club showed him the door.

That appeared to end his managerial career, until Major League Baseball itself rather unexpectedly became the custodial owner of the Expos. They tapped Robinson, at that time the game's czar of discipline, to handle the squad. Montreal had a good farm system, but had been unable to draw fans and afford free agents for years. Felipe Alou, Robinson's predecessor, had earned accolades for his ability to harness the talent at his disposal, but ended his time in Canada with five consecutive losing seasons, including four straight 90+ loss campaigns. Upon Robinson's arrival, Montreal posted consecutive winning seasons. Both were only 83-win years, but that was a far cry better than what they had been accustomed to. After one bad season, Robinson took them to a surprisingly good 81–81 record in their inaugural Washington campaign. After one more year, Robinson's career concluded.

In his various stops, Frank Robinson had painfully little frontline talent. His clubs featured some stars—such as Cal Ripken in Baltimore and Vlad Guerrero in Montreal—but the overall quality of starting lineups and main pitchers was dreadful. Since he possessed few dependable players, he did not rely on his core, instead using everyone as best he could. The Tendencies Database can confirm this. Chapter 2 contained two studies to see which managers relied the most and least on their core players. For hitters, the database looked at percentage of team plate appearances gobbled up by the starters, and for pitchers it noted the chunk of innings gobbled up by the team's top three pitchers. When combined, these stats tell us which managers who lasted at least a decade depended the least on their teams' cores:

Depending the Least on Frontline Players

Frank Robinson	2.712
Jim Fregosi	2.550
Paul Richards	2.331
Frank Chance	2.324
Casey Stengel	2.288

Among those who qualify for the chart, Robinson wins handily (though Gil Hodges scores 2.978 in his nine-year career). Robinson's score was largely a product of his team's lack of talent.

Robinson had the unwanted knack of being hired almost exclusively by teams without talent. His career hit differential — hits by his batters minus hits allowed by his staffs — demonstrates the historically dreadful nature of the clubs he managed:

Worst Hit Differentials

Frank Robinson	-1,170 hits
Billy Barnie	-1,150 hits
Zach Taylor	-954 hits
Gene Mauch	-949 hits
Art Howe	-924 hits

The totals are imperfect because of partial seasons, but only one man is even close to Robinson, and he was a nineteenth-century business manager who would never land a dugout job these days. Normally these differential lists shed light on the manager and his proclivities, but in this case it demonstrates what Robinson had to contend with. It's possible no one else has managed so many years with so many franchises yet had so little to work with as Frank Robinson.

One of Robinson's great managerial strengths was his force of character. As a player, he was always the hardest and toughest man on the field. He was the fiercest slider, the outfielder most willing to run into walls. Though older, he retained that toughness, giving him an innate sense of authority. Current Giants broadcasters Duane Kuiper and Mike Krukow, both of whom played for Robinson at different spells, never tire of telling stories about how he was as tough as nails. Some managers treat their players hard, but Robinson *was* hard.

With his unmistakable presence, Robinson had the confidence to make moves others would not. For example, with the Giants he brilliantly handled outfielder Jeffrey Leonard, who — like Robinson — was a tough kid from the inner city. Nicknamed "Penitentiary Face," Leonard liked to demonstrate that no one had authority over him. Most managers would see Leonard as a threat, but Frank Robinson recognized a kindred spirit. He made the young hitter team captain, corralling Leonard's independent streak to aid the team. This is exactly what a good manager should do — handle the players in a way that best helps the team.

CHUCK TANNER

> **W/L Record:** 1,352–1,381 (.495)
> **Managed:** Full Seasons: Chicago (AL) 1971–75; Oakland 1976; Pittsburgh
> 1977–85; Atlanta 1986–87
> Majority in: (none)
> Minority of: Chicago (AL) 1970; Atlanta 1988

Birnbaum Database: -193 runs
                  Individual Hitters: +47 runs
                  Individual Pitchers: -114 runs
                  Pythagenpat Difference: -57 runs
                  Team Offense: -128 runs
                  Team Defense: +59 runs

Team Characteristics: Tanner liked to bunt. His offenses hit for average, which compensated for their troubles drawing walks. He usually relied on his bullpens, which were generally one of his teams' strong points.

Whitey Herzog receives attention for helping to popularize the stolen base, but Chuck Tanner played a vital role as well. From 1918 to 1974, no team stole more than 200 bases in major league baseball. In 1976, Chuck Tanner's club stole 340 bases. The next year, his squad swiped 260 bases. In the 1970s, no other team stole more than 220. In the last 90 years, Tanner and Herzog are the only managers whose teams stole 600 bases in two years.

The above actually underestimates how much Tanner liked to have his teams run because in the 1976–77 off-season he switched teams. The A's stole 340 and then (after a bizarre manager-for-player trade of Tanner for Manny Sanguillen) the Pirates swiped 260. In 1976, Tanner's only year with the club, the A's stole almost as many bases as the 1975 and 1977 squads combined. Eight men had at least twenty steals for the 1976 club. Sal Bando, at age 32, stole twenty — more than he had from 1971 to 1975 combined. The 1977 Pirates had more thefts than the combined sum of the 1973 to 1976 Pirates. In 1978, the Pirates became the first team in sixty years to have consecutive 200 stolen base seasons. From 1976 to 1982, Tanner's teams averaged nearly two attempted swipes per game, a feat only Herzog matched since 1920.

Yet, strangely, Tanner backed away from the stolen base after 1982. While Herzog became the nation's leading proponent of the stolen base, Tanner's clubs frequently found themselves near the bottom of the league in willingness to steal. Admittedly, he ran some slow teams in the 1980s, but this was the man who once unleashed Sal Bando on the bases.

Tanner's consistency was not in a specific strategy, but in extreme adoptions of strategies. As White Sox skipper he had another remarkable trend — he ran his main starting pitchers harder than any other manager in the last 100 years. In 1972, Wilbur Wood and Stan Bahnsen combined to start 90 games. That last happened in 1904, when Christy Mathewson and Joe McGinnity performed the trick for the Giants. In fact, due to a brief players strike in 1972 and some makeup games in 1904, Tanner's Sox actually played fewer games than McGraw's Giants. Tanner's third starter, Tom Bradley, accounted for 40 more starts in 1972. Those three accounted for over 64 percent of the team's innings, the most by any team since the 1923 Reds, helmed by Pat Moran.

Proving it was no fluke, in 1973 Wood and Bahnsen combined for another 90 starts. Most memorably, Tanner made Wood a legend on May 28, 1973. Wood was the scheduled starter against the Indians that day, but before the game could begin some unfinished business had to be taken care of. A game between those clubs two days earlier had gone into extra innings, and ran into the league's curfew after sixteen frames. Since Wood had a rubber arm and Tanner did not expect the game to take long to complete, he had Wood finish it. Wood allowed one unearned run in five innings to gain the victory, and then he threw a complete game shutout in his start. It is as close as you could come to starting both ends of a double-header without actually doing it. Much like the stolen base, Tanner's élan for pushing his starters hard was merely a phase for him. After Chicago, he spread out the innings in a normal fashion.

Still, none of this is why people remember Tanner. As noted in this chapter's intro, his rise and fall in Pittsburgh defined his career. Tanner initially basked in the glow of media adulation when the Pirates won a world title, but the team's ensuing drug problems left a stain on his reputation that has not washed away. A 1980s legal trial focusing on drugs in baseball took place in Pittsburgh because the squad Tanner managed featured the league's worst problems with addiction. Not only did players abuse illegal substances, but they invited drug dealers into the clubhouse and on to team flights. Eventually a drug ring began operating out of Three Rivers Stadium itself. Tanner first responded to the public discovery of drug problems in the Pirate clubhouse with surprised ignorance. Bill James, in a blistering account of Tanner's managerial style, noted that while the press let Tanner get away with this approach, when the manager tried it on the witness stand of the Pittsburgh drug trial, the judge upbraided him for playing dumb.

After the drug debacle, everything that had been held up as a positive about Tanner could easily be reinterpreted. His backers always contended that Tanner's easy-going, non-disciplinary style helped his teams by allowing him to relate to the modern player. Suddenly, Tanner's impact on the players looked far from benign. Instead, critics could easily make the case that he was not forceful enough. Aside from the drug problems, they could note that the two teams Tanner ran the longest, the White Sox and Pirates, both had trouble with players staying in shape under his watch (most notably Chicago's Wilbur Wood and Pittsburgh's Dave Parker), indicating Tanner let even the most basic facets of his authority slide.

It certainly did not help Tanner that when he went to Atlanta, he suffered through failed seasons. Instead of delivering success to a floundering franchise, he once butted heads with a public relations assistant with the club who Tanner felt was not saying enough good things about the squad. Though respected enough to manage for seventeen consecutive years — a genuinely impressive achievement — the image of Chuck Tanner in retrospect is far less flattering.

BOBBY VALENTINE

> **W/L Record:** 1,117–1,072 (.510)
> **Managed:** Full Seasons: Texas 1986–91; New York (NL) 1997–2002
>   Majority in: Texas 1985, 1992
>   Minority of: New York (NL) 1996
> **Birnbaum Database:** +356 runs
>   Individual Hitters: +76 runs
>   Individual Pitchers: +151 runs
>   Pythagenpat Difference: +237 runs
>   Team Offense: -18 runs
>   Team Defense: -90 runs
> **Team Characteristics:** Bobby Valentine loved to make in-game changes. His bench players had a good chance to be called on as a pinch-hitter or defensive replacement. Even if they did not receive many starts, Valentine ensured they would not become rusty. His pitchers struck out plenty of opponents.

Bobby Valentine was the anti–Cito Gaston: he loved to tinker. Valentine specialized in using pinch-hitters. Just looking at raw numbers does not do him justice because he spent most of his career in a designated hitter league (where fewer pinch-hitters are called on). Since the Tendencies Database adjusts for that, here is how Valentine ranks with other managers of the Retrosheet period:

Most Pinch-Hitters

Bobby Valentine	0.370
Tom Kelly	0.444
Gene Mauch	0.465
Al Dark	0.616
Art Howe	0.616

Valentine dominates this list as five times he used the most pinch-hitters in the league, and he finished second in another five seasons. In 1990, the Rangers used 247 pinch-hitters while no other team in a DH league has ever employed more than 223. Actually, Valentine did not begin his career enamored with pinch-hitting. From 1989 onward, though, he came in first or second every year except 2001, when he was "only" fourth. In the last ten years of his career, his Tendencies Database score with pinch-hitters is 0.211, which would be the most extreme mark in any category for anyone in this book if Valentine maintained that pace over his entire career.

While Valentine grew into the use of pinch-hitters, he always liked replacing his position players during a game. In his first year, his position players had fewer complete games than those on any other team. Valentine largely kept the same pace up his entire career, as the Tendencies Database, which possesses this information since 1956, reveals:

Fewest Complete Games by Position Players

Bobby Valentine	1.607
Phil Garner	1.534
Tony LaRussa	1.533
Tommy Lasorda	1.474
Art Howe	1.386
Charlie Dressen	1.386

Five times Valentine's position players completed the fewest games in the league.

He positively adored displays of in-game strategy. Valentine's managerial actions complement his public image perfectly. He always had a substantial ego. While managing he gave the impression that he thought he was smarter than everyone else. If someone really believes he is that brilliant, he should be that much more willing to prove it by outfoxing the opponents with his numerous in-game decisions. That was Valentine.

The most interesting thing about the above list is the presence of both Valentine and Charlie Dressen. Valentine is the closest thing to Dressen in recent decades. Both had sizable egos that were made for the New York media market. Both went to the World Series in the Big Apple, though neither won. Dressen was certain he could guide his teams to victory by making the right moves, just like Valentine. Both had unusual career trajectories. Dressen went more than a decade without getting hired as manager, while Valentine left the western hemisphere to manage in Japan. One key distinction exists—Valentine's career was consistently more successful. Dressen roamed from failure to failure after the Dodgers let him move on, but Valentine prospered wherever he has gone. In 2005, he even became the first white manager to lead a team to victory in Japan's World Series. Perhaps Valentine's talents are as sizable as his ego, but it is more likely he possessed better players to work with than Dressen.

BILL VIRDON

W/L Record: 995–921 (.519)
Managed: Full Seasons: Pittsburgh 1972; New York (AL) 1974; Houston 1976–81;
Montreal 1983

Majority in: Pittsburgh 1973; New York (AL) 1975; Houston 1982;
 Montreal 1984
Minority of: Houston 1975
Birnbaum Database: -38 runs
Individual Hitters: -17 runs
Individual Pitchers: +157 runs
Pythagenpat Difference: -9 runs
Team Offense: -129 runs
Team Defense: -40 runs
Team Characteristics: Virdon relied as much as he possibly could on his start-
ing pitchers, particularly his best ones. The top of his order had very
good OBP, and he made sure his worst hitters were at the very bot-
tom. He rarely bunted, and his hitters rarely struck out or walked.
Due to their aversion to take pitches, Virdon is (with the exception
of Cal McVey) the only manager in the book who never had a hitter
qualify for the batting title with an OBP of .400 or better. Virdon
was the last manager who served over a decade to never preside over
a 30-save performance. Jeff Reardon had 23 for him in 1984, the most
by any of his closers.

Virdon is one of the game's most deceptive managers. On the face of it, there was nothing especially distinctive about him. He presided over no remarkable achievements, and
appeared to be just a bland, well-traveled manager forgotten by history. The Tendencies Database thinks otherwise. He constantly appears on its leaderboards for one statistic after another.
It would take too long to highlight all his distinctive features, so here are some of the more
important and extreme.

Virdon's most indelible trait as manager was his disinterest in relievers. As noted in
Chapter 2, according to the Tendencies Database he used fewer relievers per game relative to
his peers than any other manager in baseball history. Though the bullpen was an established
part of baseball before Virdon began managing and its importance continued to rise throughout his career, Virdon steadfastly held aloof from it. In his first season on the job, his bullpen
accounted for only 24 percent of Pittsburgh's innings pitched. Even in 1972 that was a low
figure. A decade later, in Virdon's last complete campaign, his relievers threw only 27 percent of the team's innings, which was Virdon's fifth straight season where his relievers
accounted for the league's smallest percentage of innings.

Not only did he rarely use his bullpen, but he generally had ineffective ones. The 1982
Astros had the dubious distinction of having both the least used and the worst (in terms of
park-adjusted ERA) bullpens. No other team has been able to make that claim in the quarter-century since then. Over Virdon's career, he received less from his bullpens than any other
manager that team splits are available for. After adding together the Tendencies Database's
score for bullpen innings, and park-adjusted ERA, here are the managers whose relievers did
the least:

Least Value from Bullpens

Bill Virdon	2.639
Tommy Lasorda	2.596
John McNamara	2.462
Earl Weaver	2.353
Red Schoendienst	2.292

Virdon usually trusted one reliever, and allotted that individual the bullpen's clutch moments. With the Yankees it was Sparky Lyle, with Houston Joe Sambito, and with Montreal Jeff Reardon. All were very good, but the rest of Virdon's bullpens were dross. That makes sense: a manager who rode his starters hard and relied on one fireman would have little need (and hence minimal interest) in middle relievers. They were eminently fungible.

On offense, Virdon liked hitters who went to the plate looking for a pitch to hit and made contact with it. Virdon's offenses constantly ranked among the bottom of the league in walks drawn. In his full managerial seasons, none of his men ever drew 100 walks and only three times did someone get as high as 75. They also rarely fanned at the plate. In Virdon's nine full seasons, he had only one 100 strikeout season, 129 by Willie Stargell in 1972. The year before, under a different manager, Stargell whiffed 154 times. In Virdon's half-dozen full seasons in Houston, the most anyone struck out was 84 by Enos Cabell in 1980. The NL in those years had 97 different occasions where someone went down on strikes at least 85 times. The Tendencies Database declares Virdon's teams the hardest to fan in baseball history.

Virdon also emphasized the importance of strikeouts with his staffs. In Houston, for example, power pitchers J. R. Richard and Nolan Ryan dominated opposing hitters. When combining hitter and pitcher strikeout scores in the Tendencies Database, Virdon again comes in first:

All Strikeouts

Bill Virdon	1.183
Walt Alston	1.324
Steve O'Neill	1.401
Wilbert Robinson	1.415
Bill Terry	1.444

Virdon only had one full season where his offenses suffered more strikeouts than his pitchers doled out. In the games he managed (and this includes only the games he personally managed in his partial seasons), his hitters struck out 9,100 times while his pitchers fanned 10,257. That amounts to an advantage of nearly 100 strikeouts per 162 games. In 1982, the Astros had a +72 strikeout advantage when he managed them, but were -3 after the team fired Virdon two-thirds of the way through the season.

DON ZIMMER

W/L Record: 885–858 (.508)

Managed: Full Seasons: San Diego 1973; Boston 1977–79; Texas 1981; Chicago (NL) 1988–90

Majority in: San Diego 1972; Boston 1980; Texas 1982

Minority of: Boston 1976; Chicago (NL) 1991

Birnbaum Database: +150 runs

Individual Hitters: +37 runs

Individual Pitchers: -151 runs

Pythagenpat Difference: +174 runs

Team Offense: -52 runs

Team Defense: +142 runs

Team Characteristics: He went with a starting lineup and did not like to take his players out in the middle of a game or use pinch-hitters. His hitters rarely walked but his pitchers partially made up for it by having good control.

Zimmer gained a poor reputation as manager, which the Tendencies Database confirms in numerous ways. First, he had a historic disinterest in offensive platoon advantage. Add all plate appearances in which a team had left-handed hitters face right-handed pitchers together with right-handed batters squaring off against southpaws, then divide that sum by the team's total plate appearances. Then rank all teams in a particular league from highest to smallest frequency of plate appearances with the platoon edge. Based on that, these managers had the least regard for this bit of baseball strategy:

Lowest Offensive Platoon Advantage

Don Zimmer	1.708
Jack McKeon	1.436
Al Dark	1.371
Lou Piniella	1.308
Danny Murtaugh	1.282

In eleven seasons in the database, Zimmer's offenses had the lowest platoon advantages five times, second least four times, and third-worst once. The 1981 Rangers ranked tenth out of fourteen teams for his highest rank ever.

Many fine reasons exist to avoid platooning or minimize interest in the platoon advantage, such as preferring a set lineup. Zimmer's score indicates something quite a bit deeper, however. When a manager's hitters constantly are least or second least likely to have a platoon advantage, either everyone else exaggerates the importance of this edge or he underestimates it. Color me skeptical that Zimmer was in the right. It is possible to use a regular starting eight and still shade toward the platoon advantage on occasion.

The best example of how Zimmer ignored the platoon advantage came from his Boston stint. Before he arrived, the team had several years when it was in the middle of the pack in platoon advantage. One reason for this was left-handed backup outfielder and pinch-hitter Bernie Carbo. According to former Red Sox pitcher, Bill Lee, Zimmer did not get along with the hitter, however, so he avoided playing Carbo. Eventually, the team decided to get some value for him and sold him to Cleveland. Under Zimmer, Boston fell to the bottom of the league in platoon advantage, where they remained until Ralph Houk became manager.

Zimmer also did a dreadful job filling out his lineup card. Using the same method described in the Sparky Anderson comment at the beginning of this chapter, Zimmer was historically inept at deciding who should bat in the top two slots in his batting order:

Worst at Putting OBP in Top 2 Slots

Don Zimmer	1.521
Danny Murtaugh	1.400
Johnny Oates	1.360
Dusty Baker	1.267
Phil Garner	1.216

Not only did he do the worst job ever, but no one else is particularly close to him. To put it in perspective, for all of Zimmer's clubs, here are the on-base percentages for the entire team as well as the top two slots for each squad:

Team	Team	#1	#2
1972 SDP	.283	.268	.287
1973 SDP	.296	.292	.350
1977 BOS	.345	.342	.319
1978 BOS	.336	.296	.315

Team	Team	#1	#2
1979 BOS	.349	.318	.315
1980 BOS	.341	.344	.311
1981 TEX	.329	.303	.320
1982 TEX	.311	.310	.302
1988 CHC	.310	.294	.311
1989 CHC.	319	.314	.344
1990 CHC	.314	.336	.341

In five years both slots were below the team average. In all of baseball, less than one in every seven teams does that. On three other occasions Zimmer's teams narrowly avoided this feat. Meanwhile, in eleven years, the OBP from both top slots beat the team OBP exactly once, in 1990.

Even the only slot in which Zimmer consistently placed above-average OBP, Chicago's #2 hole, can be held against him. Zimmer placed Hall of Fame second baseman Ryne Sandberg in that spot while first baseman Mark Grace hit third. That order should have been reversed. Sandberg had much more power — as evidenced by a 40 home run performance in 1990 — while Grace was a high-OBP hitter with solid doubles power. However, Sandberg was the second baseman and Grace the first baseman. By baseball stereotype, you bat them two and three. Admittedly, Sandberg batted second before and after Zimmer, but others' wrongs do not make him right.

Reasons other than OBP exist to have a person bat at the top of the order. A player who can steal should have an extra edge. However, that does not describe Zimmer's table-setters, who generally did not steal many bases. Aside from Chicago, his leadoff men topped twenty steals only once. The same is true of his number two hitters. Even when they tried to steal, their success rate was so poor it ruined the point. In Boston his #1 slot hitters stole 57 bases in 111 attempts, barely a 50 percent success rate.

Zimmer also had problems elsewhere on his lineup card. Once in Boston and another time in Texas the bottom third of his batting order had a better OPS than the entire team. That was inexcusable. The OPS from the 1981 Rangers' #8 slot was more than 60 points higher than any other part of the lineup. Is it really that hard to figure out who the worst hitters are and put them where they belong? It apparently was for Zimmer.

He also had a terrible reputation with pitchers. His problems in Boston are most famous. The Red Sox blew a huge lead in the 1978 pennant race, in part because starters such as Mike Torrez wore down as the season progressed. Red Sox starting pitcher Bill Lee openly belittled Zimmer for decades afterwards because of his handling of the pitching staff. Zimmer's difficulty with hurlers was not unique to Boston, however. He also showed his liabilities with the 1990 Cubs rotation. Though the Cubs had a terrible year, quickly falling out of the running, the club had some bright spots, such as a young pitcher named Mike Harkey. Though he did not have the strongest arm in the world, Harkey was very good when healthy. At the All-Star break, with the team hopelessly out of pennant contention, Zimmer decided to shift the team to a four-man rotation. Harkey initially pitched great, but rather predictably he broke down. He missed almost all of September and never was very good after that. Riding a pitcher hard is not necessarily a bad thing, but you have to be careful, especially when the season is already over.

9

Contemporary Managers,
1998–2008

The year 1998 very quietly marked the culmination of a nearly century-long trend delineating the duties between manager and front office. At the beginning of the twentieth century, managers controlled almost all functions now considered to be within the front office's realm. With the rise of Branch Rickey and the development of the modern general manager in the 1920s, the separation of duties began. The responsibilities of front office and manager became further differentiated as the GM took full control of roster construction by mid-century. Yet it was not until the end of the twentieth century that these spheres separated completely.

In 1998, Tommy Lasorda stepped down as interim Dodger GM, which, in and of itself was not especially important. However, Lasorda was the only former manager serving as general manager in the late 1990s, and since then no one else has leapt from dugout to front office. For most of the twentieth century, men frequently won promotion from one level to the next. For example, Joe Cronin left the Red Sox dugout to run the team's front office after World War II. Paul Richards cut short his potential Hall of Fame managerial career to become a GM for Houston and Atlanta. Some individuals even simultaneously held the roles of GM and skipper (including Richards for a bit in Baltimore). Even as the roles of manager and GM became increasingly distinct, movement from the dugout to front office was common.

As late as the 1980s managers continued winning promotions to GM. Whitey Herzog was GM for part of his managerial stint in St. Louis. Bobby Cox moved from dugout to front office and back. It was not just big names who moved from one position to the other, either. For example, when the Cubs earned their first postseason appearance in almost 40 years in 1984, their general manager was former and future dugout boss Dallas Green. That team's manager, Jim Frey, later succeeded Green as Cub GM.

In the early 1990s, this movement from dugout to GM ebbed. Cox, after briefly serving as manager and GM for the Braves simultaneously, voluntarily stepped down from the latter role after 1990. He was the last person to hold both jobs at the same time. The next year Frey was shown the door in Chicago. By the mid–1990s, the only former manager working as a GM was Herzog, who served exclusively in the front office with the Angels. When he stepped down in 1994, there were no ex-managers employed as GMs. Lasorda's brief tenure with the Dodgers would be the only other time a former or future manager has held that job. The roles of GM and manager have become so specialized that teams source entirely different pools of talent to fill them. A century ago a manager could reasonably hope to work his ways into the ownership ranks, but a ceiling presently prevents any possible movement from the dugout to front office. Even if an individual manager breaks through, the overall trend will remain in place. Teams reserve their main centers of authority for those who never managed in the dugout.

In fact, if anything, the new ceiling is even more extensive than the above indicates. In the early 21st century, managers are still recruited from the ranks of former players, but former players are rarely hired as key front office figures. The last former major league baseball player to be hired as a GM for any major sports team was Danny Ainge. Please note Ainge is not a baseball GM; a former two-sport player, Ainge runs an NBA basketball front office. In the new millennium only two baseball teams have hired ex-big leaguers as GMs: the White Sox with Kenny Williams, and the Orioles with both Mike Flanagan and Jim Beattie.

This transformation mirrors broader national trends. For example, in many museums and historical societies—especially those with hefty budgets—Ph.D.s are decreasingly likely to run the place. Instead, MBAs, who have been trained for large-scale administrative work, are brought in to handle executive responsibilities. The logic behind this change is understandable, and if anything it is surprising this change did not come to the national pastime earlier given the vast sums of cash baseball generates.

Managers have not only lost authority to the front office, they have essentially lost the chance to hold executive positions ever again.

FELIPE ALOU

> **W/L Record:** 1,033–1,021 (.503)
> **Managed** Full Seasons: Montreal 1993–2000, San Francisco 2003–06
> Majority in: Montreal 1992
> Minority of: Montreal 2001
> **Birnbaum Database:** +202 runs
> Individual Hitters: -14 runs
> Individual Pitchers: +182 runs
> Pythagenpat Difference: +228 runs
> Team Offense: +11 runs
> Team Defense: -205 runs
> **Team Characteristics:** Alou liked to bunt and make in-game replacements for his position players, but detested intentional walks. His hitters did not draw many walks. Though Alou generally had very good starting pitchers, he leaned heavily on his bullpen. He hated to steal when the game was out of reach, best demonstrated by his teams going three straight years (1995–97) without attempting a steal when his team was either up or down by five or more runs.

Racism cost Felipe Alou a chance at enshrinement in Cooperstown for his managerial career. Such a provocative statement should not be uttered lightly, but three related pieces of circumstantial evidence support it: how old Alou was when he first became a big league skipper, why he had to wait so long to get the job, and his record compared to others of that age.

First, Felipe Alou began managing ten days after his 57th birthday. In comparison, John McGraw was 59 when he *stopped* managing. Well, in those days the entire game was younger. However, more recently Dick Williams, who managed six different squads, left at age 59. Aside from Alou, the oldest debuts of noteworthy managers were 48-year-olds Tommy Lasorda and Roger Craig.

Second, one factor explains what took so long for baseball to hire him. Alou is a dark-skinned Latino, who never would have played major league ball before Jackie Robinson. As noted in the Cito Gaston commentary in the last chapter, baseball began hiring black managers with the speed of a glacier. At the end of 1989, when Alou was 54, only one black (Frank Robinson) had managed a full season. There was no grand conspiracy among baseball types to exclude blacks as managers. With men like Al Campanis making these decisions that was unnecessary. When baseball finally made a serious push to increase minority hirings in the late 1980s, Alou was one of the first to reap the benefits despite his advanced age.

No smoking-gun proof exists to explain Alou's otherwise inexplicably delayed entrance, but the circumstantial evidence is strong. Baseball teams avoided hiring any black managers when he was at an age someone would normally break into the ranks. Adding to this impression, black managers as a whole are older when first hired than white ones. Even in the twenty-first century a disproportionate number of the eldest rookie managers are black, including Ron Washington (age 55), Cecil Cooper (57), and Willie Randolph (50).

Third, once Alou got the job, he became one of game's greatest elderly managers. Here are the ten managers with the most victories from their age 57 season onward (through 2008 for those still active):

Managers Aged 57+	Wins
Connie Mack	2,057
Casey Stengel	1,324
Joe Torre	1,069
Felipe Alou	1,033
Bobby Cox	1,015
Wilbert Robinson	930
Tommy Lasorda	912
Jack McKeon	752
Walter Alston	721
Tony LaRussa	634

Eight are either in Cooperstown or will be immediately upon retirement; only Alou and McKeon will not. McKeon will not make it because he interrupted his managerial career by serving as San Diego's GM for a decade. In other words, he vaulted past a position Alou could not attain. Also, Alou not only makes the above list, but he also lands near the top. Mack won over 2,000 games because he owned the team while Stengel and Torre both benefited from running very talent-rich squads. Alou possessed no similar advantage.

Hall of Famers not only dominate the above list, but most also earned their plaques before turning 57. Even Lasorda, despite his late start, won three pennants before turning 57. Others polished off their resumes at age 57, including Robinson, who won his second and final pennant at that age, and Torre, who managed the Yankees through their magical 114-win season in 1998 at that point in his life. Alou and Stengel are the only real late bloomers.

Managing involves tremendous pressure and demands considerable concentration. These strains can be too taxing for someone in his sunset years, causing careers to frequently end when Alou's began. Earl Weaver was only 55 when he stopped. Al Lopez's last full season was at age 56, as was that of Charlie Grimm. Davey Johnson's last stand came at age 57, and Whitey Herzog voluntarily left the dugout at 58. Billy Martin managed only 60 games after he was 57. Bucky Harris and Bill McKechnie left the trenches at age 59. Even Sparky Anderson, who seemingly lasted forever, was only 61 when he retired.

To sum up then: Alou waited an extremely long time to get hired, his race appears to be the reason he could not break into the profession, and once he began he was as good as anyone. Racism cost Felipe Alou a plaque in Cooperstown.

Furthermore, Alou had a superlative reputation when he managed the Expos. Commanding a young team, he effectively broke in numerous young players, including Vladimir Guerrero, Orlando Cabrera, Mark Grudzielanek, Cliff Floyd, Michael Barrett, Jose Vidro, Mike Lansing, Rondell White, Javier Vazquez, Tony Armas Jr., Dustin Hermanson, Ugueth Urbina,

Carl Pavano, and Kirk Reuter. When pitch counts became fashionable in the late 1990s, Alou won huzzahs for rarely letting his starters last beyond 120 pitches, which was especially important, because Alou managed Pedro Martinez in the ace's formative years. Starters are never more fragile than when trying to establish themselves, and Martinez, who had occasional arm problems throughout his career, flourished under Alou. With a different manager, things might not have worked out as well for him. Alou had his shortcomings, as his hitters typically seemed unwilling to work the count, but he earned high marks overall.

Alou's managerial style was decidedly non-rah-rah. He intentionally maintained a cool, professional demeanor with his players, in which he made his authority plain if need be, but otherwise would rely on his coaches to handle the players. The players were to do their job so he could do his. Alou presented himself as the boss, and was accepted on those terms. Players respected him because he treated them like adults.

Alou's win-loss record was amazingly good considering the teams he ran. After 1994, the Expos collapsed as they could neither afford to re-sign their stars nor produce enough from the farm system to stay competitive. Alou's San Francisco roster consisted of Barry Bonds, Jason Schmidt, and 23 middling players. They won 100 games in 2003 — the franchise's third highest total since the days of Christy Mathewson — even though the second most dangerous bat was 36-year-old Marquis Grissom and only one pitcher aside from Schmidt tossed 140 innings. As great as Bonds was, only one of his other clubs won 100 games in a season, though several had considerably more impressive supporting casts than the pedestrian 2003 bunch.

Alou was notable disinterested in using pinch-hitters. The Tendencies Database confirms this, using Retrosheet's splits. The following list shows which managers had the fewest pinch-hit plate appearances in a season compared to the rest of the league:

Least Likely to Pinch Hit

Felipe Alou	1.703
Cito Gaston	1.613
Danny Murtaugh	1.479
Davey Johnson	1.392
Dusty Baker	1.390

Alou's squads used the fewest number of pinch-hitters eight times in thirteen seasons. Since 1990, only three NL teams have had fewer than 200 pinch-hit plate appearances in a full season. Alou managed two: the 1997 Expos and the 2003 Giants.

DUSTY BAKER

> **W/L Record:** 1,236–1,129 (.523)
> **Managed:** Full Seasons: San Francisco 1993–2002; Chicago (NL) 2003–6;
>   Cincinnati 2008
>   Majority in: (none)
>   Minority of: (none)
> **Birnbaum Database:** -103 runs
>   Individual Hitters: +119 runs
>   Individual Pitchers: -62 runs
>   Pythagenpat Difference: +87 runs
>   Team Offense: -93 runs
>   Team Defense: -154 runs
> **Team Characteristics:** His teams win with hitting, especially power. Baker has
>   overseen middling pitchers who allow more walks than normal. He

frequently uses relievers on back-to-back days. Only five teams in baseball history with more than fifteen saves had one reliever record all of them; Baker managed three: Rod Beck with the 1996 Giants, Robb Nen with the 2002 Giants, and Francisco Cordero with the 2008 Reds.

Much of the commentary on managers (including, admittedly, much of this book) presents a reductionist view of their job, portraying a skipper as someone who has the same impact on all environments at all times. In reality, managers are better at some parts of the job than at others. Place a man in a situation that fits his strengths, and he will look like a savant. Put that same individual on a team that highlights his weaknesses and people will call him a dullard. Dusty Baker's experiences with the Giants and Cubs provided ample evidence of this phenomenon.

With the Giants, Baker was exceptionally well regarded. He won three Manager of the Year Awards in eight seasons, and the venerable Leonard Koppett argued in his book *The Man in the Dugout* that Dusty Baker was "as close to perfect as one could find" in modern baseball. Numerous players did far better under his care than one could possibly have imagined, including Ellis Burks, Jeff Kent, Benito Santiago, Rich Aurilia, Brent Mayne, and J. T. Snow. People skills were Baker's strong point, and positive feelings were the trademark of his Bay Area tenure. In ten years in San Francisco, he never had a public dispute with a player. The team handled those matters in house. Jeff Kent and Barry Bonds publicly feuded with one another, but neither ever dragged Baker into it, and he did not let it disrupt the rest of the squad.

Baker's experience with the Cubs was very different, as the Bay Area's genius became the Windy City's idiot. After a strong start, nearly taking the Cubs to the World Series in 2003, things devolved into increasing acrimony. During the 2004 pennant race, the Cubs acted completely unfocused. They concerned themselves with petty details—disputes with reporters, an on-field brawl with the Astros, and most embarrassingly some players complained the Cubs' TV broadcasters said too many nice things about the opposition. A talented roster failed to reach the postseason because of asinine distractions.

Baker's critics became louder the longer he stayed in charge, and the situation cratered completely in the first half of 2006. In a four-week period, the Cubs went 5–23, appearing completely disheartened in the process. They set a franchise record for ineptitude, scoring thirteen runs in an eleven-game stretch. During that death spiral, Baker made some curious statements. Sounding openly morose, he said he felt depressed, and did not know what to do about the situation. That is the last thing a leader should say. In any line of work the boss's attitude rubs off on his underlings. Baker's Eeyore the Donkey impression did not cause the tailspin, but it amplified and extended it. The Cubs played like a team expecting to lose, finding reasons to falter, blowing game after game. When Baker left Chicago amid howls of fan discontent, his reputation lay in tatters.

The difference in Baker's performance in the two towns had more to do with the fit than with Baker himself. Five factors accounted for the difference: player age, the emphasis placed on pitching, athlete sensitivity to criticism, the players' interest in drawing walks, and the batboys (yes, really). These factors showcased Baker's strengths in San Francisco and his weaknesses with the Cubs.

First, the Giants had a veteran team, which perfectly suited Baker. He was more at ease dealing with known quantities, which made San Francisco the perfect franchise for him as team GM Brian Sabean badly neglected his farm system, building the team with established talent instead. The quality players who gurgled up from the minors, such as Rich Aurilia, were rare enough so that even Baker felt comfortable incorporating them.

In contrast, Chicago had a youth movement when they hired Baker. *Baseball America* claimed the Cubs had baseball's best farm system shortly before Baker's Wrigley Field debut. He unhesitatingly incorporated superlative young pitchers Mark Prior and Carlos Zambrano into the rotation as the Cubs could always use another starting pitcher. However, whenever Baker had to choose between starting a veteran position player or a prospect, Baker reflexively chose the veteran. Most vexingly, when the Cubs fell out of the pennant race in 2005, Baker refused to give prospect Ronny Cedeno a shot because that would mean benching Neifi Perez. Though Perez was a horrible offensive player, Baker praised him as a standout presence. Similar situations played out with unproven players like Matt Murton and Jason DuBois. Maybe they were not good enough to make it, but Baker rejected them without giving them a chance. A familiar routine developed. GM Jim Hendry would talk about wanting to see how the latest call up would do. Shortly afterward, Baker would caution against overburdening the youngster, and then bench him. Hendry had to trade veterans away in order to get Baker to play a few youngsters.

A second difference existed between Baker's Giants and Cubs squads: San Francisco's teams did not revolve around pitching. Instead, they won with offense, the part of the game at which Baker, a former hitting coach, excelled. His starting pitchers were generally just innings eaters. In fact, over the course of his entire career, he had subpar starters. According to the Tendencies Database, the following managers had the worst starting rotation ERA (available thanks to Retrosheet) adjusted for park:

Worst Starting Pitcher Park-Adjusted ERA

Frank Robinson	1.282
Dusty Baker	1.221
Johnny Oates	1.173
Gene Mauch	1.142
Bruce Bochy	1.129

In San Francisco, Baker had men like Kirk Reuter, Mark Gardner, Russ Ortiz — fine pitchers, but nothing special. This was fortunate because hitters were Baker's forte, not pitchers. The strengths of the roster and manager meshed. Chicago's best players were pitchers, most notably their young trio of starters Mark Prior, Kerry Wood, and Carlos Zambrano. In the most commonly noted criticism of Baker's time in Chicago, Wood and Prior went down with injuries after experiencing heavy workloads. Frankly, this critique is overblown as Wood had already experienced numerous injuries and one never knows if Prior would have stayed healthy, Baker or not. Nevertheless, Baker had them pitch needlessly deep in several games. He lacked the same feel for pitchers that he possessed for hitters; it was not his strength.

Third, Baker's teams in Chicago were noticeably thin-skinned. Numerous players went out of their way to complain about the media and any criticism they received. This tactic merely created more backlash against them and further distracted the team from the game. Aside from the players complaining about the broadcasters, several — including Jacque Jones, LaTroy Hawkins, and Moises Alou — developed personal media feuds.

This had not been the case in San Francisco. The key difference lay with the best player, Barry Bonds. Aside from being the Giants biggest star, Bonds was their most criticized player. Even before BALCO, critics assailed him for everything from his attitude to having a big chair in the clubhouse. Bonds never let it faze him. Think how that affected his teammates: were they really going to complain about a scathing article when the man ten times more talented received worse abuse? No. Bonds's existence meant Baker had to do minimal disciplinary work to keep the team focused. Baker's interpersonal skills focused on a kinder gentler approach with players anyway, so this fit his style. The Cubs needed someone who would kick them in the butt instead.

Fourth, the Giants' hitters minimized and Chicago's offense maximized Baker's blind spot for the base on balls. While with the Cubs, Baker publicly derided walks as things that clog bases. If it were just a press conference comment it would not matter. However, the team drew fewer free passes under his watch. In his first year, Chicago's walks declined by 93, and their walks dropped further each season he was there. In his final year, the Cubs had their worst walks-per-game rate since 1921. However, in 1921 the NL averaged 2.1 walks per nine innings, versus 3.3 in 2006. In context, that year's Cub hitters did the worst job in franchise history working the count. The 2006 Cubs drew 292 fewer walks than they allowed, the worst differential in National League history. In Baker's four years, they averaged 158 more walks allowed than drawn per year, easily the worst stretch in franchise history. The year after Baker left, Chicago's hitters drew 105 more walks than the year before. In San Francisco, though, walks were not an issue. Bonds, the game's all-time leader in walks, had his offensive philosophy. Baker was not going to make the multiple MVP winner radically alter his approach, making him generally more tolerant of walks.

The fifth crucial distinction was the different batboys Baker had in San Francisco and Chicago. That sounds frivolous, but it mattered. With the Giants, Baker made the players' children team batboys in an attempt to foster a positive atmosphere. Baker firmly believed happier teams play better. Fathers who could go weeks without seeing their kids got to spend the day hanging out with them. Someone who committed an error or struck out three times could still return to the smiling face of their child, which shone through all of the crowd's boos. A bench player could more easily endure his lack of playing time if his son was with him. The batboys motivated the players, putting them in the best frame of mind to win: enjoy the game, have fun, and do not sweat the small stuff. It not only made them happier and better focused, but it also put the players' priorities in order. First comes family, then the job you do to support it, and after that everything seems insignificant. Also, the kids made sure the adults remained on their best behavior without Baker having to say a word.

Unfortunately, in the 2002 World Series Baker's own son nearly got run over at the plate, causing Bud Selig to issue guidelines for hiring batboys. The Cubs had generic batboys and considerably less fun. If ever a team could benefit from hearing a child's laughter, it was the 2004 Cubs, who constantly sweated the small stuff.

One other concern should be noted. There is no profession where people's talents and abilities stay fixed forever. As Baker got older, he likely declined. His style centered on empathizing with his players. The older one gets, the more difficult it is to relate to twenty-somethings. Baker was neither as bad as he appeared in Chicago nor as good as he seemed in San Francisco. What happens in Cincinnati will determine his managerial legacy.

BRUCE BOCHY

> **W/L Record:** 1,094–1,156 (.486)
> **Managed:** Full Seasons: San Diego 1995–2006; San Francisco 2007–08
>   Majority in: (none)
>   Minority of: (none)
> **Birnbaum Database:** +354 runs
>   Individual Hitters: +270 runs
>   Individual Pitchers: -43 runs
>   Pythagenpat Difference: +155 runs
>   Team Offense: +87 runs
>   Team Defense: -115 runs

Team Characteristics: Bochy's teams win with hitting and lose with pitching and defense, though park factor might make it appear otherwise. His offenses do a good job hitting singles and drawing walks, but hit into numerous double plays. Surprisingly for the manager of Trevor Hoffman, his bullpens are generally below average. Bochy does a very good job putting OBP at the top of his lineup.

Pop quiz: without looking, how long did Bruce Bochy manage the Padres? Ready for the answer — no peeking unless you have a guess — twelve seasons. A dozen years! That was longer than Whitey Herzog lasted in St. Louis. It was more games than Casey Stengel ran the Yankees. Switching sports, Bochy lasted longer than Bill Walsh's entire NFL coaching career. In his tenure, Bochy had a losing record overall, and went to only one World Series, in which the Yankees swept his club. Bochy's other postseason trips saw San Diego face St. Louis in three different NLDS, in which the Padres won only one out of ten games. The Padres had not been so abjectly powerless before the Cardinals since the time of Pope Innocent III. He is a good manager, but not many last twelve years with such scant qualifications. He is Tom Kelly without the rings, and Wilbert Robinson without the personality. If Bruce Bochy fell in the woods, he would not make a sound. Has anyone ever lasted so long with one franchise and done so little to draw attention to himself?

Looking at it a bit more seriously, Bochy is one of only 22 men to last at least a dozen years on the job with one team. In their extended stints, that bunch won over 30,000 games with a .548 winning percentage while claiming 95 pennants and 44 world titles. Only four had losing records — Connie Mack, Tom Kelly, Jimmy Dykes, and Bochy. Mack merely claimed nine pennants in his first 31 seasons. Kelly delivered Minnesota its first two world championships in his first five seasons. Only Dykes had a less impressive tenure than Bochy. Even there a catch exists. Dykes made it to a dozen years during World War II, a time when teams were unusually reluctant to fire their managers.

Bochy lasted as long as he did because he is a quality manager. As noted in Chapter 1, the Birnbaum Database lists him as the greatest manager in history with a losing record: a dubious distinction, but impressive nonetheless. Not only has Bochy attained a losing record, but he garnered little attention for himself in San Diego. People rarely mentioned him as one of the most prominent managers, and rarely even noted him as an underrated one. Though it is largely inevitable someone with a poor record would gain minimal acclaim, Bochy did not even receive the credit given to other prominent sub -.500 managers such as George Stallings and Gene Mauch, who also score quite well in the Birnbaum Database.

Bochy's problem (aside from losing) was that he never did the things that cause the public to notice skippers. The best way for a manager to gain popular acclaim is postseason success. Stallings's 1914 October glory cemented his reputation, for instance. However, the Padres lost two-thirds of their postseason games under Bochy. Many fans will gravitate to a manager who makes brilliant in-game strategic decisions, as was the case with Gene Mauch. Bochy rarely engaged in intense levels of in-game strategy. In fact, as Chapter 2 showed, he is the game's all-time opponent of the bunt. Finally, many people laud managers who are especially willing to work with young talent. While Bochy did a very good job handling young pitchers in San Diego, ranging from the highly touted Jake Peavy to the little-heralded Brian Lawrence, his record with young hitters is rather poor. Well-regarded prospects Ben Davis and D'Angelo Jimenez floundered and most notably super-prospect Sean Burroughs flopped. In a dozen years with the Padres, Bochy developed only one position player, Khalil Greene. The things the general public most readily notices were not Bochy's strengths.

Yet the Padres did far better than they should have under Bochy. They posted a .494 winning percentage under his watch — equivalent to a 80–82 single-season record — despite possessing very little talent. Bochy's San Diego lineups centered on players like Mark Loretta, Ryan Klesko, Phil Nevin, Ken Caminiti, Chris Gomez, and Damian Jackson. All were useful, but they make a rather meager all-star lineup over a dozen-year period. Tony Gwynn and Rickey Henderson were the only great players Bochy had, but both were in their late 30s under him. That collection of second-tier hitters was supported by an even less impressive group of starting pitchers. Aside from a sole spectacular season by Kevin Brown in 1998, Bochy relied on a flock of journeymen in his starting rotation. Only seven pitchers started 70 games for San Diego in Bochy's dozen years there: Andy Ashby, Brian Lawrence, Jake Peavy, Woody Williams, Adam Eaton, Joey Hamilton, and Sterling Hitchcock. Peavy is a great talent and Ashby had his moments, but the rest were just innings eaters. On the whole, Bochy presided over an inferior stable of starters with the Padres. San Diego possessed a terrific reliever in Trevor Hoffman, who was not only in his prime, but also with the franchise for every season of Bochy's tenure. However, getting to Hoffman could be a chore as San Diego's middle relief was routinely a shambles. From 1995 to 2006, San Diego's non–Hoffman relievers posted a combined ERA of 4.30. In those same years, the overall bullpen ERA for the rest of the NL was 3.85. Admittedly, that is not quite a fair comparison as the closer's numbers were removed from San Diego but not the rest of the league. Since the relief ace should be the best arm in the bullpen, that should cause the remainder of San Diego's relief corps to underachieve. However, it does not explain a nearly half-point difference in ERA. Actually, that underestimates how bad San Diego's middle relievers are because the Padres' parks (first Qualcomm and then Petco) suppress scoring. Adjust for park factor, and San Diego's middle relievers would have posted an ERA of 4.66.

Thus in his dozen years in southern California, Bochy possessed a corps of solid but generally unimpressive hitters, journeymen starting pitchers, toxic middle relievers, and a superlative closer. Yet that bunch played .494 ball for him from 1995 to 2006. Somehow, 75-win talent transformed into 80-win results. Though below average, it was still an impressive achievement. Bruce Bochy's ultimate season was probably 2001. The Padres finished a hair under .500 for him despite an offense centered on 30-year-olds Phil Nevin and Ryan Klesko while the ace of the starting rotation was Kevin Jarvis, whose main claim to fame is having fewer career Win Shares than any hurler who ever started 100 games.

Bochy produced those results because he had an impressively effective track record coaxing unexpectedly strong performances from veteran hitters. Ryan Klesko came to San Diego in his early 30s, yet defied the aging curve to improve. Phil Nevin erupted under Bochy. Mark Kotsay had two of his three best seasons for him. Upon arrival in San Diego at age 33, Mike Cameron probably had his best offensive season in five years. Wally Joyner had a nice resurgence in his mid–30s, as did Mark Loretta. Tony Gwynn, 35 when Bochy arrived, won batting titles in three of the four seasons he had enough plate appearances to qualify for one. Ken Caminiti's steroid-fueled MVP occurred under Bochy. This does not mean Bochy waved a magic wand that made all veterans suddenly improve, but enough did for Bochy to score +270 runs in the Birnbaum Database's individual hitter component, one of the best marks of all time.

Since joining the Giants, Bochy has found himself mired in the second division, but the roster the front office assembled made that inevitable. Before Bochy arrived, the Giants were an aging and subpar team relying too heavily on stars Barry Bonds, Moises Alou, and Jason Schmidt. The team lost Schmidt and Alou the same off-season Bochy became manager; under the circumstances, it was an achievement that they only declined by five games. What happened in 2008 was more impressive. Despite losing Bonds, easily their best player, they improved by a game. Forecast by many to be one of the worst teams in all of baseball, the Giants narrowly missed placing third in the NL West.

Home runs have been Bochy's Achilles heel as his teams lack power. Only six times has someone hit 30 homers in a season for him, while the entire NL contained 249 such performances since 1995. Meanwhile, his pitchers give up their share of long balls. While his hitters have only had 22 different twenty-homer seasons, individual pitchers have allowed 20+ homers 29 times. That difference is especially distinctive because across baseball as a whole, individual hitters are more likely to bash twenty homers than specific pitchers allow that many. When the results from the Tendencies Database's results for hitting and allowing home runs are added together, Bochy's teams are historically bad:

Combined Home Runs

Tom Kelly	2.836
Jimmy Dykes	2.728
Phil Garner	2.574
Bruce Bochy	2.555
Jimmy McAleer	2.545

Bochy's offenses have never hit more than 161 homers in a season while his pitchers have allowed greater than 161 long balls eight times. Only twice have his hitters blasted more long balls than his staff has allowed. Overall, his pitchers have allowed 393 more homers than his hitters have allowed; only Kelly and Dykes have a larger negative split. The 2003 Padres gave up 203 while hitting a mere 123, the worst differential in National League history.

BOBBY COX

W/L Record: 2,327–1,854 (.557)
Managed: Full Seasons: Atlanta 1978–1981, 1991–2008; Toronto 1982–85
Majority in: Atlanta 1990
Minority of: (none)
Birnbaum Database: +655 runs
Individual Hitters: -141 runs
Individual Pitchers: +607 runs
Pythagenpat Difference: +264 runs
Team Offense: +69 runs
Team Defense: -144 runs
Team Characteristics: Cox's teams are built around pitching. They have good control, keep the ball in the park and strike out opponents. According to Win Shares and Defensive Efficiency Ratio, they have strong defenses aiding them. His offenses revolve around home runs. Cox prefers a set lineup and keeps his players in the same slot in the batting order. He used 47 batting orders with the 1993 Braves, one of the lowest totals ever in a 162-game schedule.

Not surprisingly, Bobby Cox scores tremendously well with pitchers in the Birnbaum Database. In particular, he has presided over world class starting rotations, something the Tendencies Database can attest to. Retrosheet's team splits provide the ERA for all rotations. Plugging park-adjusted starting rotation ERAs into the database, the following managers oversaw the best starting pitching since 1956:

Park Adjusted Starter ERA

Tommy Lasorda	0.519
Bobby Cox	0.527
Jimy Williams	0.527
Walt Alston	0.590
Earl Weaver	0.622

Cox would be first overall, but his last few seasons with the Braves hurt his overall score. His Braves finished first in this category for eleven straight seasons. That would be an impressive feat in an eight-team league; doing it in a league normally containing fourteen or sixteen teams is unfathomable.

Two factors account for Cox's success with starters. First and most importantly, his teams featured talented pitchers. This was most obvious in the 1990s Braves, who contained Greg Maddux, Tom Glavine, and John Smoltz. Never before have a trio of Cooperstown-caliber hurlers regularly pitched alongside each other for so many years. Second, Cox knows how to handle his pitchers. He maintained the delicate balance between getting the most innings he can from his arms without ruining them. Smoltz was the only member of Atlanta's trinity to eventually break down, but only after a full decade of use. According to Peter Bendix and Matt Gallagher's presentation at SABR's 2005 national convention, "The Leo Mazzone Effect," the Braves once went five years without a hurler missing a start due to injury.

Throughout his career, Cox has worked his aces hard with surprisingly few injuries, a fact evident in his first managerial opportunity. Cox pushed his one dependable starter, Phil Niekro, exceptionally hard. In 1978, the 39-year-old knuckleballer achieved personal bests in complete games (22), and innings pitched (334.3). Cox worked him even more in 1979, en route to a 21–20 record, making him the first National League pitcher to win and lose 20 games in a season since 1905. In 1978–79, only two pitchers in baseball were within 125 of Niekro's 676.3 innings. He started 86 games and faced 2,825 men in those two years, the most by any senior circuit hurler since Pete Alexander. Despite that heavy use, Niekro remained an effective and durable starter for years to come.

In Toronto, Cox continued pushing his starters hard. In 1982, Blue Jays pitcher Jim Clancy became the last non-knuckleballer to start 40 games, and teammate Dave Stieb led the league in batters faced. Under Cox, Stieb threw 1,098.3 innings from 1982 to 1985, more than any other pitcher. In terms of quality he was among the best as well, capped by a 1985 ERA title. In Toronto, however, Cox was least able to maintain the health of his starters. Clancy's ERA ballooned in 1984 and he missed part of the season the next year, though he later recovered. Stieb remained one of the game's great pitchers under Cox, but beginning in 1986 he clearly lost some of his stuff, and was never the same.

When Cox resumed the field manager role with Braves, though he no longer used his starters quite as heavily, he still distinguished himself from his peers. Instead of a standard five-man rotation, Cox adopted more of a four-and-a-half man order in which he was less likely to give his starters an extra rest when the schedule gave the team a day off. The last NL pitcher to start 36 games was Greg Maddux in 2003. Tom Glavine started 36 in 2002. Conversely, no non–Cox NL hurler has reached 36 starts since 1993. Since 1991, an Atlanta pitcher led or tied for the lead in starts thirteen different times. From 1991 to 2007, NL pitchers started at least 35 games 64 times; 22 were with the Braves. The next three highest ranking teams combined did not have that many.

Cox's habit of pushing his starters has hamstrung his teams in the postseason. On twenty different occasions, Cox asked one of his pitchers to start on three days rest in October. They responded by allowing 5.42 runs per nine innings, causing Atlanta to go 7–13 (.350) in those contests. (Please note Atlanta possessed a .533 winning percentage in their other games.) Atlanta had eight consecutive short-rest starts without logging any quality starts. Tom Glavine's performances on short rest were the worst, as he allowed 48 baserunners in 31 innings for a 6.10 ERA when starting after three days off. In his postseason starts with adequate rest his ERA was 2.98. Steve Avery thrice started on short rest, throwing a total of 10.3 innings. Greg Maddux allowed a run per inning (and nearly two hits per inning) in his three-days-rest October starts. John Smoltz pitched well with less rest (2.45 ERA in five starts), but he was the exception. Atlanta's best postseasons came when they used a four-man rotation.

They had one in 1995 when they won it all and also in 1996 when they nearly repeated. However, when Cox lacked four pitchers he trusts completely, he refused to use his fourth starter in the postseason. Unfortunately, October proved to be a very poor time to retrain his starters, who were obviously unaccustomed to such short rest. That was one reason the Braves won only one world title despite appearing in every postseason from 1991 to 2005.

Postseason problems notwithstanding, Cox's Braves achieved an impressive track record with reclamation projects, especially in the bullpen. In 2002, they took a flyer on Chris Hammond, a 36-year-old who had neither thrown a pitch in the majors in four years nor had a good season in seven. In 63 appearances, he posted an ERA of 0.95. Fellow 36-year-old Atlanta reliever Darren Holmes, who posted a 13.03 ERA with three separate squads the year before, achieved a 1.81 ERA in 55 games for Cox's 2002 bullpen. A third 36-year-old reliever, southpaw Mike Remlinger, worked alongside them. He had been a mediocre journeyman before coming to the Braves in 1999, but posted a 2.65 ERA in nearly 300 appearances and an All-Star selection while with Cox. Every year or two the Braves have received great work from a reliever plucked from the scrap heap, including hurlers Juan Berenguer, Marvin Freeman, Steve Bedrosian, Mike Bielecki, Juan Cruz, Kyle Farnsworth, Rudy Saenz, Antonio Alfonseca, Chad Paronto, and Will Ohman.

Atlanta's homegrown products also show Cox's ability to get quality from seemingly unremarkable pitchers. Cox also wrung tremendous production from numerous pitchers who did not even make the majors until they were 26 or older. First there was Greg McMichael, a reject from Cleveland's farm system whom Atlanta took a flyer on. From 1993 to 1996 he was one of the game's superior setup men, providing 80 innings a year with an ERA around three. After leaving Atlanta, he had only one more quality season. His departure was fine for Atlanta, because in 1997 a new 26-year-old emerged, Independent League refugee Kerry Ligtenberg. He spent the next five years duplicating McMichael's performance, in slightly fewer innings per season. Shortly before he left, the club discovered 28-year-old Kevin Gryboski, who established himself as an above average reliever for four seasons. After Atlanta traded him, Gryboski failed to keep his ERA under eleven. A few years later, Australia's Peter Moylan emerged as the latest overlooked gem. After getting his feet wet in 2006 at age 27, the next year he blossomed to a 1.80 ERA in 90 innings. Almost every season for fifteen straight years, the Braves got a quality arm in the bullpen from otherwise overlooked quadruple–A relievers. While pitching coach Leo Mazzone certainly deserves considerable credit, divorcing the manager from this sustained success is as foolish as giving him all the credit. Developing, coaching, and handling pitchers to ensure they produce at their fullest is a team effort, and Cox has played a vital part in it.

Atlanta's success with late-inning arms is especially noteworthy because Bobby Cox has spent his entire career on the cutting edge of reliever-usage patterns. Two dominant trends in reliever usage pervade the last 50 years: bullpens eat an increasing share of innings and innings per relief appearance keep declining. Bobby Cox is as responsible for the latter change as anyone. The Red Schoendienst commentary in Chapter 7 listed the teams that set records for fewest innings per relief appearance (IP/RA) from the 1950s to the 1980s. Finishing where that table left off, Cox's impact on reliever workloads is clear:

Year	Team	IP/RA	Manager
1989	STL	1.243	Whitey Herzog
1991	OAK	1.152	Tony LaRussa
1992	STL	1.114	Joe Torre
1993	ATL	1.054	Bobby Cox
1994	ATL	1.037	Bobby Cox
1995	CHC	0.996	Jim Riggleman

Year	Team	IP/RA	Manager
1997	ATL	0.987	Bobby Cox
2001	STL	0.961	Tony LaRussa
2002	ARI	0.917	Bob Brenly
2004	SFG	0.912	Felipe Alou
2005	STL	0.911	Tony LaRussa
2008	NYM	0.885	Willie Randolph and Jerry Manuel

Cox and Tony LaRussa led the charge for specialized relief pitchers over the last twenty years. When the A's shattered the 1.2 barrier in 1991, both Cox's Braves and Torre's Cardinals joined them. Rather tellingly, they are the three most successful managers of their generation. Furthermore, Cox might deserve more responsibility than even LaRussa for modern reliever patterns. When IP/RA is put into the Tendencies Database, here are the leaders among those with 10+ seasons managed since 1956:

Fewest IP/RA

Red Schoendienst	1.719
Bobby Cox	1.614
Whitey Herzog	1.557
Tony LaRussa	1.334
Danny Murtaugh	1.321

Cox has always had his relievers pitch comparatively short outings. His relievers tossed the fewest outs per game ten times—including twice in his initial Atlanta experience and two more times in Toronto. LaRussa receives the most attention for changing reliever usage because of his time with Oakland's fantastic bullpen from 1989 to 1991, but Cox also played a vital role. Cox's consistent pressure to lower individual reliever workload while trotting out pitching-heavy perennial division winners caused other teams to change how they used relievers.

The early 1990s was not the first time Cox helped shift bullpen usage patterns. His Toronto tenure stimulated a change in how AL managers used relievers. Ever since the creation of the designated hitter in 1973, relievers in the junior circuit went longer per outing. While NL relievers threw 1.5 to 1.6 innings per appearance, their AL counterparts tossed around 1.9 per outing. During Cox's Toronto sojourn, the difference between the two leagues diminished noticeably. Cox, with his NL background, often had his relievers face among the fewest batters per appearance. By the time he left Canada, the difference between the two leagues was one-tenth of an inning per appearance. Cox did not single-handedly cause this transformation, but he was a main catalyst for it.

Along with reliever strategy, part of Atlanta's success has been due to superior fielding. Though Cox has never had as strong a glove fetish as Bill McKechnie, his teams consistently have good defenders. The Braves experienced a historic one-year improvement in their fielding from 1990 to 1991. Going by Defensive Efficiency Ratio, they had the worst fielding team in the NL at .676, letting almost one-third of all balls in play fall for hits. In 1991, behind a revamped defense, they boasted the best DER in the league, .713. Fielding Win Shares shows a defensive improvement worth seven games from 1990 to 1991. The Blue Jays came in first or second in Fielding Win Shares in all but one of Cox's four seasons (when they placed fourth).

Cox's hitters rely on power. In part, that is a product of playing in the thin air of the plateau Atlanta rests on, but it is more than that. His batters have launched over 800 more homers than his pitchers have allowed, a mark only Joe McCarthy can top. No other manager has a homer differential better than +530. Only three of Cox's squads allowed more long balls than they hit.

TERRY FRANCONA

W/L Record: 755–703 (.518)

Managed: Full Seasons: Philadelphia 1997–2000; Boston 2004–08

Majority in: (none)

Minority of: (none)

Birnbaum Database: -195 runs

Individual Hitters: -11 runs

Individual Pitchers: -193 runs

Pythagenpat Difference: +115 runs

Team Offense: -92 runs

Team Defense: -14 runs

Team Characteristics: Francona has no interest in the intentional walk. He relies on his starting position players, but is willing to make mid-game replacements. His teams steal infrequently but generally have a fine success rate when they try. Only five AL bullpens have ever averaged less than an inning per relief appearance: Francona managed two of them.

Terry Francona is an interesting case for the Birnbaum Database. It does not think much of him, but I know a few Red Sox fans who rave about him. Normally I do not put much stock in fan opinion, but in this case I make an exception. It is not that Red Sox fans are especially brilliant, but the rift between Francona's reputation and the numbers is different from the normal discrepancy.

Gather up a handful of fans from all 30 franchises and ask them about their teams' managers. Rooters from ten teams will tell you their manager is baseball's biggest idiot. Another ten will explain that their skipper is merely a dullard. About five will admit through gritted teeth that their guy is not too terrible. The other five will shockingly have something nice to say. The crowd rarely gives managers much credit.

A structural element causes skippers to suffer excessive disrespect. A manager's job consists of many elements: handling individual players and their egos, maintaining clubhouse order, dealing with the rest of the organization, working with the media, instructing the players, delegating authority to other coaches while maintaining personal authority, enforcing discipline, motivating players, taking care of in-game tactics, and coping with miscellaneous internal matters and problems. Most of these elements take place largely or entirely behind the scenes, causing the easiest part for fans to see — the in-game strategy — to dominate popular impressions of managers. People usually only notice a managerial decision when it goes wrong. If a decision goes wrong, the public neither forgives nor forgets it. Managing is like umpiring — silence is the sign of a job well done. Thus managers do not get the respect they deserve. A person who cannot find Twins fans on the baseball blogosphere moaning about Ron Gardenhire is not looking. Gardenhire consistently turns 80–85 win squads into 90–95 win seasons, but his main problems occur in the most public elements of the job. A host of other managers take their licks as well.

This makes Francona quite interesting. Instead of fans saying he was worse than evidence indicates, he is one of those lucky few who earns good ratings from the fan base. This does not mean the fans are right. They could unfairly be giving him credit for simply not screwing up what the front office has accomplished. However, it is unusually hazardous to dismiss their opinions.

The numbers say one thing, but sometimes you have to go against them. The Birnbaum Database is good enough, but not perfect. I never understood why someone should turn their brain off after getting the data. Analysis is less in the generating of numbers than in the interpretation of them. I have always thought sabermetrics is more art than science. Therefore, I am willing to overrule the math on occasion.

Regardless of what the Birnbaum Database or any other mathematical system says, Francona has a very good chance to make Cooperstown. He already possesses two world titles. In baseball history, only Joe Torre has won three and not gained enshrinement, and obviously he will eventually go in.

In a way, Francona resembles Walter Alston. The similarity has nothing to do with tactical preferences, in which they are quite different. Alston's Dodgers played for one run, stealing and bunting. Francona's Boston teams play for the big inning, winning with walks and homers. Both, however, have a career arc that caused them to be underestimated. Neither had been especially distinguished before coming to the big league squads that made their reputations: the Dodgers and Red Sox respectively. Alston had been a minor leaguer few took seriously. Francona had a rocky experience as leader of the Phillies. Each was hired to manage a franchise that was already quite successful and backed by considerable financial resources. They both worked for widely publicized front offices that received considerable attention for their clubs' successes: Alston reported to the O'Malleys in Brooklyn, and Boston's Theo Epstein garnered quite a bit of ink for himself. However, though the pre–Alston Dodgers and pre–Francona Red Sox had been quite successful, neither had quite found what they were looking for. The Dodgers had never won a World Series, and the Red Sox last claimed a world championship in 1918, over 80 years previously.

That points to the most important similarity between Alston and Francona: they both had the uncanny knack to win when they needed to. Heading into the 1955, 1959, and 1963 seasons, nothing less than a world championship would save Alston's job. In 1955, fans thought he was a minor leaguer in over his head. Prior to 1959, many unfairly blamed Alston for the team's decline. In 1963, fans faulted him for Los Angeles's blowing a late season lead the previous year to the archrival Giants. In all three cases, Alston delivered a world title to save his job.

Francona has never had his job on the line, but his team consistently plays its best with its back to the wall. In 2004, they dropped the first three games of the ALCS to the Yankees, who scored twice as many runs as Boston in the process. The Red Sox then became the first team ever to rally from the greatest of all deficits en route to the franchise's first world title in 86 years. In 2007, Boston lost three of the first four contests in the ALCS to the Indians— only to win the last three games and then sweep the Rockies in the World Series. In 2008, the Red Sox again dropped three of the first four games in the ALCS, this time to Tampa Bay. In Game 5, they trailed 7–0 with only nine outs left in their season. Improbably, they won that game 8–7, and claimed Game 6 as well. Though Boston lost Game 7, they had once again proven their grit. Francona's Red Sox are 9–2 in must-win postseason games, an unparalleled record in major league baseball.

Alston's strengths were steadiness and unflappability. That allowed his teams to minimize the drama around them and focus on winning. Francona has been similarly able to keep the team focused on day-to-day needs without panicking. That should be more challenging in the postseason, as October's intense pressure causes many to overmanage. That in turn can lead to both poor decisions by the manager and pressing by the players. Francona trusts his players. It helps that he has great veteran leaders in David Ortiz and Curt Schilling who perform well in the clutch, but as the manager Francona is by definition the most veteran leader in the clubhouse. Like Alston, he deserves considerable credit for his teams' success when it matters most.

It will be interesting to see how long Francona lasts. He was only 38 when he joined the managerial ranks in 1997, and men with multiple world championships generally stay in the profession as long as they want. He could become one of the few managers in baseball history to work in five different decades.

RON GARDENHIRE

> **W/L Record:** 622–512 (.549)
> **Managed:** Full Seasons: Minnesota 2002–08
> > Majority in: (none)
> > Minority of: (none)
> **Birnbaum Database:** +430 runs
> > Individual Hitters: +38 runs
> > Individual Pitchers: +164 runs
> > Pythagenpat Difference: +187 runs
> > Team Offense: -25 runs
> > Team Defense: +66 runs
> **Team Characteristics:** Gardenhire possesses the best W/L record in extra inning games of anyone in this book. Through 2008, his Twins are 69–47 (.595) in them. Next best is Sparky Anderson at 198–148 (.572). Gardenhire wins with the classic Comiskey run prevention formula of pitchers with control backed up by fielders who know what they are doing.

Ron Gardenhire is the Rodney Dangerfield of contemporary baseball. He does not receive the accolades of other managers despite his teams regularly exceeding projections. In seven years, he took the Twins to October on four occasions, with at least 90 wins each time. That is as many 90-win campaigns as Minnesota saw in its previous 32 years. Gardenhire receives less credit than he deserves because his weak points are at the most publicly visible portions of the job and his strengths lay behind the scene.

Gardenhire's weaknesses are real. When he has a choice between a name veteran and a young kid, he chooses the graybeard. That is not inherently bad, except that many of the vets have proven to be worn out prior to their arrival in Minnesota. For example, in 2007 the Twins signed journeymen pitchers Ramon Ortiz and Sidney Ponson to fill out their starting rotation. The former had been a replacement-level pitcher for the previous two seasons, and the latter was even worse. Predictably, they were terrible for Minnesota, combining for a 6.22 ERA over seventeen starts. At that time, the club had a trio of arms— Scott Baker, Kevin Slowey, and Matt Garza — all 25 or younger, squeezed out of the rotation. When the Ortiz-Ponson debacle finally ended, the kids combined for 51 starts and an ERA of 4.20. This was not an isolated incident. Minnesota has signed several other used-up commodities—including Livan Hernandez, Tony Batista, Craig Monroe, Rondell White — whom Gardenhire readily played. While the front office deserves the blame more than Gardenhire, one can only wonder what input Gardenhire, given his apparent preference for known quantities, offers when management fills roster holes.

He also engages in frustrating lineup constructions. For him, the #2 slot in the batting order belongs to the scrappy guy with bat control. Cristian Guzman was his ideal second hitter. However, he was such a bad hitter that for three straight years Minnesota recorded worse OPSs from the #2 hole than from any other slot. Losing Guzman to the Nationals in the 2004–05 off-season is one of the best things that could have happened to the Twins. Now their performance from that slot is merely subpar.

Beneath those errors, however, lay an impressive record of achievement. The Twins won three consecutive division titles from 2002–04 when the best OPSs came from Lew Ford,

Corey Koskie, and Torii Hunter. Prior to the emergence of Johan Santana, Gardenhire's best pitchers were Rick Reed and Brad Radke. Fine players all, but teams with that level of talent rarely compete in the playoffs four times in five years. In 2006, they won two-thirds of the games over the last four months despite injuries to two of their best starting pitchers. In 2008, the Twins were supposed to finish well out of the running as they went 79–83 the year before, and proceeded to lose both perennial All-Star Hunter and staff ace Santana in the off-season. Instead, Minnesota came within one game of Gardenhire's fifth division title in seven years.

Perhaps Gardenhire's most impressive season was 2005. Everything went wrong that season as both Torii Hunter and catching sensation Joe Mauer missed time to injury, and Justin Morneau experienced significant growing pains in his first full campaign. No one played 150 games, and only three topped 135. The best hitter of that trio was—God help Minnesota—Jacque Jones. Their normal lineup consisted of silly string, cardboard bits, and Nick Punto held together by duct tape and a generous spackling of Lew Ford. And this squad, ladies and gentlemen, won over half its games. Neat trick. Augmenting the Lineup of the Damned was Johan Santana, who was great, but he cannot pitch every day. Elsewhere in the rotation, Kyle Lohse and Brad Radke were pedestrian, while Joe Mays was an automatic loss. The Twins made up for this two ways: by possessing the best bullpen in baseball and the work of starting pitcher Carlos Silva—who walked nine men in nearly 190 innings.

Those performances were not just flukes (admittedly, Silva's season was a fluke, but not just a fluke). They demonstrated the main strengths of Gardenhire's squads. Silva's performance was bizarrely extreme—it was the fewest walks per inning by a pitcher since 1900—but Gardenhire's staffs constantly find the strike zone. They have had the best control in the league four times and been runner-up twice. In 2005–06, they walked 20 percent fewer batters than any of baseball's 29 other teams. From 2002–08, the Twins surrendered 2,802 walks while the other 29 clubs averaged nearly 1,000 more base on balls allowed, and no other squad was under 3,200. The Twins had good control prior to Gardenhire, but nothing that impressive. Pitching coach Rick Anderson deserves credit, but a pitching coach is not a magic bullet. The working relationship between the manager and coach is crucial.

More importantly, the bullpen has always been Gardenhire's greatest strength. Eighteen men have thrown at least 40 innings of relief work in a season for him, and their record is worthy of Cox/Mazzone. Since Gardenhire has been there the Twins have brought up a half-dozen relief pitchers—Jesse Crain, Juan Rincon (technically he came up earlier but for only a handful of innings), Matt Guerrier, Pat Neshek, Brian Bass, and Willie Eyre. Each has had bad times, but most also had tremendous stretches. Crain received support in the 2005 Rookie of the Year voting, rather rare for a middle reliever. Aside from an injury-damaged 2007, he has been terrific for the Twins. From 2003–06, Rincon had an ERA of 2.93 while striking out a man per inning. Guerrier, whom the team plucked from waivers, also pitched brilliantly for several years. Neshek may have been the best middle reliever in baseball until suffering an injury. Bass and Eyre both stunk, but neither has achieved anything away from Gardenhire either.

The same pattern of improved performances continues with the relievers Gardenhire inherited from Tom Kelly, his predecessor in Minnesota. J. C. Romero was a lousy reliever who just happened to have a major breakthrough when Gardenhire showed up. Through 2008, he possesses a 4.86 ERA away from Gardenhire, but a 3.37 ERA with him. LaTroy Hawkins, who had previously failed as a starter and closer, became one of the best setup relievers in baseball when Gardenhire gave him that role. He left Minnesota shortly afterwards and has not been nearly as good since. Notice a trend? Eddie Guardado, who had established himself as a terrific reliever before Gardenhire arrived, improved anyway. The two best years of Guardado's career, according to innings pitched and ERA, were his only seasons under Gardenhire. The manager also inherited Bob Wells, who declined. Then again, Wells was a middling reliever in his mid–30 on the verge of involuntary retirement.

Finally, Gardenhire used Johan Santana primarily as a reliever in 2002–03. Santana transformed from a prospect into one of baseball's best pitchers when Gardenhire arrived. His metamorphosis began in the minors, so Gardenhire cannot take full credit. While Santana's performance was brilliant, a controversy lingered over how he was used. Some clamored for Gardenhire to make him a starter long before he did. Personally, I have limited sympathy for that argument. Please understand, I am a Cubs fan and have seen super-prospects Kerry Wood and Mark Prior arrive in the majors with trumpets sounding and rose petals laid at their feet — only to see both break down with repeated injury. People who complain that their superlative young pitcher was not worked hard enough at ages 22–23 have a serious lack of real problems to moan about. Besides, since Minnesota won the division every year that Santana spent time in the bullpen, Gardenhire's usage of Santana did not hurt the club. Gardenhire's overall record with his inherited relievers was phenomenal.

As good as his record was with the above relievers, Gardenhire's record really shines when one focuses on the veterans who have arrived in Minnesota under his watch. Mike Jackson, at age 37 and coming off a poor season, became in Twin in 2002. Jackson had a nice comeback season with the Twins, left, suffered through a final substandard season, then retired. Tony Fiore and Joe Roa each had only one good season in their careers; both came under Gardenhire. Funny how that works. Terry Mulholland was rather pedestrian for the Twins in 2004–05, but that was quite an achievement given that he was in his 40s with only one good season in the previous decade. In his only season as a full-time reliever for the Twins, he posted his best ERA in seven years. Maybe Gardenhire had nothing to do with it. Perhaps the southpaw snuck off to the Mayo Clinic for craftiness injections. Mulholland's career ended almost immediately after leaving Minnesota. Aaron Fultz was that rarest of creatures: a reliever who did not improve under Gardenhire. In 2004, his sole season in the Twin Cities, he had a typical season. Next year, in Philadelphia, he had the best year of his career. However, in his big 2005 campaign, Fultz posted routine strikeout, walk, and homer rates; his improvement came from fortune smiling on his balls in play. In 2006, the law of Voros McCracken turned him back into a pumpkin. Dennys Reyes came to Minnesota in 2006 with over 500 innings pitched in his career and a below average ERA. Under Gardenhire he posted an ERA of 0.89 that year. Not bad. From 2006–08, Reyes's Minnesota ERA is half his pre–Gardenhire ERA. Finally, Joe Nathan had been a quality middle reliever for the Giants before Minnesota traded for him. Gardenhire assigned him the closer role, and since then Nathan as been arguably the best bullpen ace this side of Mariano Rivera.

Tallying up: out of eighteen relievers the downsides were Wells's disintegrating corpse, Fultz pitching like himself, and pitiful performances from Eyre and Bass. Even these guys did not underachieve: they merely failed to experience the performance spike all of Gardenhire's other relievers went through. Folks, Ron Gardenhire has not been simply good at handling a bullpen. In all the decades since the bullpen has been an established part of the major league roster, no manager has ever had a seven-year stretch like this in getting the best production from his relievers.

The above praise should be qualified, however. Minnesota's bullpen performance declined in 2007–08. Not only was Bass bad, but Gardenhire often put him in key situations, costing Minnesota victories. Perhaps more worryingly, Gardenhire has worn down some of his arms through overuse, as Pat Neshek's injury was a direct result of Gardenhire's handling. Odds are Gardenhire's record with relievers will decline as he goes on, but that is not an insult. He may not be able to keep up the greatest stretch of bullpen performances in baseball history, but he is still the one who presided over it.

It is hard to imagine the Twins doing any better over the last seven years than they did. That is the highest compliment you can give a manager.

Phil Garner

> **W/L Record**: 985–1,054 (.483)
> **Managed**: Full Seasons: Milwaukee 1992–98; Detroit 2000–01; Houston 2005–06
> Majority in: Milwaukee 1999; Houston 2007
> Minority of: Detroit 2002; Houston 2004
> **Birnbaum Database**: +188 runs
> Individual Hitters: -35 runs
> Individual Pitchers: +106 runs
> Pythagenpat Difference: -134 runs
> Team Offense: +151 runs
> Team Defense: +100 runs
> **Team Characteristics**: Garner likes grinder baseball as his teams stole, bunted, and put the ball in play, but had no power. His hitters avoided double plays, while the defenders knew how to turn them. Control was the strong point for Garner's pitching staffs and strikeouts was their weakest trait.

Phil Garner is the Jimmy Dykes of his generation: rarely have two skippers appeared so similar as this pair. Like Dykes, Garner cut his teeth managing floundering franchises. (Though unlike Dykes, Garner received a chance to manage a team with real talent and won a pennant.) Both men were respected enough to be hired repeatedly as managers, despite their substandard win-loss record.

Also, both overcame lackluster career winning percentages to score admirably in the Birnbaum Database. Not only does Garner have an overall score of +188 runs, but he has positive marks with every squad: +90 runs with Milwaukee, +47 with Detroit, and +51 with Houston (through 2006). Garner achieved these marks by turning teams around upon arrival. In his Milwaukee debut, the team improved by nine games, enjoying their winningest season from 1983 to 2008 (and counting). Detroit improved by ten wins for their best mark from 1994 to 2005. The Astros had played .500 ball prior to his arrival in 2004, then suddenly won two-thirds of their games the rest of the way. All told, in his first full season, Houston captured their first pennant. In Garner's first full seasons with his trio of clubs, he scores +186 runs. That leaves him +2 runs the rest of his career, which is exceptionally good considering his teams had a .469 winning percentage in those years (not including post–2006 seasons which are not in the Birnbaum Database yet). The database contains five managers with career win-loss percentages in the .460s, and they averaged -172 runs.

Garner made the most of the weak hands fates dealt him. Milwaukee and Detroit were doomed no matter who managed them. The Brewers had only one winning record with him, but they only once lost more than 88 games. In their first five years without him they dropped 89, 94, 106, 94 and 94 contests. Garner lost 96 games in Detroit's 2001 campaign, but the next season (when the club fired Garner a week into it) they dropped 106, followed by 119 losses in 2002.

Garner also shared a strategic affinity with Dykes: both loved contact hitters. The commentary on Dykes in Chapter 6 listed the managers with the toughest teams to strike out. Dykes ranked fourth and Garner fifth in it. Under Garner, the Brewers were generally one of the hardest teams to fan, but as soon as he left, they immediately became one of the easiest. Detroit, who routinely led the league in most times struck out in the 1990s, suddenly improved at making contact when Garner ran them in 2000–01. When he left in 2002, they reverted to their traditional ways. His two years there were the Tigers' only full seasons since 1990 with fewer than 1,000 strikeouts.

This offensive philosophy contains a pitching corollary as Garner's hurlers rarely struck out opposing hitters. In fact, compared to their peers, they rank among the weakest power pitchers in baseball history, as the Tendencies Database makes clear:

Fewest K/9IP

Whitey Herzog	1.508
Jim Leyland	1.388
Hughie Jennings	1.381
Phil Garner	1.376
Johnny Oates	1.360

Dykes narrowly misses this list with a score of 1.246. Garner's staffs ranked last in strike-outs per inning four times, and thrice finished next-to-last. In the years he managed at least half a campaign, he never had a pitcher fan 200 batters. There have been 91 such achieve-ments in those years across all of baseball.

On both offense and defense, Garner's teams revolved around putting balls in play. He wanted to put pressure on the opposing teams' gloves while allowing his pitchers to depend on the fielders behind him. The Tendencies Database can show how important this approach was to Garner by combining the fewest strikeouts per nine innings list with the hardest offenses to whiff. (Actually, there is one catch. The teams whose hitters have the fewest strikeouts have the lowest score while the pitchers with the fewest strikeouts have the highest score. One of those scores has to be flipped around. Fortunately, as noted in Chapter 2, it is relatively easy to flip a result from the Tendencies Database. To make the results below fit better with the K/9IP tables just given, this will up end the batter strikeout results.) Based on that, the fol-lowing managers most relied on balls in play:

Most Dependent on Defenses

Whitey Herzog	2.892
Hughie Jennings	2.770
Phil Garner	2.692
Jimmy Dykes	2.618
Danny Murtaugh	2.570

Garner and Dykes—together again. They are separated across time, but not in their approach to the game. The affinity Garner and Dykes shared for balls in play contained an Achilles heel: both managers suffered terribly from home runs. Looking at the seasons in the Tendencies Database, Dykes's teams surrendered 594 more homers than they blasted; the sec-ond worst differential in history. Phil Garner has a homer differential of -362; the fifth worst ever. Adjusting for partial seasons would alter the results for both, but not significantly.

OZZIE GUILLEN

W/L Record: 433–378 (.534)
Managed: Full Seasons: Chicago (AL) 2004–08
          Majority in: (none)
          Minority of: (none)
Birnbaum Database: Guillen's career began in 2004, and the database is only
          complete through 2006. That leaves Guillen with fewer than 500

games Birnbaum-ized, which is not enough to make the data particularly meaningful. For what it is worth, through three years and 486 games, his score is +246 runs overall. The White Sox's dismal 2007 season will certainly hurt Guillen's mark once it enters the Birnbaum Database, but he will remain well above zero.

Team Characteristics: Guillen has veteran hitters who are better at slugging than getting on base. He likes using pinch-hitters, and believes in the intentional walk. All but one of his nineteen starting pitchers who qualified for the ERA title had league-average or better control. He relies on his bullpen less than any other 21st century manager. Only five AL bullpens in history have averaged less than an inning per relief appearance: Guillen managed three.

Guillen is controversial, but he gets as much out of his players as possible. Virtually no one outside the organization expected the White Sox to win it all in 2005, but they did. Many expected them to fall back the next year. Instead the Sox enjoyed consecutive 90-win seasons for the first time in 40 years. In 2008, the smart money decreed they would have a losing record, yet they won the division. Five factors explain Guillen's success: unquestioned authority, accountability, loyalty, creating an "us vs. them" unity, and sound decisions.

The club does not feature any confusion emerging over divided centers of power as Guillen has always unquestionably been in charge. Being hired by the White Sox was ideal for Guillen. Fans loved him from his days as an All-Star shortstop, the media loved him because he gave them good quotes, and most importantly owner Jerry Reinsdorf trusted him. Reinsdorf has always put a premium on loyalty, and one team official said Guillen was the last manager the aging Reinsdorf expected to hire. This loyalty goes two ways. For all Guillen's memorable outbursts, he never insults Reinsdorf.

Further strengthening his position, Guillen possesses a strong working relationship with GM Kenny Williams. A story from Guillen's rookie season reveals how this partnership helps Guillen. Veteran reliever Mike Jackson was unhappy with how Guillen used him. When an irked Guillen reported to Williams that one of his pitchers was causing problems, the GM had a simple solution. He did not want to know the man's name. Instead, Williams said Guillen should inform the pitcher to clean out his locker — he was through with the club. Then Williams wanted Guillen to tell the entire team what Williams had just told him, including how Williams did not even know the man's name in order to make sure they got the message not to complain about the manager. Only then did Williams learn the newly unemployed's identity.

Perhaps the most important element of Guillen's authority is his personality. His often profane utterances indicate a key character trait: he does not worry about ruffling feathers. If he is upset about something, he will make it known. Guillen does not operate out of fear of dangers. Living on the balls of your feet rather than your heels creates an innate sense of authority. Players know that he will confront them if he wants to, just as they know the GM, owner, the media and most of the fans support him. These elements bolstered Guillen's standing *before* winning the World Series. Obviously, capturing Chicago's first world title in 87 years further strengthened his position. Guillen possesses as much security as any manager can wish for, and most can only dream of.

Authority is good only if used appropriately, and Guillen uses his clout to create and enforce expectations for his players. His dumping of closer Shingo Takatsu illustrates this point. Though the Japanese import provided quality work as closer in 2004, finishing second in the Rookie of the Year Award voting, he started 2005 terribly. A month into the season, Guillen demoted him from the closer role, despite the lack of a proven replacement. Three months later the Sox waived Takatsu outright, in what Guillen described as the hardest decision he ever helped make. It did not matter how good Takatsu was last year, or even that Guillen personally liked him — a player had to help the team win. A series of young players under Guillen have done as well as anyone could have hoped — Carlos Quentin, Joe Crede, John Danks, Gavin Floyd, Bobby Jenks, and others. Their roles are laid out for them, and they have to fulfill them. Guillen figures if players cannot meet the pressure from him, how can they survive before 50,000 people? Though Guillen did not personally come up with the club's 2005 slogan "Win or Die Trying," it fits his approach perfectly.

Guillen demands accountability from himself as well. In 2005, the White Sox nearly blew a massive lead down the stretch, when a once mighty fifteen-game lead evaporated into a meager one and a half game advantage. He made it clear that he should be blamed if they missed the postseason. Guillen bluntly told the media several times that if the team missed the playoffs, he should be fired. That demonstrated to his players that he practices what he preaches, and lessened the scrutiny of his players at the most pressure-packed portions of the season.

Furthermore, Guillen uses loyalty with his players to run the squad efficiently. His willingness to take the blame during Chicago's near-collapse in 2005 was one example of this. He will stand up for the guys he believes helped the team win, as demonstrated by his relationship with catcher A. J. Pierzynski. Prior to his arrival in Chicago, Pierzynski had a reputation as a horrible teammate. After trading him to San Francisco, the Twins told the world that he was a terminal clubhouse cancer. The Giants released him outright after one year, further darkening his name. In Chicago, Guillen has had no complaints about him. He once told reporters that everyone hates A. J., but A. J. does not care, that is just the way Pierzynski is. As long as he performs up to expectations, Guillen does not care, nor should anyone else on the squad. That set the tone for the team: do not worry about your teammates, just go about your business. As a result of this approach, Guillen turned a potential minus into a plus. If any veteran has to respect Guillen's authority, it is Pierzynski. He cannot afford to be driven off by a third team, especially one in which the manager backed him.

However, Guillen's loyalty is not unconditional. His players must perform or go the way of Takatsu. However, a player feels like he is more than just a disposable commodity with Guillen. Just because he will break a personal connection with a player that does not mean the bond is not there.

Guillen establishes this sense of belonging by building an "us vs. them" mentality. Nothing makes men band together like having something to rally against. Many of Guillen's outbursts aid this. Whenever the Sox go to the North Side to play the Cubs, he blasts Wrigley Field. He raised hell in Oakland because the Athletics banned liquor in the visitor's clubhouse. Guillen also plays up a rivalry with the Twins. For example, in Minnesota's last home game of 2007, it was open knowledge that longtime local hero Torii Hunter was leaving for greener pastures as a free agent that off-season, making it his final game before the hometown crowd. Late in the contest, which was against Guillen's White Sox, with Minnesota safely ahead, Hunter strode to the plate for his last Twins at-bat. Fans cheered, hoping for a farewell home run. Instead, Guillen ordered him intentionally walked. Guillen was not thinking game strategy; he wanted polarization.

Guillen gets his players to buy into this polarization because he has done a good job making decisions. The 2005 closer situation demonstrates this. First, he removed Takatsu for Dustin Hermanson, a ten-year veteran who had served as a major league closer for only a half-season previous to 2005. Guillen was not worried about his limited major league experience as closer. He thought Hermanson had the best stuff, and the veteran rewarded this faith by performing admirably until felled by an injury late in the season. Guillen responded by making Bobby Jenks — a rookie who had just been called up from the minors — the closer. Many would shirk from giving a rookie that most sensitive bullpen assignment, but Guillen did it in the midst of a pennant race his team appeared to be choking away. Jenks immediately established himself as an effective relief ace. Where others would fear danger, Guillen recognized opportunity.

Guillen's tactics sometimes backfire. In 2006 he nicknamed the Twins piranhas, in an apparent attempt to fire up his team. Instead, the phrase became a rallying cry for Minnesota, and they roared down the stretch trying to live up to that statement. The Twins clinched the division on the last day of the season, appropriately by beating the White Sox.

Also, when the Sox hired Guillen one anonymous baseball official said Guillen would help a good team win some more games, but cause a bad one to lose more. Guillen demonstrated the veracity of that statement in 2007, when the Sox went 72–90. He did the same things that he normally did, but with a very different effect. He sought to light a fire under his team with outrageous comments, tried building rivalries with other teams—all the button-pushing tricks that previously worked. Alas, the team did not have the talent to rise up. Guillen resorted to the same dramatic maneuver he made in 2005: holding himself accountable, he said the team should fire him if he could not make the squad win. Saying this once or twice, as in 2005, gets people's attention. However, because the team kept losing, Guillien spent all summer repeating it. A motivational technique transformed into a cry for help. Instead of buckling down, the team flailed about. When a team lacks what it takes, sometimes the best course for a manager is to be patient and try to get the team ready for the next year. Guillen does not take it easy; patience is not his virtue. It is win or die trying, not win or die waiting.

Guillen is the closest thing we have these days to Billy Martin. Guillen is not as extreme as Martin (no one is) but they have similar tendencies. They only care about winning, have no interest in second place, and combine a ruthless pursuit of victory with a touch of humanity for their players. Both make their teams play as well as possible.

MIKE HARGROVE

> **W/L Record:** 1,188–1,173 (.503)
> **Managed:** Full Seasons: Cleveland 1992–99; Baltimore 2002–03; Seattle 2005–06
>   Majority in: Cleveland 1991
>   Minority of: Seattle 2007
> **Birnbaum Database:** +48 runs
>   Individual Hitters: -77 runs
>   Individual Pitchers: -38 runs
>   Pythagenpat Difference: +9 runs
>   Team Offense: -28 runs
>   Team Defense: +182 runs
> **Team Characteristics:** Hargrove's offenses usually stole more than their share
>   of bases, and he did not like to take his position players out in the
>   middle of a game. He is one of only two managers to last ten or more
>   years with no pitchers ever starting 35 games in a season. The starting
>   players (including the designated hitter) on the 1991 Indians gobbled up only 57.9 percent of all team plate appearance, the lowest
>   ever by a DH team. Exclude the DH, and the remaining eight starters
>   accumulated 50.3 percent of the team's trips to the plate, the fourth
>   lowest total ever.

Distinguishing Hargrove from his teams is especially difficult. He found tremendous success in Cleveland, but they also had Manny Ramirez, Kenny Lofton, Albert Belle, Jim

Thome, Roberto Alomar, Omar Vizquel, Eddie Murray, and Bartolo Colon. Alternately, Hargrove had serious difficulties in Baltimore, but they have consistently churned out rotten teams for a decade. The 2007 Mariners greatly exceeded expectations for him, but Hargrove retired mid-season that year. The Indians fired him after five consecutive titles, indicating they gave him limited credit for their success. Then again, he found work as a manager as long as he wanted it, showing the game as a whole respected his judgment. Hargrove's career record is almost precisely .500, but he never had .500 teams. He had only one team in sixteen seasons with a winning percentage between .470 and .530; normally one club in four falls between those marks.

Despite Hargrove's early success he ended his career with a reputation as a generic veteran manager rather than someone great. In part that is because he helmed weaker teams toward the end of his career, rubbing out the memory of his former glory. It is also due to the relative paucity of tangible hardware — he never hoisted the world championship trophy.

One wonders how Hargrove's reputation might have been different if he had experienced greater postseason success in Cleveland. The 1994 squad appeared headed for the postseason, but the strike ended the season in August. In 1995, when Cleveland faced Atlanta in the World Series, whoever lost that Series would become one of the best clubs to never win it all. The Braves beat the Indians, but it was an incredibly tight series, with one run deciding five of the six contests. The Torre-era Yankee dynasty began in 1996, limiting the chances for everyone else. Still, the only team to beat New York in the postseason from 1996 to 2000 was Hargrove's 1997 Indians. Despite being Cleveland's worst team from 1994 to 1999, they came one inning from the world championship. In 1998, the Indians faced the 114-win Yankees in the ALCS. Cleveland lost the series in six games, which sounds better when you realize that the Yankee dynamo swept their other postseason opponents. It is not difficult to imagine a scenario where Hargrove's Indians won a world championship or two, which would have raised his stature considerably. The Indians continually did 90–95 percent of what they needed to do to win it all, but never achieved that last little bit.

Hargrove had one pronounced trait — his pitchers consistently had the platoon advantage over hitters. According to the Tendencies Database, these post–1956 managers rank the best at making sure this part of the game worked in their favor:

Best Pitcher Platoon Matches

Gene Mauch	0.511
Mike Hargrove	0.516
Tony LaRussa	0.610
Bill Virdon	0.615
Frank Robinson	0.625

Hargrove used his southpaw relievers as platoon specialists. Six lefties pitched in at least 55 games for the Indians from 1992 to 1999. Combined, they averaged fewer than 0.8 innings per appearance, and each individually threw under an inning per game. American League relievers on the whole averaged 1.25 innings per appearance in those years. In Hargrove's full managerial seasons, 22 lefty relievers appeared in at least 30 games; only three averaged at least one inning per game. Combined, they threw 957 innings in 1224 games; 0.78 innings per appearance.

ART HOWE

W/L Record: 1,129–1,137 (.498)
Managed: Full Seasons: Houston 1989–93; Oakland 1996–2002; New York (NL) 2003–4

          Majority in: (none)

          Minority of: (none)

Birnbaum Database: +212 runs

          Individual Hitters: -8 runs

          Individual Pitchers: -63 runs

          Pythagenpat Difference: +65 runs

          Team Offense: +124 runs

          Team Defense: +94 runs

Team Characteristics: Despite managing many years for Billy Beane's Athletics (who opposed small ball tactics), Howe actually bunted a bit more than average over the course of his career. He was a firm believer in the intentional walk. Art Howe and Jim Fregosi are the only managers to last a decade in the profession despite never having a pitcher toss 240 innings in a season.

For better and for worse, Howe's managerial career is best remembered for his tenure with the Oakland A's: for better because they posted consecutive 100+ win seasons in 2001–02, and for worse because Michael Lewis's book *Moneyball* presented Howe as a nearly irrelevant figurehead. In one passage Lewis noted that GM Billy Beane told the manager how to position himself during the game. Howe preferred to sit in the back of the dugout, but Beane thought he looked more commanding when perched on the dugout steps. Clearly Oakland did not think too much of Howe, because they let him go after winning 205 games in his last pair of seasons there.

Nevertheless, the Birnbaum Database loves Howe. He scores +52 runs in Houston, despite their 392–418 (.484) record under him. He was +279 runs in seven years in Oakland with a .530 winning percentage. His Mets tenure was his only negative mark.

New York appears to have been a bad fit for Howe. They were a veteran team, while he achieved his best results with younger players. The A's featured a very well publicized youth boom when he served there, and Houston also reaped a farm system harvest when he was there. A fine All-Star team of prospects who bloomed under Howe can be created:

All-Howe Team

C	Ramon Hernandez
1B	Jeff Bagwell
2B	Craig Biggio
SS	Miguel Tejeda
3B	Eric Chavez
OF	Luis Gonzalez
OF	Eric Byrnes
OF	Ben Grieve
DH	Jason Giambi
SP	Darryl Kile
SP	Tim Hudson
SP	Mark Mulder
SP	Barry Zito
SP	Shane Reynolds

Howe possessed everything but a closer. Biggio and Giambi both had some major league experience before Howe, but it was barely 50 games in each case. Biggio was a catcher until Howe moved him to second. Bagwell and Grieve both won Rookie of the Year Awards under

Howe's watch. Terence Long, Mark Bellhorn, Scott Spiezio, Scott Servais, Aaron Harang, and Eric Anthony provide the bench players. On the Mets, Howe had Jose Reyes and David Wright — both spectacular talents — but neither played 100 games in a season for him. A notion exists that player development only occurs in the minors, but the jump to the majors might be the most important part of the process. Kids rarely crumpled under Howe.

While his teams lost as often as they won, when they lost it was because of balls in play. There are two parts to balls in play — catching those hit by opposing teams, and making it safely to first (or beyond) on the ones you hit. The best measure of the former is Defensive Efficiency Ratio, which is outs from balls in play divided by all balls in play. The best way to gauge the latter is BABIP (batting average on balls in play). Plug them into the Tendencies Database, add their results together for the following combination:

Worst at Balls in Play

Billy Barnie	2.746
Art Howe	2.512
Frank Robinson	2.427
Patsy Donovan	2.385
Jimmy McAleer	2.323

Howe's .498 career winning percentage sticks out like a sore thumb as the others led dreadful squads.

Howe's teams never hit for average. The A's featured Howe's best offense, but they emphasized drawing walks and hitting homers at the expense of batting average. Going just by BABIP, Howe actually has the worst score of anyone who lasted at least a decade, 1.451. His Defensive Efficiency Ratio was about average overall. The A's punted defense in the late 1990s. In 1997 they had Jason Giambi and Ben Grieve, both immobile posts, stationed in the outfield corners. They were last in the league in DER, an almost impossible achievement with Oakland's acres of foul territory.

Tony LaRussa

W/L Record: 2,461–2,146 (.534)
Managed: Full Seasons: Chicago (AL) 1980–85; Oakland 1987–95; St. Louis
         1996–2008
         Majority in: (none)
         Minority of: Chicago (AL) 1979, 1986; Oakland 1986
Birnbaum Database: +1,012 runs
         Individual Hitters: +240 runs
         Individual Pitchers: +455 runs
         Pythagenpat Difference: +138 runs
         Team Offense: +297 runs
         Team Defense: -118 runs
Team Characteristics: LaRussa likes the decision-making parts of the game —
         pinch-hitters, bringing in relievers, bunting, stealing bases. However, he avoids intentional walks. His teams are pretty well rounded as they either score above average in nearly all the categories in the Birnbaum Database, or at least fare only slightly worse than a typical team.

Appropriately for someone who finished law school and passed the bar exam, LaRussa has a reputation as one of baseball's smartest managers. The Tendencies Database can test that. For example, look at one part of the job—filling out the lineup card. Thanks to Retrosheet, information on batting orders exists for all teams in the last half-century. Based on that, one can see how LaRussa fares versus other skippers.

There are three main parts of any lineup. The top two slots of the order are supposed to get on base. After them, the team's best hitters are supposed to drive them in while batting in the heart of the order, generally slots three to six. Finally, the worst hitters usually end up at the bottom of the order, where they will collect fewer plate appearances. Baseball-Reference.com makes studying these Retrosheet-generated splits much easier by providing combined offensive data for these three groups for all teams.

On-base percentage is the best metric to measure top of the order hitters because their main job is to get on base. Specifically, for reasons mentioned in last chapter's Sparky Anderson commentary, take the cumulative OBP of the two top slots and divide it by the team's overall OBP. For the remaining two sections, the stat of choice is tOPS+, a Baseball-Reference invention that compares the OPS for a given split compared to the team's overall OPS. If a team with an 800 OPS had an OPS of 1200 from the heart of its order, they would have a tOPS+ of 150 because the split was 50 percent better than the squad as a whole. For the middle of the order, a higher tOPS+ indicates the manager did a good job filling out his lineup card. A lower tOPS+ for the bottom of the order is desired because that means he made sure his worst hitters were in the appropriate slots. Put all three of these splits through the Tendencies Database, add the results together, and determine who is best at creating batting orders.

However, a snag affects this plan. Everyone puts their best hitters in the heart of the order. That is not the case in the top or bottom of the order as some managers put speedsters who cannot steal first in the leadoff slot or walk machines at the bottom of the order, but every manager treats the middle the same. Ranking tOPS+ for the #3 -6 hitters simply determines which clubs had the most impressive offensive core. There is little reason to give someone credit for realizing Barry Bonds should not bat eighth.

That split tells us little about managers, but the others can be quite illuminating. Add them together and see who has done the best job with a pencil and empty lineup card. This is not a perfect system, but it works tolerably well:

Best Job Creating a Batting Order

Bill Virdon	1.455
Tony LaRussa	1.511
Sparky Anderson	1.610
Red Schoendienst	1.612
Earl Weaver	1.663
John McNamara	1.663

Virdon bests LaRussa, but they both have a comfortable lead on anyone else.

Also, LaRussa has a pet strategy with his batting orders that further shows he knows what he is doing: batting the pitcher eighth. While this confounds baseball tradition, a study in *The Book: Playing the Percentages in Baseball*, Andy Dolphin, Mitchel Lichtman, and Tom Tango revealed that placing the pitcher eighth in the batting order creates runs for a team. Those researchers have some problems with LaRussa's lineups (they think the fourth- or fifth-best hitter belongs in the #3 hole, where LaRussa puts Mark McGwire and Albert Pujols) but they agree with his signature batting order maneuver.

Do not let his genius reputation fool you, though. At heart, Tony LaRussa is a redass. Normally people associate the term "redass" with a manager like Larry Bowa, who knows only one gear—full steam ahead, which can wear a team down. LaRussa performs an internal balancing act between his heart and head. In other words he continually fights an internal battle between the burning desire to push for victory in every game with the recognition of long-term interests. Essentially, he embodies a redass version of the serenity prayer — he has the desire to push for it every game, the willpower to hold back as needed, and the intelligence to know when to push and when to hold back. One story about LaRussa demonstrated the stress this inner war placed on him. In mid–2007, LaRussa told reporters he was not about to retire because there were still games "when you've got a five-run lead, when it's tense and I can't swallow. I've got a headache, and I'm afraid I'm going to throw up. You only feel this stuff because you're anxious about the outcome." That is what happens when a person continually reins himself in.

LaRussa wants his players to feel the same drive. If one lacks that passion, even if it is a star like Scott Rolen or J. D. Drew, LaRussa cannot abide him. He sent both packing, and has had as many feuds with players as any prominent manager in recent times. In dealing with a particular player these feuds may be shortsighted, but they send a message to the rest of the team. If Scott Rolen is not safe, everyone else knows they need to play relentlessly. This ensures LaRussa's teams give their maximum effort.

In this regard, a parallel exists between Tony LaRussa and Joe McCarthy. The former Yankees skipper also strongly emphasized proper conduct while possessing a deep desire to win. Even as a rookie skipper, McCarty dumped all-time great Pete Alexander for his approach to the game. Furthermore, McCarthy, like LaRussa, also experienced head-vs.-heart conflict. McCarthy handled it by drinking his way into alcoholism. More recently, authorities arrested LaRussa in early 2007 for driving while intoxicated. It is difficult to cope with the internal pressure for decades.

Nonetheless, both managers consistently had their teams play as well as possible. In 30 years, LaRussa ran only one last-place team, while overseeing eleven first-place squads. In fact, in full seasons his teams have had the best record in the league more times than they had losing records (seven to six). Such an achievement requires talented players, but it also demands a manager who handles them appropriately. LaRussa has done a good job finding the best roles for his players, making sure everyone knows their job, and performs their best.

The most striking example of LaRussa's ability to get the most out of his players occurred in Oakland, where he assembled the greatest bullpen in baseball history from 1988 to 1990. In that three-year period, Oakland's relievers posted a combined ERA of 2.60. In contrast, the best single-season ERA by any other AL relief unit in that span was 2.82 by the 1988 Brewers. The table below compares Oakland's bullpens to the rest of the AL in defense-independent stats walks, strikeouts, and home runs allowed from 1988 to 1990. Oakland's domination is obvious:

Bullpens	BB/9IP	K/9IP	HR/9IP
Oakland	3.04	6.51	0.52
The Rest	3.67	6.10	0.75

This relief corps's performance was especially remarkable because its core members were poorly regarded prior to arriving in Oakland. The club had three bullpen mainstays in those years: Dennis Eckersley, Rick Honeycutt, and Gene Nelson. Both Eckersley and Honeycutt appeared to be washed up starters before LaRussa moved them to the bullpen. Honeycutt was so poorly thought of that Oakland acquired him for a player-to-be-named later. Nelson previously played for LaRussa in Chicago, and had done adequately, but no more than that. The Sox shipped him along with another player to Oakland for a forgettable middle infielder. The A's augmented this bunch with more of the league's unwanted. Oakland swiped Joe Klink, who had a great year for them in 1990, from Minnesota for a minor league player-to-be-named-later. Mike Norris, a starter for Billy Martin in the early 1980s for the A's, was an internal reclamation project who also prospered in 1990. LaRussa converted Eric Plunk from a flop starter into a solid reliever.

With these castoffs, LaRussa constructed a bullpen that was not only spectacularly effective, but extremely influential. He used more specialized roles for his relief pitcher than had been common, subsequently affecting how other teams construct and utilize their bullpens. This opens up several thorny questions. Some contend that LaRussa's impact on contemporary bullpen usage is a mark against him. Specialization may have done more harm than good because it causes contemporary relief aces, nominally the best arms in the bullpen, to be used far less than the firemen of yore. However, one should not automatically assume that LaRussa was as influential in this area as conventional wisdom makes him out to be. As noted earlier in this chapter, Bobby Cox also helped create hyper-specialized relievers.

To examine the issue further, first one needs to tackle the issue of LaRussa's influence before assigning credit or blame. When the record is examined, the 1988–90 A's bullpen appears to have been a way-station between how relievers were used and how they have since been handled. Relief aces were already throwing fewer innings as managers like Cox reduced innings per appearance. For instance, whereas four closers threw over 100 innings in 1985 and five more did so in 1986, none tossed that many in 1987 — only three broke 90 innings. Still, the A's amplified this trend. Nothing breeds imitation like success and Oakland's glory run provided the most successful bullpen in baseball history. Innings per relief outing dropped by 20 percent in the AL from 1987 to 1993. That was the sharpest reduction in league history, and it came when LaRussa's bullpen was at its height. Still, reliever roles were not as starkly defined then as they later became. Eckersley entered the game in the eighth inning twenty times a year from 1988 to 1990, far more than a present day closer would. LaRussa pointed the way forward and others went even further along.

Since LaRussa had an impact, that leads to the next question: was his influence benign or malignant? As critics of the 21st century bullpen usage rightly note, current relief aces throw considerably fewer innings than their pre–Eckersley ancestors. Instead of throwing 100 innings or more, contemporary closers are likely to toss around 60. It seems counterintuitive that an approach that limits the usage of the bullpen's most important player would be beneficial.

While true, the old-fashioned system featured a noticeable downside. If a team brought in its fireman to throw a few innings, he could not pitch for the next day or two. The current approach increases managerial flexibility, allowing closers to be available to close more games. Also, by minimizing the quantity of innings, managers can maximize quality of innings thrown from the most important bullpen arm. In a study in his book *Winners*, Dayn Perry argued modern closers are actually better leveraged than their predecessors. This flies in the face of a main criticism of current bullpen usage. People remember how Goose Gossage or Mike Marshall came into the seventh inning of tie games with the bases loaded and help the team out while moderns hold three-run leads in the ninth. Both scenarios existed, but neither described a typical outing for relief aces before or after Eckersley. Many seventh-inning appearances from the 1970s did not come in highly dangerous scenarios and current closers hold plenty of one-run leads.

Ultimately, however, a moderate uptick in improved leveraging does not necessarily account for a considerable drop in innings. Though it has its advantages, the Oakland bullpen lessens the relief ace's importance.

However, paradoxical as it might sound, the new model bullpen does a better overall job utilizing the entire relief corps. The old version made sense provided a club had one trustworthy reliever, but normally a gigantic difference in quality between the two top arms in a bullpen does not exist. Thus if a manager spreads out the most important innings between them, and does it in a way that allows them to be called on more frequently, that helps his team's overall performance in close and late situations. Reserving roles by inning might be arbitrary and reductionist, but it has the advantage of ensuring that pitchers know their particular roles. If ever a team should have adopted this reliever strategy, it was LaRussa's Athletics. Since they featured numerous relievers pitching great, spreading out the key innings amongst them was sensible. LaRussa's handling of the Oakland relief corps was both cause and effect of their incredible quality.

Though that great bullpen was the most obvious example of LaRussa adeptly handling his talent, it was not the only one. A more recent example came with the 2008 Cardinals. St. Louis experienced a terrific stretch in the mid–2000s built around a core of Albert Pujols, Jim Edmonds, Scott Rolen, and Chris Carpenter. By 2008, only Pujols remained (well, St. Louis still had Carpenter but he was too badly injured to be of any value). The team especially lacked dependable starting pitchers. They featured mediocre journeyman Kyle Lohse, and reclamation project Joel Pineiro backed up by two converted relievers—Braden Looper and Todd Wellemeyer. Their most reliable hurler was Adam Wainwright, a 26-year-old with only 32 major league starts in his career. That was a prayer, not a stable starting rotation. LaRussa made it work, and the Cards ended the year with an unexpectedly strong 86–76 record despite playing in the NL's toughest division.

LaRussa has made a career of getting more than one would expect from his starters. He had numerous quality staffs despite rarely having elite starting pitchers. Chris Carpenter had a great stretch, but it was brief before injuries felled him. Besides, though Carpenter had been promising, he had never established himself before joining St. Louis. Tom Seaver is the only established great pitcher LaRussa has ever had, but he was at the end of his career when he came to LaRussa's White Sox. LaRussa is more likely to get good production from veteran pitchers who never wowed anyone before. The prototypical LaRussa success story was Dave Stewart. A struggling reliever before LaRussa got a hold of him, Stewart posted four consecutive twenty-win seasons for the A's. LaRussa also oversaw revivals from Darryl Kile, Woody Williams, Kent Bottenfield, Mike Moore, Floyd Bannister, Garrett Stephenson, Todd Stottlemyre, Jason Marquis, Jeff Suppan, and Bob Welch.

However, LaRussa has not had much success with young pitchers. The White Sox featured a flock of young arms emerge under him, almost all of who had disappointing careers. While drug addiction took their toll on Cy Young Award winner LaMarr Hoyt, and Britt Burns's career foundered due to a degenerative hip, Richard Dotson, who went 22–7 in 1983 at age 24, blew out his arm. Ross Baumgarten earned some Rookie of the Year votes in 1979, but won only seven more games in his career. Super-prospect Todd Van Poppel was a disaster in Oakland. Bud Smith came up with the Cards in 2001 and despite throwing a no-hitter, was out of baseball by his 23rd birthday. Matt Morris was runner-up in the Rookie of the Year voting in 1997, and survived an arm injury to win 22 games in 2001, but then faded out. Rick Ankiel suffered an epic mental meltdown in the 2000 playoffs, and his pitching career never recovered.

Tony LaRussa is not only baseball's best manager since Joe McCarthy, but he is on the verge of doing something unthinkable—passing John McGraw on the all-time wins list. LaRussa merely needs to survive four more seasons, averaging 76 wins per campaign. His teams won 78 or more games in each of the last nine years.

Jack McKeon

W/L Record: 1,011–940 (.518)
Managed: Full Seasons: Kansas City 1973–74; San Diego 1989; Cincinnati
1998–2000; Florida 2004–05

> Majority in: Kansas City 1975; Oakland 1978; San Diego 1988; Florida
> 2003
> Minority of: Oakland 1977; San Diego 1990; Cincinnati 1997

Birnbaum Database: +381 runs
> Individual Hitters: +5 runs
> Individual Pitchers: +206 runs
> Pythagenpat Difference: +176 runs
> Team Offense: -15 runs
> Team Defense: +9 runs

Team Characteristics: McKeon kept his relievers in games for longer stretches
> than practically any manager in recent times. He oversaw good pitch-
> ing staffs backed up by adequate offenses. His squads played for one
> run, bunting and stealing to make up for their typical lack of power.
> His teams played better in the second half.

Jack McKeon is the profession's greatest fireman. McKeon has been hired as a mid-season replacement four times, by four different franchises in four different decades. Overall,
teams generally did much better after adding McKeon, as the table below shows.

Manager	Oak 1978	SD 1988	Cin 1997	Fla 2003	Combined Totals
Pre–JM	24–15 (.615)	16–30 (.348)	43–56 (.434)	17–22 (.421)	99–123 (.416)
With JM	45–78 (.366)	67–48 (.583)	33–30 (.524)	74–49 (.605)	220–205 (.518)

That is a nice improvement overall, but one can argue that these improvements do not
mean anything. After all, teams are usually underachieving when they fire their manager in
mid-season, and what looks like better play might be nothing more than the ball finally starting to bounce their way. Three advancements out of four are well within the range of random happenstance. However, digging into the details makes it clear that these improvements
were not merely the luck of the draw. Each of the three improvements was substantial. Aside
from the 1978 A's, winning percentages improved by 40 percent with the hiring of McKeon:
.410 before his arrival and .579 afterwards.

The Oakland experience was the strangest story in the bunch. By 1978, owner Charles
Finley's dynasty had collapsed as he could not financially compete with the introduction of
free agency. The A's started that year exceptionally well, going 19–5, deluding Finley into
hopes of contending. They then cooled off, so Finley switched managers, bringing in McK-
eon. Alas, the team's hot streak had been a fluke. Not only did they go 45–78 under McKeon
but the next year (with yet another new manager) they declined even more, finishing 54–108.
McKeon was not to blame for the 249-point gap in winning percentage before and after his
hiring in 1978.

When McKeon took over the 1988 Padres, he spurred the club on by deftly handling both
the clubhouse and the game on the field. Their previous manager, Larry Bowa, was the most
intense skipper in baseball, and his emotionalism rubbed the team raw. The Padres began the
year on a down note and, unable to relax, were 16–30 when Bowa received his pink slip. Upon
McKeon's arrival, the players could take a deep breath and enjoy themselves. The new boss
complemented the new atmosphere by making sensible moves. Veteran infielder Tim Flannery, in Bowa's dugout for a poor 1987, rotted on the bench. McKeon put the left-handed Flannery in a platoon arrangement, and Flannery responded with one of his best offensive seasons
to date. This move allowed McKeon to limit the playing time for infielder Chris Brown, who
was hitting poorly. The team contained a good relief pitcher in Mark Davis to whom McK-

eon gave a more prominent role. Davis responded by posting a 2.01 ERA that year and winning the Cy Young Award in 1989. Most importantly, McKeon refused to overdo it. He refrained from making wholesale change for its own sake, instead engaging in only necessary modifications, identifying the right talent, and trusting his players. The Padres ended 1988 with a winning record.

McKeon again presided over an improvement when he managed Cincinnati for the last two months of 1997. Common sense remained his secret ingredient. Rather than force himself on the situation, McKeon took opportunities to improve the club as they came. The team desperately needed offense, so he addressed that problem. Thirty-two-year-old Hal Morris, a fixture at first base for the club for several years, had rapidly declined that year. As it happened, almost immediately after McKeon arrived, an injury felled Morris. Super-sub Eduardo Perez became the regular first baseman, and performed well. Center fielder Deion Sanders also lost his spot on the team, first by landing on the disabled list, and then by returning to his main job, which was playing football. McKeon plugged the hole with Jon Nunnally, who hit .318 with power.

The 1997 Reds also featured poor starting pitching. McKeon immediately jettisoned underperforming veterans Dave Burba and John Smiley from the rotation, replacing them with rookie Brett Tomko and southpaw reliever Mike Remlinger. Tomko responded with eight quality starts in eleven tries while Remlinger was one of the Reds' better starters down the stretch. Though McKeon's changes left Cincinnati without a dependable left-handed pitcher in the bullpen, he figured it did not make any difference what happened late if the game was lost early. Once McKeon's rotation had been stabilized, the ERA for Cincinnati's starters dropped significantly in September. Other managers might hesitate to replace proven veterans, even if they were suffering, for a reliever and an unproven kid, but not McKeon.

Florida was McKeon's most famous turnaround, because after playing below .500 for half the year, the Marlins won it all. McKeon kept them mentally focused and did not panic when they hit a few bumps over the season. His patience was particularly vital because no immediate turnaround occurred upon his arrival. He arrived in the midst of a 4–14 stretch for the club. Less than a week after he began Florida entered a losing streak that dropped them to 19–29 on the year. Despite their troubles, McKeon never gave his club a sense that they were merely playing out the season. He found a balance between setting goals for the club without putting excess pressure on them. Perhaps McKeon's gutsiest move was one he did not make: upon arrival, he left the lineup intact. Normally, making some sort of change, any change, is a way to bolster a manager's authority. In this case McKeon's quiet confidence in the talent at hand aided the notion that the young Marlins could win. It was not until he had been with the Marlins for six weeks that McKeon made his first serious change, benching outfielder Todd Hollandsworth in favor of newly called up rookie Miguel Cabrera. The prospect began his career by hitting below .230 in his first month, but McKeon continued putting him out there every day. The way McKeon handled Cabrera encapsulated his approach to the entire ball club: with a player full of promise, do not overreact — just relax and let the talent bring victory.

This subtle strategy underscores why fans often underrate managers. Making good decisions seems so obvious — in hindsight. Since the overwhelming majority of decisions do not require shocking brilliance, managers rarely receive credit for what they do right. For example, the decision to bolster Flannery's role with the 1988 Padres appeared crystal clear in retrospect, but the year before he had been one of the worst offensive players in baseball. Letting him rot on the bench also would have seemed prudent. Someone who consistently makes solid decisions about routine matters will be a good manager. McKeon combined that with an understanding of the human element, giving players the right environment so they could be in the best frame of mind to play the game. A combination of sound in-game decisions and an appropriate mental outlook in dealing with his players continually brought nice rewards for McKeon.

Lou Piniella

> **W/L Record:** 1,701–1,561 (.521)
> **Managed:** Full Seasons: New York (AL) 1986–87; Cincinnati 1990–92; Seattle 1993–2002; Tampa Bay 2003–05; Chicago (NL) 2007–08
> Majority in: New York (AL) 1988
> Minority of: (none)
> **Birnbaum Database:** +50 runs
> Individual Hitters: +300 runs
> Individual Pitchers: -85 runs
> Pythagenpat Difference: +12 runs
> Team Offense: -233 runs
> Team Defense: +56 runs
> **Team Characteristics:** Piniella's offenses are good at almost everything: they can slug, steal, hit for average, and draw walks. The worst that can be said about his offenses is that they are average at striking out. Piniella presided over four 50-double seasons, the most by any manager in baseball history. His pitching staffs do not always have good control, but they strike hitters out.

The Tendencies Database contains information on teams with the best and worst scores at both hitting and pitching platoon advantage. In 1998 and 1999, Piniella's teams were last in the league in both hitting and pitching platoon advantage. When combining the results of these two inquiries, the Tendencies Database claims the following managers had the least interest in gaining the left/right advantage:

Least Overall Interest in Platoon Advantage

Lou Piniella	2.696
Jack McKeon	2.517
Al Dark	2.474
Don Zimmer	2.449
Tom Kelly	2.435

His score is especially interesting because Piniella had been a platoon player, an experience he positively *loathed*. His disgust clearly left a lifelong mark on him as not only does he top the list, but he also blows away the competition. Runner-up Jack McKeon is closer to seventh place (Dick Williams at 2.381) than to Piniella.

Piniella's experience with platooning helps solve a longtime riddle. The golden age of platooning began with George Stallings's extensive use of the tactic with the 1914 Miracle Braves, and lasted for about fifteen years. In his study on platooning from the original *Historical Baseball Abstract*, Bill James noted that it fell into disfavor around 1930, despite being a sound strategy. James reckoned its decline stemmed from player backlash, as individuals — just like Piniella a half-century later — detested working in a part-time capacity. The decline of platooning, however, came right when the Great Depression fueled a wave of player-managers into the profession. The players of the 1920s had become managers, and like Piniella, they wanted to end this practice. Now that they filled out the lineup cards, they had the power to do it.

Offensive platooning partially, but not fully, explains why Piniella has such a poor overall platoon ranking. He was fourth least likely to platoon his hitters, but scored even worse with pitchers, as the following list reveals:

Least Interest in Pitching Platoon Advantage

Earl Weaver	1.402
Lou Piniella	1.388
Tom Kelly	1.324
Walter Alston	1.311
Al Lopez	1.299

In part, disdain for pitcher platooning can translate into antipathy toward using any player — hitter or pitcher — specifically for platoon advantage. However, another factor explains this score — Piniella's use of relievers. He generally kept them in longer than his peers. This can be demonstrated by flipping around the innings per relief appearance list mentioned in the Bobby Cox commentary. Starting from 2008 and working backwards, the following men had the longest average innings per relief appearances:

Year	Team	IP/RA	Manager
2008	TEX	1.252	Ron Washington
2007	TEX	1.268	Ron Washington
2005	TBD	1.287	Lou Piniella
2004	ANA	1.429	Mike Scioscia
2003	TBD	1.465	Lou Piniella
2002	TBD	1.510	Hal McRae
1992	KCR	1.621	Hal McRae
1990	DET	1.683	Sparky Anderson
1989	TOR	1.744	Cito Gaston
1988	NYY	1.809	Lou Piniella
1987	CAL	2.066	Gene Mauch
1984	KCR	2.075	Dick Howser
1982	BOS	2.510	Ralph Houk
1974	DET	2.727	Ralph Houk

Piniella makes the list three times, more than anyone else. Though his reliever workloads have declined, he has always been at the upper end of contemporary patterns. By leaving his hurlers in a little longer, he becomes less likely to gain the platoon advantage.

As a rookie manager in 1986, Piniella handled Dave Righetti, who threw over 100 innings, one of the last times any closer has done that. The next year two Yankee relievers, including Righetti, threw over 90 innings; only a handful of teams used their main relievers that much in 1987. In Cincinnati, Piniella used the "Nasty Boys" bullpen of Rob Dibble, Randy Myers, and Norm Charlton to great effect, capturing a surprise world championship. He used them as much as he wanted to, working Dibble especially hard. Only three hurlers in either league threw more innings from the bullpen than Dibble in 1990. In Tampa, Travis Harper averaged an inning and a half per appearance, rather unorthodox in the early 21st century. With the Cubs, Piniella has used superlative middleman Carlos Marmol as much as he could. Oddly, Seattle, where Piniella spent half his managerial career, was an exception to this overall trend. In part that was because the team contained either no trustworthy arms (as was the case in the late 1990s) or a bounty of reliable relievers (which existed in Seattle in the new millennium).

As both player and manager, "Sweet Lou" has always been known for his temper. Former umpire Ron Luciano claimed Piniella once screamed at a pitching machine during spring training so he could get in practice for the regular season. As manager, Piniella has thrown several memorable temper tantrums, most notably a time with Cincinnati when he threw a base into the outfield. Piniella turns his anger into a managerial asset. Fear of angering him can motivate people. Bill James once noted something about Whitey Herzog that applies to Lou Piniella. James said Herzog recognized that sports was ultimately about confrontation, and hence had no qualms about confronting players. A person who backed down was all wrong for the sport, but one who did not back down then had to rise to meet the expectations placed on him. Few people are as comfortable with confrontation as Piniella.

He also channels his temper to relieve pressure on the team. In 2007, for example, he suffered only one ejection all year, but that tossing was a combination of acting mixed with genuine anger. Early that season everything went wrong for the Cubs. The team, which expected to compete for the division when the season began, was well under .500 a third of the way through the campaign. Their season bottomed out on June 1 when, in the midst of their fifth straight loss, ace pitcher Carlos Zambrano and starting catcher Michael Barrett engaged in a fistfight that resulted in Barrett needing medical attention. The next day, after the would-be tying run was thrown out at third in the eighth inning on a close play, Piniella engaged in a full-scale meltdown. He cussed, threw his hat off, kicked dirt, and put on quite a show. When the cameras panned the dugout, they showed a bunch of grinning, laughing players enjoying the fireworks. They needed that. Instead of getting a bunch of questions after the game about another loss and the previous day's fisticuffs, a distraction grabbed everyone's attention. Finally able to relax, they went on a 29–13 tear. A team on the verge of coughing up the entire year made the postseason. Piniella helped the team by combining his emotions with self-awareness.

Piniella has received tremendous offensive production from his players thanks to a two-fold flexibility on his part. First, Piniella is flexible in finding playing time for all his batters. He keeps everyone involved so they do not get rusty while ensuring all his quality starters get plenty of playing time. While in Seattle, he led the league in pinch-hitters used multiple times. With the 2007 Cubs he had a lineup full of corner outfielders—Matt Murton, Cliff Floyd, Daryle Ward, Alfonso Soriano, Jacque Jones—but he juggled them to make sure they had some playing time.

Second, Piniella is flexible in his offensive philosophy. Some managers wed themselves to a single approach—whether it is drawing walks, bunting, or anything else—and their teams come to personify the skipper's particular pet strategy. That is not Piniella's way; instead he accentuates his players' strong points, whatever they may be. Stolen bases are the best example of his fluid approach. In Piniella's managerial career, a hitter has qualified for the batting title without ever stealing a base twelve times; this is the sixth highest total for any manager in baseball history. Conversely, one of Piniella's players has stolen 30 or more bases seventeen times, the eighth largest total for any manager since 1920. Virtually no managers have as wide a variation in their approach to the running game. Of the five skippers with more than a dozen steal-less hitters, only one (Sparky Anderson, another manager with multifaceted offenses) had more than five 30+ stolen base occurrences. Since Piniella does not prioritize any single offensive strategy, his teams reap solid offensive performances in nearly every category over his career. Ultimately, he fixates on only one concern: scoring.

However, Piniella has had problems filling out the top of his lineup card. Taking the on-base percentage from the leadoff slot for every team in the last half-century and dividing it by team OBP, the worst job any team did prioritizing leadoff OBP was Piniella's 1994 Mariners. On a club with a .333 OBP, their first batters managed a minuscule .270 OBP. Admittedly, OBP is not the only factor that a manager should look for in a leadoff hitter, but there is no excuse for coming in last place among 1,300+ teams. Added bonus: the second worst score ever was the 1999 Mariners. Impressively, there was virtually no overlap in leadoff hitters between the 1994 and 1999 squads. When presented with an obvious leadoff hitter, such as Ichiro Suzuki in Seattle or Rickey Henderson with the Yankees, Piniella puts the right man at the top of the order. Otherwise, look out.

MIKE SCIOSCIA

> **W/L Record:** 803–655 (.551)
> **Managed:** Full Seasons: Anaheim (in all its various names) 2000–08
> >   Majority in: (none)
> >   Minority of: (none)
> **Birnbaum Database:** +312 runs
> >   Individual Hitters: +89 runs
> >   Individual Pitchers: +214 runs
> >   Pythagenpat Difference: +1 runs
> >   Team Offense: -38 runs
> >   Team Defense: +46 runs
> **Team Characteristics:** Scioscia centers his offenses around batting average. His batters bunt but his runners rarely steal. He is the only manager in this book who has never had a pitcher throw 225 innings in a season.

Scioscia prefers certain things from his hitters. Aside from 2000, which appears to be a transitional year where he settled into the job, the Angels have had the same basic offensive approach under Scioscia: do not worry about home runs and walks, just make contact and put the ball in play. From 2001–08, they were always in the bottom of the league in homers. Their highest rank was 2008's ninth best. Similarly, they never finished higher than ninth in walks drawn over those same eight years.

Instead, Scioscia's Angels put the ball in play, grinding out hits from them. In the 21st century, only twelve teams have struck out fewer than 900 times; Scioscia managed four of them. The 2002 Angels struck out 805 times, the fewest by any team in a full season since the early 1990s. The Angels' hitters thrice struck out the fewest times, and were in the AL's bottom four every year from 2002–08. The guys who whiff the most are often high priced imports like Torii Hunter or Gary Matthews Jr. The men whose offensive styles and playing time Scioscia most controls are the least likely to fan. Homegrown hitters who whiff frequently, such as Dallas McPherson and Brandon Wood, struggle for playing time. Batting average is the centerpiece of Anaheim's offense. They have led the league in batting average twice and almost always finish in the top half of the league in that category.

Though Scioscia's Angels feature a consistent approach at the plate, they are not an especially fearsome offensive unit. They are typically solid, but not spectacular. Only twice did they finish higher than seventh in the league in runs scored. However, high-contact offenses should produce rather consistent run production on a day-in, day-out basis. They do not blow out many opponents with their muted power, but making contact means balls should drop in each game. Hitters do not win many games for Anaheim, but the relentless crack-crack-crack of their bats keeps the team in most contests, allowing the pitchers and fielders a chance to claim victory.

That is just what the arms and gloves do. The Angels are consistently one of the best clubs in the league at run prevention. Scioscia's team was among the top five teams in the AL in fewest runs allowed every year from 2001–08. They allowed the fewest runs in the AL once, and twice came in second place.

Over the years, however, a shift has occurred in how Anaheim stops opponents. The

Angels used to be a defense-first team. Every year from 2001–05 they ranked higher in total runs allowed than in ERA, indicating a comparative paucity in error-forced runs. In 2004, for example, they were fourth in ERA and second in fewest runs allowed. Scioscia loves position players who can not only put the ball in play when batting, but also snap up the opposition's batted balls. In his first three years as manager the Angels led the league in Defensive Efficiency Ratio twice and were runner-up the other season.

The glove work was vital, because from 2000–03 Anaheim's pitching staffs performed rather poorly in defense-independent statistics. They never finished better than sixth in homers allowed, ranked higher than seventh in walks only once, and were always in the bottom half of the league in strikeouts. Scioscia was content to field a starting rotation full of dependable if unspectacular pitchers like Jarrod Washburn and Ramon Ortiz, as long as athletes like Adam Kennedy, Darin Erstad, and David Eckstein manned the defense. Neither the position players nor pitchers were spectacular on their own, but they complemented one another quite nicely. Though Anaheim contained few superlative starting pitchers, their rotations featured exceptional depth. The 2001 Angels had five men throw enough innings to qualify for the ERA title, and the next year four threw at least 160. Few staffs achieve that. Their starting pitchers, like the hitters, kept Anaheim in the game.

Beginning in 2004, Anaheim's run prevention pendulum swung toward pitching. They led the league in batters struck out three straight years from 2004–06 before coming in second in 2007. They were normally third or fourth best in the league in walks allowed. In 2006, they allowed the fewest homers of any AL staff. John Lackey emerged as a genuine ace starter, and Kelvim Escobar has pitched very well. And while the defense remained solid, Scioscia could not lean on it as much as he had in the past as their Defensive Efficiency Ratio drifted toward the pack.

The newfound prioritization of pitcher strikeouts, combined with the perennial concern over batters putting the ball into play, has given Scioscia great benefit from the strikeout. If you compare total pitcher and batter strikeouts for every manager in baseball history, the following managers possess the most advantageous differentials:

Best Strikeout Differential

Walter Alston	+2,931 strikeouts
Tommy Lasorda	+1,493 strikeouts
Wilbert Robinson	+1,441 strikeouts
Jim Mutrie	+1,303 strikeouts
Mike Scioscia	+1,246 strikeouts

The 2005 Angels struck out 848 times while fanning 1,126 opposing hitters. Their +278 differential is the second best by an AL squad since 1990. In the new millennium, Scioscia has the second, third, sixth, and ninth best single season strikeout differentials by an American League squad. In all of baseball history, only 40 rosters have posted a +250 or better strikeout differential. Scioscia managed three of them; no one has ever managed four.

However, the real key to the franchise's success has been Scioscia's bullpen, as his teams routinely feature one of the best relief units this side of Ron Gardenhire. A disproportionately large number of Anaheim's best players have been relievers as Scioscia inherited star closer Troy Percival, and moved young stud Francisco Rodriguez into the role when Percival left. Anaheim's middle relievers have included a stable of other highly effective relievers such as Ben Weber, Scot Shields, Alan Levine, Brendan Donnelly, and Shigetoshi Hasegawa. The Angels possessed five of the twenty best American League bullpen ERAs since 2000. This unit is especially adept at striking out hitters— the 2004 bunch is the only AL bullpen that has ever fanned more than a batter per inning.

As it happens, Scioscia's playing career occurred entirely under Tommy Lasorda, who used his bullpen sparingly. Though Scioscia has retained the pitching-first flavor of those old Dodger squads, he flips the relative importance of those who start and those who finish. Then again, both managers gained considerable advantage from strikeouts. Lasorda is second all-time on the strikeout differential list, and an excellent chance exists that Scioscia will pass him.

When reviewing Scioscia's entire roster, an overarching philosophy of baseball emerges. With their consistent hitting and deep starting pitching, the Angels are designed to stay close in most games until the late innings. Then Scioscia brings in his all-world bullpen to shut down the opposition while singles and doubles continue to drop in for his gritty hitters. It is similar to Whitey Herzog's brand of baseball, without the stolen bases. That sounds strange because Herzog was famous for steals, but the other elements are all the same — eschew power hitting, win with relief pitching, and ensure complementary team strengths. For this approach to work, Scioscia needs to make sure he keeps everyone motivated and playing hard, and handle his bullpen effectively. He is perfectly capable of that.

BUCK SHOWALTER

> **W/L Record:** 882–833 (.514)
>
> **Managed:** Full Seasons: New York 1992–95; Arizona 1998–2000; Texas 2003–06
> > Majority in: (none)
> > Minority of: (none)
>
> **Birnbaum Database:** -34 runs
> > Individual Hitters: +111 runs
> > Individual Pitchers: 0 runs
> > Pythagenpat Difference: -89 runs
> > Team Offense: -17 runs
> > Team Defense: -39 runs
>
> **Team Characteristics:** Showalter does not like small ball: his batters do not bunt and his runners do not steal. Since baseball began tracking sacrifice hits in 1894, he is the only manager to last a decade while never having a player collect ten sacrifice hits in a season. Instead, Showalter lives and dies on the big blast. Among managers who lasted at least ten years since 1920, he possesses the worst record in one-run games: 220–244 (.474).

The ultimate Buck Showalter moment came in the bottom of the ninth on May 28, 1998. His Arizona squad, up 8–6, was only one out from victory, but the bases were loaded with Barry Bonds at the plate. Showalter made the highly unorthodox move to have Bonds intentionally walked, forcing a run home and putting the tying run 90 feet from the plate. The move worked, as the next batter, Brett Mayne, lined out. It is the sort of move few would consider, let alone dare attempt.

Showalter had enough courage in his convictions to make a move he believed proper, without worrying about what anyone else thought. That exemplified Showalter — love or hate him, everyone knew who was in charge. As a result, he received considerable credit for his team's victories, and equal blame for their defeats. Not surprisingly, his managerial reputation has waxed and waned over the years.

At one time, the conventional wisdom considered Showalter to be one of baseball's sharpest and toughest minds. In 1995, he took the Yankees to their first postseason appearance in over a decade. The Yankees immediately dismissed him for losing in the first round of the playoffs, a move the public blamed on mercurial owner George Steinbrenner. By serving four years in New York, Showalter had lasted longer under the Bronx boss than any previous manager. When Showalter took over the newly established expansion Diamondbacks, his stature earned him an unusually large degree of authority for a manager. Aided by the owner's generous spending, the team won 100 games in its second year of existence. They fell back the next year, causing Showalter to be fired, but he remained a well-respected field general. He combined a genuine air of authority with a track record of improving teams.

Showalter's reputation began to dim shortly afterwards. The Diamondbacks won the World Series immediately after firing him, just as the Yankees had done in 1996, their first year without Showalter. His luster had lessened, but had not fully dissipated.

In Texas, however, Showalter's reputation took a severe hit. People expected Showalter to take charge, and spend a year sorting out whom he did and did not like, just as he had done in New York and Arizona. The Rangers did markedly improve in his second season, but soon fell backwards. Instead of flaying at 70 wins, they muddled at 80 wins: an improvement, but still disappointing. Amplifying the discontent, Showalter's controlling tendencies appeared to short circuit the team. He butted heads with superstar Alex Rodriguez, and the franchise traded him to the Yankees for slugging second baseman Alfonso Soriano. However, Soriano's production dropped instead of improving. Showalter thought that someone with Soriano's power should hit in the heart of the order, not near the top where he was accustomed to performing. Though the second baseman protested, Showalter figured the slugger would become accustomed to the new role. Nine times out of ten a manager would be right, but this was the tenth. Frustrated with yet another star infielder, Texas traded Soriano to Washington for Brad Wilkerson and some bit parts. Soriano hit 46 homers in Washington while Wilkerson hit under .230 in 2006–07. A pair of Showalter-driven trades had turned the league's best player into one of its worst outfielders. It was as though Brett Mayne had slugged a grand slam.

Showalter may still live up to his early promise. He is still fairly young (only 50 when Texas fired him after 2006), and has done a good job with two of his three squads. However, if his next team does not prosper, Showalter might have a hard time getting hired again. Once someone gains a reputation as a journeyman manager, hiring opportunities erode.

Showalter generally did a good job making sure his hitters had the platoon advantage. According to the Tendencies Database, the following managers ranked the highest at having their squads bat with the platoon advantage:

Most Likely to Hit with Platoon Advantage

Whitey Herzog	0.476
Gene Mauch	0.587
Bruce Bochy	0.588
Buck Showalter	0.699
Billy Martin	0.706

Showalter had a few switch-hitters at his disposal — Bernie Williams, Devon White, Mark Teixeira — but not an exceptional number. He makes this leaderboard despite never leading the league in this stat.

JOE TORRE

W/L Record: 2,151–1,848 (.538)
Managed: Full Seasons: New York (NL) 1978–81; Atlanta 1982–84; St. Louis
1991–94; New York (AL) 1996–2007; Los Angeles 2008

             Majority in: New York (NL) 1977

             Minority of: St. Louis 1990, 1995

    Birnbaum Database: +475 runs

             Individual Hitters: +166 runs

             Individual Pitchers: +121 runs

             Pythagenpat Difference: +278 runs

             Team Offense: -6 runs

             Team Defense: -84 runs

    Team Characteristics: Torre's team tendencies are obviously influenced by his lengthy tenure with the Yankees. As a result the Tendencies Database notes he presided over tremendous veteran offenses and pitching staffs. His hitters' best attribute has been drawing walks. Torre has used pitchers on consecutive days quite a bit. The 2003 Yankees had the greatest walk differential in baseball history at +309 (684 taken, 375 given out). No other team is within 50 of that.

Joe Torre won more games as Yankee manager than Casey Stengel (though that is because baseball's regular season is longer than during Stengel's time), and achieved a higher winning percentage with the franchise than Miller Huggins. Despite his achievements, Torre became the target of increasing criticism toward the end of his reign. In some ways he was the victim of his own success. After winning four titles in his first five years, there was nowhere to go but down. Also, some said Torre was the right man for the young team of the mid-to-late 1990s, but stayed on too long.

However, some critics made more sweeping claims, alleging Torre's contributions to the 1996–2000 Yankee dynasty were slim, at best. They point out that Torre came to a team with a great core of young talent that would have had an impressive glory run with or without him. As far as his naysayers are concerned, Torre was simply lucky enough to be brought aboard when New York's wave crested. Finally, those opposed to Torre note his record prior to the Yankees appears distinctly underwhelming, as his career win-loss record more than 100 games below .500 (894–1003) as a result of a trio of NL managerial stints.

This critique sorely underestimates Torre's achievements over his career. He always helped his teams live up to their potential, including his pre–Yankee teams with such poor records. The Birnbaum Database gives Torre a score of–10 runs for his pre–Yankees days, a remarkable figure given that his teams possessed a .471 winning record. Among all managers with at least 1,000 games managed in the Birnbaum Database, only one combines a sub -.475 winning percentage with a positive score (Gil Hodges).

Torre's first managerial assignment with the New York Mets best exemplified his ability to get the most out of his teams. If the 1996 Yankees were the ideal setup for a manager, the 1977 Mets were the worst. Under the reign of Mets honcho M. Donald Grant, the franchise reacted as poorly to free agency as possible. The front office acted personally offended by players negotiating their services on an open market. Grant preferred to think of them as serfs on his reserve clause plantation, not as people who could conceivably join the same country clubs he did. Due to their disdain for current labor relations, the Mets were not about to competitively bid for the right players. Columnists such as Dick Young (the most anti-players-union man in the national press corps) lauded Grant, encouraging this disposition.

The tale of Tom Seaver best illustrates how perverse the Mets' priorities had become, and how writers like Young helped make the situation impossible. During the 1977 season (when Torre became manager), Seaver read a Young column that crossed the line. Seaver had grown accustomed to Young routinely bashing the players, but this time Young took it a step further, bringing Seaver's wife into it. The sportswriter reported that recent contentious contract negotiations between the Mets and Seaver were because Tom Terrific's spouse wanted more money. Technically, the Mets were not making this claim as Dick Young was not the team's employee and the franchise had no oversight on his column. However, Grant had so poisoned the relationship with his players that Seaver believed Grant and/or his underlings had trash-talked his wife to the most anti-union writer in the press, who gleefully publicized their beliefs. One cannot fault Seaver for viewing the column as a slam coming from Mets' management; that was undoubtedly what happened. After this article, Seaver *demanded* a trade. Immediately. The Mets fulfilled his request barely two weeks after Torre filled out his first lineup card as the team's manager.

Since Grant refused to recognize the game's changes, Torre's first squad was stuffed with nobodies and castoffs. The Mets picked up has-beens no one else wanted, such as Frank Taveras—a slowing speedster unable to steal first base. The best acquisition Torre could hope for was someone like Lenny Randle, who came to the Mets after physically assaulting his manager in Texas. The organizational torpor affected New York's farm system too, as the late 1970s saw few usable parts gurgle up to the major leagues. Their best prospects were batters like Lee Mazzilli, John Stearns, and Steve Henderson. They performed rather well under Torre, but were hardly the backbone of a franchise renaissance. Once longtime Met stalwarts Seaver and Jerry Koosman left, Torre had to cobble together staffs from remainders like Craig Swan, Pete Falcone, and Pat Zachary. One Mets fan summed it up best by coming to Shea Stadium with a sign proclaiming "Welcome to Grant's Tomb." Torre had a wretched record there, but that was inevitable.

Torre prevented the Mets from losing 100 games in a season, which normally would be unimpressive, but under the circumstances it was a tremendous achievement. A brief comparison reveals how much worse the Grant's Tomb period could have been for the Mets. From 1977 to 1983, when the Mets went through their franchise hell, an American League team was stuck in the doldrums—the Mariners. Seattle suffered through three seasons with at least 102 defeats during this period as well as two more 95+ loss campaigns. The Mets did not feature appreciably better talent than the Mariners, but they consistently achieved slightly better results when Torre plied his trade in Shea Stadium. However, as always happens, the manager took the ax for the team's troubles, and the Mets fired Torre after the 1981 season.

In a sign of how much baseball respected Torre despite his dismal win-loss record, the Braves immediately snapped him up. He replaced Bobby Cox, and the team improved markedly, from a .472 (50–56) mark in 1981 to a .549 (89–73) record the next year. Then they won 88 games in 1983, for the franchise's best back-to-back performance since the late 1950s. Their success was not a result of any managerial brilliance on Torre's part. He merely had enough sense to trust the talent already on hand. Atlanta was an extremely young club as three of its infielders were not old enough to rent a car and only one regular position player was older than 27. All had already received considerable playing time under Cox.

It should be the easiest situation to step into—show up and get out of the players' way—yet for that very reason it is a scenario many managers fumble. When a new boss takes over, he often asserts his own authority. Torre, demonstrating traits he later made famous with the Yankees, possessed enough inner calm and confidence to stay his predecessor's course. He trusted his players, allowing them to develop. He could have taken issue with shortstop Rafael Ramirez's defense, or second baseman Glenn Hubbard's .248 batting average, but he did not. The only kid Torre benched in 1982 was outfielder Brett Butler, who hit .217 in a pennant race with only two extra base hits in 240 at bats. (Even still, the next year Torre had him play in more than 150 games.) Torre's major accomplishment in Atlanta was the absence of noteworthy errors. A decidedly unglamorous accomplishment, but please realize that avoiding mishaps is always easier in theory than in practice. Torre's Atlanta experience provided a dress rehearsal for his Yankee days.

Despite their youth and potential, Atlanta fell to 80–82 under Torre in 1984. Third base slugger Bob Horner, showing a lack of interest in conditioning that later ruined his career, spent most of the year injured. Shortstop Ramirez entered into an offensive funk from which he never really recovered. Catcher Bruce Benedict got old quickly — even by catchers' standards. Also, the bench fell apart. The team dumped Torre after 1984, but declined by another 14 games in 1985. Whatever their problem was, it was larger than him as the franchise averaged 98 losses per season from 1985 to 1990.

After briefly serving as Angels' broadcaster, the Cardinals selected Torre to replace Whitey Herzog, who resigned in mid–1990. (Technically Torre replaced Red Schoendienst, but Schoendienst was only a stopgap.) The Runnin' Redbirds had lost their step in the late 1980s, playing generally below-average ball after 1987. Torre oversaw the team's transition to a new day. By Torre's first full season in 1991, Ozzie Smith was the only key position player remaining from the Herzog years. St. Louis was not especially talented in Torre's four years with the franchise as their All-Star selections consisted of Felix Jose, Tom Pagnozzi, Bob Tewksbury, Gregg Jefferies, Ozzie Smith, and Lee Smith. Neither Smith was really that great by the early 1990s (Ozzie's selections were essentially lifetime achievement picks), and the others were hardly world-beaters.

Despite the lack of frontline talent, the Cardinals finished over .500 in each of Torre's first three full seasons. Jefferies, once a Mets' super-prospect, made the All-Star squad in each of his two years in St. Louis. Those were the only seasons he ever lived up to his potential. In 1993, with a lineup anchored by Jefferies and Bernard Gilkey, and a starting rotation led by Tewksbury, Donovan Osborne, and Rene Arocha, Torre kept the Cardinals playing over their heads, as they remained in the playoff hunt through late July. Thinking they possessed the winning formula, the Cardinals' front office brought back much of the core for 1994. When management's hopes proved delusional, Torre became the fall guy.

In 1996, Torre came to the Yankees to run a supremely talented team. People who saw him operate in Atlanta should not have been surprised that the low-key but self-assured Torre brought this team to the next level. Perhaps the most striking aspect of his performance, especially in his first season, was his patience. Think about it — here was a man who had been in the majors since 1960 but had never appeared in a World Series. At age 55, he was the oldest World Series rookie skipper between Roger Craig in 1989 and Jack McKeon in 2003. Torre's craving for postseason success could have caused anxious overmanaging, but he had the internal fortitude to avoid excessively fretting.

When the Braves won the first two games of the 1996 World Series, he stood his ground. A story recounted in the book *The Yankee Years* (which Torre produced with veteran sportswriter Tom Verducci) revealed his management style. After losing Game 1 of the Fall Classic 12–1 to the Braves, team owner George Steinbrenner, who had a reputation for constantly firing managers, met with Torre. The skipper told his boss that they had lost and might even lose the next game, but assured the mercurial owner the Yankees would not lose the Series. A manager's confidence can rub off on players, and the quieter the confidence, the more effective it can be. The players already had enough noise and pressure on them from Steinbrenner and the media while also coping with their own World Series inexperience. Sometimes a manager who personifies an even keel can best help his players' mental focus when they experience troubled times. The Yankees won the World Series in six games.

As had been the case with Joe McCarthy's Yankees more than a half-century earlier, Joe Torre's teams achieved a postseason record that boggles the mind. Capturing three consecutive world titles from 1998 to 2000, while remarkable, is not as impressive as the manner in which they were won. Consider this: in nine postseason series, the Yankees played in exactly *one* game that could have eliminated them. In that affair, the fifth and final game of the 2000 ALDS against the A's, the Yankees scored six runs in the top of the first inning, immediately icing the contest. During their three successive titles, the Yankees went an astonishing 33–8 while playing baseball's best clubs. In 25 postseason series, Torre's Yankees went 76–47 (.617), which was even better than their .605 regular-season winning percentage. A 123-game sample size is difficult to dismiss as a fluke. In short, Torre had his men playing as well as they possibly could in the postseason. He engaged in one famous tactic to help ensure this incredible October winning percentage: bringing ace closer Mariano Rivera into the game earlier than normal to ensure these most important of games would be won. The Yankees' success went beyond Rivera, though—the entire team played up to their fullest under Torre.

Admittedly, Torre's disappointing performances in his final seasons as Yankee skipper indicate he was past his prime. The hallmark of his early success, that quiet, patient confidence, vanished. For example, with his team facing elimination in the 2006 ALDS, Torre moved slumping Alex Rodriguez to the eighth slot in the batting order. That was just aimless thrashing.

In 2009, after losing his job with the Yankees, Torre furthered this disconnect between his recent actions and general reputation with *The Yankee Years*, which created headlines for the unflattering information it provided of players such as Alex Rodriguez and Kevin Brown. This sort of talk would be less surprising coming from skippers such as Ozzie Guillen or Leo Durocher, who always possessed a combative, controversial nature. Torre, however, was renowned for his quiet demeanor and the book itself contends that his managerial style was centered on creating trust between himself and his players. Yet this work came out when he was still an active manager, largely negating this notion of trust. He is the last manager one would expect to create a book like this.

Searching for a reason to explain this discrepancy leads me to believe Torre was just worn out. Forget his age for a second—he had spent a dozen years helming the most high-pressured franchise in major league sports. That must wear on a person, no matter how phlegmatic his disposition. In fact, it is worth noting that all the great Yankee managers—Miller Huggins, Joe McCarthy, Casey Stengel, and Torre—roughly lasted about as long on the job. Aside from McCarthy, they all lasted twelve seasons, and McCarthy only made it a few years more than that. Admittedly, Huggins died, but it is interesting how similar the lengths of their tenures were.

In this regard, a parallel exists with the Notre Dame Fighting Irish college football program. The Yankees and Notre Dame both expect to not only compete, but also win every year, decade after decade. If a person cannot bring home a title, he does not last long with either squad. Like the Bronx Bombers, the Fighting Irish have four main coaches in their history: Knute Rockne, Frank Leahy, Ara Parseghian, and Lou Holtz. Leahy, Parseghian, and Holtz all lasted eleven seasons with the institution, almost the same length as the typical tenure for Yankee legends. Rockne, like McCarthy, lasted a little longer, but only a little longer. In both cases, the first coach to bring glory to the institution died on the job.

It is very difficult to last for longer than a dozen years when leading such organizations. If one succeeds early, that should create the sort of job security that would come in other places. In fact, just the opposite occurs as the pressure to win it all next year becomes increasingly acute. Maintaining that level of success is virtually impossible. A team can hope to compete every year, but sports are too random to ensure perpetual championships, even if one's squad is the best. My hunch is that the situation gradually wore Torre down. Combined with Father Time's continual march, Torre was not the man he once was, causing his actions to change. No one stays in his prime forever.

Then again, in his first year in Los Angeles, Torre successfully guided the Dodgers to their first successful postseason series in twenty years, so perhaps he was not through. However, the overall history of baseball managers indicates that someone who has been on the job for 30 years should not be expected to claim glory consistently.

JIMY WILLIAMS

W/L Record: 910–790 (.535)

Managed: Full Seasons: Toronto 1986–88; Boston 1997–2000; Houston 2002–03

Majority in: Boston 2001; Houston 2004

Minority of: Toronto 1989

Birnbaum Database: +14 runs

Individual Hitters: +31 runs

Individual Pitchers: +305 runs

Pythagenpat Difference: -254 runs

Team Offense: -86 runs

Team Defense: +18 runs

Team Characteristics: His teams based themselves on run prevention. Williams gathered pitchers with good control and the ability to strike men out and placed them before good defenders. Also, he did not push his starters too hard, relying as much as he dared on his bullpen. He is the only manager in this book who never had a player with a sub - .300 OBP qualify for the batting title.

There are two types of quality starting rotations: those that eat plenty of innings and those managed by Jimy Williams. In 2000, his Boston Red Sox bunch featured the best park-adjusted ERA of any starting rotation in the AL while also averaging fewer innings per start than any team in the league. It was the only starting staff to do that since 1956. Only one other league leader in park-adjusted ERA even came close: that was the 1999 Red Sox whom Williams, of course, also managed. That team's starters were next-to-last in innings pitched. Those teams were not aberrations, either. Every rotation Williams managed for at least half the season finished in the bottom half of the league in innings thrown per start. Only once did any of his teams rank higher than eleventh. Yet they were good rotations. They finished the top half of park-adjusted ERA every year but one, and in the top three a half-dozen times.

Normally when a person veers that far from accepted practice, he is doing something quite questionable. After all, playing up one's strength is generally a good thing. In Williams's case what he did made sense for two reasons. First, Williams's gentle touch was one reason why his hurlers pitched so well on a per-inning basis, because it made sure they did not get fatigued. In the years when pitch counts came into vogue, Williams was one of the poster boys for how to handle a rotation. More important than pitch counts, his teams performed better as the year went on. In eight of the nine campaigns, his teams had a better second-half record than in the first half. Williams paced his clubs by keeping everyone as fresh as he could. Below are his total first- and second-half records in his nine full managerial seasons:

When	W-L	Pct
First Half	413–375	.524
Second Half	376–294	.561

Second, Williams could do this because he oversaw terrific bullpens. Three times his relievers claimed the best park-adjusted ERA. In 2000, they possessed both the greatest share of innings thrown and the best park-adjusted ERA. In 2003, his Astros relievers were tops in quantity and second best in quality. Williams gained tremendous value from his bullpen, a fact that the Tendencies Database illuminates. Take both park-adjusted ERA and percentage of team's innings thrown, run them through the database, and add their results together. Based on that, the following skippers owed the most to their relief units:

Got the Most from the Bullpen

Jimy Williams	1.030
Frank Robinson	1.514
Chuck Tanner	1.647
Bill Rigney	1.663
Gene Mauch	1.679

Williams does not just lead this category, he blows everyone away. He ought to. Examining park-adjusted bullpen ERA alone, Williams comes in first. When looking specifically at innings pitched, he again tops all comers. By finishing first in quality *and* quantity, Williams assuredly dominates the competition in terms of overall bullpen results.

Williams presided over stellar bullpen performances wherever he managed. In Williams's inaugural managerial season, rookie Mark Eichhorn post a 1.72 ERA while tossing 157 innings from the bullpen, the heaviest workload by any reliever in the last quarter-century. The next year Williams reduced his bullpen workhorse to "only" 127.7 innings, but Eichhorn still pitched well. When an injury (predictably) felled Eichhorn in 1988, Williams unleashed Duane Ward on the American League, who threw 111.7 innings with a superior ERA. Tom Henke proved to be a tremendous closer to Williams's Canadian squads. In Boston, Williams lessened the workloads on his relievers, but still pushed them more than most managers. In 1999, Derek Lowe tossed 109.3 innings in relief, one of the highest totals by any reliever in recent years. Instead, Williams relied on a larger band of bullpen specialists, gaining quality work over the years from Lowe, Rich Garces, Tom Gordon, Rod Beck, Jim Corsi, Rheal Cormier, and Hipolito Pichardo. In Houston, Williams had another brilliant bullpen, anchored by Billy Wagner, Octavio Dotel, and Brad Lidge. Both Lidge and Dotel threw over 90 innings in a season for Williams, near the uppermost limit any manager allocates to a 21st century reliever.

Appendix I. The Birnbaum Database
by Phil Birnbaum

I created the "Birnbaum Database," as Chris describes it, back in 2005. The idea was to figure out how much of a team's performance was due to luck. (To see the algorithms Chris mentioned in Chapter 1, skip to the end of the appendix. However, I do think it is important to discuss the ideas that went into its formulation first.)

A team doesn't always perform exactly to its talent. Teams and players have good games, and they have bad games. Similarly, they have good seasons, and they have bad seasons.

If you assume a team has a certain amount of talent at the beginning of the season, and any difference from that in the standings is due to luck, then that luck can be broken down into five separate categories. They are:

1. Batters having better (or worse) statistics than expected. For example, maybe Albert Pujols is really a .330 hitter who got lucky and hit .357 in 2008. Maybe he hit a few more home runs than his talent suggested, or grounded into a few less double plays. Perhaps he happened to face worse pitchers than average, just because of how the schedule worked out.

2. Pitchers having better (or worse) statistics than expected. This is the reverse of the Pujols example; it refers to the other team's batters. Maybe a pitcher happened to get lucky and have Ryan Howard swing through a hanging slider, when he "should have" hit it out of the park. Or maybe they faced better batters than expected, again because of the randomness of the schedule, and their statistics wind up worse than their talent suggested.

3. Team clutch hitting. Two teams can have identical batting lines, but vastly different numbers of runs scored. That is because runs score more easily if hits (and walks) are bunched together. One hit an inning for nine innings might score a run or two, but nine hits in a single inning will probably score six or seven runs. The ability to hit better in bunches—which usually means with runners on base—is conventionally referred to as "clutch hitting." The overwhelming evidence, in my opinion, shows that clutch hitting is random; the evidence suggests there aren't players or teams that can be shown to have a specific talent for it. However, a team could have a good clutch season by luck alone, and that would cause them to score more runs.

4. Opposition clutch hitting. This is the reverse of the previous point. If pitchers gave up hits in bunches, their WHIP might look pretty good, but they will have given up a lot of runs. And vice versa.

5. Scoring runs when they're most important. If a team scores 750 runs and gives up 750 runs in a season, they should finish 81–81, but could easily finish better or worse. Losing a lot of 15–1 games (still while going 750–750 overall), will cause their record to be better than .500. Two runs were enough for them to lose that 15–1 game; the other 13 runs they gave up didn't affect their record. Effectively, it is as if they gave up only 738 runs. Of course, they might have *won* a few games 15–1, but if they won most of their close games but lost most of the blowouts, their record will be better than expected. Again, the vice versa is equally true.

There are long-established ways of computing the last three points. In the early 1980s, Bill James created Runs Created, which estimates how many runs a team would be expected to score based on their overall batting line. A team that exceeded its estimate was theoretically lucky; if it fell short, it was unlucky. To measure clutch hitting on both sides, compare the actual runs scored and allowed to the Runs Created (and Component ERA) estimates, and attribute the difference to luck (or to the manager, as Chris does). That takes care of points three and four. For point five another Bill James creation — the Pythagorean Projection — takes a team's runs scored and runs allowed, and estimates what winning percentage should result from that. Falling short or exceeding this estimate is normally attributed to luck.

So it's a bit misleading when Chris calls these three points part of the Birnbaum Database. Yes, I did the calculations, but you could too. I think of them more as coming from a theoretical Bill James database, not from me.

In the last few paragraphs, I've been talking about these differences between expected and actual and saying the discrepancies are due to random chance, an interpretation which is longstanding conventional wisdom in sabermetrics. Chris doesn't think it is all luck; he suggests managers may play a role as well. If that is true — and Chris makes an interesting case that it is — that would be new knowledge. For years, we've been thinking that when a team beats its Pythagorean estimate by (say) six games, that has nothing to do with any of the actual characteristics of the team. Indeed, there is a hypothesis that Bill James named the "Johnson Effect," after a Toronto sportswriter, which says that when a team beats its Pythagoras this year, it shouldn't be expected to do so again next year.

At any rate, that leaves the first two points listed above: evaluating whether the pitchers and hitters had a "lucky" year. In 2005, I tried to come up with a method to estimate that. The idea is to look at a player's season and a couple of years before or after that particular campaign in order to see if he did something unexpected. One classic case is Norm Cash, who had a 1961 that was way beyond anything he did before or since:

Year	AB	H	2B	3B	HR	R	RBI	AVG	OBP	SLG
1959	104	25	0	1	4	16	16	0.240	0.372	0.375
1960	353	101	16	3	18	64	63	0.286	0.402	0.501
1961	535	193	22	8	41	119	132	0.361	0.487	0.662
1962	507	123	16	2	39	94	89	0.243	0.382	0.513
1963	493	133	19	1	26	67	79	0.270	0.386	0.471

Cash was a good hitter for most of his career, but 1961 dwarfs the surrounding seasons. That year, he posted an RC27 (a measure of how many runs per game a team would score if it had 9 Norm Cashes in the lineup) of 13 runs per game; his career average was 6.73 with only two other seasons above 7.

My estimate is that a player who hit like Norm Cash did in 1959, 1960, 1962, and 1963, should have created only 6.46 runs per game; far less than his actual achievement.

This system works by finding the averages of the previous two seasons and subsequent two seasons (giving double weight to the one-year-offs than to the two-year-offs). Then, my formula moves the result closer to the mean. This is done because when the four surrounding seasons are extreme — too high or too low — it is likely that they resulted somewhat from luck. Thus that little bit of luck should be adjusted for.

It is possible that when I regressed to the mean I overdid it. In fact, I think I did overcompensate a bit (and I'll explain why I think that a little bit later). More importantly, the results are still pretty reasonable. Here are Cash's five seasons in terms of actual runs above average:

1959	(part time)	1962	+28
1960	+20	1963	+26
1961	+83		

If 1961 were adjusted to make it fit right in, it would probably be about +25, right? That makes the difference between estimate and reality +58 runs. My system expects Cash to be worth +21 runs, which he exceeded by +62. Intuitively, I may have over-regressed, but not by that much.

The real question is: does the system work? Well, though I haven't done any formal testing (and I'm sure the system could be improved substantially), it gives pretty reasonable results. In most cases, however, the algorithm's estimates are pretty close to what you'd guess by looking at a copy of *Total Baseball*. For instance, let me open the book to a random page: take Ed Kirkpatrick in 1971. Here are his surrounding stats:

1969	+8	1972	+13
1970	-2	1973	-5
1971	?		

How would you fill in 1971? The algorithm puts him at +5, which is pretty reasonable. He was actually–8 that year, 13 runs beneath that.

Do this for every player on a team and add them up to get an idea how lucky (or well managed, according to Chris's approach) the team was.

The Algorithms

So, that's the system. All I have left to do is show you the algorithms. Again, I warn you that the system should not be considered perfect — the calculation is arbitrary, so all I can say is that the estimate should be reasonable. Creating a better system is a worthy endeavor, and maybe it's time for me to analyze and update it.

I should also add that the system is based on 1960 to 2003. I make no guarantees for its accuracy in other seasons. Actually, I make no guarantees even for those years, but I *especially* make no guarantees outside that period.

To get a player's estimate for season X:

Hitting

Add up season X-2, twice season X-1, twice season X+1, and season X+2. This gives the equivalent of six seasons. Count the number of "outs made" (roughly AB-H, adjusted for GIDP, etc.).

"Top up" the outs made by adding in enough league-average performance to get the outs made up to 2,100. However, do not add more than 900, or fewer than 100.

If the outs made (before topping up) was less than 800, add another 200 outs of league-average performance. If the outs made (before topping up) was less than 400, add another 200 outs of league-average performance.

To this new total of outs made, add 10% to the total top-up (which has a maximum of 1300) for each run by which the six-season RC27 is different from the league average.

Compute the new RC27 for the new total with the added "top up" plate appearances. Note that all seasons should be adjusted for year and park (with a further 5% adjustment for the war years).

If the original (six season) outs made was less than 800, subtract .06 runs per game for each 100 outs below 800.

If the original (six season) outs made was greater than 1600, add a flat 0.5.

Pitching

Add up season X-2, twice season X-1, twice season X+1, and season X+2. This gives you the equivalent of six seasons. Count up the number of "outs made" (IP multiplied by 3).

"Top up" the outs made by adding a quantity of league-average performance as follows: if the original (six season) outs made was less than 400, add 400. If it was greater than 900, add 900. If it was between 400 and 900, add the actual number of outs made.

Compute the Component ERA for this total of six seasons plus league-average performance. All seasons should be adjusted for year and park (with a further 5% adjustment for the war years). Add 0.45 for a starter (70% starts or more), 0.35 for a reliever. This is your projection for now.

Temporarily add this year's outs made to the total of the six-season outs and topped-up outs. If the temporary total is less than 1200, add .06 to the projection for each 100 outs below 1200.

That becomes the projection. There are two exceptions to the above:

If the player did not pitch in the two years before or two years after, use the league average as the projection.

If the "six season" sum is less than 300 outs, but the current season is more than 300 outs, the projection cannot be higher than the league average.

Appendix II. The Tendencies Database

Below are the inquiries performed in the Tendencies Database that came in handy for the book's commentary on managers. Most of these results were given in the course of the book, but not all. Here they are in one centralized location for your perusal. The inquiries are divided into the following sections:

- Offensive stats
- Pitching stats
- Fielding stats
- Team stats
- Combinations of multiple inquiries.

Offensive Stats

SACRIFICE HIT FREQUENCY: Chapter 2 presents the results for this inquiry, which is figured as: SH/(H+BB+ROE+HB-HR-2B-3B). The statistic exists since 1894, so 72 managers are under examination.

Most Frequent		Least Frequent	
Gene Mauch	0.440	Bruce Bochy	1.655
Billy Southworth	0.463	Buck Showalter	1.606
Tommy Lasorda	0.517	Tom Kelly	1.547
Felipe Alou	0.554	Jimmy McAleer	1.455
Joe Cronin	0.563	John McGraw	1.443

STOLEN BASE FREQUENCY: Tabulated as (SB+CS)/(H+BB+HB+ROE-HR-2B-3B), this determines how often teams attempted to steal based on opportunity. Stolen base data goes back to 1886, so 73 managers are in the sample. Some stats (like caught steals and reached on error) do not exist as far back as 1886, but are used when available. The results for this study are listed in Chapter 2.

Most Frequent		Least Frequent	
Whitey Herzog	0.358	Bill Terry	1.600
Red Schoendienst	0.491	Danny Murtaugh	1.506
Walter Alston	0.507	Jimy Williams	1.500
Clark Griffith	0.538	Johnny Oates	1.493
Mike Hargrove	0.569	Buck Showalter	1.442

STOLEN BASE SUCCESS RATE: This formula is SB/(SB+CS). This can be determined only when caught steals are known. In the AL it is from 1914–15, and 1920–onward. In the NL it is 1915, 1920–25, and 1951–onward. This inquiry looks at 53 managers. The results are listed in the Bucky Harris and Lou Boudreau commentary in the book.

Most Successful		Least Successful	
Cito Gaston	0.347	Bobby Valentine	1.305
Red Schoendienst	0.457	Miller Huggins	1.293
Whitey Herzog	0.465	Ralph Houk	1.274
Bucky Harris	0.587	Lou Boudreau	1.250
Jim Fregosi	0.632	Frank Robinson	1.237

HIT AND RUN: The formula is: GIDP/(ROE+BB+HB+H-2B-3B-HR-SH-SB-CS). Chapter 2 explains the logic behind it and presents its results. This study only exists for periods when ground into double play data is known, which is since 1933 in the NL, and 1939 in the AL. Altogether, this inquiry looks at 54 managers.

Most Interest in Hit-and-Run		Least Interest in Hit-and-Run	
Birdie Tebbetts	0.548	Tom Kelly	1.467
Billy Southworth	0.606	Connie Mack	1.389

Al Lopez	0.639	Frank Robinson	1.323
Sparky Anderson	0.647	Mike Hargrove	1.316
Davey Johnson	0.664	Bill McKechnie	1.302

WALK RATE: This inquiry contains all 77 managers. Its Tendencies Database formula is: (BB-IW)/(AB+BB+SF). The numerator is the times a batter earns his walk. The denominator is the times the batter could conceivably be walked. Excluding sacrifice hits and hit by pitches were judgment calls. Sacrifice hits were left out on the premise that the batter is not looking for a pitch to hit, but to move the runner over, and hence is swinging more freely. Hit by pitches are a byproduct of excessively wild pitching. This is not perfect as batters can draw walks when they attempt to sacrifice and some will lean into pitches, taking the HBP as a de facto walk. Generally, however, that is not the case. If HBP and SH were included in the denominator, scores would change slightly, but not substantially. Results are given in the George Stallings and Danny Murtaugh commentaries.

Most Walks		*Least Walks*	
Joe McCarthy	0.354	Danny Murtaugh	1.665
Sparky Anderson	0.447	Tom Kelly	1.484
George Stallings	0.502	Don Zimmer	1.407
Earl Weaver	0.538	Felipe Alou	1.400
Art Howe	0.599	Bill Virdon	1.396

STRIKEOUT RATE: This formula is K/(AB-H). Dividing strikeouts by plate appearances or at-bats would give an edge to teams that did a superior job getting on base, but all squads need to make three outs per inning. Batter strikeouts were not recorded in various periods in the nineteenth and early twentieth centuries, so only 70 managers qualify for this inquiry. Results are given in the Jimmy Dykes and Miller Huggins commentary sections.

Hardest to Whiff		*Most Ks*	
Bill Virdon	0.402	Miller Huggins	1.634
Felipe Alou	0.476	Sparky Anderson	1.450
Jimmy Dykes	0.592	Joe McCarthy	1.374
Phil Garner	0.635	Burt Shotton	1.356
Bill Terry	0.644	Art Howe	1.335

HITTER AGE: This information comes from Baseball-Reference.com, which lists an average age for all offenses, rounded to the nearest tenths decimal All 77 managers qualify, with results listed in the Jimmy Dykes and Burt Shotton commentary sections.

Youngest Hitters		*Oldest Hitters*	
Burt Shotton	0.467	Jimmy Dykes	1.632
Dick Williams	0.580	Al Lopez	1.499
Art Howe	0.656	Earl Weaver	1.490
Miller Huggins	0.667	Dusty Baker	1.456
Lou Boudreau	0.694	Wilbert Robinson	1.427

BATTING AVERAGE: This is hits divided by at-bats. Since it is readily available for all baseball history, all 77 managers who lasted at least ten years qualify for this inquiry. Results are given in the Bill McKechnie and Billy Southworth commentary sections.

Highest Batting Averages		*Lowest Batting Averages*	
John McGraw	0.490	Art Howe	1.526
Billy Southworth	0.519	Billy Barnie	1.461
Hughie Jennings	0.540	Frank Robinson	1.297
Danny Murtaugh	0.550	George Stallings	1.282
Red Schoendienst	0.607	Bill McKechnie	1.266

SLUGGING PERCENTAGE: Surprisingly, this is never given in the book. Since both batting average and isolated power are given separately, slugging percentage itself was redundant.

Highest Slugging Percentages		Lowest Slugging Percentages	
Joe McCarthy	0.455	Paul Richards	1.500
John McGraw	0.538	Bruce Bochy	1.490
Hughie Jennings	0.540	Billy Barnie	1.475
Davey Johnson	0.543	Jimmy Dykes	1.410
Cap Anson	0.592	Phil Garner	1.402

ISOLATED POWER: This is batting average minus slugging percentage; in other words extra bases divided by at-bats. It exists for all 77 managers who served at least ten years. Results are given in the Cap Anson and Paul Richards commentary sections.

Highest Isolated Power		Lowest Isolated Power	
Joe McCarthy	0.364	Bruce Bochy	1.565
Sparky Anderson	0.478	Jimmy McAleer	1.535
Jimy Williams	0.486	Paul Richards	1.516
Cap Anson	0.529	Phil Garner	1.441
Hughie Jennings	0.556	Jimmie Dykes	1.417

RUNS SCORED, ADJUSTED FOR PARK: This is runs scored per game, adjusted by Baseball-Reference.com's batter park factors. All 77 managers qualify for this study in the Tendencies Database and results are given in the Joe McCarthy and Jimmy McAleer commentary sections.

Most Runs Scored		Fewest Runs Scored	
Joe McCarthy	0.404	Jimmy McAleer	1.333
Hughie Jennings	0.429	Jimmie Dykes	1.290
Davey Johnson	0.460	Billie Barnie	1.281
John McGraw	0.478	Paul Richards	1.280
Sparky Anderson	0.591	Felipe Alou	1.261

GIDP: The formula here is: GIDP/(H+BB+HBP+ROE-2B-3B-HR). Things like stolen bases and sacrifice hits, which can move a player off of first base (and thus reducing the possibility of a GIDP), are excluded because those plays are often initiated with the intent of eliminating a potential double play. This inquiry wants to know which managers are most/least prone to having their hitters avoiding GIDPs. The results are given in the Connie Mack and Billy Southworth commentary sections. Fifty-four managers are examined by this facet of the Tendencies Database.

Fewest GIDP		Most GIDP	
Billy Southworth	0.505	Connie Mack	1.426
Birdie Tebbetts	0.570	Tom Kelly	1.413
Al Lopez	0.606	Danny Murtaugh	1.365
Whitey Herzog	0.632	Frank Robinson	1.317
Davey Johnson	0.657	Don Zimmer	1.225

BABIP: It stands for batting average on balls in play. The formula for this inquiry is: (H-HR)/(AB-HR-K). Since batter strikeouts are not known for all of baseball history, only 70 managers with at least ten years on the job are studied by this inquiry. The results on the left are given in the Danny Murtaugh commentary section. The results on the right are not given at all.

Highest BABIP		Lowest BABIP	
Danny Murtaugh	0.403	Art Howe	1.451
Red Schoendiest	0.451	Billy Barnie	1.401
Billy Southworth	0.500	Felipe Alou	1.373
Hughie Jennings	0.556	Dusty Baker	1.314
John McGraw	0.557	Bill Terry	1.289
Whitey Herzog	0.557		

OBP: #1–2 SLOTS: This relies on team splits information, so only the 39 managers who lasted at least a decade since 1956 qualify. Take the aggregate OBP from all hitters assigned the top two slots in a squad's batting order, and divide by the club's overall OBP to see which managers most and least prioritized getting on base from their main table-setters. The results are given in Chapter 8's commentary on Sparky Anderson and Don Zimmer.

Best OBP, Top Slots		*Worst OBP, Top Slots*	
Sparky Anderson	0.572	Don Zimmer	1.521
Red Schoendienst	0.613	Danny Murtaugh	1.400
Bruce Bochy	0.753	Johnny Oates	1.360
Buck Showalter	0.801	Dusty Baker	1.267
John McNamara	0.814	Phil Garner	1.216

TOPS+: #7–9 SLOTS: This is not used in the book, but it helped in the calculation of batting order ends mentioned in the Tony LaRussa commentary. I am skeptical of the value of the list on the right. Many of those managers prioritized a running game and de-emphasized power. As a result, slugging percentage across the batting order would be more consistent, leading to more even OPSs and those a closer bunching of tOPS+ as well. Thirty-nine managers qualify for this inquiry.

Lowest tOPS+		*Highest tOPS+*	
Tony LaRussa	0.638	Felipe Alou	1.332
Bill Virdon	0.686	Dick Williams	1.323
Dusty Baker	0.731	Walt Alston	1.244
Lou Piniella	0.741	Art Howe	1.238
Gene Mauch	0.764	Whitey Herzog	1.220

OFFENSIVE PLATOON ADVANTAGE: Add the number of plate appearances left-handed hitters face right-handed pitchers with the times right-handed hitters faces southpaws, and divide that sum by a team's total plate appearances. This inquiry relies on team splits information, so only 39 mangers qualify for it. The results are given in the Don Zimmer and Buck Showalter sections.

Most Frequent Platoon Advantage		*Least Frequent Platoon Advantage*	
Whitey Herzog	0.476	Don Zimmer	1.708
Gene Mauch	0.587	Jack McKeon	1.436
Bruce Bochy	0.588	Al Dark	1.371
Buck Showalter	0.699	Lou Piniella	1.308
Billy Martin	0.706	Danny Murtuagh	1.282

TRIPLES: The results of this inquiry are not listed in the book, but were used to help determine the most dynamic offenses. The formula is 3B/AB.

Most Triples		*Fewest Triples*	
Danny Murtaugh	0.352	Birdie Tebbetts	1.610
Whitey Herzog	0.358	Charles Comiskey	1.561
Cito Gaston	0.440	Tommy Lasorda	1.560
Red Schoendienst	0.492	Earl Weaver	1.476
Fred Clarke	0.561	Jimmy McAleer	1.455

HITTING WIN SHARES: This is not listed in the book because the results were redundant of park-adjusted runs scored. However, this information was used for the commentary on several managers. All 77 managers qualify for this list:

Most HWS		*Least HWS*	
Joe McCarthy	0.414	Jimmy McAleer	1.475
Davey Johnson	0.464	Phil Garner	1.301
John McGraw	0.467	Billy Barnie	1.275
Hughie Jennings	0.492	Jimmy Dykes	1.267
Earl Weaver	0.528	Paul Richards	1.253

Home Runs: The results for this are not given in the book, but are used for several combinations, including the static offenses, and Beane Count studies. The formula is HR/AB. All 77 managers qualify.

Most Home Runs		Fewest Home Runs	
Bill Terry	0.333	Whitey Herzog	1.682
Joe McCarthy	0.354	Red Schoendienst	1.589
Sparky Anderson	0.466	Bruce Bochy	1.519
Miller Huggins	0.510	Tom Kelly	1.467
Davey Johnson	0.536	Bill Virdon	1.456

OBP: This is the formula for on-base percentage. All 77 managers qualify, and the results are listed in the Joe McCarthy and Billy Barnie sections.

Highest OBP		Lowest OBP	
Joe McCarthy	0.414	Billy Barnie	1.401
Hughie Jennings	0.476	Felipe Alou	1.349
John McGraw	0.526	Bill McKechnie	1.324
Burt Shotton	0.578	Jimmy McAleer	1.273
Billy Southworth	0.593	Patsy Donovan	1.268

Singles: The formula is (H-2B-3B-HR)/AB. The results for this particular inquiry are not given in the book, but are used in compiling the dynamic offenses study. All 77 managers qualify for it.

Most Singles		Fewest Singles	
Red Schoendienst	0.487	Art Howe	1.505
Tom Kelly	0.524	Cito Gaston	1.453
Hughie Jennings	0.540	Lee Fohl	1.374
John McGraw	0.543	Bill McKechnie	1.285
Tommy Lasorda	0.581	Lou Boudreau	1.278

Pinch-Hitters: This is just the number of pinch-hitters used in a season. Results are given in the Bobby Valentine and Felipe Alou sections. Thirty-nine managers qualify for this inquiry in the Tendencies Database.

Most Pinch-Hitters		Fewest Pinch-Hitters	
Bobby Valentine	0.370	Felipe Alou	1.703
Tom Kelly	0.444	Cito Gaston	1.613
Gene Mauch	0.465	Danny Murtaugh	1.479
Art Howe	0.616	Davey Johnson	1.392
Al Dark	0.616	Dusty Baker	1.390

Starter–Catcher: A variation on the starter percentage inquiry, this is number of plate appearances by a starting catcher. Though it was run through the Tendencies Database, it never appears in the book (until now). It was used in the commentary for some of the managers listed below, such as Terry and Frisch. All 77 managers qualify for this inquiry.

Least Rested Catchers		Most Rested Catchers	
Red Schoendienst	0.376	Frankie Frisch	1.348
Bill Terry	0.489	Frank Robinson	1.298
Gus Schmelz	0.514	Jimmy McAleer	1.273
Sparky Anderson	0.534	Mike Hargrove	1.236
Johnny Oates	0.560	Buck Showalter	1.208

Position Player Complete Games: This stat is based on the information generated by Retrosheet. That website notes how many complete games each team had for all positions combined. The Tendencies Database subtracts the pitchers and divides the rest by games played. The database contains only Retrosheet-based information from 1956–onward, so 39 managers qualify. The results are given in the commentary sections on Jim Fregosi and Bobby Valentine.

Fewest CG		*Most CG*	
Bobby Valentine	1.607	Danny Murtaugh	0.311
Phil Garner	1.534	Cito Gaston	0.320
Tony LaRussa	1.533	Ralph Houk	0.389
Tommy Lasorda	1.474	Jim Fregosi	0.503
Art Howe	1.386	Don Zimmer	0.607
Charlie Dressen	1.386		

Pitching Stats

INTENTIONAL WALKS ISSUED: This stat has been recorded since 1954 in the NL and 1955 in the AL. As a result, the Tendencies Database inquiry involves 43 managers. The database's formula is IW/IP. Results are given in the commentary on Danny Murtaugh and Davey Johnson.

Most IW		*Fewest IW*	
Danny Murtaugh	0.383	Davey Johnson	1.736
Frank Robinson	0.435	Casey Stengel	1.602
Art Howe	0.464	Tom Kelly	1.556
Sparky Anderson	0.465	Felipe Alou	1.512
Don Zimmer	0.527	Tony LaRussa	1.479

RELIEF PITCHERS USED: This is the total number of relief appearances divided by the team's games played. Results are in Chapter 2. All 77 managers who served at least a decade qualify for this inquiry.

Most Relievers		*Fewest Relievers*	
Burt Shotton	0.378	Bill Virdon	1.609
Jimy Williams	0.440	Ralph Houk	1.608
Lou Boudreau	0.458	Earl Weaver	1.566
Whitey Herzog	0.551	Jimmie Dykes	1.522
Joe Cronin	0.607	Cito Gaston	1.520

PITCHING PLATOON ADVANTAGE: Add together the number of plate appearances left-handed pitchers face right-handed hitters with the times right-handed pitchers face left-handed hitters, and divide that sum by total batters faced by the team. Only 39 managers qualify for this study because it relies on the availability of team splits data. Results are given in the Mike Hargrove and Lou Piniella sections.

Most Frequent Platoon Advantage		*Least Frequent Platoon Advantage*	
Gene Mauch	0.511	Earl Weaver	1.402
Mike Hargrove	0.516	Lou Piniella	1.388
Tony LaRussa	0.610	Tom Kelly	1.324
Bill Virdon	0.615	Walt Alston	1.311
Frank Robinson	0.625	Al Lopez	1.299

TOP THREE PITCHERS: The results for this are in Chapter 2. It is the innings pitched from the top three workhorses for all rotations divided by total team innings pitched. For the first decade of baseball, when teams sometimes used three or fewer pitchers in the course of a season, tiebreakers are used. The first tiebreaker is innings by the top two pitchers divided by the team, and the other tiebreaker is the ace's innings divided by the team's total. All 77 managers qualify for this Tendencies Database inquiry.

Lean Heaviest on Them		*Spread Innings Around*	
Tommy Lasorda	0.429	Frank Robinson	1.331
Earl Weaver	0.435	Gus Schmelz	1.322

Lean Heaviest on Them (continued)		*Spread Innings Around* (continued)	
Bobby Cox	0.443	Jack McKeon	1.285
Al Lopez	0.588	Jimy Williams	1.279
Frank Selee	0.599	Frank Chance	1.273

WALKS ALLOWED: This inquiry is (BB-IW)/IP*9. All 77 managers who lasted at least a decade are under examination. Intentional walks are used when available, though that does not cover all managers. Results are given in the John McGraw and Burt Shotton commentaries.

Best Control		*Worst Control*	
Patsy Tebeau	0.476	Burt Shotton	1.600
John McGraw	0.514	Casey Stengel	1.387
Al Lopez	0.537	Dusty Baker	1.351
Tom Kelly	0.587	Jim Fregosi	1.350
Fred Clarke	0.596	Lou Boudreau	1.292

STRIKEOUTS: This is K/IP*9. Results are given in the Wilbert Robinson and Phil Garner sections. All 77 managers are eligible for this study.

Most Strikeouts		*Fewest Strikeouts*	
Jimy Williams	0.460	Whitey Herzog	1.508
Davey Johnson	0.484	Jim Leyland	1.388
Walter Alston	0.498	Hughie Jennings	1.381
Bobby Valentine	0.506	Phil Garner	1.376
Wilbert Robinson	0.538	Johnny Oates	1.360

PITCHER AGE: This information comes from Baseball-Reference.com, which lists an average age for all pitching staffs, rounded to the nearest tenths decimal All 77 managers qualify, with results listed in the Bill McKechnie and Steve O'Neill commentary sections.

Youngest Staffs		*Oldest Staffs*	
Burt Shotton	0.378	Al Lopez	1.564
Patsy Donovan	0.522	Wilbert Robinson	1.427
Steve O'Neill	0.598	Bill McKechnie	1.420
Billy Barnie	0.644	Bobby Valentine	1.384
Felipe Alou	0.666	Joe Torre	1.383

SAVES: The Tendencies Database figures this as saves divided by wins. Technically, all 77 managers are eligible for it, but it is essentially useless for the game's primordial managers. In the early days, most teams had no saves and those that did contained so few as to defeat the purpose of the inquiry. This is one occasion where ties really do become a serious problem, as at times seven teams would be tied for second place. Worse yet, they were tied with zero saves. Depending on how those ties sort out, Harry Wright belongs on the list on the left (the Tendencies Database gives him a score of 0.630). Frankly, putting him on would seem absurd. Ultimately, I made a judgment call to exclude Wright and all other managers who spent less than ten seasons in *leagues* that had less than ten saves. The results for this are in the commentaries for John McGraw and Tommy Lasorda.

Most Wins Saved		*Fewest Wins Saved*	
Bruce Bochy	0.546	Tommy Lasorda	1.499
Burt Shotton	0.578	Billy Southworth	1.481
John McGraw	0.600	Charlie Grimm	1.429
Felipe Alou	0.673	John McNamara	1.411
Bill Rigney	0.679	Earl Weaver	1.392

RUNS ALLOWED, ADJUSTED FOR PARK: This is runs allowed per game, adjusted by Baseball-Reference.com's pitcher park factors. All 77 managers qualify for this study in the Tendencies Database, and results are in the Hughie Jennings and Charles Comiskey commentary sections.

Best Run Prevention		*Worst Run Prevention*	
Frank Selee	0.408	Hughie Jennings	1.365
Charles Comiskey	0.415	Patsy Donovan	1.336
Al Lopez	0.513	Frank Robinson	1.278
Bobby Cox	0.527	Billy Barnie	1.253
Cito Gaston	0.560	Bruce Bochy	1.218

BULLPEN IP: This is based on team split information, so only 39 managers qualify for this inquiry. It is innings thrown by the bullpen divided by the team's total innings. The results on the right are not listed in any manager's commentary, but the numbers on the left are listed in Bill Rigney's section.

Most Bullpen IP		*Fewest Bullpen IP*	
Jimy Williams	0.389	Tommy Lasorda	1.574
Frank Robinson	0.556	Bill Virdon	1.562
Bill Rigney	0.696	Earl Weaver	1.465
Felipe Alou	0.716	Red Schoendienst	1.462
Tom Kelly	0.720	Cito Gaston	1.400

PARK-ADJUSTED BULLPEN ERA: This is bullpen ERA adjusted by Baseball-Reference's pitcher park factor. The John McNamara and Johnny Oates commentaries give the results. Since this data relies on team split information, only 39 managers qualify for it.

Best Bullpen ERA		*Worst Bullpen ERA*	
Jimy Williams	0.641	John McNamara	1.357
Cito Gaston	0.653	Jim Leyland	1.307
Danny Murtaugh	0.685	Bruce Bochy	1.151
Johnny Oates	0.693	Al Dark	1.096
Al Lopez	0.697	Tom Kelly	1.093

PARK-ADJUSTED STARTER ERA: This is the ERA for starting rotations, adjusted by Baseball-Reference.com's pitcher park factor. Since this inquiry relies on team splits information, only the 39 managers who lasted at least a decade since 1956 qualify. The results are given in the commentary sections for Bobby Cox and Dusty Baker.

Best Starter ERA		*Worst Starter ERA*	
Tommy Lasorda	0.519	Frank Robinson	1.282
Bobby Cox	0.527	Dusty Baker	1.221
Jimy Williams	0.527	Johnny Oates	1.173
Walt Alston	0.590	Gene Mauch	1.142
Earl Weaver	0.622	Bruce Bochy	1.129

INNINGS PITCHED ON NO REST: This adds together two bits of team splits information innings thrown by a pitcher who appeared the day before, and innings thrown in the second game of a doubleheader by a hurler who pitched in the first game. The results are given in the Ralph Houk and Billy Martin sections of the book. Thirty-nine managers qualify for this inquiry.

Most IP on No Rest		*Least IP on No Rest*	
Billy Martin	0.574	Ralph Houk	1.625
Al Dark	0.586	Jim Leyland	1.589
Frank Robinson	0.659	Earl Weaver	1.560
Dusty Baker	0.674	Cito Gaston	1.453
Jimy Williams	0.731	Buck Showalter	1.397

HOMERS ALLOWED: The results for this are never given, but are used in several combinations, including pitcher peripherals, and Beane Count studies. The formula, HR/IP*9, includes all baseball history, thus involving 77 managers.

Fewest HR Allowed		*Most HR Allowed*	
Danny Murtaugh	0.415	Burt Shotton	1.578
Tommy Lasorda	0.438	Sparky Anderson	1.440
Bill Virdon	0.473	Bill Terry	1.378
Paul Richards	0.511	Tom Kelly	1.369
Felipe Alou	0.589	Frank Selee	1.365

COMPLETE GAMES: In the Tendencies Database, this is determined as CG/G. Results on the right were given in the Clark Griffith commentary. Results on the left were never mentioned. All 77 managers qualified for this survey.

Most Starts Completed		*Fewest Starts Completed*	
Tommy Lasorda	0.388	Jimy Williams	1.523
Earl Weaver	0.436	Burt Shotton	1.489
Billy Southworth	0.500	Gus Schmelz	1.366
Patsy Tebeau	0.590	Clark Griffith	1.357
Al Lopez	0.603	Bill Rigney	1.335

INNINGS PITCHED PER RELIEF APPEARANCE: This relies on team splits data, and thus only 39 managers qualify for this Tendencies Database inquiry. It is the innings pitched by relievers divided by a team's total number of relief appearances. Results are listed in the Ralph Houk and Bobby Cox sections of the book.

Longest Relief Appearances		*Shortest Relief Appearances*	
Ralph Houk	0.325	Red Schoendienst	1.719
Jack McKeon	0.551	Bobby Cox	1.614
Davey Johnson	0.585	Whitey Herzog	1.557
Lou Piniella	0.598	Tony LaRussa	1.334
Walter Alston	0.600	Danny Murtaugh	1.321

PITCHING WIN SHARES: This is not listed in the book because the results were redundant of park-adjusted runs allowed. However, this information was used for the commentary on several managers. All 77 managers qualify for this list:

Most PWS		*Fewest PWS*	
Frank Selee	0.388	Patsy Donovan	1.309
Charles Comiskey	0.422	Billy Barnie	1.262
Steve O'Neill	0.513	Dusty Baker	1.250
Al Lopez	0.528	Charlie Dressen	1.234
Bobby Cox	0.532	Bruce Bochy	1.201

Fielding Stats

DER: Defensive Efficiency Ratio is the percentage of balls in play turned into outs. This stat was lifted directly from Baseball-Reference.com. Results are given in the Frank Selee and Frankie Frisch commentaries. All 77 managers qualify for this study in the Tendencies Database.

Best DER		*Worst DER*	
Earl Weaver	0.410	Don Zimmer	1.437
Frank Selee	0.458	Frankie Frisch	1.393
Frank Chance	0.505	Billy Barnie	1.345
Bill McKechnie	0.589	George Stallings	1.257
Joe McCarthy	0.596	Burt Shotton	1.244

FIELDING PERCENTAGE: This is chances fielded without error divided by total chances. Results are given in the commentary for Frankie Frisch and Birdie Tebbetts. All 77 managers qualify for this study.

Best Fielding Percentage		Worst Fielding Percentage	
Earl Weaver	0.365	Art Howe	1.373
Tom Kelly	0.516	Wilbert Robinson	1.357
Birdie Tebbetts	0.530	Patsy Donovan	1.329
Charles Comiskey	0.532	Frankie Frisch	1.319
Al Lopez	0.558	Clark Griffith	1.275

DOUBLE PLAYS: This is based on the formula: DP/(H-2B-3B-HR+BB+HB-SH-SB-CS). Basically, it is double plays divided by times a person is on first base. Results are given in the commentary sections for Hughie Jennings and Gene Mauch. It covers all 77 managers who lasted at least ten years.

Most DP Turned		Fewest DP Turned	
Danny Murtaugh	0.497	Hughie Jennings	1.540
Earl Weaver	0.531	Wilbert Robinson	1.439
Gene Mauch	0.591	Al Dark	1.357
Casey Stengel	0.667	Felipe Alou	1.276
Whitey Herzog	0.670	Bobby Valentine	1.264

FIELDING WIN SHARES: This is not listed in the book for two reasons. First, it was a bit redundant of other fielding stats. Second and most importantly, once I decided not to include the results for Pitching and Hitting Win Shares, it seemed awkward to include Fielding Win Shares. All 77 managers qualify for this list:

Most FWS		Fewest FWS	
Charles Comiskey	0.388	Patsy Donovan	1.356
Earl Weaver	0.498	Billy Barnie	1.252
Al Lopez	0.540	Hughie Jennings	1.238
Frank Selee	0.564	Bruce Bochy	1.238
Bobby Cox	0.592	Art Howe	1.210

Team Stats

STARTER PERCENTAGE: This is plate appearances by the starting eight batters (or starting nine in a league with a designated hitter) divided by total team plate appearances. All 77 managers are eligible for his inquiry. The results are given in Chapter 2.

Most Reliant on Starters		Most Reliant on Bench	
Frank Selee	0.580	George Stallings	1.387
Dick Williams	0.584	Frank Robinson	1.381
Danny Murtaugh	0.600	Jim Fregosi	1.290
Joe McCarthy	0.657	Paul Richards	1.258
Ralph Houk	0.658	Casey Stengel	1.242

PACE: This is winning percentage in the first half divided by winning percentage in the second half. The lower scores belong to teams that improved as the year went on. This inquiry in the Tendencies Database exists for all baseball history. All 77 managers qualify for the leaderboards. The results are given in Chapter 2.

Got Better Later		Got Worse Later	
Al Lopez	0.646	Joe Cronin	1.393
Frank Chance	0.667	Bill Terry	1.289
Jimy Williams	0.734	Johnny Oates	1.280
Ned Hanlon	0.734	Danny Murtaugh	1.222
Billy Martin	0.744	Miller Huggins	1.216

EVEN PACE: Take a team's winning percentage in the first and second halves of the season, and see which ones had the smallest and largest differences. The results are given in the Ned Hanlon and George Stallings commentary in Chapter 5. All 77 managers who lasted at least ten years in the profession qualify for this query.

Most Even Pace		Most Uneven Pace	
Charles Comiskey	0.562	Don Zimmer	1.258
Frank Selee	0.702	George Stallings	1.226
Bill Virdon	0.757	Paul Richards	1.207
Ned Hanlon	0.758	Jimmie Dykes	1.162
Fred Clarke	0.765	Bill Terry	1.156

ONE-RUN GAMES: Baseball-Reference.com lists each team's win-loss record in one-run contests. This ranks teams by their winning percentage in those affairs. The Tendencies Database results for this inquiry were not given in the book, but the information did provide insight for some comments in the Team Characteristics section for many managers. All 77 managers qualified for this study.

Best in One-Run Games		Worst in One-Run Games	
Earl Weaver	0.548	Jimmy McAleer	1.253
Joe Cronin	0.637	Billy Barnie	1.238
Al Lopez	0.660	Gus Schmelz	1.199
Bruce Bochy	0.664	Buck Showalter	1.184
Harry Wright	0.667	Frank Robinson	1.163

BATTING ORDER: This stat notes which managers filled out the largest and smallest number of different batting orders over the course of a season. It is based on Baseball-Reference.com's usage of Retrosheet's data. It goes back to 1956, and thus only 39 managers qualify for it. This study does not include pitchers in the batting order. The results are given in Chapter 2.

Fewest Batting Orders		Most Batting Orders	
Cito Gaston	0.320	Felipe Alou	1.520
Bobby Cox	0.448	Tom Kelly	1.449
Dick Williams	0.522	Tony LaRussa	1.435
Johnny Oates	0.573	Bill Rigney	1.314
Ralph Houk	0.637	Al Dark	1.302

Combinations

SMALL BALL: This combines sacrifice hit frequency and stolen base frequency. The results are listed in Chapter 2, and 73 managers are under scrutiny.

Pro-Small Ball		Anti-Small Ball	
Walter Alston	1.133	Buck Showalter	3.048
Frank Chance	1.334	Jimy Williams	2.927
Whitey Herzog	1.345	Jimmy McAleer	2.849
Paul Richards	1.348	Ralph Houk	2.698
Jack McKeon	1.455	Johnny Oates	2.693

SMALL BALL WITH HIT-AND-RUN: This combines the studies for stolen base frequency, sacrifice hit frequency, and hit-and-run frequency. It examines 54 managers and the results are in Chapter 2.

Pro-Small Ball		Anti-Small Ball	
Whitey Herzog	2.105	Jimy Williams	4.028
Billy Southworth	2.106	Danny Murtaugh	3.931
Walter Alston	2.201	Buck Showalter	3.929
Al Lopez	2.229	Tom Kelly	3.787
Birdie Tebbetts	2.293	Ralph Houk	3.780

VETS VS. KIDS: Based on hitter and pitcher ages. This inquiry includes all 77 managers and the results are listed in the Al Lopez and Dick Williams sections.

Youngest Teams		Oldest Teams	
Burt Shotton	0.844	Al Lopez	3.063
Patsy Donovan	1.261	Wilbert Robinson	2.854
Dick Williams	1.389	Earl Weaver	2.809
Felipe Alou	1.394	Jimmy Dykes	2.789
Frank Robinson	1.467	Bill McKechnie	2.686

STATIC OFFENSES: Based on a study by Clay Davenport in the Baseball Prospectus book *It Ain't Over 'til It's Over*, this attempts to find out which managers had the greatest disposition towards playing for the big inning. It is a combination of three inquiries in the Tendencies Database: offensive walks, strikeouts, and home runs. Seventy of the 77 managers that lasted at least a decade in the profession qualify for this. The results on the left are given in the Sparky Anderson commentary, those on the right are not given at all.

Most Static Offenses		Least Static Offenses	
Joe McCarthy	1.374	Bill Virdon	4.426
Sparky Anderson	1.447	Red Schoendienst	4.280
Gus Schmelz	1.799	Tom Kelly	4.276
Miller Huggins	1.804	Felipe Alou	4.068
Earl Weaver	1.901	Danny Murtaugh	4.010

DYNAMIC OFFENSES: Also based Clay Davenport's work in *It Ain't Over 'til It's Over*, this attempts to find out which managers had the greatest disposition towards playing for one run. It is a combination of three inquiries in the Tendencies Database: triples, singles, and stolen bases. Seventy-three of the 77 managers that lasted at least a decade in the profession qualify for this. The results on the left are given in the Whitey Herzog commentary, those on the right are not given at all.

Most Dynamic Offenses		Least Dynamic Offenses	
Whitey Herzog	1.316	Art Howe	4.089
Red Schoendienst	1.470	Jimmy McAleer	3.798
Tom Kelly	1.910	Earl Weaver	3.780
Hughie Jennings	1.952	Bill Terry	3.778
Clark Griffith	2.152	John McNamara	3.759

BEANE COUNT: This combines studies on home runs hit, walks taken, homers surrendered, and walks allowed. The results are presented in the Joe McCarthy and Tom Kelly commentary sections. All 77 managers qualify.

Best Beane Count		Worst Beane Count	
Joe McCarthy	2.505	Tom Kelly	4.907
Earl Weaver	2.641	Burt Shotton	4.533
Al Lopez	2.937	Jimmie Dykes	4.529
Jimy Williams	3.004	Fred Hutchinson	4.516
Tommy Lasorda	3.021	Jimmy McAleer	4.505

BALLS IN PLAY: This adds together the Tendencies Database's results for DER and BABIP. It shows which teams are most and least dependent on balls in play. The results on the right are listed in Art Howe's commentary. The results on the left are never given. All 77 managers qualify for this inquiry.

Most Balls in Play		Fewest Balls in Play	
Whitey Herzog	1.215	Billy Barnie	2.746
Billy Southworth	1.241	Art Howe	2.512
Frank Selee	1.261	Frank Robinson	2.427
John McGraw	1.287	Patsy Donovan	2.385
Fred Clarke	1.337	Jimmy McAleer	2.323

ALL WALKS: This combines the walks allowed and walks drawn queries. All 77 managers who lasted at least ten years in the profession qualify for this study. The results are given in the commentary sections for George Stallings and Casey Stengel.

Best at Walks		Worst at Walks	
Patsy Tebeau	1.162	Patsy Donovan	2.549
Al Lopez	1.191	Lou Boudreau	2.472
Earl Weaver	1.280	Bill Virdon	2.462
Joe McCarthy	1.293	Casey Stengel	2.448
George Stallings	1.368	Bill Rigney	2.434

FRONTLINE PLAYERS: This looks at which managers depended the most on their main starters and who relied the most on their rosters' depth. It combined the top three starting pitcher and starter percentage inquiries. All managers qualify for this combination. Results are given in the Frank Selee and Frank Robinson portions of the book.

Most Reliant on Frontline		Least Reliant on Frontline	
Frank Selee	1.179	Frank Robinson	2.712
Earl Weaver	1.278	Jim Fregosi	2.550
Bobby Cox	1.364	Paul Richards	2.331
Tommy Lasorda	1.379	Frank Chance	2.324
Al Lopez	1.397	Casey Stengel	2.288

ALL DOUBLE PLAYS: This combines the results for the Tendencies Database's inquiries for double plays turned and grounded into. This contains 54 managers. Results are given in the Casey Stengel and Connie Mack commentary sections.

Best at Double Plays		Worst at Double Plays	
Whitey Herzog	1.261	Connie Mack	2.625
Billy Southworth	1.357	Bobby Valentine	2.431
Al Lopez	1.415	Bruce Bochy	2.421
Casey Stengel	1.419	Frank Robinson	2.413
Gene Mauch	1.453	Tom Kelly	2.409

ALL PLATOON ADVANTAGE: This adds together the results of the pitching and offensive platoon advantage inquiries. The results are given in the Gene Mauch and Lou Piniella commentary sections. Only 39 managers qualify for these lists.

Most Frequent Platoon Advantage		Least Frequent Platoon Advantage	
Gene Mauch	1.098	Lou Piniella	2.696
Bruce Bochy	1.332	Jack McKeon	2.517
Whitey Herzog	1.354	Al Dark	2.474
Frank Robinson	1.402	Don Zimmer	2.449
Bill Virdon	1.420	Tom Kelly	2.435

ALL STARTING PITCHERS: This combines the results from the Tendencies Database's park-adjusted starter ERA and starter innings pitched inquiries. Thirty-nine managers qualify. The results on the right were not given prior to this appendix, and the results on the left are in the Tommy Lasorda commentary.

Most Valuable Starting Pitching		Least Valuable Starting Pitchers	
Tommy Lasorda	0.945	Frank Robinson	2.726
Bobby Cox	1.155	Gene Mauch	2.368
Earl Weaver	1.157	Tom Kelly	2.347
Cito Gaston	1.213	Sparky Anderson	2.314
Bill Virdon	1.266	Bill Rigney	2.273

ALL STRIKEOUTS: This combines the Tendencies Database's results for batting and pitching strikeouts. It includes 70 managers in all. Results on the left are given in Bill Virdon's commentary. Results on the right were not mentioned prior to now.

Best Combined Strikeouts		Worst Combined Strikeouts	
Bill Virdon	1.183	Sparky Anderson	2.674
Walt Alston	1.324	Art Howe	2.493
Steve O'Neill	1.401	Frankie Frisch	2.459
Wilbert Robinson	1.415	Miller Huggins	2.458
Bill Terry	1.444	George Stallings	2.429

ALL HOME RUNS: This combines the Tendencies Database's studies on home runs allowed and home runs hit. It includes all 77 managers with at least ten years under their belts. The results are given in the Tommy Lasorda and Bruce Bochy commentaries.

Best at Home Runs		Worst at Home Runs	
Joe McCarthy	1.212	Tom Kelly	2.836
Tommy Lasorda	1.278	Jimmy Dykes	2.728
Bobby Cox	1.291	Phil Garner	2.574
Davey Johnson	1.330	Bruce Bochy	2.555
Jimy Williams	1.338	Jimmy McAleer	2.545

STOLEN BASES COMBINED: This adds together the result of the Tendencies Database's inquiries on the frequency and success rate of stolen bases. As a result, 54 managers are under survey. The list on the left is included in Cito Gaston's commentary while the one on the right is not given in the book at all. It is not clear to me if the right side tells you very much. These are men who had poor success in stolen base attempts but also rarely stole. While high marks on both categories indicate the manager attained the most from stolen bases, the flip side is not necessarily true. The managers who got the least from stolen base would be those who combined a poor success rate in numerous opportunities. At least the batch listed below on the right had sense to limit the damage stolen bases caused their teams by rarely calling for them.

Greatest Value from SB		Least Value (?) from SB	
Whitey Herzog	0.833	Jimy Williams	2.685
Red Schoendienst	0.948	Johnny Oates	2.653
Cito Gaston	1.080	Danny Murtaugh	2.650
Walt Alston	1.286	Ralph Houk	2.621
Mike Hargrove	1.396	John McNamara	2.569

DEFENSIVE DEPENDENCY: This reveals how dependent teams were on balls in play. It does not mean they made balls in play work for them necessarily, but that strikeouts did not determine who won their games. This combines the Tendencies Database's inquiries on pitcher and batter strikeouts. The results on the left are listed in the Phil Garner section; the results on the right are not in the book. Offensive strikeouts have been flipped around to make this combination work. Seventy managers qualify for this.

Highest Defensive Dependency		Least Defensive Dependency	
Whitey Herzog	2.892	Miller Huggins	1.203
Hughie Jennings	2.770	Joe McCarthy	1.242
Phil Garner	2.692	Bobby Valentine	1.288
Jimmy Dykes	2.618	Cito Gaston	1.400
Danny Murtaugh	2.570	Frank Chance	1.434

BEST OVERALL BATTING ORDER: This combines how managers fare in two inquiries: OBP from the top two slots in a batting order and tOPS+ from the bottom three spots in the order. This is used to determine which managers did the best and worst overall job determining their batting order. The results on the left are given in Tony LaRussa's commentary in Chapter 9. (That section also explains why the heart of the order is not included in this combinative inquiry.) The results on the right are not given in the book.

Best Batting Orders		Worst Batting Orders	
Bill Virdon	1.455	Don Zimmer	2.758
Tony LaRussa	1.511	Danny Murtaugh	2.492
Sparky Anderson	1.610	Dick Williams	2.471
Red Schoendienst	1.612	Whitey Herzog	2.435
Earl Weaver	1.663	Art Howe	2.383
John McNamara	1.663		

PITCHER PERIPHERALS: This adds together scores for strikeouts, walks, and home runs allowed per inning. All 77 managers qualify for this combination. The results are given in the Steve O'Neill and Sparky Anderson sections.

Best Pitcher Peripherals		Worst Pitcher Peripherals	
Jimy Williams	1.758	Burt Shotton	4.067
Tommy Lasorda	1.772	Jim Leyland	3.640
Steve O'Neill	2.000	Dusty Baker	3.616
Paul Richards	2.093	Sparky Anderson	3.614
Davey Johnson	2.187	Patsy Donovan	3.559

ALL BULLPEN: This combines the queries for bullpen innings and park-adjusted ERA. Results are given in the Bill Virdon and Jimy Williams commentary sections. Thirty-nine managers qualify for this combination.

Most Valuable Bullpens		Least Valuable Bullpens	
Jimy Williams	1.030	Bill Virdon	2.639
Frank Robinson	1.514	Tommy Lasorda	2.596
Chuck Tanner	1.647	John McNamara	2.462
Bill Rigney	1.663	Earl Weaver	2.353
Gene Mauch	1.679	Red Schoendienst	2.292

Appendix III. LPA for Years and Managers

Listed below are the LPAs (which Chapter 3 explained) for every season from 1876 to 1969. Information from 1970–onward is not included here because I did not calculate the AOWP+ for every pitcher with at least ten starts in a season from 1970–onward. (Some were done, but all need to be tabulated in order to properly determine LPA.)

First, however, a very important qualifier should be noted: the way I calculated AOWP (which serves as the basis for AOWP+, LPA, and LPA+) caused some errors to corrupt the data. The errors are not substantial, but they should be noted.

Determining AOWP depended on my computer skills, which are generally effective, but frankly limited. When tabulating AOWP, I first went to Retrosheet and cut-and-pasted their gamelogs into Microsoft Excel. When determining the AOWP for a given pitcher, I first sorted the Excel file by starting pitchers and then did a secondary sort for opposing teams. That part went fine.

The fun began when I tabulated the information. I took a sheet of paper, and wrote the information on it. I created a grid on the previously blank page in which a bunch of rows, each one of which represented an opposing team, and several columns— one for each year in a pitcher's career. In each box I put a pitcher's starts versus the opposing team in that year, along with the opponent's winning percentage for that season. Obviously, that was a rather low-tech approach. From there, I typed up the starts and winning percentages into a different Excel file, and let it figure the math behind AOWP.

The opening stages where I put Retrosheet into Excel, and the last bit, where I used Excel to figure AOWP, each worked fine. The middle parts introduced the possibility of error. I could write down the wrong winning percentage. Perhaps I misread my own numbers when typing it into Excel. Or I could have committed a typo.

When looking at each individual pitcher, I think the odds of any of the above occurring were extremely remote. I am pretty good at monitoring myself, and got into a rhythm with this method. However, the sheer quantity of data examined makes it laughable to assume no errors were made. The AOWP database includes 10,380 different pitcher seasons altogether. If I did 99 percent of it perfectly, that is still 104 errors. Frankly, I doubt my success rate was 99 percent. Maybe 95 percent, but not 99 percent. The only way to gather this data with 100 percent accuracy would be to rely on computers for every step of the way, and that is beyond my capabilities. (I did use Excel to turn AOWP into AOWP+ and then LPA and LPA+, so no further errors should have been introduced.)

Ultimately, two consequences stem from the imperfect way I tabulated AOWP. First, not only are some of the LPAs listed below incorrect, but *all years* may be off by a little bit. This most certainly should be noted.

Second, and far more importantly, the errors ultimately make minimal difference. That may sound strange, especially to the more detail-orientated readers, but think it through. Say, for example, 1923's LPA of 2.72 is incorrect and should really be 2.88. Either way, that means there was less leveraging in that year than was normally the case prior to the 1960s. The same holds true for other years: the exact details may be off, but it provides a very effective overall picture. Even if every single number down below is off, this information still illuminates far more than it obscures. The exact numbers are less important than the overall trends and what they tell us about how teams used their pitchers over the decades. My sabermetric saving grace is that I gravitate toward issues that have not yet been investigated. Hopefully, someone with better computer skills than mine will come around and figure it out with 100 percent accuracy. This work can be improved upon.

That said, the list below contains the LPA for every year that it was worth calculating this information:

Year	LPA	Year	LPA	Year	LPA
1876	4.75	1902	2.42	1928	4.23
1877	3.95	1903	4.07	1929	4.26
1878	2.58	1904	3.90	1930	4.77
1879	5.06	1905	4.07	1931	4.86
1880	3.88	1906	3.96	1932	3.99
1881	2.58	1907	4.96	1933	3.71
1882	3.77	1908	4.94	1934	4.60
1883	4.14	1909	6.48	1935	5.17
1884	6.02	1910	5.27	1936	4.65
1885	3.48	1911	4.51	1937	5.17
1886	4.62	1912	4.77	1938	5.14
1887	4.67	1913	3.79	1939	5.93
1888	3.88	1914	2.61	1940	4.18
1889	4.73	1915	3.91	1941	4.13
1890	5.67	1916	3.97	1942	7.07
1891	3.77	1917	3.15	1943	3.06
1892	3.25	1918	2.72	1944	2.46
1893	2.91	1919	5.71	1945	4.29
1894	4.93	1920	3.22	1946	5.58
1895	4.57	1921	3.53	1947	4.24
1896	3.87	1922	3.23	1948	4.41
1897	4.38	1923	2.72	1949	5.56
1898	3.27	1924	3.72	1950	4.80
1899	4.48	1925	3.66	1951	4.25
1900	2.14	1926	3.35	1952	4.21
1901	3.52	1927	3.85	1953	6.24

Year	LPA	Year	LPA	Year	LPA
1954	7.07	1960	4.00	1966	1.68
1955	5.37	1961	4.02	1967	1.89
1956	4.34	1962	3.62	1968	1.85
1957	3.91	1963	2.77	1969	3.32
1958	2.03	1964	3.52		
1959	2.17	1965	2.46		

Two oddities should be explained. First, though I claimed in Chapter 3 that leveraging ended in the mid–1960s, a spike clearly appears in 1969, when major league baseball possessed an overall LPA of 3.32. This does not jibe with my contention that the practice had already died.

An underlying variable skews the data very badly for that year: team win-loss records. Leagues with many extreme win-loss records tend to produce especially dramatic AOWP+s and LPAs. For example, if half the teams in a league won only a fourth of their games while the other half won three-fourths, a pitcher could have an AOWP noticeably different from his squad's TOWP just by randomly having a few extra starts against either the first or second division squads. Real life never has leagues that look like that, but from year to year the gap between best and worst teams changes, affecting the likelihood of gaining noteworthy LPAs.

One of those years with exceptionally extreme win-loss records was 1969. That season, for the first and only time in baseball history, two different squads lost 110 games. In comparison, no single squad lost that many again until 2003. Also in 1969, the Orioles won 109 games, which ties the most by any club between 1954 and 1998. With so many incredible win-loss records, AOWP+s that would normally be 101s became 102s, and 102s became 103s. That is why the scores that year are higher. Even so, 1969's score is still lower than all non–World War II seasons from 1924 to 1957. If leveraging existed in a league with so many impressive win-loss records, the yearly LPA should have been higher than it was in 1969.

The second oddity was that the numbers indicate that leveraging appeared to decline in 1958–59, which goes against the storyline I presented in Chapter 3. Frankly, I am at a loss to explain this. In part, this was a reversal of what happened in 1969. In that two-year period, only one team had a winning percentage over .600 (and barely that, with the 1959 White Sox posting a .610 mark) and only one other under .400 (the 1958 Senators at .396). Normally, marks are more extreme than that. However, this does not fully explain the lower scores.

I have one other theory that can explain the 1958–59 drop. I have done a little bit of research on doubleheaders, and though I cannot make any definitive statements, I believe the overall number of doubleheaders appears to have declined in the late 1950s. Leveraging depended on fluid use of pitchers, and doubleheaders forced teams to be fluid in deploying their pitchers. Moving away from them would allow starters to work in a more regimented fashion as they could have more regular rest. Perhaps a decline in doubleheaders caused the decline in LPA in 1958–59. Whatever caused it, virtually every team in baseball saw a notable decline in their LPA in the late 1950s.

Hurting the doubleheader theory, LPAs bounced back upward in 1960. If the boom in LPA happened in 1961, it could be attributed (like 1969) to unusually disparate win-loss records, as five clubs won or lost 100 games that year. In 1960, however, no team won or lost more than 97 games. I really cannot say what caused the 1958–59 downward trend, but it appears as a blip in the numbers, while a clear trend in declining LPAs occurred in the 1960s.

Below are the LPA and LPA+ for every manager who lasted at least six seasons as a team's primary manager from 1876 to 1965. (Chapter 3's LPA and LPA+ leaderboards are drawn from these 75 names.) Please note that if a skipper managed outside the years in question, the numbers below do *not* reflect his entire career, only the portions that came during the age of leveraging. Also, the same errors that infect yearly LPAs also affect managerial scores.

Manager	LPA	LPA+	Manager	LPA	LPA+
Walter Alston	3.11	82	Lou Boudreau	4.50	93
Cap Anson	4.46	107	Al Buckenberger	5.02	125
Frank Bancroft	2.95	70	Donie Bush	4.47	110
Billy Barnie	3.63	84	Bill Carrigan	3.77	99

Manager	LPA	LPA+	Manager	LPA	LPA+
Frank Chance	7.78	178	Connie Mack	3.44	81
Jack Chapman	5.64	120	Jimmy McAleer	3.38	77
Fred Clarke	3.62	89	Joe McCarthy	3.89	86
Ty Cobb	3.98	118	John McGraw	4.51	111
Jimmy Collins	3.00	81	Bill McKechnie	4.23	98
Charles Comiskey	5.20	122	Fred Mitchell	3.11	90
Joe Cronin	4.68	100	Pat Moran	2.27	63
Patsy Donovan	4.71	110	Danny Murtaugh	4.02	129
Charlie Dressen	4.83	112	Jim Mutrie	3.45	75
Hugh Duffy	3.94	98	Steve O'Neill	4.18	90
Leo Durocher	5.35	107	Mel Ott	5.91	132
Jimmy Dykes	4.45	97	Roger Peckinpaugh	3.72	85
Buck Ewing	4.81	111	Horace Phillips	2.63	60
Bob Ferguson	2.90	76	Paul Richards	5.56	129
Lee Fohl	3.27	91	Branch Rickey	4.10	118
Frankie Frisch	5.88	126	Bill Rigney	2.59	79
Clark Griffith	4.31	107	Wilbert Robinson	4.44	118
Charlie Grimm	5.07	104	Gus Schmelz	4.01	87
Fred Haney	3.50	79	Frank Selee	4.04	106
Ned Hanlon	3.51	89	Luke Sewell	2.69	61
Bucky Harris	3.97	86	Burt Shotton	3.34	74
Jack Hendricks	3.39	92	Mayo Smith	2.96	85
Pinky Higgins	3.03	82	Billy Southworth	5.40	119
Rogers Hornsby	4.26	94	Tris Speaker	2.81	84
Dan Howley	3.42	79	George Stallings	4.45	110
Miller Huggins	3.20	89	Casey Stengel	5.33	120
Fred Hutchinson	3.71	90	Birdie Tebbetts	4.69	120
Arthur Irwin	3.95	92	Patsy Tebeau	3.47	93
Hughie Jennings	5.46	127	Bill Terry	3.84	82
Walter Johnson	6.13	137	Pie Traynor	6.60	130
Fielder Jones	4.54	110	Bill Watkins	4.91	126
Bill Killefer	5.49	143	Jimmie Wilson	4.19	86
Tom Loftus	2.65	70	Harry Wright	5.15	123
Al Lopez	4.11	104			

Glossary

The following statistics are used in the course of the book. Below is a list of what their statistical abbreviations mean. For the more complicated items that are discussed at length in the course of the book, a brief overview is provided below with a reference on where in the book to find more information about their mathematical foundations.

2B: Doubles.

3B: Triples.

A: Assists.

AOWP: Average Opponent Winning Percentage. It is the average winning percentage of all opposing teams a pitcher faces in a given season. This stat is explained in Chapter 3.

AOWP+: AOWP divided by TOWP times 100, rounded to the nearest integer. It notes how much a pitcher was leveraged in the course of a season. The higher the score, the more often he faced the best opposing clubs. An AOWP+ of 100 indicates an average usage pattern. This stat is explained in Chapter 3.

BABIP: Batting average on balls in play.

BATTING AVERAGE: Hits divided by at-bats.

BB: Base on balls.

BIRNBAUM DATABASE: A database featuring five main components designed by Phil Birnbaum to determine how much a team under/overachieved in the course of a full season. Though designed to examine luck, my contention is that with a larger sample size (at least three or four years) its findings reveal more about the manager than luck. Chapter 1 describes this database in detail; its algorithms are listed in Appendix I.

CG: Complete games.

COMPONENT ERA: This is used in the Birnbaum Database. Bill James debuted this stat in his *Win Shares* book, describing it as the Runs Created of opposing hitters against a particular pitcher. Like Runs Created, it consists of three factors. The first two are multiplied together and then divided by the third. The first factor is hits plus walks plus hit batsmen. For the second factor, begin with hits minus home runs, multiple the result by four, add four times home runs. Multiply the sum of all that by 0.89, then add 0.56 of the sum of walks and hit batsmen. The third factor is hit batsmen.

CS: Caught steals.

DER: There seems to be some disagreement what this acronym stands for. This work uses the one given in the glossary for The Hardball Times website: Defensive Efficiency Ratio. Bill James introduced the stat in his 1980s Abstracts under the name Defensive Efficiency Record, and I have also encountered it as Defensive Efficiency Rating, and Defensive Efficiency Report. Some sites, such as Baseball-Reference.com, try to avoid the issue by referring to it as "Def Eff." Whatever its name, it reveals what percentage of balls in play were converted into outs by a team's defense. All DER information used in this book comes from Baseball-Reference.com.

DP: Double plays.

ERA: Earned run average: $ER/(IP \times 9)$.

ERA+: ERA adjusted by Baseball-Reference's pitcher park factor and league-average ERA, centered at 100 and rounded to the nearest integer.

FIELDING PERCENTAGE: Percentage of balls in play handled successfully. (A+PO)/(A+PO+E).

GIDP: Ground into double play.

HB: Hit batters.

HBP: Hit by pitch. While HB is a pitching stat, HBP is a hitter stat.

HR: Home runs.

IP: Innings pitched.

ISOLATED POWER (ISO): Slugging average minus batting average.

IW: Intentional walks.

K: Strikeouts.

LP: Leverage points. This allows us to gauge how much overall leveraging occurred within a given subset. A subset can be an entire year, a series of years, a particular manager, or something else. This is explained in Chapter 3.

LPA: Leverage points average. Figures out the average leverage points received by pitchers in a given subset. This is explained in Chapter 3.

LPA+: This is the main stat used to gauge which managers engaged in the most or least leveraging of their starting pitchers, relative to their peers. It is the LPA for a manager divided by the overall LPA for the period he managed in, times 100 and rounded to the nearest integer.

OBP (ON-BASE PERCENTAGE): Percentage of plate appearance a hitter reaches base divided by times he tries to reach base: (H+BB+HBP)/(AB+BB+SF+HBP).

OPS: On-base percentage plus slugging average.

OPS+: OPS adjusted for park and league average, rounded to nearest integer and centered at 100.

PA: Plate appearances.

PARK FACTOR: Determines how a particular ballpark affected run scoring in a given season, relative to the other parks in the league. This book uses the park factors available at Baseball-Reference.com.

PK: Pickoffs.

PO: Putouts.

PYTHAGENPAT: This is a variation of the old Pythagorean projections first created by Bill James. It is an attempt to gauge expected wins and losses based on runs scored and allowed. James initially created it as: $(X^2)/[(X^2)+(Y^2)]$ in which X equals runs scored (or runs scored per game) and Y stands for runs allowed (or per game). However, James noted two was not the optimal exponent, but merely the most convenient since he had to calculate the number with a calculator in the pre–Microsoft Excel days. An internet sabermetrician who calls himself Patriot came up with a variant that is widely acclaimed as the best version. It uses a variable exponent, custom made to fit any individual run environment. The customized variable is determined by the following formula: $(X+Y)^{.287}$. In this formula, X and Y refer to runs scored and allowed per game. The result is plugged into the classic Pythagorean system in place of the exponent two. The Birnbaum Database uses this system.

RA: Relief appearances.

ROE: Reached on error.

RUNS CREATED: This is one of Bill James's most famous stats, and is central to the Birnbaum Database. It is an approximation of the offensive value of a player or a team. It consists of three factors, in which the first two are multiplied together, then divided by the third. The first factor is: (H+W-CS+HBP-GIDP). The second factor is {TB+[.26×(TBB-IBB+HBP)]+[.52×(SH+SF+SB)]}. The third factor is (AB+BB+HBP+SH+SF). For earlier periods in history, when not all the above stats exist, James created modified versions of Runs Created, fourteen variants in all. They are listed from pages 278 to 292 in the original *Bill James Historical Abstract*.

SB: Stolen bases.

SF: Sacrifice flies.

SH: Sacrifice hits.

SLUGGING PERCENTAGE: A relative gauge of a hitter's power. It is total bases divided by at-bats.

SV: Saves.

TENDENCIES DATABASE: This is essentially the heart of the book. This takes any stat, notes how a team ranks in it, and adjusts it for league size. Taking all the teams a particular manager ran gives you an idea how his teams fared in any given statistical category. A single query in the Tendencies Database is always centered at one. This is discussed in greater detail in Chapter 2.

tOPS+: This is a team's overall OPS+ compared to OPS+ in a given split. The split can be how a team hits in the eighth slot in the batting order, how they do in the third inning, with runners on base — anything an offensive split can be generated for. This is a statistic created by Baseball-Reference.com and is discussed in the Tony LaRussa commentary section of Chapter 9.

TOTAL BASES: H+2B+(2×3B)+(3×HR).

TOWP: Team's Opponent Winning Percentage. It is the average winning percentage of all opposing teams a team faces in a given season. This stat is explained in Chapter 3.

WIN SHARES: This was Bill James's most ambitious statistic; an attempt to boil down a player's hitting, fielding, and pitching contributions into one number. The formula is explained in his book, *Win Shares*. Three Win Shares are worth one game. The stat is broken into hitting, fielding, and pitching sections.

Bibliography

Books

Barber, Red. *1947: When All Hell Broke Loose in Baseball.* Garden City, N.Y.: Doubleday, 1982.

Baseball Prospectus Team of Experts. *Baseball Between the Numbers: Why Everything You Know about the Game is Wrong.* New York: Basic Books, 2006.

_____. *Baseball Prospectus 2003.* Washington: Brassey's Sports, 2003.

_____. *It Ain't Over 'til It's Over.* New York: Basic Books, 2007.

Bradbury, J. C. *The Baseball Economist: The Real Game Exposed.* New York: Dutton, 2007.

Cash, Jon David. *Before They Were Cardinals: Major League Baseball in Nineteenth Century St. Louis.* Columbia: University of Missouri Press, 2002.

Dewey, Donald, and Nicholas Acocella. *The New Biographical History of Baseball.* Chicago: Triumph Books, 2002.

Durocher, Leo, with Ed Linn. *Nice Guys Finish Last.* New York: Simon and Schuster, 1975.

Eig, Jonathan. *Opening Day: The Story of Jackie Robinson's First Season.* New York: Simon and Schuster, 2007.

Einstein, Charles. *Willie's Time: A Memoir.* New York: Lippincott, 1979.

Felber, Bill. *A Game of Brawl: The Orioles, the Beaneaters and the Battle for the 1897 Pennant.* Lincoln: University of Nebraska Press, 2007.

Fussman, Cal. *After Jackie, Pride, Prejudice, and Baseball's Forgotten History: An Oral History.* New York: ESPN Books, 2007.

Gay, Timothy M. *Tris Speaker: The Rough-and-Tumble Life of a Baseball Legend.* Lincoln: University of Nebraska Press, 2005.

Gillette, Gary, and Pete Palmer, eds. *ESPN Baseball Encyclopedia.* Fifth Edition. New York: Sterling, 2008.

Heidenry, Jack. *The Gashouse Gang: How Dizzy Dean, Leo Durocher, Branch Rickey, Pepper Martin, and Their Colorful Come-from-Behind Ballclub Won the World Series and America's Heart during the Great Depression.* New York: Public Affairs, 2007.

Honig, Donald. *Baseball When the Grass Was Real: Baseball from the Twenties to the Forties Told by the Men Who Played It.* New York: Coward, McCann, & Geoghegan, 1975.

James, Bill. *The Bill James Guide to Managers from 1870 to Today.* New York: Scribner, 1997.

_____. *The Bill James Historical Abstract.* New York: Villard Books, 1985.

_____. *The New Bill James Historical Baseball Abstract.* New York: The Free Press, 2001.

James, Bill, with Jim Henzler. *Win Shares.* Morton Grove, Ill.: STATS, 2002.

Koppett, Leonard. *The Man in the Dugout: Baseball's Top Mangers and How They Got That Way.* Expanded Edition. Philadelphia: Temple University Press, 2000.

_____. *The Thinking Fan's Guide to Baseball.* Hall of Fame Edition. Wilmington, Del: Sports Media Publishing, 2004.

Lee, Bill, with Richard Lally. *The Wrong Stuff.* New York: Penguin Books, 1985.

Luciano, Ron, with David Fisher. *The Umpire Strikes Back.* New York: Bantam Books, 1982.

Macht, Norman. *Connie Mack and the Early Years of Baseball.* Lincoln: University of Nebraska Press, 2007.

Morris, Peter. *A Game of Inches: The Stories Behind the Innovations that Shaped Baseball: The Game Behind the Scenes.* Chicago: Ivan R. Dee, 2006.

_____. *A Game of Inches: The Stories Behind the Innovations that Shaped Baseball: The Game on the Field.* Chicago: Ivan R. Dee, 2006.

Murphy, Cait. *Crazy '08: How a Cast of Cranks, Rogues, Boneheads, and Magnates Created the Greatest Year in Baseball History.* New York: Smithsonian/Collins, 2007.

Nemec, David. *The Great Encyclopedia of 19th-Century Major League Baseball.* New York: D. I. Fine Books, 1997.

Neft, David S., Richard M. Cohen, and Michael L. Neft, eds. *The Sports Encyclopedia: Baseball 2007.* New York: St. Martin's Press, 2007.

Neyer, Rob. *Rob Neyer's Big Book of Baseball Blunders.* New York: Simon and Schuster, 2006.

_____. *Rob Neyer's Big Book of Baseball Legends.* New York: Simon and Schuster, 2008.

Neyer, Rob, and Eddie Epstein. *Baseball Dynasties:*

The Greatest Teams of All-Time. New York: Norton, 2000.

Palmer, Pete, and John Thorn. *The Hidden Game of Baseball: A Revolutionary Approach to Baseball and Its Statistics.* Garden City, N.Y.: Doubleday, 1984.

Perry, Dayn. *Winners: How Good Baseball Teams Become Great Ones (And It's Not the Way You Think).* New York: John Wiley & Sons, 2006.

Rosengren, John. *Hammerin' Hank, George Almighty, and the Say Hey Kid: The Year That Changed Baseball Forever.* Naperville, Ill.: Sourcebooks, 2008.

Schwartz, Alan: *The Numbers Game: Baseball's Lifelong Fascination with Statistics.* New York: Thomas Dunne Books, 2004.

Seymour, Harold. *Baseball: The Early Years.* New York: Oxford University Press, 1960.

_____. *Baseball: The Golden Age.* New York: Oxford University Press, 1971.

Shechter, Leonard. *Jocks.* Indianapolis: Bobbs-Merrill, 1969.

Skipper, John C. *A Biographical Dictionary of Major League Baseball Managers.* Jefferson, N.C.: McFarland, 2003.

Society for American Baseball Research. *Deadball Stars of the American League.* Dulles, Va.: Potomac Books, 2006.

Society for American Baseball Research. *Deadball Stars of the National League.* Dulles, Va.: Potomac Books, 2004.

Society for American Baseball Research. *Nineteenth Century Stars.* Kansas City: Society for American Baseball Research, 1989.

Stein, Fred. *And the Skipper Bats Cleanup: A History of the Baseball Player-Manager, with Biographies of 42 Men Who Filled the Dual Role.* Jefferson, N.C.: McFarland, 2002.

Studenmund, Dave, ed. *The Hardball Times Baseball Annual 2008.* Skokie, Ill.: Acta Sports, 2007.

Tango, Tom M., Mitchel G. Lichtman, and Andrew E. Dolphin. *The Book: Playing the Percentages in Baseball.* Washington: Potomac Books, 2007.

Thompson, Dick. *The Ferrell Brothers of Baseball.* Jefferson, N.C.: McFarland, 2005.

Torre, Joe, and Tom Verducci. *The Yankee Years.* New York: Doubleday, 2009.

Veeck, Bill, and Ed Linn. *Veeck — As in Wreck: The Autobiography of Bill Veeck.* Evanston, Ill.: Holtzman Press, 1962.

Research Presentations

Angus, Jeff. "Punctuated Equilibrium in the Bullpen: The 2005 World Champion Chicago White Sox Blend Sabermetrics & Sociology to Deliver a Successful Innovation." Research presentation at the annual meeting of the Society for American Baseball Research, Seattle, July 1, 2006.

Bendix, Peter, and Matt Gallagher. "The Leo Mazzone Effect." Research presentation at the annual meeting of the Society for American Baseball Research, Toronto, August 5, 2005.

Birnbaum, Phil. "Were the 1994 Expos Just Lucky?" Research presentation at the annual meeting of the Society for American Baseball Research, Toronto, August 4, 2005.

Giacalone, Anthony. "'They Must Think We're a Bunch of (Censored)': Gussie Busch, Paternalism, and the Collapse of the Cardinals Dynasty." Research presentation at the annual meeting of the Society for American Baseball Research, St. Louis, July 28, 2007.

Morris, Peter. "Origin of the Pitching Rotation." Research presentation at the annual meeting of the Society for American Baseball Research, Toronto, August 4, 2005.

Websites

Baseball-Reference. <http://www.baseball-reference.com.>

Retrosheet. <http://www.retrosheet.org.>

Index

Profile pages are shown in **bold**.